2009

W9-APM-271

PHOTOGRAPHER'S MARKET®

From the Editors of Writer's Digest Books

BISHOP MUELLER LIBRARY
Briar Cliff University
SIOUX CITY, IA 51104

W

WRITER'S DIGEST BOOKS
CINCINNATI, OH

If you are an editor, art director, creative director, art publisher or gallery director and would like to be considered for a listing in the next edition of *Photographer's Market*, send your request for a questionnaire to *Photographer's Market*, 4700 East Galbraith Road, Cincinnati, Ohio 45236, or e-mail photomarket@fw pubs.com.

Editorial Director, Writer's Digest Books: Jane Friedman
Managing Editor, Writer's Digest Market Books: Alice Pope

Photographer's Market Web page: www.photographersmarket.com
Writer's Market Web site: www.writersmarket.com
Writer's Digest Web site: www.writersdigest.com
F + W Media Bookstore: http://fwmedia.com

2009 Photographer's Market. Copyright © 2008 by Writer's Digest Books. Published by F + W Media, Inc., 4700 East Galbraith Rd., Cincinnati, Ohio 45236. Printed and bound in the United States of America. All rights reserved. No part of this book may be reproduced in any form or by any electronic or mechanical means including information storage and retrieval systems without written permission from the publisher. Reviewers may quote brief passages to be printed in a magazine or newspaper.

Distributed in Canada by Fraser Direct
100 Armstrong Ave.
Georgetown, ON, Canada L7G 5S4
Tel: (905) 877-4411

Distributed in the U.K. and Europe by David & Charles
Brunel House, Newton Abbot, Devon, TQ12 4PU, England
Tel: (+44) 1626 323200, Fax: (+44) 1626 323319
E-mail: postmaster@davidandcharles.co.uk

Distributed in Australia by Capricorn Link
P.O. Box 704, Windsor, NSW 2756, Australia
Tel: (02) 4577-3555

Distributed in New Zealand by David Bateman Ltd.
P.O. Box 100-242, N.S.M.C., Auckland 1330, New Zealand
Tel: (09) 415-7664, Fax: (09) 415-8892

Distributed in South Africa by Real Books
P.O. Box 1040, Auckland Park 2006, Johannesburg, South Africa
Tel: (011) 837-0643, Fax: (011) 837-0645
E-mail: realbook@global.co.za

ISSN: 0147-247X
ISBN-13: 978-1-58297-546-7
ISBN-10: 1-58297-546-9

Cover design by Claudean Wheeler
Interior design by Clare Finney
Production coordinated by Greg Nock

Attention Booksellers: This is an annual directory of F + W Media, Inc.
Return deadline for this edition is December 31, 2009.

192079534

Contents

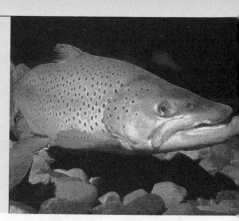

© Eric Engbretson

BUSINESS BASICS

© Charles Needle

INTERVIEWS WITH PROS

MARKETS

© Gerry Lemmo

© Michelle Turner

RESOURCES

© Steve Ahrens

INDEXES

© Gerry Lemmo

From the Editor

've always believed that the forces of the universe, whatever they may be, have a way of guiding us down the right paths, steering us in the right directions, and parking us in the right lots. That's a New Age-y way of saying many of us fall into a niche that really fits.

As I read the feature interviews in this edition of *Photographer's Market*, I was struck by the fact that all of the photographers we interviewed were specialized. But the direction of their careers was more often than not a result of serendipity rather than planning.

Michelle Turner (page 30) started out photographing children and families. "But," she says, "it wasn't until a friend asked me to photograph her wedding that I truly fell in love with the profession." Later, a bridesmaid from a wedding she had shot asked Turner to photograph her wedding abroad, and from there Turner's destination wedding business bloomed. She now shoots 90 percent destination weddings, and garners most of her business through word of mouth.

For Eric Engbretson (page 35), his photography career began as an offshoot of his love of fishing. "What fisherman doesn't wonder what it all looks like down there?" he says. Then he moved to a home on a lake in northern Wisconsin in 1990, began snorkeling, and wanted to share the amazing world he saw below the surface of the water. He started taking pictures, and later began selling to magazines. Today he makes his living as an underwater photographer.

Charles Needle's (page 41) interest in nature, and, ultimately his career as a nature photographer, developed as he recovered from Chronic Fatigue Syndrome. "I now view my illness as a gift, because it literally forced me to slow down and notice the beauty in small things," he says. Nearly bed-ridden for a year, Needle surrounded himself with as much nature as he could, whether observing what was outside his window or studying nature photography. Once he became stronger physically, he ventured outdoors with his camera. Today Needle not only works as a professional nature photographer, he also writes and teaches numerous workshops.

Whether you've settled into your own specialty or are still exploring your options, the *2009 Photographer Market* is here to help you get moving and keep moving just like our featured photographers. In addition to our interviews, you'll find useful information on selling your work and running your business, as well as up-to-date listings for everything from publications and publishers to stock photo agencies and art fairs.

Alice Pope
Managing Editor
Writer's Digest Market Books
photomarket@fwpubs.com

2009 Reader Survey:
Tell us about yourself!

1. How often do you purchase *Photographer's Market*?

◯ Every year
◯ Every other year
◯ This is my first edition

2. What type of photography do you do?

_____
_____
_____
_____

3. Do you have suggestions for improving *Photographer's Market*?

_____
_____
_____
_____
_____

4. Would you like to see an online version of *Photographer's Market*?

◯ Yes
◯ No

Name: _____
Address: _____
City: _____ State: _____ Zip: _____
Phone: _____ E-mail: _____
Web site: _____

Fax to Photographer's Market: (513)531-2686; mail to Photographer's Market, 4700 East Galbraith Road, Cincinnati, OH 45236; or e-mail photomarket@fwpubs.com.

How to Use This Book

The first thing you'll notice about most of the listings in this book is the group of symbols that appears before the name of each company. Scanning the listings for symbols can help you quickly locate markets that meet certain criteria. (You'll find a quick-reference key to the symbols on the front and back inside covers of the book.) Here's what each symbol stands for:

N   This photo buyer is new to this edition of the book.

   This photo buyer is located in Canada.

   This photo buyer is located outside the U.S. and Canada.

A   This photo buyer uses only images created on assignment.

S   This photo buyer uses only stock images.

   This photo buyer accepts submissions in digital format.

   This photo buyer uses film or other audiovisual media.

   This art fair is a juried event; a juror or committee of jurors views applicants' work and selects those whose work fits within the guidelines of the event.

Complaint Procedure

Important

If you feel you have not been treated fairly by a company listed in *Photographer's Market*, we advise you to take the following steps:

- First, try to contact the listing. Sometimes one phone call, e-mail or letter can quickly clear up the matter.

- Document all your correspondence with the listing. If you write to us with a complaint, provide the details of your submission, the date of your first contact with the listing, and the nature of your subsequent correspondence.

- We will enter your letter into our files.

- The number and severity of complaints will be considered in our decision whether to delete the listing from the next edition.

PAY SCALE

We asked photo buyers to indicate their general pay scale based on what they typically pay for a single image. Their answers are signified by a series of dollar signs before each listing. Scanning for dollar signs can help you quickly identify which markets pay at the top of the scale. However, not every photo buyer answered this question, so don't mistake a missing dollar sign as an indication of low pay rates. Also keep in mind that many photo buyers are willing to negotiate.

$ Pays $1-150

$ $ Pays $151-750

$ $ $ Pays $751-1,500

$ $ $ $ Pays more than $1,500

OPENNESS

We also asked photo buyers to indicate their level of openness to freelance photography. Looking for these symbols can help you identify buyers who are willing to work with new-comers, as well as prestigious buyers who only publish top-notch photography.

◯ Encourages beginning or unpublished photographers to submit work for consideration; publishes new photographers. May pay only in copies or have a low pay rate.

◑ Accepts outstanding work from beginning and established photographers; expects a high level of professionalism from all photographers who make contact.

◕ Hard to break into; publishes mostly previously published photographers. May pay at the top of the scale.

◉ Closed to unsolicited submissions.

SUBHEADS

Each listing is broken down into sections to make it easier to locate specific information. In the first section of each listing you'll find mailing addresses, phone numbers, e-mail and Web site addresses, and the name of the person you should contact. You'll also find general information about photo buyers, including when their business was established and their publishing philosophy. Each listing will include one or more of the following subheads:

Needs. Here you'll find specific subjects each photo buyer is seeking. (You can find an index of these subjects starting on page 504 to help you narrow your search.) You'll also find the average number of freelance photos a buyer uses each year, which will help you gauge your chances of publication.

Audiovisual Needs. If you create images for media such as filmstrips or overhead transparencies, or you shoot videotape or motion picture film, look here for photo buyers' specific needs in these areas.

Specs. Look here to see in what format the photo buyer prefers to receive accepted images. Many photo buyers will accept both digital and film (slides, transparencies, prints) formats. However, many photo buyers are reporting that they accept digital images only, so make sure you can provide the format the photo buyer requires before you send samples.

Exhibits. This subhead appears only in the Galleries section of the book. Like the Needs subhead, you'll find information here about the specific subjects and types of photography a gallery shows.

Making Contact & Terms. When you're ready to make contact with a photo buyer, look

Frequently Asked Questions

1 How do companies get listed in the book?

No company pays to be included—all listings are free. Every company has to fill out a detailed questionnaire about their photo needs. All questionnaires are screened to make sure the companies meet our requirements. Each year we contact every company in the book and ask them to update their information.

2 Why aren't other companies I know about listed in this book?

We may have sent these companies a questionnaire, but they never returned it. Or if they did return a questionnaire, we may have decided not to include them based on our requirements.

3 Some publishers say they accept photos with or without a manuscript. What does that mean?

Essentially, the word manuscript means a written article that will be published by a magazine. Some magazines will only consider publishing your photos if they accompany a written article. Other publishers will consider publishing your photos alone, without a manuscript. In previous editions, the word manuscript was abbreviated to ms. In this edition, we spell out the word manuscript whenever it occurs.

4 I sent a CD with large digital files to a photo buyer who said she wanted to see my work. I have not heard from her, and I am afraid that my photos will be used without my permission and without payment. What should I do?

Do not send large, printable files (300 dpi or larger) unless you are sure the photo buyer is going to use them, and you know what you will be paid for their usage and what rights the photo buyer is requesting. If a photo buyer shows interest in seeing your work in digital format, send small JPEGs at first so they can "review" them—i.e., determine if the subject matter and technical quality of your photos meet their requirements. Until you know for sure that the photo buyer is going to license your photos and you have some kind of agreement, do not send high-resolution files. The exception to this rule would be if you have dealt with the photo buyer before or perhaps know someone who has. Some companies receive a large volume of submissions, so sometimes you must be patient. It's a good idea to give any company listed in this book a call before you submit anything and be sure nothing has changed since we contacted them to gather or update information. This is true whether you submit slides, prints or digital images.

5 A company says they want to publish my photographs, but first they will need a fee from me. Is this a standard business practice?

No, it is not a standard business practice. You should never have to pay to have your photos reviewed or to have your photos accepted for publication. If you suspect that a company may not be reputable, do some research before you submit anything or pay their fees. The exception to this rule is contests. It is not unusual for some contests listed in this book to have entry fees (usually minimal—between five and 20 dollars).

here to find out exactly what they want to see in your submission. You'll also find what the buyer usually pays and what rights they expect in exchange. In the Stock section, this subhead is divided into two parts, Payment & Terms and Making Contact, because this information is often lengthy and complicated.

Handles. This subhead appears only in the Photo Representatives section. Some reps also represent illustrators, fine artists, stylists, make-up artists, etc., in addition to photographers. The term "handles" refers to the various types of "talent" they represent.

Tips. Look here for advice and information directly from photo buyers in their own words.

EASY-TO-USE REFERENCE ICONS

SPECIFIC PHOTO NEEDS

DETAILED SUBMISSION GUIDELINES

E-MAIL AND WEB SITE INFORMATION

WHO TO CONTACT

HOW MUCH THEY PAY

$ $ DUCKS UNLIMITED

One Waterfowl Way, Memphis TN 38120. (901)758-3864. E-mail: jhoffman@ducks.org. Web site: www.ducks.org. **Contact:** John Hoffman, photo editor. Circ. 580,000. Estab. 1937. Bimonthly association magazine of Ducks Unlimited, a nonprofit organization. Emphasizes waterfowl hunting and conservation. Readers are professional males, ages 40-50. Sample copy available for $3. Photo guidelines available on Web site, via e-mail or with SASE.

Needs Buys 84 photos from freelancers/issue; 504 photos/year. Needs images of wild ducks and geese, waterfowling and scenic wetlands. Special photo needs include waterfowl hunters, dynamic shots of waterfowl interacting in natural habitat.

Specs Accepts images in digital format. Send via CD as TIFF, JPEG, EPS files at 300 dpi; include thumbnails.

Making Contact & Terms Send only top-quality portfolio of not more than 40 transparencies (35mm or larger) with SASE for consideration. Responds in 1 month. Previously published work OK, if noted. Pays $100 for thumbnails; $125 for quarter page or less; $150 for images less than half page; $185 for half page; $240 for full page; $400 for 2-page spread; $850 for cover. Pays on publication. Credit line given. Buys one-time rights "plus permission to reprint in our Mexican and Canadian publications."

How to Start Selling Your Work

I f this is your first edition of *Photographer's Market*, you're probably feeling a little overwhelmed by all the information in this book. Before you start flipping through the listings, read the 11 steps below to learn how to get the most out of this book and your selling efforts.

1. Be honest with yourself. Are the photographs you make of the same quality as those you see published in magazines and newspapers? If the answer is yes, you may be able to sell your photos.

2. Get someone else to be honest with you. Do you know a professional photographer who would critique your work for you? Other ways to get opinions about your work: join a local camera club or other photo organization; attend a stock seminar led by a professional photographer; attend a regional or national photo conference or a workshop where they offer daily critiques.

- You'll find workshop and seminar listings beginning on page 431.
- You'll find a list of photographic organizations on page 469.
- Check your local camera store for information about camera clubs in your area.

3. Get Organized. Create a list of subjects you have photographed and organize your images into subject groups. Make sure you can quickly find specific images and keep track of any sample images you send out. You can use database software on your home computer to help you keep track of your images. (See page 26 for more information.)

Other Resources:

- *Photo Portfolio Success* by John Kaplan, Writer's Digest Books.
- *Sell and Re-Sell Your Photos* by Rohn Engh, Writer's Digest Books.
- *Sellphotos.com* by Rohn Engh, Writer's Digest Books.
- *The Photographer's Travel Guide* by William Manning, Writer's Digest Books.

4. Consider the format. Are your pictures color snapshots, black & white prints, color slides or digital captures? The format of your work will determine, in part, which markets you can approach. Below are some general guidelines for where you can market various photo formats. Always check the listings in this book for specific format information.

- **black & white prints**—galleries, art fairs, private collectors, literary/art magazines, trade magazines, newspapers, some book publishers
- **color prints**—newsletters, very small trade or club magazines
- **large color prints**—galleries, art fairs, private collectors
- **color slides** (35mm)—most magazines, newspapers, some greeting card and calendar publishers, some book publishers, textbook publishers, stock agencies
- **color transparencies** ($2\frac{1}{4} \times 2\frac{1}{4}$ and 4×5)—magazines, book publishers, calendar publishers, ad agencies, stock agencies. Many of these photo buyers have begun to accept only digital photos, especially stock agencies.

Business Basics

- **digital**—newspapers, magazines, stock agencies, ad agencies, book and greeting card publishers. (All listings that accept digital work are marked with a ▣ symbol.)

5. Do you want to sell stock images or accept assignments? A stock image is any photograph you create on your own and then sell to a publisher. An assignment is a photograph created at the request of a specific buyer. Many of the listings in *Photographer's Market* are interested in both stock and assignment work.

- Listings that are only interested in stock photography are marked with a ▣ symbol.
- Listings that are only interested in assignment photography are marked with a ▣ symbol.

6. Start researching. Generate a list of the publishers that might buy your images— check the newsstand, go to the library, search the Web, read the listings in this book. Don't forget to look at greeting cards, stationery, calendars and CD covers. Anything you see with a photograph on it, from a billboard advertisement to a cereal box, is a potential market.

- See page 5 for instructions about how to read the listings in this book.
- If you shoot a specific subject, check the Subject Index on page 504 to simplify your search.

7. Check the publisher's guidelines. Do you know exactly how the publisher you choose wants to be approached? Check the listings in this book first. If you don't know the format, subject and number of images a publisher wants in a submission, you should check their Web site first. Often, guidelines are posted there. Or you can send a short letter with a self-addressed, stamped envelope (SASE) or e-mail asking those questions. A quick call to the receptionist might also yield you the answers.

8. Check out the market. Get in the habit of reading industry magazines.

- You'll find a list of useful magazines on page 472.

9. Prepare yourself. Before you send your first submission, make sure you know how to respond when a publisher agrees to buy your work.

Pay Rates:

Most magazines and newspapers will tell you what they pay, and you can accept or decline. However, you should become familiar with typical pay rates. Ask other photographers what they charge—preferably ones you know well or who are not in direct competition with you. Many will be willing to tell you to prevent you from devaluing the market by undercharging. (See page 17 for more information.)

Other Resources:

- *Pricing Photography: The Complete Guide to Assignment and Stock Prices* by Michal Heron and David MacTavish, Allworth Press.
- *fotoQuote*, a software package that is updated each year to list typical stock photo and assignment prices, (800)679-0202, www.cradoc.com.
- *Negotiating Stock Photo Prices* by Jim Pickerell, 110 Frederick Ave., Suite A, Rockville MD 20850, (301)251-0720.

Copyright:

You should always include a copyright notice on any slide, print or digital image you send out. While you automatically own the copyright to your work the instant it is created, the notice affords extra protection. The proper format for a copyright notice includes the word or symbol for copyright, the date and your name: © 2008 Donna Poehner. To fully protect your copyright and recover damages from infringers, you must register your copyright with the Copyright Office in Washington. (See page 26 for more information.)

Rights:

In most cases, you will not actually be selling your photographs, but rather, the rights to publish them. If a publisher wants to buy your images outright, you will lose the right to resell those images in any form or even display them in your portfolio. Most publishers will buy one-time rights and/or first rights. (See page 27 for more information.)

Other Resources:

- *Legal Guide for the Visual Artist* by Tad Crawford, Allworth Press.

Contracts:

Formal contract or not, you should always agree to any terms of sale in writing. This could be as simple as sending a follow-up letter restating the agreement and asking for confirmation, once you agree to terms over the phone. You should always keep copies of any correspondence in case of a future dispute or misunderstanding. (See page 26 for more information.)

Other Resources:

- *Business and Legal Forms for Photographers* by Tad Crawford, Allworth Press.

10. Prepare your submission. The number one rule when mailing submissions is: "Follow the directions." Always address letters to specific photo buyers. Always include a SASE of sufficient size and with sufficient postage for your work to be safely returned to you. Never send originals when you are first approaching a potential buyer. Try to include something in your submission that the potential buyer can keep on file, such as a tearsheet and your résumé. In fact, photo buyers prefer that you send something they don't have to return to you. Plus, it saves you the time and expense of preparing a SASE. (See page 12 for more information.)

Other Resources:

- *Photo Portfolio Success* by John Kaplan, Writer's Digest Books.

11. Continue to promote yourself and your work. After you've made that first sale (and even before), it is important to promote yourself. Success in selling your work depends in part on how well and how often you let photo buyers know what you have to offer. This is known as self-promotion. There are several ways to promote yourself and your work. You can send postcards or other printed material through the mail; send an e-mail with an image and a link to your Web site if you have one; and upload your images to a Web site that is dedicated to showcasing your work and your photographic services. (See page 24 for more information.)

Running Your Business

Photography is an art that requires a host of skills, some which can be learned and some which are innate. To make money from your photography, the one skill you can't do without is a knowledge of business. Thankfully, this skill can be learned. What you'll find on the following pages are the basics of running a photography business. We'll cover:

- Submitting Your Work, page 12
- Digital Submission Guidelines, page 13
- Using Essential Business Forms, page 15
- Stock List, page 17
- Charging for Your Work, page 17
- Figuring Small Business Taxes, page 22
- Self-Promotion, page 24
- Organizing and Labeling Your Images, page 26
- Protecting Your Copyright, page 26

SUBMITTING YOUR WORK

Editors, art directors and other photo buyers are busy people. Many only spend 10 percent of their work time actually choosing photographs for publication. The rest of their time is spent making and returning phone calls, arranging shoots, coordinating production and a host of other unglamorous tasks that make publication possible. They want to discover new talent, and you may even have the exact image they're looking for, but if you don't follow a market's submission instructions to the letter, you have little chance of acceptance.

To learn the dos and don'ts of photography submissions, read each market's listing carefully and make sure to send only what they ask for. Don't send prints if they only want slides. Don't send color if they only want black & white. Check their Web site or send for guidelines whenever they are available to get the most complete and up-to-date submission advice. When in doubt, follow these 10 rules when sending your work to a potential buyer:

1. Don't forget your SASE—Always include a self-addressed, stamped envelope whether you want your submission back or not. Make sure your SASE is big enough, has enough packaging, and has enough postage to ensure the safe return of your work.

2. Don't over-package—Never make a submission difficult to open and file. Don't tape down all the loose corners. Don't send anything too large to fit in a standard file.

3. Don't send originals—Try not to send things you must have back. Never, ever send originals unsolicited.

4. Label everything—Put a label directly on the slide mount or print you are submitting. Include your name, address and phone number, as well as the name or number of the image. Your slides and prints will almost certainly get separated from your letter.

5. Do your research—Always research the places to which you want to sell your work. Request sample issues of magazines, visit galleries, examine ads, look at Web sites, etc. Make sure your work is appropriate before you send it out. A blind mailing is a waste of postage and a waste of time for both you and the art buyer.

6. Follow directions—Always request submission guidelines. Include a SASE for reply. Follow *all* the directions exactly, even if you think they're silly.

7. Include a business letter—Always include a cover letter, no more than one page, that lets the potential buyer know you are familiar with their company, what your photography background is (briefly), and where you've sold work before (if it pertains to what you're trying to do now). If you send an e-mail, follow the same protocol as you would for a business cover letter and include the same information.

8. Send to a person, not a title—Send submissions to a specific person at a company. When you address a cover letter to Dear Sir or Madam, it shows you know nothing about the company you want to buy your work.

9. Don't forget to follow through—Follow up major submissions with postcard samples several times a year.

10. Have something to leave behind—If you're lucky enough to score a portfolio review, always have a sample of your work to leave with the art director. Make it small enough to fit in a file but big enough not to get lost. Always include your contact information directly on the leave-behind.

DIGITAL SUBMISSION GUIDELINES

Digital images can come from scanned slides, negatives or prints, or from digital cameras. Today, almost every publisher of photographs will accept digital images. Some still accept "analog" images (slides and prints) as well as digital images, but some accept *only* digital images. And, of course, there are those who still do not accept digital images at all, but their number is decreasing.

Previews

Photo buyers need to see a preview of an image before they can decide if it will fit their needs. In the past, photographers mailed slides or prints to prospective photo buyers so they could review them, determine their quality, and decide whether or not the subject matter was something they could use. Or photographers sent a self-promotion mailer, often a postcard with one or more representative images of their work. Today, preview images can be e-mailed to prospective photo buyers, or they can be viewed on a photographer's Web site. This eliminates the hassle and expense of sending slides through the mail and wondering if you'll ever get them back.

The important thing about digital preview images is size. They should be no larger than 3 by 5 inches at 72 dpi. E-mailing larger files to someone who just wants a peek at your work could greatly inconvenience them if they have to wait a long time for the files to open or if their e-mail system cannot handle larger files. If photo buyers are interested in using your photographs, they will definitely want a larger, high-resolution file later, but don't overload their systems and their patience in the beginning with large files. Another option is sending a CD with preview images. This is not as efficient as e-mail or a Web site since the photo buyer has to put the CD in the computer and view the images one by one. If you send a CD, be sure to include a printout of thumbnail images: If the photo buyer does not have time to put the CD in the computer and view the images, she can at least glance at the printed thumbnails. CDs and DVDs are probably best reserved for high-resolution photos you know the photo buyer wants and has requested from you.

Starting a Business

For More Info

To learn more about starting a business:

- Take a course at a local college. Many community colleges offer short-term evening and weekend courses on topics like creating a business plan or finding financial assistance to start a small business.

- Contact the Small Business Administration at (800)827-5722 or check out their Web site at www.sba.gov. "The U.S. Small Business Administration was created by Congress in 1953 to help America's entrepreneurs form successful small enterprises. Today, SBA's program offices in every state offer financing, training and advocacy for small firms."

- Contact the Small Business Development Center at (202)205-6766. The SBDC offers free or low-cost advice, seminars and workshops for small business owners.

- Read a book. Try *The Business of Commercial Photography* by Ira Wexler (Amphoto Books) or *The Business of Studio Photography* by Edward R. Lilley (Allworth Press). The business section of your local library will also have many general books about starting a small business.

Size and Quality

Size and quality might be the two most important aspects of your digital submission. If the quality is not there, photo buyers will not be interested in buying your image regardless of its subject matter. Find out what the photo buyer needs. If you scan your slides or prints, make sure your scanning quality is excellent: no dirt, dust or scratches. If the file size is too small, they will not be able to do much with it either. A resolution of 72 dpi is fine for previews, but if a photo buyer wants to publish your images, they will want larger, high-resolution files. While each photo buyer may have different needs, there are some general guidelines to follow. Often digital images that are destined for print media need to be 300 dpi and the same size as the final, printed image will be (or preferably a little larger). For example, for a full-page photo in a magazine, the digital file might be 8 by 10 inches at 300 dpi. However, always check with the photo buyer who will ultimately be publishing the photo. Many magazines, book publishers, and stock photo agencies post digital submission guidelines on their Web sites or will provide copies to photographers if they ask. Photo buyers are usually happy to inform photographers of their digital guidelines since they don't want to receive images they won't be able to use due to poor quality.

Note: Many of the listings in this book that accept digital images state the dpi they require for final submissions. They may also state the size they need in terms of megabytes (MB). See subhead "Specs" in each listing.

Formats

When you know that a photo buyer is definitely going to use your photos, you will then need to submit a high-resolution digital file (as opposed to the low-resolution 72-dpi JPEGs used for previews). Photo buyers often ask for digital images to be saved as JPEGs or TIFFs. Again, make sure you know what format they prefer. Some photo buyers will want you to send them a CD or DVD with the high-resolution images saved on it. Most photo buyers appreciate having a printout of thumbnail images to review in addition to the CD. Some may allow you to e-mail images directly to them, but keep in mind that anything larger than 9 megabytes is usually too large to e-mail. Get the permission of the photo buyer before you attempt to send anything that large via e-mail.

Another option is FTP (file transfer protocol). It allows files to be transferred over the Internet from one computer to another. This option is becoming more prevalent.

Note: Most of the listings in this book that accept digital images state the format they require for final digital submissions. See subhead "Specs" in each listing.

Color space

Another thing you'll need to find out from the photo buyer is what color space they want photos to be saved in. RGB (red, green, blue) is a very common one. You might also encounter CMYK (cyan, magenta, yellow and black). Grayscale is for photos that will be printed without any color (black & white). Again, check with the photo buyer to find out what color space they require.

USING ESSENTIAL BUSINESS FORMS

Using carefully crafted business forms will not only make you look more professional in the eyes of your clients; it will make bills easier to collect while protecting your copyright. Forms from delivery memos to invoices can be created on a home computer with minimal design skills and printed in duplicate at most quick-print centers. When producing detailed contracts, remember that proper wording is imperative. You want to protect your copyright and, at the

Forms for Photographers

For More Info

To learn more about forms for photographers, try the following:

- EP (Editorial Photographers), www.editorialphoto.com.

- *Business and Legal Forms for Photographers* by Tad Crawford (Allworth Press).

- *Legal Guide for the Visual Artist* by Tad Crawford (Allworth Press).

- *ASMP Professional Business Practices in Photography* (Allworth Press).

- The American Society of Media Photographers offers traveling business seminars that cover issues from forms to pricing to collecting unpaid bills. Write to them at 14 Washington Rd., Suite 502, Princeton Junction NJ 08550, for a schedule of upcoming business seminars, or visit www.asmp.org.

- The Volunteer Lawyers for the Arts, 1 E. 53rd St., 6th Floor, New York NY 10022, (212)319-2910. The VLA is a nonprofit organization, based in New York City, dedicated to providing all artists, including photographers, with sound legal advice.

same time, be fair to clients. Therefore, it's a good idea to have a lawyer examine your forms before using them.

The following forms are useful when selling stock photography, as well as when shooting on assignment:

Delivery Memo

This document should be mailed to potential clients along with a cover letter when any submission is made. A delivery memo provides an accurate count of the images that are enclosed, and it provides rules for usage. The front of the form should include a description of the images or assignment, the kind of media in which the images can be used, the price for such usage, and the terms and conditions of paying for that usage. Ask clients to sign and return a copy of this form if they agree to the terms you've spelled out.

Terms & Conditions

This form often appears on the back of the delivery memo, but be aware that conditions on the front of a form have more legal weight than those on the back. Your terms and conditions should outline in detail all aspects of usage for an assignment or stock image. Include copyright information, client liability, and a sales agreement. Also be sure to include conditions covering the alteration of your images, transfer of rights, and digital storage. The more specific your terms and conditions are to the individual client, the more legally binding they will be. If you create your forms on your computer, seriously consider altering your standard contract to suit each assignment or other photography sale.

Invoice

This is the form you want to send more than any of the others, because mailing it means you have made a sale. The invoice should provide clients with your mailing address, an explanation of usage, and the amount due. Be sure to include a reasonable due date for payment, usually 30 days. You should also include your business tax identification number or social security number.

Model/Property Releases

Get into the habit of obtaining releases from anyone you photograph. They increase the sales potential for images and can protect you from liability. A model release is a short form, signed by the person(s) in a photo, that allows you to sell the image for commercial purposes. The property release does the same thing for photos of personal property. When photographing children, remember that a parent or guardian must sign before the release is legally binding. In exchange for signed releases, some photographers give their subjects copies of the photos; others pay the models. You may choose the system that works best for you, but keep in mind that a legally binding contract must involve consideration, the exchange of something of value. Once you obtain a release, keep it in a permanent file. (You'll find a sample property release on page 17 and a sample model release on page 18.)

You do not need a release if the image is being sold editorially. However, magazines now require such forms in order to protect themselves, especially when an image is used as a photo illustration instead of as a straight documentary shot. You always need a release for advertising purposes or for purposes of trade and promotion. In works of art, you only need a release if the subject is recognizable. When traveling in a foreign country, it is a good idea to carry releases written in that country's language. To translate releases into a foreign language, check with an embassy or a college language professor.

PROPERTY RELEASE

In consideration of $_____ and/or _____
_____, receipt of which is acknowledged, I being the legal owner of
or having the right to permit the taking and use of photographs of certain property designated as _____, do hereby
give _____, his/her assigns, licensees, and legal representatives the irrevocable right to use this image in all forms and media and in
all manners, including composite or distorted representations, for advertising,
trade, or any other lawful purposes, and I waive any rights to inspect or approve
the finished product, including written copy that may be created in connection
therewith.

Short description of photographs: _____
_____
_____

Additional information: _____

I am of full age. I have read this release and fully understand its contents.

Please Print:

Name _____

Address _____

City _____ State _____ Zip Code _____

Sample property release

STOCK LIST

Some market listings in this book ask for a stock list, so it is a good idea to have one on
hand. Your stock list should be as detailed and specific as possible. Include all the subjects
you have in your photo files, breaking them into logical categories and subcategories. On
page 19 is a sample stock list that shows how you might categorize your stock images to
create a list that will be easy for photo buyers to skim. This sample list only hints at what a
stock list might include. Create a list that reflects your unique collection of images.

CHARGING FOR YOUR WORK

No matter how many books you read about what photos are worth and how much you
should charge, no one can set your fees for you. If you let someone try, you'll be setting
yourself up for financial ruin. Figuring out what to charge for your work is a complex task
that will require a lot of time and effort. But the more time you spend finding out how much
you need to charge, the more successful you'll be at targeting your work to the right markets
and getting the money you need to keep your business, and your life, going.

Keep in mind that what you charge for an image may be completely different from what

MODEL RELEASE

In consideration of $ _____ and/or _____,
receipt of which is acknowledged, I, _____, do
hereby give _____, his/her assigns, licensees, and
legal representatives the irrevocable right to use my image in all forms and
media and in all manners, including composite or distorted representations, for
advertising, trade, or any other lawful purposes, and I waive any rights to inspect or approve the finished product, including written copy that may be created in connection therewith. The following name may be used in reference to
these photographs:

My real name, or _____

Short description of photographs: _____

_____

Additional information: _____

Please print:

Name _____

Address _____

City _____ State _____ Zip code _____

Country _____

CONSENT

(If model is under the age of 18) I am the parent or guardian of the minor named
above and have the legal authority to execute the above release. I approve the
foregoing and waive any rights in the premises.

Please print:

Name _____

Address _____

City _____ State _____ Zip code _____

Country _____

Signature _____

Witness _____ Date _____

Sample model release

STOCK LIST

INSECTS
Ants
Aphids
Bees
Beetles
Butterflies
Grasshoppers
Moths
Termites
Wasps

PROFESSIONS
Bee Keeper
Biologist
Firefighter
Nurse
Police Officer
Truck Driver
Waitress
Welder

LANDMARKS
Asia
  Angkor Wat
  Great Wall of China

Europe
  Big Ben
  Eiffel Tower
  Louvre
  Stonehenge

United States
  Empire State Building
  Grand Canyon
  Liberty Bell
  Mt. Rushmore
  Statue of Liberty

TRANSPORTATION
Airplanes and helicopters
Roads
  Country roads
  Dirt roads
  Interstate highways
  Two-lane highways

WEATHER
Clouds
  Cumulus
  Cirrus
  Nimbus
  Stratus
Flooding
Lightning
Snow and Blizzards
Storm Chasers
Rainbows
Tornadoes
Tornado Damage

Sample stock list

a photographer down the street charges. There is nothing wrong with this if you've calculated your prices carefully. Perhaps the photographer works in a basement on old equipment and you have a brand new, state-of-the-art studio. You'd better be charging more. Why the disparity? For one thing, you've got a much higher overhead, the continuing costs of running your business. You're also probably delivering a higher-quality product and are more able to meet client requests quickly. So how do you determine just how much you need to charge in order to make ends meet?

Setting your break-even rate

All photographers, before negotiating assignments, should consider their break-even rate—the amount of money they need to make in order to keep their studios open. To arrive at the actual price you'll quote to a client, you should add onto your base rate things like usage, your experience, how quickly you can deliver the image, and what kind of prices the market will bear.

Start by estimating your business expenses. These expenses may include rent (office, studio), gas and electric, insurance (equipment), phone, fax, Internet service, office supplies, postage, stationery, self-promotions/portfolio, photo equipment, computer, staff salaries, taxes. Expenses like film and processing will be charged to your clients.

Next, figure your personal expenses, which will include food, clothing, medical, car and home insurance, gas, repairs and other car expenses, entertainment, retirement savings and investments, etc.

Before you divide your annual expenses by the 365 days in the year, remember you won't be shooting billable assignments every day. A better way to calculate your base fee is by billable weeks. Assume that at least one day a week is going to be spent conducting office business and marketing your work. This amounts to approximately 10 weeks. Add in days for vacation and sick time, perhaps three weeks, and add another week for workshops and seminars. This totals 14 weeks of nonbillable time and 38 billable weeks throughout the year.

Now estimate the number of assignments/sales you expect to complete each week and multiply that number by 38. This will give you a total for your yearly assignments/sales. Finally, divide the total overhead and administrative expenses by the total number of assignments. This will give you an average price per assignment, your break-even or base rate.

As an example, let's say your expenses come to $65,000 per year (this includes $35,000 of personal expenses). If you complete two assignments each week for 38 weeks, your average price per assignment must be about $855. This is what you should charge to break even on each job. But, don't forget, you want to make money.

Establishing usage fees

Too often, photographers shortchange themselves in negotiations because they do not understand how the images in question will be used. Instead, they allow clients to set prices and prefer to accept lower fees rather than lose sales. Unfortunately, those photographers who shortchange themselves are actually bringing down prices throughout the industry. Clients realize if they shop around they can find photographers willing to shoot assignments at very low rates.

There are ways to combat low prices, however. First, educate yourself about a client's line of work. This type of professionalism helps during negotiations because it shows buyers that you are serious about your work. The added knowledge also gives you an advantage when negotiating fees because photographers are not expected to understand a client's profession.

For example, if most of your clients are in the advertising field, acquire advertising rate cards for magazines so you know what a client pays for ad space. You can also find print ad rates in the Standard Rate and Data Service directory at the library. Knowing what a client is willing to pay for ad space and considering the importance of your image to the ad will give you a better idea of what the image is really worth to the client.

For editorial assignments, fees may be more difficult to negotiate because most magazines have set page rates. They may make exceptions, however, if you have experience or if the assignment is particularly difficult or time-consuming. If a magazine's page rate is still too low to meet your break-even price, consider asking for extra tearsheets and copies of the issue in which your work appears. These pieces can be used in your portfolio and as mailers, and the savings they represent in printing costs may make up for the discrepancy between the page rate and your break-even price.

There are still more ways to negotiate sales. Some clients, such as gift and paper product manufacturers, prefer to pay royalties each time a product is sold. Special markets, such as galleries and stock agencies, typically charge photographers a commission of 20 to 50 percent for displaying or representing their images. In these markets, payment on sales comes from the purchase of prints by gallery patrons, or from fees on the "rental" of photos by clients of stock agencies. Pricing formulas should be developed by looking at your costs and the current price levels in those markets, as well as on the basis of submission fees, commissions and other administrative costs charged to you.

Bidding for jobs

As you build your business, you will likely encounter another aspect of pricing and negotiating that can be very difficult. Like it or not, clients often ask photographers to supply bids for jobs. In some cases, the bidding process is merely procedural and the assignment will go to the photographer who can best complete it. In other instances, the photographer who submits the lowest bid will earn the job. When asked to submit a bid, it is imperative that you find out which bidding process is being used. Putting together an accurate estimate takes time, and you do not want to waste your efforts if your bid is being sought merely to meet some budget quota.

If you decide to bid on a job, it's important to consider your costs carefully. You do not want to bid too much on projects and repeatedly get turned down, but you also don't want to bid too low and forfeit income. When a potential client calls to ask for a bid, consider these dos and don'ts:

1. Always keep a list of questions by the telephone so you can refer to it when bids are requested. The answers to the questions should give you a solid understanding of the project and help you reach a price estimate.
2. Never quote a price during the initial conversation, even if the caller pushes for a "ballpark figure." An on-the-spot estimate can only hurt you in the negotiating process.
3. Immediately find out what the client intends to do with the photos, and ask who will own copyrights to the images after they are produced. It is important to note that many clients believe if they hire you for a job they'll own all the rights to the images you create. If they insist on buying all rights, make sure the price they pay is worth the complete loss of the images.
4. If it is an annual project, ask who completed the job last time, then contact that photographer to see what he or she charged.
5. Find out who you are bidding against and contact those people to make sure you received the same information about the job. While agreeing to charge the same price is illegal, sharing information about reaching a price is not.
6. Talk to photographers not bidding on the project and ask them what they would charge.
7. Finally, consider all aspects of the shoot, including preparation time, fees for assistants and stylists, rental equipment, and other materials costs. Don't leave anything out.

Pricing Information

For More Info

Where to find more information about pricing:

- *Pricing Photography: The Complete Guide to Assignment and Stock Prices* by Michal Heron and David MacTavish (Allworth Press).

- *ASMP Professional Business Practices in Photography* (Allworth Press).

- *fotoQuote*, a software package produced by the Cradoc Corporation, is a customizable, annually updated database of stock photo prices for markets from ad agencies to calendar companies. The software also includes negotiating advice and scripted telephone conversations. Call (800)679-0202, or visit www.fotoquote.com for ordering information.

- Stock Photo Price Calculator, a Web site that suggests fees for advertising, corporate and editorial stock, http://photographersindex.com/stockprice.htm.

- EP (Editorial Photographers), www.editorialphoto.com.

FIGURING SMALL BUSINESS TAXES

Whether you make occasional sales from your work or you derive your entire income from your photography skills, it's a good idea to consult with a tax professional. If you are just starting out, an accountant can give you solid advice about organizing your financial records. If you are an established professional, an accountant can double-check your system and maybe find a few extra deductions. When consulting with a tax professional, it is best to see someone who is familiar with the needs and concerns of small business people, particularly photographers. You can also conduct your own tax research by contacting the Internal Revenue Service.

Self-employment tax

As a freelancer it's important to be aware of tax rates on self-employment income. All income you receive over $400 without taxes being taken out by an employer qualifies as self-employment income. Normally, when you are employed by someone else, the employer shares responsibility for the taxes due. However, when you are self-employed, you must pay the entire amount yourself.

Freelancers frequently overlook self-employment taxes and fail to set aside a sufficient amount of money. They also tend to forget state and local taxes. If the volume of your photo sales reaches a point where it becomes a substantial percentage of your income, then you are required to pay estimated tax on a quarterly basis. This requires you to project the amount of money you expect to generate in a three-month period. However burdensome this may be in the short run, it works to your advantage in that you plan for and stay current with the various taxes you are required to pay. Read IRS publication #505 (Tax Withholding and Estimated Tax).

Deductions

Many deductions can be claimed by self-employed photographers. It's in your best interest to be aware of them. Examples of 100-percent-deductible claims include production costs of résumé, business cards and brochures; photographer's rep commissions; membership dues; costs of purchasing portfolio materials; education/business-related magazines and books; insurance; and legal and professional services.

Additional deductions can be taken if your office or studio is home-based. The catch here is that your work area must be used only on a professional basis; your office can't double as a family room after hours. The IRS also wants to see evidence that you use the work space on a regular basis via established business hours and proof that you've actively marketed your work. If you can satisfy these criteria, then a percentage of mortgage interests, real estate taxes, rent, maintenance costs, utilities and homeowner's insurance, plus office furniture and equipment, can be claimed on your tax form at year's end.

In the past, to qualify for a home-office deduction, the space you worked in had to be "the most important, consequential, or influential location" you used to conduct your business. This meant that if you had a separate studio location for shooting but did scheduling, billing and record keeping in your home office, you could not claim a deduction. However, as of 1999, your home office will qualify for a deduction if you "use it exclusively and regularly for administrative or management activities of your trade or business and you have no other fixed location where you conduct substantial administrative or management activities of your trade or business." Read IRS publication #587, Business Use of Your Home, for more details.

If you are working out of your home, keep separate records and bank accounts for personal and business finances, as well as a separate business phone. Since the IRS can audit tax records as far back as seven years, it's vital to keep all paperwork related to your business. This includes invoices, vouchers, expenditures and sales receipts, canceled checks, deposit slips, register tapes and business ledger entries for this period. The burden of proof will be on you if the IRS questions any deductions claimed. To maintain professional status in the eyes of the IRS, you will need to show a profit for three years out of a five-year period.

Tax Information

For More Info

To learn more about taxes, contact the IRS. There are free booklets available that provide specific information, such as allowable deductions and tax rate structure:

- Tax Guide for Small Businesses, #334
- Travel, Entertainment, Gift and Car Expenses, #463
- Tax Withholding and Estimated Tax, #505
- Business Expenses, #535
- Accounting Periods and Methods, #538
- Business Use of Your Home, #587

To order any of these booklets, phone the IRS at (800)829-3676. IRS forms and publications, as well as answers to questions and links to help, are available on the Internet at www.irs.gov.

Business Basics

Sales tax

Sales taxes are complicated and need special consideration. For instance, if you work in more than one state, use models or work with reps in one or more states, or work in one state and store equipment in another, you may be required to pay sales tax in each of the states that apply. In particular, if you work with an out-of-state stock photo agency that has clients over a wide geographic area, you should explore your tax liability with a tax professional.

As with all taxes, sales taxes must be reported and paid on a timely basis to avoid audits and/or penalties. In regard to sales tax, you should:

- Always register your business at the tax offices with jurisdiction in your city and state.
- Always charge and collect sales tax on the full amount of the invoice, unless an exemption applies.
- If an exemption applies because of resale, you must provide a copy of the customer's resale certificate.
- If an exemption applies because of other conditions, such as selling one-time reproduction rights or working for a tax-exempt, nonprofit organization, you must also provide documentation.

SELF-PROMOTION

There are basically three ways to acquaint photo buyers with your work: through the mail, over the Internet, or in person. No one way is better or more effective than another. They each serve an individual function and should be used in concert to increase your visibility and, with a little luck, your sales.

Self-promotion mailers

When you are just starting to get your name out there and want to begin generating assignments and stock sales, it's time to design a self-promotion campaign. This is your chance to do your best, most creative work and package it in an unforgettable way to get the attention of busy photo buyers. Self-promotions traditionally are sample images printed on card stock and sent through the mail to potential clients. If the image you choose is strong and you carefully target your mailing, a traditional self-promotion can work.

But don't be afraid to go out on a limb here. You want to show just how amazing and creative you are, and you want the photo buyer to hang onto your sample for as long as

Ideas for Great Self-Promotions

For More Info

Where to find ideas for great self-promotions:

- *HOW* magazine's self-promotion annual (October issue).
- *Self-Promotion Online* by Ilise Benun (North Light Books).
- *Photo District News* magazine's self-promotion issue (April).
- *The Photographer's Guide to Marketing & Self-Promotion* by Maria Piscopo (Allworth Press).
- *Marketing Guidebook for Photographers* by Mary Virginia Swanson, available at www.mvswanson.com or by calling (520)742-6311.

possible. Why not make it impossible to throw away? Instead of a simple postcard, maybe you could send a small, usable notepad with one of your images at the top, or a calendar the photo buyer can hang up and use all year. If you target your mailing carefully, this kind of special promotion needn't be expensive.

If you're worried that a single image can't do justice to your unique style, you have two options. One way to get multiple images in front of photo buyers without sending an overwhelming package is to design a campaign of promotions that builds from a single image to a small group of related photos. Make the images tell a story and indicate that there are more to follow. If you are computer savvy, the other way to showcase a sampling of your work is to point photo buyers to an online portfolio of your best work. Send a single sample that includes your Internet address, and ask buyers to take a look.

Web sites

Web sites are steadily becoming more important in the photographer's self-promotion repertory. If you have a good collection of digital photographs—whether they have been scanned from film or are from a digital camera—you should consider creating a Web site to showcase samples of your work, provide information about the type of work you do, and display your contact information. The Web site does not have to be elaborate or contain every photograph you've ever taken. In fact, it is best if you edit your work very carefully and choose only the best images to display on your Web site. The benefit of having a Web site is that it makes it so easy for photo buyers to see your work. You can send e-mails to targeted photo buyers and include a link to your Web site. Many photo buyers report that this is how they prefer to be contacted. Of course, your URL should also be included on any print materials, such as postcards, brochures, your business cards and stationery. Some photographers even include their URL in their credit line.

Portfolio presentations

Once you've actually made contact with potential buyers and piqued their interest, they'll want to see a larger selection of your work—your portfolio. Once again, there's more than one way to get this sampling of images in front of buyers. Portfolios can be digital—stored on a disk or CD-ROM, or posted on the Internet. They can take the form of a large box or binder and require a special visit and presentation by you. Or they can come in a small binder and be sent through the mail. Whichever way(s) you choose to showcase your best work, you should always have more than one portfolio, and each should be customized for potential clients.

Keep in mind that your portfolios should contain your best work (dupes only). Never put originals in anything that will be out of your hands for more than a few minutes. Also, don't include more than 20 images. If you try to show too many pieces you'll overwhelm the buyer, and any image that is less than your best will detract from the impact of your strongest work. Finally, be sure to show only work a buyer is likely to use. It won't do any good to show a shoe manufacturer your shots of farm animals or a clothing company your food pictures. For more detailed information on the various types of portfolios and how to select which photos to include and which ones to leave out, see *Photo Portfolio Success* by John Kaplan (Writer's Digest Books).

Do you need a résumé?

Some of the listings in this book say to submit a résumé with samples. If you are a freelancer, a résumé may not always be necessary. Sometimes a stock list or a list of your clients may suffice, and may be all the photo buyer is really looking for. If you do include a résumé, limit the details to your photographic experience and credits. If you are applying for a position teaching photography or for a full-time photography position at a studio, corporation, newspaper, etc., you will need the résumé. Galleries that want to show your work may also want to see a résumé, but, again, confine the details of your life to significant photographic achievements.

ORGANIZING AND LABELING YOUR IMAGES

It will be very difficult for you to make sales of your work if you aren't able to locate a particular image in your files when a buyer needs it. It is imperative that you find a way to organize your images—a way that can adapt to a growing file of images. There are probably as many ways to catalog photographs as there are photographers. However, most photographers begin by placing their photographs into large, general categories such as landscapes, wildlife, countries, cities, etc. They then break these down further into subcategories. If you specialize in a particular subject—birds, for instance—you may want to break the bird category down further into cardinal, eagle, robin, osprey, etc. Find a coding system that works for your particular set of photographs. For example, nature and travel photographer William Manning says, "I might have slide pages for Washington, DC (WDC), Kentucky (KY), or Italy (ITY). I divide my mammal subcategory into African wildlife (AWL), North American wildlife (NAW), zoo animals (ZOO)."

After you figure out a coding system that works for you, find a method for captioning your slides. Captions with complete information often prompt sales: Photo editors appreciate having as much information as possible. Always remember to include your name and copyright symbol © on each photo. Computer software can make this job a lot easier. Programs such as Emblazon (www.planettools.com), formerly CaptionWriter, allow photographers to easily create and print labels for their slides.

The computer also makes managing your photo files much easier. Programs such as FotoBiz (www.fotobiz.net) and StockView (www.hindsightltd.com) are popular with freelance assignment and stock photographers. FotoBiz has an image log and is capable of creating labels. FotoBiz can also track your images and allows you to create documents such as delivery memos, invoices, etc. StockView (www.hindsightltd.com/stockview/stoc kview.ht ml) also tracks your images, has labeling options, and can create business documents.

Image Organization and Storage

For More Info

To learn more about selecting, organizing, labeling and storing images, see:

- *The Photographer's Travel Guide* by William Manning (Writer's Digest Books).
- *Photo Portfolio Success* by John Kaplan (Writer's Digest Books).
- *Sell & Re-Sell Your Photos* by Rohn Engh, 5th edition (Writer's Digest Books).

PROTECTING YOUR COPYRIGHT

There is one major misconception about copyright: Many photographers don't realize that once you create a photo it becomes yours. You (or your heirs) own the copyright, regardless of whether you register it for the duration of your lifetime plus 70 years.

The fact that an image is automatically copyrighted does not mean that it shouldn't be registered. Quite the contrary. You cannot even file a copyright infringement suit until you've registered your work. Also, without timely registration of your images, you can only recover actual damages—money lost as a result of sales by the infringer plus any profits the infringer earned. For example, recovering $2,000 for an ad sale can be minimal when weighed against the expense of hiring a copyright attorney. Often this deters photographers from filing lawsuits if they haven't registered their work. They know that the attorney's fees will be more than the actual damages recovered, and, therefore, infringers go unpunished.

Registration allows you to recover certain damages to which you otherwise would not be legally entitled. For instance, attorney fees and court costs can be recovered. So too can statutory damages—awards based on how deliberate and harmful the infringement was. Statutory damages can run as high as $100,000. These are the fees that make registration so important.

In order to recover these fees, there are rules regarding registration that you must follow. The rules have to do with the timeliness of your registration in relation to the infringement:

- **Unpublished images** must be registered before the infringement takes place.
- **Published images** must be registered within three months of the first date of publication or before the infringement began.

The process of registering your work is simple. Contact the Register of Copyrights, Library of Congress, Washington, DC 20559, (202)707-9100, and ask for Form VA (works of visual art). Registration costs $30, but you can register photographs in large quantities for that fee. For bulk registration, your images must be organized under one title, for example, ''The works of John Photographer, 1990-1995.''

The copyright notice

Another way to protect your copyright is to mark each image with a copyright notice. This informs everyone reviewing your work that you own the copyright. It may seem basic, but in court this can be very important. In a lawsuit, one avenue of defense for an infringer is ''innocent infringement''—basically the ''I-didn't-know'' argument. By placing a copyright notice on your images, you negate this defense for an infringer.

The copyright notice basically consists of three elements: the symbol, the year of first publication, and the copyright holder's name. Here's an example of a copyright notice for an image published in 1999: © 1999 John Q. Photographer. Instead of the symbol ©, you can use the word ''Copyright'' or simply ''Copr.'' However, most foreign countries prefer © as a common designation.

Also consider adding the notation ''All rights reserved'' after your copyright notice. This phrase is not necessary in the U.S. since all rights are automatically reserved, but it is recommended in other parts of the world.

Know your rights

The digital era is making copyright protection more difficult. As this technology grows, more and more clients will want digital versions of your photos. Don't be alarmed, just be careful. Your clients don't want to steal your work. When you negotiate the usage of your work, consider adding a phrase to your contract that limits the rights of buyers who want digital versions of your photos. You might want them to guarantee that images will be removed from their computer files once the work appears in print. You might say it's okay to perform limited digital manipulation, and then specify what can be done. The important thing is to discuss what the client intends to do and spell it out in writing.

It's essential not only to know your rights under the Copyright Law, but also to make sure that every photo buyer you deal with understands them. The following list of typical image rights should help you in your dealings with clients:

- **One-time rights.** These photos are "leased" or "licensed" on a one-time basis; one fee is paid for one use.
- **First rights.** This is generally the same as purchase of one-time rights, though the photo buyer is paying a bit more for the privilege of being the first to use the image. He may use it only once unless other rights are negotiated.
- **Serial rights.** The photographer has sold the right to use the photo in a periodical. This shouldn't be confused with using the photo in "installments." Most magazines will want to be sure the photo won't be running in a competing publication.
- **Exclusive rights.** Exclusive rights guarantee the buyer's exclusive right to use the photo in his particular market or for a particular product. A greeting card company, for example, may purchase these rights to an image with the stipulation that it not be sold to a competing company for a certain time period. The photographer, however, may retain rights to sell the image to other markets. Conditions should always be put in writing to avoid any misunderstandings.
- **Electronic rights.** These rights allow a buyer to place your work on electronic media such as CD-ROMs or Web sites. Often these rights are requested with print rights.
- **Promotion rights.** Such rights allow a publisher to use a photo for promotion of a publication in which the photo appears. The photographer should be paid for promotional use in addition to the rights first sold to reproduce the image. Another form of this—agency promotion rights—is common among stock photo agencies. Likewise, the terms of this need to be negotiated separately.
- **Work for hire.** Under the Copyright Act of 1976, section 101, a "work for hire" is defined as: "(1) a work prepared by an employee within the scope of his or her employment; or (2) a work . . . specially ordered or commissioned for use as a contribution to a collective, as part of a motion picture or audiovisual work or as a supplementary work . . . if the parties expressly agree in a written instrument signed by them that the work shall be considered a work made for hire."

Protecting Your Copyright

For More Info

How to learn more about protecting your copyright:

- Call the Copyright Office at (202)707-3000 or check out their Web site, http://lcweb.loc.gov/copyright, for forms and answers to frequently asked questions.
- ASMP (American Society of Media Photographers), www.asmp.org/commerce/legal/copyright.
- EP (Editorial Photographers), www.editorialphoto.com.
- *Legal Guide for the Visual Artist* by Tad Crawford, Allworth Press.
- *SPAR* (Society of Photographers and Artists Representatives), (212)779-7464.

- **All rights.** This involves selling or assigning all rights to a photo for a specified period of time. This differs from work for hire, which always means the photographer permanently surrenders all rights to a photo and any claims to royalties or other future compensation. Terms for all rights—including time period of usage and compensation—should only be negotiated and confirmed in a written agreement with the client.

It is understandable for a client not to want a photo to appear in a competitor's ad. Skillful negotiation usually can result in an agreement between the photographer and the client that says the image(s) will not be sold to a competitor, but could be sold to other industries, possibly offering regional exclusivity for a stated time period.

Michelle Turner

*Shooting Fashionable
Destination Weddings*

© Critsey Rowe

by Donna Poehner

Fun. Funky. Fashionable. That is the declaration in the welcome paragraph of Michelle Turner's blog. Turner, the proprietor of a Maine-based photography business specializing in wedding and lifestyle portraiture has been in business since 2002. Her style *is* fun, funky, and fashionable. Her compositions are often bold and graphic; her use of color, unique and exciting; her camera angles, sometimes askew; her choice of locations and backgrounds, unorthodox. Looking at her wedding photographs is like looking at a fashion magazine spread.

Turner's career as a professional photographer began after college as she began photographing families and children, which she really enjoyed. "But," she says, "it wasn't until a friend asked me to photograph her wedding that I truly fell in love with the profession." Weddings make up 90 percent of Turner's business, and she has traveled to many locales outside and within the United States to photograph them. Turner also offers seminars to photographers who want to develop their wedding photography style and learn how to take great images even in the most unattractive of wedding venues. Here Turner gives us a view into her successful destination wedding photography business and how she's branching out.

To see Michelle Turner's wedding images, visit www.michelleturner.com. To learn about her seminars and to see images taken during her seminars, see www.michelleturnerseminars.com.

You categorize your business as a "boutique studio." What makes your studio a "boutique studio?"

The type of service that I offer my clients. From the hand-written notes, to the packaging, to the service on the day of the wedding, I try to offer a completely unique and luxurious experience to each of my clients.

How did your "fun, funky, fashionable" style develop?

My style is constantly evolving. I don't think I really became 'fun, funky, and fashionable,' though, until a few years ago when I stopped caring what the norm for wedding photography was, and I started doing my own thing.

What are modern couples looking for in a wedding photographer?

I think modern couples are looking for a bit of fashion to be incorporated into their shoot. At least in my experience, most of them don't want the standard portraits; rather, they want a combination of candids and interesting poses and/or environmental portraiture.

DONNA POEHNER is a writer and photographer who lives in Cincinnati, Ohio.

Do your wedding clients hire you primarily for your style?

Absolutely. I think my Web site clearly showcases my particular style. The slideshows that they see upon inquiry reinforce it, and by the time they are ready to book, my clients have a very clear understanding of how I approach a wedding.

How do you promote your wedding business?

I actually do very little advertising. Almost 100 percent of my business comes from vendor referrals or client referrals. I make sure that I treat my vendors well and my past clients even better. I am very attentive to the photographic needs of my vendors as well as those of the clients. For example, if a vendor just remodeled a certain area, I try to take shots that will showcase that area for them.

Tell me about the destination wedding part of your business. How did you get started in that?

I got started with destination weddings when a bridesmaid from a past wedding asked me to photograph her wedding abroad. I draw clients from all over the United States, although the majority tends to come from Chicago, New York, or Los Angeles. They find out about me through client referrals, vendor referrals, chat boards, and after seeing some of my published photographs. Destination weddings are a large part of my business. Out of the 40 weddings I shoot a year, 90 percent are actually destination weddings (weddings in which the couple is traveling to New England to have a destination wedding or weddings in which the couple is flying me out to shoot the wedding). Of those, 50 percent are outside of the country. We

Interviews with Pros

© Michelle Turner

This wedding photo, taken in a bar with natural light in Mexico, was a bit of a happy accident for photographer Michelle Turner. "I cropped in close in order to get rid of the distracting background," she says. "My original intention was to cut both of their faces in half, but I tripped the shutter while focusing on her eye. It was this accidental shot that I liked better than the original."

have traveled to a lot of different places to photograph weddings—Belize, Guatemala, several places in Mexico, and several destinations in the United States (Chicago, New York City, Aspen).

Do you work with a partner or assistant?

I work with a second shooter if my clients pay for it. I am equally comfortable shooting on my own or with a second photographer. I would say that half of my weddings I shoot by myself and the other half I have a second shooter.

What is your method for shooting a wedding?

For 95 percent of the day I am a documentary wedding photographer: I photograph the moments, unobtrusively, as they are happening. For the remaining five percent, I am heavily involved with setting up my clients. I tend to prompt rather than pose my clients. I will suggest to them that they walk along the beach or that they kiss by a certain set of rocks. However, if the light isn't hitting them right, or if I don't feel the scene looks as it should, I am not afraid to tell them to change.

Tell me a little about your post-processing. Do you do it yourself or does an employee do it?

I'm a bit of a control freak where my images are concerned, so I do all of my post-processing myself. The first pass is done in Lightroom, where I cull out the photographs and make minor color/brightness adjustments. Then I select a handful of my favorites and I work them up in Photoshop.

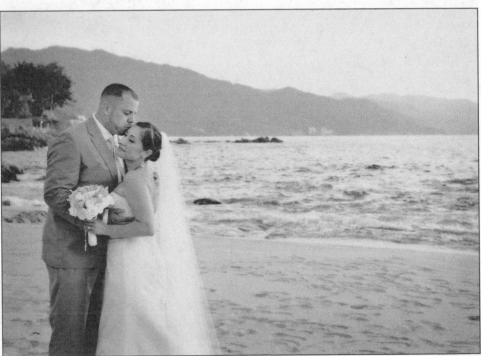

© Michelle Turner

This photo by Michelle Turner was taken on a beach in Conchas Chinas, Mexico. "I told them to cuddle into one another while I composed the photograph," she says. "They were stiff while looking at the camera, but wonderfully relaxed when they weren't, so this was a good 'pose' for this couple."

© Michelle Turner

Interviews with Pros

Michelle Turner seeks out unexpected locations for her wedding photography. This shot, she says ''was taken on the side of a Wal-Mart building during a destination wedding. I wanted to highlight the interesting outfit that she had chosen, and create an interesting juxtaposition between the clean white linen and the grungy, cracked wall.''

Do you have any tips for streamlining the wedding photography workflow?

Find what works for you. There is no one way to streamline your workflow. I experimented with several programs before I landed on Lightroom.

On your Web site you mention some actions and textures you like to use. How do your clients respond to the photographs you've created using these techniques? Do you find that the clients who hire you like a more artsy look than some other wedding photographers provide?

My clients love the look of those photographs, although realistically only about two or three percent of their photographs receive that kind of treatment. It's like anything—you can have too much of a good thing. I don't necessarily think that my image manipulation is more artsy than other photographers, but it does help me define my particular style, which sets me apart.

Could you describe your typical client?

My typical client places a high value on their wedding photographs. Most of them are willing to give me total artistic freedom during the wedding, and I have gotten to a point where they rarely second-guess my choice of locations (even when I choose to take their photographs in a back alley rather than in the park). I think this is because I tell them where some of the photographs on my Web site were taken. Sure, I have a lot of beach photographs, but there are also several in alleys, in front of painted plywood, and in parking garages.

Tell me about your seminars for photographers. How did you start doing them?

After having other photographers e-mail and ask for advice for years (on anything from choosing a location to post-processing), I finally decided to speak at my first convention—

the DWF (Digital Wedding Forum, www.digitalweddingforum.com) convention in Tampa this year. I had so many people come up to me after the session and ask me to do a multi-day workshop, that I started offering them.

You've written a book, *Wedding Photography Now*. How did this come about—how did you find your publisher, Ilex Press (or did they find you)?

I was actually called by the publisher and asked to write a book on contemporary wedding photography. They said they found me online, through a referral. They gave me complete freedom to include what I wanted. The only guidance they gave me was that the book had to be geared toward the advanced-beginner or intermediate photographer. Clients can read about it on my blog or Web site. It adds a bit of prestige.

Do you do portraits of children and families?

I do. I don't really advertise family/children portraits at this point, but I do approximately 30 portrait sessions a year. I plan to add a portrait section to my Web site in the near future, but at this point I don't plan to take on any more portrait sessions than I am currently photographing.

What are some of the challenges of balancing work (as a wedding photographer) and family?

I think the hardest part of balancing wedding photography and my family is the weekend commitment. It is really difficult for me to attend my children's weekend soccer games and family reunions. Of course, during the week I have total scheduling freedom, which is nice!

What is the best thing about being a wedding photographer?

The thing I like best about being a wedding photographer is the fact that every wedding is different, and every couple is unique!

Eric Engbretson

A True Passion for Underwater Photography

© Eric Engbretson

by Lynn Haller

Having trouble getting a sharp image or good lighting? Try photographing underwater—that's what Eric Engbretson does six months out of the year; since 1993, he's been photographing freshwater wildlife for his business, Engbretson Underwater Photography (www.underwaterfishphotos.com). His work has been featured extensively in fishing publications, as well as calendars, posters, advertising—even interpretive displays. Here Engbretson discusses how he turned a life-long interest in underwater wildlife and fishing into a profitable photography business.

How did you get started in underwater photography? What was your biggest motivator—love of marine life, love of scuba diving, or love of photography?

I'd say it was a combination of my love for fish and a burning desire to get out of the career I was in at the time so that I could spend my time doing something that wouldn't seem like work.

When I was growing up, my father had several aquariums in the house. I remember staring into them for hours watching the fish and imagining what it would be like to be in the tank with them. Later, I became an avid fisherman—and what fisherman doesn't wonder what it all looks like down there? When I moved to a home on a lake in northern Wisconsin in 1990, I began snorkeling and got my first glimpse into the underwater world. It was fantastic! I wanted to share the amazing world I was seeing, so I started taking pictures with a $10 underwater camera. The pictures were dreadful. One day, quite by accident, I discovered that magazines actually pay for pictures they use. It occurred to me that if I could get some really good shots of the fish I encountered, they would probably be well received by fishing magazines. I bought a better camera, and I sold my first fish picture about a year later in 1994.

Once I started to make a little money at it, it occurred to me that it might be possible to make a living at it. The idea of working for myself and not answering to a boss really appealed to me. I was working in broadcasting at the time as a rock-n-roll radio DJ and was basically burned out and looking for another career. The idea of getting paid to do something you

---

LYNN HALLER is a literary agent for The Salkind Agency (a subsidiary of Studio B Productions), a nonfiction literary agent specializing in working with authors of computer books. As former acquisitions editor for HOW Books, she acquired and edited a wide variety of graphic design books and featured the work of or collaborated with hundreds of designers around the world. She is author or co-author of six books about design, the latest of which is *Design Secrets: Products 2* (Rockport). She is also an amateur photographer who goes by the moniker carrienation on Flickr.

really love, something that's really fun, was seductive. But it took a very long time to get to this point. In the beginning, I took pictures on weekends and after work and whenever else I had free time. I worked at other non-photography jobs in those days, gradually working less and less as the years went by and devoting more and more time to my photography. I dreamed of a day when I could just take pictures and I wouldn't need any other job to pay the bills. Eventually, after many years, I was just working weekends in my regular job and taking pictures during the week. Finally, I got to a point where I was able to make enough money with the pictures that I didn't need to have a regular job.

What resources did you find most valuable when you were just starting to learn about this kind of photography?

I bought many books on stock photography and underwater photography and I read as much as I could. I subscribed to a few photo magazines as well. One of the key resources in those early days was *Photographer's Market*. It was a great starting point and I learned a great deal about *how* editors want to receive submissions. I bought *Photographer's Market* every year for about 10 years. Then, I began to assemble my own target market list. Using the Internet, I was able to research and find out what magazines might be interested in the kind of material I was generating. I also subscribed to a few market newsletters, like the *Guilfoyle Report*. It was great because it listed markets that were actively seeking pictures. I knew there were hundreds of markets that might buy my pictures so I was very interested in any publications or services that could put me in direct contact with the buyers, whoever they were.

I still think today that picture sellers and buyers have a hard time connecting with each other. The Internet has certainly made things easier, but my sense is that some really good work is going unpublished. This is because when it comes to specialized subjects, photogra-

© Eric Engbretson, www.underwaterfishphotos.com.

One of his newer photos, this shot of a muskellunge by Eric Engbretson sold to a magazine soon after it was taken and will be published in early 2009. Engbretson always shoots fish from below. "I've found that this angle really makes a fish look more imposing," he says. He also shoots most of his underwater subjects from about two feet away, but had a little more distance on this musky since it's such a large fish.

phers don't know who's looking for a picture and buyers don't always know where they can buy a picture they need.

What was your first big break when starting your business, and how did you get it?

I don't know if I can point to a single big break. There have certainly been some milestones along the way that told me things were going well. If I were pressed, I would point to my first sale, my first sale in a really large national magazine, and my first cover shot.

Something else that stands out is the first time I was approached by an ad agency. There's a startling difference between advertising and editorial photos when it comes to revenue. But again, there doesn't seem to be a really good system in place to marry the picture buyers with the shooters. I think anyone who can get into that loop will do very well.

Perhaps my biggest break overall was the explosion of the Internet. Seemingly overnight, it became possible not only to communicate with virtually every single picture buyer and but also to send images electronically using FTP servers. This made reaching buyers easier, faster and cheaper than ever.

What would you say are the unique challenges of shooting underwater, as opposed to other kinds of photography?

Conditions underwater are hostile to a photographer. The lakes and rivers where I shoot are generally very cold. Currents can be strong and visibility is always an issue. Underwater photography is inherently tricky. Water is 800 times thicker than air, and there are always particles, algae and other obstacles floating around, so you're never going to get the really clean look you can get by shooting through air. Besides that, the fish can be

© Eric Engbretson, www.underwaterfishphotos.com.

This bass image is a consistent seller for Eric Engbretson, having appeared in magazines and calendars numerous times demonstrating that "a single image can provide a substantial income over the course of its lifetime by selling and reselling," he says.

Interviews with Pros

elusive, and you've got to be concerned about your air supply, so there's a lot to think about. The light underwater is poor too, so I often have to carry bulky underwater strobes to illuminate subjects in deeper water. Then there's finding the fish. Sometimes that can be hard too. If you can imagine taking photos above-ground on a dark, cold, foggy, and windy day, then you know something about the everyday conditions of my underwater working environment.

What makes one of your images especially saleable?

Most of the picture buyers I've worked with like photos of fish doing something or other. A picture of a fish eating another fish will always sell. Schools of fish are also popular. Pictures of fish spawning or guarding their young usually do well. Portraits can sell well too if they do a good job of showing fish in their actual habitat. It's also good to have several elements in the frame like underwater plants, rocks, and trees. People like seeing what's down there, so including as many elements from the underwater habitat as possible almost always makes for interesting and saleable pictures. Other highly saleable pictures depict rare, threatened, or endangered species. Or they just show species that are hard to photograph in their natural habitat, like lampreys, American eels, and sturgeon. Finally, photos of exceptionally large and healthy individual fish are very popular and sell rather easily.

What percentage of your business is editorial, shot to order, and what percentage of your business is stock? Is selling your art framed a substantial amount of your business yet?

I haven't done any assignment photography or shoot-to-order work. I'd say about 75 percent of my business is editorial or magazine and book photography, and the remaining 25 percent

Interviews with Pros

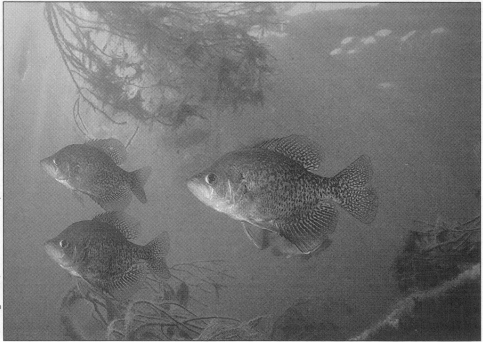

© Eric Engbretson, www.underwaterfishphotos.com.

Eric Engbretson says schools of fish, like this group of crappie, are popular with his buyers. Also good sellers are photos featuring a fish eating another fish, fish spawning, or fish guarding their young. "Most of the picture buyers I've worked with like photos of fish doing something or other," he says.

© Eric Engbretson, www.underwaterfishphotos.com.

This portrait of a brown trout is a steady seller for Eric Engbretson. "Portraits can sell well if they do a good job of showing fish in their actual habitat," he says. "It's also good to have several elements in the frame like underwater plants, rocks, and trees."

goes to things like calendars, reports, interpretive displays, catalogs, Web sites, advertising, and promotional material. I also work with several stock photo agencies that market and sell images for me at the standard 50-percent commission.

How much of your business consists of clients coming to you, and how much of it is you going to clients? In the first case, explain how clients find you; in the second case, how do you find and market yourself to new clients?

About 25 to 30 percent of my business comes from clients who contact me. They reach me through my Web site. These clients are unknown to me initially and they typically include ad and design firms, small groups, or government agencies. About 75 percent of my business comes from regular markets I've developed a relationship with over the years. I usually stay in close contact with these clients to see what they have coming up and what their picture needs are. They also tend to contact me if they need anything. I can't emphasize enough the importance of these working relationships. One piece of advice I'd really stress to new photographers is that these relationships *mean everything*. Concentrate on building relationships and the sales will take care of themselves. When I started out, my attitude was something like, "Who can I sell to?" But once I changed my mantra to, "Who can I be of service to?" it made all the difference in the world. Don't get me wrong: it's still a business and the goal is earning money, but I've found that if you put your own goals aside and focus more on service and helping your clients with their needs, you'll notice dramatic results.

A few times a year, I spend several days doing research on the Internet to identify new markets that might be interested in my specialty. I add them to my target list and usually approach them with a simple e-mail and some samples of my pictures. They don't always respond, but I keep them on my list and come back to them. Every year I'm able to turn a few of the ones who ignored me into new customers. One thing I'd like to point out is that you don't need a lot of clients. My target list has fewer than 300 clients. And only about a third buy from me every year. Admittedly, my specialty isn't going to appeal to a large number of picture buyers, but my point is that if your goal is to make, say, $70,000 a year, that means you only need to sell $700 worth of pictures to 100 clients. A friend of mine has an ad agency, and he makes a great living by super-serving just 12 clients. He says if he took on any more, he wouldn't have the time he needs to devote to each one. I think this is an interesting idea of less being more. So, basically, if you're doing a good job servicing your clients, and building those relationships, you absolutely don't need thousands of clients.

Your Web site says you spend several months of the year shooting; how do you arrange your schedule to maximize your shooting time, and what do you do in the off-season, when it's too cold to shoot?

Since I don't do any photography under the ice, the off season for me is wintertime. I don't do any shooting from November through March, but that doesn't mean I'm not busy. Since magazines typically work six months ahead, winter is the time when they are working on spring fishing articles and looking for pictures. So my office gets very busy during the winter. It's all indoor work, handling submissions and doing the actual selling and marketing. From May through October, I'm shooting under water almost every day, but clearly all the money is made in the office, not in the field. In the warmer months, I'm still talking to clients and selling pictures, but I don't usually initiate contact during that time of year.

What advice would you give anyone who wants to start out in setting up an underwater photography business?

There's always room for more good photographers, and I think interest in underwater subjects will continue. I'd encourage beginners to learn about their subjects. Become an expert on the life and behavior of your animal subjects. Become a steward of their habitat. Think of yourself as a PR person for those particular animals. If you do this, you'll show them in the best light, you'll be mindful of disturbing them, and your work will automatically show these creatures at their most magnificent. Don't just sell pictures. Instead, fall in love with your subjects and sell that love. And instead of exploiting your subjects for personal profit, you'll become partners with them by calling attention to their inherent beauty, their value in the ecosystem, and the special problems each one of them faces in an increasingly crowded world.

Where do you want to take your business next? Any types of projects that you haven't done yet that you hope to do?

I honestly don't think about that much. I see how miserable other people are at their daily jobs, and I still remember what it was like to work that way. I'm thankful and appreciative for what I have and the niche I've carved out. I guess my only goals are to be able to get up tomorrow morning and do the same thing all over again. For people lucky enough to have a career that brings them genuine joy, it's indescribable. You'd do it for free because you're so passionate about it. It's like being on vacation every day. When there's no distinction between work and play, you know you're there. What more could anyone want?

Charles Needle

Capturing Nature with Heart,
Sensitivity & Unique Vision

© Ruth Hoyt

by Deb Heneghan

As a professional fine art and editorial nature photographer and writer, Charles Needle finds beauty in all his photography subjects, whether they are in the wild or a man-made garden. He has always felt connected to nature and feels most creative and inspired when outdoors. "If you approach your subjects with an open mind and an open heart, gifts appear and subjects find you, rather than the other way around." He has carved his niche teaching workshops and classes on flower photography at botanical gardens. His unique approach to photography encompasses the healing effect of nature's photos—both for the photographer and the observer.

"It is important for me to feel in tune with my subjects, whether they are landscapes, animals, plants, flowers, people, or architecture," he says. "Before I pick up my camera I immerse myself in the environment and study the subtleties of light. I try to awaken all my senses by practicing a silent mini-meditation. Unless you truly know your subject and are open to receiving its gifts, then I believe it's difficult to fully capture the essence of a particular subject."

Connecting with nature and nature photography were a big part of Needle's recovery from Chronic Fatigue Syndrome. "I now view my illness as a gift, because it literally forced me to slow down and notice the beauty in small things," says Needle. "I was almost bed-ridden for a year, and during that time, I surrounded myself with as much nature as possible, either sitting beside a window or studying nature photography. As I became stronger physically, I ventured outdoors with my camera and discovered the magic of close-up/macro photography in my own backyard. Wearing knee-pads, crawling on the ground, I soon realized that some of the best images and most elegant beauty were right in my own backyard.

"During my recovery, I came across several scientific studies that had proven how views of nature—both real and simulated in the form of photographs or paintings—in hospital settings could help improve patient outcomes and boost staff morale," he says "One study showed that patients whose rooms overlooked a courtyard window view recovered faster from surgery, took less pain medication, and left the hospital sooner than patients whose hospital rooms overlooked brick walls or parking lots. I began researching this idea further and found a few photographers who were marketing their work to hospitals. Some had unique, high-tech ideas like backlit ceiling transparencies, large wall murals, and simulated backlit windows that changed from darkness to light, according to the time of day, for patients in intensive-care units.

"I did manage to sell some of my work to hospitals and tried marketing backlit windows,

---

DEB HENEGHAN is a freelance writer and photographer based in Madison, Wisconsin.

but that is a tough market," he says. "You have to convince hospitals to purchase high-end artwork when their budgets typically allow for poster art. Much of it also depends on cultivating contacts with interior designers and other decision-makers within the healthcare setting, which is not always easy."

So Needle began giving his slide show presentation, "The Healing Power of Nature," in local hospitals, senior centers, and nursing homes. He attended holistic healthcare practitioner conferences where he would show his multi-image nature slide show with two carousel projectors, a dissolve unit, and sound system. People were so moved by the music and visual imagery that they started asking for video and DVD versions. He also has worked with cancer patients, their families, and caregivers, helping them see beauty through the viewfinder as art therapy.

Then Bernie Siegel, nationally known doctor, pioneer in mind-body medicine, and author of numerous books, including *Love, Medicine & Miracles*, saw Needle's multi-image program. He so believed in the healing power of Needle's presentation, that he offered to endorse him and encouraged him to market his program in airports, hotels, and other public places.

These days most of Needle's income comes from teaching workshops and classes. He teaches beginning and advanced flower photography classes twice a year at the Atlanta Botanical Garden, which manages the promotion and registration. Other garden locations such as Callaway Gardens in Pine Mountain, Ga. or the Bellevue Botanical Garden in Seattle do not handle promotions or registrations.

"It's a nice balance for me having both, because it frees me from having to do all of the marketing myself," says Needle. "However, while I generate more profit on workshops I

© Charles Needle

Photographer Charles Needle holds workshops in his backyard "Garden Studio" just north of Atlanta, Georgia. "I offer one-day classes in the spring and early fall, as well as a five-day 'Creative Macro Intensive' workshop in late May for those photographers who want to immerse themselves into the exciting world of creative close-up photography," he says. "My yard features a multitude of colorful annuals and perennials, as well as a 15-foot waterfall. You can see numerous 'props,' including old wooden window frames and fencing that I like to incorporate into some of my photographs and several potted plants that you can move around to control backgrounds, lighting, depth of field, etc."

promote myself, I also need to factor in costs for classroom space rental and any food and beverage minimums when calculating tuition. Plus, handling all the logistics requires being extremely organized and focused. It takes at least a year to organize a workshop that includes coordinating the registrations, curriculum development, and handout materials. Currently, I'm in the process of looking for a part-time office manager to help with some of the workshop planning.''

One of Needle's current opportunities developed through a friend who teaches painting. ''He told me about a Florida-based company that offers workshops in Monet's Garden with private access without any tourists. I approached them and asked if I could teach some photography workshops, and they were delighted,'' says Needle.

''I like to give lots of one-on-one instruction, and public gardens offer a wide variety of subject matter in a small, concentrated space. There's usually plenty of room for everyone to spread out and discover their own corner of beauty. Private gardens are unique and usually more intimate and typically offer something special for my students. My favorite garden is my own, since it was designed specifically with photography in mind,'' says Needle. ''I have many potted plants that can be moved around for background color. Usually, you cannot do this in a public garden, which limits the creative possibilities.''

His backyard garden studio features a 15-foot waterfall surrounded by colorful annuals and perennials, and various macro photography props, including colored papers, Mylar, stained glass, and old wooden window frames and fencing. Needle encourages nature photographers who want to further their macro and flower photography skills to shoot in local public and private gardens for the experience.

Needle sells products at his workshops including macro photography accessories such as lamps, flash brackets, close-up lenses, reflectors, diffusers, small spray bottles, right-angle

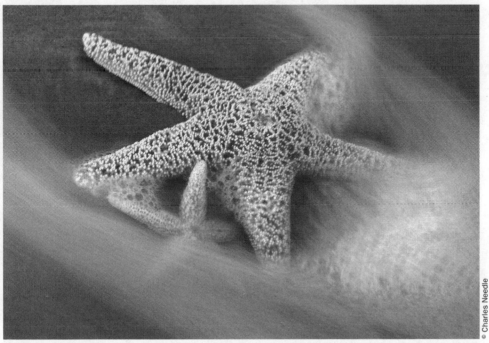

© Charles Needle

Charles Needle's image entitled ''Starcrossed Lovers'' was taken on the beach at Hilton Head Island, South Carolina, using a two-second exposure to create the soft swirl of ocean water. ''I had to work very quickly to keep my tripod legs from sinking into the already-moist sand,'' he says. ''Right after I clicked the shutter, a huge wave came crashing and caused the two starfish to separate and wash ashore!''

Interviews with Pros

viewfinders, and multi-colored flashlights. Additional income come from fine art print sales and specialty product sales including his "Healing Power of Nature" DVD, various macro photography equipment accessories, and his new eBook, entitled *Creative Macro Photography: Professional Tips & Techniques*.

In terms of his philosophy as a photographer, "I think of the camera as a 'magic box' that allows me to create whatever I envision—truly a metaphor for life and living," says Needle. "I always remind my students that photography is 'painting with light.' My particular interest is in more abstract, impressionistic nature photography that's created via camera movement techniques, multiple exposures, and montaging two or more images."

To promote his work and his workshops, Needles relies on his own Web site and others. "The Internet has helped establish my credibility and create a presence among other working professionals more than anything else," he says. "Prospective workshop students have found me by conducting Internet searches, and I have made a few product sales online. Having my workshops listed on sites such as Shaw Guides and Outdoor Photographer magazine also has directed traffic to my site. In addition, having an online gallery of images in conjunction with my REI outdoor gear and clothing store exhibits generated income that might not have occurred. I'm planning to implement a more automated payment method for course registrations in the future, and the Internet will also help make that run more efficiently."

Several years ago, Needle switched from film to digital. "When I am teaching, I like to emphasize that making great images requires a good eye, mind, and heart—and that it's not about the technology. Digital is just another means of capturing a personal vision. It is a

© Charles Needle

"I call this one 'River of Blue.' It was taken this past spring at Keukenhof Garden in Lisse, Holland (about an hour south of Amsterdam) at the peak of tulip bloom (during a rainstorm!)," says Charles Needle. "The foreground color is created by thousands of blue hyacinth, all planted around the daffodil and tulip bulbs." Needle will be teaching a workshop at Keukenhof in April 2010. "Truly, it's an amazing place," he says. "Thousands of absolutely picture-perfect bulbs with rich, saturated colors—and not a weed or brown flower petal to be found anywhere in the place!"

wonderful teaching tool, because it allows students to immediately see and correct problems in exposure, lighting or composition.

"The potential downside I see as a photography instructor, however, is that digital can cause some photographers to be complacent and lazy—thinking it can all be fixed later in PhotoShop," continues Needle. "In terms of overall image quality, I don't see much difference between film and digital. Much depends on one's skill level in post-production. I do think film can still be a valuable creative tool for those who wish to explore techniques such as slide montages."

He confesses: "My Nikon F4 is still in one of my camera bags, and I keep a freezer in my garage full of bricks of Fujichrome Velvia transparency film! While I haven't shot film in three years, I suppose it's my security blanket!"

Needle has donated framed prints and "Healing Power of Nature" DVDs to local charities such as The Wellness Community-Atlanta Northside and Visiting Nurses/Hospice in Atlanta. He donates a portion of his profits from teaching workshops at the Georgia Aquarium back to the aquarium, and he gives a scholarship donation to the North American Nature Photography Association (NANPA) annually. He also gives his time to NANPA's annual "Pro for the Day" summit, working in the field and classroom with high school scholarship program students who are budding nature photographers.

Needle finds being a charter member of NANPA is an extremely valuable networking resource. He also is a member of several local camera clubs, which also helps promote his workshops via their respective Web sites and through regular pro-bono speaking engagements and photo contest judging opportunities."

He also belongs to the Sierra Club, Wilderness Society, and Nature Conservancy. "Because I shoot for fine art purposes, membership in these groups does not really add to my credibility because I don't advertise that I'm a member to potential clients," he says.

Needle won the 2008 Nature's Best magazine Backyards Photo Contest with four of his images. His work has been featured on the cover of *The Loupe* magazine and in *Outdoor Photographer* magazine, *SELF* magazine, *Woman's World*, *The Chicago Tribune*, and *The Atlanta Journal-Constitution*.

Patience and persistence, he says, are two of the most important ingredients for success. "Create a realistic marketing plan, stay focused and don't give up. It takes time to cultivate client contacts and receive name recognition. Don't be surprised if it takes several years to begin turning a profit. In order to maximize your earning potential, choose multiple income streams such as print sales, products, teaching, licensing of images, and so on. It can also be a challenge trying to balance time in the office with time in the field. Professional nature photographer and author John Shaw once said to remember you're not making money in the field. He also said 'Don't quit your day job!'"

INTERVIEWS WITH PROS

Steve Ahrens

Creating Unforgettable Portraits
with North Light

© Steve Ahrens

by Donna Poehner

Steve Ahrens, M.Photog.Cr., of Ahrens Photography in Fond du Lac, Wisconsin, learned a lot about the craft of photography while growing up in the family business. However, he credits PPA (Professional Photographers of America, www.ppa.com) with helping him become the skilled photographer and successful studio proprietor he is today. Through the training and education offered by PPA, Ahrens has become a Master photographer, adept at creating professional portraits: beautifully composed, skillfully lit, and flattering to the subject.

Over the years, Ahrens has won numerous awards for excellence in his craft. In 2008 he was one of six photographers chosen as PPA's Diamond Photographers of the Year—their highest honor. He was also named Wisconsin Photographer of the Year for both 2007 and 2008—which he proudly heralds on the home page of his Web site (www.theahrensimage.com). In addition, Ahrens had the honor of being the only member of the Wisconsin Professional Photographer Association to have two scores of 100 awarded to the same photographer within the same print competition. In 2006, Ahrens won Kodak's Gallery Elite Award for a portrait of one of his clients. According to the Kodak judges, "it rivaled Rembrandt and was worthy of hanging in any museum."

Winning these awards is, of course, an honor for Ahrens, but it goes beyond that. He feels that striving to attain excellence through winning print competitions motivates him to improve his photography on a daily basis as he creates portraits for his clients in his studio. "It's always in the back of your mind," he says, "that maybe this is an image I can use for competition." He also thinks that people do recognize the importance of the awards, and they add prestige to his business. "People like to be associated with the winner," he says.

Fond du Lac has a population of 45,000, and with the smaller communities around it, Ahrens has a population of 60,000 to 70,000 from which to draw his clients. Ahrens says his studio doesn't have a "typical client." While most photography studios establish themselves as either a high-volume or a high-end studio, Ahrens Photography is a hybrid. Ahrens takes care of the high-end clients himself—the high school seniors, children, and families who are looking for something a little different. He employs two additional photographers and keeps them busy with the lower-end business—undergraduates, daycares, nursery schools.

Even with these high-volume clients, though, Ahrens tries to retain that high-end look and give the client more than they were expecting. "Go the extra mile to make sure the prints

DONNA POEHNER is a writer and photographer who lives in Cincinnati, Ohio.

look that much better so that people are more apt to order—which they tend to do. You won't look like you're a run-of-the-mill school photographer," he says. His staff photographers also service what he calls his medium market—family programs where the clients come in on a regular basis. Ahrens also employs a custom framer and three employees who answer the phone and process orders.

NORTH LIGHT STUDIO

Ahrens describes his style as "updated traditional." He is very excited about his north light studio—a large camera room with a bank of windows that fill the room with natural, north light, which is very flattering. Instead of *creating* a lighting pattern with strobes, Ahrens *looks for* the lighting pattern in the light coming from the windows. He still has to meter, of course, but he doesn't have to worry about flash and irritating those people whose eyes are sensitive to it. "The north light room has developed into the camera room I really want to use because it is so simple. What you see, is what you get," he says. When Ahrens first started using the north light room, clients were not familiar with the style, and so he had to educate them a bit. "But now, it's my style," he says, "so that is what people are expecting." And while Ahrens Photography still uses strobes for its high-volume work—preschools, undergraduate, sports, etc.—99 percent of their portraits are made in the north light room, including many of his award-winning photographs.

In addition to the north light from the windows, a rip-stop nylon reflector stands on the shadow side of the subject. Ahrens uses a 30-by-40 inch kicker on the highlight side,

© Steve Ahrens

This portrait of a high school senior is part of Ahrens Photography's "Eclectic" series. "After the image was photographed, textures and graphic elements were added in PhotoShop," Steve Ahrens says. Ahrens shoots high-end clients like seniors himself, and employs two additional photographers to take care of the lower-end business like undergraduates, daycares, and nursery schools. To see more examples of senior portraits, visit www.theahrensimage.com.

Interviews with Pros

which an assistant hand-holds to get light into the subject's eyes. "For high school seniors or families that added kicker just gives a little extra spark. At first we just used the window light, and then over the years we added the kicker reflector and subtractive lighting on the background as well as on the subject. We use large 4-by-8 foot insulation boards that can be used as gobos, but also have a shiny side for reflecting. So they can be used to reduce light on the background, or they can reshape the windows, by making them smaller and creating more contrasty and dramatic lighting. This works better for seniors who can sit still for longer periods of time. But for children it's easier to use the open window because they move around so much."

Using an assistant in the studio is key, Ahrens says, especially when photographing a child. "If you need a special pose, and the child moves—the assistant can help to get them back into that basic pose, so you can stay focused and talking to the child, getting their expression." Assistants can also help with props, backgrounds and holding reflectors.

Ahrens has a lot of experience working with children and has some useful advice. First of all, talk to the parents ahead of time and advise them not to pump the child to smile by saying "cheese" or "smile." "Parents may come into the camera room thinking they have to have a big smile, but once they start looking at the images in the sales appointment, they go with something that has more feeling. Without a big smile, the eyes are open a little bit more. I don't go for the big smile, just a hint of a smile or a little bit of a serious expression—it has more of a lasting quality. I think you tire of the big smile over time, when the portrait is on the wall."

Also, it helps to have an assistant or parent nearby when shooting, especially with younger kids. Make sure the child is being photographed at a time of day that is good for the child. For example, you don't want a baby to be hungry or tired. "It's hard to get a serious expression from a child you've gotten all riled up, so start the session with a serious pose and expression," says Ahrens. Some of the best expressions, he says, come toward the end of the session, when the child is getting tired.

© Steve Ahrens

This image titled "Read All About It!" was created as part of a display to benefit Operation Smile (www.operationsmile.org). "As new images are created they are added to the display via an unveiling we hold at local banks, art galleries or wherever we can display the images," says Steve Ahrens. "Our goal is to introduce four new images at each unveiling." Ahrens believes events like this are definitely a win-win situation for the photographer and the charity, and help to build a positive image for the photographer in the community.

SALES & MARKETING

Most portrait photographers know that projecting their images (on a screen or a wall) during the sales appointment generally leads to bigger sales. Ahrens Photography has been projecting their images since the 1980s, long before digital. At that time, they had slides made from their film, and they used a slide projector synched to music on cassette tapes so their clients could view a touching presentation of their "proofs."

Today, Ahrens Photography still uses projection in the sales room but of course the process is now all digital. They project images onto a 4-by-8-foot frame hung on the wall and with the use of special software Ahrens' clients can see their images projected in the various print sizes available. Projecting, says Ahrens, boosts the sales number: "It takes people up at least one size," he says. Those who started out thinking they wanted to order an 11-by-14 print, might now order a 16-by-20 or even a 20-by-24.

When it comes to ordering large wall portraits, Ahrens' clients have a few things to take into consideration. Cost, of course, is a factor, but also the available space they have in their home to hang the portrait. "There are not a lot of huge homes in this area," says Ahrens. Typically, the client will order a 24-by-30-inch print of a family; a 16-by-20-inch print of a child; and a 20-by-24-inch print of a group of children. "Some order bigger if they have a bigger home and the income to go along with it." But what is most important to Ahrens is repeat business, so he doesn't feel the need to sell a huge wall portrait to a family if that means they are not going to come back next year or the year after that to have another portrait made.

Ahrens says it is crucial to market to the right people—those you want coming through your studio doors—or else you are wasting your marketing dollar. He does a lot of direct mail, and says that it works for certain things, such as high school seniors. But it is getting harder to snag those clients through direct mail since they are inundated with mail from many photographers. Ahrens sees all marketing as an ongoing effort—you can't just send out one promo piece and leave it at that. "People have to see your name out there," he says.

© Steve Ahrens

"River Princess," like other Ahrens Photography images created for a display to benefit Operation Smile, features a child who was helped by the organization. "Operation Smile volunteers perform surgeries on children who have facial deformities like cleft lip or palate. The surgeries are performed free of charge to the families with these children," explains Ahrens. "Our goal with the display is to inform people about Operation Smile and the work that they do. To date, we have raised enough money through the display to cover the surgeries of nearly nine children who were born with facial deformities."

Displaying your portrait work in malls and other public places is a good way to get your name (and images) in front of potential clients. You can also do a third-party promotion—hook up with other businesses that sell products that appeal to your clients. Ahrens, for example, has had success partnering with a car dealership. The car dealership gives the client a gift certificate to Ahrens Photography where they'll receive a discount on a portrait session.

Ahrens is particularly pleased with a special project he did that combines marketing with benefiting a worthwhile charity. Operation Smile is an organization whose volunteer medical professionals repair childhood facial deformities throughout the world. Ahrens held an event to raise money for the organization. He held a wine-and-cheese party at a local bank after hours, and there unveiled wall portraits he had done of some children who had benefited from the surgery. Anyone who donated $240 to Operation Smile received a $100 gift card to Ahrens Photography. Ahrens believes events like this are definitely a win-win situation for the photographer and the charity, and help to build a positive image for the photographer in the community.

In the end, Ahrens believes, you're marketing all the time, in everything you do. "You're educating the customer," he says. "When people call—it's how you answer the telephone and the types of things you say to them. You have to let them know what is unique about your business, you have to promote that or market that or tell the people about that. We do that with our north light studio because that is what is unique about us."

RUNNING A SUCCESSFUL STUDIO

If you want to run a successful portrait business, Ahrens says you first have to learn the photography skills, of course. Being involved in PPA at the state and regional level helped him greatly when he was first learning. "Local groups are really important. Work on the print crew," he says. If your city hosts a PPA convention, volunteer to be a host and pick the speakers up at the airport—this gives you the opportunity to have a private audience with them to pick their brains. Entering print competitions helps you develop your style, and then people come to recognize your style and work—including other photographers with whom you can develop friendships and from whom you can continue to learn.

But, as every successful photographer knows, photography skills are not enough to keep a business alive and thriving. Business skills are just as important. "If you don't know how to do something, find people who can help you," says Ahrens. Also, keep regular business hours, even if you are just starting out and only running your business on a part-time basis. He also believes that customer service is vital: If you promise something, you have to deliver.

Gerry Lemmo

Capturing the Nuances of the Natural World

© Lynne Lemmo

by Deb Heneghan

As a young child growing up alongside a major highway in the suburbs of New York City, Gerry Lemmo first came in contact with nature by lifting up rocks in his backyard. His fascination observing ants, beetles, and other tiny creatures he uncovered sparked a lifelong obsession with the natural sciences. As a teen, Lemmo joined an entomology club and went on summer field trips to places like Arizona and the U.S. Virgin Islands. "While my hunger to travel began with my fascination with insects, my interest in photography developed from the desire to capture insects and then set them free," he says.

Today Lemmo is a well-known wildlife photographer in the Adirondack Mountains of upstate New York. Slide programs, lectures, and publishing are a major source of his income. Lemmo has been widely published in magazines including *National Geographic World*, *Audubon*, *The Nature Conservancy*, *Ranger Rick*, *Adirondack Life*, *Birds & Blooms* and *Caribbean Travel & Life*, among others. He believes it's not just his photos that have helped him create this following, but rather it's a combination of his love and respect of nature; his ability to express that through a combination of clear, compelling images; a keen knowledge of the natural world; and great enthusiasm.

You might call Lemmo a purist—he still prefers film. "As a lifelong user of film, from black and white to color negative and color reversal types, I've always found my greatest reward to be viewing my images as color slides," he says. While photographing weddings for more than 25 years, Lemmo's constant companions were his manual film advance camera bodies, manual focus lenses, and manually set flash guns. He depended on his knowledge of various photographic techniques and the basic use of lighting to produce quality images.

"Though I have the ability to PhotoShop an image, I rarely tamper with my photos, which, up until very recently, have all originated on film," says Lemmo. "Being a perfectionist of sorts, I always strive to get a clean shot right from the start, even though I have often missed many a shot, using that ideology. My main use of PhotoShop is in the removal of dirt particles that sometimes appear on my digitized images. Even my nifty slide scanner misses a spot occasionally."

Lemmo thinks that one who is both technically skilled and gifted with an ability to use light and composition to their advantage is apt to be a superior photographer and artist. This is true of those who shoot with either film or digital cameras. Though digital photography

DEB HENEGHAN is a freelance writer and photographer based in Madison, Wisconsin.

appeals to many, and may eventually even win over diehards like Lemmo, it all boils down to producing images that others want to see and perhaps purchase.

"My wife, who is also a photographer, and I decided to end our wedding business recently due to several factors," says Lemmo. "It takes a lot of energy to photograph the average eight-hour wedding day from start to finish, and the quality of the photos—plus our reputation—were always our priorities. The increased stress incurred from the wedding business and, especially, the development of digital photography were our deciding factors. During the past 10 years, digital cameras have become ubiquitous and wedding photographers have multiplied like rabbits. Thus the transition from wedding photography to slide lectures and publishing came rather quickly."

© Gerry Lemmo

Gerry Lemmo's photo of an American marten is from a series of images he took of this uncommon member of the weasel family during zero degree weather in the wilds of New York's Adirondack Mountains. Various poses of the same untamed marten have been used by *Adirondack Life* magazine and *The New York State Conservationist*. A 24 × 36 permanent enlargement of the marten, along with a number of Lemmo's other Adirondack wildlife images, was selected for wall decor in one of three rustic rest areas he has helped to furnish along a major New York State highway leading into the Adirondack region. The photos frequently provide sales through his Web site, gerrylemmo.com, which is posted at each rest area.

SHOOTING NATURE

With his focus on nature photography, Lemmo prefers to shoot his subjects in their natural environment. But when photographing insects and other small natural items it is sometimes better to stage those shoots indoors. A true naturalist, Lemmo always releases his ''studio insects'' back into their native environment. He believes that as long as natural surroundings have been used properly on a small scale it shouldn't matter if the photo was taken indoors, so long as the scene depicts real life, and looks as though it would have as a natural outdoor environment. Many close-up photos seen in scientific publications are obtained in this manner.

On outdoor shoots, Lemmo often uses a blind so he can immerse himself in nature undetected. ''It's one of the greatest ways of taking in the sights and sounds of a forest, pond, or meadow,'' he says. ''There are innumerable nuances of the natural world to be experienced this way without the wildlife sensing your presence.''

You must always keep your wits about you in the wild, says Lemmo, especially without that blind. Once, while sitting against a tree in New York's Adirondacks wearing camouflage, his human scent masked, Lemmo patiently waited three hours for a bear to appear. ''I was unexpectedly approached from my side by a 400-pound bear,'' he says. ''I had no idea I was sitting right in its path. The bear actually brought its snout over my thighs, and kept it there for roughly 20 seconds, sniffing the warm summer air. I felt its breath on me, and those 20 seconds felt like an eternity. I was afraid to move and startle the animal, but it finally turned and walked away. It was one of the most thrilling and potentially dangerous wildlife encounters I've ever experienced. I never got the chance to take a photo of the surprise visitor, but its intimate image is indelibly marked upon my memory.''

While in Alaska shooting tufted puffins on a rugged, rain-drenched island, Lemmo feared for his life as he descended a steep, wet cliff side of sharp volcanic rock hauling 50 pounds of gear. ''I was all too painfully aware that there wasn't another human within 15 miles of the island. I came away with some great shots as well as some very vivid memories of my adventure.''

Sites that are environmentally sensitive like the puffin nesting colony often require photographers to obtain permits. Lemmo was allowed to camp on the island for three consecutive nights. He also has received special permission from timber companies to enter their wilderness properties in search of wildlife and to photograph the landscape for promotional use within their brochures and in-house calendars.

DOING BUSINESS

Lemmo, who has been selling his work to publishers for more than 25 years, has developed a unique approach to marketing. He will often write an accompanying article to go with his photographs. ''When it comes to the newsstand, editors are like new car salesmen,'' says Lemmo. ''I mean this to be complimentary! They not only want to push a great looking design; they also want a product that takes the reader for a smooth ride. A well-written article can do that. When I sell a total package to an editor, they can pass that great deal on to the consumer.''

Lemmo's Web site also serves as a great marketing tool for his work. He can easily point potential clients such as magazine and book photo editors and art directors directly to work samples and photo credits. Organizations and clubs can read a summary of and view available slide presentations. All of his Web site images are displayed in low resolution and are watermarked.

Treat your Web site clients the same as those you meet in-person meeting, says Lemmo. Be sincere, friendly and inquisitive. When speaking with clients in person, make eye contact.

Interviews with Pros

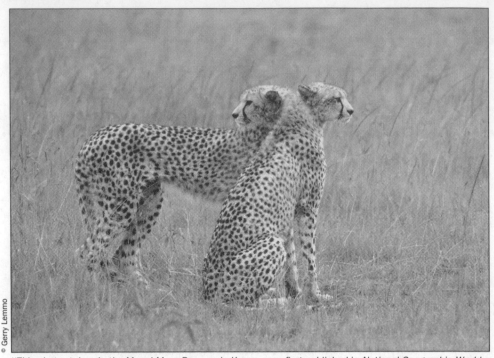

© Gerry Lemmo

"This photo, taken in the Masai Mara Reserve in Kenya, was first published in *National Geographic World*, both in the English language version, as well as in the Japanese version," says Gerry Lemmo. "It has also been used in *The Journal of Vision*, prompted by a study through Colorado University in Fort Collins." The image, having significant scientific merit, has been named "Lemmo's Cheetahs," and is now being compared to established optical illusions used in psychology tests, such as Rubin's face/vase and Schroder's staircase. Most recently, the cheetahs were published in a college textbook *Fundamentals of Human Neuropsychology*.

When dealing with Web site clients whom you have only communicated with through letters or e-mail, a phone call can only help build that professional relationship.

Most publications, Lemmo notes, have set rates for the use of photos. While one magazine might pay $400 for a cover, another may pay $150. Payment for the use of photos inside a magazine is usually determined by the size in which it is printed, yet book publishers usually have a set fee for interior use.

Lemmo is a veteran slide show presenter and he strives to meet the individual needs of each organization. He determines his fee based on the organization's rates. Fees for presentations tend to be higher than publication sales, due to the additional expenses. Travel, food, and lodging are sometimes necessary. "Most organizations have budgets, and I work with each to determine the best possible outcome for them and for me," he says.

Lemmo firmly believes that "captivating an audience and being in charge is critical, especially when giving a lecture during a slide show presentation—just as it is while photographing bridal parties. If you come across as vulnerable, you might as well pack it in."

For photographers just starting out, Lemmo advises beginning by photographing anything and everything that appeals to you. "The more variety you have at hand, even if it's only of one subject, the greater your chances will be for selling your work," he says. "By building a collection of images first, you will have a smorgasbord of visual treats that will catch the eyes of clients and their varied preferences and needs. Give them a feast to choose from."

If you do prefer to specialize—in sports photography, for instance—aim your sights on local newspapers and small publications, says Lemmo. "Once you get your feet wet, and you gain some photo credits, try progressively bigger clients. Although editors' rejection notices can be a part of your growth as a photographer, the effort you put forward to finding and approaching new contacts, and a level-headed persistence will eventually begin to pay off. These factors are a must to adhere to for the transformation from amateur status to professional. Your first big sale will make you feel 10-feet tall. I know mine did, as did my wife's, much more recently.'' (Lynne Lemmo's Alaskan aerial photo was published in *Alaska Magazine*—see the listing on page 58.)

"Though I grew up in a large city, I have never tried selling printed photos at galleries or to the affluent market," says Lemmo. "If you think your work is salable, it can't hurt to try some galleries. What may not be right for one, may be a real money maker for another."

If you'd like to enter shows to compete for cash, prizes or recognition or to make sales, by all means, go for it, advises Lemmo. It can be very time consuming, as well as very expensive, matting and framing prints for display, however. "Your pricing should reflect the amount of effort, materials, and travel time expended for a show," he says. "By explaining the complexities of how your work was accomplished, either in brochures, on noticeable placards on site or through personal contact with potential buyers that are browsing through your display you can best impress the viewers with your knowledge of your subjects and passion for your work."

While Lemmo doesn't think club membership necessarily impresses potential clients, membership might work for networking and business opportunities. "I actually don't belong to any organizations, yet my affiliation with many clubs, as a regular speaker, allows me to make many contacts, both for business and for local wildlife photo opportunities."

© Gerry Lemmo

"It took over six hours to get this image of a well-placed yellowjacket, along with several honeybees, on film," says Gerry Lemmo. "By focusing on the single jewelweed blossom, patience paid off." Although this image makes its debut in *Photographer's Market*, a nearly identical honeybee photo from the same photo shoot has been used to illustrate a scientific study at The California Institute of Technology on how honeybees fly. MSNBC also used the image to announce the Caltech findings.

Consumer Publications

Research is the key to selling any kind of photography. If you want your work to appear in a consumer publication, you're in luck. Magazines are the easiest market to research because they're available on newsstands and at the library and at your doctor's office and . . . you get the picture. So, do your homework. Before you send your query or cover letter and samples, and before you drop off your portfolio on the prescribed day, look at a copy of the magazine. The library is a good place to see sample copies because they're free, and there will be at least a year's worth of back issues right on the shelf.

Once you've read a few issues and feel confident your work is appropriate for a particular magazine, it's time to hit the keyboard. Most first submissions take the form of a query or cover letter and samples. So what kind of letter do you send? That depends on what kind of work you're selling. If you simply want to let an editor know you're available for assignments or have a list of stock images appropriate for the publication, send a cover letter, a short business letter that introduces you and your work and tells the editor why your photos are right for the magazine. If you have an idea for a photo essay or plan to provide the text and photos for an article, you should send a query letter, a 1- to 1½-page letter explaining your story or essay idea and why you're qualified to shoot it. You can send your query letter through the U.S. postal system, or you can e-mail it along with a few JPEG samples of your work. Check the listing for the magazine to see how they prefer to be contacted initially. (You'll find a sample query letter on the next page.)

Both kinds of letters can include a brief list of publication credits and any other relevant information about yourself. Both also should include a sample of your work—a tearsheet, a slide or a printed piece, but never an original negative. Be sure your sample photo is of something the magazine might publish. It will be difficult for the editor of a biking magazine to appreciate your skills if you send a sample of your fashion work.

If your letter piques the interest of an editor, he or she may want to see more. If you live near the editorial office, you might be able to schedule an appointment to show your portfolio in person. Or you can inquire about the drop-off policy—many magazines have a day or two each week when artists can leave their portfolios for art directors to review. If you're in Wichita and the magazine is in New York, you'll have to send your portfolio through the mail. Consider using FedEx or UPS; both have tracking services that can locate your book if it gets waylaid on its journey. If the publication accepts images in a digital format (most do these days), you can send more samples of your work via e-mail or on a CD—whatever the publication prefers. Make sure you ask first. Better yet, if you have a Web site, you can provide the photo buyer with the link.

To make your search for markets easier, consult the Subject Index on page 504. The index is divided into topics, and markets are listed according to the types of photographs they want to see.

Sample Query Letter

February 6, 2009

You may also include your Web site in your contact information.

Alicia Pope
2984 Hall Avenue
Cincinnati, OH 45206
e-mail: amp@shoot.net

Make sure to address letter to the current photo contact.

Connie Albright
Coastal Life
1234 Main Street
Cape Hatteras, NC 27954

Dear Ms. Albright:

Show that you are familiar with the magazine.

I enjoy reading *Coastal Life*, and I'm always impressed with the originality of the articles and photography. The feature on restored lighthouses in the June 2004 edition was spectacular.

Briefly explain your reason for querying.

Enclose copies of relevant work or direct them to your Web site. Never send originals.

I have traveled to many regions along the eastern seaboard and have photographed in several locations along the coast. I have enclosed samples of my work, including 20 slides of lighthouses, sea gulls, sand castles, as well as people enjoying the seaside at all times of the year. I have included vertical shots that would lend themselves to use on the cover. I have also included tearsheets from past assignments with *Nature Photographer*. You may keep the tearsheets on file, but I have enclosed a SASE for the return of the slides when you are done reviewing them.

Always include a self-addressed, stamped envelope for the magazine's reply.

If you feel any of these images would be appropriate for an upcoming issue of *Coastal Life*, please contact me by phone or e-mail. If you would like to see more of my coast life images, I will be happy to send more.

I look forward to hearing from you in the near future.

Sincerely,

Alicia Pope

Consumer Publications

$⬛ ⬛ ⬛ AAA MIDWEST TRAVELER

Auto Club of Missouri, 12901 N. Forty Dr., St. Louis MO 63141. (314)523-7350. Fax: (314)523-6982. E-mail: dreinhardt@aaamissouri.com. Web site: www.aaa.com/traveler. **Contact:** Deborah Reinhardt, managing editor. Circ. 500,000. Bimonthly. Emphasizes travel and driving safety. Readers are members of the Auto Club of Missouri. Sample copy and photo guidelines free with SASE (use large manila envelope) or on Web site.

Needs Buys 3-5 photos/issue. "We use four-color photos inside to accompany specific articles. Our magazine covers topics of general interest, historical (of Midwest regional interest), profile, travel, car care and driving tips. Our covers are full-color photos mainly corresponding to an article inside. Except for cover shots, we use freelance photos only to accompany specific articles." Model release preferred. Photo captions required.

Specs Accepts images in digital format. Send via Zip as TIFF files at minimum of 300 dpi.

Making Contact & Terms Send query letter with résumé of credits and list of stock photo subjects. Does not keep samples on file; include SASE for return of material. Responds in 1 month. Simultaneous submissions and previously published work OK. Pays $400 for color cover; $75-200 for color inside. **Pays on acceptance.** Credit line given. Buys first, second and electronic rights.

Tips "Send an 8½×11 SASE for sample copies and study the type of covers and inside work we use. Photo needs driven by an editoral calendar/schedule. Write to request a copy and include SASE."

ADVENTURE CYCLIST

P.O. Box 8308, Missoula MT 59807. (406)721-1776, ext. 222. Fax: (406)721-8754. E-mail: editor@adventurecycling.org. Web site: www.adventurecycling.org/mag. **Contact:** Mike Deme, editor. Circ. 44,000. Estab. 1974. Publication of Adventure Cycling Association. Magazine published 9 times/year. Emphasizes bicycle touring and travel. Sample copy and photo guidelines free with 9×12 SAE and 4 first-class stamps. Guidelines also available on Web site.

Needs Cover and inside photos. Model release preferred. Photo captions required.

Making Contact & Terms Query first by e-mail to obtain permission to submit samples or portfolio for review. Responds in 6-9 weeks. Simultaneous submissions and previously published work OK. Payment negotiable. Pays on publication. Credit line given. Buys one-time rights.

$ $⬛ ALASKA: Exploring Life on The Last Frontier

301 Arctic Slope Ave., Suite 300, Anchorage AK 99518. (907)272-6070. Web site: www.alaskamagazine.com. **Contact**: Rachel Steer, assistant director. Circ. 140,000. Estab. 1935. Monthly magazine. Readers are people interested in Alaska. Sample copy available for $4. Photo guidelines free with SASE or on Web site.

Needs Buys 500 photos/year, supplied mainly by freelancers. Photo captions required.

Making Contact & Terms Send carefully edited, captioned submission of 35mm, 2¼×2¼ or 4×5 transparencies. Include SASE for return of material. Also accepts images in digital format; check guidelines before submitting. Responds in 1 month. Pays $50 maximum for b&w photos; $75-500 for color photos; $300 maximum/day; $2,000 maximum/complete job; $300 maximum/full page; $500 maximum/cover. Buys limited rights, first North American serial rights and electronic rights.

Consumer Publications

Tips "Each issue of Alaska features a 4- to 6-page photo feature. We're looking for themes and photos to show the best of Alaska. We want sharp, artistically composed pictures. Cover photo always relates to stories inside the issue."

▣ ◪ ALTERNATIVES JOURNAL: Canadian Environmental Ideas & Action

Faculty of Environmental Studies, University of Waterloo, Waterloo ON N2L 3G1 Canada. (519)888-4545. Fax: (519)746-0292. E-mail: mruby@fes.uwaterloo.ca. Web site: www.alternativesjournal.ca. **Contact:** Marcia Ruby, production coordinator. Circ. 5,000. Estab. 1971. Bimonthly magazine. Emphasizes environmental issues. Readers are activists, academics, professionals, policy makers. Sample copy free with 9×12 SAE and 2 first-class stamps.

- *"Alternatives* is a nonprofit organization whose contributors are all volunteer. We are able to give a small honorarium to artists and photographers. This in no way should reflect the value of the work. It symbolizes our thanks for their contribution to *Alternatives*."

Needs Buys 4-8 photos from freelancers/issue; 48-96 photos/year. Subjects vary widely depending on theme of each issue. "We need action shots of people involved in environmental issues." Check Web site for upcoming themes. Reviews photos with or without a manuscript. Photo captions preferred; include who, when, where, environmental significance of shot.

Specs Accepts images in digital format. Send via CD, e-mail as JPEG files at 300 dpi.

Making Contact & Terms "E-mail your Web address/electronic portfolio." Simultaneous submissions and previously published work OK. Pays on publication. Buys one-time rights; negotiable.

Tips "*Alternatives* covers Canadian and global environmental issues. Strong action photos or topical environmental issues are needed—preferably with people. We also print animal shots. We look for positive solutions to problems and prefer to illustrate the solutions rather than the problems. Freelancers need a good background understanding of environmental issues. You need to know the significance of your subject before you can powerfully present its visual perspective."

▣ AMERICAN ARCHAEOLOGY

The Archaeological Conservancy, 5301 Central NE #902, Albuquerque NM 87108. (505)266-9668. Fax: (505)266-0311. E-mail: tacmag@nm.net. Web site: www.americanarchaeology.org. **Contact:** Vicki Singer, art director. Circ. 35,000. Estab. 1997. Quarterly consumer magazine. Sample copies available.

Specs Uses 35mm, 2¼×2¼, 4×5 transparencies. Accepts images in digital format. Send via CD at 300 dpi or higher.

Making Contact & Terms Send query letter with résumé, photocopies and tearsheets. Provide résumé, business card, self-promotion piece to be kept on file for possible future assignments. Responds in 2 months to queries. Previously published work OK. Pays $50 and up for occasional stock images; assigns work by project (pay varies); negotiable. **Pays on acceptance.** Credit line given. Buys one-time rights.

Tips "Read our magazine. Include accurate and detailed captions."

$ $▨ ▣ AMERICAN FORESTS MAGAZINE

734 15th St. NW, 8th Floor, Washington DC 20005. (202)737-1944, ext. 203. Fax: (202)737-2457. E-mail: mrobbins@amfor.org. Web site: www.americanforests.org. **Contact:** Mi-

chelle Robbins, editor. Circ. 25,000. Estab. 1895. Quarterly publication of American Forests. Emphasizes use, enjoyment and management of forests and other natural resources. Readers are "people from all walks of life, from rural to urban settings, whose main common denominator is an abiding love for trees, forests or forestry." Sample copy and photo guidelines free with magazine-sized envelope and 7 first-class stamps.

Needs Buys 32 photos from freelancers/issue; 128 photos/year. Needs woods scenics, wildlife, woods use/management, and urban forestry shots. "Also shots of national champion trees; contact editor for details." Photo captions required; include who, what, where, when and why.

Specs Uses 35mm or larger. Accepts images in digital format. Send link to viewing platform, or send via CD or FTP as TIFF files at 300 dpi.

Making Contact & Terms "We regularly review portfolios from photographers to look for potential images for upcoming issues or to find new photographers to work with." Send query letter with résumé of credits. Include SASE for return of material. Responds in 4 months. Pays $500 for color cover; $90-200 for color inside; $75-100 for b&w inside; $250-2,000 for text/photo package. **Pays on acceptance.** Credit line given. Buys one-time rights and rights for use in online version of magazine.

Tips "Please identify species in tree shots if possible."

$ ⑤ ▣ THE AMERICAN GARDENER

American Horticultural Society, 7931 E. Boulevard Dr., Alexandria VA 22308-1300. (703)768-5700. Fax: (703)768-7533. E-mail: editor@ahs.org. Web site: www.ahs.org. **Contact:** Mary Yee, art director/managing editor. Circ. 30,000. Estab. 1922. Bimonthly magazine. Sample copy available for $5. Photo guidelines free with SASE or via e-mail request.

Needs Uses 35-50 photos/issue. Needs photos of plants, gardens, landscapes. Reviews photos with or without a manuscript. Photo captions required; include complete botanical names of plants including genus, species and botanical variety or cultivar.

Specs Prefers color, 35mm slides and larger transparencies or high-res JPEG or TIFF files with a minimum size of 5×7 inches at 300 dpi. Digital images should be submitted on a CD.

Making Contact & Terms Send query letter with samples, stock list. Photographer will be contacted for portfolio review if interested. Does not keep samples on file; include SASE for return of material. Pays $350 maximum for color cover; $80-130 for color inside. Pays on publication. Credit line given. Buys one-time North American and nonexclusive rights.

Tips "Lists of plant species for which photographs are needed are sent out to a selected list of photographers approximately 10 weeks before publication. We currently have about 20 photographers on that list. Most of them have photo libraries representing thousands of species. Before adding photographers to our list, we need to determine both the quality and quantity of their collections. Therefore, we ask all photographers to submit both some samples of their slides (these will be returned immediately if sent with a SASE) and a list indicating the types and number of plants in their collection. After reviewing both, we may decide to add the photographer to our photo call for a trial period of 6 issues (1 year)."

$ $▣ AMERICAN HUNTER

NRA, 11250 Waples Mill Rd., Fairfax VA 22030. (703)267-1336. Fax: (703)267-3971. E-mail: AMERICANHUNTER@nrahq.org. Web site: www.nrapublications.org. **Contact:** J. Scott Olmsted, editor-in-chief. Circ. 1 million. Monthly magazine of the National Rifle Association. Sample copy and photo guidelines free with 9×12 SAE.

Needs Uses wildlife shots and hunting action scenes. Photos purchased with or without accompanying manuscript. Seeks general hunting stories on North American game. Model release required "for every recognizable human face in a photo." Photo captions preferred.
Specs Uses 35mm color transparencies. Accepts images in digital format. Send via CD as TIFF, GIF, JPEG files at 300 dpi. Vertical format required for cover.
Making Contact & Terms Send material by mail for consideration; include SASE for return of material. Responds in 3 months. Pays $125-600/transparency; $1000 for color cover; $400-1400 for text/photo package. Pays on publication. Credit line given. Buys one-time rights.
Tips "Most successful photographers maintain a file in our offices so editors can select photos to fill holes when needed. We keep files on most North American big game, small game, waterfowl, upland birds, and some exotics. We need live hunting shots as well as profiles and portraits in all settings. Many times there is not enough time to call photographers for special needs. This practice puts your name in front of the editors more often and increases the chances of sales."

ANIMAL TRAILS

2660 Petersborough St., Herndon VA 20171. E-mail: animaltrails@yahoo.com. Quarterly publication.
Needs Needs photos of environmental, landscapes/scenics, wildlife, architecture, cities/urban, gardening, interiors/decorating, pets, religious, rural, performing arts, agriculture, product shots/still life—as related to animals. Interested in alternative process, avant garde, documentary, fashion/glamour, fine art, historical/vintage, seasonal. Reviews photos with or without a manuscript. Model/property release preferred.
Specs Uses glossy or matte color and/or b&w prints.
Making Contact & Terms Send query letter via e-mail. Provide résumé, business card, self-promotion piece to be kept on file for possible future assignments. "A photograph or two is requested but not required. Illustrations and artwork are also accepted." Responds within 1 month to queries; 1 week to portfolios. Simultaneous submissions and previously published work OK. **Pays on acceptance.** Credit line given. Buys one-time rights, first rights; negotiable.

ⓃAPERTURE

547 W. 27th St., 4th Floor, New York NY 10001. (212)505-5555. E-mail: editorial@aperture.org. Web site: www.aperture.org. **Contact:** Michael Famighetti, managing editor. Circ. 30,000. Quarterly. Emphasizes fine-art and contemporary photography, as well as social reportage. Readers include photographers, artists, collectors, writers.
Needs Uses about 60 photos/issue; biannual portfolio review. Model release required. Photo captions required.
Making Contact & Terms Submit portfolio for review in January and July; include SASE for return of material. Responds in 2 months. No payment. Credit line given.
Tips "We are a nonprofit foundation. Do not send portfolios outside of January and July."

$⊘▣ AQUARIUM FISH INTERNATIONAL

P.O. Box 6050, Mission Viejo CA 92690. Fax: (949)855-3045. E-mail: aquariumfish@bowtieinc.com. Web site: www.aquariumfish.com. **Contact:** Patricia Knight, managing editor. Es-

Consumer Publications

tab. 1988. Monthly magazine. Emphasizes aquarium fish. Readers are both genders, all ages. Photo guidelines free with SASE, via e-mail or on Web site.

Needs Buys 30 photos from freelancers/issue; 360 photos/year. Needs photos of aquariums and fish, freshwater and saltwater; ponds.

Specs Uses 35mm slides, transparencies. Accepts digital images—"but digital image guidelines must be strictly followed for submissions to be considered."

Making Contact & Terms Send slides, transparencies, original prints (no laser printouts) or CDs (no DVDs) by mail for consideration; include SASE for return of material. Pays $200 for color cover; $15-150 for color inside. Pays on publication. Credit line given. Buys first North American serial rights.

$ $🔲🅰🔲 ATLANTA HOMES & LIFESTYLES

1100 Johnson Ferry Rd. NE, Suite 595, Atlanta GA 30342. (404)252-6670. Web site: www.atl antahomesmag.com. **Contact:** Rachel Cardina, creative director. Editor: Clinton Ross Smith. Circ. 34,000. Estab. 1983. Monthly magazine. Covers residential design (home and garden); food, wine and entertaining; people, lifestyle subjects in the metro Atlanta area. Sample copy available for $3.95.

Needs Needs photos of homes (interior/exterior), people, decorating ideas, products, gardens. Model/property release required. Photo captions preferred.

Specs Uses 35mm, $2^1/_4 \times 2^1/_4$, 4×5 transparencies. Accepts images in digital format.

Making Contact & Terms Contact creative director to review portfolio. Provide résumé, business card, brochure, flier or tearsheets to be kept on file for possible future assignments. Responds in 2 months. Simultaneous submissions and previously published work OK. Pays $150-750/job. **Pays on acceptance.** Credit line given. Buys one-time rights.

🔲🔲 ATLANTA LIFE MAGAZINE

2500 Hospital Blvd., Suite 370, Roswell GA 30076.(707) 664-6466. Fax: (707) 664-6465. E-mail: graphics@atlantalifemag.com. Web site: www.atlantalifemag.com. **Contact:** Natalie Sokol. Estab. 2006. Monthly consumer magazine. "We are an upscale lifestyle magazine covering north metro Atlanta. We cover a variety of topics, including sports, fashion, travel, health, finances, home design."

Needs Needs photos of architecture, cities/urban, gardening, interiors/decorating, entertainment, food/drink, health/fitness/beauty, performing arts, sports, travel. Interested in lifestyle. Reviews photos with or without a manuscript. Model release required. Captions required: include identification of subjects.

Specs Accepts images in digital format. Send JPEG or GIF files.

Making Contact & Terms Payment negotiated. Pays on publication. Credit line given. Buys one-time rights, Web usage rights.

Tips "Have high-resolution photo support if you are also submitting a manuscript."

$🔲🔲 AUTO RESTORER

P.O. Box 6050, Mission Viejo CA 92690. (949)855-8822, ext. 3412. Fax: (949)855-3045. E-mail: tkade@bowtieinc.com. Web site: www.autorestorermagazine.com. **Contact:** Ted Kade, editor. Circ. 60,000. Estab. 1989. Monthly magazine. Emphasizes restoration of collector cars and trucks. Readers are 98% male, professional/technical/managerial, ages 35-65.

Needs Buys 47 photos from freelancers/issue; 564 photos/year. Needs photos of auto restoration projects and restored cars. Reviews photos with accompanying manuscript only. Model/property release preferred. Photo captions required; include year, make and model of car; identification of people in photo.

Specs Prefers images in high-resolution digital format. Send via CD at 240 dpi with minimum width of 5 inches. Uses transparencies, mostly 35mm, 2¼×2¼.

Making Contact & Terms Submit inquiry and portfolio for review. Provide résumé, business card, brochure, flier or tearsheets to be kept on file for possible future assignments. Responds in 1 month. Simultaneous submissions OK. Pays $50 for b&w cover; $35 for b&w inside. Pays on publication. Credit line given. Buys first North American serial rights.

Tips Looks for "technically proficient or dramatic photos of various automotive subjects, auto portraits, detail shots, action photos, good angles, composition and lighting. We're also looking for photos to illustrate how-to articles such as how to repair a damaged fender or how to repair a carburetor."

🄽 $ $ ⬛ ▣ BACKPACKER MAGAZINE

2520 55th St., Suite 210, Boulder CO 80301. (610)967-8371. Fax: (610)967-8181. Web site: www.backpacker.com. **Contact:** Jackie Ney, photo editor. Photo Assistant: Genny Wright (genny.wright@rodale.com; (610)967-7754). Magazine published 9 times/year. Readers are male and female, ages 35-45. Photo guidelines available on Web site or free with SASE marked Attn: Guidelines.

• *Backpacke*r will be moving to Colorado in late 2007.

Needs Buys 80 photos from freelancers/issue; 720 photos/year. Needs transparencies of people backpacking, camping, landscapes/scenics. Reviews photos with or without a manuscript. Model/property release required.

Specs Accepts images in digital format. Send via CD, Zip, e-mail as JPEG files at 72 dpi for review (300 dpi needed to print).

Making Contact & Terms Send query letter with résumé of credits, photo list and example of work to be kept on file. Sometimes considers simultaneous submissions and previously published work. Pays $500-1,000 for color cover; $100-600 for color inside. Pays on publication. Credit line given. Rights negotiable.

⬛ ▣ BASEBALL

2660 Petersborough St., Herndon VA 20171. E-mail: shannonaswriter@yahoo.com. Quarterly magazine covering baseball. Photo guidelines available by e-mail request.

Needs Wants photos of baseball scenes featuring children and teens; photos of celebrities, couples, multicultural, families, parents, environmental, landscapes/scenics, wildlife, agriculture—as related to the sport of baseball. Interested in alternative process, avant garde, documentary, fine art, historical/vintage, seasonal. Reviews photos with or without a manuscript.

Specs Uses glossy or matte color and/or b&w prints.

Making Contact & Terms Send query letter via e-mail. "If possible, please do not include photographs in files if they are sent through e-mail. A disk with your photographs is acceptable. If you plan to send a disk, photographs or portfolio, please send an e-mail stating this." Provide résumé, business card, self-promotion piece to be kept on file for possible future assignments. "Photographs sent with CDs are requested but not required. Illustrations and artwork are also accepted." Responds within 1 month to queries; 1 week to portfolios. Simultaneous submissions and previously published work OK. **Pays on acceptance.** Credit line given. Buys one-time, first rights; negotiable.

Consumer Publications

$☑ ▣ THE BEAR DELUXE MAGAZINE

Orlo, P.O. Box 10342, Portland OR 97296. (503)242-1047. E-mail: bear@orlo.org. Web site: www.orlo.org. **Contact:** Kristen Rogers, art director. Circ. 20,000. Estab. 1993. Quarterly magazine. "We use the arts to focus on environmental themes." Sample copy available for $3. Photo guidelines available for SASE.

Needs Buys 10 photos from freelancers/issue; 40 photos/year. Needs photos of environmental, landscapes/scenics, wildlife, adventure, political. Reviews photos with or without a manuscript. Model release required (as needed); property release preferred. Photo captions preferred; include place, year, photographer, names of subjects.

Specs Uses 8×10 matte b&w prints. Accepts images in digital format. Send via CD, Zip, or low-res e-mail files.

Making Contact & Terms Send query letter with résumé, slides, prints, photocopies. Portfolio may be dropped off by appointment. Provide résumé, self-promotion piece to be kept on file for possible future assignments. Responds in 6 months to queries; 2 months to portfolios. Only returns materials if appropriate SASE included. Not liable for submitted materials. Simultaneous submissions and previously published work OK as long as it is noted as such. Pays $200 for b&w cover; $30-50 for b&w inside. Pays approximately 3 weeks after publication. Credit line given. Buys one-time rights; negotiable.

Tips "Read the magazine. We want unique and unexpected photos, not your traditional nature or landscape stuff."

$☑ ⑤ BIRD WATCHER'S DIGEST

149 Acme St., Marietta OH 45750. (740)373-5285. E-mail: editor@birdwatchersdigest.com. Web site: www.birdwatchersdigest.com. **Contact:** Bill Thompson III, editor. Circ. 99,000. Bimonthly; digest size. Emphasizes birds and bird watchers. Readers are bird watchers/birders (backyard and field, veterans and novices). Sample copy available for $3.99. Photo guidelines available on Web site.

Needs Buys 25-35 photos from freelancers/issue; 150-210 photos/year. Needs photos of North American species.

Specs Accepts high-resolution (300 dpi) digital images via CD or DVD. "We appreciate quality thumbnails to accompany digital images."

Making Contact & Terms Send query letter with list of stock photo subjects, samples, SASE. Responds in 2 months. *Work previously published in other bird publications should not be submitted.* Pays $75 for color inside. Pays on publication. Credit line given. Buys one-time rights.

Tips "Query with slides to be considered for photograph want-list. Send a sample of at least 20 slides for consideration. Sample will be reviewed and responded to in 8 weeks."

Ⓝ $☑ Ⓐ ▣ ⊕ BIRD WATCHING MAGAZINE

Bauer Active, Media House Lynchwood, Peterborough PE2 6EA United Kingdom. (44)(733)264-666. Fax: (44)(733)465-376. E-mail: sue.begg@emap.com. Web site: www.birdwatching.co.uk. **Contact:** Sue Begg, photo researcher. Circ. 22,000. Estab. 1986. Monthly hobby magazine for bird watchers. Sample copy free for SAE with first-class postage/IRC.

Needs Needs photos of "wild birds photographed in the wild, mainly in action or showing interesting aspects of behavior. Also stunning landscape pictures in birding areas and images of people with binoculars, telescopes, etc." Also considers travel, hobby and gardening shots related to bird watching. Reviews photos with or without a manuscript. Photo captions preferred.

Specs Uses 35mm, 2¼×2¼ transparencies. Accepts images in digital format. Send via CD, e-mail as TIFF, EPS, JPEG files at 200 dpi.

Making Contact & Terms Provide résumé, business card, self-promotion piece or tearsheets to be kept on file for possible future assignments. Returns unsolicited material if SASE enclosed. Responds in 1 month. Simultaneous submissions OK. Pays £70-100 for color cover; £15-120 for color inside. Pays on publication. Buys one-time rights.

Tips "All photos are held on file here in the office once they have been selected. They are returned when used or a request for their return is made. Make sure all slides are well labeled: bird, name, date, place taken, photographer's name and address. Send sample of images to show full range of subject and photographic techniques."

$ $⊘ Ⓢ ▣ BIRDS & BLOOMS

Reiman Media Group, Inc., 5400 S. 60th St., Greendale WI 53129. Fax: (414)423-8463. E-mail: photocoordinator@reimanpub.com. Web site: www.birdsandblooms.com. **Contact:** Trudi Bellin, photo coordinator. Estab. 1994. Bimonthly magazine. Celebrates "the beauty in your own backyard." Readers are male and female, ages 40-70 (majority), who prefer to spend their spare time in their "outdoor living room." Heavy interest in "amateur" gardening, backyard bird-watching and bird-feeding. Sample copy available for $2.

  • *Birds & Blooms EXTRA* is published in the months between regular issues. Content and guidelines are the same.

Needs Buys 50 photos from freelancers/issue; 600 photos/year. Needs photos of gardening, backyard birds, landscapes, outdoor hobbies and seasonal.

Specs Prefers color transparencies, all sizes. Accepts images in digital format: TIFF or high-quality JPEG files at 300 dpi for up to 9×11 reproduction. Embedded metadata is recommended. Send via lightboxes or on removable media. Or send CD/DVD with printed thumbnails and caption sheet. E-mail if first review selection is small (12 images or less).

Making Contact & Terms Send query letter with résumé of credits, stock list. Send unsolicited photos by mail for consideration. Keeps samples on file (tearsheets; no dupes); include SASE for return of material. Responds in 3 months for first review. Simultaneous submissions and previously published work OK. Buys stock only. Pays $100-300 for inside; $300 for cover; $200 for color back cover. Pays on publication. Credit line given. Buys one-time rights to stock photos; all rights to assignments. "Magazine generates an annual book; you can count on most images appearing again in the annual at a re-use rate."

Tips "Technical quality is extremely important; focus must be sharp (no soft focus), and colors must be vivid so they 'pop off the page.' Study our magazine thoroughly—we have a continuing need for sharp, colorful images, and those who can supply what we need can expect to be regular contributors. Very interested in photos of people involved in typical backyard activities."

Ⓝ ◯ Ⓐ ▣ ↺ BLACKFLASH

Buffalo Berry Press, P.O. Box 7381, Station Main, Saskatoon SK S7K 4J3 Canada. (306)374-5115. E-mail: editor@blackflash.ca. Web site: www.blackflash.ca. **Contact:** Lissa Robinson, managing editor. Circ. 1,700. Estab. 1983. Canadian journal of photo-based and electronic arts published 3 times/year.

Needs Looking for lens-based and new media contemporary fine art and electronic arts practitioners." Reviews photos with or without a manuscript.

Specs Accepts images in digital format. Send via CD, Zip, e-mail as TIFF, EPS, BMP, JPEG files at 300 dpi.

Making Contact & Terms Send query letter with résumé, digital images. Does not keep samples on file; will return material with SASE only. Simultaneous submissions OK. Pays when copy has been proofed and edited. Credit line given. Buys one-time rights.

Tips "We need alternative and interesting contemporary photography. Understand our mandate and read our magazine prior to submitting."

$⊘ ▣ BLUE RIDGE COUNTRY

P.O. Box 21535, Roanoke VA 24018. (540)989-6138. Fax: (540)989-7603. E-mail: photos@le isurepublishing.com. Web site: www.blueridgecountry.com. **Contact:** Cara Ellen Modisett, editor. Circ. 60,000. Estab. 1988. Bimonthly magazine. Emphasizes outdoor scenics, recreation, travel destinations in 9-state Blue Ridge Mountain region. Photo guidelines available for SASE or on Web site.

Needs Buys 20-40 photos from freelancers/issue; 100-300 photos/year. Need photos of travel, scenics and wildlife. Seeking more scenics with people in them. Model release preferred. Photo captions required.

Specs Uses 35mm, $2\frac{1}{4} \times 2\frac{1}{4}$, 4×5 transparencies. Accepts images in digital format. Send via CD, e-mail, or FTP (contact editor for information) at 300 dpi; low-res images okay for initial review, but accepted images must be high-res.

Making Contact & Terms Send query letter with list of stock photo subjects, samples with caption info and SASE. Responds in 2 months. Pays $150 for color cover; $40-150 for color inside. Pays on publication. Credit line given. Buys one-time rights.

$◻ Ⓢ ▣ BOROUGH NEWS MAGAZINE

2941 N. Front St., Harrisburg PA 17110. (717)236-9526. Fax: (717)236-8164. E-mail: caccurti @boroughs.org. Web site: www.boroughs.org. **Contact:** Courtney Accurti, editor. Circ. 6,000. Estab. 2001. Monthly magazine of Pennsylvania State Association of Boroughs. Emphasizes borough government in Pennsylvania. Readers are officials in municipalities in Pennsylvania. Sample copy free with 9×12 SAE and 5 first-class stamps.

Needs Number of photos/issue varies with inside copy. Needs "color photos of scenics (Pennsylvania), local government activities, Pennsylvania landmarks, ecology—for cover photos only; authors of articles supply their own photos." Special photo needs include street and road maintenance work; wetlands scenic. Model release preferred. Photo captions preferred; include identification of place and/or subject.

Specs Uses color prints and 35mm transparencies. Accepts images in digital format. Send via CD, Zip, e-mail as TIFF, EPS, JPEG, PSD files at 300 dpi.

Making Contact & Terms Send query letter with résumé of credits and list of stock photo subjects. Send unsolicited photos by mail for consideration; include SASE for return of material. Provide résumé, business card, brochure, flier or tearsheets to be kept on file for possible future assignments. Responds in 1 month. Pays $30 for color cover. Pays on publication. Buys one-time rights.

Tips "We're looking for a variety of scenic shots of Pennsylvania for front covers of the magazine, especially special issues such as engineering, street/road maintenance, downtown revitalization, technology, tourism and historic preservation, public safety and economic development, and recreation."

$ $BOWHUNTER

6385 Flank Dr., Harrisburg PA 17112. (717)695-8083. E-mail: bowhunter_magazine@inter mediaoutdoors.com. Web site: www.bowhunter.com. **Contact:** Mark Olszewski, art director. Editor: Dwight Schuh. Publisher: Jeff Waring. Circ. 180,067. Estab. 1971. Published 9 times/year. Emphasizes bow and arrow hunting. Sample copy available for $2. Submission guidelines free with SASE.

Needs Buys 50-75 photos/year. Wants scenic (showing bowhunting) and wildlife (big and small game of North America) photos. "No cute animal shots or poses. We want informative, entertaining bowhunting adventure, how-to and where-to-go articles." Reviews photos with or without a manuscript.

Specs Digital submissions preferred—300 dpi, RAW, JPG, or TIFF format; CMYK preferred, provided on CD or DVD named in a simple and logical system with accompanying contact sheet. Also uses 5×7, 8×10 glossy b&w and/or color prints, both vertical and horizontal format; 35mm and 2¼×2¼ transparencies; vertical format preferred for cover.

Making Contact & Terms Send query letter with samples, SASE. Responds in 2 weeks to queries; 6 weeks to samples. Pays $50-125 for b&w inside; $75-300 for color inside; $600 for cover, "occasionally more if photo warrants it." Pays on acceptance. Credit line given. Buys one-time publication rights.

Tips "Know bowhunting and/or wildlife and study several copies of our magazine before submitting any material. We're looking for better quality, and we're using more color on inside pages. Most purchased photos are of big game animals. Hunting scenes are second. In b&w we look for sharp, realistic light, good contrast. Color must be sharp; early or late light is best. We avoid anything that looks staged; we want natural settings, quality animals. Send only your best, and, if at all possible, let us hold those we indicate interest in. Very little is taken on assignment; most comes from our files or is part of the manuscript package. If your work is in our files, it will probably be used."

◯ 🔀 BRIARPATCH

2138 McIntyre St., Regina SK S4P 2R7 Canada. (306)525-2949. E-mail: editor@briarpatchmagazine.com. Web site: www.briarpatchmagazine.com. **Contact:** Dave Mitchell, editor. Circ. 3,000. Estab. 1973. Magazine published 8 times/year. Emphasizes Canadian and international politics, labor, environment, women, peace. Readers are left-wing political activists. Sample copy available for $4.95 plus shipping.

Needs Buys 15-30 photos from freelancers/issue; 150-300 photos/year. Needs photos of Canadian and international politics, labor, environment, women, peace and personalities. Model/property release preferred. Photo captions preferred; include name of person(s) in photo, etc.

Specs Minimum 3×5 color or b&w prints.

Making Contact & Terms Send query letter with samples or link to online portfolio. Do not send slides. Provide resume, business card, brochure, flier, or tearsheets to be kept on file for possible future assignments. Include SASE for return of material. Responds in 1 month. Simultaneous submissions and previously published work OK. Pays $20 per published photo and $100 for cover. Credit line given. Buys one-time rights.

$◩ ▣ BRIDAL GUIDES

2660 Petersborough St., Herndon VA 20171. E-mail: BridalGuides@yahoo.com. Estab. 1998. Quarterly. Photo guidelines available by e-mail request.

Needs Buys 12 photos from freelancers/issue; 48-72 photos/year. Needs photos of babies/children/teens, celebrities, couples, multicultural, families, parents, cities/urban, environmental, landscapes/scenics, wildlife, architecture, gardening, interiors/decorating, pets,

Consumer Publications

religious, rural, adventure, entertainment, events, food/drink, health/fitness, performing arts, travel, agriculture—as related to weddings. Interested in alternative process, avant garde, documentary, fashion/glamour, fine art, historical/vintage, seasonal. Also wants photos of weddings "and those who make it all happen, both behind and in front of the scene." Reviews photos with or without a manuscript. Model/property release preferred. **Specs** Uses glossy or matte color and/or b&w prints.

Making Contact & Terms Send query letter via e-mail. "If possible, please do not include photographs in files if they are sent through e-mail. A disk with your photographs is acceptable. If you plan to send a disk, photographs or portfolio, please send an e-mail stating this." Provide résumé, business card or self-promotion piece to be kept on file for possible future assignments. "A photograph or two sent with CD is requested but not required. Illustrations and artwork are also accepted." Responds within 1 month to queries; 1 week to portfolios. Simultaneous submissions and previously published work OK. **Pays on acceptance.** Credit line given. Buys one-time rights, first rights; negotiable.

$◫ THE BRIDGE BULLETIN

American Contract Bridge League, 2990 Airways Blvd., Memphis TN 38116-3847. (901)332-5586. Fax: (901)398-7754. E-mail: editor@acbl.org. Web site: www.acbl.org. Circ. 154,000. Estab. 1937. Monthly association magazine for tournament/duplicate bridge players. Sample copies available.

Needs Buys 4-5 photos/year. Reviews photos with or without a manuscript.
Specs Prefers high-res digital images, color only.
Making Contact & Terms Query by phone. Responds only if interested; send nonreturnable samples. Previously published work OK. Pays $100 or more for suitable work. Pays on publication. Credit line given. Buys all rights.
Tips Photos must relate to bridge. Call first.

◩ ◫ BVM: Beach Volleyball Magazine

STN Media Co., 700 Torrance Blvd. Suite C, Redondo Beach CA 90277. (310)792-2226. Fax: (310)792-2231. E-mail: vince@bvmag.com, ryan@bvmag.com. Web site: www.bvmag.com. **Contact:** Vince Rios, art director. Circ. 30,000. Estab. 2006. Consumer magazine published 6 times/year focusing on the lifestyle of beach volleyball; features news about the beach volleyball community nationwide, including exclusive interviews with top AVP players, major association news, junior volleyball coverage, and major tournament coverage.
Needs Needs lifestyle photos of beach volleyball, travel. Reviews photos with or without manuscript. Model release required. Captions required, including identification of subjects.
Specs Accepts images in digital format. Send JPEG or GIF files. Also reviews contact sheets.
Making Contact & Terms Payment negotiated. Pays on publication. Credit line given. Buys all rights.

◫ $CALLIOPE: Exploring World History

Cobblestone Publishing, 30 Grove St., Peterborough NH 03458. (603)924-7209. Fax: (603)924-7380. E-mail: cfbakeriii@meganet.net. Web site: www.cobblestonepub.com. **Contact:** Rosalie Baker, editor. Circ. 13,000. Estab. 1990. Magazine published 9 times/year (May/June, July/August, November/December). Emphasis on non-United States history. Readers are children ages 10-14. Sample copies available for $5.95 with 9×12 or larger SAE and 5 first-class stamps. Photo guidelines available on Web site or free with SASE.

Needs Needs contemporary shots of historical locations, buildings, artifacts, historical reenactments and costumes. Reviews photos with or without accompanying manuscript. Model/property release preferred.

Specs Uses b&w and/or color prints; 35mm transparencies.

Making Contact & Terms Send query letter with stock photo list. Provide résumé and, if desired, business card, brochure, flier or tearsheets to be kept on file for possible future assignments. Responds within 5 months. Simultaneous submissions and previously published work OK. Pays $15-100 for inside; cover (color) photo payment negotiated. Pays on publication. Credit line given. Buys one-time rights; negotiable.

Tips "Given our young audience, we like to have pictures that include people, both young and old. Pictures must be dynamic to make history appealing. Submissions must relate to themes in each issue."

⬛ $⬛ ⬛ ⬛ CANADA LUTHERAN

302-393 Portage Ave., Winnipeg MB R3B 3H6 Canada. (204)984-9172. Fax: (204)984-9185. E-mail: canaluth@elcic.ca. Web site: www.elcic.ca/clweb. **Contact:** Trina Gallop, manager of communications. Circ. 14,000. Estab. 1986. Monthly publication of Evangelical Lutheran Church in Canada. Emphasizes faith/religious content, Lutheran denomination. Readers are members of the Evangelical Lutheran Church in Canada. Sample copy available for $5 Canadian (includes postage).

Needs Buys 1-2 photos from freelancers/issue; 12-24 photos/year. Needs photos of people in worship, at work/play, diversity, advocacy, youth/young people, etc. Canadian sources preferred.

Specs Accepts images in digital format. Send via CD, e-mail as JPEG files at 300 dpi minimum.

Making Contact & Terms Send sample prints and photo CDs by mail (include SASE for return of material) or send low-resolution images by e-mail. Pays $75-125 for color cover, $15-50 for b&w inside. Prices are in Canadian dollars. Pays on publication. Credit line given. Buys one-time rights.

Tips "Give us many photos that show your range. We prefer to keep them on file for at least a year. We have a short-term turnaround and turn to our file on a monthly basis to illustrate articles or cover concepts. Changing technology speeds up the turnaround time considerably when assessing images, yet forces publishers to think farther in advance to be able to achieve promised cost savings. U.S. photographers—send via U.S. mail. We sometimes get wrongly charged duty at the border when shipping via couriers."

$⬛ ⬛ ⬛ CANADIAN HOMES & COTTAGES

2650 Meadowvale Blvd., Unit 4, Mississauga ON L5N 6M5 Canada. (905)567-1440. Fax: (905)567-1442. E-mail: editorial@homesandcottages.com. Web site: www.homesandcotta ges.com. **Contact:** Steven Chester, managing editor. Circ. 79,099. Bimonthly. Canada's largest building, renovation and home improvement magazine. Photo guidelines free with SASE.

Needs Needs photos of landscapes/scenics, architecture, interiors/decorating.

Making Contact & Terms Does not keep samples on file; cannot return material. Responds only if interested; send nonreturnable samples. **Pays on acceptance.** Credit line given.

▣ ⬓ THE CANADIAN ORGANIC GROWER

Canadian Organic Growers, 129 Beech Hill Rd., Weldon NB E4H 4N5 Canada. E-mail: janet@cog.ca. Web site: www.cog.ca. **Contact:** Janet Wallace, managing editor. Circ. 4,000. Estab. 1975. Quarterly consumer magazine for organic gardeners, farmers and consumers in Canada.

Needs Needs photos of gardening, rural, agriculture, organic gardening and farming in Canada. Reviews photos with or without accompanying manuscript. Captions required; include identification of subjects.

Specs Accepts images in digital format. Send JPEG or GIF files

Making Contact & Terms Pays on publication. Credit line given. Buys one-time rights.

⬚ $⬓ CANADIAN YACHTING

800-2 St. Clair Ave. E., Toronto ON M4T 2T5 Canada. (416)703-7167. Fax: (416)513-0348. E-mail: eakerr@kerrwil.com. Web site: www.cymagazine.ca. **Contact:** Elizabeth A. Kerr, publisher. Circ. 31,000. Estab. 1976. Bimonthly magazine. Emphasizes sailing (and power-boats). Readers are mostly male, highly educated, high income, well read. Sample copy free with upon request.

Needs Buys 28 photos from freelancers/issue; 168 photos/year. Needs photos of all sailing/boating-related (keelboats, dinghies, racing, cruising, etc.). Model/property release preferred. Photo captions preferred.

Making Contact & Terms Submit portfolio for review or query with SASE, stock photo list and transparencies. Responds in 1 month. Simultaneous submissions and previously published work OK. Pays $150-350 for color cover; $30-70 for b&w or color inside. Pays on publication. Buys one-time rights.

$ $⬚ ⬚ ▣ CANOE & KAYAK

P.O. Box 3146, Kirkland WA 98083-3146. (425)827-6363. Fax: (425)827-1893. E-mail: photos@canoekayak.com. Web site: www.canoekayak.com. **Contact:** Art Director. Circ. 63,000. Estab. 1973. Bimonthly magazine. Emphasizes a variety of paddle sports, as well as how-to material and articles about equipment. For upscale canoe and kayak enthusiasts at all levels of ability. Also publishes special projects. Sample copy free with 9×12 SASE.

Needs Buys 25 photos from freelancers/issue; 150 photos/year. Needs photos of canoeing, kayaking, ocean touring, canoe sailing, fishing when compatible to the main activity, canoe camping but not rafting. No photos showing disregard for the environment, be it river or land; no photos showing gasoline-powered, multi-hp engines; no photos showing unskilled persons taking extraordinary risks to life, etc. Accompanying manuscripts for ''editorial coverage striving for balanced representation of all interests in today's paddling activity. Those interests include paddling adventures (both close to home and far away), camping, fishing, flatwater, whitewater, ocean kayaking, poling, sailing, outdoor photography, how-to projects, instruction and historical perspective. Regular columns feature paddling techniques, conservation topics, safety, interviews, equipment reviews, book/movie reviews, new products and letters from readers.'' Photos only occasionally purchased without accompanying manuscript. Model release preferred ''when potential for litigation.'' Property release required. Photo captions preferred.

Specs Uses 5×7, 8×10 glossy b&w prints; 35mm, 2¼×2¼, 4×5 transparencies; color transparencies for cover; vertical format preferred. Accepts images in digital format. Send via CD, Zip as TIFF, EPS, JPEG files at 300 dpi.

Making Contact & Terms Interested in reviewing work from newer, lesser-known photographers. Query or send material. "Let me know those areas in which you have particularly strong expertise and/or photo file material. Send best samples only and make sure they relate to the magazine's emphasis and/or focus. (If you don't know what that is, pick up a recent issue before sending me unusable material.) We will review dupes for consideration only. Originals required for publication. Also, if you have something in the works or extraordinary photo subject matter of interest to our audience, let me know! It would be helpful to me if those with substantial reserves would supply indexes by subject matter." Include SASE for return of material. Responds in 1 month. Simultaneous submissions and previously published work OK, in noncompeting publications. Pays $500-700 for color cover; $75-200 for b&w inside; $75-350 for color inside. Pays on publication. Credit line given. Buys one-time rights, first serial rights and exclusive rights.

Tips "We have a highly specialized subject, and readers don't want just any photo of the activity. We're particularly interested in photos showing paddlers' *faces*; the faces of people having a good time. We're after anything that highlights the paddling activity as a lifestyle and the urge to be outdoors." All photos should be "as natural as possible with authentic subjects. We receive a lot of submissions from photographers to whom canoeing and kayaking are quite novel activities. These photos are often clichéd and uninteresting. So consider the quality of your work carefully before submission if you are not familiar with the sport. We are always in search of fresh ways of looking at our sport. All paddlers must be wearing life vests/PFDs."

$THE CAPE ROCK

Southeast Missouri State University, Cape Girardeau MO 63701. (573)651-2500. E-mail: hhecht@semo.edu. Web site: http://cstl-cla.semo.edu/hhecht/caperock.htm. **Contact:** Harvey Hecht, editor-in-chief. Circ. 1,000. Estab. 1964. Semiannual. Emphasizes poetry and poets for libraries and interested persons. Photo guidelines available on Web site.

Needs Uses 11 photos/issue (at least 9 of which must be "portrait format." A cover photo is usually color; the others are printed in b&w. "We feature a single photographer each issue. Submit 25-30 thematically organized black-and-white glossies (at least 5×7), or send 5 pictures with plan for complete issue. We favor a series that conveys a sense of place, e.g., an issue featuring Chicago might show buildings or other landmarks, people of the city (no nudes), travel or scenic. No how-to or products. Sample issues and guidelines provide all information a photographer needs to decide whether to submit to us." Model release not required, "but photographer is liable." Photo captions not required, "but photographer should indicate where series was shot."

Making Contact & Terms Send query letter with list of stock photo subjects, actual photos or a high quality digital file for review; include SASE for return of material. Response time varies. Pays $100 and 10 copies of publication. Credit line given. Buys all rights, but will release rights to photographer on request.

Tips "We don't give assignments, but we look for a unified package put together by the photographer. We may request additional or alternative photos when accepting a package."

CARLSBAD MAGAZINE

Wheelhouse Media, 2917 State St., Suite 210, Carlsbad CA 92008. (760)729-9010. Fax: (760)729-9011. E-mail: carly@carlsbadmagazine.com. Web site: www.clickoncarlsbad.com; www.carlsbadmagazine.com. **Contact:** Carly Bartkiewicz, managing editor. Circ.

Consumer Publications

37,000. Estab. 2004. Bimonthly consumer magazine covering the people, places, events and arts in Carlsbad, California. "We are a regional magazine highlighting all things pertaining specifically to Carlsbad. We focus on history, events, people and places that make Carlsbad interesting and unique. Our audience is both Carlsbad residents and visitors or anyone interested in learning more about Carlsbad." Sample copy available for $2.31.

Needs Needs photos of gardening, entertainment, events, performing arts. Interested in historical/vintage, lifestyle. "People, places, events, arts in Carlsbad, California."

Specs Accepts images in digital format. Send as GIF or JPEG files.

Making Contact & Terms Pays $15-400/photo. Pays on publication. Credit line given. Buys one-time rights.

Tips "E-mail is the preferred method for queries."

$▣ CHESS LIFE FOR KIDS

U.S. Chess Federation, P.O. Box 3967, Crossville TN 38557. (732)252-8388. E-mail: gpeterse n@uschess.org. Web site: www.uschess.org. **Contact:** Glenn Petersen, editor. Estab. 2006. Circ. 28,000. Bimonthly association magazine geared for the young reader, age 12 and under, interested in chess; fellow chess players; tournament results; and instruction. Sample copy available with SAE and first-class postage. Photo guidelines available via e-mail.

Needs Wants photos of babies/children/teens, celebrities, multicultural, families, senior citizens, events, humor. Some aspect of chess must be present: playing, watching, young/old contrast. Reviews photos with or without a manuscript. Property release is required. Captions required.

Specs Accepts images in digital format. Send via Zip or e-mail. Contact Frankie Butler at fbutler@uschess.org for more information on digital specs. Uses glossy color prints.

Making Contact & Terms E-mail query letter with link to photographer's Web site. Provide self-promotion piece to be kept on file. Responds in 1 week to queries and portfolios. Simultaneous submissions and previously published work OK. Pays $150 minimum/$300 maximum for color cover. Pays $35 for color inside. Pays on publication. Credit line given. Rights are negotiable. Will negotiate with a photographer unwilling to sell all rights.

Tips "Read the magazine. What would appeal to *your* 10-year-old? Be original. We have plenty of people to shoot headshots and award ceremonies. And remember, you're competing against proud parents as well."

◑ ▣ ✂ CHICKADEE MAGAZINE

10 Lower Spadina Ave., Suite 400, Toronto ON M5V 2Z2 Canada. (416)340-2700. Fax: (416)340-9769. E-mail: deb@owlkids.com. Web site: www.owlkids.com. **Contact:** Debbie Yea, photo researcher. Circ. 92,000. Estab. 1979. Published 10 times/year. A discovery magazine for children ages 6-9. Sample copy available for $4.95 with 9×12 SAE and $1.50 money order to cover postage. Photo guidelines available for SAE or via e-mail.

- *chickaDEE* has received Magazine of the Year, Parents' Choice, Silver Honor, Canadian Children's Book Centre Choice and several Distinguished Achievement awards from the Association of Educational Publishers.

Needs Photo stories, photo puzzles, children ages 6-10, multicultural, environmental, wildlife, pets, adventure, events, hobbies, humor, performing arts, sports, travel, science, technology, animals in their natural habitats. Interested in documentary, seasonal. Model/property release required. Photo captions required.

Specs Prefers images in digital format. E-mail as TIFF, JPEG files at 72 dpi; 300 dpi required for publication.

Making Contact & Terms Previously published work OK. Credit line given. Buys one-time rights.

⬤ ▣ ⬆ CHIRP MAGAZINE

10 Lower Spadina Ave., Suite 400, Toronto ON M5V 2Z2 Canada. (416)340-2700. Fax: (416)340-9769. E-mail: deb@owlkids.com. Web site: www.owlkids.com. **Contact:** Debbi Yea, photo researcher. Circ. 85,000. Estab. 1997. Published 10 times/year. A discovery magazine for children ages 3-6. Sample copy available for $4.95 with 9×12 SAE and $1.50 money order to cover postage. Photo guidelines available for SAE or via e-mail.

• *Chirp* has received Best New Magazine of the Year, Parents' Choice, Canadian Children's Book Centre Choice and Distinguished Achievement awards from the Association of Educational Publishers.

Needs Photo stories, photo puzzles, children ages 5-7, multicultural, environmental, wildlife, adventure, events, hobbies, humor, animals in their natural habitats. Interested in documentary, seasonal. Model/property release required. Photo captions required.

Specs Prefers images in digital format. Send via CD, e-mail as TIFF, JPEG files at 72 dpi; 300 dpi required for publication.

Making Contact & Terms Previously published work OK. Credit line given. Buys one-time rights.

$ $⬤ ▣ CLEVELAND MAGAZINE

Great Lakes Publishing, 1422 Euclid Ave., #730, Cleveland OH 44115. (216)771-2833. Fax: (216)781-6318. E-mail: kessen@clevelandmagazine.com. Web site: www.clevelandmagazine.com. **Contact:** Jennifer Kessen, art director. Circ. 50,000. Estab. 1972. Monthly consumer magazine emphasizing Cleveland, Ohio. General interest to upscale audience.

Needs Buys 50 photos from freelancers/issue; 600 photos/year. Needs photos of people (babies/children/teens, celebrities, couples, multicultural, parents, families, senior citizens), environmental, landscapes/scenics, architecture, education, gardening, interiors/decorating, adventure, entertainment, events, food/drink, health/fitness, hobbies, humor, performing arts, sports, travel, business concepts, industry, medicine, political, product shots/still life, technology/computers. Interested in documentary, fashion/glamour, seasonal. Reviews photos with or without a manuscript. Model release required for portraits; property release required for individual homes. Photo captions required; include names, date, location, event, phone.

Specs Prefers images in digital format. Send via CD, e-mail as TIFF, JPEG files at 300 dpi. Also uses color and b&w prints; 35mm, $2^{1}/_{4} \times 2^{1}/_{4}$, 4×5, 8×10 transparencies.

Making Contact & Terms Provide self-promotion piece or tearsheets to be kept on file for possible future assignments. Responds only if interested. Pays on publication. Credit line given. Buys one-time publication, electronic and promotional rights.

$⬛ ▣ COMPANY MAGAZINE

P.O. Box 60790, Chicago IL 60660-0790. (773)761-9432. Fax: (773)761-9443. E-mail: editor@companymagazine.org. Web site: www.companymagazine.org. **Contact:** Martin McHugh, editor. Circ. 114,000. Estab. 1983. Quarterly magazine published by the Jesuits (Society of Jesus). Emphasizes Jesuit works/ministries and the people involved in them. Sample copy available for 9×12 SAE.

Needs Needs photos and photo-stories of Jesuit and allied ministries and projects. Reviews photos with or without manuscript. Photo captions required.

Specs Accepts images in digital format. Send via CD, Zip, e-mail "at screen resolution as long as higher-res is available."

Making Contact & Terms Query with samples; include SASE for return of material. Provide résumé, business card, brochure, flier or tearsheets to be kept on file for possible future assignments. Responds in 1 month. Pays $50-100 for individual photos; $300 for color cover; up to $750 for photo story. Pays on publication. Credit line given. Buys one-time rights; negotiable.

Tips "Avoid large-group, 'smile-at-camera' photos. We are interested in people/activity photographs that tell a story about Jesuit ministries."

$⊡ CONFRONTATION MAGAZINE

English Dept., C.W. Post Campus of Long Island University, 720 Northern Blvd., Brookville NY 11548. (516)299-2391. Fax: (516)299-2735. E-mail: martin.tucker@liu.edu. **Contact:** Martin Tucker, editor. Circ. 2,000. Estab. 1968. Semiannual literary magazine. Readers are college-educated lay people interested in literature. Sample copy available for $3.

Needs Reviews photos with or without manuscript. Photo captions preferred.

Making Contact & Terms Send query letter with résumé of credits, stock list. Responds in 1 month. Simultaneous submissions OK. Pays $100-300 for b&w or color cover; $40-100 for b&w inside; $50-100 for color inside. Pays on publication. Credit line given. Buys first North American serial rights; negotiable.

▣ CONTEMPORARY BRIDE MAGAZINE

216 Stelton Rd., Unit D-1, Piscataway NJ 08854. (732)968-0123. Fax: (732)968-0220. E-mail: gary@contemporarybride.com. Web site: www.contemporarybride.com. **Contact:** Gary Paris, publisher. Circ. 120,000. Estab. 1994. Biannual bridal magazine with wedding planner; 4-color publication with editorial, calendars, check-off lists and advertisers. Sample copy available for first-class postage.

Needs Needs photos of travel destinations, fashion, bridal events. Reviews photos with accompanying manuscript only. Model/property release preferred. Photo captions preferred; include photo credits.

Specs Accepts images in digital format. Send as high-res files at 300 dpi.

Making Contact & Terms Send query letter with samples. Art director will contact photographer for portfolio review if interested. Provide b&w and/or color prints, disc. Keeps samples on file; cannot return material. Responds only if interested; send nonreturnable samples. Simultaneous submissions and previously published work OK. Payment negotiable. Buys all rights, electronic rights.

Tips "Digital images preferred with a creative eye for all wedding-related photos. Give us the *best* presentation."

$☐ ⑤ CONTINENTAL NEWSTIME

501 W. Broadway, Plaza A, PMB #265, San Diego CA 92101-3802. (858)492-8696. E-mail: ContinentalNewsService@yahoo.com. Web site: www.ContinentalNewsService.com. **Contact:** Gary P. Salamone, editor-in-chief. Estab. 1987. Twice-monthly general interest magazine of news and commentary on U.S. national and world news, with travel columns, entertainment features, humor pieces, comic strips, general humor panels, and editorial

cartoons. Covers the unreported and under-reported national (U.S.) and international news. Sample copy available for $4 in US and $6 CAN/foreign.

Needs Buys variable number of photos from freelancers. Needs photos of celebrities, public figures, U.S. and foreign government officials/cabinet ministers, newsworthy events, breaking/unreported/under-reported news. Reviews photos with or without a manuscript. Model/property release required. Photo captions required.

Specs Uses 8×10 color and/or b&w prints.

Making Contact & Terms Send query letter with résumé, photocopies, tearsheets, stock list. Provide résumé to be kept on file for possible future assignments. Responds only if interested; send nonreturnable samples. Simultaneous submissions OK. Pays $10 minimum for b&w cover. Pays on publication. Credit line given. Buys one-time rights.

Tips "Read our magazine to develop a better feel for our photo applications/uses and to satisfy our stated photo needs."

ⓝ Ⓩ COSMOPOLITAN

Hearst Communications, Inc., 224 W. 57th St., 8th Floor, New York NY 10019. (212)649-2000. E-mail: cosmopolitan@hearst.com. Web site: www.cosmopolitan.com. *Cosmopolitan* targets young women for whom beauty, fashion, fitness, career, relationships and personal growth are top priorities. It includes articles and columns on nutrition and food, travel, personal finance, home/lifestyle and celebrities. *Query before submitting.*

$ $Ⓩ Ⓢ ▣ COUNTRY

Reiman Media Group, Inc., 5400 S. 60th St., Greendale WI 53129. Fax: (414)423-8463. E-mail: photocoordinator@rcimanpub.com. Web site: www.country-magazine.com. **Contact:** Trudi Bellin, photo coordinator. Estab. 1987. Bimonthly magazine. "For those who live in or long for the country." Readers are rural-oriented, male and female. "*Country* is supported entirely by subscriptions and accepts no outside advertising." Sample copy available for $2. Photo guidelines free with SASE.

● *Country EXTRA* is published in the months between regular issues. Content and guidelines are the same.

Needs Buys 40 photos from freelancers/issue; 480 photos/year. Needs photos of families, senior citizens, gardening, travel, agriculture, country scenics, animals, rural and small-town folk at work or wholesome play. Interested in historical/vintage, seasonal. Photo captions preferred; include season, location.

Specs Prefers color transparencies, all sizes. Accepts images in digital format: TIFF or high-quality JPEG files at 300 dpi for up to 9×11 reproduction. Embedded metadata is recommended. Send via lightboxes or on removable media. Or send CD/DVD with printed thumbnails and caption sheet. E-mail if first review selection is small (12 images or less).

Making Contact & Terms Send query letter with résumé of credits, stock list. Send unsolicited photos by mail for consideration. Keeps samples on file (tearsheets, no dupes); include SASE for return of material. Responds in 3 months. Previously published work OK. Buys stock only. Pays $300 for color cover; $200 for color back cover; $100-300 for color inside. Pays on publication. Credit line given. Buys one-time rights to stock photos; all rights to assignment.

Tips "Technical quality is extremely important; focus must be sharp (no soft focus), and colors must be vivid so they 'pop off the page.' Study our magazine thoroughly—we have a continuing need for sharp, colorful images, especially those taken along the backroads of rural North America. Photographers who can supply what we need can expect to be regular contributors. Submissions are on spec and should cover only one season.''

$⊘ ▣ CYCLE CALIFORNIA! MAGAZINE

1702-L Meridian Ave., #289, San Jose CA 95125. (888)292-5323. Fax: (408)292-3005. E-mail: bmack@cyclecalifornia.com. Web site: www.cyclecalifornia.com. **Contact:** Bob Mack, publisher. Circ. 30,000. Estab. 1995. Monthly magazine providing readers with a comprehensive source of bicycling information, emphasizing the bicycling life in northern California and Nevada; promotes bicycling in all its facets. Sample copy available for 9×12 SAE with $1.31 first-class postage. Photo guidelines available for 37¢ SASE.

Needs Buys 3-5 photos from freelancers/issue; 45 photos/year. Needs photos of recreational bicycling, bicycle racing, triathalons, bicycle touring and adventure racing. Cover photos must be vertical format, color. All cyclists must be wearing a helmet if riding. Reviews photos with or without manuscript. Model release required; property release preferred. Photo captions preferred; include when and where photo is taken; if an event, include name, date and location of event; for nonevent photos, location is important.

Specs High-resolution TIFF images preferred (2000×3000 pixel minimum). Cover photos are 7×9 inches. Uses 4×6 matte color and b&w prints.

Making Contact & Terms Send query letter with slides, prints or CD/disk. Keeps usable images on file; include SASE for return of material. Responds in 3 weeks. Simultaneous submissions OK. Pays $125 for color cover; $25 for b&w inside; $50 for color inside. Pays on publication.

Tips ''We are looking for photographic images that depict the fun of bicycle riding. Your submissions should show people enjoying the sport. Read the magazine to get a feel for what we do. Label images so we can tell what description goes with which image.''

⊘ ▣ DANCE

2660 Petersborough St., Herndon VA 20171. E-mail: shannonaswriter@yahoo.com. Quarterly publication featuring international dancers.

Needs Needs photos of babies/children/teens, celebrities, couples, multicultural, families, parents, senior citizens, environmental, landscapes/scenics, wildlife, architecture, cities/urban, gardening, interiors/decorating, pets, religious, rural, performing arts, agriculture, product shots/still life—as related to international dance for children and teens. Interested in alternative process, avant garde, documentary, fashion/glamour, fine art, historical/vintage, seasonal. Reviews photos with or without a manuscript. Model/property release preferred.

Specs Uses glossy or matte color and/or b&w prints.

Making Contact & Terms Send query letter via e-mail. Provide résumé, business card, self-promotion piece to be kept on file for possible future assignments. ''Photographs sent along with CDs are requested but not required. Artwork and illustrations also accepted.'' Responds within 1 month to queries; 1 week to portfolios. Simultaneous submissions and previously published work OK. **Pays on acceptance.** Credit line given. Buys one-time rights, first rights; negotiable.

$⊘ ▣ 🌐 DIGITAL PHOTO

Bauer Active, Media House, Lynchwood, Peterborough Business Park, Peterborough PE2 6EA United Kingdom. +44 1733 468 546. Fax: +44 1733 468 387. E-mail: dp@bauerconsu mer.co.uk. Circ. 70,000. Estab. 1997. Monthly consumer magazine. "The UK's best-selling photography and imaging magazine—learn how to use your digital camera the right way and enhance the results in Photoshop and Elements software—we make it easy!"

Needs Stunning, digitally manipulated images of any subject and Photoshop, Elements, or Paint Shop Pro step-by-step tutorials of any subject. Reviews photos with or without a manuscript. Model/property release preferred. Photo captions preferred.

Specs Uses up to A4 glossy color and/or b&w prints. Accepts images in digital format. Send via CD as PSD, TIFF, JPEG files at 300 dpi.

Making Contact & Terms Send query letter with résumé, tearsheets, contact prints and CD with high-res files. Provide SAE for eventual return. Responds in 1 month to queries. Rates negotiable. Pays on publication. Credit line given. Buys first rights.

Tips "Read magazine to check the type of images we use, and send a sample of images you think would be suitable. The broader your style, the better for general acceptance, while individual styles appeal to our Gallery section. Step-by-step technique pieces must be formatted to house style, so check magazine before submitting. Supply a contact sheet or thumbnail of all the images supplied in electronic form to make it easier for us to make a quick decision on the work."

🅽 $⊘ ⚏ DOGS IN CANADA

Apex Publishing Ltd., 200 Ronsone Dr., Suite 401, Etobicoke ON M9W 5Z9 Canada. (416)798-9778. Fax: (416)798-9671. E-mail: photos@dogsincanada.com. Web site: www.dogsincanada.com. **Contact:** Kelly Caldwell, editor-in-chief/art director. Circ. 41,769. Estab. 1889. Monthly consumer magazine. "*Dogs in Canada* magazine is a reliable and authoritative source of information about dogs. Our mix of editorial content and photography must satisfy a diverse readership, including breed fanciers and those who simply have a beloved family pet. Photography is of central importance." Sample copy available for $4.95 and 8×10 SAE with postage. Request photo guidelines via e-mail.

Needs Buys 10-30 photos/year. Needs photos from any category as long as there is a dog in the shot. Reviews photos with or without a manuscript. Model/property release preferred. Photo captions preferred; include breed of dog.

Specs Prefers images in digital format. Send via CD as TIFF or ESP files at 300 dpi.

Making Contact & Terms E-mail query letter with link to photographer's Web site and JPEG samples at 72 dpi. Send query letter with slides, prints. Provide résumé, business card, self-promotion piece to be kept on file for possible future assignments. Responds only if interested; send nonreturnable samples. Considers previously published work. Pays $80-600 for b&w or color cover; $50-300 for b&w or color inside. Pays net 30 days. Credit line given. Buys first rights, electronic rights.

Tips "Well-composed, high-quality photographs are expected. A creative approach catches our eye. Photos that capture a moment in time and the essence of a dog are preferred to a staged portrait."

$ $⊟ DUCKS UNLIMITED

One Waterfowl Way, Memphis TN 38120. (901)758-3864. E-mail: jhoffman@ducks.org. Web site: www.ducks.org. **Contact:** John Hoffman, photo editor. Circ. 700,000. Estab. 1937. Bimonthly association magazine of Ducks Unlimited, a nonprofit organization. Emphasizes waterfowl hunting and conservation. Readers are professional males, ages 40-50. Sample copy available for $3. Photo guidelines available on Web site, via e-mail or with SASE.

Consumer Publications

Needs Buys 84 photos from freelancers/issue; 504 photos/year. Needs images of wild ducks and geese, waterfowling and scenic wetlands. Special photo needs include waterfowl hunters, dynamic shots of waterfowl interacting in natural habitat.

Specs Accepts images in digital format. Send via CD as TIFF, JPEG, EPS files at 300 dpi; include thumbnails.

Making Contact & Terms Send only top-quality portfolio of not more than 40 transparencies (35mm or larger) with SASE for consideration. Responds in 1 month. Previously published work OK, if noted. Pays on publication. Credit line given. Buys one-time rights "plus permission to reprint in our Mexican and Canadian publications."

$ $⨂ Ⓢ ▣ E/THE ENVIRONMENTAL MAGAZINE

28 Knight St., Norwalk CT 06851. (203)854-5559. Fax: (203)866-0602. E-mail: bbelli@emag azine.com. Web site: www.emagazine.com. **Contact:** Brita Belli, editor, photos editor. Trudy Hodenfield, art director. Circ. 60,000. Estab. 1988. Nonprofit consumer magazine. Emphasizes environmental issues. Readers are environmental activists, people concerned about the environment. Sample copy available for 9×12 SAE and $5. Photo guidelines free with SASE or via e-mail.

Needs Buys 20 photos from freelancers/issue. Needs photos of threatened landscapes, environmental leaders, people and the environment, pollution, transportation, energy, wildlife and activism. Photo captions required; include location, identities of people in photograph, date, action in photograph.

Specs Accepts images in digital format. Send via CD, Zip, e-mail as TIFF, EPS, JPEG files at 300 dpi and at least 3×4 print size.

Making Contact & Terms Send query letter with résumé of credits and list of stock photo subjects, specialties or accompanying story ideas. Keeps printed samples on file. Responds in 6 weeks. Simultaneous submissions and previously published work OK. Pays up to $500 for color cover; up to $250 for color inside. Pays several weeks after publication. Credit line given. Buys print and Web version rights.

Tips Wants to see "straightforward, journalistic images. Abstract or art photography or landscape photography is not used." In addition, "please do not send manuscripts with photographs. These can be addressed as queries to the managing editor."

$ $⨂ Ⓢ ▣ THE ELKS MAGAZINE

425 W. Diversey Pkwy., Chicago IL 60614-6196. (773)755-4894. Fax: (773)755-4792. E-mail: cheryls@elks.org. Web site: www.elks.org/elksmag. **Contact:** Cheryl T. Stachura, editor/publisher. Circ. nearly 1 million. Estab. 1922. Magazine published 10 times/year. Mission is to provide news of Elks to all 1 million members. "In addition, we have general interest articles. Themes: Americana; history; wholesome, family info; sports; industries; adventure; technology. We do not cover religion, politics, controversial issues." Sample copy free.

Needs Buys 10 cover photos/year; mostly from stock photo houses; approximately 20 photos/month for interior use. "Photographs of Elks in action are particularly welcome." Reviews photos with or without a manuscript. Photo captions required; include location.

Specs Accepts high-resolution digital images. Uses 35mm, $2^{1}/_{4} \times 2^{1}/_{4}$, 4×5, 8×10 transparencies.

Making Contact & Terms Send query letter with samples. Does not keep samples on file; include SASE for return of material. Responds in 2 months to queries. Simultaneous submissions OK. Pays $475 for color cover. Pays on publication. Credit line given. Buys one-time rights.

Tips "Artistry and technical excellence are as important as subject matter. We are now purchasing 90 percent of our photographs from photographic stock houses."

$ $⊘ ▣ ENTREPRENEUR

2445 McCabe Way, Suite 400, Irvine CA 92614. (949)261-2325. E-mail: rolson@entrepreneu r.com. Web site: www.entrepreneur.com. **Contact:** Richard R. Olson, design director. Circ. 650,000. Estab. 1977. Monthly magazine emphasizing business. Readers are existing and aspiring small business owners.

Needs Uses about 40 photos/issue; about 10% supplied by freelance photographers; 80% on assignment; 10% from stock. Needs "people at work, home office, business situations. I want to see colorful shots in all formats and styles." Model/property release preferred. Photo captions required; include names of subjects.

Specs Accepts images in digital format and film. Send via Zip, CD, e-mail as TIFF, EPS, JPEG files at 300 dpi.

Making Contact & Terms Provide résumé, business card, brochure, flier or tearsheets to be kept on file for possible future assignments. Pays $2,000 for color cover; $700 for color inside. **Pays on acceptance.** Credit line given. Buys one-time North American rights; negotiable.

Tips "I am looking for photographers who use the environment creatively; I do not like blank walls for backgrounds. Lighting is also important. I prefer medium-format for most shoots. I think photographers are going back to the basics—a good, clean shot, different angles and bright colors. I also like gelled lighting. I prefer examples of your work—promo cards and tearsheets—along with business cards and résumés."

$◻ ▣ ⊕ EOS MAGAZINE

Robert Scott Publishing Ltd., The Old Barn, Ball Lane, Tackley, Kidlington, Oxfordshire 0X5 3AG United Kingdom. (44)(186)933-1741. Fax: (44)(186)933-1641. E-mail: editorial@eos-magazine.com. Web site: www.eos-magazine.com. **Contact:** Angela August, editor. Circ. 20,000. Estab. 1993. Quarterly consumer magazine for all users of Canon EOS cameras. Photo guidelines free.

Needs Looking for quality stand-alone images as well as photos showing specific photographic techniques and comparison pictures. All images must be taken with EOS cameras but not necessarily with Canon lenses. Model release preferred. Photo captions required; include technical details of photo equipment and techniques used.

Specs Accepts images in digital format exclusively.

Making Contact & Terms E-mail to request 'Notes for Contributors' (Put this in the subject line). You will be e-mailed with further information about how to submit images, current requirements, and rates of payment. Pays on publication. Credit line given. Buys one-time rights.

Tips "We are more likely to use images from photographers who submit a wide selection of top-quality images (40-60 images)."

$ $⊘ ▣ ⬙ FAITH TODAY

Evangelical Fellowship of Canada, MIP Box 3745, Markham ON L3R 0Y4 Canada. (905)479-6071, ext 241. Fax: (905)479-4742. E-mail: FTeditor@efc-canada.com. Web site: www.faith

today.ca. **Contact:** Bill Fledderus, senior editor. Circ. 18,000. Estab. 1983. Bimonthly consumer publication. Sample copy free for SAE.

Needs Buys 3 photos from freelancers/issue; 18 photos/year. Needs photojournalism of Canadian religious events and photos of multicultural, families, senior citizens, education, religious. Interested in religious historical/vintage. Also looking for scenes of church life: people praying, singing, etc. Reviews photos with or without a manuscript. Photo captions required.

Specs Uses color prints. Accepts images in digital format. Send via e-mail as TIFF, EPS, JPEG files at 266 dpi.

Making Contact & Terms Send query letter with photocopies, stock list. Does not keep samples on file; include SASE for return of material. Responds only if interested; send nonreturnable samples. Simultaneous submissions and previously published work OK. Pays $25-400 for color cover; $25-150 for color inside. Pays on publication. Credit line given ''if requested.'' Buys one-time rights.

Tips ''We emphasize Canada and so generally use photos that are clearly Canadian. Our Web site does not adequately represent our use of photos but does list sample articles, so you can see the kind of topics we cover. We also commission illustrations and welcome queries on that. Many of our photos come via DesignPics.com.''

$ $⊘ ⑤ ▣ FARM & RANCH LIVING

Reiman Media Group, Inc., 5400 S. 60th St., Greendale WI 53129. Fax: (414)423-8463. E-mail: photocoordinator@reimanpub.com. Web site: www.farmandranchliving.com. **Contact:** Trudi Bellin, photo coordinator. Estab. 1978. Bimonthly magazine. ''Concentrates on families who love the land.'' Readers are full-time farmers and ranchers. *''Farm & Ranch Living* is supported entirely by subscriptions and accepts no outside advertising.'' Sample copy available for $2. Photo guidelines free with SASE.

Needs Buys 30 photos from freelancers/issue; 160 photos/year. Needs photos of beautiful or warmhearted agricultural scenes, lifestyle images of farmers and ranchers (riding, gardening, restoring tractors, handling livestock, hobbies, pets, etc.). Looks for everything from colorful close-ups of produce to panoramic vistas of crops and pastures in a scenic environment. Especially interested in great seasonal shots of agriculture: harvests, feeding cattle in winter, planting, mowing hay. ''Shots that are creative, pretty, idyllic or have a warmhearted human interest quality have the best chance of being used.'' Photo captions preferred; include season and location, and identify subject (type of crop, livestock, etc.).

Specs Prefers color transparencies, all sizes. Accepts images in digital format: TIFF or high-quality JPEG files at 300 dpi for up to 9×11 reproduction. Embedded metadata is recommended. Send via lightboxes or on removable media with printed thumbnails and caption sheet. E-mail if first review selection is small (12 images or less).

Making Contact & Terms Send query letter with samples or list of stock photo subjects; include SASE for return of material. ''We review one season at a time; we work one season in advance.'' Responds in 3 months. Previously published work OK. Buys stock only. Pays $300 for color cover; $200 for color back cover; $100-300 for inside. Pays on publication. Buys one-time rights to stock photos; all rights to assignments.

Tips ''Technical quality is extremely important; focus must be sharp (no soft focus), and colors must be vivid so they 'pop off the page.' Study our magazine thoroughly. We have a continuing need for sharp, colorful images. Those who supply what we need can expect to be regular contributors.''

Consumer Publications

$□ FELLOWSHIP

P.O. Box 271, Nyack NY 10960. (845)358-4601, ext. 42. Fax: (845)358-4924. E-mail: editor@ forusa.org. Web site: www.forusa.org. **Contact:** Ethan Vesely-Flad, editor. Circ. 6,000. Estab. 1935. Publication of the Fellowship of Reconciliation; quarterly magazine (36-52 pages) published 4 times/year. Emphasizes peace-making, social justice, nonviolent social change. Readers are interested in peace, justice, nonviolence and spirituality. Sample copy available for $7.50.

Needs Buys 1-2 photos from freelancers/issue; 4-10 photos/year. Needs stock photos of people, civil disobedience, demonstrations—Middle East, Latin America, Caribbean, prisons, anti-nuclear, children, gay/lesbian, human rights issues, Asia/Pacific. Other needs include landscapes/scenics, disasters, environmental, wildlife, religious, humor. Interested in fine art; b&w only. Captions required.

Making Contact & Terms Provide résumé, business card, brochure, flier or tearsheets to be kept on file for possible future assignments. ''Call on specs.'' Responds in 4-6 weeks. Simultaneous submissions and previously published work OK. Pays $100 for color cover; $35 for b&w inside. Pays on publication. Credit line given. Buys one-time rights.

Tips ''You must want to make a contribution to peace movements. Money is simply token.''

$☑ ▣ FIELD & STREAM

2 Park Ave., New York NY 10016. (212)779-5238. Fax: (212)779-5114. Web site: www.field andstream.com. **Contact:** Amy Berkley, photo editor. Circ. 1.5 million. Broad-based service magazine published 11 times/year. Editorial content ranges from very basic ''how it's done'' filler stories that tell in pictures and words how an outdoor technique is accomplished or device is made, to feature articles of penetrating depth about national conservation, game management and resource management issues; also recreational hunting, fishing, travel, nature and outdoor equipment. Photo guidelines available.

Needs Photos using action and a variety of subjects and angles in color and occasionally b&w. ''We are always looking for cover photographs, in color, vertical or horizontal. Remember: a cover picture must have room for cover lines.'' Also looking for interesting photo essay ideas related to hunting and fishing. Query photo editor by mail. Needs photo information regarding subjects, the area, the nature of the activity and the point the picture makes. First Shots: these photos appear every month (2/issue). Prime space, 2-page spread. One of a kind, dramatic, impactful images, capturing the action and excitement of hunting and fishing. Great beauty shots. Unique wildlife images. See recent issues. ''Please do not submit images without reviewing past issues and having a strong understanding of our audience.''

Specs Uses 35mm slides. Will also consider large-format photography. Accepts images in digital format. Send via CD, e-mail as JPEG files at 300 dpi.

Making Contact & Terms Submit photos by registered mail. Send slides in $8\frac{1}{2} \times 11$ plastic sheets, and pack slides and/or prints between cardboard. Include SASE for return of material. Drop portfolios at receptionist's desk, ninth floor. Buys first North American serial rights.

$□ ▣ FIFTY SOMETHING MAGAZINE

1168 Beachview Dr., Willoughby OH 44094. (440)951-2468. Fax: (440)951-1015. E-mail: linde@apk.net. **Contact:** Linda Lindeman-DeCarlo, publisher. Circ. 10,000. Estab. 1990. Quarterly consumer magazine targeted to the 50-and-better reader. Sample copy available

Consumer Publications

for 9×12 SAE with $1.35 first-class postage. Photo guidelines available for #10 SASE.

Needs Buys 2 photos from freelancers/issue; 8 photos/year. Needs photos of celebrities, couples, families, parents, senior citizens, disasters, environmental, landscapes/scenics, architecture, gardening, interiors/decorating, pets, rural, medicine, military, political, product shots/still life, adventure, entertainment, events, health/fitness/beauty, hobbies, humor, sports, travel. Interested in alternative process, avant garde, documentary, fashion/glamour, fine art, historical/vintage, seasonal. Reviews photos with or without a manuscript. Model/property release preferred. Photo captions preferred.

Specs Uses 4×6 glossy color and/or b&w prints; 35mm, 8×10 transparencies. Accepts images in digital format. Send via CD as TIFF, EPS, JPEG files at 300 dpi.

Making Contact & Terms Send query letter with résumé, slides, prints, photocopies, tearsheets, transparencies, stock list. Or direct us to your Web site. Provide résumé, business card, self-promotion piece to be kept on file for possible future assignments. Responds in 2 months. Simultaneous submissions and previously published work OK. Pays $10-100. Pays on publication. Credit line given. Buys one-time rights.

Tips "Looking for photos that are clear and colorful. Need material for historical and nostalgic features. Anything that is directed toward the over-50 reader."

▣ FLY FISHERMAN

Intermedia Outdoors, Inc., 6385 Flank Dr., Harrisburg PA 17112. (717)657-9555. Fax: (717)657-9552. Web site: www.flyfisherman.com. **Contact:** David Siegfried, art director: Editor/publisher: John Randolph. Circ. 130,000. Magazine published 6 times/year. Emphasizes all types of fly fishing for readers who are "80% male, 83% college-educated, 98% married; average household income is $138,000, and 49% are managers or professionals; 68% keep their copies for future reference and spend 33 days/year fishing." Sample copy available via Web site or for $4.95 with 9×12 SAE and 4 first-class stamps. Photo guidelines available on Web site or free with SASE.

Needs Buys 36 photos from freelancers/issue; 216 photos/year. Needs shots of "fly fishing and all related areas—scenics, fish, insects, how-to." Photo captions required.

Making Contact & Terms Send 35mm, 2¼×2¼, 4×5 or 8×10 color transparencies by mail with SASE for consideration. Accepts color digital images on CD or via e-mail for submissions. Responds in 6 weeks. Payment negotiable. Pays on publication. Credit line given. Buys one-time or all rights.

$ $ FOOD & WINE

American Express Publishing Corporation, 1120 Avenue of the Americas, New York NY 10036. (212)382-5600. Web site: www.foodandwine.com. **Contact:** Fredrika Stjarne, director o f photography. Circ. 950,000. Estab. 1978. Monthly magazine. Emphasizes food and wine. Readers are "upscale people who cook, entertain, dine out and travel stylishly."

Needs Uses about 25-30 photos/issue; 85% freelance photography on assignment basis; 15% freelance stock. "We look for editorial reportage specialists who do restaurants, food on location, and travel photography." Model release required. Photo captions required.

Making Contact & Terms Drop off portfolio on Wednesday (attn: Rebecca Jacobs). Call for pickup. Submit fliers, tearsheets, etc., to be kept on file for possible future assignments and stock usage. Pays $450/color page; $100-450 for color photos. **Pays on acceptance.** Credit line given. Buys one-time world rights.

$ $▣ FORTUNE

Rockefeller Center, Time-Life Bldg., 1271 Avenue of the Americas, New York NY 10020. (212)522-8021. Fax: (212)467-1213. E-mail: scott_thode@fortunemail.com. Web site: www .fortune.com. **Contact:** Scott Thode, deputy picture editor. Emphasizes analysis of news in the business world for management personnel.

Making Contact & Terms Picture Editor reviews photographers' portfolios on an overnight drop-off basis. Photos purchased on assignment only. Day rate on assignment (against space rate): $500; page rate for space: $400; minimum for b&w or color usage: $200.

ℕ $⬰ ⑤ 🖥 ⊕ FRANCE MAGAZINE

Archant House, Oriel Rd., Cheltenham, Gloucestershire GL50 1BB United Kingdom. (44)(124)221-6050. Fax: (44)(124)221-6076. E-mail: editorial@francemag.com. Web site: www.francemag.com. **Contact:** Stephanie Sheldrake. Circ. 40,000. Estab. 1990. Monthly magazine about France. Readers are male and female, ages 45 and over; people who holiday in France.

Needs Needs photos of France and French subjects: people, places, customs, curiosities, produce, towns, cities, countryside. Photo captions required; include location and as much information as is practical.

Specs Uses 35mm, medium-format transparencies; high-quality digital.

Making Contact & Terms "E-mail in the first instance with list of subjects. Please do not send digital images. We will add you to our photographer list and contact you on an ad-hoc basis for photographic requirements."

⬰ ⑤ FREEFALL

Undead Poets Press, 15735 Kerstyn St., Taylor MI 48180-4891. E-mail: mauruspoet@yahoo. com. **Contact:** Marc Maurus, publisher. Estab. 1997. Circ. 250. Poetry journal "that uses standard snapshot-sized photos, one on the front cover and one on the back." Photo guidelines available with #10 SASE.

Needs Buys 1 or 2 photos from freelancers/issue; 6 photos/year. Needs photos of babies/ children/teens, couples, multicultural, families, parents, senior citizens, architecture, cities/urban, gardening, interiors/decorating, rural, agriculture, industry, medicine, product shots/still life, science, landscapes/scenics, wildlife, hobbies, humor, performing arts, travel. Interested in fine art, seasonal. Model/property release required.

Specs Uses 4×6 glossy or matte color or b&w pritns.

Making Contact & Terms Send query letter with prints. Does not keep samples on file; include SASE for return of material. Credit line given.

Tips "We look for quality composition in artistic work. Our magazine is edgy as often as it is pondering, and we like our photos to be varied as well."

$⬰ 🖥 FT. MYERS MAGAZINE

15880 Summerlin Rd., Suite 189, Ft. Myers FL 33908. E-mail: ftmyers@optonline.net. **Contact:** Andrew Elias, director. Circ. 20,000. Estab. 2002. Magazine published every 2 months for southwest Florida, focusing on local and national arts and lifestyle. *Ft. Myers Magazine* is targeted at successful, educated and active residents of southwest Florida, ages 20-60, as well as guests at the best hotels and resorts on the Gulf Coast. Media columns and features include: books, music, video, films, theater, Internet, software (news, previews, reviews, interviews, profiles). Lifestyle columns and features include: art & design, house

& garden, food & drink, sports & recreation, health & fitness, travel & leisure, science & technology (news, previews, reviews, interviews, profiles). Sample copy available for $3 including postage & handling.

Needs Buys 3-6 photos from freelancers/year. Needs photos of celebrities, architecture, gardening, interiors/decorating, medicine, product shots/still life, environmental, landscapes/scenics, wildlife, entertainment, events, food & drink, health/fitness/beauty, performing arts, sports, travel. Interested in alternative process, avant garde, documentary, fashion/glamour, fine art, historical/vintage. Also needs beaches, beach scenes/sunsets over beaches, boating/fishing, palm trees. Reviews photos with or without a manuscript. Model release required. Photo captions preferred; include description of image and photo credit.

Specs Uses 4×5, 8×10 glossy or matte color and/or b&w prints; 35mm, 2×2, 4×5, 8×10 transparencies ("all are acceptable, but we prefer prints or digital"). Accepts images in digital format. Send via CD, floppy disk, Zip, e-mail (preferred) as TIFF, EPS, PICT, JPEG, PDF files (prefers TIFF or JPEG) at 300-600 dpi.

Making Contact & Terms Send query letter via e-mail with digital images and stock list. Provide résumé, business card, self-promotion piece to be kept on file. Responds only if interested; send nonreturnable samples. Simultaneous submissions and previously published work OK. Pays $100 for b&w or color cover; $25-100 for b&w or color inside. Pays on publication. Credit line given. Buys one-time rights.

Ⓝ $ FUR-FISH-GAME

A.R. Harding Publishing, 2878 E. Main St., Columbus OH 43212. Web site: www.furfishgame.com. **Contact:** Mitch Cox, editor. Monthly outdoor magazine emphasizing hunting, trapping, fishing and camping.

Needs Buys 4 photos from freelancers/issue; 50 photos/year. Needs photos of freshwater fish, wildlife, wilderness and rural scenes. Reviews photos with or without a manuscript. Photo captions required; include subject.

Specs Uses color and/or b&w prints; 35mm transparencies.

Making Contact & Terms Send query letter "and nothing more." Does not keep samples on file; include SASE for return of material. Responds in 1 month to queries. Simultaneous submissions and previously published work OK. Pays $35 minimum for b&w and color inside. Pays on publication. Credit line given. Buys one-time rights.

Ⓝ $ $ ⬚ GEORGIA STRAIGHT

1701 W. Broadway, Vancouver BC V6J 1Y3 Canada. (604)730-7000. Fax: (604)730-7010. E-mail: photos@straight.com. Web site: www.straight.com. **Contact:** Charlie Smith, editor. Circ. 117,000. Estab. 1967. Weekly tabloid. Emphasizes entertainment. Readers are generally well-educated people, ages 20-45. Sample copy free with 10×12 SASE.

Needs Buys 7 photos from freelancers/issue; 364 photos/year. Needs photos of entertainment events and personalities. Photo captions essential.

Making Contact & Terms Send query letter with list of stock photo subjects. Provide résumé, business card, brochure, flier or tearsheets to be kept on file for possible future assignments. Responds in 1 month. Simultaneous submissions and previously published work OK. Include SASE for return of material. Pays $250-300 for cover; $100-200 for inside. Pays on publication. Credit line given. Buys one-time rights.

Tips "Almost all needs are for in-Vancouver assigned photos, except for high-quality portraits of film stars. We rarely use unsolicited photos, except for Vancouver photos for our content page.''

$◻ ▣ GERMAN LIFE MAGAZINE

1068 National Hwy., LaVale MD 21502. (301)729-6190. Fax: (301)729-1720. E-mail: mslider @germanlifc.com. Web site: www.germanlife.com. **Contact:** Mark Slider, editor. Circ. 40,000. Estab. 1994. Bimonthly magazine focusing on history, culture, and travel relating to German-speaking Europe and German-American heritage. Sample copy available for $5.95.

Needs Limited number of photos purchased separate from text articles.

Specs Queries welcome for specs.

Making Contact & Terms Payment varies. Pays on publication. Credit line given. Buys one-time rights.

▣ GHOST TOWN

2660 Petersborough St., Herndon VA 20171. E-mail: shannonaswriter@yahoo.com. Estab. 1998. Quarterly magazine. Photo guidelines available by e-mail request.

Needs Buys 12 photos from freelancers/issue; 48-72 photos/year. Needs photos of babies/ children/teens, celebrities, couples, multicultural, families, parents, disasters, environmental, landscapes/scenics, wildlife, architecture, cities/urban, education, gardening, interiors/ decorating, pets, religious, rural, adventure, events, food/drink, sports, travel, agriculture, medicine, military, political, product shots/still life, science, technology—as related to archaeology and ghost towns. Interested in alternative process, avant garde, documentary, fashion/glamour, fine art, historical/vintage, seasonal. Wants photos of archaeology sites and excavations in progress of American ghost towns. ''Would like photographs of artifacts and Paleobiology.'' Reviews photos with or without a manuscript. Model/property release preferred.

Specs Uses glossy or matte color and/or b&w prints.

Making Contact & Terms Send query letter via e-mail. ''If possible, please do not include photographs in files if they are sent through e-mail. A CD sent with your photographs is acceptable.'' Provide résumé, business card or self-promotion piece to be kept on file for possible future assignments. ''Photographs sent with CDs are requested but not required. Illustrations and artwork are also accepted.'' Responds within 1 month to queries; 1 week to portfolios. Simultaneous submissions and previously published work OK. **Pays on acceptance.** Credit line given. Buys one-time rights, first rights; negotiable.

$▨ ▣ ▣ GRIT MAGAZINE

1503 SW 42nd St., Topeka KS 66609. (785)274-4300. Fax: (785)274-4305. E-mail: grit@grit. com. Web site: www.grit.com. **Contact:** Hank Will, editor. Circ. 150,000. Estab. 1882. Bimonthly magazine. Emphasizes small town life, country lifestyle or ''hobby'' farm-oriented material. Readership is national. Sample copy available for $4.

Needs Buys 24 + photos/year with accompanying stories or articles; 90% from freelancers. Needs, on a regular basis, photos of small-farm livestock, animals, farm labor, gardening, produce and related images. ''Be certain pictures are well composed, properly exposed and pin sharp. Must be *shot* at high resolution (no less than 300 dpi). No cheesecake. No pictures that cannot be shown to any member of the family. No pictures that are out of focus or over- or under-exposed. No ribbon-cutting, check-passing or hand-shaking pictures. Story subjects include all aspects of the hobby or country lifestyle farm, such as livestock, farm dogs, barn cats, sowing and hoeing, small tractors, fences, etc." Photo captions required. "Any image that stands alone must be accompanied by 50-100 words of meaningful caption information."

Specs Uses 35mm, slides and high-resolution digital images. Send digital images via CD, Zip as JPEG files at 300 dpi.

Making Contact & Terms Study the magazine. "We use a beautiful country scene for 'Reverie', the last page in each issue. Take a look at previous issues to get a sense of the sort of shot we're looking for." Send material by mail with SASE for consideration. Responds ASAP. Pay is negotiable up to $1,000 for color cover; $35-200 for color inside; $25-100 for b&w inside. Rarely uses b&w, and only if "irresistibly atmospheric." Pays on publication. Buys shared rights; negotiable.

Tips "This is a relaunch of an old title. You must study the new publication to make sure your submissions are appropriate to *Grit*'s new direction."

$ $ 🖵 HARPER'S MAGAZINE

Harper's Magazine Foundation, 666 Broadway, 11th Floor, New York NY 10012. (212)420-5720. Fax: (212)228-5889. E-mail: alyssa@harpers.org. Web site: www.harpers.org. **Contact:** Alyssa Coppelman, assistant art director. Circ. 250,000. Estab. 1850. Monthly literary magazine. "The nation's oldest continually published magazine providing fiction, satire, political criticism, social criticism, essays."

Needs Buys 8-10 photos from freelancers/issue; 120 photos/year. Needs photos of human rights issues, environmental, political. Interested in alternative process, avant garde, documentary, fine art, historical/vintage. Model/property release preferred.

Specs Uses any format. Accepts images in digital format. Send preferably via e-mail to alyssa@harpers.org or on CD; TIFF, EPS, JPEG files at 300 dpi.

Making Contact & Terms Send query letter with résumé, slides, prints, photocopies, tearsheets, transparencies. Portfolio may be dropped off last Wednesday of the month. Provide self-promotion piece to be kept on file for possible future assignments. Responds in 1 week. Pays $200-800 for b&w/color cover; $250-400 for b&w/color inside. Pays on publication. Credit line given. Buys one-time rights; negotiable.

Tips "*Harper's* is geared more toward fine art photos or artist's portfolios than to 'traditional' photo usages. For instance, we never do fashion, food, travel (unless it's for political commentary), lifestyles or celebrity profiles. A good understanding of the magazine is crucial for photo submissions. We consider all styles and like experimental or nontraditional work. Please don't confuse us with *Harper's Bazaar*!"

$ 🖵 HIGHLIGHTS FOR CHILDREN

803 Church St., Honesdale PA 18431. (570)253-1080. Web site: www.highlights.com. **Contact:** Cindy Faber Smith, art director. Circ. around 2.5 million. Monthly magazine for children ages 2-12. Sample copy free.

    • *Highlights* is currently expanding photographic needs.

Needs Buys 100 or more photos/year. "We will consider outstanding photo essays on subjects of high interest to children." Reviews photos with accompanying manuscript only. Wants no single photos without captions or accompanying manuscript.

Specs Accepts images in digital format. Send via CD at 300 dpi. Also accepts transparencies of all sizes.

Making Contact & Terms Send photo essays with SASE for consideration. Responds in 7 weeks. Pays $30 minimum for b&w photos; $50 minimum for color photos; $100 minimum for manuscript. Buys all rights.

Tips "Tell a story that is exciting to children. We also need mystery photos, puzzles that use photography/collage, special effects, anything unusual that will visually and mentally challenge children."

$ $ ☑ Ⓢ ▣ HIGHWAYS, The Official Publication of The Good Sam Club

Affinity Group Inc., 2575 Vista Del Mar Dr., Ventura CA 93001-3920. (805)667-4003. Fax: (805)667-4122. E-mail: vlaw@affinitygroup.com. Web site: www.goodsamclub.com/high ways. **Contact:** Valerie Law, editorial director. Circ. 975,000. Estab. 1966. Monthly consumer magazine. "Your authoritative source for information on issues of concern to all RVers, as well as your link to the RV community." Sample copy free with 8½×11 SAE.

Specs Accepts images in digital format. Send via CD or e-mail at 300 dpi.

Making Contact & Terms Editorial director will contact photographer for portfolio review if interested. Pays $500 for cover; $75-350 for inside. Buys one-time rights.

$ $ HOOF BEATS

750 Michigan Ave., Columbus OH 43215. (614)224-2291. Fax: (614)222-6791. E-mail: hoofb eats@ustrotting.com. Web site: www.hoofbeatsmagazine.com. **Contact:** Nicole Kraft, executive editor. Art Director/Production Manager: Gena Gallagher. Circ. 13,500. Estab. 1933. Monthly publication of the U.S. Trotting Association. Emphasizes harness racing. Readers are participants in the sport of harness racing. Sample copy free.

Needs Buys 6 photos from freelancers/issue; 72 photos/year. Needs "artistic or striking photos that feature harness horses for covers; other photos on specific horses and drivers by assignment only."

Making Contact & Terms Send query letter with samples; include SASE for return of material. Responds in 3 weeks. Simultaneous submissions OK. Pays $150 minimum for color cover; $25-150 for b&w inside; $50-200 for color inside; freelance assignments negotiable. Pays on publication. Credit line given if requested. Buys one-time rights.

Tips "We look for photos with unique perspective and that display unusual techniques or use of light. Send query letter first. Know the publication and its needs before submitting. Be sure to shoot pictures of harness horses only, not thoroughbred or riding horses. We always need good night racing action or creative photography."

Ⓝ $ $ ☑ ▣ HORIZONS MAGAZINE

P.O. Box 1091, Bismarck ND 58502. (701)335-4458. Fax: (701)223-4645. E-mail: ndhorizons @btinet.net. Web site: www.ndhorizons.com. **Contact:** Andrea W. Collin, editor. Estab. 1971. Quality regional magazine. Photos used in magazines, audiovisual, calendars.

Needs Buys 50 photos/year; offers 25 assignments/year. Needs scenics of North Dakota events, places and people. Also needs wildlife, cities/urban, rural, adventure, entertainment, events, hobbies, performing arts, travel, agriculture, industry. Interested in historical/vintage, seasonal. Model/property release preferred. Photo captions preferred.

Specs Prefers images in digital format. Send via CD, as TIFF, EPS files at 600 dpi.

Making Contact & Terms Prefers email query letter. Pays by the project, varies ($300-500); negotiable. Pays on usage. Credit line given. Buys one-time rights; negotiable.

Tips "Know North Dakota events, places. Have strong quality of composition and light."

Consumer Publications

$HORSE ILLUSTRATED

Fancy Publications, BowTie Magazines, P.O. Box 8237, Lexington KY 40533. (859)260-9800. Fax: (859)260-1154. E-mail: horseillustrated@bowtieinc.com. Web site: www.horseil lustrated.com. **Contact:** Elizabeth Moyer, editor. Circ. 192,000. Readers are "primarily adult horsewomen, ages 18-40, who ride and show mostly for pleasure, and who are very concerned about the well being of their horses. Editorial focus covers all breeds and all riding disciplines." Sample copy available for $4.50. Photo guidelines free with SASE.

Needs Buys 30-50 photos from freelancers/issue. Needs stock photos of riding and horse care. "Photos must reflect safe, responsible horsekeeping practices. We prefer all riders to wear protective helmets; prefer people to be shown only in action shots (riding, grooming, treating, etc.). We like all riders—especially those jumping—to be wearing protective headgear."

Specs Prefer digital images—high resolution JPEGs on a CD with printout of thumbnails.

Making Contact & Terms Send by mail for consideration. Responds in 2 months. Pays $250 for color cover; $65-250 for color inside. Credit line given. Buys one-time rights.

Tips "Looks for clear, sharp color shots of horse care and training. Healthy horses, safe riding and care atmosphere is standard in our publication. Send SASE for a list of photography needs, photo guidelines, and to submit work. Photo guidelines are also available on our Web site."

☐ Ⓢ ILLOGICAL MUSE

P.O. Box 63, Buchanan MI 49107-1424. E-mail: illogicalmuse@yahoo.com. Web site: www. geocities.com/illogicalmuse. **Contact:** Amber Rothrock, editor. Estab. 2004. Quarterly literary magazine. Online journal publishing fiction, poetry, reviews, essays and artwork. Photo guidelines available on Web site.

Needs Wants photos of babies/children/teens, couples, multicultural, parents, senior citizens, architecture, cities/urban, gardening, pets, religious, rural, agriculture, disasters, environmental, wildlife, hobbies, performing arts; interested in avant garde, historical/vintage, seasonal. Does not want to see anything pornographic; mild erotica is fine. "I am open to all schools and styles but tend to lean toward the more experimental and avant garde." Reviews photos with or without a manuscript. Model release preferred. Property release preferred. Photo captions preferred.

Specs Accepts images in digital format only. Send JPEG or GIF files via CD or e-mail.

Making Contact & Terms E-mail query letter with link to photographer's Web site, JPEG samples at 72 dpi. "Send a cover letter with a brief, publishable bio. An exceptionally long list of prior achievements is not necessary. Tell me a little bit about yourself and the work you do." Does not keep samples on file; include SASE for return of material. Responds in 1 month to queries; 6 months to portfolios. Simultaneous submissions and previously published work OK. All rights remain with the photographer.

Tips "Visit the Web site to see if it appeals to you. It's hard to say what I am specifically looking for as I try to keep an open mind with every submission. Just send your best."

▣ IMMIGRANT ANCESTORS

2660 Petersborough St., Herndon VA 20171. E-mail: immigrantancestors@yahoo.com. Estab. 2005. Quarterly magazine, "searching for immigrants and immigrant ancestors." Photo guidelines available by e-mail request.

Needs Buys 12-24 photos/year. Needs photos of babies/children/teens, multicultural, families, parents, disasters, environmental, landscapes/scenics, wildlife, cities/urban, educa-tion, religious, rural, adventure, events, food/drink, sports, travel, agriculture, medicine, military, political, product shots/still life, science, technology-as related to early immigra-tion and those who made its history. Interested in alternative process, avant garde, docu-mentary, fashion/glamour, fine art, historical/vintage, seasonal. Reviews photos with or without manuscript. Model/property release preferred.

Specs Uses glossy or matte color and/or b&w prints.

Making Contact & Terms Send query letter via e-mail. "If possible, please do not include photographs in files if they are sent through e-mail. A disk with your photographs is accept-able." Provide résumé, business card or self-promotion piece to be kept on file for possible future assignments. Responds within 1 month to queries; 1 week to portfolios. Simultaneous submissions and previously published work OK. **Pays on acceptance.** Credit line given. Buys one-time rights, first rights; negotiable.

$ $☐ INDIANAPOLIS MONTHLY

40 Monument Circle, Suite 100, Indianapolis IN 46204. (317)237-9288. Web site: www.india napolismonthly.com. **Contact:** Art Director. Monthly regional magazine. Readers are ups-cale, well-educated. Circ. 50,000. Sample copy available for $4.95 and 9×12 SASE.

Needs Buys 10-12 photos from freelancers/issue; 120-144 photos/year. Needs seasonal, human interest, humorous, regional; subjects must be Indiana- or Indianapolis-related. Model release preferred. Photo caption information required.

Specs Glossy prints; transparencies, digital. Send via CD, e-mail as TIFF, EPS, JPEG files at 300 dpi at actual size.

Making Contact & Terms Send query letter with samples, SASE. Responds in 1 month. Previously published work on occasion OK, if different market. Pays $300-1,200 for color cover; $75-350 for b&w inside; $75-350 for color inside. Pays on publication. Credit line given. Buys first North American serial rights.

Tips "Read publication. Send photos similar to those you see published. If you see nothing like what you are considering submitting, it's unlikely we will be interested. We are always interested in photo essay queries if they are Indiana-specific."

$ $☐ INSIGHT MAGAZINE

Review and Herald Publishing Association, 55 W. Oak Ridge Dr., Hagerstown MD 21740-7390. (301)393-3000. Fax: (301)393-4055. E-mail: insight@rhpa.org. Web site: www.insigh tmagazine.org. **Contact:** Jason Diggs, art director. Circ. 20,000. Estab. 1970. Weekly Sev-enth-Day Adventist teen magazine. "We print teens' true stories about God's involvement in their lives. All stories, if illustrated by a photo, must uphold moral and church organiza-tion standards while capturing a hip, teen style." Sample copy free.

Needs "Send query letter with photo samples so we can evaluate style." Model/property release required. Photo captions preferred; include who, what, where, when.

Making Contact & Terms Send query letter with samples. Provide résumé, business card, self-promotion piece or tearsheets to be kept on file for possible future assignments. Re-sponds only if interested; send nonreturnable samples. Simultaneous submissions and pre-viously published work OK. Pays $200-300 for color cover; $200-400 for color inside. Pays 30-45 days after receiving invoice and contract. Credit line given. Buys first rights.

Consumer Publications

$ ☑ ▣ THE IOWAN MAGAZINE

218 Sixth Ave., Suite 610, Des Moines IA 50309. (515)246-0402. Fax: (515)282-0125. E-mail: editor@iowan.com or artdirector@iowan.com. Web site: www.iowan.com. **Contact:** Beth Wilson, editor; Bobbie Russie, art director. Circ. 22,000. Estab. 1952. Bimonthly magazine. Emphasizes ''Iowa's people, places, events, nature and history.'' Readers are over age 40, college-educated, middle-to-upper income. Sample copy available for $4.50 + shipping/handling; call the Distribution Center toll-free at (877)899-9977. Photo guidelines available on Web site or via e-mail.

Needs ''We print only Iowa-related images from Iowa photographers, illustrators, and artists. Show us Iowa's residents, towns, environmental, landscape/scenics, wildlife, architecture, rural, entertainment, events, performing arts, travel.'' Interested in Iowa heritage, historical/vintage, seasonal. Accepts unsolicited stock photos related to above. Editorial stock photo needs available on Web site or via e-mail. Model/property release preferred. Photo captions required.

Specs Digital format preferred on clearly labeled CD/DVD with submission form, printed contact sheet, and image reference. See Web site for details. Press resolution is 300 dpi at 9×12. Digital materials will not be returned. Uses 35mm, color transparencies, which will be returned following press deadline.

Making Contact & Terms Pays $50-250 for stock photo one-time use, depending on size printed; pays on publication. Contract rates run $200-500/day for assigned editorials; pays within 60 days of receipt of invoice.

$ $ ☑ ▣ ISLANDS, The Leading Guide to Island Travel

460 N. Orlando Ave., Suite 200, Winter Park FL 32789. (407) 571- 4930. Fax: (407) 628-7061. E-mail: lori-barbely@ bonniercorp.com. Web site: www.islands.com. **Contact:** Lori Barbely, photography editor. Circ. 200,000. Bimonthly. Emphasizes travel.

Needs Buys 50 photos from freelancers/issue; 400 photos/year. Needs photos of island travel. Reviews photos with or without a m anus cript. Model/property release preferred. Detailed captions required (please use metadata); include name, phone, address, subject information.

Specs Prefers images in digital format. Send via CD, e-mail, Web gallery, FTP site as JPEG files at 72 dpi (must have 300 dpi file available if image is selected for use). Film is not desired.

Making Contact & Terms Send query letter with tearsheets. Provide résumé, business card, self-promotion piece or tearsheets to be kept on file for possible future assignments. You will be contacted if additional information or a portfolio is desired. Keeps samples on file. Simultaneous submissions OK. Pays $600-1,000 for color cover; $100-350 for inside. Pays 30 days after publication. Credit line given. Buys one-time rights.

$ ☑ ▣ ITALIAN AMERICA

219 E St. NE, Washington DC 20002. (202)547-2900. Fax: (202)547-0121. E-mail: ddesanctis @osia.org. Web site: www.osia.org. **Contact:** Dona De Sanctis, editor-in-chief. Circ. 65,000. Estab. 1996. Quarterly. ''*Italian America* is the official publication of the Order Sons of Italy in America, the nation's oldest and largest organization of American men and women of Italian heritage. *Italian America* strives to provide timely information about OSIA, while reporting on individuals, institutions, issues and events of current or historical significance in the Italian American community.'' Sample copy and photo guidelines free.

Needs Buys 5-10 photos from freelancers/issue; 25 photos/year. Needs photos of travel, history, personalities; anything Italian or Italian-American. Reviews photos with or without a manuscript. Special photo needs include travel in Italy. Model release preferred. Photo captions required.

Specs Accepts images in digital format. Send via CD, e-mail as TIFF, EPS, PICT, BMP, GIF, JPEG files at 400 dpi.

Making Contact & Terms Send query letter with tearsheets. Provide resume, business card, self-promotion piece or tearsheets to be kept on file for possible future assignments. Art director will contact photographer for portfolio review if interested. Portfolio should include color tearsheets. Responds only if interested; send nonreturnable samples. Simultaneous submissions OK. Pays $250 for b&w or color cover; $50-250 for b&w or color inside. Pays on publication. Credit line given. Buys one-time rights.

$ $⊘ KANSAS!

1000 SW Jackson St., Suite 100, Topeka KS 66612-1354. (785)296-3479. Fax: (785)296-6988. Web site: www.kansmag.com. **Contact:** Becky Blake, director. Circ. 40,000. Estab. 1945. Quarterly magazine published by the Travel & Tourism Development Division of the Kansas Department of Commerce. Emphasizes Kansas travel, scenery, arts, recreation and people. Photo guidelines available on Web site.

Needs Buys 60-80 photos from freelancers/year. Subjects include animal, human interest, nature, seasonal, rural, scenic, sport, travel, wildlife, photo essay/photo feature, all from Kansas. No b&w, nudes, still life or fashion photos. Reviews photos with or without a manuscript. Model/property release preferred. Photo captions required; include subject and specific location.

Specs Uses 35mm, 2¼×2¼ or 4×5 transparencies.

Making Contact & Terms Send material by mail for consideration. Previously published work OK. Pays on acceptance. Credit line given. Buys one-time or limited universal rights.

Tips Kansas-oriented material only. Prefers Kansas photographers. "Follow guidelines, submission dates specifically. Shoot a lot of seasonal scenics."

$◻ ▣ KENTUCKY MONTHLY

106-C St. James Court, Frankfort KY 40601-0559. (502)227-0053. Fax: (502)227-5009. E-mail: steve@kentuckymonthly.com. Web site: www.kentuckymonthly.com. **Contact:** Stephen Vest, editor. Circ. 40,000. Estab. 1998. Monthly magazine focusing on Kentucky and/or Kentucky-related stories. Sample copy available for $3.

Needs Buys 10 photos from freelancers/issue; 120 photos/year. Needs photos of celebrities, wildlife, entertainment, landscapes. Reviews photos with or without a manuscript. Model release required. Photo captions preferred.

Specs Uses glossy prints; 35mm transparencies. Accepts images in digital format. Send via CD, e-mail at 300 dpi.

Making Contact & Terms Send query letter. Provide self-promotion piece to be kept on file for possible future assignments. Responds in 1 month. Simultaneous submissions OK. Pays $25 minimum for inside photos. Pays the 15th of the following month. Credit line given. Buys one-time rights.

$ $⊠ ▣ KNOWATLANTA, The Premier Relocation Guide

New South Publishing, 1303 Hightower Trail, Suite 101, Atlanta GA 30350. (770)650-1102. Fax: (770)650-2848. E-mail: editor1@knowatlanta.com. Web site: www.knowatlanta.com.

Consumer Publications

Contact: Judy Putnam, editor-in-chief. Circ. 48,000. Estab. 1986. Quarterly magazine serving as a relocation guide to the Atlanta metro area with a corporate audience. Photography reflects regional and local material as well as corporate-style imagery.

Needs Buys more than 10 photos from freelancers/issue; more than 40 photos/year. Needs photos of cities/urban, events, performing arts, business concepts, medicine, technology/computers. Reviews photos with or without a manuscript. Model release required; property release preferred. Photo captions preferred.

Specs Uses 8×10 glossy color prints; 35mm, $2\frac{1}{4} \times 2\frac{1}{4}$ transparencies. Accepts images in digital format. Send via CD, Zip, e-mail as TIFF, EPS, JPEG files at 300 dpi.

Making Contact & Terms Send query letter with photocopies. Provide résumé, business card, self-promotion piece to be kept on file for possible future assignments. Responds only if interested; send nonreturnable samples. Pays $600 maximum for color cover; $300 maximum for color inside. Pays on publication. Credit line given. Buys first rights.

Tips "Think like our readers. What would they want to know about or see in this magazine? Try to represent the relocated person if using subjects in photography."

ℕ $◯ 🅰 ▣ LACROSSE MAGAZINE

113 W. University Pkwy., Baltimore MD 21210. (410)235-6882. Fax: (410)366-6735. E-mail: pkrome@uslacrosse.org. Web site: www.laxmagazine.com. **Contact:** Paul Krome, editor. Circ. 160,000. Estab. 1978. Publication of US Lacrosse. Monthly magazine. Emphasizes sport of lacrosse. Readers are male and female lacrosse enthusiasts of all ages. Sample copy free with general information pack.

Needs Buys 15-30 photos from freelancers/issue; 120-240 photos/year. Needs lacrosse action shots. Photo captions required; include rosters with numbers for identification.

Specs Accepts images in digital format. Send via disc. Original RAW/NEF files or 300 dpi TIFFs.

Making Contact & Terms Send unsolicited photos by mail with SASE for consideration. Provide résumé, business card, brochure, flier or tearsheets to be kept on file for possible future assignments. Responds in 3 weeks. Simultaneous submissions and previously published work OK. Pays $250 for color cover; $75-150 inside. Pays on publication. Credit line given. Buys one-time rights.

ℕ $ $ LADIES HOME JOURNAL

125 Park Ave., 20th Floor, New York NY 10017. (212)455-1033. Fax: (212)455-1313. Web site: www.lhj.com. **Contact:** Sabrina Regan, photo associate. Circ. 6 million. Monthly magazine. Features women's issues. Readership consists of women with children and working women in 30s age group.

Needs Uses 90 photos/issue; 100% supplied by freelancers. Needs photos of children, celebrities and women's lifestyles/situations. Reviews photos only without manuscript. Model release preferred. Photo captions preferred.

Making Contact & Terms Provide résumé, business card, brochure, flier or tearsheet to be kept on file for possible assignment. "Do not send slides or original work; send only promo cards or disks." Responds in 3 weeks. Pays $500/page. **Pays on acceptance.** Credit line given. Buys one-time rights.

$◯ ▣ LAKE COUNTRY JOURNAL

Evergreen Press, P.O. Box 465, Brainerd MN 56401. (218)828-6424. Fax: (218)825-7816. E-mail: andrea@lakecountryjournal.com. Web site: www.lakecountryjournal.com. **Contact:**

Andrea Baumann, art director. Estab. 1996. Bimonthly regional consumer magazine focused on northern Minnesota. Sample copy and photo guidelines available for $5 and 9×12 SAE.

Needs Buys 35 photos from freelancers/issue; 210 photos/year. Needs photos of environmental, landscapes, wildlife, architecture, gardening, decorating, rural, entertainment, events, food/drink, health/fitness/beauty, hobbies, humor, sports, agriculture, medicine. Interested in documentary, fine art, historical/vintage, seasonal; Minnesota outdoors. Reviews photos with or without a manuscript. Model release preferred. Photo captions preferred; include who, where, when.

Specs Prefers images in digital format. Send via CD, DVD as TIFF, EPS files at 300 dpi. Also accepts 35mm slides.

Making Contact & Terms Send query letter with résumé, slides, prints, tearsheets, transparencies, stock list. Provide résumé, business card or self-promotion piece to be kept on file for possible future assignments. Responds in 3 weeks to queries. Previously published work OK. Pays $180 for cover; $35-150 for inside. Pays on publication. Credit line given. Buys one-time rights; negotiable.

$ LAKE SUPERIOR MAGAZINE

Lake Superior Port Cities, Inc., P.O. Box 16417, Duluth MN 55816-0417. (218)722-5002. Fax: (218)722-4096. E-mail: edit@lakesuperior.com. Web site: www.lakesuperior.com. **Contact:** Konnie LeMay, editor. Circ. 20,000. Estab. 1979. Bimonthly magazine. "Beautiful picture magazine about Lake Superior." Readers are male and female, ages 35-55, highly educated, upper-middle and upper-management level through working. Sample copy available for $4.95 plus $5.95 S&H. Photo guidelines free with SASE or via Web site.

Needs Buys 21 photos from freelancers/issue; 126 photos/year. Also buys photos for calendars and books. Needs photos of landscapes/scenics, travel, wildlife, personalities, boats, underwater—all Lake Superior-related. Photo captions preferred.

Specs Uses 5×7, 8×10 glossy b&w and color-corrected prints; 35mm, $2\frac{1}{4} \times 2\frac{1}{4}$, 4×5, 8×10 transparencies. Accepts images in digital format. Send via CD with at least thumbnails on a printout.

Making Contact & Terms Send unsolicited photos by mail with SASE for consideration. Provide résumé, business card, brochure, flier or tearsheets to be kept on file for possible future assignments. Responds in 2 months. Simultaneous submissions OK. Pays $150 for color cover; $50 for b&w or color inside. Pays on publication. Credit line given. Buys first North American serial rights; reserves second rights for future use.

Tips "Be aware of the focus of our publication—Lake Superior. Photo features concern only that. Features with text can be related. We are known for our fine color photography and reproduction. It has to be 'tops.' We try to use images large; therefore, detail quality and resolution must be good. We look for unique outlook on subject, not just snapshots. Must communicate emotionally. Some photographers send material we can keep in-house and refer to, and these will often get used."

LEFT BEHIND: A Journal of Shock Literature

832 Shasta Dr, Colton CA 92324. E-mail: jeffe@myleftbehind.com. Web site: http://www.myleftbehind.com. **Contact:** Jeff Green, editor. Estab. 2008. Circ. 1,000. Quarterly literary magazine of poetry, short stories, short plays, screenplays, essays, and visual art. "We want the work you thought was too racy to ever admit you wrote. The blasphemous, erotic,

misanthropic, politically incorrect, homoerotic, homophobic, homo-habilis, scatalogical, you know, the good stuff. Pseudonyms welcome. The serious and dark are encouraged, but the humorous is prized. Make us blush and say, 'jeez, did we print that?' Imagine you're Mapplethorpe but without the soft touch.''

Needs *"Left Behind* desperately needs cover art featuring the left buttock; both color and b/w art inside (model releases required).'' Buys 10 photos from freelancers/issue; 40 photos/year. Senior Citizens, outdoor and environmental disasters, cities and urban scenes, pets, religious, humor. Interested in alternative process and avante garde, documentary, erotic, fine art, historical/vintage, and lifestyle photos. Reviews photos with or without a manuscript. Model release is required, photo captions preferred.

Specs Accepts 35 mm prints of any size in glossy, matte, color, or b&w; accepts 4×5 digital images via CD, zip, e-mail, as TIFF, GIF, or JPEG files at $+300$ dpi.

Making Contact and Terms Email query letter with link to photographer's Web site or JPEG samples at 72 dpi or send query letter with slides, prints, photocopies, or transparencies. Does not keep samples on file; include SASE for return of material. Responds in 2 months. Considers simultaneous submissions and previously published work. Pays 2 copies minimum. Pays on publication, credit line given. Buys one-time and electronic rights, will negotiate with photographer.

Advice "Shock us; don't be boring.''

⬛ $◻ 🖳 LIVING FREE

P.O. Box 969, Winnisquam NH 03289. (603)455-7368. E-mail: free@natnh.com. Web site: www.natnh.com/lf/mag.html. **Contact:** Tom Caldwell, editor-in-chief. Quarterly electronic magazine succeeding Naturist Life International's Online e-zine. Emphasizes nudism. Readers are male and female nudists. Sample copy available on CD for $10. Photo guidelines free with SASE. We periodically organize naturist photo safaris to shoot nudes in nature.

Needs Buys 36 photos from freelancers/issue; 144 photos/year. Needs photos depicting family-oriented nudist/naturist work, recreational activity and travel. Reviews photos with or without a manuscript. Model release required (including Internet use) for recognizable nude subjects. Photo captions preferred.

Specs Prefers digital images submitted on CD or via e-mail; 8×10 glossy color and/or b&w prints.

Making Contact & Terms Send query letter with résumé of credits. Send unsolicited photos by mail or e-mail for consideration; include SASE for return of material. Provide résumé, business card, brochure, flier or tearsheets to be kept on file for possible future assignments. Responds in 2 weeks. Pays $50 for color cover; $10-25 for others. Pays on publication. Credit line given. "Prefer to own all rights but sometimes agree to one-time publication rights.''

Tips "The ideal photo shows ordinary-looking people of all ages doing everyday activities, in the joy of nudism. We do not want 'cheesecake' glamour images or anything that emphasizes the erotic.''

$◻ 🖳 MISSOURI LIFE

Missouri Life, Inc., 515 E. Morgan St., Boonville MO 65233. (660)882-9898. Fax: (660)882-9899. E-mail: info@missourilife.com. Web site: www.missourilife.com. **Contact:** Shea Bryant, art dirctor. Circ. 20,000. Estab. 1973. Bimonthly consumer magazine. *"Missouri Life* celebrates Missouri people and places, past and present, and the unique qualities of our great state with interesting stories and bold, colorful photography.'' Sample copy available for $4.50 and SASE with $2.44 first-class postage. Photo guidelines available on Web site.

Needs Buys 80 photos from freelancers/issue; more than 500 photos/year. Needs photos of environmental, seasonal, landscapes/scenics, wildlife, architecture, cities/urban, rural, adventure, historical sites, entertainment, events, hobbies, performing arts, travel. Reviews photos with or without manuscript. Model/property release required. Photo captions required; include location, names and detailed identification (including any title and hometown) of subjects.

Specs Prefers images in high-res digital format (minimum 300 ppi at 8×10). Send via e-mail, CD, Zip as EPS, JPEG, TIFF files.

Making Contact & Terms Send query letter with résumé, stock list. Provide self-promotion piece to be kept on file for possible future assignments. Responds in 1 month. Pays $100-150 for color cover; $50 for color inside. Pays on publication. Credit line given. Buys first rights, nonexclusive rights, limited rights.

Tips ''Be familiar with our magazine and the state of Missouri. Provide well-labeled images with detailed caption and credit information.''

$⬜ Ⓢ ⬛ MUZZLE BLASTS

P.O. Box 67, Friendship IN 47021. (812)667-5131. Fax: (812)667-5137. E-mail: mblastdop@ seidata.com. Web site: www.nmlra.org. **Contact:** Terri Trowbridge, director of publications. Circ. 20,000. Estab. 1939. Publication of the National Muzzle Loading Rifle Association. Monthly magazine emphasizing muzzleloading. Sample copy free. Photo guidelines free with SASE.

Needs Interested in muzzleloading, muzzleloading hunting, primitive camping. ''Ours is a specialized association magazine. We buy some big-game wildlife photos but are more interested in photos featuring muzzleloaders, hunting, powder horns and accoutrements.'' Model/property release required. Photo captions preferred.

Specs Accepts images in digital format. Send via e-mail or on a CD in JPEG or TIFF format. Also accepts 3×5 color transparencies, quality color and b&w prints; sharply contrasting 35mm color slides are acceptable.

Making Contact & Terms Send query letter with stock list. Keeps samples on file; include SASE for return of material. Responds in 2 weeks. Simultaneous submissions OK. Pays $300 for color cover; $25-50 for b&w inside. Pays on publication. Credit line given. Buys one-time rights.

$⬜ ⬛ NA'AMAT WOMAN

350 Fifth Ave., Suite 4700, New York NY 10118. (212)563-5222. Fax: (212)563-5710. E-mail: judith@naamat.org. Web site: www.naamat.org. **Contact:** Judith A. Sokoloff, editor. Circ. 20,000. Estab. 1926. Quarterly organization magazine focusing on issues of concern to contemporary Jewish families and women. Sample copy free with SAE and $1.35 first-class postage.

Needs Buys 5-10 photos from freelancers/issue; 50 photos/year. Needs photos of Jewish themes, Israel, women, babies/children/teens, families, parents, senior citizens, landscapes/scenics, architecture, religious, travel. Interested in documentary, fine art, historical/vintage, seasonal. Reviews photos with or without manuscript. Photo captions preferred.

Specs Uses color and/or b&w prints. Accepts images in digital format. Contact editor before sending.

Making Contact & Terms Provide résumé, business card, self-promotion piece or tearsheets to be kept on file for possible future assignments. Art director will contact photographer for portfolio review if interested. Keeps samples on file; include SASE for return of material. Responds in 6 weeks. Pays $250 maximum for cover; $35-75 for inside. Pays on publication. Credit line given. Buys one-time, first rights.

⊘ ☺ NATIONAL GEOGRAPHIC

National Geographic Society, 1145 17th St. NW, Washington DC 20036. Web site: www.nati onalgeographic.com. **Contact:** Susan Smith, deputy director of photography. Director of Photography: David Griffin. Circ. 7 million. Monthly publication of the National Geographic Society.

- This is a premiere market that demands photographic excellence. *National Geographic* does not accept unsolicited work from freelance photographers. Photography internships and faculty fellowships are available. Contact Susan Smith, deputy director of photography, for application information.

$⊘ ▣ NATIVE PEOPLES MAGAZINE

5333 N. Seventh St., Suite C-224, Phoenix AZ 85014. (602)265-4855. Fax: (602)265-3113. E-mail: artdirector@nativepeoples.com. Web site: www.nativepeoples.com. **Contact:** Kevin Coochwytewa, art director. Circ. 50,000. Estab. 1987. Bimonthly magazine. "Dedicated to the sensitive portrayal of the arts and lifeways of the Native peoples of the Americas." Photo guidelines free with SASE or on Web site.

Needs Buys 20-50 photos from freelancers/issue; 120-300 photos/year. Needs Native American lifeways photos (babies/children/teens, celebrities, couples, multicultural, families, parents, senior citizens, events). Also uses photos of entertainment, performing arts, travel. Interested in fine art. Model/property release preferred. Photo captions preferred; include names, location and circumstances.

Specs Uses transparencies, all formats. Accepts images in digital format. Send via CD, Zip, e-mail as TIFF, JPEG, EPS files at 300 dpi.

Making Contact & Terms Submit portfolio for review. Send unsolicited photos by mail for consideration; include SASE for return of material. Responds in 1 month. Pays $250 for color cover; $45-150 for color or b&w inside. Pays on publication. Buys one-time rights.

Tips "Send samples, or, if in the area, arrange a visit with the editors."

$⊘ ⓢ ▣ NATURE FRIEND, Helping Children Explore the Wonders of God's Creation

4253 Woodcock Lane, Dayton VA 22821. (540)867-0764. Fax: (540)867-9516. **Contact:** Kevin Shank, editor. Circ. 13,000. Estab. 1982. Monthly children's magazine. Sample copy available for $5 plus $2 first-class postage.

Needs Buys 5-10 photos from freelancers/issue; 100 photos/year. Needs photos of wildlife, wildlife interacting with each other, humorous wildlife, all natural habitat appearance. Reviews photos with or without manuscript. Model/property release preferred. Photo captions preferred.

Specs Prefers images in digital format. Send via CD or DVD as TIFF files at 300 dpi at 8×10 size; provide color thumbnails when submitting photos. "Transparencies are handled and stored carefully; however, we do not accept liability for them so discourage submissions of them."

Making Contact & Terms Responds in one month to queries; 2 weeks to portfolios. "Label

Consumer Publications

contact prints and digital media with your name, address, and phone number so we can easily know how to contact you if we select your photo for use." Please send articles rather than queries. We try to respond within 4-6 months. Simultaneous submissions and previously published work OK. Pays $75 for front cover; $50 for back cover; $15-25 for inside photos. Pays on publication. Credit line given. Buys one-time rights.

Tips "We're always looking for photos of wild animals doing something unusual or humorous . Please label every sheet of paper or digital media with name, address and phone number. We may need to contact you on short notice, and you do not want to miss a sale. Also, photos are selected on a monthly basis, after the articles. What this means to a photographer is that photos are secondary to writings and cannot be selected far in advance. High-resolution photos in our files the day we are making selections will stand the greatest chance of being published."

$⊡ NATURE PHOTOGRAPHER

P.O. Box 220, Lubec ME 04652. (207)733-4201. Fax: (207)733-4202. E-mail: nature_photogr apher@yahoo.com. Web site: www.naturephotographermag.com. **Contact:** Helen Longest-Saccone, editor-in-chief/photo editor. Circ. 35,000. Estab. 1990. Quarterly 4-color, high-quality magazine. Emphasizes "conservation-oriented, low-impact nature photography" with strong how-to focus. Readers are male and female nature photographers of all ages. Sample copy available for 10 × 13 SAE with 6 first-class stamps.

• *Nature Photographer* charges $79.50/year to be a "field contributor."

Needs Buys 90-120 photos from freelancers/issue; 400 photos/year. Needs nature shots of "all types—abstracts, animals/wildlife, flowers, plants, scenics, environmental images, etc. Shots must be in natural settings; no set-ups, zoo or captive animal shots accepted." Reviews photos (slides or digital images on CD) with or without ms 4 times/year: May (for fall issue); August (for winter issue); November (for spring issue); and January (for summer issue). Photo captions required; include description of subject, location, type of equipment, how photographed. "This information published with photos."

Making Contact & Terms Contact by e-mail or with SASE for guidelines before submitting images. Prefers to see 35mm transparencies or CD of digital images. "Send digital images via CD; please do not e-mail digital images." Does not keep samples on file; include SASE for return of material. Responds within 4 months, according to deadline. Simultaneous submissions and previously published work OK. Pays $100 for color cover; $20 for b&w inside; $25-40 for color inside; $75-150 for photo/text package. Pays on publication. Credit line given. Buys one-time rights.

Tips Recommends working with "the best lens you can afford and slow-speed slide film; or, if shooting digital, using the RAW mode." Suggests editing with a 4× or 8× loupe (magnifier) on a light board to check for sharpness, color saturation, etc. "Color prints are not normally used for publication in our magazine. When editing digital captured images, please enlarge to the point that you are certain that the focal point is tack sharp. Also avoid having grain in the final image."

$⟳ ⌷ NECROLOGY MAGAZINE

Isis International, P.O. Box 510232, St. Louis MO 63151. (314)315-5200. E-mail: editor@nec rologymag.com. Web site: www.necrologymag.com. **Contact:** John Ferguson, editor Circ. 1,000. Estab. 2006. Quarterly consumer magazine. "Necrology is a publication of science fiction, fantasy, horror, and Lovecraftian-type fiction." Sample copy available for $5. Photo guidelines available with #10 SASE. Request photo guildelines via e-mail.

Consumer Publications

Needs Buys 1-2 photos from freelancers/issue; 4-8 photos/year. Needs photos of architecture, cities/urban, religious, landscapes/scenics; interested in alternative process, avant garde, fine art, historical/vintage, seasonal. Cemeteries, crypts, and anything that might relate to the magazine. Reviews photos with or without a manuscript. Model release required. Property release preferred. Photo captions preferred; include subject, location.

Specs Uses b&w prints. Accepts images in digital format. E-mail query letter with link to photographer's Web site. Send via CD, Zip or e-mail as JPEG, GIF or Photoshop files, grayscale. File size must be under 100k.

Making Contact & Terms Does not keep samples on file; include SASE for return of material. Responds in 2 weeks to queries and portfolios. Pays $1-20 for b&w cover or inside. **Pays on acceptance.** Credit line given. Buys one-time rights.

Tips "Read our magazine. We publish horror and fantasy. Photos should have something dark, edgy, and relate to our fiction. Follow guidelines. We prefer e-mail or CD submissions; other types of submissions may not be reviewed."

$ $ 🖥 NEW MEXICO MAGAZINE

495 Old Santa Fe Trail, Santa Fe NM 87501. (505)827-7447. Fax: (505)827-6496. E-mail: artdirector@nmmagazine.com. Web site: www.nmmagazine.com. **Contact:** Fabian West, art editor. Circ. 123,000. Monthly magazine for affluent people ages 35-65 interested in the Southwest or who have lived in or visited New Mexico. Sample copy available for $4.95 with 9×12 SAE and 3 first-class stamps. Photo guidelines available on Web site.

Needs Buys 10 photos from freelancers/issue; 120 photos/year. Needs New Mexico photos only—landscapes, people, events, architecture, etc. "Most work is done on assignment in relation to a story, but we welcome photo essay suggestions from photographers. Cover photos usually relate to the main feature in the magazine." Model release preferred.

Specs Uses 300 dpi digital files with contact sheets (8-9 per page). Photo captions required; include who, what, where.

Making Contact & Terms Submit portfolio to Steve Larese; include SASE for return of material. Pays $450/day; $300 for color or b&w cover; $60-100 for color or b&w stock. Pays on publication. Credit line given. Buys one-time rights.

Tips "*New Mexico Magazine* is the official magazine for the state of New Mexico. Photographers should know New Mexico. We are interested in the less common stock of the state. The magazine is editorial driven, and all photos run directly related to a story in the magazine."

$◯ 🖥 NEWWITCH, Cutting Edge Paganism

BBI Media, Inc., P.O. Box 641, Point Arena CA 95468-0641. (707)882-2052. Fax: (707)882-2793. E-mail: meditor@newwitch.com. Web site: www.newwitch.com. **Contact:** Anne Niven, editor-in-chief. Circ. 15,000. Estab. 2002. Quarterly consumer magazine. "*newWitch* aims to break the stereotypes about wicca being boring—we are hip, active and irreverent." Sample copy and photo guidelines available for SAE.

Needs Buys 10 photos from freelancers/issue; 40 photos/year. Interested in alternative process, avant garde, seasonal. Reviews photos with or without a manuscript. Model release preferred.

Specs Uses 5×7 or larger matte color or b&w prints. Accepts images in digital format. Send via CD, Zip, e-mail as TIFF, JPEG files at 400 dpi.

Making Contact & Terms "Request a sample copy (we send them free!) first, to see if our style and subject matter meet your interests.'' Provide self-promotion piece to be kept on file for possible future assignments. Responds in 10 weeks to queries; 1 month to portfolios. Responds only if interested; send nonreturnable samples. Simultaneous submissions and previously published work OK. Pays $100-200 for color cover; $10-100 for b&w inside. Pays on publication. Credit line given. Buys one-time rights, all rights; negotiable.

Tips ''You should be aware of pagan/wiccan culture (you do *not* need to be a witch). We like contemporary, edgy work and extreme closeups, mostly of people ages 18-34.''

$⬛ 🖥 NORTH AMERICAN WHITETAIL MAGAZINE

P.O. Box 741, Marietta GA 30061. (770)953-9222. Fax: (770)933-9510. E-mail: ron.sinfelt@imoutdoors.com. Web site: www.northamericanwhitetail.com. **Contact**: Ron Sinfelt, photo editor. Circ. 130,000. Estab. 1982. Published 8 times/year (July-February) by Primedia. Emphasizes trophy whitetail deer hunting. Sample copy available for $3. Photo guidelines free with SASE.

Needs Buys 8 photos from freelancers/issue; 64 photos/year. Needs photos of large, live whitetail deer, hunter posing with or approaching downed trophy deer, or hunter posing with mounted head. Also uses photos of deer habitats and signs. Model release preferred. Photo captions preferred; include when and where scene was photographed.

Specs Accepts images in digital format. Send via CD at 300 dpi with output of 8×12 inches. Also uses 8×10 b&w prints; 35mm transparencies.

Making Contact & Terms Send query letter with résumé of credits and list of stock photo subjects. Will return unsolicited material in 1 month if accompanied by SASE. Simultaneous submissions not accepted. Pays $400 for color cover; $75 for color inside; $25 for b&w inside. Tearsheets provided. Pays 60 days prior to publication. Credit line given. Buys one-time rights.

Tips ''In samples we look for extremely sharp, well-composed photos of whitetailed deer in natural settings. We also use photos depicting deer hunting scenes. Please study the photos we are using before making submission. We'll return photos we don't expect to use and hold the remainder for potential use. Please do not send dupes. Use an 8×10 envelope to ensure sharpness of images, and put name and identifying number on all slides and prints. Photos returned at time of publication or at photographer's request.''

$🖥 NORTH CAROLINA LITERARY REVIEW

East Carolina University, Greenville NC 27858-4353. (252)328-1537. Fax: (252)328-4889. E-mail: rodmand@ecu.edu. Web site: www.ecu.edu/nclr. **Contact:** Diane Rodman, art acquisitions editor. Circ. 750. Estab. 1992. Annual literary magazine with North Carolina focus. *NCLR* publishes poetry, fiction and nonfiction by and interviews with NC writers, and articles and essays about NC literature, literary history and culture. Photographs must be NC-related. Sample copy available for $15. Photo guidelines available for SASE or on Web site.

Needs Buys 3-6 photos from freelancers/issue. Model/property release preferred. Photo captions preferred.

Specs Uses b&w prints; 4×5 transparencies. Accepts images in digital format. Inqure first; request, submit TIFF, GIF files at 300 dpi to nclruser@ecu.edu.

Making Contact & Terms Send query letter with Web site address to show sample of work. Portfolios may be dropped off. Provide résumé, business card, self-promotion piece to be kept on file for possible future assignments. Send nonreturnable samples or include SASE

Consumer Publications

for return of material. Responds in 2 months to queries. Pays $50-250 for cover; $5-100 for b&w inside. Pays on publication. Credit line given. Buys first rights.

Tips "Look at our publication—1998-present back issues. See our Web site."

$ $☑ 🖵 NORTHEAST BOATING MAGAZINE

(formerly Offshore), Offshore Communications, Inc., 500 Victory Rd., Marina Bay, North Quincy MA 02171. (617)221-1400. Fax: (617)847-1871. E-mail: dauerd@northeastboating.net. Web site: www.northeastboating.net. **Contact:** Dave Dauer, director of creative services. Monthly magazine. Focuses on recreational boating in the Northeast region of U.S., from Maine to New Jersey. Sample copy free with 9×12 SASE.

Needs Buys 35-50 photos from freelancers/issue; 420-600 photos/year. Needs photos of recreational boats and boating activities. "Boats covered are mostly 20-50 feet; mostly power, but some sail, too." Photo captions required; include location.

Specs Accepts slides or digital images only. "Cover photos should be vertical format and have strong graphics and/or color."

Making Contact & Terms "Please call before sending photos." Simlultaneous submissions and previously published work OK. Pays $400 for color cover; $75-250 for color inside. Pays on publication. Credit line given. Buys one-time rights.

$🖵 NORTHERN WOODLANDS: A New Way of Looking at the Forest

P.O. Box 471, Corinth VT 05039-9900. (802)439-6292. Fax: (802)439-6296. E-mail: anne@northernwoodlands.org. Web site: www.northernwoodlands.org. **Contact:** managing editor. Circ. 17,000. Estab. 1994. Quarterly consumer magazine "created to inspire landowners' sense of stewardship by increasing their awareness of the natural history and the principles of conservation and forestry that are directly related to their land; to encourage loggers, foresters, and purchasers of raw materials to continually raise the standards by which they utilize the forest's resources; to increase the public's awareness and appreciation of the social, economic, and environmental benefits of a working forest; to raise the level of discussion about environmental and natural resource issues; and to educate a new generation of forest stewards." Sample copies available for $5. Photo guidelines available on Web site.

Needs Buys 10-50 photos from freelancers/year. Needs photos of forestry, environmental, landscapes/scenics, wildlife, rural, adventure, travel, agriculture, science. Interested in historical/vintage, seasonal. Other specific photo needs: vertical format, photos specific to assignments in northern New England and upstate New York. Reviews photos with or without a manuscript. Model release preferred. Photo captions required.

Specs Uses glossy or matte color and b&w prints; 35mm, 2¼×2¼ transparencies. Prefers images in digital format. Send via CD, Zip, e-mail as TIFF, EPS files at 300 dpi minimum. No e-mails larger than 10 MB.

Making Contact & Terms Send query letter with slides. Provide self-promotion piece to be kept on file for possible future assignments. Responds only if interested; send nonreturnable samples. Previously published work OK. Pays $150 for color cover; $25-75 for b&w inside. "We might pay upon receipt or as late as publication." Credit line given. Buys one-time rights.

Tips "Read our magazine or go to our Web site for samples of the current issue. We're always looking for high-quality cover photos on a seasonal theme. Vertical format for covers is essential. Also, note that our title goes up top, so photos with some blank space up top

Consumer Publications

are best. Please remember that not all good photographs make good covers—we like to have a subject, lots of color, and we don't mind people. Anything covering the woods and people of Vermont, New Hampshire, Maine, northern Massachusetts or northern New York is great. Unusual subjects, and ones we haven't run before (we've run lots of birds, moose, large mammals, and horse-loggers), get our attention. For inside photos we already have stories and are usually looking for regional photographers willing to shoot a subject theme.''

$NORTHWEST TRAVEL MAGAZINE

4969 Hwy. 101, Suite 2, Florence OR 97439. (800)348-8401. Fax: (541)997-1124. E-mail: barb@ohwy.com. Web site: www.northwestmagazines.com. **Contact:** Barbara Grano, photo editor. Circ. 50,000. Estab. 1991. Bimonthly consumer magazine emphasizing travel in Oregon, Washington, Idaho, western Montana, and British Columbia, Canada. Readers are middle-class, middle-age. Sample copy available for $6. Photo guidelines free with SASE or on Web site.

Needs Buys 3-5 photos from freelancers/issue; 18-30 photos/year. Wants seasonal scenics. Model release required. Photo captions required; include specific location and description. ''Label all slides and transparencies with captions and photographer's name.''

Specs Uses 35mm, $2\frac{1}{4}\times2\frac{1}{4}$, 4×5 positive transparencies. ''Do not e-mail images.''

Making Contact & Terms We recommend acquiring model releases for any photos that include people, but we don't require releases except for photos used on covers or in advertising. Prefers positive transparences, 35 mm to 4×5. Photos must be current, shot within the last five years. Digital photos must be sent on CDs as high resolution (300 dpi) TIFF, JPEG, or EPS files without compression. Images should be $8\frac{1}{2}\times11\frac{1}{2}$. Include clear, color contact sheets of all images (no more than 8 per page). CDs are not returned. To be considered for calendars, photos must have horizontal formats. The annual deadline for Calendars is June 15. Responds in 1 month. Pays $425 for color cover; $100 for calendar usage; $25-50 for b&w inside; $25-100 for color inside; $100-250 for photo/text package. Credit line given. Buys one-time rights. Note: we do not sign personal delivery memoms. SASE or return postage required.

Tips ''Send slide film that can be enlarged without graininess (50-100 ASA). We don't use color filters. Send 20-40 slides. Protect slides with sleeves put in plastic holders. Don't send in little boxes. We work about 3 months ahead, so send spring images in winter, summer images in spring, etc.''

$ ⊠ Ⓢ ▣ NORTHWOODS JOURNAL, a magazine for working writers

Conservatory of American Letters, P.O. Box 298, Thomaston ME 04861. (207) 226-7528. E-mail: cal@americanletters.org. Web site: www.americanletters.org. **Contact:** Robert Olmsted, editor. Circ. 100-200. Estab. 1992. Quarterly literary magazine. ''We are a magazine for writers—a showcase, not a how-to.'' Sample copy available for $6.50 and 6×9 SAE with $1.04 postage.

Needs Sometimes buys 1 photo from freelancers/issue; at least 4 photos/year. Needs photos of landscapes/scenics, wildlife, rural. Reviews photos with or without a manuscript. Model release required.

Specs Uses 5×7 glossy color and/or b&w prints. No digital images. Send via mail.

Making Contact & Terms Send query letter with prints. Does not keep samples on file; include SASE for return of material. Responds in 1 week to queries. Pays $5-20 for b&w cover; $20-50 for color cover. **Pays on acceptance**. Credit line given. Buys one-time rights.

Tips "We're a small, tough market. We buy a seasonal color cover photo for each issue of the magazine, and occasional color covers for books. Our subject matter usually does not suggest interior photos."

$OREGON COAST MAGAZINE

4969 Hwy. 101, Suite 2, Florence OR 97439. (800)348-8401. Fax: (541)997-1124. E-mail: barb@ohwy.com. Web site: www.northwestmagazines.com. **Contact:** Barbara Grano, photo editor. Circ. 50,000. Estab. 1982. Bimonthly magazine. Emphasizes Oregon coast life. Readers are middle-class, middle-aged. Sample copy available for $6, including postage. Photo guidelines available with SASE or on Web site.

Needs Buys 3-5 photos from freelancers/issue; 18-30 photos/year. Needs scenics. Especially needs photos of typical subjects—waves, beaches, lighthouses—with a fresh perspective. Needs mostly vertical format. Model release required. Photo captions required; include specific location and description. "Label all slides and transparencies with captions and photographer's name."

Making Contact & Terms We recommend acquiring model releases for any photos that include people, but we don't require releases except for photos used on covers or in advertising. Prefers positive transparences, 35 mm to 4×5. Photos must be current, shot within the last five years. Digital photos must be sent on CDs as high resolution (300 dpi) TIFF, JPEG, or EPS files without compression. Images should be $8^{1}/_{2} \times 11^{1}/_{5}$. Include clear, color contact sheets of all images (no more than 8 per page). CDs are not returned. To be considered for calendars, photos must have horizontal formats. The annual deadline for Calendars is June 15. Responds in 1 month. Pays $425 for color cover; $100 for calendar usage; $25-50 for b&w inside; $25-100 for color inside; $100-250 for photo/text package. Credit line given. Buys one-time rights. Note: we do not sign personal delivery memoms. SASE or return postage required.

Tips "Send only the very best. Use only slide film that can be enlarged without graininess. Don't use color filters. An appropriate submission would be 20-40 slides. Protect slides with sleeves—put in plastic holders. Don't send in little boxes."

$ $ ⬜ ▣ ⬖ OUTDOOR CANADA

25 Sheppard Ave. W., Suite 100, Toronto ON M2N 6S7 Canada. (416)218-3697. Fax: (416)227-8296. E-mail: scheung@outdoorcanada.ca. Web site: www.outdoorcanada.ca. **Contact:** Sandra Cheung, associate art director. Art Director: Robert Biron. Circ. 100,000. Estab. 1972. Magazine published 8 times/year. Photo guidelines free with SASE (or SAE and IRC), via e-mail or on Web site.

Needs Buys 200-300 photos/year. Needs photos of wildlife; fishing, hunting, ice-fishing; action shots. **"Canadian content only."** Photo captions required; include identification of fish, bird or animal.

Specs Accepts images in digital format.

Making Contact & Terms "Send a well edited selection of transparencies with return postage for consideration. E-mail/CD portfolios also accepted." Responds in 1 month. Pays $550 for cover; $75-400 for color inside, depending on size used (all payable in Canadian funds). Pays on invoice. Buys one-time rights.

$▣ OVER THE BACK FENCE

Long Point Media, LLC, 2947 Interstate Pkwy., Brunswick OH 44212. (330)220-2483. Fax: (330)220-3083. E-mail: RockyA@LongPointMedia.com. Web site: www.backfencemagazin

Consumer Publications

e.com. **Contact:** Rocky Alten, creative director. Estab. 1994. Bimonthly magazine. *"Over the Back Fence* is a regional magazine serving southern and central Ohio. We are looking for photos of interesting people, events and history of our area." Sample copy available for $5. Photo guidelines available on Web site.

Needs Buys 50 photos from freelancers/issue; 200 photos/year. Needs photos of scenics, attractions, food (specific to each issue), historical locations in region (call for specific counties). Model release required for identifiable people. Photo captions preferred; include location, description, names, date of photo (year), and if previously published, where and when.

Specs Prefers images in digital format. Review guidelines before submitting.

Making Contact & Terms Send query letter with stock list and résumé of credits. Provide résumé, business card, brochure, flier or tearsheets to be kept on file for possible future assignments. Responds in 3 months. Simultaneous submissions and previously published work OK, "but you must identify photos used in other publications." Pays $100 for cover; $25-100 for inside. "We pay mileage fees to photographers on assignments. See our photographer's rates and guidelines for specifics." Pays on publication. Credit line given "except in the case of ads, where it may or may not appear." Buys one-time rights.

Tips "We are looking for sharp, colorful images and prefer using digital files or color transparencies over color prints when possible. Nostalgic and historical photos are usually in black and white."

◨ ▣ ↕ OWL MAGAZINE

10 Lower Spadina Ave., Suite 400, Toronto ON M5V 2Z2 Canada. (416)340-2700. Fax: (416)340-9769. E-mail: deb@owlkids.com. Web site: www.owlkids.com. **Contact:** Debbie Yea, photo researcher. Circ. 80,000. Estab. 1976. Published 10 times/year. A discovery magazine for children ages 9-13. Sample copy available for $4.95 and 9 × 12 SAE with $1.50 money order for postage. Photo guidelines free with SAE or via e-mail.

Needs Photo stories, photo puzzles, photos of children ages 12-14, extreme weather, wildlife, science, technology, environmental, pop culture, multicultural, events, adventure, hobbies, humor, sports and extreme sports. Interested in documentary, seasonal. Model/property release required. Photo captions required. Will buy story packages.

Specs Accepts images in digital format. E-mail as TIFF, JPEG files at 72 dpi. "For publication, we require 300 dpi."

Making Contact & Terms Accepts no responsibility for unsolicited material. Previously published work OK. Credit line given. Buys one-time rights.

Tips "Photos should be sharply focused with good lighting, and engaging for kids. We are always on the lookout for humorous, action-packed shots; eye-catching, sports, animals, bloopers, etc. Photos with a 'wow' impact."

$ ◨ ▣ PADDLER MAGAZINE

Paddlesport Publishing, Inc., 12040 98th Ave. NE, Suite 205, Kirkland WA 98033. (425)814-4140. Fax: 425)814-4042. E-mail: jason@paddlermagazine.com. Web site: www.paddlermagazine.com. **Contact:** Jason Mohr, art director. Circ. 50,000. Estab. 1990. Bimonthly magazine. Emphasizes kayaking, rafting, canoeing and sea kayaking. Sample copy available for $3.50. Photo guidelines free with SASE.

Needs Buys 27-45 photos from freelancers/issue; 162-270 photos/year. Needs photos of scenics and action. Model/property release preferred. Photo captions preferred; include location.

Consumer Publications

Specs Prefers images in digital format. Send via CD, Zip, e-mail as TIFF, EPS, JPEG files at 300 dpi. Digital submissions should be accompanied by a printed proof sheet. Also accepts 35mm transparencies.

Making Contact & Terms Send query letter with stock list. Send unsolicited photos by mail with SASE for consideration. Keeps samples on file. Responds in 2 months. Pays $250-350 for color cover; $50 for inset color cover; $125 for color full page inside. Pays on publication. Credit line given. Buys first North American serial rights; negotiable.

Tips "Send innovative photos of canoeing, kayaking and rafting, and let us keep them on file."

▣ PAKN TREGER

National Yiddish Book Center, 1021 West St., Amherst MA 01002. E-mail: bwolfson@bikher .org. Web site: www.yiddishbookcenter.org. **Contact:** Betsey Wolfson, designer. Circ. 30,000. Estab. 1980. Literary magazine published 3 times/year; focuses on modern and contemporary Yewish and Yiddish culture.

Needs Needs photos of families, parents, senior citizens,education, religious, humor, historical/vintage, Jewish and Yiddish culture. Reviews photos with or without a manuscript. Captions required; include identification of subjects.

Specs Accepts images in digital format. Send JPEG or GIF files.

Making Contact & Terms Negotiates payment. Pays on publication. Credit line given. Buys one-time rights.

$▣ PENNSYLVANIA

P.O. Box 755, Camp Hill PA 17011. (717)697-4660. E-mail: editor@pa-mag.com. Web site: www.pa-mag.com. **Contact:** Matthew K. Holliday, editor. Circ. 30,000. Bimonthly. Emphasizes history, travel and contemporary topics. Readers are 40-70 years old, professional and retired; average income is $59,000. Sample copy available for $2.95. Photo guidelines free with SASE or via e-mail.

Needs Uses about 40 photos/issue; most supplied by freelancers. Needs include travel, wildlife and scenic. All photos must be taken in Pennsylvania. Reviews photos with or without accompanying manuscript. Photo captions required.

Making Contact & Terms Send query letter with samples. Send digital submissions of 5.0 MP or higher (OK on CD-ROM with accompanying printout with image file references); 5×7 and larger color prints; 35mm and 2¼×2¼ transparencies (duplicates only, in camera or otherwise, no originals) by mail for consideration; include SASE for return of material. Responds in 1 month. Simultaneous submissions and previously published work OK with notification. Pays $100-150 for color cover; $35 for color inside; $50-500 for text/photo package. Credit line given. Buys one-time, first rights or other rights as arranged.

Tips Look at several past issues and review guidelines before submitting.

Ⓝ $ $▣ PENNSYLVANIA ANGLER & BOATER

P.O. Box 67000, Harrisburg PA 17106-7000. (717)705-7844. Fax: (717)705-7831. Web site: www.fish.state.pa.us. **Contact:** editor. Bimonthly. *"Pennsylvania Angler & Boater* is the Keystone State's official fishing and boating magazine, published by the Pennsylvania Fish & Boat Commission." Readers are anglers and boaters in Pennsylvania. Sample copy and photo guidelines free for 9×12 SAE and 9 oz. postage, or via Web site.

Needs Buys 8 photos from freelancers/issue; 48 photos/year. Needs "action fishing and boating shots." Model release required. Photo captions required.

Making Contact & Terms "Don't submit without first considering contributor guidelines, available on Web site. Then send query letter with résumé of credits. Send 35mm or larger transparencies by mail for consideration; include SASE for return of material. Send low-res images on CD; we'll later request high-res images of those shots that interest us." Responds in several weeks. Pays $400 maximum for color cover; $30 minimum for color inside; $50-300 for text/photo package. Pays between acceptance and publication. Credit line given.

$ ⑤ ▣ PHI DELTA KAPPA

408 N. Union St., P.O. Box 789, Bloomington IN 47402. Web site: www.pdkintl.org/kappan. htm. **Contact:** Carol Bucheri, design director. Estab. 1915. Produces *Phi Delta Kappa* magazine and supporting materials. Photos used in magazine, fliers and subscription cards. Photo guidelines available online at www.pdkintl.org/kappan/khpsubmi.htm.

Needs Uses high-quality royalty-free, model-released stock phots on education topics. Especially interested in photos of educators and students at all levels, pre-D through university depicting a variety of people in different educational settings; teacher-to-teacher interactions with or without students (e.g., teachers' meetings, in-service, professional development settings). Reviews stock photos. Model release required. Photo caption required; include who, what, when, where.

Specs Uses 8×10 b&w and color prints; occasionally uses color. Accepts images in digital format. Send e-mail inquiries to cbucheri@pdkintl.org.

Making Contact & Terms Send query letter with list of education-related stock photo subjects before sending samples, or send URL for online portfolio. Provide photocopies, brochure or flier to be kept on file for possible future assignments. Responds in 3 weeks. Credit line and tearsheets given. Buys one-time rights.

Tips "We will definitely consider purchasing collections of royalty-free, copyright-free, model-released stock work if the majority of the photos are relevant."

$ ▣ Ⓐ ▣ ▣ PHOTO LIFE

Apex Publications, 185 St. Paul St., Quebec QC G1K 3W2 Canada. (800)905-7468. Fax: (800)664-2739. Web site: www.photolife.com. **Contact:** Anita Dammer, editor. Circ. 60,000. Magazine published 6 times/year. Readers are amateur, advanced amateur and professional photographers. Sample copy free with SASE. Photo guidelines available on Web site.

Needs Buys 70 photos from freelancers/issue; 420 photos/year. Needs landscape/wildlife shots, fashion, scenics, b&w images and so on. Priority is given to Canadian photographers.

Specs Accepts images in digital format. Send via CD at 300 dpi.

Making Contact & Terms Send query letter with résumé of credits, SASE. Pays on publication. Buys first North American serial rights and one-time rights.

Tips "Looking for good writers to cover any subject of interest to the amateur and advanced photographer. Fine art photos should be striking, innovative. General stock and outdoor photos should be presented with a strong technical theme."

$ $ ▣ ▣ PHOTO TECHNIQUES

Preston Publications, 6600 W. Touhy Ave., Niles IL 60714. (847)647-2900. Fax: (847)647-1155. E-mail: slewis@phototechmag.com. Web site: www.phototechmag.com. **Contact:**

Scott Lewis, editor. Circ. 25,000. Estab. 1979. Bimonthly magazine for advanced traditional and digital photographers. Sample copy available for $6. Photo guidelines free with SAE or available on Web site.

Needs Publishes expert technical articles about photography. Needs photos of rural, landscapes/scenics, "but if extensively photographed by others, ask yourself if your photo is sufficiently different." Also "some urban or portrait if it fits theme of article." Especially needs digital ink system testing and coloring and alternative processes articles. Reviews photos with or without a manuscript. Photo captions required; include technical data.

Specs Uses any and all formats.

Making Contact & Terms "E-mail queries work best." Send article or portfolio for review. Portfolio should include b&w and/or color prints, slides or transparencies. Keeps samples on file; include SASE for return of material. "Prefer that work not have been previously published in any competing photography magazine; small, scholarly, or local publication OK." Pays $300 for color cover; $100-150/page. Pays on publication. Credit line given. Buys one-time rights.

Tips "We need people to be familiar with our magazine before submitting/querying. Include return postage/packaging. Also, we much prefer complete, finished submissions. When people ask, 'Would you be interested in...?', often the answer is simply, 'We don't know! Let us see it.' Most of our articles are written by practicing photographers and use their work as illustrations."

PHOTOGRAPHER'S FORUM MAGAZINE

Serbin Communications, Inc., 813 Reddick St., Santa Barbara CA 93103. (805)963-0439 or (800)876-6425. Fax: (805)965-0496. E-mail: julie@serbin.com. Web site: www.serbin.com. **Contact:** Julie Simpson, managing editor. Quarterly magazine for the serious student and emerging professional photographer. Includes feature articles on historic and contemporary photographers, interviews, book reviews, workshop listings, new products. (See separate listings for annual photography contests in the Contests section.)

�[N] $⬚ ⬚ PILOT MAGAZINE

Archant Specialist, The Mill, Bearwalden Business Park, Wendens Ambo Saffron Walden, Essex CB11 4GB United Kingdom. (44)(179)954-4200. Fax: (44)(179)954-4201. E-mail: dave .calderwood@pilotweb.co.uk. Web site: www.pilotweb.co.uk. **Contact:** Dave Calderwood, editor-in-chief. Circ. 25,048. Estab. 1968. Monthly consumer magazine. Photo guidelines available.

Needs Needs photos of aviation. Reviews photos with or without a manuscript. Photo captions required.

Specs Uses glossy, color prints; 35mm, $2^{1}/_{4} \times 2^{1}/_{4}$, 4×5, 8×10 transparencies. Accepts images in digital format. Send via CD, Zip as JPEG files at 300 dpi.

Making Contact & Terms Does not keep samples on file; include SASE for return of material. Previously published work OK. Pays £30 for color inside. Pays on publication. Credit line given. Buys one-time rights.

Tips "Read our magazine. Label all photos with name and address. Supply generous captions."

⬚ POETS & WRITERS MAGAZINE

90 Broad Street, 2100, New York NY 10004. (212)226-3586. Fax: (212)226-3963. E-mail: editor@pw.org. Web site: www.pw.org/magazine. Circ. 60,000. Estab. 1987. Bimonthly

literary trade magazine. "Designed for poets, fiction writers and creative nonfiction writers. We supply our readers with information about the publishing industry, conferences and workshop opportunities, grants and awards available to writers, as well as interviews with contemporary authors."

Needs Needs photos of contemporary writers: poets, fiction writers, writers of creative nonfiction. Photo captions required.

Specs Digital format.

Making Contact & Terms Provide URL, self-promotion piece or tearsheets to be kept on file for possible future assignments. Managing editor will contact photographer for portfolio review if interested. Pays on publication. Credit line given.

Tips "We seek photographs to accompany articles and profiles. We'd be pleased to have photographers' lists of author photos."

$☐ ⑤ ▣ ⊠ THE PRAIRIE JOURNAL, A Magazine of Canadian Literature

P.O. Box 61203, Brentwood PO, Calgary AB T2L 2K6 Canada. E-mail: prairiejournal@yahoo .com. Web site: www.geocities.com/prairiejournal. Circ. 600. Estab. 1983. Literary magazine published twice/year. Features mainly poetry and artwork. Sample copy available for $6 and $7 \times 8^{1}/_{2}$ SAE. Photo guidelines available for SAE and IRC.

Needs Buys 4 photos/year. Needs literary only, artistic.

Specs Uses b&w prints. Accepts images in digital format. Send via e-mail "if your query is successful."

Making Contact & Terms Send query letter with photocopies only (no originals) by mail. Provide self-promotion piece to be kept on file. Responds in 6 months, only if interested; send nonreturnable samples. Pays $10-50 for b&w cover or inside. Pays on publication. Credit line given. Buys first rights.

Tips "Black & white literary, artistic work preferred; not commercial. We especially like newcomers. Read our publication or check out our Web site. You need to own copyright for your work and have permission to reproduce it. We are open to subjects that would be suitable for a literary arts magazine containing poetry, fiction, reviews, interviews. We do not commission but choose from your samples."

$☐ Ⓐ ▣ THE PROGRESSIVE

409 E. Main St., Madison WI 53703. (608)257-4626. E-mail: photos@progressive.org. Web site: www.progressive.org. **Contact:** Nick Jehlen, art director. Circ. 68,000. Estab. 1909. Monthly political magazine. "Grassroots publication from a left perspective, interested in foreign and domestic issues of peace and social justice." Photo guidelines free and on Web site.

Needs Buys 5-10 photos from freelancers/issue; 50-100 photos/year. Looking for images documenting the human condition and the social/political environments of contemporary society. Special photo needs include "labor activities, environmental issues and political movements." Photo captions required; include name, place, date, credit information.

Specs Accepts low-resolution JPEGs via e-mail.

Making Contact & Terms Send query letter with photocopies; include SASE. Provide stock list to be kept on file for possible future assignments. Art director will contact photographer for portfolio review if interested. Responds once every month. Simultaneous submissions and previously published work OK. Pays $50-150 for b&w inside. Pays on publication. Credit line given. Buys one-time rights. All material returned with SASE.

Consumer Publications

Tips "Most of the photos we publish are of political actions. Interesting and well-composed photos of creative actions are the most likely to be published. We also use 2-3 short photo essays on political or social subjects per year." For detailed photo information, see Web site at www.art.progressive.org.

$⬚ ⬚ RACQUETBALL MAGAZINE

1685 W. Uintah, Colorado Springs CO 80904-2906. (719)635-5396. Fax: (719)635-0685. E-mail: jhiser@usra.org. Web site: www.usaracquetball.com. **Contact:** Jim Hiser, executive director. Circ. 30,000. Estab. 1990. Bimonthly magazine of USA Racquetball. Emphasizes racquetball. Sample copy available for $4.50. Photo guidelines available.

Needs Buys 6-12 photos from freelancers/issue; 36-72 photos/year. Needs photos of action racquetball. Model/property release preferred. Photo captions required.

Specs Accepts images in digital format. Send via CD as EPS files at 900 dpi.

Making Contact & Terms Provide résumé, business card, brochure, flier or tearsheets to be kept on file for possible future assignments. Responds in 1 month. Previously published work OK. Pays $200 for color cover; $3-5 for b&w inside; $25-75 for color inside. Pays on publication. Credit line given. Buys all rights; negotiable.

$⬚ ⬚ THE RAMBLER

Rambler Publications, LLC, P.O. Box 5070, Chapel Hill NC 27514-5001. (919)545-9789. Fax:(919)545-0921. E-mail: art@ramblermagazine.com. Web site: www.ramblermagazine.com. **Contact:** Elizabeth Oliver, managing editor. Circ. 4,000. Bimonthly literary magazine. Sample copy available. Photo guidelines are free with an SASE or on the Web site.

Needs Buys 125 freelance photos/year. Needs photos of cities/urban, environmental, people. Interested in avant garde, documentary, fine art, color, and b&w. Reviews photos with or without a manuscript. Model/property release preferred.

Specs Uses 8×10 prints. Accepts images in digital format. Send TIFF files at 300 dpi via CD or e-mail.

Making Contact & Terms E-mail query letter with link to photographer's Web site, JPEG samples at 72 dpi. Does not keep samples on file; include SASE for return of material. Simultaneous submissions and previously published work OK. Pays $100 maximum for b&w cover; $100 maximum for color cover. Pays $25 maximum for b&w inside; $25 maximum for color inside. Pays on publication. Credit line given. Buys one-time rights.

$ $⬚ RANGER RICK

11100 Wildlife Center Dr., Reston VA 20190-5362. (703)438-6525. Fax: (703)438-6094. E-mail: mcelhinney@nwf.org. Web site: www.nwf.org/rangerrick. **Contact:** Susan McElhinney, photo editor. Circ. 500,000. Estab. 1967. Monthly educational magazine published by the National Wildlife Federation for children ages 8-12. Photo guidelines free with SASE.

Needs Needs photos of children, multicultural, environmental, wildlife, adventure, science.

Specs Uses transparencies or digital capture; dupes or lightboxes OK for first edit.

Making Contact & Terms Send nonreturnable printed samples or Web site address. *Ranger Rick* space rates: $300 (quarter page) to $1,000 (cover).

Tips "Seeking experienced photographers with substantial publishing history only."

REFORM JUDAISM

633 Third Ave., 7th Floor, New York NY 10017-6778. (212)650-4240. E-mail: rjmagazine@urj.org. Web site: www.reformjudaismmag.org. **Contact:** Joy Weinberg, managing editor.

Circ. 305,000. Estab. 1972. Quarterly publication of the Union for Reform Judaism. Offers insightful, incisive coverage of the challenges faced by contemporary Jews. Readers are members of Reform congregations in North America. Sample copy available for $3.50. Photo guidelines available via e-mail or on Web site.

Needs Buys 3 photos from freelancers/issue; 12 photos/year. Needs photos relating to Jewish life or Jewish issues, Israel, politics. Model release required. Photo captions required.

Making Contact & Terms Provide résumé, business card, brochure, flier or tearsheets to be kept on file for possible future assignments. Responds in 1 month. Simultaneous submissions and previously published work OK. Include self-addressed, stamped postcard for response. Pays on publication. Credit line given. Buys one-time rights, first North American serial rights.

Tips Wants to see "excellent photography: artistic, creative, evocative pictures that involve the reader."

$⃠ ⊡ Ⓢ ▣ REMINISCE

Reiman Media Group, Inc., 5400 S. 60th St., Greendale WI 53129. Fax: (414)423-8463. E-mail: photocoordinator@reimanpub.com. Web site: www.reminisce.com. **Contact:** Trudi Bellin, photo coordinator. Estab. 1990. Bimonthly magazine. "The magazine that brings back the good times." Readers are males and females interested in nostalgia, ages 55 and over. Sample copy available for $2. Photo guidelines free with SASE.

- *Reminisce EXTRA* is published in the months between regular issues. Content and guidelines are the same.

Needs Buys 11 photos from freelancers/issue; 130 photos/year. Needs good-quality b&w and color vintage photography; has occasional use for high-quality color shots of memorabilia. Photo captions preferred; include season, location.

Specs Accepts images in digital format: TIFF or high-quality JPEG files at 300 dpi for up to 9×11 reproduction. Embedded metadata is recommended. Send via lightboxes or on removable media. Or send CD/DVD with printed thumbnails and caption sheet. E-mail if first review selection is small (12 images or less). Will preview sharp photocopies to judge possible use; or color transparencies/b&w prints.

Making Contact & Terms Send query letter with list of stock photo subjects. Send unsolicited photos by mail for consideration. Submit seasonally. Keeps samples on file (tearsheets, no dupes); include SASE for return of material. Responds in 3 months. Previously published work OK. Buys stock only. Pays $150-300 for cover; $50-150 for inside. Pays on publication. Credit line given. Buys one-time rights, occasionally needs nonprint electronic rights.

Tips "We are continually in need of authentic color taken in the 1940s, 1950s and 1960s, and black & white stock photos. Technical quality is extremely important; focus must be sharp (no soft focus); we can work with shifted color on vintage photos. Study our magazine thoroughly—we have a continuing need for vintage color and black &white images, and those who can supply what we need can expect to be regular contributors."

▣ REVOLUTIONARY WAR TRACKS

2660 Petersborough St., Herndon VA 20171. E-mail: revolutionarywartracks@yahoo.com. Estab. 2005. Quarterly magazine, "bringing Revolutionary War history alive for children and teens." Photo guidelines available by e-mail request.

Needs Buys 12-24 photos/year. Needs photos of babies/children/teens, multicultural, fami-

Consumer Publications

Consumer Publications

lies, parents, disasters, environmental, landscapes/scenics, wildlife, cities/urban, education, religious, rural, adventure, events, food/drink, sports, travel, agriculture, medicine, military, political, product shots/still life, science, technology—as related to Revolutionary War history. Interested in alternative process, avant garde, documentary, fashion/glamour, fine art, historical/vintage, seasonal. Reviews photos with or without a manuscript. Model/property release preferred.

Specs Uses glossy or matte color and/or b&w prints.

Making Contact & Terms Send query letter via e-mail. "If possible, please do not include photographs in files if they are sent through e-mail. A disk with your photographs is acceptable." Provide résumé, business card or self-promotion piece to be kept on file for possible future assignments. "Photographs sent with CDs are requested but not required." Responds within 1 month to queries; 1 week to portfolios. Simultaneous submissions and previously published work OK. **Pays on acceptance.** Credit line given. Buys one-time rights, first rights; negotiable.

◙ ▣ RHODE ISLAND MONTHLY

Rhode Island Monthly Communications, Inc., 280 Kinsley Ave., Providence RI 02903-1017. (401)277-8174. Fax: (401)277-8080. Web site: www.rimonthly.com. **Contact:** Ellen Dessloch, art director. Circ. 40,000. Estab. 1988. Monthly regional publication for and about Rhode Island.

Needs Buys 15 photos from freelancers/issue; 200 photos/year. "Almost all photos have a local slant: portraits, photo essays, food, lifestyle, home, issues."

Specs Uses glossy b&w prints; 35 mm, $2\frac{1}{4} \times 2\frac{1}{4}$, 4×5 transparencies. Accepts images in digital format.

Making Contact & Terms Send query letter with tearsheets, transparencies. Portfolio may be dropped off. Provide self-promotion piece to be kept on file for possible future assignments. Will return anything with SASE. Responds in 2 weeks. Pays "about a month after invoice is submitted." Credit line given. Buys one-time rights.

Tips "Freelancers should be familiar with *Rhode Island Monthly* and should be able to demonstrate their proficiency in the medium before any work is assigned."

$◙ Ⓐ ▣ THE ROANOKER

P.O. Box 21535, Roanoke VA 24018. (540)989-6138. Fax: (540)989-7603. E-mail: lloria@leisurepublishing.com. Web site: www.theroanoker.com. **Contact:** Leonard Loria, creative director. Circ. 14,000. Estab. 1974. Bimonthly. Emphasizes Roanoke region and western Virginia. Readers are upper-income, educated people interested in their community. Sample copy available for $3.

Needs Buys 30 photos from freelancers/issue; 180 photos/year. Needs photos of couples, multicultural, families, parents, senior citizens, architecture, cities/urban, education, interiors/decorating, entertainment, events, food/drink, health/fitness/beauty, performing arts, sports, travel, business concepts, medicine, technology/computers, seasonal. Needs "travel and scenic photos in western Virginia; color photo essays on life in western Virginia." Model/property release preferred. Photo captions required.

Making Contact & Terms Accepts digital format. Send via CD, e-mail as TIFF, EPS, JPEG files at 300 dpi, minimum print size 8×10 with cutlines and thumbnails. Responds in 1 month. Simultaneous submissions and previously published work OK. Pays $100-150 for color cover; $15-25 for b&w inside, $25-100 for color inside; $100/day. Pays on publication. Credit line given. Rights purchased vary; negotiable.

ROCKFORD REVIEW

P.O. Box 858, Rockford IL 61105. Web site: http://writersguild1.tripod.com. **Contact:** David Ross, editor. Circ. 750. Estab. 1982. Association publication of Rockford Writers' Guild. Published twice/year (summer and winter). Emphasizes poetry and prose of all types. Readers are of all stages and ages who share an interest in quality writing and art. Sample copy available for $9.

- This publication is literary in nature and publishes very few photographs. However, the photos on the cover tend to be experimental (e.g., solarized images, photograms, etc.).

Needs Uses 1-5 photos/issue; all supplied by freelancers. Needs photos of scenics and personalities. Model/property release preferred. Photo captions preferred; include when and where, and biography.

Specs Uses 8×10 or 5×7 glossy b&w prints.

Making Contact & Terms Send unsolicited photos by mail for consideration. Does not keep samples on file; include SASE for return of material. Responds in 6 weeks. Simultaneous submissions OK. Payment is one copy of magazine, but work is eligible for *Review*'s $25 Editor's Choice prize. Pays on publication. Credit line given. Buys first North American serial rights.

Tips "Experimental work with a literary magazine in mind will be carefully considered. Avoid the 'news' approach."

ROCKY MOUNTAIN SPORTS MAGAZINE

Windy City Publishing, Inc., P.O. Box 3036, Boulder CO 80211. (303) 477-9770. Fax: (303)477-9747. E-mail: rheaton@rockymountainsports.com. Web site: www.rockymountainsports.com. **Contact:** Rebecca Heaton. Estab. 1986. Circ. 95,000. Monthly consumer magazine covering running, mountain biking, road racing, snowboarding, both alpine and Nordic skiing, kayaking, hiking, climbing, mountaineering, and other individual sports.

Needs Needs photos of adventure, running, mountain biking, road racing, snowboarding, both alpine and Nordic skiing, kayaking, hiking, climbing, mountaineering, and other individual sports. Interested in lifestyle. Editorial calendar: March: running; April: adventure; May: triathlon; June: climbing/paddling/mountain biking; July: summer travel; August: organic; September: women; October: gym/fitness; November: snow sports; December: snow sports. Reviews photos with or without a manuscript. Model release required. Captions required; include identification of subjects.

Specs Accepts images in digital format. Send JPEG or TIFF files at 300 dpi minimum.

Making Contact & Terms Payment negotiated. Pays on publication. Credit line given. Buys one-time rights.

Tips "Think fun. Don't be afraid to try something new. We like new."

ROLLING STONE

Wenner Media, 1290 Avenue of the Americas, 2nd Floor, New York NY 10104. (212)484-1616. Fax: (212)767-8203. Web site: www.rollingstone.com. **Contact:** Jodi Peckman, director of photography. Circ. 1,254,148. Estab. 1967. Biweekly consumer magazine. Emphasizes film, CD reviews, music groups, celebrities, fashion. Readers are young adults interested in news of popular music, politics and culture.

Needs Needs photos of celebrities, political, entertainment, events. Interested in alternative process, avant garde, documentary, fashion/glamour.

Specs Accepts images in digital format. Send as TIFF, JPEG files at 300 dpi.

Making Contact & Terms Portfolio may be dropped off every Wednesday and picked up on Friday afternoon. Provide business card, self-promotion piece to be kept on file for possible future assignments. Responds only if interested; send nonreturnable samples.

Tips "It's not about a photographer's experience, it's about a photographer's talent and eye. Lots of photographers have years of professional experience but their work isn't for us. Others might not have years of experience, but they have this amazing eye."

$▣ RURAL HERITAGE

P.O. Box 2067, Cedar Rapids IA 52406-2067. (319)362-3027. E-mail: publisher@ruralheritag e.com. Web site: www.ruralheritage.com. **Contact:** Joe Mischka, publisher. Circ. 8,500. Estab. 1976. Bimonthly journal in support of modern-day farming and logging with draft animals (horses, mules, oxen). Sample copy available for $8 ($10 outside the U.S.). Photo guidelines available on Web site or via e-mail.

Needs "Quality photographs of draft animals working in harness."

Specs "For interior pages we use glossy color prints, high-quality slides, or high-resolution images (300 dpi or greater) shot with a quality digital camera. For covers we use 5×7 glossy color prints, large-format transparencies, or high-resolution images shot with a quality digital camera. Digital images must be original (not resized, cropped, etc.) files from a digital camera; scans unacceptable."

Making Contact & Terms Send query letter with samples. "Please include SASE for the return of your material, and put your name and address on the back of each piece." Pays $100 for color cover; $10-25 for b&w inside. Also provides 2 copies of issue in which work appears. Pays on publication.

Tips "Animals usually look better from the side than from the front. We like to see all the animal's body parts, including hooves, ears and tail. For animals in harness, we want to see the entire implement or vehicle. We prefer action shots (plowing, harvesting hay, etc.). Watch out for shadows across animals and people. Please include the name of any human handlers involved, the farm, the town (or county), state, and the animals' names (if possible) and breeds. You'll find current guidelines in the 'Business Office' of our Web site."

$▣ RUSSIAN LIFE MAGAZINE

P.O. Box 567, Montpelier VT 05601. (802)223-4955. E-mail: editors@russianlife.com. Web site: www.russianlife.com. **Contact:** Paul Richardson, publisher. Estab. 1956. Bimonthly magazine.

Needs Uses 25-35 photos/issue. Offers 10-15 freelance assignments/year. Needs photojournalism related to Russian culture, art and history. Model/property release preferred.

Making Contact & Terms Works with local freelancers only. Send query letter with samples. Send 35mm, 2¼×2¼, 4×5, 8×10 transparencies; 35mm film; digital format. Include SASE "or material will not be returned." Responds in 1 month. Pays $20-50 (color photo with accompanying story), depending on placement in magazine. Pays on publication. Credit line given. Buys one-time and electronic rights.

$▣ ▣ SANDLAPPER MAGAZINE

P.O. Box 1108, Lexington SC 29071. Fax: (803)359-0629. E-mail: aida@sandlapper.org. Web site: www.sandlapper.org. **Contact:** Aida Rogers, editor. Estab. 1989. Quarterly magazine. Emphasizes South Carolina topics *only*.

Needs Uses about 10 photographers/issue. Needs photos of anything related to South Carolina in any style, "as long as they're not in bad taste." Model release preferred. Photo captions required; include places and people.

Specs Uses 8×10 color and b&w prints; 35mm, 2¼×2¼, 4×5, 8×10 transparencies. Accepts images in digital format. Send via CD, Zip as TIFF, JPEG files at 300 dpi. "Do not format exclusively for PC. RGB preferred. Submit low-resolution and high-resolution files, and label them as such. Please call or e-mail Elaine Gillespie with any questions" about digital submissions: (803)779-2126; elaine@thegillespieagency.com.

Making Contact & Terms Send query letter with samples. Keeps samples on file; include SASE for return of material. Responds in 1 month. Pays $150 for color cover; $50-100 for color inside. Pays 1 month *after* publication. Credit line given. Buys first rights plus right to reprint.

Tips "We see plenty of beach sunsets, mountain waterfalls, and shore birds. Would like fresh images of people working and playing in the palmetto state."

$ 🖳 SCHOLASTIC MAGAZINES

568 Broadway, New York NY 10012. (212)343-7147. Fax: (212)343-7799. E-mail: sdiamond @scholastic.com. Web site: www.scholastic.com. **Contact**: Steven Diamond, executive director of photography. Estab. 1920. Publication of magazines varies from weekly to monthly. "We publish 27 titles on topics from current events, science, math, fine art, literature and social studies. Interested in featuring high-quality, well-composed images of students of all ages and all ethnic backgrounds."

Needs Needs photos of various subjects depending upon educational topics planned for academic year. Model release required. Photo captions required. "Images must be interesting, bright and lively!"

Specs Accepts images in digital format. Send via CD, e-mail.

Making Contact & Terms Send query letter with résumé, business card, brochure, flier or tearsheets to be kept on file for possible future assignments. Material cannot be returned. Previously published work OK. Pays on publication.

Tips Especially interested in good photography of all ages of student population. All images must have model/property releases.

$ $ 🖉 🅰 🖳 SEATTLE HOMES AND LIFESTYLES

Network Communications, Inc., 1221 E. Pike St., Suite 305, Seattle WA 98122. (206)322-6699. Fax: (206)322-2799. E-mail: swilliams@seattlehomesmag.com. Web site: www.seattl ehomesmag.com. **Contact:** Shawn Williams, art director. Circ. 30,000. Estab. 1996. Magazine published 10 times/year. Emphasizes interior home design, gardens, architecture, lifestyles (food, wine, entertaining). Sample copy available for $3.95 and SAE.

Needs Buys 35-60 photos from freelancers/issue; 200 photos/year. Needs photos of architecture, interior design, gardens, food, wine, entertaining. All work is commissioned specifically for magazine. Model release required. Photo captions required. "Do not send photos without querying first."

Specs Accepts images in digital format.

Making Contact & Terms No phone calls please. Send query letter with résumé, photocopies, tearsheets. Provide self-promotion piece to be kept on file for possible future assignments. Responds only if interested; send nonreturnable samples. Payment varies by assignment, $140-900, depending on number of photos and complexity of project. **Pays on**

Consumer Publications

acceptance. Credit line given. Buys exclusive one-time rights, first rights for one year; includes Web usage for one year.

Tips "Assignments contracted to experienced architectural and interior photographers for home-design and garden features. Photographers must be in Seattle area."

$☑ ▣ SHARING THE VICTORY

Fellowship of Christian Athletes, 8701 Leeds Rd., Kansas City MO 64129. (816)921-0909. Fax: (816)921-8755. E-mail: stv@fca.org. Web site: www.sharingthevictory.com. **Contact:** Jill Ewert, managing editor. Circ. 80,000. Estab. 1982. Monthly association magazine featuring stories and testimonials of prominent athletes and coaches in sports who proclaim a relationship with Jesus Christ. Sample copy available for $1 and 9×12 SAE. No photo guidelines available.

Needs Needs photos of sports. "We buy photos of persons being featured in our magazine. We don't buy photos without story being suggested first." Reviews photos with accompanying manuscript only. "All submitted stories must be connected to the FCA Ministry." Model release preferred; property release required. Photo captions preferred.

Specs Uses glossy or matte color prints; 35mm, 2¼×2¼ transparencies. Accepts images in digital format. Send via CD, Zip, e-mail as TIFF, JPEG files at 300 dpi.

Making Contact & Terms Contact through e-mail with a list of types of sports photographs in stock. Do not send samples. Simultaneous submissions OK. Pays $150 maximum for color cover; $100 maximum for color inside. Pays on publication. Credit line given. Buys one-time rights.

Tips "We would like to increase our supply of photographers who can do contract work."

$☑ ▣ SHINE BRIGHTLY

P.O. Box 7259, Grand Rapids MI 49510. (616)241-5616. Fax: (616)241-5558. E-mail: sara@g emsgc.org. Web site: www.gemsgc.org. **Contact:** Sara Hilton, senior editor. Circ. 15,500. Estab. 1970. Monthly publication of GEMS Girls' Club. Emphasizes "girls ages 9-14 in action. The magazine is a Christian girls' publication that inspires, motivates, and equips girls to become world changers." Sample copy and photo guidelines available for $1 with 9×12 SASE.

Needs Uses about 5-6 photos/issue. Needs "photos suitable for illustrating stories and articles: photos of babies/children/teens, multicultural, religious, girls aged 9-14 from multicultural backgrounds, close-up shots with eye contact." Model/property release preferred.

Specs Uses 5×7 glossy color prints. Accepts images in digital format. Send via Zip, CD as TIFF, BMP files at 300 dpi.

Making Contact & Terms Send 5×7 glossy color prints by mail (include SASE), electronic images by CD only (no e-mail) for consideration. Will view photographer's Web site if available. Responds in 2 months. Simultaneous submissions OK. Pays $50-75 for cover; $35 for color inside. Pays on publication. Credit line given. Buys one-time rights.

Tips "Make the photos simple. We prefer to get a spec sheet or CDs rather than photos, and we'd really like to hold photos sent to us on speculation until publication. We select those we might use and send others back. Freelancers should write for our annual theme update and try to get photos to fit the theme of each issue." Recommends that photographers "be concerned about current trends in fashions, hair styles, and realize that all girls don't belong to 'families.' Please, no slides, no negatives and no e-mail submissions."

⊘ ▣ SHOTS

P.O. Box 27755, Minneapolis MN 55427-0755. E-mail: shotsmag@juno.com. Web site: www.shotsmag.com. **Contact:** Russell Joslin, editor/publisher. Circ. 2,000. Quarterly fine art photography magazine. "We publish black-and-white fine art photography by photographers with an innate passion for personal, creative work." Sample copy available for $6. Photo guidelines free with SASE or on Web site.

Needs Fine art photography of all types accepted for consideration (but not bought). Reviews photos with or without a manuscript. Model/property release preferred. Photo captions preferred.

Specs Uses 8×10 b&w prints. Accepts images in digital format. Send via CD as TIFF files at 300 dpi. "See Web site for further specifications."

Making Contact & Terms Send query letter with prints. There is a **$15 submission fee for nonsubscribers** (free for subscribers). Include SASE for return of material. Responds in 3 months. Credit line given. Does not buy photographs/rights.

⊘ SMITHSONIAN

MRC 513, P.O. Box 37012, Washington DC 20013-7012. (202)633-6090. Fax: (202)633-6095. Web site: www.smithsonianmagazine.com. **Contact:** Jeff Campagna, art department administrator. Monthly magazine. *Smithsonian* chronicles the arts, environment, sciences and popular culture of the times for today's well-rounded individuals with diverse, general interests, providing its readers with information and knowledge in an entertaining way. Visit Web site for photo submission guidelines. *Does not accept unsolicited photos or portfolios. Call or query before submitting.*

▣ SOUTHCOMM PUBLISHING COMPANY, INC.

2600 Abbey Court, Alpharetta GA 30004. (678)624-1075. Fax: (678)624-1079. E-mail: cwwalker@southcomm.com. Web site: www.southcomm.com. **Contact:** Carolyn Williams-Walker, managing editor. Estab. 1985. "We publish approximately 35 publications throughout the year. They are primarily for chambers of commerce throughout the Southeast (Georgia, Tennessee, South Carolina, North Carolina, Alabama, Virgina, Florida). We are expanding to the Northeast (Pennsylvania) and Texas. Our publications are used for tourism, economic development and marketing purposes. We also are a custom publishing company, offering brochures and other types of printed material."

Needs "We are only looking for photographers who can travel to the communities with which we're working as we need shots that are specific to those locations. We will not consider generic stock-type photos. Images are generally for editorial purposes; however, advertising shots sometimes are required." Model/property release preferred. Photo captions required. "Indentify people, buildings and as many specifics as possible."

Specs Prefers images in digital format. Send via CD, saved as TIFF, GIF or JPEG files for Mac at no less than 300 dpi. Uses matte color prints. "We prefer digital photography for all our publications."

Making Contact & Terms Send query letter with résumé and photocopies. Keeps samples on file; provide résumé, business card. Responds only if interested; send nonreturnable samples. Pays $40 minimum; $60 maximum for color inside. "Payment per photo varies per project. However, rates are mainly toward the minimum end of the range. We pay the same rates for cover images as for interior shots because, at times, images identified for the cover cannot be used as such. They are then used in the interior instead." **Pays on**

acceptance. Credit line given. "Photos that are shot on assignment become the property of SouthComm Publishing Company, Inc. They cannot be released to our clients or another third party. We will purchase one-time rights to use images from photographers should the need arise." Will negotiate with a photographer unwilling to sell all rights.

Tips "We are looking for photographers who enjoy traveling and are highly organized and can communicate well with our clients as well as with us. Digital photographers *must* turn in contact sheets of all images shot in the community, clearly identifying the subjects."

$ $⑤ ▣ SOUTHERN BOATING

Southern Boating & Yachting, Inc., 330 N. Andrews Ave., Ft. Lauderdale FL 33301. (954)522-5515. Fax: (954)522-2260. E-mail: marilyn@southernboating.com. Web site: www.southernboating.com. **Contact:** Marilyn Mower, editor. Circ. 40,000. Estab. 1972. Monthly magazine. Emphasizes "powerboating and cruising in the southeastern U.S., Bahamas and the Caribbean." Readers are "concentrated in 30-60 age group, mostly male, affluent, very experienced boat owners." Sample copy available for $7.

Needs Number of photos/issue varies; many supplied by freelancers. Seeks "boating lifestyle" cover shots. Buys stock only. No "assigned covers." Model release required. Photo captions required.

Specs Accepts images in digital format. Send via CD, floppy disk, e-mail as JPEG, TIFF files, minimum 4×6 in. at 300 dpi.

Making Contact & Terms Send query letter with list of stock photo subjects, SASE. Response time varies. Simultaneous submissions and previously published work OK. Pays $500 minimum for color cover; $70 minimum for color inside; photo/text package negotiable. Pays within 30 days of publication. Credit line given. Buys one-time print and electronic/Web site rights.

Tips "We want lifestyle shots of saltwater cruising, fishing or just relaxing on the water. Lifestyle or family boating shots shots are actively sought."

$ $ $▨ ▣ SPORT FISHING

Bonnier Corporation, LLC, 460 N. Orlando Ave., Suite 200, Winter Park FL 32789. (407)628-4802. Fax: (407)628-7061. E-mail: editor@sportfishingmag.com or stephanie.pancratz@bonniercorp.com. Web site: www.sportfishingmag.com. **Contact:** Stephanie Pancratz, managing editor. Circ. 150,000 (paid). Estab. 1986. Publishes 10 issues/year. Emphasizes saltwater sport fishing. Readers are upscale boat owners and affluent fishermen. Sample copy available for $2.50, 9×12 SAE and 6 first-class stamps. Photo guidelines available on Web site, via e-mail or with SASE.

Needs Buys 50% or more photos from freelancers/issue. Needs photos of saltwater fish and fishing—especially good action shots. "Are working more from stock—good opportunities for extra sales on any given assignment." Model release not generally required.

Specs Prefers images in RAW, unaltered/undoctored digital format, especially for the option to run images very large, with accompanying low-res JPGs for quick review. Original 35 mm (or larger) transparencies are accepted for smaller images, but no longer for the cover. All guidelines, rates, suggestions available on Web site; click on "Editorial Guidelines" at bottom of home page.

Making Contact & Terms Send query letter with samples. Send unsolicited photos by mail or low resolution digitals by e-mail for consideration. Provide business card, brochure, flier or tearsheets to be kept on file for possible future assignments. Responds in 3 weeks. Pays

$1,000 for cover; $75-400 for inside. Buys one-time rights unless otherwise agreed upon. **Tips** ''Sharp focus critical; avoid 'kill' shots of big game fish, sharks; avoid bloody fish in/ at the boat. The best guideline is the magazine itself. Know your market. Get used to shooting on, in or under water. Most of our needs are found there. If you have first-rate photos and questions, e-mail us.''

☑ SPORTS ILLUSTRATED

AOL/Time Warner, Time Life Building, 135 W. 50th St., New York NY 10020. (212)522-1212. Web site: www.si.com. **Contact:** James Colton, photography editor. *Sports Illustrated* reports and interprets the world of sports, recreation and active leisure. It previews, analyzes and comments on major games and events, as well as those noteworthy for character and spirit alone. In addition, the magazine has articles on such subjects as fashion, physical fitness and conservation. *Query before submitting.*

$☐ ▣ STICKMAN REVIEW: An Online Literary Journal

721 Oakwater Lane, Port Orange, FL 32128. (928)913-0869. E-mail: art@stickmanreview.c om. Web site: www.stickmanreview.com. **Contact:** Anthony Brown, editor. Estab. 2001. Biannual literary magazine publishing fiction, poetry, essays and art for a literary audience. Sample copies available on Web site.
Needs Buys 2 photos from freelancers/issue; 4 photos/year. Interested in alternative process, avant garde, documentary, erotic, fine art. Reviews photos with or without a manuscript.
Specs Accepts images in digital format. Send via e-mail as JPEG, GIF, TIFF, PS D files at 72 dpi (500K maximum).
Making Contact & Terms Contact through e-mail only. Does not keep samples on file; cannot return material. Do not query, just submit the work you would like considered. Responds 2 months to portfolios. Simultaneous submissions OK. Pays $25-50. **Pays on acceptance.** Credit line given. Buys electronic rights.
Tips ''Please check out the magazine on our Web site. We are open to anything, so long as its intent is artistic expression.''

$▨ SUB-TERRAIN MAGAZINE

P.O. Box 3008, MPO, Vancouver BC V6B 3X5 Canada. (604)876-8710. Fax: (604)879-2667. E-mail: subter@portal.ca. Web site: www.subterrain.ca. **Contact:** Brian Kaufman, editor-in-chief. Estab. 1988. Literary magazine published 3 times/year.
Needs Uses ''many'' unsolicited photos. Needs ''artistic'' photos. Photo captions preferred.
Specs Uses color and/or b&w prints.
Making Contact & Terms Submit portfolio for review. Send unsolicited photos by mail for consideration. Keeps samples on file ''sometimes.'' Responds in 6 months. Simultaneous submissions OK. Pays $25-100/photo. Also pays in contributor's copies. Pays on publication. Credit line given. Buys one-time rights.

$☑ ▣ THE SUN

107 N. Roberson St., Chapel Hill NC 27516. (919)942-5282. Fax: (919)932-3101. Web site: www.thesunmagazine.org. **Contact:** Art Director. Circ. 70,000. Estab. 1974. Monthly literary magazine featuring personal essays, interviews, poems, short stories, photos and photo essays. Sample copy available for $5. Photo guidelines free with SASE or on Web site.

Needs Buys 10-30 photos/issue; 200-300 photos/year. Needs " slice of life" photographs of people and environments. "We also need photographs that relate to political, spiritual, and social themes. We consider documentary-style images. Most of our photos of people feature unrecognizable individuals, although we do run portraits in specific places, including the cover."

Model/property release strongly preferred.

Specs Uses 4×5 to 11×17 glossy or matte b&w prints. Slides are not accepted, and color photos are discouraged. "We cannot review images via e-mail or Web site. If you are submitting digital images, please send high-quality digital prints first. If we accept your images for publication, we will request the image files on CD or DVD media (Mac or PC) in uncompressed TIFF grayscale format at 300 dpi or greater."

Making Contact & Terms Send query letter with prints. Portfolio may be dropped off Monday-Friday. Does not keep samples on file; include SASE for return of material. Responds in 3 months. Simultaneous submissions and previously published work OK. "Submit no more than 30 of your best b&w prints. Please do not e-mail images." Pays $500 for b&w cover; $100-300 for b&w inside. Pays on publication. Credit line given. Buys one-time rights.

Tips "We're looking for artful and sensitive photographs that aren't overly sentimental. We're open to unusual work. Read the magazine to get a sense of what we're about. Send the best possible prints of your work. Our submission rate is extremely high; please be patient after sending us your work. Send return postage and secure return packaging."

☒ ⊘ ⒜ ▣ SURFACE MAGAZINE: American Avant Garde

55 Washington St., Suite 419, Brooklyn NY 11201. (718)488-0650. Fax: (718)488-0651. E-mail: avantguardian@surfacemag.com. Web site: www.surfacemag.com. Circ. 112,000. Estab. 1994. Consumer magazine published 6 times/year.

Needs Buys 200 photos from freelancers/issue; 1,600 photos/year. Needs photos of environmental, landscapes/scenics, architecture, cities/urban, interiors/decorating, performing arts, travel, product shots/still life, technology. Interested in avant garde, fashion, portraits, fine art, seasonal.

Specs Uses 11×17 glossy matte prints; 35mm, $2^1/_4 \times 2^1/_4$, 4×5, 8×10 transparencies. Accepts images in digital format. Send via CD, Zip as TIFF, JPEG files at 300 dpi.

Making Contact & Terms Contact through rep or send query letter with prints, photocopies, tearsheets. Provide self-promotion piece to be kept on file for possible future assignments. "Portfolios are reviewed on Friday each week. Submitted portfolios must be clearly labelled and include a shipping account number or postage for return. Please call for more details." Responds only if interested; send nonreturnable samples. Simultaneous submissions OK. Credit line given.

$▣ TEXAS GARDENER MAGAZINE

P.O. Box 9005, Waco TX 76714-9005. (254)848-9393. Fax: (254)848-9779. E-mail: info@texasgardener.com. Web site: www.texasgardener.com. **Contact:** Chris S. Corby, editor/publisher. Circ. 25,000. Bimonthly. Emphasizes gardening. Readers are "51% male, 49% female, home gardeners, 98% Texas residents." Sample copy available for $4.

Needs Buys 18-27 photos from freelancers/issue; 108-162 photos/year. Needs "color photos of gardening activities in Texas." Special needs include "cover photos shot in vertical format. Must be taken in Texas." Photo captions required.

Consumer Publications

Specs Prefers high-resolution digital images. Send via e-mail as JPEG files at 300 dpi.

Making Contact & Terms Send query letter with samples, SASE. Responds in 3 weeks. Pays $100-200 for color cover; $25-100 for color inside. Pays on publication. Credit line given. Buys one-time rights.

Tips "Provide complete information on photos. For example, if you submit a photo of watermelons growing in a garden, we need to know what variety they are and when and where the picture was taken."

$☐ ▣ THEMA

THEMA Literary Society, P.O. Box 8747, Metairie LA 70011-8747. (504)940-7156. E-mail: thema@cox.net. Web site: http://members.cox.net/thema. **Contact:** Virginia Howard, manager/editor. Circ. 300. Estab. 1988. Literary magazine published 3 times/year emphasizing theme-related short stories, poetry and art. Sample copy available for $10.

Needs Photo must relate to one of *THEMA*'s upcoming themes (indicate the target theme on submission of photo). Upcoming themes (submission deadlines in parenthesis); Put It In Your Pocket, Lillian (March 1, 2009); The Dean's Cat (July 1, 2009); Math & Music (November 1, 2009). Reviews photos with or without a manuscript. Model/property release preferred. Photo captions preferred.

Specs Uses 5×7 glossy color and/or b&w prints. Accepts images in digital format. Send via Zip as TIFF files at 200 dpi.

Making Contact & Terms Send query letter with prints, photocopies. Does not keep samples on file; include SASE for return of material. Responds in 1 week to queries; 3 months to portfolios. Simultaneous submissions and previously published work OK. Pays $25 for cover; $10 for b&w inside. **Pays on acceptance.** Credit line given. Buys one-time rights.

Tips "Submit only work that relates to one of *THEMA*'s upcoming themes. Contact by snail mail preferred."

THIN AIR MAGAZINE

Northern Arizona University, P.O. Box 6032, Flagstaff AZ 86011. (928)523-6743. Fax: (928)523-7074. Web site: www.thinairmagazine.com. **Contact:** Art Editor. Circ. 400. Estab. 1995. Annual literary magazine. Emphasizes arts and literature—poetry, fiction and essays. Readers are collegiate, academic, writerly adult males and females interested in arts and literature. Sample copy available for $6.

Needs Buys 2-4 photos from freelancers/issue; 4-8 photos/year. Needs scenic/wildlife shots and b&w photos that portray a statement or tell a story. Looking for b&w or color cover shots. Model/property release preferred. Photo captions preferred; include name of photographer, date of photo.

Specs Uses 8×10 b&w prints.

Making Contact & Terms Send unsolicited photos by mail with SASE for consideration. Photos accepted August through May only. Keeps samples on file. Responds in 3 months. Simultaneous submissions and previously published work OK. Pays 2 contributor's copies. Credit line given. Buys one-time rights.

N̲ $▣ TIKKUN

2342 Shattack Ave., #1200, Berkeley CA 94704. (510)644-1200. Fax: (510)644-1255. E-mail: magazine@tikkun.org. Web site: www.tikkun.org. **Contact:** Dave Belden, managing editor. Circ. 25,000. Estab. 1986. "A bimonthly Jewish and interfaith critique of politics, culture and society.'' Readers are 60% Jewish, professional, middle-class, literary people ages 30-60.

Needs Uses 15 photos/issue; 30% supplied by freelancers. Needs political, social commentary; Middle East and U.S. photos. Reviews photos with or without a manuscript.

Specs Uses b&w and color prints. Accepts images in digital format for Mac (Photoshop EPS). Send via CD.

Making Contact & Terms Send prints or good photocopies. Keeps samples on file; include SASE for return of material. Response time varies. ''Turnaround is 4 months, unless artist specifies other.'' Previously published work OK. Pays $50 for b&w inside. Pays on publication. Credit line given. Buys all rights; negotiable.

Tips ''Look at our magazine and suggest how your photos can enhance our articles and subject material. Send samples.''

$○ ▣ ⊕ TIMES OF THE ISLANDS: The International Magazine of the Turks & Caicos Islands

Times Publications Ltd., Southwinds Plaza, Box 234, Providenciales, Turks & Caicos Islands, British West Indies. (649)946-4788. E-mail: timespub@tciway.tc. Web site: www.timespub.tc. **Contact:** Kathy Borsuk, editor. Circ. 14,000. Estab. 1988. Quarterly magazine focusing on in-depth topics specifically related to Turks & Caicos Islands. Targeted beyond mass tourists to homeowners/investors/developers and others with strong interest in learning about these islands. Sample copy available for $6. Photo guidelines available on Web site.

Needs Buys 5 photos from freelancers/issue; 20 photos/year. Needs photos of environmental, landscapes/scenics, wildlife, architecture, adventure, travel. Interested in historical/vintage. Also scuba diving, islands in TCI beyond main island of Providenciales. Reviews photos with or without a manuscript. Photo captions required; include specific location, names of any people.

Specs Prefers images in high resolution digital format. Send via CD or e-mail as JPEG files.

Making Contact & Terms Send query e-mail with photo samples. Provide business card, self-promotion piece to be kept on file for possible future assignments. Responds in 6 weeks to queries. Simultaneous submissions and previously published work OK. Pays $100-300 for color cover; $50-100 for inside. Pays on publication. Credit line given. Buys one-time rights; negotiable.

Tips ''Make sure photo is specific to Turks & Caicos and location/subject accurately identified.''

$☑ Ⓐ ▣ ⊕ TOTAL 911

9Publishing Limited, P.O. Box 6815, Matlock DE4 4WZ United Kingdom. (44)(845)450-6464. E-mail: editorial@total911.co.uk. Web site: www.total911.com. **Contact:** Philip Raby, publishing editor. Estab. 2005. Monthly consumer magazine. ''A high-quality magazine for enthusiasts of the Porsche 911 in all its forms. Sold all around the world.'' Request photo guildelines via e-mail.

Needs Needs photos of automobiles, Porsche 911.

Specs Accepts images in digital format.

Making Contact & Terms E-mail query letter with link to photographer's Web site, JPEG samples at 72 dpi. Pays 30 days after publication. Credit line given. Buys one-time rights.

Tips ''Do not contact us unless you are a professional photographer who can produce

Consumer Publications

outstanding work using top-quality digital equipment. Especially keen to contact good photographers in the United States.''

$ ☑ ▣ TRACK & FIELD NEWS

2570 El Camino Real, Suite 606, Mountain View CA 94040. (650)948-8188. Fax: (650)948-9445. E-mail: editorial@trackandfieldnews.com. Web site: www.trackandfieldnews.com. **Contact:** Jon Hendershott, associate editor (features/photography). Circ. 25,000. Estab. 1948. Monthly magazine. Emphasizes national and world-class track and field competition and participants at those levels for athletes, coaches, administrators and fans. Sample copy free with 9 × 12 SASE. Photo guidelines free.

Needs Buys 10-15 photos from freelancers/issue; 120-180 photos/year. Wants, on a regular basis, photos of national-class athletes, men and women, preferably in action. ''We are always looking for quality pictures of track and field action, as well as offbeat and different feature photos. We always prefer to hear from a photographer before he/she covers a specific meet. We also welcome shots from road and cross-country races for both men and women. Any photos may eventually be used to illustrate news stories in *T&FN*, feature stories in *T&FN*, or may be used in our other publications (books, technical journals, etc.). Any such editorial use will be paid for, regardless of whether material is used directly in *T&FN*. About all we don't want to see are pictures taken with someone's Instamatic or Polaroid. No shots of someone's child or grandparent running. Professional work only.'' Photo captions required; include subject name, meet date/name.

Specs Images must be in digital format. Send via CD, e-mail at 300 dpi.

Making Contact & Terms Send query letter with samples, SASE. Responds in 10-14 days. Pays $225 for color cover; $25 for b&w inside; $50 for color inside ($100 for interior color, full page; $175 for interior 2-page poster/spread). Payment is made monthly. Credit line given. Buys one-time rights.

Tips ''No photographer is going to get rich via *T&FN*. We can offer a credit line, nominal payment and, in some cases, credentials to major track and field meets to enable on-the-field shooting. Also, we can offer the chance for competent photographers to shoot major competitions and competitors up close, as well as being the most highly regarded publication in the track world as a forum to display a photographer's talents.''

Ⓝ $ $ ☑ ▣ TRAIL RUNNER, The Magazine of Running Adventure

Big Stone Publishing, 417 Main St., Unit N, Carbondale CO 81623. (970)704-1442. Fax: (970)963-4965. E-mail: mbenge@bigstonepub.com. Web site: www.trailrunnermag.com. **Contact:** Mike Benge, editor. Circ. 22,000. Estab. 1999. Bimonthly magazine. The nation's only 4-color glossy magazine covering all aspects of trail running. Sample copy available for 9 × 12 SAE with $1.65 postage. Photo guidelines available for SASE or on Web site.

Needs Buys 50-75 photos from freelancers/issue; 300-500 photos/year. Needs photos of landscapes/scenics, adventure, health/fitness, sports, travel. Interested in anything related to running on trails and the outdoors. Reviews photos with or without a manuscript. Model/property release preferred. Photo captions required.

Specs Uses glossy color prints; 35mm transparencies. Accepts images in digital format. Send via CD, e-mail as TIFF files at 600 dpi.

Making Contact & Terms Send query letter with slides, stock list. Contact photo editor for appointment to drop off portfolio. Provide résumé, business card or self-promotion piece to be kept on file for possible future assignments. Responds in 3 weeks. Simultaneous

Consumer Publications

submissions OK. Pays $50-300 for b&w cover; $500 for color cover; $50-200 for b&w inside; $50-250 for color inside; $350 for spread (color). Pays 30 days from date of publication. Credit line given. Buys one-time rights, first rights; negotiable.

Tips ''Read our magazine. Stay away from model shots, or at least those with make-up and spandex clothing. No waving at the camera.''

☑ TRAVEL + LEISURE

1120 Avenue of the Americas, 10th Floor, New York NY 10036. (212)382-5600. Fax: (212)382-5877. Web site: www.travelandleisure.com. **Contact:** Photo Department. Circ. 1.2 million. Monthly magazine. Emphasizes travel destinations, resorts, portraits, dining and entertainment.

Needs Does not accept unsolicited photos. Model release required. Photo captions required.

Making Contact & Terms ''If mailing a portfolio, include a self-addressed stamped package for its safe return. You may also send it by messenger Monday through Friday between 11 a.m. and 5 p.m. We accept work in book form exclusively—no transparencies, loose prints, nor scans on CD, disk or e-mail. Send photocopies or photo prints, not originals, as we are not responsible for lost or damaged images in unsolicited portfolios. We do not meet with photographers if we haven't seen their book. However, please include a promo card in your portfolio with contact information, so we may get in touch with you if necessary.''

$▣ ⊕ TRAVELLER

45-49 Brompton Rd., London SW3 1DE United Kingdom. (44)(207)589-0500. Fax: (44)(207)581-8476. E-mail: traveller@wexas.com. Web site: www.traveller.org.uk. **Contact:** Amy Sohanpaul, editor. Circ. 25,000. Quarterly. Readers are predominantly male, professional, ages 35 and older. Sample copy available for £4.95.

Needs Uses 75-100 photos/issue; all supplied by freelancers. Needs photos of travel, wildlife, tribes. Reviews photos with or without a manuscript. Photo captions preferred.

Making Contact & Terms Send at least 20 original color slides or b&w prints. Or send at least 20 low-res scans by e-mail or CD (include printout of thumbnails); high-res (300 dpi) scans will be required for final publication. Does not keep samples on file; include SASE for return of material. Responds in 3 months. Pays £150 for color cover; £80 for full page; £50 for other sizes. Pays on publication. Buys one-time rights.

Tips Look at guidelines for contributors on Web site.

$ $◻ ▣ TRICYCLE: The Buddhist Review

The Buddhist Ray, Inc., 92 Vandam St., New York NY 10013. (212)645-1143. Fax: (212)645-1493. E-mail: editorial@tricycle.com. Web site: www.tricycle.com. **Contact:** Alexandra Kaloyanides, senior editor. Circ. 60,000. Estab. 1991. Quarterly nonprofit magazine devoted to the exploration of Buddhism, literature and the arts.

Needs Buys 10 photos from freelancers/issue; 40 photos/year. Reviews photos with or without a m anus cript. Model/property release preferred. Photo captions preferred.

Specs Uses glossy b&w and color prints; 35mm transparencies. Accepts images in digital format. Send via CD, Zip, e-mail as TIFF, EPS, BMP, GIF, JPEG files at 300 dpi.

Making Contact & Terms Send query letter with tearsheets. Provide business card, self-promotion piece to be kept on file for possible future assignments. Responds in 3 months to queries. Simultaneous submissions OK. Pays $7 50 maximum for color cover; $250 maximum for b&w or color inside. Pays on publication. Credit line given. Buys one-time rights.

Tips "Read the magazine to get a sense of the kind of work we publish. We don't only use Buddhist art; we select artwork depending on the content of the piece."

$ $⬚ ▣ ◨ UP HERE

Suite 800, 4920 52nd St., Yellowknife NT X1A 2N9 Canada. (867)766-6710. Fax: (867)873-9876. E-mail: aaron@uphere.ca. Web site: www.uphere.ca. **Contact:** Jake Kennedy, editor. Circ. 35,000. Estab. 1984. Magazine published 8 times/year. Emphasizes Canada's North. Readers are educated, affluent men and women ages 30 to 60.

Needs Buys 18-27 photos from freelancers/issue; 144-216 photos/year. Needs photos of Northern Canada environmental, landscapes/scenics, wildlife, adventure, performing arts. Interested in documentary, seasonal. Purchases photos with or without accompanying manuscript. Photo captions required.

Specs Accepts images in digital format. Send via CD, e-mail. also uses color transparencies, not prints, labeled with the photographer's name, address, phone number, and caption.

Making Contact & Terms Provide résumé, business card, brochure, flier or tearsheets to be kept on file for possible future assignments. Pays $350-400 for color cover, up to $300 for color inside. Pays on publication. Credit line given. Buys one-time rights.

Tips "We are a *people* magazine. We need stories that are uniquely Northern (people, places, etc.). Few scenics as such. We approach local freelancers for given subjects, but routinely complete commissioned photography with images from stock sources. Please let us know about Northern images you have." Wants to see "sharp, clear photos, good color and composition. We always need verticals to consider for the cover, but they usually tie in with an article inside."

⬚ VANITY FAIR

Condé Nast Building, 4 Times Square, New York NY 10036. (212)286-2860. Fax: (212)286-7787 or (212)286-6787. Web site: www.vanityfair.com. **Contact:** Susan White, photography director. Monthly magazine.

Needs Freelancers supply 50% of photos. Needs portraits. Model/property release required for everyone. Photo captions required for photographer, styles, hair, makeup, etc.

Making Contact & Terms Contact through rep or submit portfolio for review. Provide résumé, business card, brochure, flier or tearsheets to be kept on file for possible future assignments. Responds in 2 weeks. Payment negotiable. Pays on publication.

Tips "We solicit material after a portfolio drop. So, really we don't want unsolicited material."

▣ WASHINGTON TRAILS

2019 3rd Ave., Suite 100, Seattle WA 98121-2430. (206)625-1367. E-mail: editor@wta.org. Web site: www.wta.org. **Contact:** Andrew Engelson, editor. Circ. 7,000. Estab. 1966. Magazine of the Washington Trails Association, published 10 times/year. Emphasizes "backpacking, hiking, cross-country skiing, all nonmotorized trail use, outdoor equipment and minimum-impact camping techniques." Readers are "people active in outdoor activities, primarily backpacking; residents of the Pacific Northwest, mostly Washington; age group: 9-90; family-oriented; interested in wilderness preservation, trail maintenance." Photo guidelines free with SASE or on Web site.

Consumer Publications

Consumer Publications

Needs Uses 10-15 photos from volunteers/issue; 100-150 photos/year. Needs "wilderness/ scenic; people involved in hiking, backpacking, skiing, wildlife; outdoor equipment photos, all with Pacific Northwest emphasis." Photo captions required.

Making Contact & Terms Send JPEGs by e-mail, or 5×7 or 8×10 glossy b&w prints by mail for consideration; include SASE for return of material. Responds in 1-2 months. Simultaneous submissions and previously published work OK. No payment for photos. A 1-year subscription offered for use of color cover shot. Credit line given.

Tips "We are a black & white publication and prefer using black & white originals for the best reproduction. Photos must have a Pacific Northwest slant. Photos that meet our cover specifications are always of interest to us. Familiarity with our magazine would greatly aid the photographer in submitting material to us. Contributing to *Washington Trails* won't help pay your bills, but sharing your photos with other backpackers and skiers has its own rewards."

$ ☑ Ⓐ THE WATER SKIER

1251 Holy Cow Rd., Polk City FL 33868-8200. (863)324-4341. Fax: (863)325-8259. E-mail: satkinson@usawaterski.org. Web site: www.usawaterski.org. **Contact:** Scott Atkinson, editor. Circ. 28,000. Estab. 1950. Magazine of USA Water Ski, published 7 times/year. Emphasizes water skiing. Readers are male and female professionals, ages 20-45. Sample copy available for $3.50. Photo guidelines available.

Needs Buys 1-5 photos from freelancers/issue; 9-45 photos/year. Needs photos of sports action. Model/property release required. Photo captions required.

Making Contact & Terms Call first. Pays $50-150 for color photos. Pays on publication. Credit line given. Buys all rights.

Ⓝ $ $ WATERSKI

World Publications, LLC, 460 N. Orlando Ave., Suite 200, Winter Park FL 32789. (407)628-4802. Fax: (407)628-7061. E-mail: bill.doster@worldpub.net. Web site: www.waterskimag. com. **Contact**: Bill Doster, photo editor. Circ. 105,000. Estab. 1978. Published 8 times/year. Emphasizes water skiing instruction, lifestyle, competition, travel. Readers are 36-year-old males, average household income $65,000. Sample copy available for $2.95. Photo guidelines free with SASE.

Needs Buys 20 photos from freelancers/issue; 160 photos/year. Needs photos of instruction, travel, personality. Model/property release preferred. Photo captions preferred; include person, trick described.

Making Contact & Terms Query with good samples, SASE. Keeps samples on file. Responds within 2 months. Pays $200-500/day; $500 for color cover; $50-75 for b&w inside; $75-300 for color inside; $150/color page rate; $50-75/b&w page rate. Pays on publication. Credit line given. Buys first North American serial rights.

Tips "Clean, clear, tight images. Plenty of vibrant action, colorful travel scenics and personality. Must be able to shoot action photography. Looking for photographers in other geographic regions for diverse coverage."

$ ◯ ▣ ♺ WAVELENGTH MAGAZINE

2101 Cinnabar Dr., Nanaimo BC V9X 1B3 Canada. (250)244-6437. E-mail: info@wavelength magazine.com. Web site: www.wavelengthmagazine.com. **Contact:** John Kimantas, editor.

Circ. 20,000. Estab. 1991. Quarterly magazine. Emphasizes safe, ecologically sensitive paddling. For sample copy, see downloadable PDF version on Web site.

Needs Buys 10 photos from freelancers/issue ("usually only from authors"); 60 photos/year. Needs kayaking shots. Photos should have sea kayak in them. Reviews photos with or without a manuscript. Model/property release preferred. Photo captions preferred.

Specs Prefers digital submissions, but only after query. Send as low-res for assessment.

Making Contact & Terms Send query letter. Provide business card or self-promotion piece to be kept on file for possible future assignments. Responds in 2 months to queries. Absolutely no simultaneous submissions or previously published work accepted. Pays $100-200 for color cover; $25-50 for inside. Pays on publication. Credit line given. Buys one-time print rights including electronic archive rights.

Tips "Look at free downloadable version on Web site and include kayak in picture wherever possible. Always need vertical shots for cover!"

$ $⊘ ▣ WESTERN OUTDOORS, The Magazine of Western Sportfishing

Western Outdoors Publications, P.O. Box 73370, San Clemente CA 92673. (949)366-0030. Fax: (949)366-0804. E-mail: rich@wonews.com. **Contact:** Rich Holland, editor. Circ. 100,000. Estab. 1961. Magazine published 9 times/year. Emphasizes fishing and boating "for Far West states." Sample copy free. Editorial and photo guidelines free with SASE.

Needs Uses 80-85 photos/issue; 70% supplied by freelancers; 80% comes from assignments, 25% from stock. Needs photos of fishing in California, Oregon, Washington, Baja. Most photos purchased with accompanying manuscript. Model/property release preferred for women and men in brief attire. Photo captions required.

Specs Prefers images in digital format.

Making Contact & Terms Query or send photos with SASE for consideration. Responds in 3 weeks. Pays $50-150 for color inside; $300-400 for color cover; $400-600 for text/photo package. **Pays on acceptance.** Buys one-time rights for photos only; first North American serial rights for articles; electronic rights are negotiable.

Tips "Submissions should be of interest to Western fishermen, and should include a 1,120- to 1,500-word manuscript; a Trip Facts Box (where to stay, costs, special information); photos; captions; and a map of the area. Emphasis is on fishing how-to, somewhere-to-go. Submit seasonal material 6 months in advance. Query only; no unsolicited manuscripts. Make your photos tell the story, and don't depend on captions to explain what is pictured. Get action shots, live fish. In fishing, we seek individual action or underwater shots. For cover photos, use vertical format composed with action entering picture from right; leave enough left-hand margin for cover blurbs, space at top of frame for magazine logo. Add human element to scenics to lend scale. Get to know the magazine and its editors. Ask for the year's editorial schedule (available through advertising department), and offer cover photos to match the theme of an issue. In samples, looks for color saturation, pleasing use of color components; originality, creativity; attractiveness of human subjects, as well as fish; above all—sharp, sharp, sharp focus!"

⊘ ▣ WHISKEY ISLAND MAGAZINE

Department of English, Cleveland State University, Cleveland OH 44115. (216)687-2056. Fax: (216)687-6943. E-mail: whiskeyisland@csuohio.edu. Web site: www.csuohio.edu/whiskey_island. **Contact:** Editor. Circ. 1,000. Estab. 1977. Biannual literary magazine publishing extremely contemporary writing. Sample copy available for $6. Photo guidelines available for SASE.

Needs Uses 10 photos/issue; 20 photos/year. Interested in mixed media, alternative process, avant garde, fine art. Surreal and abstract are welcome. Do not send sentimental images, "rust-belt" scenes, photos of Cleveland, straight landscapes, or anything that can be viewed as "romantic." Model/property release preferred. Photo captions required; include title of work, photographer's name, address, phone number, e-mail, etc.

Specs Accepts images in digital format. Send via e-mail attachment as individual, high-resolution JPEG files. No TIFFs. No disks.

Making Contact & Terms E-mail with sample images. Do not just send your Web site link. Does not keep samples on file; responds in 3 months. Pays 2 contributor's copies and a 1-year subscription. Credit line given. Include as much contact information as possible.

$⬜ 🖳 WHOLE LIFE TIMES

Conscious Enlightenment, Inc, 1200 S. Hope St., Ste 300, Los Angeles CA 90015. (213)747-6378. Fax: (213) 747-6386. E-mail: graphics@wholelifetimes.com. Web site: www.wholelif etimes.com. Circ. 58,000. Estab. 1979. Local southern California magazine emphasizing alternative health, personal growth, environment, progressive politics, spirituality, social justice, organic food. Readers are 6 5% female, educated and active, average age 25-5 4. "Our approach is option-oriented, holistic, entertaining. " Sample copy available for $4 or on Web site.

Needs Buys 4-5 photos from freelancers/issue; 5 0 photos/year. Sometimes needs photos related to local environmental issues, food, celebrities in alignment with mission, progressive local politicians, social or political commentary cartoons , unusual beauty shots. Also seeking local photographers with unusual, edgy style. Reviews photos with or without a manuscript. Model release required; ownership release required. "Almost all photos are by local assignment."

Specs Prefers images in digital format. Send via e-mail, CD, DVD as TIFF, EPS, JPEG files at 300 dpi. Also uses 8×10 glossy or matte color prints; 35mm, $2\frac{1}{4} \times 2\frac{1}{4}$, 4×5, 8×10 transparencies.

Making Contact & Terms Send query letter with nonreturnable prints or digital files, photocopies, tearsheets, stock list. Provide business card to be kept on file for possible future assignments. Responds only if interested ; send nonreturnable samples. Simultaneous submissions and previously published work OK. Fees are negotiated for assignments. Stock usage fees comparable to online fees. Pays 30 days after publication. Credit line given "with photo and in masthead. " Buys one-time rights and one-time electronic rights.

Tips "Our readers are sophisticated but not trendy. For more info on our niche, see www.cul turalcreatives.com. Prefer vertical images for cover and require space for cover lines and masthead. Payscale is moderate. Great opportunity for exposure and expanding portfolio through our well-established, nationally recognized niche publication in business for 2 8 years. Send only your best work!"

$ $🖳 WINE & SPIRITS

2 W. 32nd St., Suite 601, New York NY 10001. (212)695-4660, ext. 15. Fax: (212)695-2920. E-mail: elenab@wineandspiritsmagazine.com. Web site: www.wineandspiritsmagazine.c om. **Contact:** Elena Bessarabova, art director. Circ. 70,000. Estab. 1982. Bimonthly magazine. Emphasizes wine. Readers are male, ages 39-60, married, parents, $70,000-plus income, wine consumers. Sample copy available for $4.95; Special issues are $4.95-6.50 each.

Needs Buys 0-30 photos from freelancers/issue; 0-180 photos/year. Needs photos of food, wine, travel, people. Photo captions preferred; include date, location.

Specs Accepts images in digital format. Send via SyQuest, Zip at 300 dpi.

Making Contact & Terms Submit portfolio for review. Provide résumé, business card, brochure, flier or tearsheets to be kept on file for possible future assignments. Responds in 2 weeks, if interested. Simultaneous submissions OK. Pays $200-1,000/job. Pays on publication. Credit line given. Buys one-time rights.

$ $⊘ ▣ WRITER'S DIGEST

F+W Media, Inc., 4700 E. Galbraith Rd., Cincinnati OH 45236. (513)531-2690, ext. 11573. Fax: (513)891-7153. E-mail: kathy.dezarn@fwpubs.com. Web site: www.writersdigest.com. **Contact:** Kathleen DeZarn, art director. Editor: Maria Schneider. Circ. 120,000. Estab. 1920. Monthly consumer magazine. "Our readers write fiction, nonfiction, plays and scripts. They're interested in improving their writing skills and the ability to sell their work, and finding new outlets for their talents." Photo guidelines free with SASE or via e-mail.

Needs Occasionally buys photos from freelancers. Needs photos of education, hobbies, writing life, business concepts, product shots/still life. Other specific photo needs: photographers to shoot authors on location for magazine cover. Model/property release required. Photo captions required; include your copyright notice.

Specs Uses 8×10 color and/or digital (resizable) images. Accepts images in digital format if hired. Send via CD as TIFF, EPS, JPEG files at 300 dpi (at hire).

Making Contact & Terms Provide business card, self-promotion piece to be kept on file for possible future assignments. Keeps samples on file. Responds only if interested; send nonreturnable samples. Pays $0-1,000 for color cover; $0-600 for color inside. Pays when billed/invoiced. Credit line given. Buys one-time rights.

Tips "Please don't submit/re-submit frequently. We keep samples on file and will contact you if interested. Submissions are considered for other Writer's Digest publications as well. For stock photography, please include pricing/sizes of black & white usage if available."

◻ THE WYOMING COMPANION MAGAZINE

P.O. Box 1111, Laramie WY 82073-1111. E-mail: editor@wyomingcompanion.com. Web site: www.wyomingcompanion.com. **Contact:** Mick McLean, editor. Online magazine.

Needs Photos should be related to the state of Wyoming: scenics, recreation, people, Yellowstone and the Tetons, sunsets.

Making Contact & Terms Contact via e-mail. Photographers retain copyright.

Tips "Photographers should see Web site for more information, or query by e-mail."

YACHTING MAGAZINE

Bonnier Corporation, 18 Marshall St., Suite 114, South Norwalk CT 06854-2237. (203)299-5900. Fax: (203)299-5901. Web site: www.yachtingnet.com. **Contact:** David Pollard, art director. Circ. 132,000. Estab. 1907. Monthly magazine addressing the interests of both sail and powerboat owners, with the emphasis on high-end vessels. Includes boating events, boating-related products, gear and how-to.

Making Contact & Terms Send query letter with tearsheets. Provide self-promotion piece to be kept on file for possible future assignments. Responds only if interested; send nonreturnable samples. Pays on publication. Buys first rights.

Tips "Read the magazine, and have a presentable portfolio."

$▣ YOUTH RUNNER MAGAZINE

P.O. Box 1156, Lake Oswego OR 97035. (503)236-2524. Fax: (503)620-3800. E-mail: dank@ youthrunner.com. Web site: www.youthrunner.com. **Contact:** Dan Kesterson, editor. Circ. 100,000. Estab. 1996. Ten issues per year. Features track, cross country and road racing for young athletes, ages 8-18. Photo guidelines available on Web site.

Needs Uses 30-50 photos/issue. Also uses photos on Web site daily. Needs action shots from track, cross country and indoor meets. Model release preferred; property release required. Photo captions preferred.

Specs Accepts images in digital format only. Send via e-mail or CD.

Making Contact & Terms Send low-res photos via e-mail first or link to gallery for consideration. Responds to e-mail submissions immediately. Simultaneous submissions OK. Pays $25 minimum. Credit line given. Buys electronic rights, all rights.

Newspapers & Newsletters

When working with newspapers, always remember that time is of the essence. Newspapers have various deadlines for each of their sections. An interesting feature or news photo has a better chance of getting in the next edition if the subject is timely and has local appeal. Most of the markets in this section are interested in regional coverage. Find publications near you and contact editors to get an understanding of their deadline schedules.

More and more newspapers are accepting submissions in digital format. In fact, most newspapers prefer digital images. However, if you submit to a newspaper that still uses film, ask the editors if they prefer certain types of film or if they want color slides or black & white prints. Many smaller newspapers do not have the capability to run color images, so black & white prints are preferred. However, color slides and prints can be converted to black & white. Editors who have the option of running color or black & white photos often prefer color film because of its versatility.

Although most newspapers rely on staff photographers, some hire freelancers as stringers for certain stories. Act professionally and build an editor's confidence in you by supplying innovative images. For example, don't get caught in the trap of shooting "grip-and-grin" photos when a corporation executive is handing over a check to a nonprofit organization. Turn the scene into an interesting portrait. Capture some spontaneous interaction between the recipient and the donor. By planning ahead you can be creative.

When you receive assignments, think about the image before you snap your first photo. If you are scheduled to meet someone at a specific location, arrive early and scout around. Find a proper setting or locate some props to use in the shoot. Do whatever you can to show the editor you are willing to make that extra effort.

Always try to retain resale rights to shots of major news events. High news value means high resale value, and strong news photos can be resold repeatedly. If you have an image with national appeal, search for larger markets, possibly through the wire services. You also may find buyers among national news magazines such as *Time* or *Newsweek*.

While most newspapers offer low payment for images, they are willing to negotiate if the image will have a major impact. Front-page artwork often sells newspapers, so don't underestimate the worth of your images.

$ ⌑ ARCHAEOLOGY

2660 Petersborough St., Herndon VA 20171. E-mail: shannonaswriter@yahoo.com. Estab. 1998. Quarterly magazine. Photo guidelines available via e-mail.

Needs Buys 12 photos from freelancers/issue; 48-72 photos/year. Needs photos of babies/children/teens, celebrities, couples, multicultural, families, parents, disasters, environmental, landscapes/scenics, wildlife, architecture, cities/urban, education, gardening, interiors/decorating, pets, religious, rural, adventure, events, food/drink, sports, travel, agriculture, medicine, military, political, product shots/still life, science, technology—as related to archaeology. Interested in alternative process, avant garde, documentary, fashion/glamour, fine art, historical/vintage, seasonal. Wants photos of archaeology sites and excavations in progress that are available for children and teens to visit. "Would like photographs of artifacts and Paleobiology." Reviews photos with or without a manuscript. Model/property release preferred.

Specs Uses glossy or matte color and/or b&w prints.

Making Contact & Terms Send query letter via e-mail. "If possible, please do not include photographs in files if they are sent through e-mail. A CD with your photographs sent to *Archaeology* is acceptable." Provide résumé, business card or self-promotion piece to be kept on file for possible future assignments. "A CD with your photographs is requested but not required. Illustrations and artwork are also accepted." Responds within 1 month to queries; 1 week to portfolios. Simultaneous submissions and previously published work OK. **Pays on acceptance**. Credit line given. Buys one-time rights, first rights; negotiable.

◯ ▣ CALIFORNIA BUCKS

Outdoor News Service, P.O. Box 9007, San Bernardino CA 92427-0007. (909) 887-3444. Fax: (909) 887-8180. E-mail: odwriter@charter.net. Web site: www.outdoornewsservice.com. **Contact:** Rick Bean, managing editor. Circ. 500. Estab. 2005. Quarterly newsletter "covers the hunting of deer in California—when, where and how."

Needs Needs photos of deer and deer hunting. Reviews photos with or without a manuscript. Model release required: include identification of subjects.

Specs Accepts images in digital format. Send JPEG or TIFF files.

Making Contact & Terms Pays $25-$50/photo, depending on size. For photos submitted with a manuscript, pays $75/printed page. Pays on publication. Credit line given. Buys one-time rights.

Tips "Request a sample copy so you can see how the newsletter is set up. Virtually the whole newsletter is broken into 'departments.'"

$ ◯ ▣ CALIFORNIA HOG HUNTER, A Newsletter Dedicated to Hunting Wild Hogs

Outdoor News Service, P.O. Box 9007, San Bernardino CA 92427-0007. (909)887-3444. Fax: (909)887-8180. E-mail: odwriter@charter.net. Web site: www.outdoornewsservice.com. **Contact:** Rick Bean, managing editor. Circ. 1,000. Estab. 1998. Quarterly newsletter "covers the hunting of wild hogs in California—when, where and how."

Needs Needs photos of wild hogs and wild-hog hunting. Reviews photos with or without a manuscript. Model release required: include identification of subjects.

Specs Accepts images in digital format. Send JPEG or TIFF files.

Making Contact & Terms Pays $25-$50/photo, depending on size. For photos submitted with a manuscript, pays $75/printed page. Pays on publication. Credit line given. Buys one-time rights.

Tips ''Request a sample copy so you can see how the newsletter is set up. Virtually the whole newsletter is broken into 'departments.' ''

Ⓝ $ Ⓢ ▣ CAPPER'S

1503 SW 42nd St., Topeka KS 66609-1265. (800)678-5779, ext. 4348. Fax: (800)274-4305. E-mail: cappers@cappers.com. Web site: www.cappers.com. **Contact:** Andrew Humphrey, associate editor. Circ. 120,000. Estab. 1879. Monthly tabloid. Emphasizes human-interest subjects. Readers are Midwesterners in small towns and on rural routes. Sample copy available for $4; contact Customer Care toll-free at (800)678-4883 for details.

Needs Buys 1-3 photos from freelancers/issue; 26-72 photos/year. ''We make no photo assignments. We select freelance photos with specific issues in mind.'' Needs photos of ''human-interest activities, nature (scenic), etc., in bright, cheery colors. We often use photos tied to the season, a holiday, or an upcoming event of general interest.'' Photo captions required.

Specs Uses 35mm color slides or larger transparencies. Prefers images in digital format. Send via CD; ''Images should be JPEGs at least 6 inches wide, with a resolution of no less than 300 dpi. Include a hard-copy sheet of thumbnails.''

Making Contact & Terms ''Send for guidelines and a sample copy. Study the types of photos in the publication, then send a sheet of 10-20 samples with caption material for our consideration. Although we do most of our business by mail, a phone number is helpful in case we need more caption information. Phone calls to try to sell us on your photos don't really help.'' Reporting time varies. Pays $40 for color cover photo; $10-30 for color inside; $5-15 for b&w inside. Pays on publication. Credit line given. Buys shared rights.

Tips ''We're looking for photos of everyday people doing everyday activities. If the photographer can present this in a pleasing manner, these are the photos we're most likely to use. Seasonal shots are appropriate for *Capper's*, but they should be natural, not posed. We steer clear of dark, mood shots; they don't reproduce well on newsprint. Most of our readers are small-town or rural southerners or midwesterners, so we're looking for photos with which they can identify. Although our format is tabloid, we don't use celebrity shots and won't devote an area much larger than approximately 5×6 (inside) or 8×7 (cover) to one photo.''

Ⓝ $ ◻ Ⓐ ▣ FULTON COUNTY DAILY REPORT

Dept. PM, 190 Pryor St. SW, Atlanta GA 30303. (404)521-1227. Fax: (404)659-4739. E-mail: jbennitt@alm.com. Web site: www.dailyreportonline.com. **Contact:** Jason R. Bennitt, art director. Daily newspaper (5 times/week). Emphasizes legal news and business. Readers are male and female professionals, age 25+, involved in legal field, court system, legislature, etc. Sample copy available for $2 with 9¾×12¾ SAE and 6 first-class stamps.

Needs Buys 1-2 photos from freelancers/issue; 260-520 photos/year. Needs informal environmental photographs of lawyers, judges and others involved in legal news and business. Some real estate, etc. Photo captions preferred; include complete name of subject and date shot, along with other pertinent information. Two or more people should be identified from left to right.

Specs Accepts images in digital format. Send via CD or e-mail as JPEG files at 200-600 dpi.

Making Contact & Terms Submit portfolio for review. Mail or e-mail samples. Keeps samples on file. Simultaneous submissions and previously published work OK. ''Freelance work generally done on an assignment-only basis.'' Pays $75-100 for color cover; $50-75 for color inside. Credit line given.

Tips Wants to see ability with ''casual, environmental portraiture, people—especially in office settings, urban environment, courtrooms, etc.—and photojournalistic coverage of people in law or courtroom settings.'' In general, needs ''competent, fast freelancers from time to time around the state of Georgia who can be called in at the last minute. We keep a list of them for reference. Good work keeps you on the list.'' Recommends that ''when shooting for *FCDR*, it's best to avoid law-book-type photos if possible, along with other overused legal clichés.''

N $⊡ PITTSBURGH CITY PAPER

650 Smithfield St., Suite 2200, Pittsburgh PA 15222. (412)316-3342. Fax: (412)316-3388. E-mail: lcunning@steelcitymedia.com. Web site: www.pghcitypaper.com. **Contact:** Lisa Cunningham, art director. Editor: Chris Potter. Circ. 80,000. Estab. 1991. Weekly tabloid. Emphasizes Pittsburgh arts, news, entertainment. Readers are active, educated adults, ages 29-54, with disposable incomes. Sample copy free with 12×15 SASE.

Needs Occasionally uses freelancers as needed. Most photography is digital. Model/property release preferred. Photo captions preferred. ''We can write actual captions, but we need all the pertinent facts.'' **Works with local photographers only.**

Making Contact & Terms Arrange a personal interview to show portfolio. Send query letter with résumé of credits. Provide résumé, business card, brochure, flier or tearsheets to be kept on file for possible future assignments. Does not keep samples on file; does not accept file photos. Include SASE for return of material. Responds in 2 weeks. Previously published work OK. Pays $25-125/job. Pays on publication. Credit line given.

Tips Provide ''something beyond the sort of shots typically seen in daily newspapers. Consider the long-term value of exposing your work through publication. In negotiating prices, be honest about your costs, while remembering there are others competing for the assignment. Be reliable and allow time for possible re-shooting to end up with the best pic possible.''

$⊘ A ⊡ STREETPEOPLE'S WEEKLY NEWS (Homeless Editorial/Business/Sports/Finance)

P.O. Box 270942, Dallas TX 75227-0942. E-mail: sw_n@yahoo.com. **Contact:** Lon G. Dorsey, Jr., publisher. Estab. 1990. Newspaper. Sample copy available by sending $ 7.35 to cover immediate handling (same day as received) and postage. Includes photo guidelines package now required. ''Also contains information about our homeless television show and photo gallery.''

• *SWN ews* wishes to establish relationships with professionals interested in homeless issues. ''Photographers may be certified by *SWN* by submitting $35 check or money order and samples of work. Photographers needed in every metropolitan city in U.S.''

Needs Wants photos of babies/children/teens, celebrities, couples, multicultural, families, parents, senior citizens, cities/urban, education, pets, religious, rural, events, food/drink, health/fitness, hobbies, humor, political, technology/computers. Interested in alternative process, documentary, fine art, historical/vintage, seasonal. Subjects include: photojournalism on homeless or street people. Model/property release required. ''All photos *must* be accompanied by *signed* model releases.'' Photo captions required.

Specs Accepts images in digital format. Send via CD, e-mail as GIF, JPEG files. Items to be considered for publishing must be in pdf. Write first to gain clearance to publisher.

Making Contact & Terms ''Hundreds of photographers are needed to show national state of America's homeless.'' Send unsolicited photos by mail for consideration with SASE for return. Responds promptly. Pays $15-450 for cover; $15-150 for inside. Pays extra for electronic usage (negotiable). Pays on acceptance or publication. Credit line sometimes given. Buys all rights; negotiable.

Tips In freelancer's samples, wants to see ''professionalism, clarity of purpose, without sex or negative atmosphere which could harm purpose of paper.'' The trend is toward ''kinder, gentler situations, the 'let's help our fellows' attitude.'' To break in, ''find out what we're about so we don't waste time with exhaustive explanations. We're interested in all homeless situations. Inquiries not answered without SASE. **All persons interested in providing photography should get registered with us.** Now using 'Registered photographers and Interns of *SW News*' for publishing and upcoming Internet worldwide awards competition. Info regarding competition is outlined in *SWN*'s photo guidelines package. Photographers not registered will not be considered due to the continuous sending of improper materials, inadequate information, wasted hours of screening matter, etc. **If you don't wish to register with us, please don't send anything for consideration.** You'll find that many professional pubs are going this way to reduce the materials management pressures which have increased. We are trying something else new—salespeople who are also photographers. So, if you have a marketing/sales background with a photo kicker, contact us!''

$ ▨ ▣ ⊕ THE SUNDAY POST

D.C. Thomson & Co. Ltd., 2 Albert Square, Dundee DD1 9QJ Scotland. (44)(1382)223131. Fax: (44)(1382)201064. E-mail: mail@sundaypost.com. Web site: www.sundaypost.com. **Contact:** Alan Morrison, picture editor. Circ. 481,000. Estab. 1919. Weekly family newspaper.

Needs Needs photos of ''UK news and news involving Scots,'' sports. Other specific needs: exclusive news pictures from the UK, especially Scotland. Reviews photos with accompanying manuscript only. Model/property release preferred. Photo captions required; include contact details, subjects, date. ''Save in the caption field of the file info, so they can be viewed on our picture desk system. Mac users should ensure attachments are PC-compatible as we use PCs.''

Specs Prefers images in digital format. Send via e-mail as JPEG files. ''We need a minimum 5MB file saved at quality level 9 or above, ideally at 200 ppi/dpi.''

Making Contact & Terms Send query letter with tearsheets, stock list. Does not keep samples on file; include SASE for return of material. Responds in 2 weeks to queries. Simultaneous submissions OK. Pays $200 (USD) for b&w or color cover; $100-150 (USD) for b&w or color inside. Pays on publication. Credit line not given. Buys single use, all editions, one date, worldwide rights; negotiable.

Tips ''Offer pictures by e-mail before sending: lo-res only, please—72 ppi, 800 pixels on the widest side; no more than 10 at a time. Make sure the daily papers aren't running the story first and that it's not being covered by the Press Association (PA). We get their pictures on our contracted feed.''

$ $ ▣ ⊠ TORONTO SUN PUBLISHING

333 King St. E., Toronto ON M5A 3X5 Canada. (416)947-2399. E-mail: torsun.photoeditor@ sunmedia.ca. Web site: www.torontosun.com. **Contact:** Jim Thomson, photo editor. Circ.

Newspapers

180,000. Estab. 1971. Daily newspaper. Emphasizes sports, news and entertainment. Readers are 60% male, 40% female, ages 25-60. Sample copy free with SASE.

Needs Uses 30-50 photos/issue; occasionally uses freelancers (spot news pics only). Needs photos of Toronto personalities making news out of town. Also disasters, beauty, sports, fashion/glamour. Reviews photos with or without a manuscript. Photo captions preferred.

Specs Accepts images in digital format. Send via CD or e-mail.

Making Contact & Terms Arrange a personal interview to show portfolio. Send any size color prints; 35mm transparencies; press link digital format. Deadline: 11 p.m. daily. Does not keep samples on file. Responds in 1-2 weeks. Simultaneous submissions and previously published work OK. Pays $125-500 for color cover; $50-500 for b&w inside. Pays on publication. Credit line given. Buys one-time and other negotiated rights.

Tips "The squeeky wheel gets the grease when it delivers the goods. Don't try to oversell a questionable photo. Return calls promptly."

Trade Publications

Most trade publications are directed toward the business community in an effort to keep readers abreast of the ever-changing trends and events in their specific professions. For photographers, shooting for these publications can be financially rewarding and can serve as a stepping stone toward acquiring future assignments.

As often happens with this category, the number of trade publications produced increases or decreases as professions develop or deteriorate. In recent years, for example, magazines involving new technology have flourished as the technology continues to grow and change.

Trade publication readers are usually very knowledgeable about their businesses or professions. The editors and photo editors, too, are often experts in their particular fields. So, with both the readers and the publications' staffs, you are dealing with a much more discriminating audience. To be taken seriously, your photos must not be merely technically good pictures, but also should communicate a solid understanding of the subject and reveal greater insights.

In particular, photographers who can communicate their knowledge in both verbal and visual form will often find their work more in demand. If you have such expertise, you may wish to query about submitting a photo/text package that highlights a unique aspect of working in a particular profession or that deals with a current issue of interest to that field.

Many photos purchased by these publications come from stock—both freelance inventories and stock photo agencies. Generally, these publications are more conservative with their freelance budgets and use stock as an economical alternative. For this reason, some listings in this section will advise sending a stock list as an initial method of contact. (See sample stock list on page 19.) Some of the more established publications with larger circulations and advertising bases will sometimes offer assignments as they become familiar with a particular photographer's work. For the most part, though, stock remains the primary means of breaking in and doing business with this market.

Trade Publications

$ AMERICAN BEE JOURNAL

51 S. Second St., Hamilton IL 62341. (217)847-3324. Fax: (217)847-3660. E-mail: abj@dada nt.com. Web site: www.dadant.com/journal. **Contact:** Joe M. Graham, editor. Circ. 13,000. Estab. 1861. Monthly trade magazine. Emphasizes beekeeping for hobby and professional beekeepers. Sample copy free with SASE.

Needs Buys 1-2 photos from freelancers/issue; 12-24 photos/year. Needs photos of beekeeping and related topics, beehive products, honey and cooking with honey. Special needs include color photos of seasonal beekeeping scenes. Model release preferred. Photo captions preferred.

Making Contact & Terms Send query letter with samples. Send 5×7 or 8½×11 color prints by mail for consideration; include SASE for return of material. Responds in 2 weeks. Pays $75 for color cover; $10 for color inside. Pays on publication. Credit line given. Buys all rights.

$ ⬚ Ⓐ ▣ AMERICAN POWER BOAT ASSOCIATION

17640 E. Nine Mile Rd., Box 377, Eastpointe MI 48021-0377. (586)773-9700. Fax: (586)773-6490. E-mail: propeller@apba-racing.com. Web site: www.apba-racing.com. **Contact:** Tana Moore, publications editor. Estab. 1903. Sanctioning body for US power boat racing; monthly magazine. Majority of assignments made on annual basis. Photos used in monthly magazine, brochures, audiovisual presentations, press releases, programs and website.

Needs Needs photos of APBA boat racing—action and candid. Interested in documentary, historical/vintage. Photo captions or class/driver ID required.

Specs Accepts images in digital format. Send via CD, e-mail as TIFF, EPS, JPEG files at 300 dpi.

Making Contact & Terms Initial personal contact preferred. Suggests initial contact by e-mail, letter or phone, possibly to be followed by evaluating samples. Provide business card to be kept on file for possible future assignments. Responds in 2 weeks when needed. Payment varies. Standard is $25 for color cover; $15 for interior pages. Credit line given. Buys one-time rights; negotiable. Photo usage must be invoiced by photographer within the month incurred.

Tips Prefers to see selection of shots of power boats in action or pit shots, candids, etc., (all identified). Must show ability to produce clear color action shots of racing events. "Send a few samples with introduction letter, especially if related to boat racing."

$ ⬚ APPALOOSA JOURNAL

Appaloosa Horse Club, 2720 W. Pullman Rd., Moscow ID 83843. (208)882-5578. Fax: (208)882-8150. E-mail: journal@appaloosa.com. Web site: www.appaloosajournal.com. **Contact:** Diane Rice, editor. Circ. 22,000. Estab. 1946. Monthly association magazine. "*Appaloosa Journal* is the official publication of the Appaloosa Horse Club. We are dedicated to educating and entertaining Appaloosa enthusiasts from around the world." Readers are Appaloosa owners, breeders and trainers, child through adult. Complimentary sample copies available. Photo guidelines free with SASE or online.

Needs Buys 3 photos from freelancers/issue; 36 photos/year. Needs photos for cover, and to accompany features and articles. Specifically wants photographs of high-quality Appaloosa horses, especially in winter scenes. Model release required. Photo captions required.

Specs Uses glossy color prints; 35 mm transparencies; digital images 300+ dpi at 5×7 inches or larger, depending on use.

Making Contact & Terms Send query letter with résumé, slides, prints, or e-mail as PDF or GIF. Keeps samples on file. Responds only if interested; send nonreturnable samples. Simultaneous submissions OK. Pays $200 for color cover; $25 minimum for color inside. **Pays on publication.** Credit line given. Buys first rights.

Tips "The Appaloosa Horse Club is a not-for-profit organization. Serious inquiries within specified budget only." In photographer's samples, wants to see "high-quality color photos of world-class, characteristic (coat patterned) Appaloosa horses in appealing, picturesque outdoor environments. Send a letter introducing yourself and briefly explaining your work. If you have inflexible preset fees, be upfront and include that information. Be patient. We are located at the headquarters; although an image might not work for the magazine, it might work for other printed materials. Work has a better chance of being used if allowed to keep on file. If work must be returned promptly, please specify. Otherwise, we will keep it for other departments' consideration."

$ $ AQUA MAGAZINE: The Business Publication for Spa & Pool Professionals

Athletic Business Publications, Inc., 4130 Lien Rd., Madison WI 53704-3602. (608)249-0186. Fax: (608)249-1153. E-mail: scott@aquamagazine.com. Web site: www.aquamagazine.com. **Contact:** Scott Maurer, art director. Circ. 15,000. Estab. 1976. Monthly magazine. "*AQUA* serves spa dealers, swimming pool dealers and/or builders, spa/swimming pool maintenance and service, casual furniture/patio dealers, landscape architects/designers and others allied to the spa/swimming pool market. Readers are qualified owners, GM, sales directors, titled personnel."

Needs Photos of swimming pools and/or spas (hot tubs) that show all or part of pool/spa. "The images may include grills, furniture, gazebos, ponds, water features." Photo captions preferred.

Making Contact & Terms "OK to send promotional literature, and to e-mail contact sheets/Web gallery or low-resolution samples, but do not send anything that has to be returned (i.e., slides, prints) unless asked for." Simultaneous submissions and previously published work OK, "but should be explained." Pays $400 for color cover (negotiable); $200 for color inside. Pays on publication. Credit line given. Buys all rights; negotiable.

Tips Wants to see "visually arresting images, high quality, multiple angles, day/night lighting situations. Photos including people are rarely published."

$ $ ATHLETIC BUSINESS: The Leading Resource for Athletic, Fitness & Recreation Professionals

Athletic Business Publications, Inc., 4130 Lien Rd., Madison WI 53704. (608)249-0186. Fax: (608)249-1153. E-mail: katy@athleticbusiness.com. Web site: www.athleticbusiness.com. **Contact:** Katy Williams, art director. Circ. 44,000. Estab. 1977. Monthly magazine. Emphasizes athletics, fitness and recreation. Readers are athletic, park and recreational directors and club managers, ages 30-65. Sample copy available for $8. The magazine can also be viewed digitally at www.athleticbusiness.com.

Needs Buys 2-3 photos from freelancers per issue; 24-26 photos/year. Needs photos of college and high school team sports, coaches, athletic equipment, recreational parks, and health club/multi-sport interiors." Model/property release preferred. Photo captions preferred.

Making Contact & Terms "Feel free to send promotional literature, but do not send anything that has to be returned (i.e., slides, prints) unless asked for." Simultaneous submissions and previously published work OK, "but should be explained." Pays $400 for color cover (negotiable); $200 for color inside. Pays on publication. Credit line given. Buys all rights; negotiable.

Tips Wants to see "visually arresting images, ability with subject and high quality photography." To break in, "shoot a quality and creative shot (that is part of our market) from more than one angle and at different depths."

$□ Ⓐ ▣ BEE CULTURE: The Magazine of American Beekeeping

A.I. Root, 623 W. Liberty St., Medina OH 44256-6677. (800)289-7668, ext. 3214 or (330)725-6677, ext. 3214. E-mail: kim@beeculture.com. Web site: www.beeculture.com. **Contact:** Kim Flottum, editor. Circ. 12,000. Estab. 1873. Monthly trade magazine emphasizing beekeeping industry—how-to, politics, news and events. Sample copies available. Photo guidelines available on Web site.

Needs Buys 1-2 photos from freelancers/issue; 6-8 photos/year. Needs photos of honey bees and beekeeping, bees on flowers, etc. Reviews photos with or without a manuscript. Model release required. Photo captions preferred.

Specs Uses 5×7 glossy or matte color prints; 35mm, 2¼×2¼, 4×5, 8×10 transparencies. Accepts images in digital format. Send via CD, e-mail as TIFF, EPS, JPEG files at 300 dpi. Low-res for review encouraged.

Making Contact & Terms Send e-mail with low-res photos. Does not keep samples on file; include SASE for return of material. "E-mail contact preferred. Send low-res samples electronically for examination." Responds in 2 weeks to queries. Payment negotiable. **Pays on acceptance.** Credit line given. Buys first rights.

Tips "Read 2-3 issues for layout and topics. Think in vertical!"

▣ BEEF TODAY

Farm Journal Media, 222 S. Jefferson St., Mexico MO 65265. (573)581-9646. Fax: (573)581-9646. E-mail: lbenne@farmjournal.com. Web site: www.agweb.com. **Contact:** Lindsey Benne, art director. Circ. 220,000. Monthly magazine. Emphasizes American agriculture. Readers are active farmers, ranchers or agribusiness people. Sample copy and photo guidelines free with SASE.

Needs Buys 5-10 photos from freelancers/issue; 180-240 photos/year. "We use studio-type portraiture (environmental portraits), technical, details, scenics." Wants photos of environmental, livestock (feeding transporting, worming cattle), landscapes/scenics (from different regions of the U.S.). Model release preferred. Photo captions required.

Specs Accepts images in digital format. Send via CD or e-mail as TIFF, EPS, JPEG files, color RGB only.

Making Contact & Terms Arrange a personal interview to show portfolio. Send query letter with résumé of credits along with business card, brochure, flier or tearsheets to be kept on file for possible future assignments. DO NOT SEND ORIGINALS. Responds in 2 weeks. Simultaneous submissions OK. Payment negotiable. "We pay a cover bonus." **Pays on acceptance.** Credit line given. Buys one-time rights.

Tips In portfolio or samples, likes to see "about 20 slides showing photographer's use of lighting and ability to work with people. Know your intended market. Familiarize yourself with the magazine and keep abreast of how photos are used in the general magazine field."

Trade Publications

$⬛🖼️ BOXOFFICE

8981 Sunset Blvd., Suite 309, West Hollywood CA 90069. (310)858-4500. Fax: (310)858-4503. E-mail: chad@boxoffice.com. Web site: www.boxoffice.com. **Contact:** Chad Greene, staff editor. Circ. 10,000. Estab. 1920. Monthly trade magazine; the official publication of the National Association of Theater Owners. Sample copy available for $10.

Needs Photo needs are very specific: "All photos must be of movie theaters and management." Reviews photos with accompanying manuscript only. Photo captions required.

Specs Uses 4×5, 8×10 glossy color and/or b&w prints; 35mm, $2\frac{1}{4} \times 2\frac{1}{4}$, 4×5 transparencies. Accepts images in digital format. Send via CD, Zip as TIFF files at 300 dpi.

Making Contact & Terms Send query letter with résumé, tearsheets. Does not keep samples on file; cannot return material. Responds in 1 month to queries. Responds only if interested; send nonreturnable samples. Previously published work OK. Pays $10/printed photo. Pays on publication. Credit line sometimes given. Buys one-time print rights and all electronic rights.

🖼️ CANADIAN GUERNSEY JOURNAL

5653 Hwy 6 N RR 5, Guelph ON N1H 6J2 Canada. (519)836-2141. Fax: (519)763-6582. E-mail: info@guernseycanada.ca. Web site: www.guernseycanada.ca. **Contact:** Doris Curran, administration. Estab. 1927. Annual journal of the Canadian Guernsey Association. Emphasizes dairy cattle, purebred and grade guernseys. Readers are dairy farmers and agriculture-related companies. Sample copy available for $15.

Needs Needs photos of guernsey cattle: posed, informal, scenes. Photo captions preferred.

Making Contact & Terms Contact through adminstration office. Keeps samples on file.

🖼️ CATHOLIC LIBRARY WORLD

100 North St., Suite 224, Pittsfield MA 01201-5109. (413)443-2CLA. Fax: (413)442-2252. E-mail: cla@cathla.org. Web site: www.cathla.org/cathlibworld.html. **Contact:** Jean R. Bostley, SSJ, executive director. Circ. 1,100. Estab. 1929. Quarterly magazine of the Catholic Library Association. Emphasizes libraries and librarians (community/school libraries; academic/research librarians; archivists). Readers are librarians who belong to the Catholic Library Association; other subscribers are generally employed in Catholic institutions or academic settings. Sample copy available for $15.

Needs Uses 2-5 photos/issue. Needs photos of authors of children's books, and librarians who have done something to contribute to the community at large. Special needs include photos of annual conferences. Model release preferred for photos of authors. Photo captions preferred.

Specs Uses 5×7 b&w prints. Accepts images in digital format. Send via e-mail, CD, Zip as PDF files at 1,200 dpi.

Making Contact & Terms Send b&w prints; include SASE for return of material. Deadlines: January 15, April 15, July 15, September 15. Responds in 2 weeks. Credit line given. Acquires one-time rights.

🖼️ CONSTRUCTION BULLETIN

15524 Highwood Dr., Minnetonka MN 55345. (952)933-3386. Fax: (952)933-5063. E-mail: ivy.chang@reedbusiness.com. Web site: www.acppubs.com. **Contact:** Ivy Chang, editor. Circ. 5,000. Estab. 1893. Weekly magazine. Emphasizes construction in Minnesota, North

Dakota and South Dakota *only*. Readers are male and female executives, ages 23-70. Sample copy available for $4.

Needs Uses 15 photos/issue; digital images only. Needs photos of construction equipment in use on Minnesota, North Dakota, South Dakota job sites. Photo captions required; include who, what, where, when.

Making Contact & Terms Send high-resolution digital images (minimum 300 dpi) for consideration. Credit line given.

Tips ''Be observant; keep camera at hand when approaching construction sites in Minnesota, North Dakota and South Dakota.''

N ⊘ A DISPLAY DESIGN IDEAS

1145 Sanctuary Pkwy., Suite 355, Alpharetta GA 30004. (770)569-1540. Fax: (770)569-5105. E-mail: rsway@ddimagazine.com. Web site: www.ddimagazine.com. **Contact:** Roxanna Sway, editor. Circ. 21,500. Estab. 1988. Monthly magazine. Emphasizes retail design, store planning, visual merchandising. Readers are retail architects, designers and retail executives. Sample copies available.

Needs Buys 7 or fewer photos from freelancers/issue; 84 or fewer photos/year. Needs photos of architecture, mostly interior. Property release preferred.

Specs Prefers digital submissions. Send as TIFF or JPG files at 300 dpi.

Making Contact & Terms Send query letter with résumé of credits. Provide résumé, business card, brochure, flier or tearsheets to be kept on file for possible future assignments. Responds in 3 weeks. Credit line given. Rights negotiable.

Tips Looks for architectural interiors, ability to work with different lighting. ''Send samples (photocopies OK) and résumé.''

$ $○ ▣ EL RESTAURANTE MEXICANO

Maiden Name Press, P.O. Box 2249, Oak Park IL 60303. (708)488-0100. Fax: (708)488-0101. E-mail: kfurore@restmex.com. Web site: www.restmex.com. **Contact:** Kathy Furore, editor. Circ. 26,000. Estab. 1997. Bimonthly trade magazine for restaurants that serve Mexican, Tex-Mex, Southwestern and Latin cuisine. Sample copies available.

Needs Buys at least 1 photo from freelancers/issue; at least 6 photos/year. Needs photos of food/drink. Reviews photos with or without a manuscript.

Specs Uses 35mm transparencies. Accepts images in digital format. Send via e-mail as TIFF, JPEG files of at least 300 dpi.

Making Contact & Terms Send query letter with slides, prints, photocopies, tearsheets, transparencies or stock list. Provide résumé, business card, self-promotion piece to be kept on file for possible future assignments. Responds in 2 months to queries. Previously published work OK. Pays $450 maximum for color cover; $125 maximum for color inside. Pays on publication. Credit line given. Buys all rights; negotiable.

Tips ''We look for outstanding food photography; the more creatively styled, the better.''

▣ ESL TEACHER TODAY

2660 Petersborough St., Herndon VA 20171. E-mail: shannonaswriter@yahoo.com. **Contact:** Shannon Murphy. Quarterly trade magazine. Photo guildelines available via e-mail.

Needs Buys 12-24 photos/year. Needs photos of babies/children/teens, multicultural, families, parents, disasters, environmental, landscapes/scenics, wildlife, cities/urban, education, religious, rural, adventure, events, food/drink, sports, travel, agriculture, medicine, military, political, product shots/still life, science, technology—as related to teaching ESL (English as a Second Language) around the globe. Interested in alternative process, avant garde, documentary, fashion/glamour, fine art, historical/vintage, seasonal. Reviews photos with or without a manuscript. Model/property release preferred.

Specs Uses glossy or matte color and/or b&w prints.

Making Contact & Terms Send query letter via e mail. "If possible, please do not include photographs in files if they are sent through e-mail. A disk with your photographs sent to *ESL Teacher Today* is acceptable." Provide résumé, business card or self-promotion piece to be kept on file for possible future assignments. Responds within 1 month to queries; 1 week to portfolios. Simultaneous submissions and previously published work OK. **Pays on acceptance.** Credit line given. Buys one-time rights, first rights; negotiable.

$ Ⓐ ▣ FIRE CHIEF

330 N. Wabash Ave., Suite 2300, Chicago IL 60611. (312)595-1080. Fax: (312)595-0295. E-mail: sundee@firechief.com. Web site: www.firechief.com. **Contact:** Sundee Koffarnus, art director. Circ. 53,000. Estab. 1956. Monthly magazine. Emphasizes fire department management and operations. Readers are primarily fire officers and predominantly chiefs of departments. Sample copy free. Photo guidelines free with SASE or on Web site.

Needs Fire and emergency response, especially leadership themes—if you do not have fire or EMS, please do not contact.

Specs Digital format preferred, filename less than 15 characters. Send via e-mail, CD, Zip as TIFF, EPS files at highest possible resolution.

Making Contact & Terms Send low-resolution JPGs for consideration along with caption, date, time, and location. Samples are kept on file. Expect confirmation/response within 1 month. Payment upon publication. Buys first serial rights; negotiable.

Tips "As our name implies, fire chief prefers images that show a leading officer (white, yellow, or red helmet) in action—on scene of a fire, disaster, accident/rescue, hazmat, etc. Other subjects: administration, communications, decontamination, dispatch, EMS, foam, heavy rescue, incident command, live fire training, public education, SCBA, water rescue, wildfire."

$ ⊘ ▣ FIRE ENGINEERING

21-00 Route 208 South, Fairlawn NJ 07410. (973)251-5040. Fax: (973)251-5065. E-mail: dianef@pennwell.com. Web site: www.fireengineering.com. **Contact:** Diane Feldman, executive editor. Estab. 1877. Training magazine for firefighters. Photo guidelines free.

Needs Uses 400 photos/year. Needs action photos of disasters, firefighting, EMS, public safety, fire investigation and prevention, rescue. Photo captions required; include date, what is happening, location and fire department contact.

Specs Accepts images in digital format. Send via CD as JPEG files at 300 dpi.

Making Contact & Terms Send unsolicited photos by mail for consideration. Responds in 3 months. Pays $300 for color cover; $35-150 for color inside. Pays on publication. Credit line given. We retain copyright.

Tips "Firefighters must be doing something. Our focus is on training and learning lessons from photos."

$ $ ⊘ Ⓢ ▣ FIREHOUSE MAGAZINE

3 Huntington Quadrangle, Suite 301N, Melville NY 11747. (631)845-2700. Fax: (631)845-7218. Web site: www.firehouse.com. **Contact:** Harvey Eisner, editor-in-chief. Circ. 90,000.

Estab. 1976. Monthly. Emphasizes "firefighting—notable fires, techniques, dramatic fires and rescues, etc." Readers are "paid and volunteer firefighters, EMTs." Sample copy available for $5 with 9×12 SASE and 7 first-class stamps. Photo guidelines free with SASE or on Web site .

Needs Buys 20 photos from freelancers/issue; 240 photos/year. Needs photos of fires, terrorism, firefighter training, natural disasters, highway incidents, hazardous materials, dramatic rescues. Model release preferred.

Specs Uses 3×5, 5×7, 8×10 matte or glossy b&w or color prints; 35mm transparencies. Accepts images in digital format. Send via CD, e-mail as TIFF, EPS, JPEG files at 300 dpi.

Making Contact & Terms "Photos must not be more than 30 days old." Include SASE. "Photos cannot be returned without SASE." Responds ASAP. Pays up to $200 for color cover; $20-100 for b&w inside; $20-200 for color inside. Pays on publication. Credit line given. Buys one-time rights.

Tips "Mostly we are looking for action-packed photos—the more fire, the better the shot. Show firefighters in full gear; do not show spectators. Fire safety is a big concern. Much of our photo work is freelance. Try to be in the right place at the right time as the fire occurs. Be sure that photos are clear, in focus, and show firefighters/EMTs at work. Firehouse encourages submissions of high-quality action photos that relate to the firefighting/EMS field. Please understand that while we encourage first-time photographers, a minimum waiting period of 3-6 months is not unusual. Although we are capable of receiving photos over the Internet, please be advised that there are color variations. Include captions. Photographers must include a SASE, and we cannot guarantee the return of unsolicited photos. Mark name and address on the back of each photo."

⊞ $ GENERAL AVIATION NEWS

P.O. Box 39099, Lakewood WA 98439-0099. (253)471-9888. Fax: (253)471-9911. E-mail: janice@GeneralAviationNews.com. Web site: www.GeneralAviationNews.com. **Contact:** Janice Wood, editor. Circ. 50,000. Estab. 1949. Biweekly tabloid. Emphasizes aviation. Readers are pilots, airplane owners and aviation professionals. Sample copy available for $3.50. Photo guidelines free with SASE.

Needs Photo captions preferred.

Making Contact & Terms Send query letter with résumé of credits. Do *not* send unsolicited prints; contact editor first. Does not keep samples on file; include SASE for return of material. Responds in 1 month. Fee varies according to subject, how/where photo is used. Pays on publication. Credit line given. Buys one-time rights.

Tips Wants to see "sharp photos of planes with good color; airshows not generally used."

▣ GEOSYNTHETICS

Industrial Fabrics Association International, 1801 County Road-B W., Roseville MN 55113. (651)222-2508 or (800)225-4324. Fax: (651)225-6966. E-mail: generalinfo@ifai.com. Web site: www.gfrmagazine.com and www.ifai.com. **Contact:** Ron Bygness, editor. Circ. 18,000. Estab. 1983. Association magazine published 6 times/year. Emphasizes geosynthetics in civil engineering applications. Readers are civil engineers, professors and consulting engineers. Sample copies available.

Needs Uses 10-15 photos/issue; various number supplied by freelancers. Needs photos of finished applications using geosynthetics; photos of the application process. Reviews photos with accompanying manuscript only . Model release required. Photo captions required; include project, type of geosynthetics used and location.

Specs Prefers images in high-res digital format.

Making Contact & Terms "Please call before submitting samples!" Keeps samples on file. Responds in 1 month. Simultaneous submissions OK. Credit line given. Buys all rights; negotiable.

$⊘ 🖥 GOVERNMENT TECHNOLOGY

e.Republic, Inc., 100 Blue Ravine Rd., Folsom CA 95630. (916)932-1300. Fax: (916)932-1470. E-mail: kmartinelli@erepublic.com. Web site: www.govtech.net. **Contact:** Kelly Martinelli, creative director. Circ. 60,000. Estab. 1987. Monthly trade magazine. Emphasizes information technology as it applies to state and local government. Readers are government executives.

Needs Buys 2 photos from freelancers/issue; 20 photos/year. Needs photos of government officials, disasters, environmental, political, technology/computers. Reviews photos with accompanying manuscript only. Model release required; property release preferred. Photo captions required.

Specs Accepts images in digital format only. Send via DVD, CD, Zip, e-mail as TIFF, JPEG files at 300 dpi.

Making Contact & Terms Send query letter with résumé, prints, tearsheets. Provide business card, self-promotion piece to be kept on file for possible future assignments. Responds only if interested; send nonreturnable samples. Simultaneous submissions and previously published work OK. Payment is dependent upon pre-publication agreement between photographer and *Government Technology*. Pays on publication. Credit line given. Buys one-time rights, electronic rights.

Tips "See some of the layout of the magazine; read a little of it."

$🖥 GRAIN JOURNAL

3065 Pershing Court, Decatur IL 62526. (217)877-9660. Fax: (217)877-6647. E-mail: ed@grainnet.com. Web site: www.grainnet.com. **Contact:** Ed Zdrojewski, editor. Circ. 10,752. Bimonthly trade magazine. Emphasizes grain industry. Readers are "elevator and feed mill managers primarily, as well as suppliers and others in the industry." Sample copy free with SASE (#10 envelope).

Needs Uses about 1-2 photos/issue. "We need photos concerning industry practices and activities. We look for clear, high-quality images without a lot of extraneous material." Photo captions preferred.

Specs Accepts images in digital format minimum 300 dpi resolution. Send via e-mail, floppy disk, Zip.

Making Contact & Terms Send query letter with samples and list of stock photo subjects. Responds in 1 week. Pays $100 for color cover; $30 for b&w inside. Pays on publication. Credit line given. Buys all rights; negotiable.

$⊘ 🆂 🖥 THE HORSE

P.O. Box 919003, Lexington KY 40591-9003. (859)276-6833. Fax: (859)276-4450. E-mail: photos@thehorse.com. Web site: www.thehorse.com. **Contact:** Megan Arszman, photo/newsletter editor. Circ. 49,000. Estab. 1995. Monthly magazine. Emphasizes equine health. Readers are equine veterinarians, hands-on horse owners, trainers and barn managers. Sample copy free with large SASE. Photo guidelines free with SASE and on Web site.

Needs Buys 20-30 photos from freelancers/issue; 240-360 photos/year. Needs generic horse

Trade Publications

shots, horse health such as farrier and veterinarian shots. "We use all breeds and all disciplines." Model/property release preferred. Photo captions preferred.

Specs Uses color transparencies. Accepts images in digital format. Send via CD, floppy disk, Zip, e-mail as TIFF, EPS, JPEG files at 300 dpi (4×6). "All photos must have metadata included in them before sending to photo editor."

Making Contact & Terms Send unsolicited photos by mail for consideration. Keeps samples on file. Previously published work OK. Pays $350 for color cover; $40-120 for color inside. Pays on publication. Buys one-time rights.

Tips "Please include name, address, and phone number of photographer; date images were sent; whether images may be kept on file or should be returned; date by which images should be returned; number of images sent. Usually 10-20 samples is adequate. Do not submit originals. E-mail photo editor before you send photos."

☑ 🖵 IGA GROCERGRAM

Pace Communications, 1301 Carolina St., Greensboro NC 27401. (336)383-5772. Fax: (336)383-5792. E-mail: chris.ferguson@paceco.com. **Contact:** Chris Ferguson, art director. Circ. 11,000. Estab. 1926. Quarterly magazine of the Independent Grocers Alliance. Emphasizes food industry. Readers are IGA retailers. Sample copy available upon request.

Needs Needs in-store shots, food (appetite appeal). Prefers shots of IGA stores. Model/property release required. Photo captions required.

Specs Accepts images in digital format. Send as TIFF files at 300 dpi.

Making Contact & Terms Send samples by e-mail or link to Web sitel for consideration. Provide résumé, business card, brochure, flier or tearsheets to be kept on file for possible future assignments. Keeps samples on file. Responds in 3 weeks. Simultaneous submissions and previously published work OK. Pay negotiable. **Pays on acceptance**. Credit line given. Buys one-time rights.

$☑ 🖵 JOURNAL OF ADVENTIST EDUCATION

General Conference of Seventh-day Adventists, 12501 Old Columbia Pike, Silver Spring MD 20904-6600. (301)680-5075. Fax: (301)622-9627. E-mail: rumbleb@gc.adventist.org. Web site: http://education.gc.adventist.org/jae. **Contact:** Beverly J. Robinson-Rumble, editor. Circ. 11,000. Estab. 1939. Published 5 times/year. Emphasizes procedures, philosophy and subject matter of Christian education. Official professional organ of the Department of Education covering elementary, secondary and higher education for all Seventh-day Adventist educational personnel (worldwide).

Needs Buys 5-15 photos from freelancers/issue; up to 75 photos/year. Needs photos of children/teens, multicultural, parents, education, religious, health/fitness, technology/computers with people, committees, offices, school photos of teachers, students, parents, activities at all levels , elementary though graduate school. Reviews photos with or without a manuscript. Model release preferred. Photo captions preferred.

Specs Uses mostly color prints; 35mm, 2¼×2¼, 4×5 transparencies. Accepts images in digital format. Send via Zip, CD-ROM (preferred), e-mail as TIFF, GIF, JPEG files at 300 dpi. Do not send large numbers of photos as e-mail attachments.

Making Contact & Terms Send query letter with prints, photocopies, transparencies. Provide self-promotion piece to be kept on file for possible future assignments. Responds in 1 month to queries. Simultaneous submissions and previously published work OK. Pays $100-350 for color cover; $50-100 for color inside. Willing to negotiate on electronic usage of photos. Pays on publication. Credit line given. Buys one-time rights for use in magazine and on website,

Tips ''Get good-quality people shots—close-ups, verticals especially; use interesting props in classroom shots; include teacher and students together, teachers in groups, parents and teachers, cooperative learning and multiage, multicultural children. Pay attention to backgrounds (not too busy) and understand the need for high res photos!''

$JOURNAL OF PSYCHOACTIVE DRUGS

Haight-Ashbury Publications, 856 Stanyan St., San Francisco CA 94117. (415)752-7601. Fax: (415)933-8674. E-mail: hajournal@comcast.net. Web site: http://www.hajpd.com. **Contact:** Terry Chambers, managing editor. Circ. 1,400. Estab. 1967. Quarterly. Emphasizes ''psychoactive substances (both legal and illegal).'' Readers are ''professionals (primarily health) in the drug abuse treatment field.''

Needs Uses 1 photo/issue; supplied by freelancers. Needs ''full-color abstract, surreal, avant garde or computer graphics.''

Making Contact & Terms Send query letter with 4×6 color prints or 35mm slides. Online and e-mail submissions are accepted. Include SASE for return of material. Responds in 2 weeks. Simultaneous submissions and previously published work OK. Pays $50 for color cover. Pays on publication. Credit line given. Buys one-time rights.

$ $ ☑ ▣ JUDICATURE

2700 University Ave., Des Moines IA 50311. (773)973-0145. Fax: (773)338-9687. E-mail: drichert@ajs.org. Web site: www.ajs.org. **Contact:** David Richert, editor. Circ. 6,000. Estab. 1917. Bimonthly publication of the American Judicature Society. Emphasizes courts, administration of justice. Readers are judges, lawyers, professors, citizens interested in improving the administration of justice. Sample copy free with 9×12 SAE and 6 first-class stamps.

Needs Buys 1-2 photos from freelancers/issue; 6-12 photos/year. Needs photos relating to courts, the law. ''Actual or posed courtroom shots are always needed.'' Interested in fine art, historical/vintage. Model/property release preferred. Photo captions preferred.

Specs Uses b&w and/or color prints. Accepts images in digital format. Send via CD, Zip, e-mail as JPEG files at 600 dpi.

Making Contact & Terms Send 5×7 glossy b&w prints or slides by mail for consideration; include SASE for return of material. Provide résumé, business card, brochure, flier or tearsheets to be kept on file for possible future assignments. Responds in 2 weeks. Simultaneous submissions and previously published work OK. Pays $250 for b&w cover; $350 for color cover; $125-250 for b&w inside; $125-300 for color inside. Pays on publication. Credit line given. Buys one-time rights.

$LANDSCAPE ARCHITECTURE

636 Eye St. NW, Washington DC 20001. (202)898-2444. E-mail: jroth@asla.org. Web site: www.asla.org. **Contact:** Jeff Roth, art director. Circ. 22,000. Estab. 1910. Monthly magazine of the American Society of Landscape Architects. Emphasizes ''landscape architecture, urban design, parks and recreation, architecture, sculpture'' for professional planners and designers.

Needs Buys 5-10 photos from freelancers/issue; 50-120 photos/year. Needs photos of landscape- and architecture-related subjects as described above. Special needs include aerial photography and environmental portraits. Model release required. Credit, caption information required.

Making Contact & Terms Send query letter with samples or list of stock photo subjects. Provide brochure, flier or tearsheets to be kept on file for possible future assignments. Response time varies. Previously published work OK. Pays $300-600/day. Pays on publication. Credit line given. Buys one-time rights.

Tips "We take an editorial approach to photographing our subjects."

$ $⊘ MARKETING & TECHNOLOGY GROUP

1415 N. Dayton, Chicago IL 60622. (312)274-2216. Fax: (312)266-3363. E-mail: qburns@me atingplace.com. Web site: www.meatingplace.com. **Contact:** Queenie Burns, vice president/design & production. Circ. 18,000. Estab. 1993. Publishes magazines that emphasize meat and poultry processing. Readers are predominantly male, ages 35-65, generally conservative. Sample copy available for $4.

Needs Buys 1-3 photos from freelancers/issue. Needs photos of food, processing plant tours, product shots, illustrative/conceptual. Model/property release preferred. Photo captions preferred.

Making Contact & Terms Provide résumé, business card, brochure, flier or tearsheets to be kept on file for possible future assignments. Submit portfolio for review. Keeps samples on file. Responds in 1 month. Simultaneous submissions and previously published work OK. Payment negotiable. Pays on publication. Credit line given.

Tips "Work quickly and meet deadlines. Follow directions when given; and when none are given, be creative while using your best judgment."

⊘ ▣ ⇅ MEETINGS AND INCENTIVE TRAVEL

Rogers Media, 1 Mount Pleasant Rd., 7th Floor, Toronto ON M4Y 2Y5 Canada. (416)764-1634. Fax: (416)764-1419. E-mail: dave.curcio@mtg.rogers.com. Web site: www.meetingsc anada.com. **Contact:** Lindsey Mrav, art director. Circ. 10,500. Estab. 1970. Bimonthly trade magazine emphasizing meetings and travel.

Needs Buys 1-5 photos from freelancers/issue; 7-30 photos/year. Needs photos of environmental, landscapes/scenics, cities/urban, interiors/decorating, events, food/drink, travel, business concepts, technology/computers. Reviews photos with or without a manuscript. Model/property release required. Photo captions required; include location and date.

Specs Uses 8×12 prints depending on shoot and size of photo in magazine. Accepts images in digital format. Send via CD as TIFF files at 300 dpi.

Making Contact & Terms Contact through rep or send query letter with tearsheets. Portfolio may be dropped off every Tuesday. Provide résumé, business card, self-promotion piece to be kept on file for possible future assignments. Responds only if interested; send nonreturnable samples. Simultaneous submissions and previously published work OK. "Payment depends on many factors." Credit line given. Buys one-time rights.

Tips "Send samples to keep on file."

ℕ ⊘ ▣ MY FOODSERVICE NEWS

(formerly Midwest Foodservice News) P.O. Box 917, Newark OH 43058. (740)345-5542. Fax: (740)345-5557. E-mail: carmen@midwestfoodnetwork.com. Web site: www.midwestf oodnework.com. **Contact:** Carmen Seward, editor. Circ. 27,000. Estab. 1976. Bi-monthly magazine. "Regional publication with a national interest and a local flair. Each edition contains state and national news, plus articles of local interest, to foster an informative dialogue between foodservice operators, their suppliers and associated businesses." Sample copy available for $3.95 with $2 first-class postage.

Needs Buys 5 or more photos from freelancers/issue; approximately 100 photos/year. Needs photos of celebrities, cities/urban, food/drink, travel, product shots/still life, photos from the restaurant and hospitality industry and foodservice companies (i.e., chefs, restaurant kitchens, dining areas, chef celebrities, etc.). Interested in historical/vintage. Reviews photos with or without ms. Model/property release required. Photo captions preferred; include description of photo plus all the names, etc., and photo credit.

Specs Accepts images in digital format only. Send via CD, e-mail as TIFF, EPS, BMP, GIF, JPEG files at 300-800 dpi.

Making Contact & Terms Send query letter with slides, prints, transparencies. Provide self-promotion piece to be kept on file for possible future assignments. Responds only if interested; send nonreturnable samples. Simultaneous submissions OK. Pay is based on experience. Pays on publication. Credit line given. Buys first rights.

$ $⊘ ▣ NAILPRO

7628 Densmore Ave., Van Nuys CA 91406-2042. (818)782-7328. Fax: (818)782-7450. E-mail: syaggy@creativeage.com. Web site: www.nailpro.com. **Contact:** Stephanie Yaggy, executive editor. Circ. 65,000. Estab. 1990. Monthly magazine publishd by Creative Age Publications. Emphasizes topics for professional manicurists and nail salon owners. Readers are females of all ages. Sample copy available for $2 with 9×12 SASE.

Needs Buys 10-12 photos from freelancers/issue; 120-144 photos/year. Needs photos of beautiful nails illustrating all kinds of nail extensions and enhancements; photographs showing process of creating and decorating nails, both natural and artificial. Also needs salon interiors, health/fitness, fashion/glamour. Model release required. Photo captions required; identify people and process if applicable.

Specs Accepts images in digital format. Send via Zip, e-mail as TIFF, EPS files at 300 dpi or better.

Making Contact & Terms Send query letter; responds only if interested. Call for portfolio review. "Art directors are rarely available, but photographers can leave materials and pick up later (or leave nonreturnable samples)." Send color prints; 35mm, 2¼×2¼, 4×5 transparencies. Keeps samples on file. Responds in 1 month. Previously published work OK. Pays $500 for color cover; $50-250 for color inside. **Pays on acceptance**. Credit line given. Buys one-time rights.

Tips "Talk to the person in charge of choosing art about photo needs for the next issue and try to satisfy that immediate need; that often leads to assignments. Submit samples and portfolios with letter stating specialties or strong points."

Ⓝ NFPA JOURNAL

1 Batterymarch Park, Quincy MA 02169. E-mail: NFPAJournal@nfpa.org. Web site: www.nfpa.org. **Contact:** David Yount, art director. Circ. 85,000. Bimonthly magazine of the National Fire Protection Association. Emphasizes fire and life safety information. Readers are fire professionals, engineers, architects, building code officials, ages 20-65. Sample copy free with 9×12 SAE or via e-mail.

Needs Buys 5-7 photos from freelancers/issue; 30-42 photos/year. Needs photos of fires and fire-related incidents. Model release preferred. Photo captions preferred.

Making Contact & Terms Send query letter with list of stock photo subjects. Provide résumé, business card, brochure, flier or tearsheets to be kept on file for possible future assignments. Send color prints and 35mm transparencies in 3-ring slide sleeve with date. Responds in 3 weeks. Payment negotiated. Pays on publication. Credit line given.

Tips "Send cover letter, 35mm color slides, preferably with manuscripts and photo captions."

$◱ ▣ 9-1-1 MAGAZINE

18201 Weston Place, Tustin CA 92780. (714)544-7776. E-mail: editor@9-1-1magazine.com. Web site: www.9-1-1magazine.com. **Contact:** Randall Larson, editor. Circ. 18,000. Estab. 1988. Published 9 times/year. Emphasizes public safety communications for police, fire, paramedic, dispatch, medical, etc. Readers are ages 20-65. Sample copy free with 9×12 SASE and 7 first-class stamps. Photo guidelines free with SASE.

Needs Buys 20-30 photos from freelancers/issue; 270 photos/year. "Primary needs include dramatic photographs of incidents and unusual situations for covers; *From the Field*, our 2-page photo department included in each issue; and to illustrate articles. We especially need communications-related photos and law enforcement images. We have an overabundance of car-crash and structure-fire images, and are only looking for the more unusual or spectacular images in those categories. We rarely use stock photos, and we insist that all photography submitted to *9-1-1 Magazine* be for our exclusive use." Photo captions required; if possible, include incident location by city and state, agencies involved, incident details.

Specs Prefers digital images but also accepts color prints; 35mm, $2\frac{1}{4} \times 2\frac{1}{4}$, 4×5, 8×10 transparencies. "Digital picture submissions should be from a (minimum) 4-megapixel camera at highest setting (or minimum resolution of 1,500 pixels wide; or 5" wide at 300 dpi). Low-res samples acceptable with query."

Making Contact & Terms Send query letter with list of stock photo subjects. "Prefer original images versus stock content." Send unsolicited photos by post or e-mail for consideration; include SASE for return of material. Responds in 3 weeks. Pays $300 for color cover; $50 for color inside, ¼ page or less; $75 for color inside, ½ page; $100 for color inside, full page. Pays on publication. Credit line given. Buys one-time rights.

Tips "We need photos for unillustrated cover stories and features appearing in each issue. See editorial calendar on Web site under 'Advertising' link. Assignments possible. Emphasis is on interesting composition, clarity and uniqueness of image."

$ $◯ Ⓢ ▣ PI MAGAZINE, Professional Investigator Magazine

(formerly PI Magazine, Journal of Professional Investigators) 4400 Rt. 9 S., Suite 1000, P.O. Box 7198, Freehold NJ 07728-7198. (732)308-3800. Fax: (732)308-3314. E-mail: jim@pimag azine.com. Web site: www.pimagazine.com. **Contact:** Jimmie Mesis, publisher. Circ. 10,000. Estab. 1987. Bimonthly trade magazine. "Our audience is 80% private investigators with the balance law enforcement, insurance investigators, and people with interest in becoming a PI. The magazine features educational articles about the profession. Serious conservative format." Sample copy available for $7.95 and SAE with $1.75 first-class postage.

Needs Buys 10 photos from freelancers/issue; 60-100 photos/year. Needs photos of technology/computers, law/crime. Reviews photos with or without a manuscript. Model/property release required. Photo captions preferred.

Specs Accepts images in digital format. Send via CD, e-mail as TIFF, EPS files at highest dpi.

Making Contact & Terms Send query letter with tearsheets, stock list. Provide résumé, business card, self-promotion piece to be kept on file for possible future assignments. Responds only if interested; send nonreturnable samples. Simultaneous submissions OK. Pays $200-500 for color cover; $50-200 for color inside. Pays on publication. Credit line given. Buys all rights; negotiable.

$ $◫ PLANNING

American Planning Association, 122 S. Michigan Ave, Chicago IL 60603. (312)431-9100. E-mail: rsessions@planning.org. Web site: www.planning.org. **Contact:** Richard Sessions, art director. Editor: Sylvia Lewis. Circ. 43,000. Estab. 1972. Monthly magazine. "We focus on urban and regional planning, reaching most of the nation's professional planners and others interested in the topic." Sample copy and photo guidelines free with 10×13 SASE with 4 first-class stamps (do not send cash or checks).

Needs Buys 4-5 photos from freelancers/issue; 60 photos/year. Photos purchased with accompanying manuscript and on assignment. Photo essay/photo feature (architecture, neighborhoods, historic preservation, agriculture); scenic (mountains, wilderness, rivers, oceans, lakes); housing; transportation (cars, railroads, trolleys, highways). "No cheesecake; no sentimental shots of dogs, children, etc. High artistic quality is very important. We publish high-quality nonfiction stories on city planning and land use. Ours is an association magazine but not a house organ, and we use the standard journalistic techniques: interviews, anecdotes, quotes. Topics include energy, the environment, housing, transportation, land use, agriculture, neighborhoods and urban affairs." Photo captions required.

Specs Uses 4-color prints; 35mm, 4×5 transparencies. Accepts images in digital format. Send via Zip, CD as TIFF, EPS, JPEG files at 300 dpi and around 5×7 in physical size.

Making Contact & Terms Send query letter with samples; include SASE for return of material. Responds in 1 month. Previously published work OK. Pays $50-100 for b&w photos; $75-200 for color photos; $375 maximum for cover; $200-600 for manuscript. Pays on publication. Credit line given.

Tips "Just let us know you exist. Eventually, we may be able to use your services. Send tearsheets or photocopies of your work, or a little self-promo piece. Subject lists are only minimally useful, as are Web site addresses. How the work looks is of paramount importance. Please don't send original slides or prints with the expectation of them being returned. Send something we can keep in our files."

$PLASTICS NEWS

1725 Merriman Rd., Akron OH 44313. (330)836-9180. Fax: (330)836-2322. E-mail: dloepp@crain.com. Web site: www.plasticsnews.com. **Contact:** Don Loepp, managing editor. Circ. 60,000. Estab. 1989. Weekly tabloid. Emphasizes plastics industry business news. Readers are male and female executives of companies that manufacture a broad range of plastics products; suppliers and customers of the plastics processing industry. Sample copy available for $1.95.

Needs Buys 1-3 photos from freelancers/issue; 52-156 photos/year. Needs photos of technology related to use and manufacturing of plastic products. Model/property release preferred. Photo captions required.

Making Contact & Terms Send unsolicited photos by mail for consideration. Provide résumé, business card, brochure, flier or tearsheets to be kept on file for possible future assignments. Send query letter with stock list. Keeps samples on file; include SASE for return of material. Responds in 2 weeks. Simultaneous submissions and previously published work OK. Pays $125-175 for color cover; $100-150 for b&w inside; $125-175 for color inside. Pays on publication. Credit line given. Buys one-time and all rights.

N $ A ■ PRODUCE MERCHANDISING

Vance Publishing Corp., 10901 W. 84th Terrace, Lenexa KS 66214. (800)255-5113. Fax: (913)438-0691. E-mail: dbabcock@producemerchandising.com. Web site: www.producem erchandising.com. **Contact:** David Babcock, chief editor. Circ. 12,000. Estab. 1988. Monthly magazine, email newsletters, and Web site. Emphasizes the retail end of the fresh produce industry. Readers are male and female executives who oversee produce operations in US and Canadian supermarkets as well as in-store produce department personnel. Sample copies available.

Needs Buys 2-5 photos from freelancers/issue; 24-60 photos/year. Needs in-store shots, environmental portraits for cover photos or display pictures. Photo captions required; include subject's name, job title and company title-all verified and correctly spelled.

Specs Accepts images in digital format. Send via email as TIFF, JPEG files.

Making Contact & Terms Email only. Response time "depends on when we will be in a specific photographer's area and have a need." Pays $500-750 for color cover; $25-50/color photo. **Pays on acceptance.** Credit line given. Buys all rights.

Tips "We seek photographers who serve as our on-site 'art director' to ensure capture of creative angles and quality images."

N ■ PROFESSIONAL PHOTOGRAPHER

Professional Photographers of America, 229 Peachtree St. NE, Suite 2200, International Tower, Atlanta GA 30303. (404)522-8600. Fax: (404)614-6406. E-mail: cbishopp@ppa.com. Web site: www.ppmag.com. **Contact:** Cameron Bishopp, director of publications. Art Director: Debbie Todd. Circ. 26,000. Estab. 1907. Monthly magazine. Emphasizes professional photography in the fields of portrait, wedding, commercial/advertising, sports, corporate and industrial. Readers include professional photographers and photographic services and educators. Approximately half the circulation is Professional Photographers of America members. Sample copy available for $5 postpaid.

● PPA members submit material unpaid to promote their photo businesses and obtain recognition. Images sent to *Professional Photographer* should be technically perfect, and photographers should include information about how the photo was produced.

Needs Buys 25-30 photos from freelancers/issue; 300-360 photos/year. "We only accept material as illustration that relates directly to photographic articles showing professional studio, location, commercial and portrait techniques. A majority are supplied by Professional Photographers of America members." Reviews photos with accompanying manuscript only. "We always need commercial/advertising and industrial success stories; how to sell your photography to major accounts, unusual professional photo assignments. Also, photographer and studio application stories about the profitable use of electronic still imaging for customers and clients." Model release preferred. Photo captions required.

Specs Prefers images in digital format. Send via CD, e-mail as TIFF, EPS, JPEG files at 72 dpi minimum. Also uses 8×10 unmounted glossy b&w and/or color prints; 35mm, $2\frac{1}{4} \times 2\frac{1}{4}$, 4×5, 8×10 transparencies.

Making Contact & Terms Send query letter with résumé of credits. "We prefer a story query, or complete manuscript if writer feels subject fits our magazine. Photos will be part of manuscript package." Responds in 2 months. Credit line given.

Ⓐ ▣ PUBLIC POWER

1875 Connecticut Ave. NW, Suite 1200, Washington, DC 20009-5715. (202)467-2948. Fax: (202)467-2910. E-mail: jlabella@appanet.org and llundstrom@appanet.org. Web site: www.appanet.org. Contact: Jeanne LaBella, editor and Laurel Lundstrom, production editor. Circ. 20,000. Bimonthly publication of the American Public Power Association. Emphasizes electric power provided by cities, towns and utility districts. Sample copy and photo guidelines free.

Needs "We buy photos on assignment only."

Specs Prefers digital images; call art director (Robert Thomas) at (202)467-2983 to discuss.

Making Contact & Terms Send query letter with samples. Provide résumé, business card, brochure, flier or tearsheets to be kept on file for possible future assignments. **Pays on acceptance.** Credit line given. Buys one-time rights.

RANGEFINDER

6059 Bristol Pkwy., Ste. 100, Culver City CA 90230. (310)846-4770 x319. Fax: (310)395-9058. E-mail: bhurter@rfpublishing.com, aronck@rfpublishing.com. Web site: www.rangefindermag.com. **Contact:** Oliver Gettell, associate editor or Abigail Ronck, assistant editor. Circ. 50,000. Estab. 1952. Monthly magazine. Emphasizes topics, developments and products of interest to the professional photographer. Readers are professionals in all phases of photography. Sample copy free with 11×14 SAE and 2 first-class stamps. Photo guidelines free with SASE.

Needs Buys very few photos from freelancers/issue. Needs all kinds of photos; almost always run in conjunction with articles. "We prefer photos accompanying 'how-to' or special interest stories from the photographer." No pictorials. Special needs include seasonal cover shots (vertical format only). Model release required; property release preferred. Photo captions preferred.

Making Contact & Terms Send query letter with résumé of credits. Keeps samples on file; include SASE for return of material. Responds in 1 month. Previously published work occasionally OK; give details. Payment varies. Covers submitted gratis. Pays on publication. Credit line given. Buys first North American serial rights; negotiable.

$▣ READING TODAY

International Reading Association, 800 Barksdale Rd., P.O. Box 8139, Newark DE 19714-8139. (302)731-1600, ext. 250. Fax: (302)731-1057. E-mail: jmicklos@reading.org. Web site: www.reading.org. **Contact:** John Micklos, Jr., editor-in-chief. Circ. 85,000. Estab. 1983. Bimonthly newspaper of the International Reading Association. Emphasizes reading education. Readers are educators who belong to the International Reading Association. Sample copies available. Photo guidelines free with SASE.

Needs Buys 4 photos from freelancers/issue; 24 photos/year. Needs classroom shots and photos of people of all ages reading in various settings. Reviews photos with or without a manuscript. Model/property release preferred. Photo captions preferred; include names (if appropriate) and context of photo.

Specs Uses $3\frac{1}{2}\times 5$ or larger color and b&w prints. Accepts images in digital format. Send via CD, e-mail as JPEG files.

Making Contact & Terms Send query letter with résumé of credits and stock list. Send unsolicited photos by mail for consideration; include SASE for return of material. Responds in 1 month. Simultaneous submissions and previously published work OK. Pays $100 for editorial use. **Pays on acceptance.** Credit line given. Buys one-time rights for print use and rights to post editorially on the IRA Web site.

$⊘ ▣ RECOMMEND MAGAZINE

Worth International Media Group, 5979 NW 151st St., Suite 120, Miami Lakes FL 33014. (305)828-0123. Fax: (305)826-6950. E-mail: janet@recommend.com. Web site: www.reco mmend.com or www.worthit.com. **Contact:** Janet Del Mastro, art director. Circ. 55,000. Estab. 1985. Monthly. Emphasizes travel. Readers are travel agents, meeting planners, hoteliers, ad agencies.

Needs Buys 16 photos from freelancers/issue; 192 photos/year. "Our publication divides the world into 7 regions. Every month we use travel destination-oriented photos of animals, cities, resorts and cruise lines; feature all types of travel photography from all over the world." Model/property release required. Photo captions preferred; identification required on every photo.

Specs Accepts images in digital format. Send via CD, Zip as TIFF, EPS files at 300 dpi minimum. "We do not accept 35mm slides or transparencies."

Making Contact & Terms "Contact via e-mail to view sample of photography." Simultaneous submissions and previously published work OK. Pays $75-150 for color cover; $50 for front cover less than 80 square inches; $25-50 for color inside. Pays 30 days after publication. Credit line given. Buys one-time rights.

Tips Prefers to see high-res digital files.

$⊘ Ⓢ ▣ REFEREE

P.O. Box 161, Franksville WI 53126. (262)632-8855. Fax: (262)632-5460. E-mail: jstern@ref eree.com. Web site: www.referee.com. **Contact:** Jeffrey Stern, senior editor. Circ. 40,000. Estab. 1976. Monthly magazine. Readers are mostly male, ages 30-50. Sample copy free with 9×12 SAE and 5 first-class stamps. Photo guidelines free with SASE.

Needs Buys 37 photos from freelancers/issue; 444 photos/year. Needs action officiating shots—all sports. Photo needs are ongoing. Photo captions required; include officials' names and hometowns.

Specs Prefers to use digital files (minimum 300 dpi submitted on CD only—no DVDs) and 35mm slides. Also uses color prints.

Making Contact & Terms Send unsolicited photos by mail for consideration. Responds in 2 weeks. Simultaneous submissions and previously published work OK. Pays $100 for color cover; $35 for color inside. Pays on publication. Credit line given. Rights purchased negotiable.

Tips "Prefer photos that bring out the uniqueness of being a sports official. Need photos primarily of officials at or above the high school level in baseball, football, basketball, softball, volleyball and soccer in action. Other sports acceptable, but used less frequently. When at sporting events, take a few shots with the officials in mind, even though you may be on assignment for another reason. Don't be afraid to give it a try. We're receptive, always looking for new freelance contributors. We are constantly looking for pictures of officials/umpires. Our needs in this area have increased. Names and hometowns of officials are required."

$ $⬛⬛ RESTAURANT HOSPITALITY

Penton Media, 1300 E. Ninth St., Cleveland OH 44114. (216)931-9942. Fax: (216)696-0836. E-mail: chris.roberto@penton.com. Web site: www.restaurant-hospitality.com. **Contact:** Chris Roberto, group creative director. Editor-in-Chief: Michael Sanson. Circ. 123,000. Estab. 1919. Monthly magazine. Emphasizes "hands-on restaurant management ideas and strategies." Readers are restaurant owners, chefs, food service chain executives.

Needs Buys 15 photos from freelancers/issue; 180 photos/year. Needs "on-location portraits, restaurant and food service interiors, and occasional food photos." Special needs include "subject-related photos; query first." Model release preferred. Photo captions preferred.

Specs Accepts images in digital format. Send via CD, FTP, e-mail as JPEG files at 300 dpi.

Making Contact & Terms Send postcard samples. Provide business card, samples or tearsheets to be kept on file for possible future assignments. Previously published work OK. Pay varies; negotiable. Cover fees on per project basis. **Pays on acceptance.** Credit line given. Buys one-time rights plus usage in all media.

Tips "Send postcard samples including your Web address for online viewing of your work."

⬛ $⬛ RETAILERS FORUM

383 E. Main St., Centerport NY 11721. (631)754-5000. Fax: (631)754-0630. E-mail: forumpublishing@aol.com. **Contact:** Martin Stevens, publisher. Circ. 70,000. Estab. 1981. Monthly magazine. Readers are entrepreneurs and retail store owners. Sample copy available for $7.50.

Needs Buys 3-6 photos from freelancers/issue; 36-72 photos/year. "We publish trade magazines for retail variety goods stores and flea market vendors. Items include jewelry, cosmetics, novelties, toys, etc. (five-and-dime-type goods). We are interested in creative and abstract impressions—not straight-on product shots. Humor a plus." Model/property release required.

Specs Uses color prints. Accepts images in digital format. Send via e-mail at 300 dpi.

Making Contact & Terms Send unsolicited photos by mail or e-mail for consideration. Does not keep samples on file; include SASE for return of material. Responds in 2 weeks. Simultaneous submissions and previously published work OK. Pays $100 for color cover; $50 for color inside. **Pays on acceptance.** Buys one-time rights.

$ $⬛⬛ SCRAP

1615 L St. NW, Suite 600, Washington DC 20036. (202)662-8547. E-mail: kentkiser@scrap.org. Web site: www.scrap.org. **Contact:** Kent Kiser, publisher and editor-in-chief. Circ. 13,000. Estab. 1988. Bimonthly magazine of the Institute of Scrap Recycling Industries. Emphasizes scrap recycling for owners and managers of recycling operations worldwide. Sample copy available for $8.

Needs Buys 0-15 photos from freelancers/issue; 15-70 photos/year. Needs operation shots of companies being profiled and studio concept shots. Model release required. Photo captions required.

Specs Accepts images in digital format. Send via CD, Zip, e-mail as TIFF files at 270 dpi.

Making Contact & Terms Provide résumé, business card, brochure, flier or tearsheets to be kept on file for possible future assignments. Previously published work OK. Pays $800-1,500/day; $100-400 for b&w inside; $200-600 for color inside. **Pays on delivery of images.** Credit line given. Rights negotiable.

Tips Photographers must possess ''ability to photograph people in corporate atmosphere, as well as industrial operations; ability to work well with executives, as well as laborers. We are always looking for good color photographers to accompany our staff writers on visits to companies being profiled. We try to keep travel costs to a minimum by hiring photographers located in the general vicinity of the profiled company. Other photography (primarily studio work) is usually assigned through freelance art director.''

$□ ▣ SMALL BUSINESS TIMES

126 N. Jefferson St., Ste. 403, Milwaukee WI 53202-6120. (414)277-8181. (414)277-8191. Web site: www.biztimes.com. **Contact**: Shelly Tabor, art director. Circ. 15,000. Estab. 1994. Biweekly business-to-business publication.

Needs Buys 2-3 photos from freelancers/issue; 200 photos/year. Needs photos of cities/urban, business men and women, business concepts. Interested in documentary.

Specs Uses various sizes of glossy color and b&w prints. Accepts images in digital format. Send via CD as TIFF files at 300 dpi.

Making Contact & Terms Provide résumé, business card, self-promotion piece to be kept on file for possible future assignments. Responds only if interested; send nonreturnable samples. Simultaneous submissions and previously published work OK. Pays $250 maximum for color cover; $80 maximum for b&w inside. **Pays on acceptance**. Credit line given.

Tips ''Readers are owners/managers/CEOs. Cover stories and special reports often need conceptual images and portraits. Clean, modern and cutting edge with good composition. Covers have lots of possibility! Approximate one-week turnaround. Most assignments are for the Milwaukee area.''

$ THOROUGHBRED TIMES

P.O. Box 8237, Lexington KY 40533. (859)260-9800. E-mail: photos@thoroughbredtimes.com. Web site: www.thoroughbredtimes.com. **Contact:** Sarah Dorroh, photo editor. Circ. 19,000. Estab. 1985. Weekly tabloid news magazine. Emphasizes Thoroughbred breeding and racing. Readers are wide demographic range of industry professionals. Photo guidelines available upon request.

Needs Buys 10-15 photos from freelancers/issue; 520-780 photos/year. Looks for photos ''only from desired trade (Thoroughbred breeding and racing).'' Needs photos of specific subject features (personality, farm or business). Model release preferred. Photo captions preferred. ''File info required.''

Making Contact & Terms Provide business card, brochure, flier or tearsheets to be kept on file for possible future assignments. Responds in 1 month. Previously published work OK. Pays $50 for b&w cover or inside; $50 for color; $250/day. Pays on publication. Credit line given. Buys one-time rights.

$ $□ ▣ VETERINARY ECONOMICS

Advanstar Veterinary Healthcare Communications, 8033 Flint, Lenexa KS 66214. (913)492-4300. Fax: (913)492-4157. Web site: www.vetecon.com. **Contact:** Alison Fulton, senior art director. Circ. 58,000. Estab. 1960. Monthly trade magazine emphasizing practice management for veterinarians. Sample copies and photo guidelines available.

Needs Photographers on an "as needed" basis for editorial portraits; must be willing to sign license agreement; 6-12 photos/year. Needs photos of business concepts and medicine. Reviews photos with or without a manuscript. Model release and license agreement required. Photo captions preferred.

Specs Prefers images in digital format. Send via CD, Zip, e-mail as TIFF, EPS, JPEG files at 300 dpi.

Making Contact & Terms Send 1 e-mail with sample image less than 2 MB; repeat e-mails are deleted. Does not keep samples on file. **Pays on acceptance.** Credit line given.

THE WHOLESALER

1838 Techny Court, Northbrook IL 60062. (847)564-1127. Fax: (847)564-1264. E-mail: editor@thewholesaler.com. Web site: www.thewholesaler.com. **Contact:** Mary Jo Martin, editor. Circ. 35,000. Estab. 1946. Monthly news tabloid. Emphasizes wholesaling/distribution in the plumbing, heating, air conditioning, piping (including valves), fire protection industry. Readers are owners and managers of wholesale distribution businesses; manufacturer representatives. Sample copy free with 11 × 15¾ SAE and 5 first-class stamps.

Needs Buys 3 photos from freelancers/issue; 36 photos/year. Interested in field and action shots in the warehouse, on the loading dock, at the job site. Property release preferred. Photo captions preferred; "Just give us the facts."

Making Contact & Terms Send query letter with stock list. Send any size glossy color and/or b&w prints by mail with SASE for consideration. Responds in 2 weeks. Simultaneous submissions and previously published work OK. Pays on publication. Buys one-time rights.

$ $▣ WINES & VINES

1800 Lincoln Ave., San Rafael CA 94901. (415)453-9700. Fax: (415)453-2517. E-mail: bridget@winesandvines.com. Web site: www.winesandvines.com. **Contact:** Bridget Holland. Circ. 5,000. Estab. 1919. Monthly magazine. Emphasizes winemaking, grape growing, and marketing in North America and internationally for wine industry professionals, including winemakers, grape growers, wine merchants and suppliers.

Needs Wants color cover subjects on a regular basis.

Specs Accepts images in digital format. Send via CD, Zip, e-mail as TIFF, or JPEG files at 400 dpi.

Making Contact & Terms Prefers e-mail query with link to portfolio; or send material by mail for consideration. Will e-mail if interested in reviewing photographer's portfolio. Provide business card to be kept on file for possible future assignments. Responds in 3 months. Previously published work considered. Pays $100-350 for color cover, or negotiable ad trade out. Pays on publication. Credit line given. Buys one-time rights.

$▣ ▣ ⊕ WORLD TOBACCO

dmg world media, Westgate House, 120/130 Station Rd., Redhill, Surrey RH1 1ET. (44)(1737)855573. E-mail: lukedodd@dmgworldmedia.com; duncanmacowan@dmgworldmedia.com. Web site: www.worldtobacco.co.uk. **Contact:** Duncan MacOwan, editor. Circ. 4,300. Trade magazine. "Focuses on all aspects of the tobacco industry from international trends to national markets, offering news and views on the entire industry from leaf farming to primary and secondary manufacturing, to packaging, distribution and marketing." Sample copies available. Request photo guildelines via e-mail.

Needs Buys 5-10 photos from freelancers/issue; agriculture, product shots/still life. "Any-

Trade Publications

thing related to tobacco and smoking. Abstract smoking images considered, as well as international images.''

Specs Accepts almost all formats. Minimum resolution of 300 dpi at the size to be printed. Prefers TIFFs to JPEGs, but can accept either.

Making Contact & Terms E-mail query letter with link to photographer's Web site, JPEG samples at 72 dpi. Provide self-promotion piece to be kept on file for possible future assignments. Pays £200 maximum for cover photo. **Pays on acceptance.** Credit line given.

Tips ''Check the features list on our Web site.''

$☐ ▣ WRITERS' JOURNAL, The Complete Writers' Magazine

Val-Tech Media, P.O. Box 394, Perham MN 56573. (218)346-7921. Fax: (218)346-7924. E-mail: writersjournal@writersjournal.com. Web site: www.writersjournal.com. **Contact:** John Ogroske, publisher. Circ. 2 2,000. Estab. 1980. Bimonthly trade magazine. Sample copy available for $6.

Needs Buys 1 photo from freelancers/issue; 6 photos/year. Needs photos of landscapes/scenics, wildlife, rural, travel. *WRITERS' Journal* offers 2 photography contests yearly. Send SASE for contest guidelines or visit Web site. Model release required (''if applicable to photo''). Photo titles preferred.

Specs Uses 8×10 color prints; 35mm or larger transparencies or slides (preferred) for non-contest photos. ''Digital images must be accompanied by a hardcopy printout.''

Making Contact & Terms Send query letter with tearsheets, stock list. Does not keep samples on file; include SASE for return of material. Responds in 2 months. Pays $50-60 for color cover. Pays on publication. Credit line given. Buys first North American rights.

Book Publishers

There are diverse needs for photography in the book publishing industry. Publishers need photos for the obvious (covers, jackets, text illustrations and promotional materials), but they may also need them for use on CD-ROMs and Web sites. Generally, though, publishers either buy individual or groups of photos for text illustration, or they publish entire books of photography.

Those in need of text illustration use photos for cover art and interiors of textbooks, travel books and nonfiction books. For illustration, photographs may be purchased from a stock agency or from a photographer's stock, or the publisher may make assignments. Publishers usually pay for photography used in book illustration or on covers on a per-image or per-project basis. Some pay photographers hourly or day rates, if on an assignment basis. No matter how payment is made, however, the competitive publishing market requires freelancers to remain flexible.

To approach book publishers for illustration jobs, send a cover letter with photographs or slides and a stock photo list with prices, if available. (See sample stock list on page 19.) If you have a Web site, provide a link to it. If you have published work, tearsheets are very helpful in showing publishers how your work translates to the printed page.

PHOTO BOOKS

Publishers who produce photography books usually publish books with a theme, featuring the work of one or several photographers. It is not always necessary to be well-known to publish your photographs as a book. What you do need, however, is a unique perspective, a salable idea and quality work.

For entire books, publishers may pay in one lump sum or with an advance plus royalties (a percentage of the book sales). When approaching a publisher for your own book of photographs, query first with a brief letter describing the project, and include sample photographs. If the publisher is interested in seeing the complete proposal, you can send additional information in one of two ways depending on the complexity of the project.

Prints placed in sequence in a protective box, along with an outline, will do for easy-to-describe, straightforward book projects. For more complex projects, you may want to create a book dummy. A dummy is basically a book model with photographs and text arranged as they will appear in finished book form. Book dummies show exactly how a book will look, including the sequence, size, format and layout of photographs and accompanying text. The quality of the dummy is important, but keep in mind that the expense can be prohibitive.

To find the right publisher for your work, first check the Subject Index on page 504 to help narrow your search, then read the appropriate listings carefully. Send for catalogs and guidelines for those publishers that interest you. You may find guidelines on publishers' Web sites as well. Also, become familiar with your local bookstore or visit the site of an online bookstore such as Amazon.com. By examining the books already published, you can find those publishers who produce your type of work. Check for both large and small publishers. While smaller firms may not have as much money to spend, they are often more willing to take risks, especially on the work of new photographers. Keep in mind that photo books are expensive to produce and may have a limited market.

$ $ Ⓐ ALL ABOUT KIDS PUBLISHING

9333 Bendow Dr., Gilroy CA 95020. (408)846-1833. Fax: (408)846-1835. Web site: www.aa kp.com. **Contact:** Linda L. Guevara, editor. Estab. 2000. Publishes children's books, including picture books and books for young readers.
Needs Uses freelance photographers on assignment only. Model/property release required.
Specs Uses 35mm transparencies.
Making Contact & Terms Submit portfolio, color samples/copies. Include cover letter, résumé, contact info. Keeps samples on file for possible future assignments; include SASE for return of material. Pays by the project, $500 minimum or royalty of 5% based on wholesale price.
Tips "Visit out our Web site for updates and submission guidelines."

$ ⊘ ▣ AMERICAN PLANNING ASSOCIATION

122 S. Michigan, Suite 1600, Chicago IL 60603. (312)431-9100. Fax: (312)431-9985. Web site: www.planning.org. **Contact:** Richard Sessions, Susan Deegan or Jessica Campbell, art directors. Publishes planning and related subjects. Photos used for text illustrations, promotional materials, book covers, dust jackets. Examples of recently published titles: *Planning* (text illustrations, cover); *PAS Reports* (text illustrations, cover). Photo guidelines and sample (*Planning*) available for $1 postage (stamps only please, no cash or checks).
Needs Buys 100 photos/year; offers 8-10 freelance assignments/year. Needs planning-related photos. Photo captions required; include what's in the photo and credit information.
Specs Uses 35mm color slides; 5×7, 8×10 b&w prints. Accepts images in digital format. Send via CD, floppy disk, Zip, e-mail as TIFF, EPS, JPEG files at 300 dpi minimum; maximum quality, lowest compression.
Making Contact & Terms Provide résumé, business card, brochure, flier, tearsheets, promo pages or good photocopies to be kept on file for possible future assignments. "Do not send original work—slides, prints, whatever—with the expectation of it being returned." Responds in 2 weeks. Simultaneous submissions and previously published work OK. Pays $350 maximum for cover; $100-150 for b&w or color inside. **Pays on receipt of invoice**. Credit line given. Buys one-time and electronic rights (CD-ROM and online).
Tips "Send a sample I can keep."

AMHERST MEDIA®: PUBLISHER OF PHOTOGRAPHY BOOKS

175 Rano St., Suite 200, Buffalo NY 14207. (716)874-4450. Fax: (716)874-4508. E-mail: submissions@amherstmedia.com. Web site: www.amherstmedia.com. **Contact:** Craig Alesse, photo book publisher. Estab. 1974. Publishes trade paperback originals and reprints. Subjects include photography how-to. Photos used for text illustrations, book covers. Examples of recently published titles: *Portrait Photographer's Handbook*; *The Best of Professional*

Digital Photography; *How to Create a High-Profit Photography Business in Any Market*. Catalog and submission guidelines free.

Needs Does not buy single photos, but accepts proposals for photography how-to books. "Looking for well-written and illustrated photo books." Reviews photos as part of a manuscript package only.

Making Contact & Terms Send query letter with book outline, 2 sample chapters and SASE. Responds in 2 months to queries. Simultaneous submissions OK. Pays 6-8% royalties on retail price; offers advance. Rights negotiable.

Tips "Our audience is made up of beginning to advanced photographers. If I were trying to market a photography book, I would fill the need of a specific audience and self-edit in a tight manner."

$ $⊘ Ⓐ ▣ APPALACHIAN MOUNTAIN CLUB BOOKS

5 Joy St., Boston MA 02108. (617)523-0655 or (800)372-1758. Fax: (617)523-0722. Web site: www.outdoors.org. **Contact:** Athena Lakri, production manager. Estab. 1876. Publishes hardcover originals, trade paperback originals and reprints. Subjects include nature, outdoors, recreation, paddlesports, hiking/backpacking, skiing in the northeast. Photos used for text illustrations, book covers. Examples of recently published titles: *Discover the White Mountains*; *Best Day Hikes* series.

Needs Looking for photos of paddlesports, skiing and outdoor recreation. Model/property release required. Photo captions preferred; include location, description of subject, photographer's name and phone number.

Specs Uses 3×5 glossy color and/or b&w prints; 35mm, 2¼×2¼ transparencies, digital format.

Making Contact & Terms Send query letter with brochure, stock list or tearsheets. Art director will contact photographer for portfolio review if interested. Keeps samples on file. Responds only if interested; send nonreturnable samples. Considers previously published work. Pays by the project, $100-400 for color cover; $50 for grayscale inside. **Pays on acceptance.** Credit line given. Buys first North American serial rights.

Ⓐ ▣ BENTLEY PUBLISHERS

1734 Massachusetts Ave., Cambridge MA 02138. (617)547-4170. Fax: (617)876-9235. E-mail: michael.bentley@rb.com and susan.lit@bentleypublishers.com. Web site: www.bentleypublishers.com. **Contact:** Michael Bentley, president. Estab. 1950. Publishes professional, technical, consumer how-to books. Photos used for text illustrations, promotional materials, book covers, dust jackets. Examples of published titles: *Porsche: Genesis of Genius;* Toyota Prius Repair and Maintenance Manual.

Needs Buys 70-100 photos/year; offers 5-10 freelance assignments/year. Looking for motorsport, automotive technical and engineering photos. Reviews stock photos. Model/property release required. Photo captions required; include date and subject matter.

Specs Uses 8×10 transparencies. Accepts images in digital format.

Making Contact & Terms Send query letter with samples. Provide résumé, business card, brochure, flier or tearsheets to be kept on file for possible future assignments. Keeps samples on file; cannot return material. Works on assignment only. Responds in 6 weeks. Simultaneous submissions and previously published work OK. Payment negotiable. Credit line given. Buys electronic and one-time rights.

▣ ◩ BOSTON MILLS PRESS

132 Main St., Erin ON N0B 1T0 Canada. (519)833-2407. Fax: (519)833-2195. Web site: www.bostonmillspress.com. **Contact:** John Denison, publisher. Estab. 1974. Publishes coffee table books, local guide books. Photos used for text illustrations, book covers and dust jackets. Examples of recently published titles: *Gift of Wings*; *Superior: Journey on an Inland Sea*.

Needs "We're looking for book-length ideas, *not* stock. We pay a royalty on books sold, plus advance."

Specs Prefers images in digital format, but will accept 35mm transparencies.

Making Contact & Terms Send query letter with résumé of credits. Does not keep samples on file; include SAE/IRC for return of material. Responds in 3 weeks. Simultaneous submissions OK. Payment negotiated with contract. Credit line given.

⬚ $CLEANING CONSULTANT SERVICES

P.O. Box 1273, Seattle WA 98111. (206)682-9748. Fax: (206)622-6876. E-mail: wgriffin@cleaningconsultants.com. Web site: www.cleaningconsultants.com. **Contact:** William R. Griffin, publisher. "We publish books on cleaning, maintenance and self-employment. Examples are related to janitorial, housekeeping, maid services, window washing, carpet cleaning and pressure washing, etc. We also publish a quarterly magazine for self-employed cleaners. For information and a free sample, visit www.cleaningbusiness.com." Photos used for text illustrations, promotional materials, book covers and all uses related to production and marketing of books.

Needs Buys 20-50 freelance photos/year; offers 5-15 freelance assignments/year. Needs photos of people doing cleaning work. "We are always looking for unique cleaning-related photos." Reviews stock (cleaning-related photos only). Model release preferred. Photo captions preferred.

Specs Uses 4×6, 5×7, 8×10 glossy color prints.

Making Contact & Terms Send query with résumé of credits, samples, list of stock photo subjects, or send unsolicited photos for consideration via e-mail. Provide résumé, business card, brochure, flier or tearsheets to be kept on file for possible future assignments. Responds in 3-4 weeks if interested. Simultaneous submissions and previously published work OK if not used in competitive publications. Pays $5-50/b&w photo; $5/color photo; $10-30/hour; $40-250/job; negotiable depending on specific project. Credit lines generally given. Buys all rights; depends on need and project.

Tips "We are especially interested in color photos of people doing cleaning work in USA and other countries for use on the covers of our publications. Be willing to work at reasonable rates. Selling 2 or 3 photos does not qualify you to earn top-of-the-line rates. We expect to use more photos, but they must be specific to our market, which is quite select. Don't send stock sample sheets that do not relate to our target audience. Send photos that fit our specific interest only. E-mail if you need more information or would like specific guidance."

$ $▣ CONARI PRESS

Red Wheel/Weiser/Conari, 500 Third St., Suite 230, San Francisco, CA 94107. E-mail: info@redwheelweiser.com. Web site: www.redwheelweiser.com. **Contact:** Art Director. Estab. 1987. Publishes hardcover and trade paperback originals and reprints. Subjects include women's studies, psychology, parenting, inspiration, home and relationships (all nonfiction titles). Photos used for text illustrations, book covers, dust jackets.

Needs Buys 5-10 freelance photos/year. Looking for artful photos; subject matter varies. Interested in reviewing stock photos of most anything except high-tech, corporate or industrial images. Model release required. Photo captions preferred; include photography copyright.

Specs Prefers images in digital format.

Making Contact & Terms Provide résumé, business card, self-promotion piece or tearsheets to be kept on file for possible future assignments. Art director will contact photographer for portfolio review if interested. Portfolio should include prints, tearsheets, slides, transparencies or thumbnails. Keeps samples on file. Simultaneous submissions and previously published work OK. Pays by the project: $400-1,000 for color cover; rates vary for color inside. Pays on publication. Credit line given on copyright page or back cover.

Tips "Review our Web site to make sure your work is appropriate."

$▣ CRABTREE PUBLISHING COMPANY

PMB 16A, 350 Fifth Ave., Suite 3308, New York NY 10118. (800)387-7650. Fax: (800)355-7166. Web site: www.crabtreebooks.com. **Contact:** Crystal Foxton and Allison Napier, photo researchers. Estab. 1978. Publishes juvenile nonfiction, library and trade. Subjects include natural science, history, geography (including cultural geography), 18th- and 19th-century North America, sports. Photos used for text illustrations, book covers. Examples of recently published titles: *Insect Homes*; *Changing Weather: Storms*; *Extreme Mountain Biking*; *Inventing the Camera*; *Sir Walter Raleigh: Founding the Virginia Colony*; *Black Holes*.

Needs Buys 400-600 photos/year. Wants photos of cultural events around the world, animals (exotic and domestic) and historical reenactments. Model/property release required for children, photos of artwork, etc. Photo captions preferred; include place, name of subject, date photographed, animal behavior.

Specs Uses color prints; 35mm, 4×5, 8×10 transparencies; high-resolution digital files (no JPEG compressed files).

Making Contact & Terms Does NOT accept unsolicited photos. Provide résumé, business card, brochure, flier or tearsheets to be kept on file for possible future assignments. Simultaneous submissions and previously published work OK. Pays $75-100 for color photos. Pays on publication. Credit line given. Buys non-exclusive rights.

Tips "Since our books are for younger readers, lively photos of children and animals are always excellent." Portfolio should be "diverse and encompass several subjects rather than just 1 or 2; depth of coverage of subject should be intense so that any publishing company could, conceivably, use all or many of a photographer's photos in a book on a particular subject."

$◻ ▣ THE CREATIVE COMPANY

Imprint: Creative Editions. 123 S. Broad St., Mankato MN 56001. (507)388-2024. Fax: (507)388-1364. E-mail: tkleist@thecreativecompany.us. Web site: www.thecreativecompany.us. **Contact:** Tricia Kleist, photo researcher. Estab. 1933. Publishes hardcover originals, textbooks for children. Subjects include animals, nature, geography, history, sports (professional and college), science, technology, biographies. Photos used for text illustrations, book covers. Examples of recently published titles: Let's Investigate Wildlife series (text illustrations, book cover); Ovations (biography) series (text illustrations, book cover). Catalog available for 9×12 SAE with $2 first-class postage. Photo guidelines free with SASE.

Needs Buys 2,000 stock photos/year. Needs photos of celebrities, disasters, environmental, landscapes/scenics, wildlife, architecture, cities/urban, gardening, pets, rural, adventure, automobiles, entertainment, health/fitness, hobbies, sports, travel, agriculture, industry, medicine, military, science, technology/computers. Other specific photo needs: NFL, NHL, NBA, Major League Baseball. Photo captions required; include photographer's or agent's name.

Specs Accepts images in digital format for Mac only. Send via CD as JPEG files.

Making Contact & Terms Send query letter with photocopies, tearsheets, stock list. Provide self-promotion piece to be kept on file for possible future assignments. Responds in 1 month to queries. Simultaneous submissions and previously published work OK. Pays $100-150 for cover; $50-150 for inside. Projects with photos and text are considered as well. Pays on publication. Credit line given. Buys one-time rights and foreign publication rights as requested.

Tips "Inquiries must include nonreturnable samples. After establishing policies and terms, we keep photographers on file and contact as needed. All photographers who agree to our policies can be included on our e-mail list for specific, hard-to-find image needs. We rarely use black-and-white or photos of people unless the text requires it. Project proposals must be for a 4-, 6-, or 8-book series for children."

$□ ▣ CREATIVE EDITIONS

The Creative Company, 123 S. Broad St., Mankato MN 56001. (507)388-2024. Fax: (507)388-1364. E-mail: tkleist@thecreativecompany.us. Web site: www.thecreativecompany.us. **Contact:** Tricia Kleist, photo researcher. Estab. 1989. Publishes hardcover originals. Subjects include photo essays, biography, poetry, stories designed for children. Photos used for text illustrations, book covers, dust jackets. Examples of recently published titles: *Little Red Riding Hood* (text illustrations, book cover, dust jacket); *Poe* (text illustrations, book cover, dust jacket). Catalog available.

Needs Looking for photo-illustrated documentaries or gift books. Must include some text. Publishes 5-10 books/year.

Specs Uses any size glossy or matte color and/or b&w prints. Accepts images in digital format for Mac only. Send via CD as JPEG files at 72 dpi minimum (high-res upon request only).

Making Contact & Terms Send query letter with publication credits and project proposal, prints, photocopies, tearsheets of previous publications, stock list for proposed project. Responds in 1 month to queries. Simultaneous submissions and previously published work OK. Advance to be negotiated. Credit line given. Buys world rights for the book; photos remain property of photographer.

Tips "Creative Editions publishes unique books for the book-lover. Emphasis is on aesthetics and quality. Completed manuscripts are more likely to be accepted than preliminary proposals. Please do not send slides or other valuable materials."

ℕ $ $□ ▣ CREATIVE HOMEOWNER

24 Park Way, Upper Saddle River NJ 07458. (201)934-7100, ext. 375. Fax: (201)934-7541. E-mail: rpoplasky@creativehomeowner.com. Web site: www.creativehomeowner.com. **Contact:** Robyn Poplasky, photo researcher. Estab. 1975. Publishes soft cover originals, mass market paperback originals. Photos used for text illustrations, promotional materials, book covers. Examples of recently published titles: *Design Ideas for Curb Appeal*; *The Smart Approach to the Organized Home*; *1,001 Ideas for Architectural Trimwork*. Catalog available. Photo guidelines available via fax.

Needs Buys 1,000 freelance photos/year. Needs photos of architecture, interiors/decorating, some gardening. Other needs include interior and exterior design photography; garden beauty shots. Photo captions required; include photographer credit, designer credit, location, small description, if possible.

Specs Accepts images in digital format. Send via CD as TIFF files at 300 dpi. Transparencies are preferred.

Making Contact & Terms Send query letter with résumé, photocopies, tearsheets, transparencies, stock list. Provide résumé, business card, self-promotion piece to be kept on file for possible future assignments. Responds in 2 weeks to queries. Simultaneous submissions and previously published work OK. Pays $800 for color cover; $100-150 for color inside; $200 for back cover. Pays on publication. Credit line given. Buys one-time rights.

Tips "Be able to pull submissions for fast delivery. Label and document all transparencies for easy in-office tracking and return."

CREATIVE WITH WORDS PUBLICATIONS (CWW)

P.O. Box 223226, Carmel CA 93922. Fax: (831)655-8627. E-mail: geltrich@mbay.net. Web site: http://members.tripod.com/CreativeWithWords. **Contact:** Brigitta Geltrich, editor. Estab. 1975. Publishes poetry and prose anthologies according to set themes. Black & white photos used for text illustrations, book covers. Photo guidelines free with SASE.

Needs Looking for theme-related b&w photos. Model/property release preferred.

Specs Uses any size b&w photos. "We will reduce to fit the page."

Making Contact & Terms Request theme list, then query with photos. Does not keep samples on file; include SASE for return of material. Responds 3 weeks after deadline if submitted for a specific theme. Payment negotiable. Pays on publication. Credit line given. Buys one-time rights.

N $ $⊘ S ▣ ⊡ ECW PRESS

2120 Queen St. E., Suite 200, Toronto ON M4E 1E2 Canada. (416)694-3348. E-mail: info@ecwpress.com. Web site: www.ecwpress.com. **Contact:** Jack David, publisher. Estab. 1974. Publishes hardcover and trade paperback originals. Subjects include entertainment, biography, sports, travel, fiction, poetry. Photos used for text illustrations, book covers, dust jackets. Examples of recently published titles: *Living the Dream: The Unofficial Story of Hannah Montana and Miley Cyrus* (text illustrations); *Finding LOST* (text illustrations).

Needs Buys hundreds of freelance photos/year. Looking for color, b&w, fan/backstage, paparazzi, action, original, rarely used. Reviews stock photos. Property release required for entertainment or star shots. Photo captions required; include identification of all people.

Specs Accepts images in digital format. Send via CD as TIFF files at 300 dpi.

Making Contact & Terms Send query letter. Provide e-mail. To show portfolio, photographer should follow up with letter after initial query. Does not keep samples on file; include SASE for return of material. Responds in 3 weeks. Pays by the project: $250-600 for color cover; $50-125 for color inside. Pays on publication. Credit line given. Buys one-time book rights (all markets).

Tips "We have many projects on the go. Query for projects needing illustrations. Please check our website before querying."

$ $⊡ FIFTH HOUSE PUBLISHERS

1511-1800 Fourth St. SW, Calgary AB T2S 2S5 Canada. (403)571-5230. Fax: (403)571-5235. E-mail: meaghan@fifthhousepublishers.ca. Web site: www.fifthhousepublishers.ca. **Con-**

tact: Meaghan Craven, managing editor. Estab. 1982. Publishes calendars, history, biography, western Canadiana. Photos used for text illustrations, book covers, dust jackets and calendars. Examples of recently published titles: *The Canadian Weather Trivia Calendar*; *Wild Alberta*; *A World Within*.

Needs Buys 15-20 photos/year. Looking for photos of Canadian weather. Model/property release preferred. Photo captions required; include location and identification.

Making Contact & Terms Send query letter with samples and stock list. Keeps samples on file. Pays $400 Canadian/calendar image. Pays on publication. Credit line given. Buys one-time rights.

ℕ $☐ FORUM PUBLISHING CO.

Imprint: Retailers Forum. 383 E. Main St., Centerport NY 11721. (631)754-5000. Fax: (631)754-0630. E-mail: forumpublishing@aol.com. Web site: www.forum123.com. **Contact:** Marti, art director. Estab. 1981. Publishes trade magazines and directories.

Needs Buys 24 freelance photos/year. Needs photos of humor, business concepts, industry, product shots/still life. Interested in seasonal. Other photo needs include humorous and creative use of products and merchandise. Model/property release preferred.

Specs Uses any size color prints; 4×5, 8×10 transparencies.

Making Contact & Terms Send query letter with prints. Does not keep samples on file; include SASE for return of material. Responds in 2 weeks to queries. Simultaneous submissions and previously published work OK. Works with local freelancers only. Pays $50-100 for color cover. **Pays on acceptance.** Credit line sometimes given. Buys one-time rights.

Tips "We publish trade magazines and directories and are looking for creative pictures of products/merchandise. Call Marti for complete details."

ℕ $▣ ✷ GUERNICA EDITIONS, INC.

P.O. Box 117, Station P, Toronto ON M5S 2S6 Canada. Fax: (416)657-8885. Web site: www.guernicaeditions.com. **Contact:** Antonio D'Alfonso, editor. Estab. 1978. Publishes adult trade (literary). Photos used for book covers. Examples of recently published titles: *Barry Callagan: Essays on His Work*, edited by Priscila Uppal; *Mary Di Michele: Essays on Her Works*, edited by Joseph Pivato; *Maria Mazziotti: Essays on Her Works*, edited by Sean Thomas Doughtery; *Mary Melfi*: *Essays on Her Works*, edited by William Anselmi.

Needs Buys varying number of photos/year; "often" assigns work. Needs life events, including characters; houses. Photo captions required.

Specs Uses color and/or b&w prints. Accepts images in digital format. Send via CD, Zip as TIFF, GIF files at 300 dpi minimum.

Making Contact & Terms Send query letter with samples. Sometimes keeps samples on file. Cannot return material. Responds in 2 weeks. Pays $150 for cover. Pays on publication. Credit line given. Buys book rights. "Photo rights go to photographers. All we need is the right to reproduce the work."

Tips "Look at what we do. Send some samples. If we like them, we'll write back."

☐ ▣ HERALD PRESS

616 Walnut Ave., Scottdale PA 15683. (724)887-8500. Fax: (724)887-3111. E-mail: merrill@mpn.net. Web site: www.mph.org. **Contact:** Design Director. Estab. 1908. Photos used for book covers, dust jackets. Examples of published titles: *Lord, Teach Us to Pray; Starting Over; Amish Cooking* (all cover shots).

Needs Buys 5 photos/year; offers occasional freelance assignments. Subject matter varies. Reviews stock photos of people and other subjects including religious, environmental. Model/property release required. Photo captions preferred; include identification information.

Specs Prefers images in digital format. Submit URL or link to Web pages or light box.

Making Contact & Terms Send query letter or e-mail with samples. Provide résumé, business card, brochure, flier or tearsheets to be kept on file for possible future assignments. Keeps samples on file. Works on assignment only or selects from file of samples. Responds in 1 month. Simultaneous submissions and previously published work OK. Payment negotiable. **Pays on acceptance.** Credit line given. Buys book rights; negotiable.

Tips "We put your résumé and samples on file. It is best to direct us to your Web site."

$ $ 🗹 🖻 HOLT, RINEHART AND WINSTON

10801 N. Mopac Expressway, Bldg. 3, Austin TX 78759-5415. (512)721-7000. Fax: (800)269-5232. E-mail: HoltInfo@hrw.com. Web site: www.hrw.com. **Contact:** Curtis Riker, director of image acquisitions. Photo Research Manager: Jeannie Taylor. Publishes textbooks in multiple formats. "The Photo Research Department of the HRW School Division in Austin obtains photographs for textbooks in subject areas taught in secondary schools." Photos are used for text illustrations, promotional materials and book covers.

Needs Uses 6,500+ photos/year. Wants photos that illustrate content for mathematics, sciences, social studies, world languages, and language arts. Model/property release preferred. Photo captions required; include scientific explanation, location and/or other detailed information.

Specs Prefers images in digital format. Send via CD or broadband transmission.

Making Contact & Terms Send a query letter with a sample of work (nonreturnable photocopies, tearsheets, printed promos) and a list of subjects in stock. Self-promotion pieces kept on file for future reference. Include promotional Web site link if available. "Do not call!" Will respond only if interested. Payment negotiable depending on format and number of uses. Credit line given.

Tips "Our book image programs yield an emphasis on rights-managed stock imagery, with a focus on teens and a balanced ethnic mix. Though we commission assignment photography, we maintain an in-house studio with 2 full-time photographers. We are interested in natural-looking, uncluttered photographs labeled with exact descriptions, that are technically correct and include no evidence of liqor, drugs, cigarettes or brand names."

🗹 🖻 HYPERION BOOKS FOR CHILDREN

114 Fifth Ave., New York NY 10011. (212)633-4400. Fax: (212)807-5880. Web site: www.hyperionchildrensbooks.com. **Contact:** Susan Masry, design coordinator. Publishes children's books, including picture books and books for young readers. Subjects include adventure, animals, history, multicultural, sports. Catalog available for 9 × 12 SAE with 3 first-class stamps.

Needs Needs photos of multicultural subjects.

Making Contact & Terms Provide résumé, business card, self-promotion piece to be kept on file for possible future assignments. Pays royalties based on retail price of book, or a flat fee.

$ $ ⊘ Ⓐ ▣ INNER TRADITIONS/BEAR & COMPANY

1 Park St., Rochester VT 05767. (802)767-3174. Fax: (802)767-3726. E-mail: peris@innertra ditions.com. Web site: www.innertraditions.com. **Contact:** Peri Ann Swan, art director. Estab. 1975. Publishes adult trade and teen self-help. Subjects include New Age, health, self-help, esoteric philosophy. Photos used for text illustrations, book covers. Examples of recently published titles: *Tibetan Sacred Dance* (cover, interior); *Tutankhamun Prophecies* (cover); *Animal Voices* (cover, interior).

Needs Buys 10-50 photos/year; offers 5-10 freelance assignments/year. Needs photos of babies/children/teens, multicultural, families, parents, religious, alternative medicine, environmental, landscapes/scenics. Interested in fine art, historical/vintage. Reviews stock photos. Model/property release required. Photo captions preferred.

Specs Uses 35mm, 4×5 transparencies. Accepts images in digital format. Send via CD, Zip as TIFF, EPS, JPEG files at 300 dpi.

Making Contact & Terms Provide résumé, business card, brochure, flier or tearsheets to be kept on file for possible future assignments. Works with freelancers on assignment only. Simultaneous submissions OK. Pays $150-600 for color cover; $50-200 for b&w and color inside. Pays on publication. Credit line given. Buys book rights; negotiable.

$ $ ⊘ Ⓐ ▣ JUDICATURE

2700 University Ave., Des Moines IA 50311. (773)973-0145. Fax: (773)338-9687. E-mail: drichert@ajs.org. Web site: www.ajs.org. **Contact:** David Richert, editor. Estab. 1917. Publishes legal journal, court and legal books. Photos used for text illustrations, cover of bimonthly journal.

Needs Buys 10-12 photos/year; occasionally offers freelance assignments. Looking for photos relating to courts, the law. Reviews stock photos. Model/property release preferred. Photo captions preferred.

Specs Uses 5×7 color and/or b&w prints; 35mm transparencies. Prefers images in digital format.

Making Contact & Terms Send query letter with samples. Works on assignment only. Keeps samples on file. Responds in 2 weeks. Simultaneous submissions and previously published work OK. Pays $250-350 for cover; $125-300 for color inside; $125-250 for b&w inside. **Pays on receipt of invoice.** Credit line given. Buys one-time rights.

$ $ ⊘ ▣ LERNER PUBLISHING GROUP, INC.

241 First Ave. N., Minneapolis MN 55401. (612)332-3344. Fax: (612)332-7615. E-mail: dwallek@igigraphics.com. Web site: www.lernerbooks.com. **Contact:** Dan Wallek, director of photo research. Estab. 1959. Publishes educational books for grades K-12. Subjects include animals, biography, history, geography, science, vehicles, and sports. Photos used for text illustrations, promotional materials, book covers. Examples of recently published titles: *Javelinas - Early Bird Nature Books* (text illustrations, book cover); *Bangladesh in Pictures* (text illustrations, book cover).

Needs Buys more than 6,000 photos/year; occasionally offers assignments. Needs photos of children/teens, celebrities, multicultural, families, disasters, environmental, landscapes/ scenics, wildlife, cities/urban, education, pets, rural, hobbies, sports, agriculture, industry, political, science, vehicles, technology/computers. Model/property release preferred when photos are of social issues (e.g., the homeless). Photo captions required; include who, where, what and when.

Specs Prefers images in digital format. Send via FTP, CD, or e-mail as TIFF or JPEG files at 300 dpi.

Making Contact & Terms Send query letter with detailed stock list by mail, fax or e-mail. Provide flier or tearsheets to be kept on file. "No calls, please." Cannot return material. Responds only if interested. Previously published work OK. Pays by the project: $150-400 for cover; $50-150 for inside. **Pays on receipt of invoice**. Credit line given. Licenses images for book based on print-run rights, electronic rights, Spanish-language rights, worldwide territory rights.

Tips Prefers crisp, clear images that can be used editorially. "Send in as detailed a stock list as you can (including fees for clearing additional rights), and be willing to negotiate price."

$ S □ MITCHELL LANE PUBLISHERS, INC.

P.O. Box 196, Hockessin DE 19707. (302)234-9426. Fax: (302)234-4742. E-mail: mitchelllane@mitchelllane.com. Web site: www.mitchelllane.com. **Contact:** Barbara Mitchell, publisher. Estab. 1993. Publishes hardcover originals for library market. Subjects include biography and other nonfiction for children and young adults. Photos used for text illustrations, book covers. Examples of recently published titles: *Meet Our New Student from Nigeria* (text illustrations and book cover); *A Backyard Flower Garden for Kids* (text illustrations, book cover).

Needs Photo captions required.

Specs Accepts images in digital format. Send via CD as TIFF, JPEG files at 300 dpi.

Making Contact & Terms Send query letter with stock list (stock photo agencies only). Does not keep samples on file; cannot return material. Responds only if interested. Pays on publication. Credit line given. Buys one-time rights.

$ ◑ S □ NICOLAS-HAYS, INC.

P.O. Box 540206, Lake Worth, FL 33454-0206. (451)798-1040. Fax: (451)798-1042. E-mail: info@nicolashays.com. Web site: www.nicolashays.com. **Contact:** Y. Paglia. Estab. 1976. Publishes trade paperback originals and reprints. Subjects include Eastern philosophy, Jungian psychology, New Age how-to. Photos used for book covers. Example of recently published title: *Dervish Yoga for Health and Longevity: Samadeva Gestual Euphony-The Seven Major Arkanas* (book cover). Catalog available upon request.

Needs Buys 1 freelance photo/year. Needs photos of landscapes/scenics.

Specs Uses color prints; 35mm, $2\frac{1}{4} \times 2\frac{1}{4}$, 4×5 transparencies. Accepts images in digital format.

Making Contact & Terms Send query letter with photocopies, tearsheets. Provide self-promotion piece to be kept on file for possible future assignments. Responds only if interested; send nonreturnable samples. Simultaneous submissions and previously pubished work OK. Pays $100-200 for color cover. **Pays on acceptance**. Credit line given. Buys one-time rights.

Tips "We are a small company and do not use many photos. We keep landscapes/seascapes/skyscapes on hand—images need to be inspirational."

$ □ PAULIST PRESS

997 Macarthur Blvd., Mahwah NJ 07430. (201)825-7300. Fax: (201)825-8345. E-mail: pmcmahon@paulistpress.com. Web site: www.paulistpress.com. **Contact:** Paul McMahon, man-

aging editor. Estab. 1857. Publishes hardcover and trade paperback originals, juvenile and textbooks. Types of books include religion, theology and spirituality including biography. Specializes in academic and pastoral theology. Recent titles include *He Said Yes, Finding Purpose in Narnia,* and *Our Daily Bread.* Publishes 90 titles/year; 5% requires freelance illustration; 5% require freelance design. Paulist Press also publishes the general trade imprint HIDDENSPRING.

Needs Works with 5 illustrators and 10 designers/year. Prefers local freelancers particularly for juvenile titles, jacket/cover, and text illustration. Prefers knowledge of QuarkXPress. Works on assignment only.

Making Contact & Terms Send query letter with brochure, résumé and tearsheets. Samples are filed. Portfolio review not required. Negotiates rights purchased. Originals are returned at job's completion if requested. Book design assigns 8 freelance design jobs/year. Jackets/Covers assigns 30 freelance design jobs/year. Pays by the project, $400-$800. Text Illustration assigns 5 freelance illustration jobs/year. Pays by the project.

Ⓝ $ $Ⓒ Ⓢ ▣ PELICAN PUBLISHING CO.

1000 Burmaster St., Gretna LA 70053. (504)368-1175. Fax: (504)368-1195. E-mail: tcallaway @pelicanpub.com. Web site: www.pelicanpub.com. **Contact:** Terry Callaway, production manager or Bridget McDowell, art director. Publishes adult trade, juvenile, textbooks, how-to, cooking, fiction, travel, science and art books; also religious inspirational and business motivational. Photos used for book covers. Books have a ''high-quality, conservative and detail-oriented'' look. Examples of published titles: *Brownies to Die For; Abraham Lincoln's Execution; Texas Zeke and the Longhorn.*

Needs Buys 8 photos/year; offers 3 freelance assignments/year. Needs photos of travel (international), cooking/food, business concepts, nature/inspirational. Reviews royalty-free stock photos of travel subjects, people, nature, etc. Model/property release required. Photo captions required.

Specs Uses 8×10 glossy color prints; 35mm, 4×5 transparencies. Accepts images in digital format. Send via CD as TIFF files at 300 dpi or higher.

Making Contact & Terms Send query letter with stock list. Provide résumé, business card, brochure, flier or tearsheets to be kept on file for possible future assignments. Responds as needed. Pays $100-500 for color photos; negotiable with option for books as payment. **Pays on acceptance.** Credit line given. Buys one-time and book rights; negotiable.

$◯ ▣ PHOTOGRAPHER'S MARKET

4700 E. Galbraith Rd., Cincinnati OH 45236. (513)531-2690, ext. 11546. Fax: (513)531-2686. E-mail: photomarket@fwpubs.com. **Contact:** Alice Pope, editor. Photo guidelines free with SASE or via e-mail.

Needs Publishes 30-35 photos/year. Uses general subject matter. Photos must be work sold to markets listed in *Photographer's Market.* Photos are used to illustrate the various types of images being sold to photo buyers listed in *Photographer's Market.* Look through this book for examples.

Specs Prefers images in digital format. Send via e-mail or CD as TIFF or JPEG files, 5×7 at 300 dpi; saved as grayscale, not RGB. Uses color and b&w (b&w preferred) prints, any size and format (5×7 or 8×10 preferred). Also uses tearsheets and transparencies, all sizes, color and b&w.

Making Contact & Terms ''Submit photos in fall and winter to ensure sufficient time to review them before our early-summer deadline. Be sure to include SASE for return of material. All photos are judged according to subject uniqueness as well as technical quality and composition. Photos are held and reviewed at close of deadline." Simultaneous submissions OK. *Work must be previously published.* Pays $75 plus complimentary copy of *Photographer's Market*. Pays when book goes to printer (September). Book forwarded in November upon arrival from printer. Credit line given. Buys second reprint rights.

Tips "Send photos with brief cover letter describing the background of the sale. If sending more than one photo, make sure that photos are clearly identified. Slides should be enclosed in plastic slide sleeves, and prints should be reinforced with cardboard. Cannot return material if SASE is not included. Tearsheets will be considered disposable unless SASE is provided and return is requested. Because photos are printed in black & white on newsprint stock, some photos (especially color shots) may not reproduce well. Photos should have strong contrast and not too much fine detail that might be lost when printed. Being able to communicate via e-mail (not just snail mail and phone) is a plus."

PRAKKEN PUBLICATIONS, INC.

832 Phoenix Dr., P.O. Box 8623, Ann Arbor MI 48107. (734)975-2800. Fax: (734)975-2787. Web site: http://techdirections.com or http://eddigest.com. **Contact**: Sharon K. Miller, art/design/production manager. Estab. 1934. Publishes *The Education Digest* (magazine), *Tech Directions* (magazine for technology and career/technical educators), text and reference books for technology and career/technical education. Photos used for text illustrations, promotional materials, book covers, magazine covers and posters. Photo guidelines available at Web site.

Needs Wants photos of education "in action," especially technology and career/technical education; prominent historical figures, technology/computers, industry. Photo captions required; include scene location, activity.

Specs Uses all media; any size. Accepts images in digital format. Send via CD, Jaz, Zip as TIFF, EPS, JPEG files at 300 dpi.

Making Contact & Terms Send query letter with samples. Send unsolicited photos by mail for consideration. Keeps samples on file. Payment negotiable. Methods of payment to be arranged. Credit line given. Rights negotiable.

Tips Wants to see "high-quality action shots in tech/career tech-ed classrooms" when reviewing portfolios. Send inquiry with relevant samples to be kept on file. "We buy very few freelance photographs but would be delighted to see something relevant."

$ $ REIMAN MEDIA GROUP, INC.

5400 S. 60th St., Greendale WI 53129. Fax: (414)423-8463. E-mail: tbellin@rd.com. Web site: www.reimanpub.com. **Contact:** Trudi Bellin, photo coordinator. Estab. 1965. Publishes consumer-cooking, people-interest, gardening, nostalgia and country themes. Examples of recently published titles: The Taste of Home Cookbook; Winning Recipes; Best of Country Salad and Sandwiches; Annual-2008 Birds & Blooms.

Needs Buys 950 photos/year. Looking for food-related images showing at-home entertaining for all seasons, family dinners, couples cooking and dining, pot lucks, table settings, food as gifts; people and backyard beauty shots. Reviews stock photos of families, senior citizens, couples (30s-60s age range), social groups, rural, rural lifestyle, scenics, birds, flowers and flower gardens. "Conservative audience means few photos published with wine, liquor or smoking elements." Model/property release required. Photo captions preferred; include season, location.

Specs Uses color transparencies, any size. Accepts images in digital format: TIFF or high-quality JPEG files at 300 dpi for up to 9×11 reproduction. Embedded metadata is recommended. Send via lightboxes or on removable media. Send CD/DVD with printed thumbnails and caption sheet. E-mail if first review selection is small (12 images or less).

Making Contact & Terms Send query letter with résumé of credits and stock list. Send unsolicited photos by mail for consideration. Keeps samples on file ("tearsheets, no duplicates"); include SASE for return of material. Responds in 3 months for first review. Simultaneous submissions and previously published work OK. Pays $300 for color cover; $100-300 for color inside. Pays on publication. Credit line given. Buys one-time rights (reprint and Web rights reserved).

Tips "Study our publications first. Keep our target audience in mind. Send well-composed and well-framed photos that are sharp and colorful. All images received on spec."

$○ ▣ SENTIENT PUBLICATIONS, LLC

1113 Spruce St., Boulder CO 80302. (303)443-2188. Fax: (303)381-2538. E-mail: cshaw@sentientpublications.com. Web site: www.sentientpublications.com. **Contact:** Connie Shaw, editor. Estab. 2001. Publishes trade paperback originals and reprints. Subjects include education, ecology, spirituality, travel, publishing, self-help, health, parenting. Photos used for book covers. Examples of recently published titles: *Mysteries of the Life Force, Roadsigns.* Catalog free with #10 SASE.

Needs Buys 8 freelance photos/year. Needs photos of babies/children/teens, landscape/scenics, religious. Interested in avant garde.

Specs Accepts images in digital format. Send via e-mail as TIFF files at 300 dpi.

Making Contact & Terms Send query letter with résumé, prints, photocopies, stock list. Provide self-promotion piece to be kept on file for possible future assignments. Responds only if interested; send nonreturnable samples. Simultaneous submissions and previously published work OK. Pays $100 maximum for color cover. Pays on publication. Credit line given. Buys one-time rights.

Tips "Look at our Web site for the kind of cover art we need."

▣ ⬑ VISITOR'S CHOICE MAGAZINE

102 E. Fourth St., Vancouver BC V5T 1G2 Canada. (604)608-5180. Fax: (604)608-5181. E-mail: editor@visitorschoice.com. Web site: www.visitorschoice.com. **Contact:** Shelley Ackerman, art director. Estab. 1977. Publishes full-color visitor guides for 16 communities and areas of British Columbia. Photos used for text illustrations, book covers, Web sites. Photo guidelines available via e-mail upon request.

Needs Looking for photos of attractions, mountains, lakes, views, lifestyle, architecture, festivals, people, sports and recreation—specific to British Columbia region. Specifically looking for people/activity shots. Model release required; property release preferred. Photo captions required—"detailed but brief."

Specs Uses color prints; 35mm transparencies. Prefers images in digital format.

Making Contact & Terms Send query letter or e-mail with samples; include SASE for return of material. Works with Canadian photographers. Keeps digital images on file. Responds in 3 weeks. Previously published work OK. Payment varies with size of photo published. Pays in 30-60 days. Credit line given.

Tips "Please submit photos that are relevant to our needs only. Photos should be specific, clear, artistic, colorful, with good lighting."

$⬜ ⬛ WAVELAND PRESS, INC.

4180 IL Rt. 83, Suite 101, Long Grove IL 60047-9580. (847)634-0081. Fax: (847)634-9501. E-mail: info@waveland.com. Web site: www.waveland.com. **Contact:** Jan Weissman, photo editor. Estab. 1975. Publishes college textbooks. Photos used for text illustrations, book covers. Examples of recently published titles: *Our Global Environment: A Health Perspective, 6th Edition*; *Juvenile Justice, 2nd Edition*.

Needs Number of photos purchased varies depending on type of project and subject matter. Subject matter should relate to college disciplines: criminal justice, anthropology, speech/communication, sociology, archaeology, etc. Needs photos of multicultural, disasters, environmental, cities/urban, education, religious, rural, health/fitness, agriculture, political, technology. Interested in fine art, historical/vintage. Model/property release required. Photo captions preferred.

Specs Accepts images in digital format. Send via CD, Zip, e-mail as TIFF, EPS, JPEG files at 300 dpi.

Making Contact & Terms Send query letter with stock list. Provide résumé, business card, brochure, flier or tearsheets to be kept on file for possible future assignments. Simultaneous submissions and previously published work OK. Pays $100-200 for cover; $50-100 for inside. Pays on publication. Credit line given. Buys one-time and book rights.

Tips "Mail stock list and price list."

$⬜ ⬛ WILSHIRE BOOK COMPANY

9731 Variel Ave., Chatsworth CA 91311-4315. (818)700-1522. Fax: (818)700-1527. E-mail: mpowers@mpowers.com. Web site: www.mpowers.com. **Contact**: Melvin Powers, president. Estab. 1947. Publishes trade paperback originals and reprints. Photos used for book covers.

Needs Needs photos of horses. Model release required.

Specs Uses 35mm, $2\frac{1}{4} \times 2\frac{1}{4}$, 4×5 transparencies. Accepts images in digital format. Send via floppy disk, e-mail.

Making Contact & Terms Send query letter with slides, prints, transparencies. Portfolio may be dropped off Monday through Friday. Does not keep samples on file; include SASE for return of material. Responds in 6 weeks. Simultaneous submissions and previously published work OK. Pays $200 for color cover. **Pays on acceptance**. Credit line given.

Greeting Cards, Posters

& Related Products

The greeting card industry takes in close to $7.5 billion per year—80 percent through the giants American Greetings and Hallmark Cards. Naturally, these big companies are difficult to break into, but there is plenty of opportunity to license your images to smaller companies.

There are more than 2,000 greeting card companies in the United States, many of which produce low-priced cards that fill a niche in the market, focusing on anything from the cute to the risqué to seasonal topics. A number of listings in this section produce items like calendars, mugs and posters, as well as greeting cards.

Before approaching greeting card, poster or calendar companies, it's important to research the industry to see what's being bought and sold. Start by checking out card, gift and specialty stores that carry greeting cards and posters. Pay attention to the selections of calendars, especially the large seasonal displays during December. Studying what you see on store shelves will give you an idea of what types of photos are marketable.

Greetings etc., published by Edgell Publications, is a trade publication for marketers, publishers, designers and retailers of greeting cards. The magazine offers industry news and information on trends, new products, and trade shows. Look for the magazine at your library; call (973)895-3300, ext. 234 to subscribe, or visit their Web site: www.edgellcommunications.com/Greetings/. Also, the National Stationery Show (www.nationalstationeryshow.com) is a large trade show held every year in New York City. It is the main event of the greeting card industry.

APPROACHING THE MARKET

After your initial research, query companies you are interested in working with and send a stock photo list. (See sample stock list on page 19.) You can help narrow your search by consulting the Subject Index on page 504. Check the index for companies interested in the subjects you shoot.

Since these companies receive large volumes of submissions, they often appreciate knowing what is available rather than actually receiving samples. This kind of query can lead to future sales even if your stock inventory doesn't meet their immediate needs. Buyers know they can request additional submissions as their needs change. Some listings in this section advise sending quality samples along with your query while others specifically request only a list. As you plan your queries, follow the instructions to establish a good rapport with companies from the start.

Some larger companies have staff photographers for routine assignments but also look for freelance images. Usually, this is in the form of stock, and images are especially desirable if they are of unusual subject matter or remote scenic areas for which assignments—even to staff shooters—would be too costly. Freelancers are usually offered assignments once they have established track records and demonstrated a flair for certain techniques, subject matter or locations. Smaller companies are more receptive to working with freelancers, though they are less likely to assign work because of smaller budgets for photography.

The pay in this market can be quite lucrative if you provide the right image at the right time for a client in need of it, or if you develop a working relationship with one or a few of the better-paying markets. You should be aware, though, that one reason for higher rates of payment in this market is that these companies may want to buy all rights to images. But with changes in the copyright law, many companies are more willing to negotiate sales that specify all rights for limited time periods or exclusive product rights rather than complete surrender of copyright. Some companies pay royalties, which means you will earn the money over a period of time based on the sales of the product.

▣ ☒ ART IN MOTION

2000 Brigantine Dr., Coquitlam BC V3K 7B5 Canada. (604)525-3900 or (800)663-1308. Fax: (604)525-6166 or (877)525-6166. E-mail: artistrelations@artinmotion.com. Web site: www.artinmotion.com. **Contact:** Artist Relations. Specializes in open edition reproductions, framing prints, wall decor and licensing.

Needs "We are publishers of fine art reproductions, specializing in the decorative and gallery market. In photography, we often look for alternative techniques such as hand coloring, polaroid transfer, or any process that gives the photograph a unique look."

Specs Accepts unzipped digital images sent via e-mail as JPEG files at 72 dpi.

Making Contact & Terms Submit portfolio for review. Pays royalties of 10%. Royalties paid monthly. "Art In Motion covers all associated costs to reproduce and promote your artwork."

Tips "Contact us via e-mail, or direct us to your Web site; also send slides or color copies of your work (all submissions will be returned)."

▨ ▣ ARTVISIONS™: FINE ART LICENSING

12117 SE 26th St., Bellevue WA 98005-4118. Web site: www.artvisions.com. Estab. 1993. Licenses "fashionable, decorative fine art photography and high-quality art to the commercial print, décor and puzzle/game markets."

Needs Handles fine art and photography licensing only. *"We're not currently seeking new talent. However, we are always willing to view the work of top-notch established artists."*

Making Contact & Terms "See Web site. Not currently seeking new talent. However, we are always willing to view the work of top-notch established artists and photographers. If you fit this category, please contact ArtVisions via e-mail and include a link to a Web site where your art can be seen. Or, you may include a few small samples attached to your e-mail as JPEG files." Exclusive worldwide representation for licensing is required. Written contract provided.

Tips "To gain an idea of the type of art we license, please view our Web site. Animals, children, people and pretty places should be generic, rather than readily identifiable (this also prevents potential copyright issues and problems caused by not having personal releases for use of a 'likeness'). We prefer that your original work be in the form of high-resolution TIFF files from a 'pro-quality' digital camera, or scans from a $2\frac{1}{4}$ square, 4×5, or larger format. Note: scans/digital files are not to be interpolated or compressed in any way. We are firmly entrenched in the digital world; if you are not, then we cannot represent you. If you need advice about marketing your art, please visit: www.artistsconsult.com.''

$ $⊘ ▣ AVANTI PRESS INC.

6 W. 18 St., 6th Floor, New York NY 10011. (212)414-1025. E-mail: artsubmissions@avanti press.com. Web site: www.avantipress.com. **Contact:** Art Submissions. Estab. 1980. Specializes in photographic greeting cards. Photo guidelines free with SASE or on Web site.

Needs Buys approximately 200 images/year; all are supplied by freelancers. Interested in humorous, narrative, colorful, simple, to-the-point photos of babies, children (4 years old and younger), mature adults, animals (in humorous situations) and exceptional florals. Has specific deadlines for seasonal material. Does NOT want travel, sunsets, landscapes, nudes, high-tech. Reviews stock photos. Model/property release required.

Specs Will work with all mediums and formats. Accepts images in digital format. Send via CD as TIFF, JPEG files.

Making Contact & Terms Request guidelines for submission with SASE or visit Web site. DO NOT submit original material. Pays on license. Credit line given. Buys 5-year worldwide, exclusive card rights.

Ⓝ ⊘ ▣ BENTLEY PUBLISHING GROUP

1410 Lesnick Lane, Walnut Creek CA 94597. (925)935-3186. Fax: (925)935-0213. E-mail: info@bentleypublishinggroup.com. Web site: www.bentleypublishinggroup.com. **Contact:** Cynthia Morales, product development coordinator. Estab. 1986. Publishes posters.

Needs Interested in figurative, architecture, cities, urban, gardening, interiors/decorating, rural, food/drink, travel—b&w, color or handtinted photography. Interested in alternative process, avant garde, fine art, historical/vintage. Reviews stock photos and slides. Model/property release required. Include location, date, subject matter or special information.

Specs Mainly uses 16×20, 22×28, 18×24, 24×30, 24×36 color and/or b&w prints; 4×5 transparencies from high-quality photos. Accepts images in digital format. Send via CD as TIFF or JPEG files.

Making Contact & Terms Submit photos or slides for review; include SASE for return of material. ''Do not call.'' Responds in 6 weeks. Simultaneous submissions and previously published work OK. Pays royalties quarterly based upon sales, 10%.

Ⓝ $⊘ Ⓢ ▣ BLUE SKY PUBLISHING

Spectrum Press, P.O. Box 19974, Boulder CO 80308-2974. (303)530-4654. E-mail: BSPinfo@ blueskypublishing.net. Web site: www.blueskypublishing.net. Estab. 1989. Specializes in fine art and photographic greeting cards.

Needs Buys 12-24 images/year; all are supplied by freelancers. Interested in Rocky Mountain winter landscapes, dramatic winter scenes featuring wildlife in mountain settings, winter scenes from the Southwest, unique and creative Christmas still life images, and scenes that express the warmth and romance of the holidays. Submit seasonal material December-April. Reviews stock photos. Model/property release preferred.

Specs Uses 35mm, 4×5 (preferred) transparencies. Accepts images in digital format.

Making Contact & Terms Submit 24-48 of your best images for review. Provide résumé, business card, self-promotion piece or tearsheets to be kept on file for possible future assignments. ''We try to respond within 1 month, but it could take 2 months.'' Simultaneous submissions and previously published work OK. Pays $150 advance against royalties of

Greeting Cards

3%. **Pays on acceptance**. Buys exclusive product rights for 5 years; negotiable.

Tips "Due to the volume of calls we receive from photographers, we ask that you refrain from calling regarding the status of your submission. We will contact you within 2 months to request more samples of your work if we are interested. We do not return unsolicited samples."

⬤ ▣ THE BOREALIS PRESS

P.O. Box 230, Surry ME 04684. (207)667-3700 or (800)669-6845. Fax: (207)667-9649. E-mail: info@borealispress.net. Web site: www.borealispress.net. **Contact:** Mark Baldwin. Estab. 1989. Specializes in greeting cards, magnets and "other products for thoughtful people." Photo guidelines available for SASE.

Needs Buys more than 100 images/year; 90% are supplied by freelancers. Needs photos of humor, babies/children/teens, couples, families, parents, senior citizens, adventure, events, hobbies, pets/animals. Interested in documentary, historical/vintage, seasonal. Photos must tell a story. Model/property release preferred.

Specs Uses 5×7 to 8×10 prints; 35mm, 2¼×2¼, 4×5, 8×10 transparencies. Accepts images in digital format. Send via CD. Send low-resolution files if e-mailing. Send images to art@borealispress.net.

Making Contact & Terms Send query letter with slides (if necessary), prints, photocopies, SASE. Send no originals on initital submissions. "Artist's name must be on every image submitted." Responds in 2 weeks to queries; 3 weeks to portfolios. Previously published work OK. Pays by the project, royalties. **Pays on acceptance**, receipt of contract.

Tips "Photos should have some sort of story, in the loosest sense. They can be in any form. We do not want multiple submissions to other card companies. Include SASE, and put your name on every image you submit."

$⬤ Ⓢ ▣ BRISTOL GIFT CO., INC.

P.O. Box 425, Washingtonville NY 10992. (845)496-2821. Fax: (845)496-2859. E-mail: bristo l6@frontiernet.net. Web site: http://bristolgift.net. **Contact:** Matthew Ropiecki, president. Estab. 1988. Specializes in gifts.

Needs Interested in religious, nature, still life. Submit seasonal material 6 months in advance. Reviews stock photos. Model/property release preferred.

Specs Uses 4×5, 8×10 color prints; 4×5 transparencies. Accepts images in digital format. Send via CD, floppy disk, Zip, e-mail as TIFF, JPEG files.

Making Contact & Terms Send query letter with samples. Keeps samples on file. Responds in 1 month. Previously published work OK. Pays $50-200/image. Buys exclusive product rights.

$◯ ▣ CENTRIC CORPORATION

6712 Melrose Ave., Los Angeles CA 90038. (323)936-2100. Fax: (323)936-2101. E-mail: centric@juno.com. Web site: www.centriccorp.com. **Contact:** Sammy Okdot, president. Estab. 1986. Specializes in products that have nostalgic, humorous, thought-provoking images or sayings on them and in the following product catergories: T-shirts, watches, pens, clocks, pillows, and drinkware.

Needs Photos of cities' major landmarks, attractions and things for which areas are well-known, and humorous or thought-provoking images. Submit seasonal material 5 months in advance. Reviews stock photos.

Specs Uses 8×12 color and/or b&w prints; 35mm transparencies. Accepts images in digital format. Send via CD as JPEG files.

Making Contact & Terms Submit portfolio for review or query with résumé of credits. Provide résumé, business card, self-promotion piece or tearsheets to be kept on file for possible future assignments. Responds in 2 weeks. Works mainly with local freelancers. Pays by the job; negotiable. **Pays on acceptance.** Rights negotiable.

$☐ COMSTOCK CARDS

600 S. Rock Blvd., Suite 15, Reno NV 89502. (775)856-9400. Fax: (775)856-9406. E-mail: info@comstockcards.com. Web site: www.comstockcards.com. **Contact:** Production Assistant. Estab. 1986. Specializes in greeting cards, invitations, notepads, games, gift wrap. Photo guidelines free with SASE.

Needs Buys/assigns 30-40 images/year; all are supplied by freelancers. Wants wild, outrageous and shocking adult humor; seductive images of men or women. Definitely does not want to see traditional, sweet, cute, animals or scenics. ''If it's appropriate to show your mother, we don't want it!'' Frontal nudity in both men and women is OK and now being accepted as long as it is professionally done—no snapshot from home. Submit seasonal material 10 months in advance. Model/property release required. Photo captions preferred.

Specs Uses 5×7 color prints; 35mm, 2¼×2¼ color transparencies. Accepts images in digital format.

Making Contact & Terms Send query letter with samples, tearsheets, SASE. Responds in 2 months. Pays $50-150 for color photos. Pays on publication. Buys all rights; negotiable.

Tips ''Submit with SASE if you want material returned.''

☐ DESIGN DESIGN, INC.

P.O. Box 2266, Grand Rapids MI 49501. (616)771-8359. Fax: (616)774-4020. E-mail: susan.b irnbaum@designdesign.us. Web site: www.designdesign.us. **Contact:** Susan Birnbaum, creative director. Estab. 1986. Specializes in greeting cards and paper-related product development.

Needs Licenses stock images from freelancers and assigns work. Specializes in humorous topics. Submit seasonal material 1 year in advance. Model/property release required.

Specs Uses 35mm transparencies. Accepts images in digital format. Send via Zip.

Making Contact & Terms Submit portfolio for review. Provide résumé, business card, self-promotion piece or tearsheets to be kept on file for possible future assignments. Do not send original work. Pays royalties. Pays upon sales. Credit line given.

⊙ Ⓐ GRAPHIC ARTS CENTER PUBLISHING COMPANY

P.O. Box 10306, Portland OR 97296-0306. (503)226-2402, ext. 306. Fax: (503)223-1410. E-mail: editorial@gacpc.com. Web site: www.gacpc.com. **Contact:** Jean Bond-Slaughter, editor. ''We are an independent book packager/producer.''

Needs Photos of environment, regional, landscapes/scenics. ''We only publish regionally focused books and calendars.'' Photo captions required.

Specs Contact the editorial department at the phone number above to receive permission to send in a submission. Upon acceptance, send bio, samples, 20-40 transparencies that are numbered, labeled with descriptions and verified in a delivery memo, return postage or a filled-out FedEx form. Responds in up to 4 months. Uses transparencies of any format, 35mm, 2¼×2¼, 4×5, but must be tack sharp and possess high reproductive quality; or

Greeting Cards

submit equivalent digital files. "Our books/calendars usually represent one photographer. We use only full-time, professional photographers and/or well-established photographic businesses. New calendar/book proposals must have large market appeal and/or have corporate sale possibilities as well as fit our company's present focus."

⊘ Ⓢ ▣ IMPACT PHOTOGRAPHICS

4961 Windplay Dr., El Dorado Hills CA 95762. (916)939-9333. Fax: (916)939-9334. Web site: www.impactphotographics.com. Estab. 1975. Specializes in calendars, postcards, magnets, bookmarks, mugs, CD-ROMs, posters, books for the tourist industry. Photo guidelines and fee schedule free with SASE.

• This company sells to specific tourist destinations; their products are not sold nationally. They need material that will be sold for at least a 5-year period.

Needs Buys stock. Buys 3,000 photos/year. Needs photos of wildlife, scenics, US travel destinations, national parks, theme parks and animals. Submit seasonal material 4-5 months in advance. Model/property release required. Photo captions preferred.

Specs Uses 35mm, $2^1/_4 \times 2^1/_4$, 4×5, 8×10 transparencies. Accepts images in digital format. Send via CD, Zip as TIFF, JPEG files at 300 dpi.

Making Contact & Terms "Must have submissions request before submitting samples. No unsolicited submissions." Send query letter with stock list. Provide business card, self-promotion piece or tearsheets to be kept on file for possible future assignments. Responds in 1 month. Simultaneous submissions and previously published work OK. Request fee schedule; rates vary by size. Pays on usage. Credit line and printed samples of work given. Buys one-time and nonexclusive product rights.

Ⓝ $ $▣ INTERCONTINENTAL GREETINGS, LTD

38 West 32nd St., Ste. 910, New York NY 10016. (212)683-5830. Fax: (212)779-8564. E-mail: intertg@intercontinental-ltd.com. Web site: www.intercontinental-ltd.com. **Contact:** Jerra Parfitt. Estab. 1967. Sells reproduction rights of designs to manufacturers of multiple products around the world. Represents artists in 50 different countries. "Our clients specialize in greeting cards, giftware, giftwrap, calendars, postcards, prints, posters, stationery, paper goods, food tins, playing cards, tabletop, bath and service ware and much more."

Needs Approached by several hundred artists/year. Seeking creative decorative art in traditional and computer media (Photoshop and Illustrator work accepted). Prefers artwork previously made with few or no rights pending. Graphics, sports, occasions (i.e., Christmas, baby, birthday, wedding), humorous, "soft touch," romantic themes, animals. Accepts seasonal/holiday material any time. Prefers artists/designers experienced in greeting cards, paper products, tabletop and giftware.

Specs Uses slides; 4×5, 8×10 transparencies. Accepts images in digital format.

Making Contact & Terms Query with samples. Send unsolicited CDs or DVDs by mail. "Please do not send original artwork." Upon request, submit portfolio for review. Provide résumé, business card, brochure, flyer, tear sheets or slides to be kept on file for possible future assignments. "Once your art is accepted, we require original color art-Photoshop files on disc (Mac, TIFF, 300 dpi); 4×5, 8×10 transparencies; 35mm slides. We will respond only if interested (will send back non-accepted artwork in SASE if provided)." Pays on publication. No credit line given. Offers advance when appropriate. Sells one-time rights and exclusive product rights. Simultaneous submissions and previously published work OK. "Please state reserved rights, if any."

Tips Recommends the annual New York SURTEX and Licensing shows. In photographer's portfolio samples, wants to see "a neat presentation, perhaps thematic in arrangement. We don't buy much photography, but it pays to be persistent. Just keep sending samples until something catches my eye."

⬛ ▣ NEW YORK GRAPHIC SOCIETY PUBLISHING GROUP

129 Glover Ave., Norwalk CT 06850-1311. (203)847-2000. Fax: (203)846-4869. E-mail: donna@nygs.com. Web site: www.nygs.com. **Contact:** Donna LeVan, vice president of publishing (contact via e-mail only, no phone calls). Estab. 1925. Specializes in fine art reproductions, prints, posters, canvases.

Needs Buys 150 images/year; 125 are supplied by freelancers. "Looking for variety of images."

Specs Prefers digital format. Send low-res JPGs via e-mail; no zip files.

Making Contact & Terms Send query letter with samples to Attn: Artist Submissions. Does not keep samples on file; include SASE for return of material. Responds in 3 months. Payment negotiable. Pays on usage. Credit line given. Buys exclusive product rights. No phone calls.

Tips "Visit website to review artist submission guidelines and to see appropriate types of imagery for publication."

$⬛ ▣ NOVA MEDIA INC.

1724 N. State St., Big Rapids MI 49307-9073. (231)796-4637. E-mail: trund@netonecom.net. Web site: www.novamediainc.com. **Contact:** Thomas J. Rundquist, president. Estab. 1981. Specializes in CD-ROMs, CDs/tapes, games, limited edition plates, posters, school supplies, T-shirts. Photo guidelines free with SASE.

Needs Buys 100 images/year; most are supplied by freelancers. Offers 20 assignments/year. Seeking art fantasy photos. Needs photos of children/teens, celebrities, multicultural, families, landscapes/scenics, education, religious, rural, entertainment, health/fitness/beauty, military, political, technology/computers. Interested in documentary, erotic, fashion/glamour, fine art, historical/vintage. Submit seasonal material 2 months in advance. Reviews stock photos. Model release required. Photo captions preferred.

Specs Uses color and/or b&w prints. Accepts images in digital format. Send via CD.

Making Contact & Terms Send query letter with samples. Accepts e-mail submissions. Responds in 1 month. Keeps samples on file; does not return material. Simultaneous submissions and previously published work OK. Payment negotiable. Pays extra for electronic usage of photos. Pays on usage. Credit line given. Buys electronic rights; negotiable.

Tips "The most effective way to contact us is by e-mail or regular mail. Visit our website."

▣ PALM PRESS, INC.

1442A Walnut St., Berkeley CA 94709. (510)486-0502. Fax: (510)486-1158. E-mail: theresa@palmpressinc.com. Web site: www.palmpressinc.com. **Contact:** Theresa McCormick, assistant art director. Estab. 1980. Specializes in greeting cards. Photo guidelines available on Web site.

Needs Buys only photographic images from freelancers. Buys 200 images/year. Wants photos of humor, nostalgia; unusual, interesting, original b&w or color images for all occasions including Christmas and Valentine's Day. Submit seasonal material 1 year in advance. Model/property release required.

Specs Accepts digital format. Submit no more than 50 photos. Send via e-mail as small files. If mailing prints or slides, include SASE for work to be returned. Pays royalties on sales. Credit line given.

Making Contact & Terms "SASE must be included for work to be returned." Responds in 3-4 weeks. Pays royalties on sales. Credit line given.

✍ 🖥 PAPER PRODUCTS DESIGN

60 Galli Dr., Novato CA 94949. (415)883-1888. Fax: (415)883-1999. E-mail: carol@paperproductsdesign.com. Web site: www.paperproductsdesign.com. **Contact:** Carol Florsheim. Estab. 1992. Specializes in napkins, plates, candles, porcelain.

Needs Buys 500 images/year; all are supplied by freelancers. Needs photos of babies/children/teens, architecture, gardening, pets, food/drink, humor, travel. Interested in avant garde, fashion/glamour, fine art, historical/vintage, seasonal. Submit seasonal material 6 months in advance. Model release required. Photo captions preferred.

Specs Uses glossy color and/or b&w prints; 35mm, $2\frac{1}{4} \times 2\frac{1}{4}$, 4×5, 8×10 transparencies. Accepts images in digital format. Send via Zip, e-mail at 350 dpi.

Making Contact & Terms Send query letter with photocopies, tearsheets. Responds in 1 month to queries, only if interested. Simultaneous submissions and previously published work OK.

✍ Ⓢ 🖥 PORTFOLIO GRAPHICS, INC.

P.O. Box 17437, Salt Lake City UT 84117. (801)424-2574. E-mail: info@portfoliographics.com. Web site: www.nygs.com. **Contact:** Kent Barton, creative director. Estab. 1986. Publishes and distributes open edition fine art prints and posters.

Needs Buys 100 images/year; nearly all are supplied by freelancers. Seeking creative, fashionable, and decorative art for commercial and designer markets. Clients include galleries, designers, poster distributors (worldwide) and framers. For posters, "keep in mind that we need decorative art that can be framed and hung in home or office." Submit seasonal material on an ongoing basis. Reviews stock photos. Photo captions preferred.

Specs Uses prints, transparencies, digital files.

Making Contact & Terms Send photos, transparencies, tearsheets or gallery booklets with SASE. Does not keep samples on file; must include SASE for return of material. Art director will contact photographer for portfolio review if interested. Responds in 3 months. Pays royalties of 10% on sales. Semi-annual royalties paid per pieces sold. Credit line given. Buys exclusive product rights license per piece.

Tips "We find artists through galleries, magazines, art exhibits and submissions. We are looking for a variety of artists, styles and subjects that are fresh and unique."

$ $✍ 🖥 ↕ POSTERS INTERNATIONAL

1180 Caledonia Rd., Toronto ON M6A 2W5 Canada. (416)789-7156. Fax: (416)789-7159. E-mail: dow@pifineart.com. Web site: www.postersinternational.net. **Contact:** Dow Marcus, art director. Estab. 1976. Specializes in posters/prints. Photo guidelines available.

Needs Needs photos of landscapes/scenics, floral, architecture, cities/urban, European, hobbies. Interested in alternative process, avant garde, fine art, historical/vintage. Interesting effects, Polaroids, painterly or hand-tinted submissions welcome. Submit seasonal material 2 months in advance. Model/property release preferred. Photo captions preferred; include date, title, artist, location.

Specs Accepts images in digital format. Send via CD, Zip, e-mail as low res JPEG files for review. Images of interest will be requested in min 300 dpi TIFF files.

Making Contact & Terms Send query letter with résumé, slides, prints, photocopies, tear-sheets, transparencies, stock list. Provide business card, self-promotion piece to be kept on file for possible future assignments. Responds in 2 weeks to queries; 5 weeks to portfolios. Simultaneous submissions OK. Pays royalties of 10% minimum. Buys worldwide rights for approximately 4-5 years to publish in poster form.

Tips "Keep all materials in contained unit. Provide easy access to contact information. Provide any information on previously published images. Submit a number of pieces. Develop a theme (we publish in series of 2, 4, 6, etc.). Black & white performs very well. Vintage is also a key genre; sepia great, too. Catalog is published with supplement 2 times/year. We show our images in our ads, supporting materials and website."

$ $⊘ Ⓢ ▣ REIMAN MEDIA GROUP, INC.

5400 S. 60th St., Greendale WI 53129. Fax: (414)423-8463. E-mail: tbellin@rd.com. Web site: www.reimanpub.com. **Contact:** Trudi Bellin, photo coordinator. Estab. 1965. Specializes in calendars; also publishes books, cards and posters. Photo guidelines free with SASE.

- Also publishes magazines, several of which are listed in the Consumer Publications section of this book.

Needs Buys more than 350 images/year; all are supplied by freelancers. Interested in humorous cow and pig photos as well as scenic North American country images including barns, churches, cabins, and lighthouses. Needs photos of landscapes/scenics, gardening, rural, travel, agriculture. Also needs backyard and flower gardens; wild birds, song birds, and hummingbirds; North American scenics by season; various cute baby animals plus kittens and puppies. All calendars reflect the seasons, even those that highlight animals. Interested in seasonal. Unsolicited calendar work must arrive September 1-15. All submissions must be limited to 40 images or less per calendar theme. No smoking, drinking, nudity. Reviews stock photos. Model/property release required. Photo captions required; include season, location; birds and flowers must include common and/or scientific names.

Specs Uses color transparencies, all sizes. Accepts images in digital format. Prefers you set up lightboxes for review, but accepts files on removable media, include files via CD or DVD with printed thumbnails and caption sheets. Embedded metadata is recommended. "Comp high-res files must be available." Published at 300 dpi for up to 11×13 reproduction.

Making Contact & Terms Send query letter with résumé of credits, stock list. Tearsheets are kept on file but not dupes. Responds in 3 months for first review. Simultaneous submissions and previously published work OK. Pays $25-400/image. Pays on publication. Credit line given. Buys one-time rights.

Tips "Most contributors have been published in our magazines first. Horizontal format is preferred for calendars. The subject of the calendar theme must be central to the photo composition. All projects look for technical quality. Focus has to be sharp (no soft focus), and colors must be vivid so they 'pop off the page.' "

▣ ⊕ SANTORO GRAPHICS LTD.

Rotunda Point, 11 Hartfield Crescent, Wimbledon, London SW19 3RL United Kingdom. (44)(208)781-1100. Fax: (44)(208)781-1101. E-mail: fbostock@santorographics.com. Web site: www.santorographics.com. **Contact:** Kathryn Clague, art director's assistant. Specializes in greeting cards, stationery, gift wrap, party supplies, school supplies.

Greeting Cards

Needs Wants "humorous, cute, retro, nostalgic and unusual pictures of animals, people and situations." Also interested in fine art imagery. "Do not submit seasonal material; we do not print it."

Specs Accepts images in digital format sent via CD or e-mail; glossy prints; 35mm transparencies.

Making Contact & Terms Send query letter/e-mail with CV, slides/prints/photocopies/digital files. Include SASE for return of material. **Pays on receipt of invoice.** Credit line not given. Rights and fees determined by negotiation.

Ⓝ $Ⓢ ▣ SUGARDADDYPHOTOS

Hanklooks Publications, P.O. box 86776, Los Angeles CA 90012. Estab. 2000. (626)627-5127. E-mail: iphotographu@charter.net. Web site: www.sugardaddyphotos.com. **Contact:** Henry Salazar, editor-in-chief. Stock agency and picture library. Clients include: advertising agencies, businesses, newspapers, postcard publishers, public relations firms, book publishers, calendar companies, audiovisual firms, magazine publishers, greeting card companies.

Needs Wants photos of babies/children/teens, celebrities, couples, multicultural, families, parents, senior citizens, architecture, cities/urban, education, gardening, interiors/decorating, pets, religious, rural, agriculture, business concepts, industry, medicine, military, political, product shots/still life, science, technology/computers, disasters, environmental, landscapes/scenics, wildlife, adventure, automobiles, entertainment, events, food/drink, health/fitness/beauty, hobbies, humor, performing arts, sports, travel, exotic locations. Interested in alternative process, avant garde, documentary, erotic, fashion/glamour, fine art, historical/vintage, lifestyle, seasonal.

Specs Uses 35 mm, $2\frac{1}{4} \times 2\frac{1}{4}$, 4×5, 8×10 transparencies. Accepts images in digital format. Send TIFF or JPEG files at 300 dpi via CD. Buys photos, film and videotape outright; pays $5-500 for b&w photos; pays $10-1,000 for color photos; pays $20-2,000 for film; pays $30-3,000 for videotape. Pay 40-50% commission. Average price per image (to clients): $1-150 for photos and videotape. Enforces strict minimum prices. "We have set prices; however, they are subject to change without notice." Photographers can choose not to sell images on discount terms. Works with photographers with or without a contract; negotiable. Offers nonexclusive contract. Statements issued quarterly. Payments made quarterly. Offers one-time rights. Informs photographers and allows them to negotiate when a client requests all rights. Model/property release required. Photo captions required; include location, city, state, country, full description, related keywords, date image was taken.

Making Contact E-mail query letter with JPEG samples at 72 dpi. Send query letter with résumé, slides, prints, tearsheets, transparencies. Provide résumé, business card, self-promotion piece to be kept on file. Expects minimum inital submission of 50 images with submissions of at least 50 images every 2 months.

Tips "Please e-mail before sending samples. We're interested in receiving submissions from new photographers. Arrange your work in categories to view. Clients expect the very best in professional-quality material."

$▢ Ⓢ ▨ TELDON

Teldon Marketing Inc., Unit 100 - 12751 Vulcan Way, Richmond BC V6V 3C8 Canada. E-mail: photo@teldon.com. Web site: www.teldonmarketing.com. **Contact:** Photo Editor. Estab. 1968. Publishes high-quality dated and nondated promotional products, including wall calendars, desk calendars, magnets, newsletters, postcards, etc. Photo guidelines free with SAE (legal size)—waiting list applies.

Needs Buys over 1,000 images/year; 70% are supplied by freelancers. Needs photos of lifestyles (babies/children/teens, couples, multicultural, families, parents, senior citizens, wildlife (North American), architecture (exterior residential homes), gardening, interiors/decorating, adventure, sports, travel (world), motivational, inspirational, landscape/scenic. Reviews stock photos. Model/property release required for trademarked buildings, residential houses, people. Photo captions required; include complete detailed description of destination, i.e., Robson Square, Vancouver, British Columbia, Canada (month picture taken also helpful).

Specs Uses 35mm, medium- and large-format (horizontal only) transparencies. "We make duplicates of what we think is possible material and return the originals within a given time frame. Originals are recalled once final selection has been made. We do not accept digital submissions at this time."

Making Contact & Terms Send query letter or e-mail. "No submissions accepted unless photo guidelines have been received and reviewed." Include SAE and IRCs for return of material. Responds in 1 month, depending on workload. Simultaneous submissions and previously published work OK. Works with freelancers and stock agencies. Pays $150 for one-time use, non-negotiable. Pays in September of publication year. Credit line and complementary calendar copies given. Photos used for one-time use in dated products, North American rights, unlimited print runs.

Tips Send horizontal transparencies only; dramatic and colorful nature/scenic/wildlife shots. City shots should be no older than 1 year. "Examine our catalog on our website carefully, and you will see what we are looking for."

$ $⊘ Ⓢ ▣ TIDE-MARK PRESS

P.O. Box 20, Windsor CT 06095. (860)683-4499, ext. 108. Fax: (860)683-4055. E-mail: scott@tide-mark.com. Web site: www.tidemarkpress.com. **Contact:** Scott Kaeser, acquisitions editor. Estab. 1979. Specializes in calendars. Photo guidelines available on website or free with SASE.

Needs Buys 1,000 images/year; 800 are supplied by freelancers. Categories: landscapes/scenics, wildlife, architecture, gardening, interiors/decorating, pets, religious, adventure, automobiles, entertainment, events, food/drink, health/fitness, hobbies, humor, performing arts, sports, travel. Interested in fine art, historical/vintage; Native American; African American. Needs "complete calendar concepts that are unique but also have identifiable markets; groups of photos that could work as an entire calendar; ideas and approach must be visually appealing and innovative but also have a definable audience. No general nature or varied subjects without a single theme." Submit seasonal material 18 months in advance. Reviews stock photos. Model release preferred. Photo captions required.

Specs Uses 35mm transparencies. Accepts los-res images in EPS or JPEG format for initial review; send high-res only on selection.

Making Contact & Terms "Offer specific topic suggestions that reflect specific strengths of your stock." Send query letter with sample images; include SASE for return of material. Editor will contact photographer for portfolio review if interested. Responds in 3 months. Pays $150-350/color image for photos; royalties on net sales if entire calendar supplied. Pays on publication or per agreement. Credit line given. Buys one-time rights.

Tips "We tend to be a niche publisher and rely on niche photographers to supply our needs.

Ask for a copy of our guidelines and a copy of our catalog so that you will be familiar with our products. Then send a query letter of specific concepts for a calendar.''

$ $☑ 🖻 THE ZOLAN COMPANY, LLC

70 Blackman Rd., Ridgefield CT 06877. (203)431-1629. Fax: (203)431-2629. E-mail: donaldz 798@aol.com. Web site: www.zolan.com. **Contact:** Jennifer Zolan, president/art director. Commercial and fine art business. Photos used for artist reference in oil paintings.

Needs Buys 16-24 images/year; assignments vary with need. Looking for candid, heartwarming and endearing photos of children (ages 1-3) with high emotional appeal, capturing the magical moments of early childhood.'' Interested in Christmas/Holiday photos. We are looking for kids in the following scenes: Hispanic kids in endearing scenes, ethnic children for inspirational themes, boys in country scenes with farm tractors, boys on the farm, girls working on the farm, girls at the beach, boys playing sports, children with dogs and puppies. Reviews stock photos. Model release preferred.

Specs Uses any size color and/or b&w prints. Prefers images in digital format. Send via e-mail, CD, Zip as TIFF, EPS, PICT, GIF, JPEG files at 72 dpi.

Making Contact & Terms Request photo guidelines by e-mail. Does not keep samples on file; include SASE for return of material. Responds in 2 months to queries. Pays $300-1,000 ''depending on the extent of photo shoot and if backgrounds are part of the assignment shoot.'' **Pays on acceptance**.

Tips ''Photos should have high emotional appeal and tell a story. Photos should look candid and natural. Call or write for free photo guidelines before submitting your work. We are happy to work with amateur and professional photographers. We are always looking for human interest types of photographs on early childhood, ages 1-3. Photos should evoke pleasant and happy memories of early childhood. Photographers should write, e-mail for guidelines before submitting their work. No submissions without receiving the guidelines.''

Stock Photo Agencies

I f you are unfamiliar with how stock agencies work, the concept is easy to understand. Stock agencies house large files of images from contracted photographers and market the photos to potential clients. In exchange for licensing the images, agencies typically extract a 50-percent commission from each use. The photographer receives the other 50 percent.

In recent years, the stock industry has witnessed enormous growth, with agencies popping up worldwide. Many of these agencies, large and small, are listed in this section. However, as more and more agencies compete for sales, there has been a trend toward partnerships among some small to mid-size agencies. Other agencies have been acquired by larger agencies and essentially turned into subsidiaries. Often these subsidiaries are strategically located to cover different portions of the world. Typically, smaller agencies are bought if they have images that fill a need for the parent company. For example, a small agency might specialize in animal photographs and be purchased by a larger agency that needs those images but doesn't want to search for individual wildlife photographers.

The stock industry is extremely competitive, and if you intend to sell stock through an agency, you must know how they work. Below is a checklist that can help you land a contract with an agency.

- Build a solid base of quality images before contacting any agency. If you send an agency 50-100 images, they are going to want more if they're interested. You must have enough quality images in your files to withstand the initial review and get a contract.
- Be prepared to supply new images on a regular basis. Most contracts stipulate that photographers must send additional submissions periodically—perhaps quarterly, monthly or annually. Unless you are committed to shooting regularly, or unless you have amassed a gigantic collection of images, don't pursue a stock agency.
- Make sure all of your work is properly cataloged and identified with a file number. Start this process early so that you're prepared when agencies ask for this information. They'll need to know what is contained in each photograph so that the images can be properly keyworded on Web sites.
- Research those agencies that might be interested in your work. Smaller agencies tend to be more receptive to newcomers because they need to build their image files. When larger agencies seek new photographers, they usually want to see specific subjects in which photographers specialize. If you specialize in a certain subject area, be sure to check out our Subject Index on page 504, which lists companies according to the types of images they need.
- Conduct reference checks on any agencies you plan to approach to make sure they conduct business in a professional manner. Talk to current clients and other contracted

photographers to see if they are happy with the agency. Also, some stock agencies are run by photographers who market their own work through their own agencies. If you are interested in working with such an agency, be certain that your work will be given fair marketing treatment.

- Once you've selected a stock agency, contact them via e-mail or whatever means they have stipulated in their listing or on their Web site. Today, almost all stock agencies have Web sites and want images submitted in digital format. If the agency accepts slides, write a brief cover letter explaining that you are searching for an agency and that you would like to send some images for review. Wait to hear back from the agency before you send samples. Then send only duplicates for review so that important work won't get lost or damaged. Always include a SASE when sending samples by regular mail. It is best to send images in digital format; some agencies will only accept digital submissions.
- Finally, don't expect sales to roll in the minute a contract is signed. It usually takes a few years before initial sales are made.

SIGNING AN AGREEMENT

There are several points to consider when reviewing stock agency contracts. First, it's common practice among many agencies to charge photographers fees, such as catalog insertion rates or image duping fees. Don't be alarmed and think the agency is trying to cheat you when you see these clauses. Besides, it might be possible to reduce or eliminate these fees through negotiation.

Another important item in most contracts deals with exclusive rights to market your images. Some agencies require exclusivity to sales of images they are marketing for you. In other words, you can't market the same images they have on file. This prevents photographers from undercutting agencies on sales. Such clauses are fair to both sides as long as you can continue marketing images that are not in the agency's files.

An agency also may restrict your rights to sign with another stock agency. Usually such clauses are designed merely to keep you from signing with a competitor. Be certain your contract allows you to work with other agencies. This may mean limiting the area of distribution for each agency. For example, one agency may get to sell your work in the United States, while the other gets Europe. Or it could mean that one agency sells only to commercial clients, while the other handles editorial work. Before you sign any agency contract, make sure you can live with the conditions, including 40/60 fee splits favoring the agency.

Finally, be certain you understand the term limitations of your contract. Some agreements renew automatically with each submission of images. Others renew automatically after a period of time unless you terminate your contract in writing. This might be a problem if you and your agency are at odds for any reason. Make sure you understand the contractual language before signing anything.

REACHING CLIENTS

One thing to keep in mind when looking for a stock agent is how they plan to market your work. A combination of marketing methods seems the best way to attract buyers, and most large stock agencies are moving in that direction by offering catalogs, CDs and Web sites.

But don't discount small, specialized agencies. Even if they don't have the marketing muscle of big companies, they do know their clients well and often offer personalized service and deep image files that can't be matched by more general agencies. If you specialize in regional or scientific imagery, you may want to consider a specialized agency.

MICROSTOCK

A relatively new force in the stock photography business is microstock. The term microstock comes from the "micro payments" that these agencies charge their clients—often as little as one dollar (the photographer gets only half of that), depending on the size of the image. Compare that to a traditional stock photo agency, where a rights-managed image could be licensed for hundreds of dollars, depending on the image and its use. Unlike the traditional stock agencies, microstock agencies are more willing to look at work from amateur photographers, and they consider their content "member generated." However, they do not accept all photos or all photographers; images must still be vetted by the microstock site before the photographer can upload his collection and begin selling. Microstock sites are looking for the lifestyle, people and business images that their traditional counterparts often seek. Unlike most traditional stock agencies, microstock sites offer no rights-managed images; all images are royalty free.

So if photographers stand to make only fifty cents from licensing an image, how are they supposed to make money from this arrangement? The idea is to sell a huge quantity of photos at these low prices. Microstock agencies have tapped into a budget-minded client that the traditional agencies have not normally attracted—the small business, nonprofit organization, and even the individual who could not afford to spend $300 for a photo for their newsletter or brochure. There is currently a debate in the photography community about the viability of microstock as a business model for stock photographers. Some say it is driving down the value of *all* photography and making it harder for all photographers to make a living selling their stock photos. While others might agree that it is driving down the value of photography, they say that microstock is here to stay and photographers should find a way to make it work for them or find other revenue streams to counteract any loss of income due to the effects of microstock. Still others feel no pinch from microstock: They feel their clients would never purchase from a microstock site and that they are secure in knowing they can offer their clients something unique.

If you want to see how a microstock site works, see the following Web sites, which are some of the more prominent microstock sites. You'll find directions on how to open an account and start uploading photos.

www.shutterstock.com (http://submit.shutterstock.com/)

www.istockphoto.com (http://www.istockphoto.com/training_manuals.php)

www.bigstockphoto.com (http://bigstockphoto.com/core.php?predupload=1)

www.fotolia.com (http://fotolia.com/Info/HowToSell)

www.dreamstime.com (http://www.dreamstime.com/sell)

DIGITAL IMAGING GUIDELINES AND SYSTEMS

The photography industry is in a state of flux as it grapples with the ongoing changes that digital imaging has brought. In an effort to identify and promote digital imaging standards, the Universal Photographic Digital Imaging Guidelines (UPDIG) were established. The objectives of UPDIG are to:

- make digital imaging practices more clear and reliable
- develop a Web resource for imaging professionals (including photo buyers, photographers and nonprofit organizations related to the photography industry)
- Demonstrate the creative and economic benefits of the guidelines to clients
- Develop industry guidelines and workflows for various types of image reproduction, including RAW file delivery, batch-converted files, color-managed master files, and CMYK with proofs.

To learn more about UPDIG, visit www.updig.org.

PLUS (Picture Licensing Universal System) is a cooperative, multi-industry initiative designed to define and categorize image usage around the world. It does not address pricing

Learn More About the Stock Industry

There are numerous resources available for photographers who want to learn about the stock industry. Here are a few of the best.

For More Info

- **PhotoSource International, (800)223-3860,** Web site: www.photosource.com. Owned by author/photographer Rohn Engh, this company produces several newsletters that can be extremely useful for stock photographers. A few of these include *PhotoStockNotes*, *PhotoDaily*, *PhotoLetter* and *PhotoBulletin*. Engh's *Sellphotos.com* (Writer's Digest Books) is a comprehensive guide to selling editorial stock photography online. Recently revised *Sell & Re-Sell Your Photos* (Writer's Digest Books) tells how to sell stock to book and magazine publishers.

- **Selling Stock, (301)251-0720,** Web site: www.pickphoto.com. This newsletter is published by one of the photo industry's leading insiders, Jim Pickerell. He gives plenty of behind-the-scenes information about agencies and is a huge advocate for stock photographers.

- ***Negotiating Stock Photo Prices*, 5th edition,** by Jim Pickerell and Cheryl Pickerell DiFrank, 110 Frederick Avenue, Suite A, Rockville MD 20850, (301)251-0720. This is the most comprehensive and authoritative book on selling stock photography.

- **The Picture Archive Council of America, (800)457-7222,** Web site: www.pacaoffice.org. Anyone researching an American agency should check to see if the agency is a member of this organization. PACA members are required to practice certain standards of professionalism in order to maintain membership.

- **British Association of Picture Libraries and Agencies, (44)(171)713-1780,** Web site: www.bapla.org.uk. This is PACA's counterpart in the United Kingdom and is a quick way to examine the track record of many foreign agencies.

- ***Photo District News,*** Web site: www.pdn-pix.com. This monthly trade magazine for the photography industry frequently features articles on the latest trends in stock photography, and publishes an annual stock photography issue.

- ***Stock Artists Alliance,*** Web site: www.stockartistsalliance.org. This trade organization focuses on protecting the rights of independent stock photographers.

or negotiations, but deals solely with defining licensing language and managing license data so that photographers and those who license photography can work with the same systems and use the same language when licensing images. To learn more about PLUS, visit www.useplus.com.

MARKETING YOUR OWN STOCK

If you find the terms of traditional agencies unacceptable, there are alternatives available. Many photographers are turning to the Internet as a way to sell their stock images without an agent and are doing very well. Your other option is to join with other photographers sharing space on the Web. Check out PhotoSource International at www.photosource.com and www.agpix.com.

If you want to market your own stock, it is not absolutely necessary that you have your own Web site, but it will help tremendously. Photo buyers often "google" the keyword they're searching for—that is, they use an Internet search engine, keying in the keyword plus "photo." Many photo buyers, from advertising firms to magazines, at one time or another, either have found the big stock agencies too unwieldy to deal with, or they simply did not have exactly what the photo buyer was looking for. Googling can lead a photo buyer straight to your site; be sure you have adequate contact information on your Web site so the photo buyer can contact you and possibly negotiate the use of your photos.

One of the best ways to get into stock is to sell outtakes from assignments. The use of stock images in advertising, design and editorial work has risen in the last five years. As the quality of stock images continues to improve, even more creatives will embrace stock as an inexpensive and effective means of incorporating art into their designs. Retaining the rights to your assignment work will provide income even when you are no longer able to work as a photographer.

▣ ▣ A+E

9 Hochgernstr., Stein D-83371 Germany. Phone: (+49)8621-61833. Fax: (+49)8621-63875. E-mail: apluse@aol.com. Web site: www.apluse.de. **Contact:** Elisabeth Pauli, director. Estab. 1987. Picture library. Has 30,000 photos in files. Clients include newspapers, postcard publishers, book publishers, calendar companies, magazine publishers.

Needs Wants photos of nature/landscapes/scenics, pets, "only your best material."

Specs Uses 35mm, 6×6 transparencies. Accepts images in digital format. Send via CD as JPEG files at 100 dpi for referencing purposes only.

Payment & Terms Pays 50% commission. Average price per image (to clients): $15-100 for b&w photos; $75-1,000 for color photos. Offers volume discounts to customers. Works with photographers on contract basis only. Offers nonexclusive contract. Subject exclusivity may be negotiated. Statements issued annually. Payment made annually. Photographers allowed to review account records in cases of discrepancies only. Offers one-time rights. Model/property release required. Photo captions preferred; include country, date, name of person, town, landmark, etc.

Making Contact Send query letter with your qualification, description of your equipment, transparencies or CD, stock list. Include SASE for return of material in Europe. Cannot return material outside Europe. Expects minimum initial submission of 100 images with annual submissions of at least 100 images. Responds in 1 month.

Tips "Judge your work critically. Technically perfect photos only—sharp focus, high colors, creative views—will attract a photo editor's attention."

▣ ACCENT ALASKA/KEN GRAHAM AGENCY

P.O. Box 272, Girdwood AK 99587. (907)783-2796. Fax: (907)783-3247. E-mail: info@accentalaska.com. Web site: www.accentalaska.com. **Contact:** Ken Graham, owner. Estab. 1979. Stock agency. Has 18,000 photos online. Clients include: advertising agencies, public relations firms, audiovisual firms, businesses, book publishers, magazine publishers, newspapers, calendar companies, greeting card companies, postcard publishers, CD-ROM encyclopedias.

Needs Wants modern stock images of Alaska, Antarctica, Hawaii and Pacific Northwest." lease do not submit material which we already have in our files."

Specs Uses images from digital cameras 8 megapixels or greater; no longer accepting film but will review and select then you return us scanned images with metadata embedded. Send via CD, Zip, e-mail lightbox URL.

Payment & Terms Pays 50% commission. Negotiates fees at industry-standard prices. Works with photographers on contract basis only. Offers nonexclusive contract. Payment made quarterly. "We are a rights managed agency."

Making Contact "See our Web site contact page. Any material must include SASE for returns." Expects minimum initial submission of 60 images. Prefers online Web gallery for initial review.

Tips "Realize we specialize in Alaska and the Northwest although we do accept images from Hawaii, Pacific, Antarctica and Europe. The bulk of our sales are Alaska-related. We are always interested in seeing submissions of sharp, colorful, and professional-quality images with model-released people when applicable. Do not want to see same material repeated in our library."

ACE STOCK LIMITED

Satellite House, 2 Salisbury Rd., Wimbledon, London SW19 4EZ United Kingdom. (44)(208)944-9944. Fax: (44)(208)944-9940. E-mail: info@acestock.com. Web site: www.a cestock.com. **Contact:** John Panton, director. Estab. 1980. Stock photo agency. Has approximately 500,000 photos in files; over 65,000 online. Clients include: ad agencies, audiovisual firms, businesses, book/encyclopedia publishers, magazine publishers, postcard companies, calendar companies, greeting card companies, design companies, direct mail companies.

Needs Photos of babies/children/teens, couples, multicultural, families, parents, senior citizens, environmental, landscapes/scenics, wildlife, pets, adventure, automobiles, food/drink, health/fitness, hobbies, humor, sports, travel, business concepts, industry, medicine, product shots/still life, science, technology/computers. Interested in alternative process, avant garde, documentary, fashion/glamour, seasonal.

Specs "Under duress will accept 35mm, 6×6 cm, 4×5, 8×10 transparencies. Prefer digital submissions saved as RGB, JPEG, Photoshop 98 color space, Quality High. Scanning resolutions for low-res at 72 dpi and high-res at 300 dpi with 30MB minimum size. Send via CD-ROM, or e-mail low-res samples."

Payment & Terms Pays 50% commission on net receipts. Average price per image (to clients): $400. Works with photographers on contract basis only. Offers limited regional exclusivity. Contracts renew automatically for 2 years with each submission. No charges for scanning. Charges $200/image for catalog insertion. Statements issued quarterly. Payment made quarterly. Photographers permitted to review sales records with 1-month written notice. Offers one-time rights, first rights or mostly nonexclusive rights. Informs photographers when client requests to buy all rights, but agency negotiates for photographer. Model/property release required for people and buildings. Photo captions required; include place, date and function. "Prefer data as IPTC-embedded within Photoshop File Info 'caption' for each scanned image."

Making Contact Send e-mail with low-res attachments or website link or FTP or send 50 sample transparencies. Alternatively, arrange a personal interview to show portfolio or post 50 sample transparencies. Responds within 1 month. Photo guidelines sheet free with SASE. Online tips sheet for contracted photographers.

Tips Prefers to see ''definitive cross-section of your collection that typifies your style and prowess. Must show originality, command of color, composition and general rules of stock photography. All people must be mid-Atlantic to sell in UK. No dupes. Scanning and image manipulation is all done in-house. We market primarily online search engines and e-mail promos. In addition, we distribute printed catalogs and CD-ROMs.''

▣ ◪ AERIAL ARCHIVES

Hangar 23, Box 470455, San Francisco CA 94147-0455. (415)771-2555. Fax: (707)769-7277. E-mail: www.aerialarchives.com/contact.htm. Web site: www.aerialarchives.com. **Contact:** Herb Lingl. Estab. 1989. Has 100,000 photos in files. Has 2,000 hours of film, video footage. Clients include: advertising agencies, public relations firms, audiovisual firms, businesses, book publishers, magazine publishers, newspapers, calendar companies.

Needs Aerial photography only.

Specs Accepts images in digital format only, *unless they are historical.* Uses $2\frac{1}{4} \times 2\frac{1}{4}$, 4×5, 9×9 transparencies; 70mm, 5″ and 9×9 (aerial film). Other media also accepted.

Payment & Terms Buys photos, film, videotape outright only in special situations where requested by submitting party. Pays on commission basis. Average price per image (to clients): $325. Enforces minimum prices. Offers volume discounts to customers. Photographers can choose not to sell images on discount terms. Works with photographers on contract basis only. Statements issued quarterly. Payment made monthly. Photographers allowed to review account records in cases of discrepancies only. Offers one-time rights, electronic media rights, agency promotion rights. Informs photographers and allows them to negotiate when client requests all rights. Property release preferred. Photo captions required; include date and location, and altitude if available.

Making Contact Send query letter with stock list. Provide résumé, business card, self-promotion piece to be kept on file. Expects minimum initial submission of 100 images with quarterly submissions of at least 50 images. Responds only if interested; send nonreturnable samples. Photo guidelines sheet available via e-mail.

Tips ''Supply complete captions with date and location; aerial photography only.''

▣ ⊕ AGE FOTOSTOCK

Buenaventura Muñoz 16, 08018 Barcelona, Spain. (34)(93)300-2552. E-mail: agency@age @agefotostock.com (New York); age@agefotostock.com (Barcelona). Web site: www.agef otostock.com. Estab. 1973. Stock agency. There is a branch office in Madrid and a subsidiary company in New York City, age fotostock america, inc. Photographers may submitt their images to Barcelona directly or through the New York office at: age fotostock america, inc., 594 Broadway, Suite 707, New York NY 10012-3257. Clients include: advertising agencies, businesses, newspapers, postcard publishers, public relations firms, book publishers, calendar companies, audiovisual firms, magazine publishers, greeting card companies.

Needs ''We are a general stock agency and are constantly uploading images onto our website. Therefore, we constantly require creative new photos from all categories.''

Specs Accepts all formats. Details available upon request, or see Web site, ''Photographers/ submitting images.''

Payment & Terms Pays 50% commission for all formats. Terms specified in photographer's contract. Works with photographers on contract basis only. Offers image exclusivity world-wide. Statements issued monthly. Payment made monthly. Photographers allowed to review account records. Model/property release required. Photo captions required.

Making Contact "Send query letter with résumé and 100 images for selection. Download the photographer's info pack from our web site."

AGSTOCKUSA INC.

25315 Arriba Del Mundo Dr., Carmel CA 93923. (831)624-8600. Fax: (831)626-3260. E-mail: edyoung@agstockusa.com. Web site: www.agstockusa.com. **Contact:** Ed Young, owner. Estab. 1996. Stock photo agency. Has 100,000 photos. Clients include: advertising agencies, graphic design firms, businesses, public relations firms, book/encyclopedia publishers, calendar companies, magazine publishers, greeting card companies.

Needs Photos should cover all aspects of agriculture worldwide: fruits, vegetables and grains in various growth stages; studio work, aerials; harvesting, processing, irrigation, insects, weeds, farm life, agricultural equipment, livestock, plant damage and plant disease.

Specs Uses 35mm, 2¼×2¼, 4×5, 6×7, 6×17 transparencies. Accepts images in digital format. Send as high-res TIFF files.

Payment & Terms Pays 50% commission for color photos. Average price per image (to clients): $ 100-25,000 for color photos. Works with photographers on contract basis only. Offers nonexclusive contract. Contracts renew automatically with additional submissions for 2 years. Charges 50% Web site insertion fee. Statements issued monthly. Payment made monthly. Photographers allowed to review account records. Offers unlimited use and buyouts if photographer agrees to sale. Informs photographer when client requests all rights; final decision made by agency. Model/property release preferred. Photo caption s required; include location of photo and all technical information (what, why, how, etc.).

Making Contact "Review our Web site to determine if work meets our standards and requirements." Submit low-res JPEGs on CD for review. Call first. Keeps samples on file; include SASE for return of material. Expects minimum initial submission of 250 images. Responds in 3 weeks. Photo guidelines available on website. Agency newsletter distributed yearly to contributors under contract.

Tips "Build up a good file (quantity and quality) of photos before approaching any agency. A portfolio of 16,000 images is currently displayed on our Web site. CD-ROM catalog with 7,600 images available to qualified photo buyers."

AKM IMAGES, INC.

109 Bushnell Place, Mooresville NC 28115. E-mail: um83@yahoo.com. Web site: www.akm images.com. **Contact:** Annie-Ying Molander. Estab. 2002. Stock agency. Has over 50,000 photos in files. Clients include: advertising agencies, book publishers, magazine publishers, newspapers, calendar companies, greeting card companies, postcard publishers.

Needs Wants photos of agriculture, cities/urban, food/wine, gardening, multicultural, religious, rural, landscapes/scenics, entertainment, bird, wildlife, macro, travel and underwater. "We also need landscape and culture from Asian countries, Nordic countries (Sweden, Norway, Finland), Alaska, Greenland, Iceland. Also need culture about Sami and Lapplander, from Nordic countries and Native American."

Specs Uses 4×6 glossy color prints; 35mm transparancies. Accepts images in digital format. Send via CD, DVD with caption. We also accept slides/negatives.

Payment/Terms Pays 50% commission for color photos. Average price per image (to clients) varies for color photos. Terms specified in photographers' contracts. Works with photographers with contract. Offers nonexclusive contract. Contracts renew automatically with additional submissions. Photographers allowed to review account records in cases of discrepancies only. Offers one-time rights. Model/property release required. Photo captions required.

Making Contact Send query letter by e-mail with images and stock list. Does not keep samples on file; include SASE for return of material. Expects minimum initial submissions of 100 images. Responds in 1 month to samples. Photo submission guidelines available free with SASE or via e-mail.

ALASKA STOCK IMAGES

2505 Fairbanks St., Anchorage AK 99503. (907)276-1343. Fax: (907)258-7848. E-mail: info @alaskastock.com. Web site: www.alaskastock.com. **Contact:** Jeff Schultz, owner. Stock photo agency. Member of the Picture Archive Council of America (PACA) and ASMP. Has 350,000 photos in files. Clients include: international and national advertising agencies; businesses; magazines and newspapers; book/encyclopedia publishers; calendar, postcard and greeting card publishers.

Needs Wants photos of everything related to Alaska, including babies/children/teens, couples, multicultural, families, parents, senior citizens involved in winter activities and outdoor recreation, wildlife, environmental, landscapes/scenics, cities/urban, pets, adventure, travel, industry. Interested in alternative process, avant garde, documentary (images which were or could have been shot in Alaska), historical/vintage, seasonal, Christmas.

Specs Uses 35mm, 2×2, 4×5, 6×17 panoramic transparencies. Accepts images in digital format. Send via CD as JPEG files at 72 dpi for review purposes. "Put together a gallery of low-res images on your Web site and send us the URL, or send via PC-formatted CD as JPEG files no larger than 9×12 at 72 dpi for review purposes." Accepted images must be 50MB minimum shot as raw originals.

Payment & Terms Pays 40% commission for color and b&w photos; minimum use fee $125. No charges for catalog, dupes, etc. Offers volume discounts to customers; inquire about specific terms. Photographers can choose not to sell images on discount terms. Works with photographers on contract basis only. Offers nonexclusive contract; exclusive contract for images in promotions. Contracts renew automatically with additional submissions; nonexclusive for 3 years. Statements issued monthly. Payment made monthly. Photographers allowed to review account records. Offers negotiable rights. Informs photographer and negotiates rights for photographer when client requests all rights. Model/property release preferred for any people and recognizable personal objects (boats, homes, etc.). Photo captions required; include who, what, when, where.

Making Contact Send query letter with samples. Does not keep samples on file; include SASE for return of material. Expects minimum initial submission of 200 images with periodic submissions of 100-200 images 1-4 times/year. Responds in 3 weeks. Photo guidelines free on request. Market tips sheet distributed 2 times/year to those with contracts. "View our guidelines online at www.alaskastock.com/prospectivephotographers.asp."

Tips "E-mailed sample images should be sent in one file, not separate images. For photographers shooting digital images, Alaska Stock assumes that you are shooting RAW format and are able to properly process the RAW image to meet our 50MB minimum standards with acceptable color, contrast and density range."

▣ ⊕ AMANA IMAGES INC.

2-2-43 Higashi Shinagawa, Shinagawa-ku, Tokyo140-0002 Japan. (81)(3)3740-4019. Fax: (81)(3)3740-4036. E-mail: planet-info@amanaimages.com. Web site: http://amanaimages. com. **Contact:** Ms. Mariko Kawashima, photographer relations. Estab. 1979. Stock photo agency. Member of the Picture Archive Council of America (PACA). Has 1,800,000 digital files and continuously growing. Clients include: advertising agencies, public relations firms, businesses, book/encyclopedia publishers, magazine publishers, newspapers, postcard publishers, calendar companies, greeting card companies, and TV stations.

Needs Wants photos of babies/children/teens, celebrities, couples, multicultural, families, parents, senior citizens, disasters, environmental, landscapes/scenics, wildlife, architecture, cities/urban, education, gardening, interiors/decorating, pets, religious, rural, adventure, automobiles, entertainment, events, food/drink, health/fitness, hobbies, humor, performing arts, sports, travel, agriculture, business concepts, medicine, military, political, industry, product shots/still life, science, technology/computers. Interested in documentary, erotic, fashion/glamour, fine art, historical/vintage, seasonal.

Specs Uses 35mm, Brownie, 4X5 transparencies. Digital format by single-lens reflex camera with more than 6 megapixel (larger than 17MB) or TIFF-RGB. Digital high-res image size: larger than 48MB for CG, 3D, etc. using editing software, e.g. Photoshop or Shade, digital change made by scanning, composed images, collage images.

Payment & Terms Based on agreement.

Making Contact Send 30-50 sample images (shorter side has to be 600 pixel as JPEG file) and your profile by e-mail. "After inspection of your images we may offer you an agreement. Submissions are accepted only after signing the agreement."

▨ AMERICAN MUSEUM OF NATURAL HISTORY LIBRARY, PHOTOGRAPHIC COLLECTION

Library Services Department, Central Park West at 79th St., New York NY 10024. (212)769-5419. Fax: (212)769-5009. E-mail: speccol@amnh.org. Web site: www.amnh.org. **Contact:** Barbara Mathe, museum archivist. Estab. 1869. Provides services for authors, film and TV producers, general public, government agencies, picture researchers, scholars, students, teachers and publishers.

Needs "We accept only donations with full rights (nonexclusive) to use; we offer visibility through credits." Model release required. Photo caption s required.

Payment & Terms Credit line given. Buys all rights.

▣ ⊕ ANDES PRESS AGENCY

26 Padbury Ct., London E2 7EH United Kingdom. (44)(0)20 7613 5417. Fax: (44)(0)20 7739 3159. E-mail: apa@andespressagency.com. Web site: www.andespressagency.com. **Contact:** Val Baker. Picture library and news/feature syndicate. Has 300,000 photos in files. Clients include: magazine publishers, businesses, book publishers, non-governmental charities, newspapers.

Needs Wants photos of multicultural, senior citizens, disasters, environmental, landscapes/scenics, architecture, cities/urban, education, religious, rural, travel, agriculture, business, industry, political. "We have color and black & white photographs on social, political and economic aspects of Latin America, Africa, Asia and Britain, specializing in contemporary world religions."

Specs Uses 35mm and digital files.

Payment & Terms Pays 50% commission for b&w and color photos. General price range (to clients): £60-300 for color photos. Works with photographers on contract basis only. Offers nonexclusive contract. Contracts renew with additional submissions. Statements issued bimonthly. Payment made bimonthly. Offers one-time rights. "We never sell all rights; photographer has to negotiate if interested." Model/property release preferred. Photo captions required.

Making Contact Send query via e-mail. Do not send unsolicited images.

Tips "We want to see that the photographer has mastered one subject in depth. Also, we have a market for photo features as well as stock photos. Please write to us first via e-mail."

▣ ANIMALS ANIMALS/EARTH SCENES

17 Railroad Ave., Chatham NY 12037. (800)392-5503 or (518)392-5500. Fax: (518)392-5550. E-mail: info@animalsanimals.com. Web site: www.animalsanimals.com. **Contact:** Nancy Carrizales. Member of Picture Archive Council of America (PACA). Has 1.5 million photos in files. Clients include: ad agencies, public relations firms, businesses, audiovisual firms, book publishers, magazine publishers, encyclopedia publishers, newspapers, postcard companies, calendar companies, greeting card companies.

Needs "We specialize in nature photography." Wants photos of disasters, environmental, landscapes/scenics, wildlife, pets, travel, agriculture.

Specs Uses 35mm, $2\frac{1}{4} \times 2\frac{1}{4}$, 4×5 transparencies. Accepts images in digital format.

Payment & Terms Pays 50% commission. Works with photographers on contract basis only. Offers exclusive contract. Charges catalog insertion fee. Photographers allowed to review account records to verify sales figures "if requested and with proper notice and cause." Statements issued quarterly. Payment made quarterly. Offers one-time rights; other uses negotiable. Informs photographers and allows them to negotiate when client requests all rights. Model release required if used for advertising. Photo captions required; include Latin names ("they must be correct!").

Making Contact Send query for guidelines by mail or e-mail. Expects minimum initial submission of 200 images with quarterly submissions of at least 200 images. Include SASE for return of material.

Tips "First, pre-edit your material. Second, know your subject."

▣ ⊕ ANT PHOTO LIBRARY

860 Derril Rd., Moorooduc, 3933 Australia. (61)(3)5978.-8877. Fax: (61)(3)5978-8144. E-mail: images@antphoto.com.au. Web site: www.antphoto.com.au. **Contact:** Peter Crawley-Boevey. Estab. 1982. Has 170,000 photos in files, with 30,000 high-res files online. Clients include: advertising agencies, public relations firms, businesses, book publishers, magazine publishers, newspapers, calendar companies, greeting card companies, postcard publishers.

Needs Wants photos of "flora and fauna of Australia, Asia and Antarctica , and the environments in which they live."

Specs "Use digital camera files supplied as a minimum of 16-bit TIFF files from a minimun of 8-megapixel SLR digital camera. Full specs on our Web site."

Payment & Terms Pays 50% commission for color photos. Offers volume discounts to customers. Discount sales terms not negotiable. Discount sales terms negotiable. Works with photographers on contract basis only. Offers limited regional exclusivity. Statements issued quarterly. Payment made quarterly. Model release required. Photo captions required;

include species, common name and scientific name on supplied Excel spreadsheet.

Making Contact Send e-mail with 10 of your best images attached (images must be relevant to our needs). Expects minimum initial submission of 200 images with regular submissions of at least 100 images. Responds in 3 weeks to samples. Photo guidelines available on website. Market tips sheet "available to all photographers we represent."

Tips "Our clients come to us for images of all common and not-so-common wildlife species from around the world particularly. Good clean shots. Good lighting and very sharp."

⊘ ▣ APPALIGHT

230 Griffith Run Rd., Spencer WV 25276. E-mail: wyro@appalight.com. Web site: www.app alight.com. **Contact:** Chuck Wyrostok, director. Estab. 1988. Stock photo agency. Has over 30,000 photos in files. Clients include advertising agencies, public relations firms, businesses, book/encyclopedia publishers, magazine publishers, calendar companies, greeting card companies, graphic designers.

- Currently not accepting submissions. This agency also markets images through the Photo Source Bank.

Needs General subject matter with emphasis on the people, natural history, culture, commerce, flora, fauna, and travel destinations of the Appalachian Mountain region and Eastern Shore of the United States. Wants photos of West Virginia, babies/children/teens, couples, multicultural, families, parents, senior citizens, disasters, environmental, landscapes, wildlife, cities/urban, education, gardening, pets, religious, rural, adventure, events, health/fitness, hobbies, humor, travel, agriculture, business concepts, industry, medicine, military, political, science, technology/computers. Interested in documentary, seasonal.

Specs Uses 8×10 glossy b&w prints; 35mm, 2¼×2¼, 4×5 transparencies and digital images.

Payment & Terms Pays 50% commission for b&w or color photos. Works with photographers on nonexclusive contract basis only. Contracts renew automatically for 2-year period with additional submissions. Payment made quarterly. Photographers allowed to review account records during regular business hours or by appointment. Offers one-time rights, electronic media rights. Model release preferred. Photo captions required.

Making Contact AppaLight is not currently accepting submissions.

Tips "We look for a solid blend of topnotch technical quality, style, content and impact. Images that portray metaphors applying to ideas, moods, business endeavors, risk-taking, teamwork and winning are especially desirable."

▣ ⊕ ARCHIVO CRIOLLO

El comercio e8-113 y Shyris Building Andre, Main Floor, Quito, Ecuador. Phone/fax: (593)(2)2469-204. E-mail: info@archivocriollo.com. Web site: www.archivocriollo.com. **Contact:** Diana Santander, administrator. Estab. 1998. Picture library. Has 20,000 photos in files. Clients include: advertising agencies, businesses, newspapers, postcard publishers, calendar companies, magazine publishers, greeting card companies, travel agencies.

Needs Wants photos of multicultural, environmental, landscapes/scenics, wildlife, architecture, cities/urban, religious, rural, adventure, travel, art and culture, photo production, photo design, press photos. Interested in alternative process, documentary, fine art, historical/vintage.

Specs Uses 35mm transparencies. Accepts images in digital format. Send via CD, Zip, e-mail or FTP as JPEG files at 300 dpi, 11 inches.

Payment & Terms Pays 50% commission for color photos. Average price per image (to clients): $50-150 for color photos; $450-750 for videotape. Enforces minimum prices. Offers volume discounts to customers; terms specified in photographers' contracts. Photographers can choose not to sell images on discount terms. Works with photographers with or without a contract; negotiable. Offers nonexclusive contract. Charges 50% sales fee. Payment made quarterly. Photographers allowed to review account records. Informs photographers and allows them to negotiate when client requests all rights. Photo captions preferred.
Making Contact Send query letter with stock list. Responds only if interested. Catalog available.

ARGUS PHOTO, LTD. (APL)

Room 2001-4 Progress Commercial Bldg., 9 Irving St., Causeway Bay, Hong Kong. (852)2890-6970. Fax: (852)2881-6979. E-mail: argus@argusphoto.com. Web site: www.argusphoto.com. **Contact:** Lydia Li, photo editor. Estab. 1992. Stock photo agency with branches in Beijing and Guangzhou. Has over 1 million searchable photos online. Clients include: advertising agencies, graphic houses, corporations, real estate developers, book and magazine publishers, postcard, greeting card, calendar and paper product manufacturers.
Needs "We cover general subject matters with constant needs of high-end lifestyle images, wellness, interior design/home decor, hospitality, garden and pool, Asian/Oriental people, and sports images. High quality feature stories with English text on travel, food and drink, architectural/interior design and celebrities are most welcome."
Specs Accepts high-quality digital images only. Send 50MB JPEG files at 300 dpi via DVD for review. English captions and keywords are required.
Payment & Terms Pays 50% commission. Average price per image (to clients): US$100-6,000. Offers volume discounts to customers. Works with photographers on contract basis only. Statements/payment made quarterly. Informs photographers and allows them to negotiate when client requests all rights. Model/property release may be required. Expects minimum initial submission of 200 images.

ARKRELIGION.COM

57 Burdon Lane, Cheam Surrey SM2 7BY United Kingdom. (44)(208)642-3593. Fax: (44)(208)395-7230. E-mail: images@artdirectors.co.uk. Web site: www.arkreligion.com. Estab. 2004. Stock agency. Has 100,000 photos in files. Clients include: advertising agencies, businesses, newspapers, postcard publishers, calendar companies, magazine publishers, greeting card companies.
Needs Wants photos of major, minor and alternative religions. This covers all aspects of religion from birth to death.
Specs Prefers digital submissions. Initial submission: 1MB JPEG. High-res requirement: 50MB TIFF. See contributors' page on Web site for full details. Uses 35mm, $2\frac{1}{4} \times 2\frac{1}{4}$, 4×5, 8×10 transparencies.
Payment & Terms Pays 50% commission for b&w or color photos when submitted digitally; pays 40% commission when film is submitted. Average price per image (to clients): $65-1,000 for b&w or color photos. Enforces strict minimum prices. Offers volume discounts to customers. Discount sales terms not negotiable. Works with photographers on contract basis only. Offers nonexclusive contract. Statements issued quarterly. Payment made quarterly. Photographers allowed to review account records in cases of discrepancies only.

Stock Photo Agencies

Offers one-time rights, electronic media rights. Model/property release preferred. Photo captions required; include as much relevant information as possible.

Making Contact Contact by e-mail. Does not keep samples on file. Expects minimum initial submission of 50 images with periodic submissions of at least 50 images. Responds in 6 weeks to queries. Photo guidelines available on Web site.

Tips "Fully caption material and follow the full requirements for digital submissions as detailed on the Web site. Will only accept slides/transparencies where these represent exceptional and/or difficult-to-obtain images."

▣ ⊕ ART DIRECTORS & TRIP PHOTO LIBRARY

57 Burdon Lane, Cheam Surrey SM2 7BY United Kingdom. (44)(208)642-3593. Fax: (44)(208)395-7230. E-mail: images@artdirectors.co.uk. Web site: www.artdirectors.co.uk. Estab. 1992. Stock agency. Has 1 million photos in files. Clients include: advertising agencies, businesses, newspapers, postcard publishers, public relations firms, book publishers, calendar companies, magazine publishers, greeting card companies.

Needs Wants photos of babies/children/teens, couples, multicultural, families, parents, senior citizens, disasters, environmental, landscapes/scenics, wildlife, architecture, cities/urban, education, gardening, interiors/decorating, pets, religious, rural, adventure, automobiles, entertainment, events, food/drink, health/fitness, hobbies, humor, performing arts, sports, travel, agriculture, business concepts, industry, medicine, military, political, product shots/still life, science, technology/computers. Interested in alternative process, avant garde, documentary, historical/vintage, seasonal.

Specs Prefers digital submissions. Initial submission: 1MB JPEG. High-res requirement: 50MB TIFF. See contributors' page on Web site for full details. Uses 35mm, $2^1/_4 \times 2^1/_4$, 4×5, 8×10 transparencies.

Payment & Terms Pays 50% commission for b&w or color photos when submitted digitally; pays 40% commission when film is submitted. Average price per image (to clients): $65-1,000 for b&w or color photos. Enforces strict minimum prices. Offers volume discounts to customers. Discount sales terms not negotiable. Works with photographers on contract basis only. Offers nonexclusive contract. Statements issued quarterly. Payment made quarterly. Photographers allowed to review account records in cases of discrepancies only. Offers one-time rights, electronic media rights. Model/property release preferred. Photo captions required; include as much relevant information as possible.

Making Contact Contact by e-mail. Does not keep samples on file. Expects minimum initial submission of 50 images with periodic submissions of at least 50 images. Responds in 6 weeks to queries. Photo guidelines available on Web site.

Tips "Fully caption material and follow the full requirements for digital submissions as detailed on the Web site. Will only accept slides/transparencies where these represent exceptional and/or difficult-to-obtain images."

▣ ART LICENSING INTERNATIONAL INC.

711 S Osprey Ave, Ste 1, Sarasota, FL 34236. (941)966-4042. Fax: (941)296-7345. E-mail: artlicensing@comcast.net. Web site: www.artlicensinginc.com; www.licensingcourse.com; www.out-of-the-blue.us. **Contact:** Michael Woodward, president. Licensing manager Jane Mason. Estab. 1986. "We represent artists, photographers and creators who wish to establish a licensing program for their work. We are particularly interested in photographic images that we can license internationally particulary for fine art posters, limited edition giclees for interior design projects and home and office decor.

Needs "We prefer concepts that have a unique look or theme and that are distinctive from the generic designs produced in-house by publishers and manufacturers. Images for prints and posters must be in pairs or sets of 4 or more with a regard for trends and color palettes related to the home décor and interrerior design trends. Nature themes are of particular interest."

Payment & Terms "Our general commission rate is 50% with no expenses to the photographer as long as the photographer provides high-resolution scans."

Making Contact Send CD/photocopies, e-mail JPEGS or details of your website. Send SASE if you want material returned.

Tips "We require substantial portfolios of work that can generate good incomes, or concepts that have wide commerical appeal."

ART RESOURCE

536 Broadway, 5th Floor, New York NY 10012. (212)505-8700. Fax: (212)505-2053. E-mail: requests@artres.com. Web site: www.artres.com. **Contact:** Diana Reeve. Estab. 1970. Stock photo agency specializing in fine arts. Member of the Picture Archive Council of America (PACA). Has access to 3 million photos. Clients include: advertising agencies, public relations firms, audiovisual firms, businesses, book/encyclopedia publishers, magazine publishers, newspapers, postcard publishers, calendar companies, greeting card companies, all other publishing.

Needs Wants photos of painting, sculpture, architecture *only*.

Specs Uses 8×10 b&w prints; 35mm, 4×5, 8×10 transparencies.

Payment & Terms Pays 50% commission. Average price per image (to client): $185-10,000 for color photos. Negotiates fees below standard minimum prices. Offers volume discounts to customers; terms specified in photographer's contract. Discount sales terms not negotiable. Offers one-time rights, electronic media rights, agency promotion and other negotiated rights. Photo captions required.

Making Contact Send query letter with stock list.

Tips "We represent European fine art archives and museums in the U.S. and Europe but occasionally represent a photographer with a specialty in photographing fine art."

ARTWERKS STOCK PHOTOGRAPHY

5045 Brennan Bend, Idaho Falls ID 83406. (208)523-1545. E-mail: photojournalistjerry@msn.com. **Contact:** Jerry Sinkovec, owner. Estab. 1984. News/feature syndicate. Has 100 million photos in files. Clients include: advertising agencies, public relations firms, businesses, book publishers, magazine publishers, calendar companies, postcard publishers.

Needs Wants photos of American Indians, ski action, ballooning, British Isles, Europe, Southwest scenery, disasters, environmental, landscapes/scenics, wildlife, adventure, events, food/drink, hobbies, performing arts, sports, travel, business concepts, industry, product shots/still life, science, technology/computers. Interested in documentary, fine art, historical/vintage, lifestyle.

Specs Uses 8×10 glossy color and/or b&w prints; 35mm, $2^{1}/_{4} \times 2^{1}/_{4}$, 4×5 transparencies. Accepts images in digital format. Send via CD, Zip as JPEG files.

Payment & Terms Pays 50% commission. Average price per image (to clients): $125-800 for b&w photos; $150-2,000 for color photos; $250-5,000 for film and videotape. Negotiates fees below stated minimums depending on number of photos being used. Offers volume discounts to customers; terms not specified in photographers' contracts. Discount sales terms not negotiable. Works with photographers with or without a contract, negotiable. Offers nonexclusive contract. Charges 100% duping fee. Statements issued quarterly. Payment made quarterly. Offers one-time rights. Does not inform photographers or allow them to negotiate when a client requests all rights. Model/property release preferred. Photo captions preferred.

Making Contact Send query letter with brochure, stock list, tearsheets. Provide résumé, business card. Portfolios may be dropped off every Monday. Agency will contact photographer for portfolio review if interested. Portfolio should include slides, tearsheets, transparencies. Works with freelancers on assignment only. Does not keep samples on file; include SASE for return of material. Expects minimum initial submission of 20 images. Responds in 2 weeks. Catalog free with SASE.

N ⊡ ⊕ ASIA IMAGES GROUP

15 Shaw Rd., #08-02, Teo Bldg., Singapore 367953. (65)6288-2119. Fax: (65)6288-2117. E-mail: info@asia-images.com. Web site: www.asia-images.com. **Contact:** Alexander Mares-Manton, founder and creative director. Estab. 2001. Stock agency. "We specialize in creating, distributing and licensing locally relevant Asian model-released lifestyle and business images. Our image collections reflect the visual trends, styles and issues that are current in Asia, home of the world's fastest growing economies. We have three major collections: Asia Images (rights managed); AsiaPix (royalty free); and PictureIndia (royalty free)." Clients include: advertising agencies, corporations, public relations firms, book publishers, calendar companies, magazine publishers.

Needs Wants photos of babies/children/teens, couples, families, parents, senior citizens, health/fitness/beauty, science, technology. "We are only interested in seeing images about or from Asia."

Specs Accepts images in digital format. "We want to see 72-dpi JPEGs for editing and 300-dpi TIFF files for archiving and selling."

Payment & Terms "We have minimum prices that we stick to unless many sales are given to one photographer at the same time." Works with photographers on image-exclusive contract basis only. "We need worldwide exclusivity for the images we represent, but photographers are encouraged to work with other agencies with other images." Statements issued monthly. Payment made monthly. Photographers allowed to review account records. Offers one-time rights, electronic media rights. Model and property releases are required for all images.

Making Contact Send e-mail with 10-20 JPEGs of your best work. No minimum submissions. Responds only if interested; send nonreturnable samples.

Tips "Asia Images Group is a small niche agency specializing in images of Asia for both advertising and editorial clients worldwide. We are interested in working closely with a small group of photographers rather than becoming too large to be personable. When submitting work, please send 10-20 JPEGs in an e-mail and tell us something about your work and your experience in Asia."

N ⊡ ⊕ AUSCAPE INTERNATIONAL

8/44-48 Bowral St., Bowral NSW 2576 Australia. (61)(024)861-6818. Fax: (61)(024)861-6838. E-mail: auscape@auscape.com.au. Web site: www.auscape.com.au. **Contact:** Sarah Tahourdin, director. Has 250,000 photos in files. Clients include: advertising agencies, book publishers, magazine publishers, newspapers, calendar companies, greeting card companies.

Stock Photo Agencies

Needs Wants photos of environmental, landscapes/scenics, wildlife, pets, health/fitness, medicine, model-released Australian lifestyle.

Specs Uses 35mm, $2\frac{1}{4} \times 2\frac{1}{4}$, 4×5, 8×10 transparencies. Accepts images in digital format. Send via CD or DVD as TIFF files at 300 dpi.

Payment & Terms Pays 50% commission for color photos. Enforces minimum prices. Offers volume discounts to customers. Works with photographers on contract basis only. Requires exclusive contract. Statements issued quarterly. Payment made quarterly. Photographers allowed to review account records. Charges scan fees for all transparencies scanned in-house; all scans placed on Web site. Offers one-time rights. Photo captions required; include scientific names, common names, locations.

Making Contact Does not keep samples on file. Expects minimum initial submission of 200 images with monthly submissions of at least 50 images. Responds in 3 weeks to samples. Photo guidelines sheet free.

Tips "Send only informative, sharp, well-composed pictures. We are a specialist natural history agency and our clients mostly ask for pictures with content rather than empty-but-striking visual impact. There must be passion behind the images and a thorough knowledge of the subject."

AUTHOR PICTURES AT LEBRECHT

3 Bolton Road, London NW8 0RJ. United Kingdom. Estab. 1992. E-mail: pictures@lebrecht. co.uk. Web site: www.authorpictures.co.uk. **Contact:** Ms. E. Lebrecht. Picture library has 65,000 high-res images online; thousands more not yet scanned.Clients include: advertising agencies, newspapers, public relations firms, book publishers, calendar companies, magazine publishers, greeting card companies.

Needs Wants photos of authors, writers, historians, plays, playwrights, philosophers, etc.

Specs Accepts images in digital format only.

Payment & Terms Pays 50% commission for b&w or color photos. Offers volume discounts to customers. Works with photographers on contract basis only. Offers limited regional exclusivity. Statements issued quarterly. Offers one-time rights. Informs photographers and allows them to negotiate when a client requests all rights. Photo captions required; include who is in photo, location, date.

Making Contact Send e-mail.

THE BERGMAN COLLECTION

Division of Project Masters, Inc., P.O. Box AG, Princeton NJ 08542-0872. (609)921-0749. Fax: (609)921-6216. E-mail: information@pmiprinceton.com. Web site: http://pmiprinceton.com. **Contact:** Victoria B. Bergman, vice president. Estab. 1980 (Collection established in the 1930s.) Stock agency. Has 20,000 photos in files. Clients include: advertising agencies, book publishers, audiovisual firms, magazine publishers.

Needs "Specializes in medical, technical and scientific stock images of high quality and accuracy."

Specs Uses color and/or b&w prints; 35mm, $2\frac{1}{4} \times 2\frac{1}{4}$ transparencies. Accepts images in digital format. Send via CD, floppy disk, Zip, e-mail as TIFF, BMP, JPEG files.

Payment & Terms Pays on commission basis. Works with photographers on contract basis only. Offers one-time rights. Model/property release required. Photo captions required; must be medically, technically, scientifically accurate.

Making Contact "Do not send unsolicited images. Call, write, fax or e-mail to be added to our database of photographers able to supply, on an as-needed basis, specialized images not already in the collection. Include a description of the field of medicine, technology or science in which you have images. We contact photographers when a specific need arises."

Tips "Our needs are for very specific images that usually will have been taken by specialists in the field as part of their own research or professional practice. A good number of the images placed by The Bergman Collection have come from photographers in our database."

▣ BIOLOGICAL PHOTO SERVICE AND TERRAPHOTOGRAPHICS

P.O. Box 490, Moss Beach CA 94038. (650)359-6219. E-mail: bpsterra@pacbell.net. Web site: www.agpix.com/biologicalphoto. **Contact:** Carl W. May, photo agent. Stock photo agency. Estab. 1980. Has 80,000 photos in files. Clients include: ad agencies, businesses, book/encyclopedia publishers, magazine publishers.

Needs All subjects in the pure and applied life and earth sciences. Stock photographers must be scientists. Subject needs include: electron micrographs of all sorts; biotechnology; modern medical imaging; marine and freshwater biology; diverse invertebrates; organisms used in research; tropical biology; and land and water conservation. All aspects of general and pathogenic microbiology, normal human biology, petrology, volcanology, seismology, paleontology, mining, petroleum industry, alternative energy sources, meteorology and the basic medical sciences, including anatomy, histology, medical microbiology, human embryology and human genetics.

Specs Uses 4×5 through 11×14 glossy, high-contrast b&w prints for EM's; 35mm, $2^{1}/_{4} \times 2^{1}/_{4}$, 4×5, 8×10 transparencies. "Dupes acceptable for rare and unusual subjects, but we prefer originals." Welcomes images in digital format as 50-100MB TIFF files.

Payment & Terms Pays 50% commission for b&w and color photos. General price range (for clients): $75-500, sometimes higher for advertising uses. Works with photographers with or without a contract, but only as an exclusive agency. Photographers may market directly on their own, but not through other agencies or portals. Statements issued quarterly. Payment made quarterly; "one month after end of quarter." Photographers allowed to review account records to verify sales figures "by appointment at any time." Offers only rights-managed uses of all kinds; negotiable. Informs photographers and allows them veto authority when client requests a buyout. Model/property release required for photos used in advertising and other commercial areas. Thorough scientific photo captions required; include complete identification of subject and location.

Making Contact Interested in receiving work from newer, lesser-known scientific and medical photographers if they have the proper background. Send query letter with stock list, résumé of scientific and photographic background; include SASE for return of material. Responds in 2 weeks. Photo guidelines free with query, résumé and SASE. Tips sheet distributed intermittently to stock photographers only. "Nonscientists should not apply."

Tips "When samples are requested, we look for proper exposure, maximum depth of field, adequate visual information and composition, and adequate technical and general information in captions. Digital files should have image information in IPTC and EXIF fields. We avoid excessive overlap among our photographer/scientists. We are experiencing an ever-growing demand for photos covering environmental problems and solutions of all sorts—local to global, domestic and foreign. Our three greatest problems with potential photographers are: 1) inadequate captions/metadata; 2) inadequate quantities of *fresh* and *diverse* photos; 3) poor sharpness/depth of field/grain/composition in photos."

CALIFORNIA VIEWS/MR. PAT HATHAWAY HISTORICAL PHOTO COLLECTION

469 Pacific St., Monterey CA 93940-2702. (831)373-3811. E-mail: hathaway@caviews.com. Web site: www.caviews.com. **Contact:** Mr. Pat Hathaway, photo archivist. Estab. 1970. Picture library; historical collection. Has 80,000 b&w images; 10,000 35mm color images in files. Clients include: advertising agencies, public relations firms, audiovisual firms, book/encyclopedia publishers, magazine publishers, museums, postcard companies, calendar companies, television companies, interior decorators, film companies.

Needs Historical photos of California from 1855 to today, including disasters, landscapes/scenics, rural, agricultural, automobiles, travel, military, portraits, John Steinbeck and Edward F. Rickets.

Payment & Terms Payment negotiable. Offers volume discounts to customers.

Making Contact "We accept donations of California photographic material in order to maintain our position as one of California's largest archives. Please do not send unsolicited images." Does not keep samples on file; cannot return material.

⌧ ⌧ ⌧ ⌧ CAMERA PRESS LTD.

21 Queen Elizabeth St., London SE1 2PD United Kingdom. (44)(207)278-1300 or (44)(207)940-9123. Fax: (44)(207)278-5126. E-mail: editorial@camerapress.com or j.wald @camerapress.com. Web site: www.camerapress.com. **Contact:** Jacqui Ann Wald, editor. Quality syndication service and picture library. Clients include: advertising agencies, public relations firms, audiovisual firms, book/encyclopedia publishers, magazine publishers, newspapers, postcard companies, calendar companies, greeting card companies and TV stations. Clients principally press but also advertising, publishers, etc.

• Camera Press sends and receives images via ISDN, FTP, and e-mail.

Needs Celebrities, world personalities (e.g., politics, sports, entertainment, arts, etc.), news/documentary, scientific, human interest, humor, women's features, stock.

Specs Accepts images in digital format as TIFF, JPEG files as long as they are a minimum of 300 dpi or 16MB.

Payment & Terms Standard payment term: 50% net commission. Statements issued every 2 months along with payments.

Tips "Camera Press, one of the oldest and most celebrated family-owned picture agencies, will celebrate its 60th anniversary in November 2007. We represent some of the top names in the photographic world but also welcome emerging talents and gifted newcomers. We seek quality celebrity images; lively, colorful features which tell a story; and individual portraits of world personalities, both established and up-and-coming. Accurate captions are essential. Remember there is a big worldwide demand for celebrity premieres and openings. Other needs include: scientific development and novelties; beauty, fashion, interiors, food and women's interests; humorous pictures featuring the weird, the wacky and the wonderful."

⌧ ⌧ ⌧ CAPITAL PICTURES

85 Randolph Ave., London W9 1DL United Kingdom. (44)(207)286-2212. Fax: (44)(207)286-1218. E-mail: sales@capitalpictures.com. Web site: www.capitalpictures.c om. Picture library. Has 80,000 photos on file. Clients include: advertising agencies, book publishers, magazine publishers, newspapers. Specializes in high-quality photographs of famous people (politics, royalty, music, fashion, film and television).

Needs "We have a lot of clients looking for 'picture of the capital.' We need very high-quality images of London—postcard-type images for international sales. Not just large files, but great content—famous landmarks photographed at the best time, from the best angle, creating interesting and evocative images. Try looking on the Internet for pictures of London for some inspiration.''

Specs High-quality digital format only. Send via CD, e-mail as JPEG files.

Payment & Terms Pays 50% commission of money received. ''We have our own price guide but will negotiate competitive fees for large quantity usage or supply agreements.'' Offers volume discounts to customers. Discount sales terms negotiable. Works with photographers with or without a contract; negotiable, whatever is most appropriate. No charges—only 50% commission for sales. Statements issued monthly. Payment made monthly. Photographers allowed to review account records. Offers any rights they wish to purchase. Informs photographers and allows them to negotiate when client requests all rights ''if we think it is appropriate.'' Photo captions preferred; include date, place, event, name of subject(s).

Making Contact Send query letter with samples. Agency will contact photographer for portfolio review if interested. Keeps samples on file. Expects minimum initial submission of 24 images with monthly submissions of at least 24 images. Responds in 1 month to queries.

■ ▨ CHARLTON PHOTOS, INC.

3605 Mountain Dr., Brookfield WI 53045. (262)781-9328. Fax: (262)781-9390. E-mail: jim@charltonphotos.com. Web site: www.charltonphotos.com. **Contact:** James Charlton, director of research. Estab. 1981. Stock photo agency. Has 475,000 photos; 200 hours of video. Clients include: ad agencies, public relations firms, audiovisual firms, businesses, book/encyclopedia publishers, magazine publishers, newspapers, calendar companies.

Needs ''We handle photos of agriculture and pets.''

Specs Uses color photos; 35mm, 2 ¼ transparencies, as well as digital. Also uses video.

Payment & Terms Pays 60/40% commission. Average price per image (to clients): $500-650 for color photos. Offers volume discounts to customers; terms specified in photographers' contracts. Works with photographers on contract basis only. Prefers exclusive contract, but negotiable based on subject matter submitted. Contracts renew automatically with additional submisions for 3 years minimum. Charges duping fee, 50% catalog insertion fee and materials fee. Statements issued monthly. Payment made monthly. Photographers allowed to review account records that relate to their work. Model/property release required for identifiable people and places. Photo captions required; include who, what, when, where.

Making Contact Query by phone before sending any material. Expects initial submission of 1,000 images. Responds in 2 weeks. Photo guidelines free with SASE. Market tips sheet distributed quarterly to contract freelance photographers; free with SASE.

Tips ''Provide our agency with images we request by shooting a self-directed assignment each month. Visit our Web site.''

■ BRUCE COLEMAN PHOTO LIBRARY

Bruce Coleman, Inc., 111 Brook St., 2nd Floor, Scarsdale NY 10583. (914)713-4821. Fax: (914)722-8347. E-mail: library@bciusa.com. Web site: www.bciusa.com. **Contact:** Norman Owen Tomalin, photo director. Estab. 1970. Stock photo agency. Has more than 1.75 million photos on file. Clients include: advertising agencies, public relations firms, audiovisual firms, businesses, book/encyclopedia publishers, magazine publishers, newspapers, postcard publishers, calendar companies, greeting card companies, zoos (installations), TV.

Needs Wants photos of babies/children/teens, couples, multicultural, families, parents, senior citizens, disasters, environmental, landscapes/scenics, wildlife, architecture, cities/ urban, pets, rural, adventure, hobbies, sports, travel, agricultural, business concepts, industry, product shots/still life, science, technology/computers.

Specs Accepts images in digital format.

Payment & Terms Pays 50% commission for color transparencies, digital files and b&w photos. Average price per image (to clients): $125 minimum for color and b&w photos. Contracts renew automatically for 5 years. Statements issued quarterly. Payment made quarterly. Does not allow photographer to review account records; any deductions are itemized. Offers one-time rights. Model/property release preferred for people, private property. Photo captions required; include location, species, genus name, Latin name, points of interest.

Making Contact Send e-mail query with résumé and URL link or a CD portfolio. "A portfolio can be uploaded to our FTP server." Photo guidelines and technical specs available online.

Tips "We look for strong dramatic angles, beautiful light, sharpness. We like photos that express moods/feelings and show us a unique eye/style. We like work to be properly captioned; the digital file should contain all vital information regarding the photograph. We are asking for natural settings, dramatic use of light and/or angles. Photographs should not be contrived and should express strong feelings toward the subject. We advise photographers to shoot a lot and edit carefully, photograph what they really love, and follow our want lists."

Ⓝ ▣ ⊕ EDUARDO COMESAÑA AGENCIA DE PRENSA/BANCO FOTOGRÁFICO

Av. Olleros 1850 4to. "F" C1426CRH Buenos Aires, Argentina. (54)(11)4771-9418. Fax: (54)(11)4771-0080. E-mail: info@comesana.com. Web site: www.comesana.com. **Contact:** Eduardo Comesaña, managing director. Estab. 1977. Stock agency, news/feature syndicate. Has 500,000 photos in files. Clients include: advertising agencies, businesses, newspapers, postcard publishers, book publishers, calendar companies, magazine publishers.

Needs Wants photos of babies/children/teens, celebrities, couples, families, parents, disasters, environmental, landscapes/scenics, wildlife, education, adventure, entertainment, events, health/fitness, humor, performing arts, travel, agriculture, business concepts, industry, medicine, political, science, technology/computers. Interested in documentary, fine art, historical/vintage.

Specs Accepts images in digital format only. Send via CD, DVD as TIFF or JPEG files at 300 dpi. By e-mail in JPEG format only.

Payment & Terms Pays 50% commission for b&w or color photos. Offers volume discounts to customers; terms specified in photographer's contracts. Photographers can choose not to sell images on discount terms. Works with photographers with or without a contract; negotiable. Offers limited regional exclusivity. Contracts renew automatically with additional submissions. Statements issued quarterly. Payment made quarterly. Photographers allowed to review account records in cases of discrepancies only. Offers one-time rights. Model release preferred; property release required.

Making Contact Send query letter with tearsheets, stock list. Provide self-promotion piece to be kept on file. Expects minimum initial submission of 200 images in low-res files with monthly submissions of at least 200 images. Responds only if interested; send nonreturnable samples.

CORBIS
902 Broadway, 3rd Floor, New York NY 10010. (212)777-6200. Fax: (212)533-4034. Web site: www.corbis.com. Estab. 1991. Stock agency, picture library, news/feature syndicate. Member of the Picture Archive Council of America (PACA). Corbis also has offices in London, Paris, Dusseldorf, Tokyo, Seattle, Chicago and Los Angeles. Clients include: advertising agencies, businesses, newspapers, public relations firms, book publishers, calendar companies, audiovisual firms, magazine publishers, greeting card companies, businesses/corporations, media companies.

Making Contact "Please check "About Corbis" on our Web site for current submission information."

▣ CUSTOM MEDICAL STOCK PHOTO
The Custom Medical Bldg., 3660 W. Irving Park Rd., Chicago IL 60618-4132. (773)267-3100. Fax: (773)267-6071. E-mail: sales@cmsp.com. Web site: www.cmsp.com. **Contact:** Mike Fisher and Henry Schleichkorn, medical archivists. Clients include: advertising agencies, magazines, journals, textbook publishers, design firms, audiovisual firms, hospitals, Web designers—all commercial and editorial markets that express interest in medical and scientific subject area.

Needs Wants photos of biomedical, scientific, healthcare environmentals and general biology for advertising illustrations, textbook and journal articles, annual reports, editorial use and patient education.

Specs "Accepting only digital submissions. Go online to www.cmsp.com/cmspweb/images for information about contacting us before submitting images, and image specifications."

Payment & Terms Pays per shot or commission. Per-shot rate depends on usage. Commission: 30% on domestic leases; 25% on foreign leases. Works with photographers on contract basis only. Contracts of 5-7 years. Royalty-free contract available. Administrative costs charged based on commission structure. Credit line given if applicable, at client's discretion. Offers one-time, electronic media and agency promotion rights; other rights negotiable. Informs photographers but does not permit them to negotiate when a client requests all rights.

Making Contact Send query letter with list of stock photo subjects or check contributor website. Call for address and submission packet. "Do not send uncaptioned, unsolicited photos by mail." Responds in 1 month on average. Photo guidelines available on website. Monthly want list available to contributors only. Model/property release required.

Tips "Our past want lists are a valuable guide to the types of images requested by our clients. Past want lists are available on the Web. Environmentals of researchers, hi-tech biomedicine, physicians, nurses and patients of all ages in situations from neonatal care to mature adults are requested frequently. Almost any image can qualify to be medical if it touches an area of life: breakfast, sports, etc. Trends also follow newsworthy events found on newswires. Photos should be good, clean images that portray a single idea, whether it is biological, medical, scientific or conceptual. Put together a minimum of 10 images for submission. Contributing to our agency can be very profitable if a solid commitment can exist."

▣ DDB STOCK PHOTOGRAPHY, LLC
P.O. Box 80155, Baton Rouge LA 70898. (225)763-6235. Fax: (225)763-6894. E-mail: info@ddbstock.com. Web site: www.ddbstock.com. **Contact:** Douglas D. Bryant, president. Estab.

1970. Stock photo agency. Member of American Society of Picture Professionals. Rights managed stock only, no RF. Currently represents 103 professional photographers. Has 550,000 transparencies in files and 20,000 high resolution digital images available for download on Web site. Clients include: text-trade book/encyclopedia publishers, travel industry, museums, ad agencies, audiovisual firms, magazine publishers, CD-ROM publishers and many foreign publishers.

Needs Specializes in picture coverage of Latin America with emphasis on Mexico, Central America, South America, and the Caribbean. Needs photos of anthropology/archeology, art, commerce, crafts, secondary and university education, festivals and ritual, geography, history, indigenous people and culture, museums, parks, political figures, religion. Also uses babies/children/teens, couples, multicultural, families, parents, senior citizens, architecture, rural, adventure, entertainment, events, food/drink, health/fitness, performing arts, business concepts, industry, military, science, technology/computers.

Specs Prefers images in TIFF digital format on DVD at 8 megapixels or higher. Prepare digital submissions per http://www.ddbstock.com/submissionguidelines.html. Accepts original 35mm transparencies.

Payment & Terms Pays 40% commission for color photos; 25% on foreign sales through foreign agents. Payment rates: $50-$20,000. Average price per image (to clients): $275. Offers volume discount to customers; terms specified in photographers' contracts. 4-year initial minimum holding period for original transparencies. Payment made quarterly. Does not allow independent audits. "We are a small agency and do not have staff to oversee audits." Offers one-time, print/electronic media, world and all language rights. Model/property release preferred for ad set-up shots. Photo captions required; include location and detailed description. "We have a geographic focus and need specific location info on captions (Geocode latitude/longitude if you carry a GPS unit, and include latitude/longitude in captions)."

Making Contact Interested in receiving work from professional photographers who regularly visit Latin America. Send query letter with brochure, tearsheets, stock list. Expects minimum initial submission of 300 digital images/original transparencies and yearly submissions of at least 500 images. Responds in 6 weeks. Photo guidelines available on website.

Tips "Speak Spanish and spend one to six months shooting in Latin America and the Caribbean every year. Follow our needs list closely. Call before leaving on assignment. Shoot digital TIFFs at 8 megapixels or larger. Shoot Fuji professional transparency film if you have not converted to digital. Edit carefully. Eliminate images with focus, framing, excessive grain/noise, or exposure problems. The market is far too competitive for average pictures and amateur photographers. Review guidelines for photographers on our website. Include coverage from at least three Latin American countries or five Caribbean Islands. No one-time vacation shots! Shoot subjects in demand listed on Web site."

🔲 🌐 DINODIA PHOTO LIBRARY

13-15 Vithoba Lane, Vithalwadi, Kalbadevi, Bombay 400 002 India. (91)(22)2240-4126. Fax: (91)(22)2240-1675. E-mail: jagdish@dinodia.com. Web site: www.dinodia.com. **Contact:** Jagdish Agarwal, founder. Estab. 1987. Stock photo agency. Has 500,000 photos in files. Clients include: advertising agencies, public relations firms, audiovisual firms, businesses, book/encyclopedia publishers, magazine publishers, newspapers, postcard companies, calendar companies, greeting card companies.

Needs Wants photos of babies/children/teens, celebrities, couples, multicultural, families, parents, senior citizens, disasters, environment, landscapes/scenics, wildlife, architecture, cities/urban, education, gardening, interiors/decorating, pets, religious, rural, adventure, automobiles, entertainment, events, food/drink, health/fitness/beauty, hobbies, humor, performing arts, sports, travel, agriculture, business concepts, industry, medicine, military, political, product shots/still life, science, technology/computers. Interested in alternative process, avant garde, documentary, erotic, fashion/glamour, fine art, historical/vintage, seasonal.

Specs "At the moment we are only accepting digital. Initially it is better to send a few nonreturnable printed samples for our review."

Payment & Terms Pays 50% commission for b&w and color photos. General price range (to clients): US $50-600. Negotiates fees below stated minimum prices. Offers volume discounts to customers; inquire about specific terms. Discount sales terms not negotiable. Works with photographers on contract basis only. Offers limited regional exclusivity; "Prefer exclusive for India." Contracts renew automatically with additional submissions for 5 years. Statement issued monthly. Payment made monthly. Photographers permitted to review sales figures. Informs photographers and allows them to negotiate when client requests all rights. Offers one-time rights. Model release preferred. Photo captions required.

Making Contact Send query letter with résumé of credits, nonreturnable samples, stock list and SASE. Responds in 1 month. Photo guidelines free with SASE. Dinodia news distributed monthly to contracted photographers.

Tips "We look for style—maybe in color, composition, mood, subject matter, whatever— but the photos should have above-average appeal." Sees trend that "market is saturated with standard documentary-type photos. Buyers are looking more often for stock that appears to have been shot on assignment."

▣ DK STOCK, INC.

3524 78th Street Ste 29A, Jackson Heights, New York NY 11372. (212)405-1891. Fax: (212)405-1890. E-mail: david@dkstock.com. Web site: www.dkstock.com. **Contact:** David Deas, photo editor. Estab. 2000. "A multicultural stock photo company based in New York City, and the first company to launch a fully searchable multiethnic website and publish an African-American stock photography catalog. Prior to launching DK Stock, its founders worked for years in the advertising industry as a creative team specializing in connecting clients to the $1.6 trillion ethnic market. This market is growing, and DK Stock's goal is to service it with model-released, well composed, professional imagery." Member of the Picture Archive Council of America (PACA). Has 10,000 photos in files. Clients include: advertising agencies, public relations firms, buisinesses, book publishers, magazine publishers, newspapers, calendar companies, greeting card companies.

Needs "Looking for contemporary lifestyle images that reflect the black and Hispanic diaspora." Wants photos of babies/children/teens, celebrities, couples, multicultural, families, parents, senior citizens, education, adventure, entertainment, health/fitness/beauty, hobbies, humor, performing arts, sports, travel, agriculture, business concepts, industry, medicine, military, political, science, technology/computers. Interested in historical/vintage, lifestyle. "Images should include models of Hispanics and/or people of African descent. Images of Caucasian models interacting with black and/or Hispanic people can also be submitted. Be creative, selective and current. Visit website to get an idea of the style and range of representative work. E-mail for a current copy of 'needs list.' "

Specs Uses 35mm, $2\frac{1}{4} \times 2\frac{1}{4}$, 4×5, 8×10 transparencies. Accepts images in digital format. Send via CD as TIFF files at 300 dpi, 50MB.

Payment & Terms Pays 50% commission for b&w or color photos. Average price per image (to clients): $100-15,000 for b&w photos or color photos. Enforces minimum prices. Offers volume discounts to customers; terms specified in photographers' contracts. Photographers can choose not to sell images on discount terms. Works with photographers on contract basis only. Offers nonexclusive contract. Contracts renew automatically with additional submissions for 5 years. Statements issued monthly. Payment made monthly. Photographers allowed to review account records. Model/property release required. Photo captions optional.

Making Contact Send query letter with slides, prints, photocopies, tearsheets, transparencies. Portfolio may be dropped off every Monday-Friday. Does not keep samples on file; include SASE for return of material. Expects minimum initial submission of 50 images with 5 times/year submissions of at least 25 images. Responds in 2 weeks to samples, portfolios. Photo guidelines free with SASE. Catalog free with SASE.

Tips "We love working with talented people. If you have 10 incredible images, let's begin a relationship. Also, we're always looking for new and upcoming talent as well as photographers who can contribute often. There is an increasing demand for lifestyle photos of multicultural people. Our clients are based in the Americas, Europe, Asia and Africa. Be creative, original and technically proficient."

▣ ⊕ DW STOCK PICTURE LIBRARY (DWSPL)

108 Beecroft Rd., Beecroft, New South Wales 2119 Australia. (61)(02)9869-0717. E-mail: info@dwpicture.com.au. Web site: www.dwpicture.com.au. Estab. 1997. Has more than 200,000 photos on file and 30,000 online. "Strengths include historical images, marine life, African wildlife, Australia, travel, horticulture, agriculture, people and lifestyles." Clients include: advertising agencies, designers, printers, book publishers, magazine publishers, calendar companies.

Needs Wants photos of babies/children/teens, families, parents, senior citizens, disasters, gardening, pets, rural, health/fitness, travel, industry. Interested in lifestyle.

Specs Accepts images in digital format. Send as low-res JPEG files via CD.

Payment & Terms Pays 50% commission. Average price per image (to clients): $200 for color photos. Enforces minimum prices. Offers volume discounts to customers. Works with photographers on contract basis only. Statements issued quarterly. Photographers allowed to review account records in cases of discrepancies only. Offers one-time rights. Model release preferred. Photo captions required.

Making Contact Send query letter with images; include SASE if sending by mail. Expects minimum initial submission of 200 images. Responds in 2 weeks to samples.

▣ ⊕ E & E PICTURE LIBRARY

Beggars Roost, Woolpack Hill, Brabourne Lees, Ashford, Kent TN25 6RR United Kingdom. E-mail: isobel@picture-library.freeserve.co.uk. Web site: www.eeimages.com and www.heritage-images.com (go to E & E Image Library); www.eeimages.co.uk. **Contact:** Isobel Sinden. Estab. 1998. Member of BAPLA (British Association of Picture Libraries and Agencies). Has 250,000 images on file. Clients include: advertisers/designers, businesses, book publishers, magazine publishers, newspapers, calendar/card companies, merchandising, TV.

Needs worldwide religion, faith, spiritual images, buildings, clergy, festivals, ceremony, objects, places, food, ritual, monks, nuns, stained glass, carvings, the unusual. Mormons,

Stock Photo Agencies

Shakers, all groups/sects, large or small. Death: burial, funerals, graves, gravediggers, green burial, commemorative. Ancient/heritage/biblelands/saints/eccentricities/festivals: curiosities, unusual oddities like follies, signs, symbols. Architecture, religious or secular. Manuscripts and illustrations, old and new, linked with any of the subjects above.

Specs Accepts images in digital format. Send via CD, JPEG files in medium-high resolution. Uses 35mm, $2\frac{1}{4} \times 2\frac{1}{4}$, 4×5 transparencies.

Payment & Terms Average price per image (to clients): $140-200 for color photos. Offers volume discounts to customers. Works with photographers on contract basis for 5 years, offering exclusive/nonexclusive contract renewable automatically with additional submissions. Offers one-time rights. Model release where necessary. Photo captions very important and must be accurate. Include what, where, any special features or connections, name, date (if possible), and religion.

Making Contact Send query letter with slides, tearsheets, transparencies/CD. Expects minimum initial submission of 40 images. Responds in 2 weeks. Photo guidelines sheet and "wants list" available via e-mail.

Tips "Decide on exact subject of image. *Get in close and then closer.* Exclude all extraneous matter. Fill the frame. Dynamic shots. Interesting angles, light. No shadows or miniscule subject matter far away. Tell us what is important about the picture. No people in shot unless they have a role in the proceedings as in a festival or service, etc."

▣ ⊕ ECOSCENE

Empire Farm, Throop Rd., Templecombe Somerset BA8 0HR United Kingdom. (44)(196)337-1700. E-mail: pictures@ecoscene.com. Web site: www.ecoscene.com. **Contact:** Sally Morgan, director. Estab. 1988. Picture library. Has 80,000 photos in files. Clients include: advertising agencies, businesses, book/encyclopedia publishers, magazine publishers, newspapers, Internet, multimedia.

Needs Wants photos of disasters, environmental, energy issues, sustainable development, wildlife, gardening, rural, health/fitness, agriculture, medicine, science, pollution, industry, energy, indigenous peoples.

Specs Accepts digital submissions only. Send via CD as 48MB (minimum) TIFF files at 300 dpi.

Payment & Terms Pays 55% commission for color photos. Average price per image (to clients): $90 minimum for color photos. Negotiates fees below stated minimum prices, depending on quantity reproduced by a single client. Offers volume discounts to customers. Discount sales terms not negotiable. Works with photographers on contract basis only. Offers nonexclusive contract. Contracts renew automatically with additional submissions, 4 years minimum. Statements issued quarterly. Payment made quarterly. Offers one-time and electronic media rights. Informs photographers and allows them to negotiate when client requests all rights. Model/property release preferred. Photo captions required; include location, subject matter, and common and Latin names of wildlife and any behavior shown in pictures.

Making Contact Send query letter with résumé of credits. Digital submissions only. Keeps samples on file; include SASE for return of material. Expects minimum initial submission of 100 images with annual submissions of at least 100 images. Responds in 3 weeks. Photo guidelines free with SASE. Market tips sheets distributed quarterly to anybody who requests, and to all contributors.

Tips Photographers should have a "neat presentation and accurate, informative captions.

Images must be tightly edited with no fillers. Photographers must be critical of their own work and check out the website to see the type of image required. Substandard work is never accepted, whatever the subject matter. Enclose return postage.''

Ⓝ ▣ 808 IMAGES, INC.

75 Kupuohi St., #102, Lahaina HI 96761. (808)573-6875. Fax: (808)573-6876. E-mail: scott@ 808images.com. Web site: www.808images.com. **Contact:** Scott Mead, production manager. Estab. 2006. Stock agency. 5,000+ images photos in files. Clients include: advertising agencies, postcard publishers, public relations firms, calendar companies, magazine publishers, greeting card companies.

Needs Needs photos of cites/urban, gardening, religious, rural, adventure, entertainment, events, food/drink, performing arts, sports, travel, product shots/still lifes, technology/ computers, environmental, landscapes/scenics, wildlife, Hawaiiana, Polynesia, tropical. Interested in fine art, lifestyle, historical/vintage, seasonal.

Specs Uses matte color and b&w prints; 35mm, $2\frac{1}{4} \times 2\frac{1}{4}$ transparencies. Accepts images in digital format. Send TIFF or JPEG files at 300 dpi via CD or FTP.

Payment & Terms Pays 50% commission for b&w and color photos; 50% for film; 50% for videotape. Average price per image (to client): $15-750 for color and b&w photos. Enforces strict minimum prices. Photographers can choose not to sell images on discount terms. Works with photographers on contract basis only. Contracts renew automatically with additional submissions each year. Statements issued quarterly. Payment made quarterly. Photographers allowed to review account records. Offers one-time rights, electronic media rights, agency promotion rights, and multi-use rights. Informs photographers and allows them to negotiate when a client requests all rights. Model/property release preferred. E-mail query letter with link to photographer's Web site; JPEG samples at 72 dpi, stock list. Send query letter with tearsheets, stock list. Provide résumé, business card, self-promotion piece to be kept on file. Expects minimum initial submission of 10 images with quarterly submission of at least 100 images. Responds in 2 months to samples; 2 weeks to portfolios. Photo guidelines sheet available online. Catalog available for $40.00.

Tips We *only* deal with Hawaiian/Polynesian images. Send only your *best* images; review for dust/artifacts prior to submission.

▣ ▨ ESTOCK PHOTO, LLC

27-28 Thomson Ave., Ste. 628 Long Island City NY 11101. (800)284-3399. Fax: (212)545-1185. E-mail: sales@estockphoto.com. Web site: www.estockphoto.com. **Contact:** Laura Diez, president. Member of Picture Archive Council of America (PACA). Has over 1 million photos in files. Clients include: ad agencies, public relations and AV firms; businesses; book, magazine and encyclopedia publishers; newspapers, calendar and greeting card companies; textile firms; travel agencies and poster companies.

Needs Wants photos of travel, destination, people, lifestyles, business.

Specs Uses 35mm, medium-format, 4×5 transparencies. Accepts images in digital format.

Payment & Terms Price depends on quality and quantity. Usually pays 50% commission. General price range (to clients): $125-6,500. Works with photographers on contract basis only. Offers exclusive and limited regional exclusive contracts. Contracts renew automatically for 3 years. Offers to clients "any rights they want to have; payment is calculated accordingly." Statements issued bimonthly and quarterly. **Payment made bimonthly and quarterly**. Photographers allowed to review account records to verify their sales figures.

Offers one-time and electronic media rights. Informs photographers and allows them to negotiate when client requests all rights; some conditions. Model release required; "depends on subject matter." Photo captions preferred.

Making Contact Send query letter with samples—"about 100 is the best way." Send query letter with list of stock photo subjects or submit portfolio for review. Response time depends; often the same day. Photo guidelines free with SASE.

Tips "Photos should show what the photographer is all about. They should show technical competence—photos that are sharp, well-composed, have impact; if color, they should show color."

ETHNO IMAGES, INC.

5966 Lofland, Frisco TX 75034. (510)773-4492. E-mail: admin@mail.ethnoimages.com. Web site: www.ethnoimages.com. **Contact:** Troy A. Jones, CEO/president; T. Lynn Jones, COO. Estab. 1999. Since its inception, Ethno Images has become the resource of choice for multicultural imagery. The Ethno collection contains lifestyle-driven images spanning traditional to contemporary to cutting edge. Clients are marketing professionals in advertising agencies, book and magazine publishers, in-house marketing departments and design shops.

Needs Wants multicultural images representing lifestyles, families, teenagers, children, couples, celebrities, sports and business. "All multicultural groups accepted; African-American images are requested frequently."

Specs Digital submissions only. Send digital images via CD, Zip as TIFF, JPEG files at 300 dpi (at least 48MB).

Payment & Terms Pays 50% commission for b&w or color photos. Average price per image (to clients): $300. Enforces minimum prices. Offers volume discounts to customers. Works with photographers on contract and freelance basis. Offers nonexclusive contract. Payment made monthly. Model release required; property release preferred. Photo captions required.

Making Contact E-mail us and send low-resolution files or a Web address for review. Photo guidelines and a current needs list provided upon request.

Tips "Caption each image and provide contact information. Prefer initial submissions on CD-ROM in JPEG format or TIFF format. Call or e-mail for more information."

EYE UBIQUITOUS/HUTCHINSON

(formerly Eye Ubiquitous), 65 Brighton Rd., Shoreham, West Sussex BN43 6RE United Kingdom. +44 (0)1273 440113. Fax: +44 (0)1273 440 116. E-mail: library@eyeubiquitous.com. Web site: www.eyeubiquitous.com. **Contact:** Stephen Rafferty, library manager. Estab. 1988. Picture library. Has 300,000 photos in files. Clients include: ad agencies, public relations firms, businesses, book/encyclopedia publishers, magazine publishers, newspapers, television companies.

Needs Wants photos of worldwide social documentary and general stock.

Specs Transparencies and 50 MB files at 300 DPI, color corrected Adobe 1998.

Payment & Terms Pays commission exclusive 40% and 35% non exclusive. Offers volume discounts to customers; inquire about specific terms. Discount sales terms not negotiable. Works with photographers on contract basis only. Offers exclusive, limited regional exclusivity and nonexclusive contracts. Contracts renew automatically with additional submissions. Charges to photographers "discussed on an individual basis." Payment made quarterly. Photographers allowed to review account records. Buys one-time, electronic media and agency promotion rights; negotiable. Does not inform photographers or allow them to negotiate when client requests all rights. Model/property release preferred for people, "particularly Americans." Photo captions required; include where, what, why, who.

Making Contact Submit portfolio for review. Works with freelancers only. Keeps samples on file. Include SASE for return. No minimum number of images expected in initial submission, but "the more the better." Responds as time allows. Photo guidelines free with SASE. Catalog free with SASE. Market tips sheet distributed to contributors "when we can"; free with SASE.

Tips "Find out how picture libraries operate. This is the same for all libraries worldwide. Amateurs can be very good photographers but very bad at understanding the industry after reading some irresponsible and misleading articles. Research the library requirements."

▣ ⊕ FAMOUS PICTURES & FEATURES AGENCY

13 Harwood Rd., London SW6 4QP United Kingdom. (44)(207)731-9333. Fax: (44)(207)731-9330. E-mail: contributors@famous.uk.com or pictures@famous.uk.com. Web site: www.famous.uk.com. **Contact:** Rob Howard. Estab. 1985. Picture library, news/feature syndicate. Has more than 500,000 photos on database. Clients include: advertising agencies, book publishers, magazine publishers, newspapers, calendar companies, postcard publishers and poster publishers.

Needs Wants photos of music, film, TV personalities; international celebrities; live, studio, party shots (paparazzi) with stars of all types.

Specs Prefers images in digital format. Send via FTP or e-mail as JPEG files at 300 dpi or higher.

Payment & Terms Pays 50% commission for color photos. Offers volume discounts to customers. Photographers can choose not to sell images on discount terms. Works with photographers with or without a contract; contracts available for all photographers. Offers limited regional exclusivity. Statements issued monthly. Payment made monthly. Photographers allowed to review account records. Offers one-time rights. Photo captions preferred.

Making Contact E-mail, phone or write, provide samples. Provide résumé, business card, self-promotion piece or tearsheets to be kept on file. Agency will contact photographer for portfolio review if interested. Keeps samples in online database. Will return material with SAE/IRC.

Tips "We are solely marketing images via computer networks. Our fully searchable archive of new and old pictures is online. Send details via e-mail for more information. When submitting work, please caption pictures correctly."

▨ ▣ FIRST LIGHT ASSOCIATED PHOTOGRAPHERS

550 Queen Street East, Ste 320, Toronto, ON M5A 1V2 Canada. (416)597-8625. Fax: (416)597-2035. E-mail: info@firstlight.com. Web site: www.firstlight.com. **Contact:** Anne Bastarache, director, photography. Estab. 1984. Stock agency and image partner of Getty Images, represents over 150 photographers and 40 rights-managed and royalty-free collections. Over one million images available online. Clients include: advertising agencies, public relations firms, audiovisual firms, businesses, book/encyclopedia publishers, magazine publishers, newspapers, calendar companies.

Needs Wants commercial imagery in all categories. Special emphasis on model-released people, lifestyle, conceptual photography and business and canadian images. "Our broad files require variety of subjects." Sister company WAVE royalty-free also requires environmentally relevant imagery; contact First Light for more information.

Specs "For initial review submission we prefer low-res JPEG files via e-mail; for final submissions we require clean 50MB (minimum) high-res TIFF files."

Payment & Terms Photographer's imagery is represented as rights-managed. 45% commission rate. Works on contract basis only, nonexclusive. Statements issued monthly. Payment made monthly. Offers one-time rights. Informs photographers and allows them to negotiate when client requests buy-out. Model releases required. IPTC embedding required for all final files. Photo captions required.

Making Contact Send query letter via e-mail.

Tips "Wants to see tightly edited submissions. Well-produced, non-candid imagery."

▣ ⊕ FOCUS NEW ZEALAND PHOTO LIBRARY LTD.

Box 84 153, Westgate, Auckland 0657 New Zealand. (64)(9)411 5416. Fax: (64)(9)411 5417. E-mail: photos@focusnewzealand.com. Web site: www.focusnewzealand.com. **Contact:** Brian Moorhead, director. Estab. 1985. Stock agency. Has 40,000 photos in files. Clients include: advertising agencies, businesses, newspapers, postcard publishers, public relations firms, book publishers, calendar companies, magazine publishers, greeting card companies, electronic graphics.

Needs Wants photos of babies/children/teens, couples, multicultural, families, parents, senior citizens, environmental, landscapes/scenics, architecture, cities/urban, education, rural, adventure, events, health/fitness/beauty, hobbies, performing arts, sports, travel, agriculture, business concepts, industry, science, technology/computers. Interested in seasonal. Also needs New Zealand, Australian and South Pacific images.

Specs Uses 35mm, medium-format and up to full-frame panoramic 6×17 transparencies. Accepts images in digital format, RGB, TIFF, 300 dpi, A4 minimum.

Payment & Terms Pays 50% commission. Offers volume discounts to customers. Discount sales terms not negotiable. Works with photographers on contract basis only. Offers nonexclusive contract. Statements issued quarterly. Payment made quarterly. Photographers allowed to review account records. Offers one-time, electronic media and agency promotion rights. Model/property release preferred. Photo captions required; include exact location, content, details, releases, date taken.

Making Contact Send query letter. Does not keep samples on file; include SASE for return of material. Expects minimum initial submission of 100 images with yearly submissions of at least 100-200 images. Responds in 3 weeks to samples. Photo guidelines sheet free with SASE or by e-mail. Catalog free on website. Market tips sheet available by mail or e-mail to contributors only.

Tips "Only submit original, well-composed, well-constructed, technically excellent work, fully captioned."

▣ FOODPIX

Jupiter Images, 99 Pasadena Ave., South Pasadena CA 91030. (800)764-7427. E-mail: aosburn@jupiterimages.com. Web site: www.jupiterimages.com. **Contact:** Amy Osburn, sr. collection director. Estab. 1994. Stock agency. Member of the Picture Archive Council of America (PACA). Has 40,000 photos in files. Clients include: advertising agencies, businesses, newspapers, book publishers, calendar companies, design firms, magazine publishers.

Needs Wants food, beverage and food/lifestyle images.

Specs Accepts analog and digital images. Review and complete the Online Submission Questionnaire on the Web site before submitting work.

Payment & Terms Enforces minimum prices. Offers volume discounts to customers; terms specified in photographers' contracts. Works with photographers on contract basis only. Offers exclusive contract only. Statements issued monthly. Payment made quarterly. Offers one-time rights. Model/property release required. Photo captions required.

Making Contact Send query e-mail with samples. Expects maximum initial submission of 50 images. Responds in 1 month. Catalog available.

▣ ⊕ FOTO-PRESS TIMMERMANN

Speckweg 34A, D-91096 Moehrendorf, Germany. (49)(9131)42801. Fax: (49)(9131)450528. E-mail: info@f-pt.com. Web site: www.f-pt.com. **Contact:** Wolfgang Timmermann. Stock photo agency. Has 750,000 photos in files. Clients include: advertising agencies, audiovisual firms, businesses, book/encyclopedia publishers, magazine publishers, newspapers, calendar companies.

Needs Wants landscapes, countries, travel, tourism, towns, people, business, nature, babies/children/teens, couples, families, parents, senior citizens, adventure, entertainment, health/fitness/beauty, hobbies, industry, medicine, technology/computers. Interested in erotic, fine art, seasonal, lifestyle.

Specs Uses $2\frac{1}{4} \times 2\frac{1}{4}$, 4×5, 8×10 transparencies (no prints). Accepts images in digital format. Send via CD, Zip as TIFF files.

Payment & Terms Pays 50% commission for color photos. Works on nonexclusive contract basis (limited regional exclusivity). First period: 3 years; contract automatically renewed for 1 year. Photographers allowed to review account records. Statements issued quarterly. Payment made quarterly. Offers one-time rights. Informs photographers and allows them to negotiate when a client requests to buy all rights. Model/property release preferred. Photo captions required; include state, country, city, subject, etc.

Making Contact Send query letter with stock list. Send unsolicited photos by mail for consideration; include SAE/IRC for return of material. Responds in 1 month.

▣ ⊕ FOTOSCOPIO

Jaramillo 3894 8° ''18'', C1430AGJ Capital Federal, Buenos Aires, Argentina. Phone/fax: (54)(114)542-3512. E-mail: info@fotoscopio.com. Web site: www.fotoscopio.com. **Contact:** Gustavo Di Pace, director. Estab. 1999. Fotoscopio is a Latin American stock photo agency. Has 50,000 photos in files. Clients include: advertising agencies, businesses, postcard publishers, book publishers, calendar companies, magazine publishers, greeting card companies.

Needs Wants photos of Hispanic people, Latin American countries, babies/children/teens, celebrities, couples, multicultural, families, senior citizens, disasters, environmental, landscapes/scenics, wildlife, architecture, cities/urban, interiors/decorating, pets, religious, adventure, automobiles, entertainment, health/fitness/beauty, hobbies, sports, travel, agriculture, business concepts, industry, product shots/still life, technology/computers. Interested in documentary, fine art, historical/vintage.

Specs Uses 35mm, $2\frac{1}{4} \times 2\frac{1}{4}$, 4×5, 8×10 transparencies. Accepts images in digital format. Send via CD, Zip, e-mail as JPEG files at 72 dpi.

Payment & Terms Average price per image (to clients): $50-300 for b&w photos; $50-800 for color photos. Negotiates fees below stated minimums. Offers volume discounts to customers; terms specified in photographer's contracts. Discount sales terms not negotiable. Works with photographers on contract basis only. Offers nonexclusive contract. Contracts renew automatically with additional submissions for 1 year. Statements issued and payment made whenever one yields rights of reproduction of his photography. Photographers allowed to review account records in cases of discrepancies only. Offers one-time and electronic media rights. Model release required; property release preferred. Photo captions preferred.

Making Contact Send query letter with résumé, slides, prints, photocopies, tearsheets, transparencies, stock list. Provide résumé, business card, self-promotion piece to be kept on file. Expects minimum initial submission of 100 images. Responds in 1 month to samples. Photo guidelines sheet free with SASE.

▣ FUNDAMENTAL PHOTOGRAPHS

210 Forsyth St., Suite 2, New York NY 10002. (212)473-5770. Fax: (212)228-5059. E-mail: mail@fphoto.com. Web site: www.fphoto.com. **Contact:** Kip Peticolas, partner. Estab. 1979. Stock photo agency. Applied for membership into the Picture Archive Council of America (PACA). Has 100,000 photos in files. Clients include: textbook/encyclopedia publishers, advertising agencies, corporate industrial.

Needs Wants photos of medicine, biology, microbiology, environmental, industry, weather, disasters, science-related business concepts, agriculture, technology/computers.

Specs Uses 35mm and all large-format transparencies. Accepts images in digital format. Send as RAW or TIFF files at 300 dpi, 11×14 size.

Payment & Terms Pays 50% commission for b&w or color photos. General price range (to clients): $100-500 for b&w photos; $150-1,200 for color photos; depends on rights needed. Enforces strict minimum prices. Offers volume discount to customers. Works with photographers on contract basis only. Offers guaranteed subject exclusivity. Contracts renew automatically with additional submissions for 2 or 3 years. Charges $5/image scanning fee; can increase to $15 if corrective Photoshop work required. Statements issued and payment made quarterly for any sales during previous quarter. Photographers allowed to review account records with written request submitted 2 months in advance. Offers one-time and electronic media rights. Gets photographer's approval when client requests all rights; negotiation conducted by the agency. Model release required. Photo captions required; include date and location.

Making Contact Arrange a personal interview to show portfolio or make contact by e-mail and arrange for digital submission. Submit portfolio for review. Send query letter with résumé of credits, samples or list of stock photo subjects. Keeps samples on file; include SASE for return of material. Expects minimum initial submission of 100 images. Photo guidelines free with SASE. Tips sheet distributed. E-mail crucial for communicating current photo needs.

Tips "Our primary market is science textbooks. Photographers should research the type of illustration used and tailor submissions to show awareness of saleable material. We are looking for science subjects ranging from nature and rocks to industrials, medicine, chemistry and physics; macro photography, photomicrography, stroboscopic; well-lit still life shots are desirable. The biggest trend that affects us is the need for images that document new discoveries in sciences and ecology."

⊕ GEOSLIDES & GEO AERIAL PHOTOGRAPHY

4 Christian Fields, London SW16 3JZ United Kingdom. (44)(208)764-6292. Fax: (44)(115)981-9418. E-mail: geoslides@geo-group.co.uk. Web site: www.geo-group.co.uk.

Contact: John Douglas, marketing director. Estab. 1968. Picture library. Has approximately 100,000 photos in files. Clients include: advertising agencies, public relations firms, audiovisual firms, businesses, book/encyclopedia publishers, magazine publishers, newspapers, calendar companies, television.

Needs Accent on travel/geography and aerial (oblique) shots. Wants photos of disasters, environmental, landscapes/scenics, wildlife, architecture, rural, adventure, travel, agriculture, industry, medicine, military, political, product shots/still life, science, technology/computers. Interested in documentary, historical/vintage.

Specs High-res digital.

Payment & Terms Pays 50% commission for b&w or color photos. General price range (to clients) $75-750. Works with photographers with or without a contract; negotiable. Offers nonexclusive contract. Charges mailing costs. Statements issued monthly. Payment made upon receipt of client's fees. Offers one-time rights and first rights. Does not inform photographers or allow them to negotiate when clients request all rights. Model release required. Photo captions required; include description of location, subject matter and sometimes the date.

Making Contact Send query letter or e-mail with résumé of credits, stock list; include SAE/IRC for return of material. Photo guidelines available for SAE/IRC. No samples until called for.

Tips Looks for "technical perfection, detailed captions, must fit our needs, especially location needs. Increasingly competitive on an international scale. Quality is important. Needs large stocks with frequent renewals." To break in, "build up a comprehensive (i.e., in subject or geographical area) collection of photographs which are well documented."

GETTY IMAGES

601 N. 34th St., Seattle WA 98103. (206)925-5000. Fax: (206)925-5001. Web site: www.getty images.com. "Getty Images is the world's leading imagery company, creating and distributing the largest and most relevant collection of still and moving images to communication professionals around the globe and supporting their work with asset management services. From news and sports photography to contemporary and archival imagery, Getty Images' products are found each day in newspapers, magazines, advertising, films, television, books and websites. Gettyimages.com is the first place customers turn to search, purchase, download and manage powerful imagery. Seattle-headquartered Getty Images is a global company with customers in more than 100 countries."

Making Contact Please visit www.gettyimages.com/contributors and select the link "Interested in marketing your imagery through Getty Images?"

GRANT HEILMAN PHOTOGRAPHY, INC.

P.O. Box 317, Lititz PA 17543. (717)626-0296. Fax: (717)626-0971. E-mail: info@heilmanph oto.com. Web site: www.heilmanphoto.com. **Contact:** Sonia Wasco, president. Estab. 1948. Member of the Picture Archive Council of America (PACA). Has one million photos in files. Now representing Photo Network Stock. Sub agents in Canada, Europe, England, Japan. Clients include: advertising agencies, public relations firms, businesses, book/textbook publishers, magazine publishers, calendar companies, greeting card companies, postcard publishers.

Needs Wants photos of environmental, landscapes/scenics, wildlife, gardening, pets, rural, agriculture, science, technology/computers. Interested in seasonal.

Specs Uses 35mm, $2\frac{1}{4} \times 2\frac{1}{4}$, 4×5 transparencies. Accepts images in digital format. Send via CD, floppy disk, Jaz, Zip, e-mail as TIFF, EPS, PICT, JPEG files.

Payment & Terms Pays on commission basis. Enforces minimum prices. Offers volume discounts to customers. Works with photographers on contract basis only. Offers guaranteed subject exclusivity (within files). Contracts renew automatically with additional submissions per contract definition. Charges determined by contract. Statements issued quarterly. Payment made quarterly. Photographers allowed to review account records. Offers one-time rights, electronic media rights, agency promotion rights. Model/property release required. Photo captions required; include all known information.

Making Contact Send query letter with résumé, slides, prints, photocopies, tearsheets, transparencies, stock list. Provide résumé, business card, self-promotion piece to be kept on file. Expects minimum initial submission of 200 images.

Tips "Make a professional presentation."

▣ ⊕ HORIZON INTERNATIONAL IMAGES LIMITED

Horizon House, Route de Picaterre, Alderney, Guernsey GY9 3UP British Channel Islands. (44)(1481)822587. Fax: (44)(1481)823880. E-mail: mail@hrzn.com. Web site: www.hrzn. com; www.e-picturelibrary.net. UK registered. Estab. 1978. Stock photo agency. Horizon sells stock image use rights (in UK and worldwide), both rights managed and royalty free, via its website and international agents.

Needs Wants photos of Lifestyle (sports, couples, multicultural, families, parents, seniors, adventure, entertainment, food/drink, health/fitness, babies/children/teens, humor); Business (meetings, small business, big business); Industry (construction, energy, manufacturing, mining, medicine, science, technology/computers). Environment (landscapes/scenics, plants, rural); Animals (farm, horses, wildlife, pets); Travel (architecture, natural landmarks, festivals/traditional costume). Particular requirements for model-released people.

Specs Accepts images in digital format. Drum-scanned from transparencies or 12-megapixel camera and above interpolated to minimum 50MB file before JPEG compression. Use factor 10 JPEG compression in current versions of Adobe Photoshop. All submitted image files must be carefully cropped to mask out rebate and retouched with clone or repair tools (do not use dust filter software). Submit via Horizon's website or send by post on CD or DVD (media nonreturnable). Transparency scanning service available—please inquire.

Payment & Terms Considering new photographers of high technical and artistic standard on 50% sales commission. See full Terms and Conditions on website.

Making Contact Register first on www.e-picturelibrary.net (click "Join Now" on the task bar). Then submit sample selection via online submission system. Horizon sometimes purchases and commissions stock (is prepared to review assignment portfolios from photographers interested in producing images of model-released people on an assigned basis).

Tips "Horizon's terms and conditions apply."

▣ HORTICULTURAL PHOTOGRAPHY™

337 Bedal Lane, Campbell CA 95008. (408)364-2015. Fax: (408)364-2016. E-mail: requests @horticulturalphoto.com. Web site: www.horticulturalphoto.com. **Contact:** Robin M. Orans, owner. Estab. 1974. Picture library. Has 200,000 photos in files. Clients include: advertising agencies, public relations firms, businesses, book publishers, magazine publishers.

Needs Wants photos of flowers, plants with botanical identification, gardens, landscapes.

Specs Uses color slides; 35mm transparencies. Accepts images in digital format. Contact prior to sending images.

Payment & Terms Pays commission for images. Average price per image (to clients): $25-

1,000 for color photos. Negotiates fees below stated minimums; depends on quantity. Offers volume discounts to customers. Discount sales terms not negotiable. Works with photographers on contract basis only; negotiable. Statements issued semiannually. Payment made semiannually. Photographers allowed to review account records in cases of discrepancies only. Offers one-time rights, electronic media rights and language rights. Photo captions required; include common and botanical names of plants, date taken, location.

Making Contact Contact through rep. Send e-mail with résumé, stock list. Does not keep samples on file. Expects minimum initial submission of 40 images with quarterly submissions of at least 100 images. Responds in 1 month to samples and portfolios. Photo guidelines available by e-mail or on Web site.

Tips "Send e-mail for guidelines."

📖 🌐 HUTCHISON PICTURE LIBRARY

65 Brighton Rd., Shoreham-by-Sea, West Sussex BN43 6RE United Kingdom. E-mail: library @hutchisonpictures.co.uk. Web site: www.hutchisonpictures.co.uk. **Contact:** Stephen Rafferty, manager. Stock photo agency, picture library. Has around 500,000 photos in files. Clients include: ad agencies, public relations firms, audiovisual firms, businesses, book/encyclopedia publishers, magazine publishers, newspapers, postcard companies, calendar companies, television and film companies.

Needs "We are a general, documentary library (no news or personalities). We file mainly by country and aim to have coverage of every country in the world. Within each country we cover such subjects as industry, agriculture, people, customs, urban, landscapes, etc. We have special files on many subjects such as medical (traditional, alternative, hospital, etc.), energy, environmental issues, human relations (relationships, childbirth, young children, etc., but all real people, not models)." We constantly require images of Spain and spanish speaking countries. Also interested in babies/children/teens, couples, multicultural, families, parents, senior citizens, disasters, architecture, education, gardening, interiors/decorating, religious, rural, health/fitness, travel, military, political, science, technology/computers. Interested in documentary, seasonal. "We are a color library."

Specs Uses 35mm transparencies. Accepts images in digital format: 50MB at 300 dpi, cleaned of dust and scratches at 100%, color corrected.

Payment & Terms Pays 40% commission for exclusive; 35% for nonexclusive. Statements issued semiannually. Payment made semiannually. Sends statement with check in June and January. Offers one-time rights. Model release preferred. Photo captions required.

Making Contact Always willing to look at new material or collections. Arrange a personal interview to show portfolio. Send letter with brief description of collection and photographic intentions. Responds in about 2 weeks, depends on backlog of material to be reviewed. "We have letters outlining working practices and lists of particular needs (they change)." Distributes tips sheets to photographers who already have a relationship with the library.

Tips Looks for "collections of reasonable size (rarely less than 1,000 transparencies) and variety; well captioned (or at least well indicated picture subjects; captions can be added to mounts later); sharp pictures, good color, composition; and informative pictures. Prettiness is rarely enough. Our clients want information, whether it is about what a landscape looks like or how people live, etc. The general rule of thumb is that we would consider a collection which has a subject we do not already have coverage of or a detailed and thorough specialist collection. Please do not send *any* photographs without prior agreement."

▣ ⊕ ▧ I.C.P. INTERNATIONAL COLOUR PRESS

Piazza Vesuvio 19, Milano 20144 Italy. (39)(024)801-3106. Fax: (39)(024)819-5625. E-mail: icp@icponline.it. Web site: www.icponline.it. **Contact:** Mr. Alessandro Marosa, CEO. Estab. 1970. Stock photo agency. Clients include: advertising agencies, public relations firms, audiovisual firms, businesses, book/encyclopedia publishers, magazine publishers, postcard publishers, calendar companies and greeting card companies.

Specs High-res digital (A3-A4, 300 dpi), keyworded (English and, if possible, Italian).

Payment & Terms Pays 50% commission for color photos. Offers volume discounts to customers; terms specified in photographer's contract. Discount sales terms not negotiable. Contracts renew automatically with additional submissions, for 3 years. Statements issued monthly. Payment made monthly. Photographers permitted to review account records to verify sales figures or deductions. Offers one-time, first and sectorial exclusive rights. Model/property release required. Photo captions required.

Making Contact Arrange a personal interview to show portfolio. Send query letter with samples and stock list. Works on assignment only. No fixed minimum for initial submission. Responds in 3 weeks, if interested.

▣ THE IMAGE FINDERS

2570 Superior Ave., Suite 200, Cleveland OH 44114. (216)781-7729. E-mail: imagefinders@ sbcglobal.net. Web site: www.theimagefinders.com. **Contact:** Jim Baron, owner. Estab. 1988. Stock photo agency. Has 500,000 photos in files. Clients include: advertising agencies, public relations firms, businesses, book/encyclopedia publishers, magazine publishers, calendar companies, greeting card companies.

Needs General stock agency. Always interested in good Ohio images. Also needs babies/children/teens, couples, multicultural, families, senior citizens, landscapes/scenics, wildlife, architecture, gardening, pets, automobiles, food/drink, sports, travel, agriculture, business concepts, industry, medicine, political, technology/computers. Interested in fashion/glamour, fine art, seasonal.

Specs Accepts digital images; see guidelines before submitting. Send via CD.

Payment & Terms Pays 50% commission for b&w and color photos. Average price per image (to clients): $50-500 for b&w photos; $50-2,000 for color photos. "This is a small agency and we will, on occasion, go below stated minimum prices." Offers volume discounts to customers; terms specified in photographers' contracts. Works with photographers on contract basis only. Contracts renew automatically with additional submissions for 2 years. Statements issued monthly if requested. Payment made monthly. Photographers allowed to review account records. Offers one-time rights; negotiable depending on what the client needs and will pay for. Informs photographers and allows them to negotiate when client requests all rights. "This is rare for us. I would inform photographer of what the client wants and work with photographer to strike the best deal." Model/property release preferred. Photo captions required; include location, city, state, country, type of plant or animal, etc.

Making Contact Send query letter with stock list or send e-mail with link to your website. Call before you send anything that you want returned. Expects minimum initial submission of 100 images with periodic submission of at least 100-500 images. Responds in 2 weeks. Photo guidelines free with SASE. Market tips sheet distributed 2-4 times/year to photographers under contract.

Tips Photographers must be willing to build their file of images. "We need more people images, industry, lifestyles, wildlife, travel, etc. Scenics and landscapes must be outstanding to be considered. Call first or e-mail. Submit at least 100 good images. Must have ability to produce more than 100-200 images per year.''

THE IMAGE WORKS

P.O. Box 443, Woodstock NY 12498. (845)679-8500. Fax: (845)679-0606. E-mail: info@thei mageworks.com. Web site: www.theimageworks.com. **Contact:** Mark Antman, president. Estab. 1983. Stock photo agency. Member of Picture Archive Council of America (PACA). Has over 1 million photos in files. Clients include: ad agencies, book/encyclopedia publishers, magazine publishers, newspapers, postcard publishers, greeting card companies, documentary video.

Needs ''We are always looking for excellent documentary photography. Our prime subjects are people-related subjects like family, education, health care, workplace issues, worldwide historical, technology, fine arts.''

Specs All images must be in digital format; contact for digital guidelines. Rarely accepts 35mm, $2\frac{1}{4} \times 2\frac{1}{4}$ transparencies and prints .

Payment & Terms Pays 50% commission for b&w and color photos. Average price per image (to clients): $200 for b&w and color photos. Works with photographers on contract basis only. Offers nonexclusive contract. Statements issued monthly. Payment made monthly. Photographers allowed to review account records to verify sales figures by appointment. Offers one-time, agency promotion and electronic media rights. Informs photographers and allows them to negotiate when clients request all rights. Model release preferred. Photo captions required.

Making Contact Send e-mail with description of stock photo archives. Responds in 1 month. Expects minimum initial submission of 500 images.

Tips ''The Image Works was one of the first agencies to market images digitally. All digital images from photographers must be reproduction-quality. When making a new submission to us, be sure to include a variety of images that show your range as a photographer. We also want to see some depth in specialized subject areas. Thorough captions are a must. We will not look at uncaptioned images. Write or call first.''

IMAGES.DE DIGITAL PHOTO GMBH

Potsdamer Str. 96, D-10785 Berlin Germany. (49)(30)25 79 28 980. Fax: (49)(30)25 79 28 999. E-mail: info@images.de. Web site: www.images.de. **Contact:** Katja Herold. Estab. 1997. News/feature syndicate. Has 50,000 photos in files. Clients include: advertising agencies, newspapers, public relations firms, book publishers, magazine publishers. ''Images.de is a service company with 10 years experience on the picture market. We offer fulfillment services to picture agencies, including translation, distribution into Fotofiner and APIS picturemaxx, customer communication, invoicing, media control, cash delivery, and usage control.''

Needs Wants photos of babies/children/teens, couples, multicultural, families, parents, senior citizens, environment, entertainment, events, food/drink, health/fitness, hobbies, travel, agriculture, business concepts, industry, medicine, political, science, technology/computers.

Specs Accepts images in digital format. Send via FTP, CD.

Payment & Terms Pays 50% commission for b&w photos; 50% for color photos. Average price per image (to clients): $50-1,000 for b&w photos or color photos. Offers volume discounts to customers. Discount sales terms not negotiable. Works with photographers with or without a contract; negotiable. Offers limited regional exclusivity. Statements issued monthly. Payment made monthly. Photographers allowed to review account records in cases of discrepancies only. Offers one-time rights, electronic media rights. Informs photographers and allows them to negotiate when client requests all rights. Model release preferred; property release required. Photo captions required.

Making Contact Send query letter with CD or link to Web site. Expects minimum initial submission of 100 images.

▣ INDEX STOCK IMAGERY, INC.

23 W. 18th St., 3rd Floor, New York NY 10011. (212)929-4644 or (800)690-6979. Fax: (212)633-1914. E-mail: editing@indexstock.com. Web site: www.indexstock.com. Corporate Web site: www.indexstockimagery.com. **Contact:** New Artist Inquiries. Estab. 1981. Stock photo agency. Member of Picture Archive Council of America (PACA). "Representation in over 70 countries worldwide, with 100,000+ images; represent 1,700 artists and smaller agencies, including the Stock Imagery and Picture Cube collections. Manage several corporate and not-for-profit archives. Offers two royalty-free subscription products-Index Open and Photos to Go Unlimited. Markets images to small business and consumers via Photos to Go."

Needs Alternative processes and stylistically creative imagery of the highest quality.

Specs Prefers images in digital format from a 10 megapixel or higher camera (no point-and-shoots: must use a professional camera with interchangeable lens). Files must be captured in RAW, converted to TIFF (no JPEG files accepted). See the Web site under "For Artists Only" for more information.

Payment & Terms Pays 40% commission for image sales. "We have competitive prices, but under special circumstances we contact photographer prior to negotiations." Works on material exclusive contract basis only. Statements and payments issued monthly. Photographers allowed to review account records. Offers one-time and electronic media rights. Informs photographer and allows them to negotiate when client requests all rights. Model/ property release required for all images. Photo captions required.

Making Contact "We are always willing to review new photographers' work. However, we prefer to see that the individual has a subject specialty or a stylistic signature that sets them apart in this highly competitive industry. Therefore, we ask that an initial submission be properly edited to demonstrate that they have a high degree of vision, creativity and style that can be relied upon on a regular basis. Quite simply, we are looking for technically superior, highly creative images."

⊠ $⑤ ▣ ⊕ INMAGINE RF & RM IMAGE SUBMISSIONS (IRIS)

Inmagine Corporation LLC, 2650 Fountain View Dr., Ste 332, Houston TX 77057. Estab. 2000. 800-810-3888. Fax: 866-234-5310. E-mail: photo@inmagine.com. Web site: http:// submission.inmagine.com. Stock agency, picture library. Member of the Picture Archive Council of America (PACA). Has 3,100,000 photos in files. Branch offices in USA, Hong Kong, Australia, Malaysia, Thailand, United Arab Emirates, Singapore, Indonesia, and China. Clients include: advertising agencies, businesses, newspapers, public relations firms, magazine publishers.

Needs Wants photos of babies, children, teens, couples, multicultural, families, parents, education, business concepts, industry, medicine, environmental and landscapes, adventure, entertainment, events, food and drink, health, fitness, beauty, hobbies, sports, travel, fashion/glamour, and lifestyle.

Specs Accepts images in digital format. Submit online via http://submission.inmagine.com or send JPEG files at 300 dpi.

Payment and Terms Pays 50% commission for color photos. Average price per image (to clients) is $100 minimum, maximum negotiable. Negotiates fees below stated minimums. Offers volume discounts to customers, terms specified in photographers' contracts. Works with photographers on a contract basis only. Offers nonexclusive contract. Payments made monthly. Photographers are allowed to view account records in cases of discrepancies only. Offers one-time rights. Model and property release required. Photo caption required.

Making Contact Photographers should contact through website. Expects minimum initial submission of 5 images. Responds in 1 week to samples. Photo guidelines available online.

Tips "Complete the steps as outlined in the IRIS submission pages. Email us if there are queries. Send only the best of your portfolio for submission, stock oriented materials only. EXIF should reside in file with keywords and captions."

Ⓐ ▣ INTERNATIONAL PHOTO NEWS

Dept. PM, 2902 29th Way, West Palm Beach FL 33407. (561)683-9090. E-mail: jkravetz1@e arthlink.net. **Contact:** Jay Kravetz, photo editor. News/feature syndicate. Has 50,000 photos in files. Clients include: newspapers, magazines, book publishers. Previous/current clients include: newspapers that need celebrity photos with story.

Needs Wants photos of celebrities, entertainment, events, health/fitness/beauty, performing arts, travel, politics, movies, music and television, at work or play. Interested in avant garde, fashion/glamour.

Specs Accepts images in digital format. Send via CD, Zip, e-mail as TIFF, JPEG files at 300 dpi. Uses 5×7, 8×10 glossy b&w prints.

Payment & Terms Pays $10 for b&w photos; $25 for color photos; 5-10% commission. Average price per image (to clients): $25-100 for b&w photos; $50-500 for color photos. Works with photographers on contract basis only. Offers nonexclusive contract. Contracts renew automatically with additional submissions; 1-year renewal. Photographers allowed to review account records. Statements issued monthly. Payment made monthly. Offers one-time rights. Model/property release preferred. Photo captions required.

Making Contact Send query letter with résumé of credits. Solicits photos by assignment only. Responds in 1 week.

Tips "We use celebrity photographs to coincide with our syndicated columns. Must be approved by the celebrity."

▣ 🌐 THE IRISH PICTURE LIBRARY

Davison & Associates Ltd., 69b Heather Rd., Sandyford Industrial Estate, Dublin 18 Ireland. (353)1295 0799. Fax: (353)1295 0705. E-mail: ipl@fatherbrowne.com. Web site: www.fath erbrowne.com/ipl. **Contact:** David Davison. Estab. 1990. Picture library. Has 60,000 photos in files. Clients include: advertising agencies, businesses, book publishers, magazine publishers, newspapers, calendar companies.

Needs Wants photos of historic Irish material. Interested in alternative process, fine art, historical/vintage.

Specs Uses any prints. Accepts images in digital format. Send via CD as TIFF, JPEG files at 400 dpi.

Payment & Terms Pays 50% commission for b&w and color photos. Average price per image (to clients): $100-1,000 for b&w and color photos. Enforces minimum prices. Offers volume discounts to customers. Photographers can choose not to sell images on discount terms. Works with photographers on contract basis only. Statements issued quarterly. Payment made quarterly. Photographers allowed to review account records. Offers one-time rights, electronic media rights. Property release required. Photo captions required.

Making Contact Send query letter with photocopies. Does not keep samples on file; include SAE/IRC for return of material.

▨ 🖳 🌐 ISOPIX

Werkhuizenstraat 7-9 Rue des Ateliers, Brussels 1080 Belgium. (32)(2)420-30-50. Fax: (32)(2)420-41-22. E-mail: pmarncf@isopix.be. Web site: www.isopix.be. **Contact:** Paul Marnef, director. Estab. 1984. News/feature syndicate. Has 2.5 million photos on website, including press (celebrities, royalty, portraits, news sports, archival), stock (contemporary and creative photography) and royalty free. Clients include: advertising agencies, public relations firms, businesses, book publishers, magazine publishers, newspapers, calendar companies, postcard publishers.

Needs Wants photos of teens, celebrities, couples, families, parents, senior citizens, disasters, environmental, landscapes/scenics, wildlife, education, religious, events, food/drink, health/fitness, hobbies, humor, agriculture, business concepts, industry, medicine, science, technology/computers. Interested in alternative process, avant garde, documentary, fashion/glamour, fine art, historical/vintage, seasonal.

Specs Accepts images in digital format; JPEG files only.

Payment & Terms Pays 60-60% commission for b&w and color photos. Enforces strict minimum prices. Works with photographers with or without a contract; negotiable. Offers limited regional exclusivity. Contracts renew automatically with additional submissions. Statements issued monthly. Payment made monthly. Photographers allowed to review account records in cases of discrepancies only. Model/property release preferred. Photo captions required.

Making Contact Contact through rep. Does not keep samples on file; include SAE/IRC for return of material. Expects minimum initial submission of 1,000 images with quarterly submissions of at least 500 images.

🖳 🌐 ISRAELIMAGES.COM

POB 60 Kammon 20112, Israel. (972)(4)908-2023. Fax: (972)(4)990-5783. E-mail: israel@isr aelimages.com. Web site: www.israelimages.com. **Contact:** Israel Talby, managing director. Estab. 1991. Has 450,000 photos in files. Clients include: advertising agencies, web designers, businesses, book publishers, magazine publishers, newspapers, calendar companies, greeting card and postcard publishers, multimedia producers, schools and universities, etc.

Needs "We are interested in everything about Israel, Judaism (worldwide) and The Holy Land."

Specs Uses digital material only, minimum accepted size 2000×3000 pixels. Send CD with low-res samples for review. "When accepted, we need TIFF or JPEG files at 300 dpi, RGB, saved at quality '11' in Photoshop."

Payment & Terms Average price per image (to clients): $50-3,000/picture. Negotiates fees below standard minimum against considerable volume that justifies it. Offers volume discounts to customers. Works with photographers on contract basis only. Offers limited regional exclusivity, nonexclusive contract. Contracts renew automatically with additional submissions. Statements issued quarterly. Payment made quarterly. Photographers allowed to review account records. Offers one-time rights, electronic media rights, agency promotion rights. Informs photographers and allows them to negotiate when a client requests all rights. Model/property release preferred. Photo captions required (what, who, when, where).

Making Contact Send query letter with CD or send low-res by e-mail. Expects minimum initial submission of 100 images. Responds in 2 weeks.

Tips ''We strongly encourage everyone to send us images to review. When sending material, a strong edit is a must. We don't like to get 100 pictures with 50 similars. Last, don't overload our e-mail with submissions. Make an e-mail query, or better yet, view our submission guidelines on the Web site. Good luck and welcome!''

▣ IVERSON SCIENCE PHOTOS

31 Boss Ave., Portsmouth NH 03801. (603)433-8484. Fax: (603)433-8484. E-mail: bruce.iverson@verizon.net. Web site: www.iversonsciencephotos.com. **Contact:** Bruce Iverson, owner. Estab. 1981. Stock photo agency. Clients include: advertising agencies, book/encyclopedia publishers, museums.

Needs Currently only interested in submissions of scanning electron micrographs and transmission electron micrographs—all subjects.

Specs Uses all photographic formats and digital imagery.

Payment & Terms Pays 50% commission for b&w and color photos. Offers nonexclusive contract. Photographer paid within 1 month of agency's receipt of payment. Offers one-time rights. Photo captions required; include magnification and subject matter.

Making Contact ''Give us a call or e-mail first. Our subject matter is very specialized.'' Responds in 2 weeks.

Tips ''We are a specialist agency for science photos and technical images.''

▣ ⊕ JAYAWARDENE TRAVEL PHOTO LIBRARY

7A Napier Road, Wembley, Middlesex HA0 UA United Kingdom. (44)(20)8795-3581. Fax: (44)(20)8795-4083. E-mail: jaytravelphotos@aol.com. Web site: www.jaytravelphotos.com. **Contact:** Rohith or Franco, partners. Estab. 1992. Stock photo agency and picture library. Has 150,000 photos in files. Clients include: advertising agencies, businesses, book/encyclopedia publishers, magazine publishers, newspapers, postcard publishers, tour operators/travel companies.

Needs Travel and tourism-related images worldwide.

Specs Uses 35mm up to 6×7cm original transparencies and digital images (see website for guidelines).

Payment & Terms Pays 50% commission. Average price per image (to clients): $125-1,000. Enforces minimum prices of $125, ''but negotiable on quantity purchases.'' Offers volume discounts to customers; inquire about specific terms. Discount sales terms not negotiable. Works with photographers on contract basis only. Offers limited regional exclusivity contract. Statements issued semiannually. Payment made semiannually, within 30 days of payment received from client. Offers one-time and exclusive rights for fixed periods. Does not inform photographers or allow them to negotiate when client requests all rights. Model/property release preferred. Photo captions required; include country, city/location, subject description.

Making Contact Send e-mail with stock list, or call. Expects a minimum initial submission of 300 images with quarterly submissions of at least 100 images. Responds in 3 weeks.

Tips "Study our guidelines on our website on what to submit. If you're planning a photo shoot anywhere, you need to give us an itinerary, with as much detail as possible, so we can brief you on what kind of pictures the library may need."

JEROBOAM

120 27th St., San Francisco CA 94110. (415)821-7098. E-mail: jeroboamster@gmail.com. **Contact:** Ellen Bunning, owner. Estab. 1972. Has 200,000 b&w photos, 200,000 color slides in files. Clients include: text and trade book, magazine and encyclopedia publishers, editorial (mostly textbooks).

Needs "We want people interacting, relating photos, artistic/documentary/photojournalistic images, especially ethnic and handicapped. Images must have excellent print quality—contextually interesting and exciting and artistically stimulating." Wants photos of babies/children/teens, couples, multicultural, families, parents, senior citizens, disasters, environmental, cities/urban, education, gardening, pets, religious, rural, adventure, health/fitness, humor, performing arts, sports, travel, agriculture, industry, medicine, military, political, science, technology/computers. Interested in documentary, historical/vintage, seasonal. Needs shots of school, family, career and other living situations. Child development, growth and therapy, medical situations. No nature or studio shots.

Specs Uses 35mm transparencies.

Payment & Terms Works on consignment only; pays 50% commission. Average price per image (to clients): $150 minimum for b&w and color photos. Works with photographers without a signed contract. Statements issued monthly. Payment made monthly. Photographers allowed to review account records to verify sales figures. Offers one-time and electronic media rights. Informs photographers and allows them to negotiate when client requests all rights. Model/property release preferred for people in contexts of special education, sexuality, etc. Photo captions preferred; include "age of subject, location, etc."

Making Contact Call if in the Bay area; if not, query with samples and list of stock photo subjects; send material by mail for consideration or submit portfolio for review. "Let us know how long you've been shooting." Responds in 2 weeks.

Tips "The Jeroboam photographers have shot professionally a minimum of 5 years, have experienced some success in marketing their talent, and care about their craft excellence and their own creative vision. New trends are toward more intimate, action shots; more ethnic images needed."

KIEFFER NATURE STOCK

4548 Beachcomber Court, Boulder CO 80301. (303)530-3357. E-mail: John@KiefferNatureStock.com. Web site: www.KiefferNatureStock.com. **Contact:** John Kieffer, president. Estab. 1986. Stock agency. Has 150,000 images on file and in keyword-searchable online database. Clients include: advertising agencies, businesses, multimedia, greeting card and postcard publishers, book publishers, calendar companies, graphic design firms, magazine publishers.

Needs "Our photos show people of all ages participating in an active and healthy lifestyle." Wants photos of babies/children/teens, couples, multicultural, families, senior citizens, recreation, environmental, landscapes/scenics, wildlife, rural, adventure, health/fitness, sports, travel, agriculture.

Specs Requires images in high-resolution digital format. Also accepts large-format film (6×7-cm and 4×5-inch); 35mm transparencies. Send low-resolution files via CD or e-mail in JPEG format at 72 dpi.

Payment & Terms Pays 50% commission for all imagery. Average price per image (to clients): $150-3,500 for all imagery. ''Tries to work with a buyer's budget.'' Offers volume discounts to customers. Offers nonexclusive contract. Payment made quarterly. Model release required; property release preferred. Photo captions required; include location, description.

Making Contact ''First review our Web site. Then send a query letter via e-mail, and include a stock list or an active link to your Web site.'' Keeps samples on file. Responds in 3 weeks.

KIMBALL STOCK

(formerly Ron Kimball Stock) 1960 Colony St., Mountain View CA 94043. (888)562-5522 or (650)969-0682. Fax: (650)969-0485. E-mail: submissions@kimballstock.com. Web site: www.kimballstock.com. **Contact:** Jeff Kimball. Estab. 1970. Has 1 million photos in files. Clients include: advertising agencies, businesses, newspapers, postcard publishers, public relations firms, book publishers, calendar companies, magazine publishers, greeting card companies.

Needs Wants photos of dogs, cats, lifestyle with cars and domestic animals, landscapes/scenics, wildlife (outside of North America). Interested in seasonal.

Specs Prefers images in digital format, minimum of 10-megapixel digital camera, although 16-megapixel is preferred. Send via e-mail as JPEG files or send CD to mailing address. Uses 35mm, 120mm, 4×5 transparencies.

Payment & Terms Pays 50% commission for color photos. Offers volume discounts to customers. Works with photographers with or without a contract; negotiable. Offers nonexclusive contract. Statements issued quarterly. Payment made quarterly. Photographers allowed to review account records. Offers one-time rights, electronic media rights. Model / property release required. Photo captions required.

Making Contact Send query letter wit h transparencies, digital files, stock list. Provide self-promotion piece to be kept on file. Expects minimum initial submission of 250 images with quarterly submissions of at least 200 images. Responds only if interested ; send nonreturnable samples. Photo guidelines available on Web site.

JOAN KRAMER AND ASSOCIATES, INC.

10490 Wilshire Blvd., Suite 1701, Los Angeles CA 90024. (310)446-1866. Fax: (310)446-1856. E-mail: ekeeeek@earthlink.net. Web site: www.home.earthlink.net/ ~ ekeeeek. **Contact:** Joan Kramer, president. Member of Picture Archive Council of America (PACA). Has 1 million photos in files. Clients include: ad agencies, magazines, recording companies, photo researchers, book publishers, greeting card companies, promotional companies, AV producers.

Needs ''We use any and all subjects! Stock slides must be of professional quality.'' Subjects on file include travel, cities, personalities, animals, flowers, lifestyles, underwater, scenics, sports and couples.

Specs Uses 8×10 glossy b&w prints; any size transparencies.

Payment & Terms Pays 50% commission. Offers all rights. Model release required.

Making Contact Send query letter or call to arrange an appointment. Do not send photos before calling.

▣ ⊕ LAND OF THE BIBLE PHOTO ARCHIVE

P.O. Box 8441, Jerusalem 91084 Israel. (972)(2)566-2167. Fax: (972)(2)566-3451. E-mail: radovan@netvision.net.il. Web site: www.biblelandpictures.com. **Contact:** Zev Radovan. Estab. 1975. Picture library. Has 50,000 photos in files. Clients include: book publishers, magazine publishers, newspapers, calendar companies, postcard publishers.

Needs Wants photos of museum objects, archaeological sites. Also multicultural, landscapes/scenics, architecture, religious, travel. Interested in documentary, fine art, historical/vintage.

Specs Uses high-resolution digital system.

Payment & Terms Average price per image (to clients): $80-700 for b&w, color photos. Offers volume discounts to customers; terms specified in photographers' contracts.

Tips "Our archives contain tens of thousands of color slides covering a wide range of subjects: historical and archaeological sites, aerial and close-up views, museum objects, mosaics, coins, inscriptions, the myriad ethnic and religious groups individually portrayed in their daily activities, colorful ceremonies, etc. Upon request, we accept assignments for in-field photography."

LIGHTWAVE

170 Lowell St., Arlington MA 02174. (781)646-1747. E-mail: paul@lightwavephoto.com. Web site: www.lightwavephoto.com. **Contact:** Paul Light. Has 250,000 photos in files. Clients include: advertising agencies, textbook publishers.

Needs Wants candid photos of people in school, work and leisure activities, lifestyle.

Specs Uses color transparencies.

Payment & Terms Pays $210/photo; 50% commission. Works with photographers on contract basis only. Offers nonexclusive contract. Contracts renew automatically each year. Statements issued annually. Payment made "after each usage." Offers one-time rights. Informs photographers and allows them to negotiate when client requests all rights. Model/property release preferred. Photo captions preferred.

Making Contact "Create a small website and send us the URL."

Tips "Photographers should enjoy photographing people in everyday activities. Work should be carefully edited before submission. Shoot constantly and watch what is being published. We are looking for photographers who can photograph daily life with compassion and originality."

▣ ⊕ LINEAIR FOTOARCHIEF, B.V.

van der Helllaan 6, Arnhem 6824 HT Netherlands. (31)(26)4456713. Fax: (31)(26)3511123. E-mail: info@lineairfoto.nl. Web site: www.lineairfoto.nl. **Contact:** Ron Giling, manager. Estab. 1990. Stock photo agency. Has 500,000 analog photos in files and more than 300,00 downloadable images available through the Web site. Clients include advertising agencies, public relations firms, book/encyclopedia publishers, magazine publishers. Library specializes in images from Asia, Africa, Latin America, Eastern Europe and nature in all forms on all continents. Member of WEA, a group of international libraries that use the same server to market each other's images, uploading only once.

Needs Wants photos of disasters, environmental, landscapes/scenics, wildlife, cities/urban, education, religious, adventure, travel, agriculture, business concepts, industry, political, science, technology/computers. Interested in everything that has to do with the development of countries all over the world, especially in Asia, Africa and Latin America.

Stock Photo Agencies

Specs Accepts images in digital format only. Send via CD as TIFF or high-quality JPEG files at 300 dpi, A4 or rather bigger size. ''Photo files need to have IPTC information!''

Payments & Terms Pays 50% commission. Average price per image (to clients): $100-500. Enforces minimum prices. Offers volume discounts to customers; inquire about specific terms. Photographers can choose not to sell images on discount terms. Works with or without a signed contract; negotiable. Offers limited regional exclusivity. Statements issued quarterly. Payment made quarterly. Photographers allowed to review account records. ''They can review bills to clients involved.'' Offers one-time rights. Informs photographers and allows them to negotiate when client requests all rights. Photo captions required; include country, city or region, description of the image.

Making Contact Submit portfolio or e-mail thumbnails (20KB files) for review. There is no minimum for initial submissions. Responds in 3 weeks. Market tips sheet available upon request. View Web site to subject matter and quality.

Tips ''We like to see high-quality pictures in all aspects of photography. So we'd rather see 50 good ones than 500 for us to select the 50 out of. Send contact sheets. We will mark the selected pictures for you to send as high-res, including the very important IPTC (caption and keywords).''

▣ ⊕ LINK PICTURE LIBRARY

41A The Downs, London SW20 8HG United Kingdom. (44)(208)944-6933. E-mail: library@l inkpicturelibrary.com. Web site: www.linkpicturelibrary.com. **Contact:** Orde Eliason. Has 100,000 photos in files. Clients include: businesses, book publishers, magazine publishers, newspapers. Specializes in images of Southern and Central Africa, Southeast Asia, China and India.

Needs Wants photos of children and teens, multicultural, cities/urban, religious, adventure, travel, business concepts, industry, military, political. Interested in documentary, historical/vintage. Especially interested in India and Africa.

Specs Accepts images in digital format. Send via CD, e-mail as TIFF, JPEG files at 300 dpi.

Payment & Terms Pays 50% commission for color photos. Average price per image (to clients): $120 minimum for b&w, color photos. Enforces minimum prices. Offers volume discounts to customers. Offers nonexclusive contract. Contracts renew automatically with additional submissions for 3 years. Statements issued semiannually. Payment made semiannually. Photographers allowed to review account records. Offers one-time rights. Photo captions required; include country, city location, subject detail.

Making Contact Provide résumé, business card, self-promotion piece to be kept on file. Expects minimum initial submission of 100 images with quarterly submissions of at least 100 images. Responds in 2 weeks to samples. Responds only if interested; send nonreturnable samples.

Tips ''Arrange your work in categories to view. Have metadate embedded in all images. Provide contact details and supply SASE for returns.''

▣ LUCKYPIX

1658 N. Milwaukee, #324, Chicago IL 60647. (773)235-2000. Fax: (773)235-2030. E-mail: info@luckypix.com. Web site: www.luckypix.com. **Contact:** Director of Photography. Estab. 2001. Stock agency. Has 9,000 photos in files (adding constantly). Clients include: advertising agencies, businesses, book publishers, design companies, magazine publishers.

Needs Wants outstanding people/lifestyle images.

Stock Photo Agencies

Specs 50 + MB TIFs, 300 DPI, 8-Bit Files. Photos for review: upload to website or e-mail info@luckypix.com. Final: CD/DVD as TIFF files.

Payment & Terms 50% commission for net revenues. Enforces minimum prices. Offers exclusivity by image and similars. Contracts renew automatically annually. Statements and payments issued quarterly. Model/property release required.

Making Contact Call or upload sample from website (preferred). Responds in 1 week. See website for guidelines.

Tips "Have fun shooting. Search the archives before deciding what pictures to send."

▣ ◪ MASTERFILE

3 Concorde Gate, 4th Floor, Toronto ON M3C 3N7 Canada. (800)387-9010. E-mail: portfolio @masterfile.com. Web site: www.masterfile.com. General stock agency offering rights-managed and royalty-free images. The combined collection exceeds 1 million images online. Clients include: major advertising agencies, broadcasters, graphic designers, public relations firms, book and magazine publishers, producers of greeting cards, calendars and packaging.

Specs Accepts images in digital format only, in accordance with submission guidelines.

Payment & Terms Pays photographers 40% royalties of amounts received by Masterfile. Contributor terms outlined in photographer's contract, which is image-exclusive. Photographer sales statements and royalty payments issued monthly.

Making Contact Refer to www.masterfile.com/info/artists/submissions.html for submission guidelines.

▧ ▨ MICHELE MATTEI PHOTOGRAPHY

1714 Wilton Place, Los Angeles CA 90028. (323)462-6342. Fax: (323)462-7568. E-mail: michele@michelemattei.com. Web site: www.michelemattei.com. **Contact:** Michele Mattei, director. Estab. 1974. Stock photo agency. Clients include: book/encyclopedia publishers, magazine publishers, television, film.

Needs Wants photos of television and film celebrities, feature stories. Written information to accompany stories needed. Does not wish to see fashion and greeting card-type scenics. Also wants environmental, architecture, cities/urban, health/fitness, science, technology/computers, lifestyle.

Payment & Terms Pays 50% commission for color and b&w photos. Offers one-time rights. Model release required. Photo captions required.

Making Contact Send query letter with résumé, samples, stock list.

Tips "Shots of celebrities and home/family stories are frequently requested." In samples, looking for "high-quality, recognizable personalities and current newsmaking material. We are interested mostly in celebrity photography. Written material on personality or event helps us to distribute material faster and more efficiently."

▣ ◪ ▨ MAXX IMAGES, INC.

711 W. 15th St., North Vancouver BC V7M 1T2 Canada. (604)985-2560. Fax: (604)985-2590. E-mail: newsubmissions@maxximages.com. Web site: www.maxximages.com. **Contact:** Dave Maquignaz, president. Estab. 1994. Stock agency. Member of the Picture Archive Council of America (PACA). Has 3.2 million images online. Has 350 hours of video footage. Clients include: advertising agencies, public relation firms, audiovisual firms, businesses,

book publishers, magazine publishers, newspapers, calendar companies, postcard publishers, video production, graphic design studios.

Needs Wants photos of people, lifestyle, business, recreation, leisure.

Specs Uses all formats.

Making Contact Send e-mail. Review submission guidelines on website prior to contact.

▣ THE MEDICAL FILE INC.

279 E. 44th St., 21st Floor, New York NY 10017. (212)883-0820 or (917)215-6301. E-mail: themedicalfile@gmail.com. Web site: www.themedicalfile.com. **Contact:** Barbara Gottlieb, president. Estab. 2005. Clients include: advertising agencies, public relations firms, businesses, book/encyclopedia publishers, magazine publishers, postcard companies, calendar companies and greeting card companies.

Needs Wants photos of any medically related imagery including fitness and food in relation to healthcare.

Specs Accepts digital format images only on CD or DVD. Images can be downloaded to FTP site.

Payment & Terms Average price per image (for clients): $250 and up. Works on exclusive and nonexclusive contract basis. Contracts renew automatically with each submission for length of original contract. Payment made quarterly. Offers one-time rights. Informs photographers when clients request all rights or exclusivity. Model release required. Photo captions required.

Making Contact Arrange a personal interview to show portfolio. Submit portfolio for review. Tips sheet distributed as needed to contract photographers only.

Tips Wants to see a cross-section of images for style and subject. "Photographers should not photograph people *before* getting a model release. The day of the 'grab shot' is over."

�Ⓝ ▣ 🌐 MUSIC & ARTS PICTURES AT LEBRECHT

3 Bolton Road, London NW8 0RJ United Kingdom. E-mail: pictures@lebrecht.co.uk. Web site: www.lebrecht.co.uk. **Contact:** Ms. E. Lebrecht. Estab. 1992. Has 65,000 high-res images online; thousands more not yet scanned. Clients include: book publishers, magazine publishers, newspapers, calendar companies, film production companies, greeting card companies, public relations firms, advertising agencies.

Needs Wants photos of arts personalities, performing arts, instruments, musicians, dance (ballet, contemporary and folk), orchestras, opera, concert halls, jazz, blues, rock, authors, artists, theatre, comedy, art and artists. Interested in historical/vintage.

Specs Accepts images in digital format only.

Payment & Terms Pays 50% commission for b&w or color photos. Offers volume discounts to customers. Works with photographers on contract basis only. Offers limited regional exclusivity. Statements issued quarterly. Offers one-time rights. Informs photographers and allows them to negotiate when a client requests all rights. Model release required. Photo captions required; include who is in photo, location, date.

Making Contact Send e-mail.

▣ 🖼 911 PICTURES

63 Gardiners Lane., East Hampton NY 11937. (631)324-2061. Fax: (631)329-9264. E-mail: 911pix@optonline.net. Web site: www.911pictures.com. **Contact:** Michael Heller, president. Estab. 1996. Stock agency. Has 3,200 photos in files. Clients include: advertising

agencies, public relations firms, audiovisual firms, businesses, book publishers, magazine publishers, calendar companies, insurance companies, public safety training facilities.

Needs Wants photos of disaster services, public safety/emergency services, fire, police, EMS, rescue, hazmat. Interested in documentary.

Specs Accepts images in digital format on CD at minimum 300 dpi, 8″ minimum short dimension. Images for review may be sent via e-mail, CD as BMP, GIF, JPEG files at 72 dpi.

Payment & Terms Pays 50% commission for b&w and color photos; 75% for film and videotape. Enforces minimum prices. Offers volume discounts to customers. Works with photographers on contract basis only. Offers nonexclusive contract. Charges any print fee (from negative or slide) or dupe fee (from slide). Statements issued/sale. Payment made/sale. Photographers allowed to review account records in cases of discrepancies only. Offers one-time rights. Informs photographers and allows them to negotiate when client requests all rights. Model release preferred. Photo captions preferred; include photographer's name, and a short caption as to what is occurring in photo.

Making Contact Send query letter with résumé, slides, prints, photocopies, tearsheets. "Photographers can also send e-mail with thumbnail (low-resolution) attachments." Does not keep samples on file; include SASE for return of material. Responds only if interested; send nonreturnable samples. Photo guidelines sheet free with SASE.

Tips "Keep in mind that there are hundreds of photographers shooting hundreds of fires, car accidents, rescues, etc., every day. Take the time to edit your own material, so that you are only sending in your best work. We are especially in need of hazmat, police and natural disaster images. At this time 911 Pictures is only soliciting work from those photographers who shoot professionally or who shoot public safety on a regular basis. We are not interested in occasional submissions of one or two images."

◼ NOVASTOCK

1306 Matthews Plantation Dr., Matthews NC 28105 2463. (888)894-8622. Fax: (704)841-8181. E-mail: Novastock@aol.com. Web site: www.creativeshake.com/novastock. **Contact:** Anne Clark, submission department. Estab. 1993. Stock agency. Clients include: advertising agencies, businesses, postcard publishers, public relations firms, book publishers, calendar companies, magazine publishers, greeting card companies, and large international network of subagents.

Needs "We need commercial stock subjects such as lifestyles, fitness, business, science, medical, family, etc. We also are looking for unique and unusual imagery. We have one photographer who burns, scratches and paints on his film." Wants photos of babies/children/teens, couples, multicultural, families, parents, senior citizens, disasters, environmental, wildlife, rural, adventure, health/fitness, travel, business concepts, military, science, technology/computers.

Specs Prefers images in digital format as follows: (1) Original digital camera files. (2) Scanned images in the 30-50MB range. "When sending files for editing, please send small files only. Once we make our picks, you can supply larger files. Final large files should be uncompressed TIFF or JPEG saved at best-quality compression. NEVER sharpen or use contrast and saturation filters. Always flatten layers. Files and disks must be readable on Windows PC."

Payment & Terms Pays 50% commission for b&w and color photos. Price range per image: $100-50,000 for b&w and color photos. "We never charge the photographer for any ex-

Stock Photo Agencies

penses whatsoever." Works with photographers on contract basis only. "We need exclusivity only for images accepted, and similars." Photographer is allowed to market work not represented by Novastock. Statements and payments are made in the month following receipt of income from sales. Informs photographers and discusses with photographer when client requests all rights. Model/property release required. Photo captions required; include who, what and where. "Science and technology need detailed and accurate captions. Model releases must be cross-referenced with the appropriate images."

Making Contact Contact by e-mail or send query letter with digital files, slides, tearsheets, transparencies. Does not keep samples on file; include SASE for return of material or personal check to cover return costs. Expects minimum initial submission of 100 images. Responds in 1 week to submissions.

Tips "Digital files on CD/DVD are preferred. All images must be labeled with caption (if necessary) and marked with model release information and your name and copyright. We market agency material through more than 50 agencies in our international subagency network. The photographer is permitted to freely market nonsimilar work any way he/she wishes. If you are unsure if your work meets the highest level of professionalism as used in current advertising, please do not contact."

▣ ⊕ OKAPIA K.G.

Michael Grzimek & Co., Postfach 645, Röderbergweg 168, Frankfurt 60385 Germany. E-mail: okapia@t-online.de. Web site: www.okapia.com. **Contact:** President. Stock photo agency and picture library. Has 700,000 photos in files. Clients include: ad agencies, book/encyclopedia publishers, magazine publishers, newspapers, postcard companies, calendar companies, greeting card companies, school book publishers.

Needs Wants photos of natural history, babies/children/teens, couples, families, parents, senior citizens, gardening, pets, adventure, health/fitness, travel, agriculture, industry, medical, science, technology/computers, general interest.

Specs Uses 35mm, $2^1/_4 \times 2^1/_4$, 4×5 transparencies. Accepts digital images. Send via DVD, CD, floppy disk as JPEG files at 355 dpi.

Payment & Terms Pays 50% commission for color photos. Average price per image (to clients): $60-120 for color photos. Enforces strict minimum prices. Offers volume discounts to customers. Discount sales terms not negotiable. Works with photographers on contract basis only. Offers nonexclusive contract, limited regional exclusivity and guaranteed subject exclusivity (within files). Contracts renew automatically for 1 year with additional submissions. Charges catalog insertion fee. Statements issued quarterly, semiannually or annually, depending on money photographers earn. Payment made quarterly, semiannually or annually with statement. Photographers allowed to review account records in cases of discrepancies only. Offers one-time, electronic media and agency promotion rights. Does not permit photographers to negotiate when client requests all rights. Model/property release preferred. Photo captions required.

Making Contact Send query letter with slides. Does not keep samples on file; include SASE for return of material. Expects minimum initial submission of 300 slides. Responds in 5 weeks. Photo guidelines free with SASE. Distributes tips sheets on request semiannually to photographers with statements.

Tips "We need every theme which can be photographed." For best results, "send pictures continuously."

▣ OMNI-PHOTO COMMUNICATIONS

10 E. 23rd St., New York NY 10010. Phone: (212) 995-0805. Fax: (212)995-0895. E-mail: info@omniphoto.com. Web site: www.omniphoto.com. **Contact:** Mary Fran Loftus, president. Estab. 1979. Stock photo and art agency. Has 100,000 photos in files. Clients include: advertising agencies, public relations firms, businesses, book/encyclopedia/magazines/calendar/greeting card companies.

Needs Wants photos of babies/children/teens, couples, multicultural, families, senior citizens, environmental, wildlife, architecture, cities/urban, religious, rural, entertainment, food/drink, health/fitness, sports, travel, agriculture, industry, medicine.

Specs Accepts images in digital format. High-resolution 30- 50MB JPEGs required for accepted digital images.

Payment & Terms Pays 50% commission. Works with photographers on contract basis only. Offers limited regional exclusivity. Contracts renew automatically with additional submissions for 4 years. Charges catalog insertion fee. Statements issued with payment on a quarterly basis. Offers one-time rights. Informs photographers and allows them to negotiate when client requests all rights. Model/property release required. Photo captions required.

Making Contact "Send low-res sample JPEGs (approximately 3×5 inches) on DVD, CD, or point us to your Web site portfolio. Only discs with SASE are returned. No e-mail attachments."

Tips "We want spontaneous-looking, professional-quality photos of people interacting with each other. Have carefully-thought-out backgrounds, props and composition, commanding use of color. Stock photographers must produce high-quality work at an abundant rate. Self-assignment is very important, as is a willingness to obtain model releases; caption thoroughly and make submissions regularly."

▣ ⊕ ONASIA

30 Cecil Street, Prudential Tower Level 15, Singapore 049712. + 66 2673 9407-8. Fax: + 66 2673 9409. E-Mail: sales@onasia.com . Web site: www.onasia.com. Contact: Peter Charlesworth or Yvan Cohen, directors. An Asia-specialized agency offering rights-managed stock, features and assignment services. Represents over 180 photographers and has over 180,000 high-resolution images available online and 400,000 photos in files. Offices in Singapore and Bangkok. Represented co-exclusively by Jupiter Images for commercial imagery. Clients include: advertising and graphic design agencies, newspapers, magazines, book publishers, calendar and gift card companies.

Needs Wants model-released Asia-related conceptual, lifestyle and business imagery as well as a broad range of nonreleased editorial imagery including current affairs, historical collections, travel and leisure, economics as well as social and political trends. Please note: We only accept images from or relating to Asia.

Specs Accepts images in digital format. Send via CD or to our FTP site as 12 × 18-inch JPEG files at 300 dpi. All files must be retouched to remove dust and dirt. Photo captions required; include dates, location, country and a detailed description of image, including names where possible.

Payment/Terms Pays 50% commission to photographers. Terms specified in photographer contracts. Photographers are required to submit on an image-exclusive basis. Statements issued monthly.

Making Contact E-mail queries to info@onasia.com with lo-res JPEG samples or a link to photographer's Web site. Does not keep samples on file; cannot return material. Expects minimum initial submission of 150 images. Photo guidelines available via e-mail.

Tips "Provide a well-edited lo-res portfolio for initial evaluation. Ensure that subsequent submissions are tightly edited, sized to Onasia's specs, retouched and submitted with full captions."

N ▣ ▣ OPCAO BRASIL IMAGENS

Rua Barata Ribeiro, No. 370 GR. 215/216, Copacabana, Rio de Janeiro, 22040-002 Brazil. Phone/fax: (55)(21)2256-9007. E-mail: opcao@opcaobrasil.com.br. Web site: www.opc aobrasil.com.br. **Contact:** Ms. Graca Machado and Mr. Marcos Machado, directors. Estab. 1993. Has 600,000 photos in files. Clients include: advertising agencies, book publishers, magazine publishers, calendar companies, postcard publishers, publishing houses.

Needs Wants photos of babies/children/teens, couples, families, parents, wildlife, health/fitness, beauty, education, hobbies, sports, industry, medicine. "We need photos of wild animals, mostly from the Brazilian fauna. We are looking for photographers who have images of people who live in tropical countries."

Specs Accepts images in digital format.

Payment & Terms Pays 50% commission for b&w or color photos. Average price per image (to clients): $100-400 for b&w photos; $200 minimum for color photos. Negotiates fees below standard minimum prices only in case of renting, at least, 20 images. Offers volume discounts to customers. Works with photographers on contract basis only. Offers limited regional exclusivity. Contracts renew automatically with additional submissions for 3 years. Charges $200/image for catalog insertion. Statements issued quarterly. Payment made quarterly. Photographers allowed to review account records in cases of discrepancies only. Offers one-time rights, electronic media rights, agency promotion rights. Model release required; property release preferred. Photo captions required.

Making Contact Initial contact should be by e-mail or fax. Explain what kind of material you have. Provide business card, self-promotion piece to be kept on file. "If not interested, we return the samples." Expects minimum initial submission of 200 images with quarterly submissions of at least 500 images. Responds in 1 month to samples.

Tips "We need creative photos presenting the unique look of the photographer on active and healthy people in everyday life at home, at gyms, at work, etc., showing modern and up-to-date individuals. We are looking for photographers who have images of people with the characteristics of Latin American citizens."

▣ OUT OF THE BLUE

711 S Osprey Ave., Ste 1, Sarasota FL 34236. (941) 966-4042. Fax: (941)296-7345. E-mail: outoftheblue.us@mac.com. Web site: www.out-of-the-blue.us. Estab. 2003. **Contact:** Michael Woodward, president or Jane Mason, licensing manager. "Here serendipity, creativity and commerce merge. We specializes in creating 'Art Brands.' We are looking for fine art photographic collections that we can license for product categories such as fine art posters, giclees on paper and canvas for interior design projects, home and office decor."

Needs "We require collections or groups of photographic images which are either decorative or have a more sophisiticated fine art look." E-mail or CD prestations preferred.

Making Contact "Commission rate is 50% with no expenses to photographers as long as photographer can provide high-resolution scans if we agree to representation." Fine artists should send short bio.

Tips ''We are interested in collections or groups of images that have commercial appeal. Posters and prints are normally sold in pairs which complement each other. Pay close attention to trends. Color palettes which reflect the words eco-friendly/environmental and 'green' are in demand.''

▣ ⊕ ▨ OXFORD SCIENTIFIC (OSF)

Oxford Scientific Films, Network House, 2nd Floor Waterside House, 9 Woodfield Rd., London W9 2BA United Kingdom. (44)(0) 20 7432 8200. Fax: (44)(0) 20 7432 8201. E-mail: uksales@osf.co.uk. Web site: www.osf.co.uk. **Contact**: Creative Director. Estab. 1968. Stock agency. Stills and footage libraries. Has 350,000 photos, over 2,000 feet of HD, film and video originated footage.Clients include: advertising agencies, design companies, audiovisual firms, book/encyclopedia publishers, magazine and newspaper publishers, merchandising companies, multimedia publishers, film production companies.

Needs Wants photos and footage of natural history: animals, plants, behavior, close-ups, life-histories, histology, embryology, electron microscopy, scenics, geology, weather, conservation, country practices, ecological techniques, pollution, special-effects, high- speed, time-lapse, landscapes, environmental, travel, sports, pets, domestic animals, wildlife, disasters, gardening, rural, agriculture, industry, medicine, science, technology/computers. Interested in seasonal.

Specs Uses 35mm and larger transparencies; 16 and 35mm film and video. Accepts images in digital format. Send via CD, e-mail at 72 dpi for initial review; 300 dpi (RGB TIFF files) for final submission. Review guidelines for details.

Payment & Terms Pays 50% commission. Negotiates fees below stated minimums on bulk deals. Average price per image (to clients) $100-2,000 for b&w and color photos; $300-4,000 for film or videotape. Offers volume discounts to regular customers; inquire about specific terms. Discount sale terms not negotiable. Works with photographers on contract basis only; needs image exclusivity. Offers image-exclusive contract, limited regional exclusivity, guaranteed subject exclusivity. Contracts renew automatically every 2 years. There is a charge for handling footage. Offers one-time, electronic media and agency promotion rights. Informs photographers and allows them to negotiate when client requests all rights. Model/property release required. Photo captions required; include common name, Latin name, behavior, location and country, magnification where appropriate, if captive, if digitally manipulated. Contact OSF for footage terms.

Making Contact Submission guidelines available on website. Expects minimum initial submission of 100 images with quarterly submissions of at least 100 images. Interested in receiving high-quality, creative, inspiring work from both amateur and professional photographers. Responds in 1 month.

Tips ''Contact via e-mail, phone or fax, or visit our website to obtain submission guidelines.'' Prefers to see ''good focus, composition, exposure, rare or unusual natural history subjects and behavioral and action shots, inspiring photography, strong images as well as creative shots. Read photographer's pack from website or e-mail/write to request a pack, giving brief outline of areas covered and specialties and size.''

⋉ ▣ PACIFIC STOCK/PRINTSCAPES.COM

Koko Marina Center, 7192 Kalanianaole Hwy., Suite G-230, Honolulu HI 96825. (808)394-5100. Fax: (808)394-5200. E-mail: pics@pacificstock.com. Web site: www.pacificstock. com and www.printscapes.com. **Contact:** Barbara Brundage, owner/president. Member of

Picture Archive Council of America (PACA). Has 100,000 photos in files; 25,000 digital images online. "Pacific Stock specializes exclusively in rights-managed imagery from throughout Hawaii, Pacific and Asia and its royalty-free collection." Clients include advertising agencies, public relations firms, book/encyclopedia publishers, magazine publishers, postcard companies, calendar companies, greeting card companies. "We also cater to the professional interior design market at our new fine art Web site, www.printscapes.com."

Needs Needs photos and fine art of Hawaii, Pacific Islands, and throughout the Pacific Rim. Subjects include: people (women, babies/children/teens, couples, multicultural, families, parents, senior citizens), culture, marine science, environmental, landscapes, wildlife, adventure, food/drink, health/fitness, sports, travel, agriculture, business concepts." e also have an extensive vintage Hawaii file as well as fine art throughout the Pacific Rim."

Specs Accepts images in digital format only. Send via Hard Drive or DVD as 16-bit TIFF files (guidelines on website at http://www.pacificstock.com/photographer_guidelines.asp).

Payment & Terms Pays 40% commission for color, black and white photos, or fine art imagery. Average price per image (to clients): $650. Works with photographers and artists on contract basis only. Statements and payments issued monthly. Contributors allowed to review account records to verify sales figures. Offers one-time or first rights; additional rights with contributor's permission. Informs contributors and allows them to negotiate when client requests all rights. Model/property release required for all people and certain properties, i.e., homes and boats. Photo captions required; include: "who, what, where." See submission guidelines for more details.

Making Contact "E-mail or call us after reviewing our Web site and our photo guidelines. Want lists distributed regularly to represented photograpehrs; free via e-mail to interested photographers."

Tips Photographer must be able to supply minimum of 500 image files (must be model-released) for initial entry and must make quarterly submissions of fresh material from Hawaii, Pacific and Asia area destinations. Image files must be captioned in File Info (i.e., IPTC headers) according to our submission guidelines. Please contact us to discuss the types of imagery that sell well for us. We are also looking for fine artists whose work is representative of Hawaii and the Pacific Rim. We are interested in working with contributors who work with us and enjoy supplying imagery requested by our valued clients."

▣ PAINET INC.

20 Eighth St. S., P.O. Box 431, New Rockford ND 58356. (701)947-5932 or (888)966-5932. Fax: (701)947-5933. E-mail: photogs@painetworks.com. Web site: www.painetworks.com. **Contact:** S. Corporation, owner. Estab. 1985. Picture library. Has 589,000 digital photos in files. Clients include: advertising agencies, magazine publishers.

Needs "Anything and everything."

Specs "Refer to www.painetworks.com/helppages/submit.htm for information on how to scan and submit images to Painet. The standard contract is also available from this page."

Payment & Terms Pays 60% commission (see contract). Works with photographers with or without a contract. Offers nonexclusive contract. Payment made immediately after a sale. Informs photographers and allows them to negotiate when client requests all rights. Provides buyer contact information to photographer by sending photographer copies of the original invoices on all orders of photographer's images.

Making Contact "Occasionally receives a list of current photo requests."

Tips ''We have added an online search engine with 532,000 images. We welcome submissions from new photographers, since we add approximately 60,000 images quarterly. Painet markets color and black & white images electronically or by contact with the photographer. Because images and image descriptions are entered into a database from which searches are made, we encourage our photographers to include lengthy descriptions that improve the chances of finding their images during a database search. We prefer descriptions be included in the IPTC (File Info area of Photoshop). Photographers who provide us their e-mail address will receive a biweekly list of current photo requests from buyers. Photographers can then send matching images via e-mail or FTP, and we forward them to the buyer. Painet also hosts Photographer's and Photo Agency Web sites. See details at http://www.painetworks.com/helppages/setupPT.htm.''

▣ PANORAMIC IMAGES

2302 Main St., Evanston IL 60202. (847)324-7000. Fax: (847)324-7004. E-mail: images@panoramicimages.com, michelle@panoramicimages.com. Web site: www.panoramicimages.com. **Contact:** Michelle Alvarado Novak, director of photography. Estab. 1987. Stock photo agency. Member of ASPP, NANPA and IAPP. Clients include: advertising agencies, magazine publishers, newspapers, design firms, graphic designers, corporate art consultants, postcard companies, calendar companies.

Needs Wants photos of lifestyles, environmental, landscapes/scenics, wildlife, architecture, cities/urban, gardening, interiors/decorating, rural, adventure, automobiles, health/fitness, sports, travel, business concepts, industry, medicine, military, science, technology/computers. Interested in alternative process, avant garde, documentary, fine art, historical/vintage, seasonal. Works only with *panoramic formats* (2:1 aspect ratio or greater). Subjects include: cityscapes/skylines, international travel, nature, tabletop, backgrounds, conceptual.

Specs Uses $2^{1}/_{4} \times 5$, $2^{1}/_{4} \times 7$ (6×12cm, 6×17cm). ''Transparencies preferred for initial submission. Call for digital submission guidelines or see Web site.''

Payment & Terms Pays 40% commission for photos. Average price per image (to clients): $600. No charge for scanning, metadata or inclusion on Web site. Statements issued quarterly. Payment made quarterly. Offers one-time, electronic rights and limited exclusive usage. Model release preferred ''and/or property release, if necessary.'' Photo captions required. Call or see Web site for submission guidelines before submitting.

Making Contact Send e-mail with stock list or low-res scans/lightbox. Responds in 1-3 months. Specific want lists created for contributing photographers. Photographer's work is represented on full e-commerce Web site and distributed worldwide through image distribution partnerships with Getty Images, National Geographic Society Image Collection, Amana, Digital Vision, etc.

Tips Wants to see ''well-exposed chromes or very high-res stitched pans. Panoramic views of well-known locations nationwide and worldwide. Also, generic beauty panoramics.''

▣ ⊕ PAPILIO NATURAL HISTORY LIBRARY

155 Station Rd., Herne Bay, Kent CT6 5QA United Kingdom. (44)(122)736-0996. E-mail: library@papiliophotos.com. Web site: www.papiliophotos.com. **Contact:** Justine Pickett. Estab. 1984. Has 120,000 photos in files. Clients include: advertising agencies, book publishers, magazine publishers, newspapers, calendar companies, greeting card companies, postcard publishers.

Needs Wants photos of wildlife.

Specs Prefers digital submissions. Uses digital shot in-camera as RAW and converted to TIFF for submission, minimum file size 17MB. See webpage for further details or contact for a full information sheet about shooting and supplying digital photos.

Payment & Terms Works with photographers on contract basis only. Offers nonexclusive contract. Statements issued quarterly. Payment made quarterly. Offers one-time rights, electronic media rights. Photo captions required; include Latin names and behavioral information and keywords.

Making Contact Send query letter with résumé. Does not keep samples on file. Expects minimum initial submission of 150 images. Responds in 1 month to samples. Returns all unsuitable material with letter. Photo guidelines sheet free with SASE.

Tips "Contact first for information about digital. Send digitial submissions on either cd or DVD disk. Supply full caption listing for all images. Wildlife photography is very competitive. Photographers are advised to send only top-quality images."

🖳 PHOTO AGORA

3711 Hidden Meadow Lane, Keezletown VA 22832. (540)269-8283. E-mail: PhotoAgora@aol.com. Web site: www.photoagora.com. **Contact:** Robert Maust. Estab. 1972. Stock photo agency. Has over 60,000 photos in files. Clients include: businesses, book/encyclopedia and textbook publishers, magazine publishers, calendar companies.

Needs Wants photos of families, children, students, Virginia, Africa and other third world areas, work situations, etc. Also needs babies/children/teens, couples, multicultural, parents, senior citizens, disasters, environmental, landscapes/scenics, wildlife, cities/urban, education, gardening, pets, religious, rural, health/fitness, travel, agriculture, industry, medicine, science, technology/computers.

Specs Prefers high-resolution digital images. Ask for password to download agreement and submission guidelines from web site.

Payment & Terms Pays 50% commission for b&w and color photos. Average price per image (to clients): $40 minimum for b&w photos; $100 minimum for color photos. Negotiates fees below standard minimum prices. Offers volume discounts to customers; inquire about specific terms. Photographers can choose not to sell images on discount terms. Works with photographers with or without a contract. Offers nonexclusive contract. Statements issued quarterly. Payment made quarterly. Photographers allowed to review account records. Offers one-time rights. Informs photographers and allows them to negotiate when client requests all rights. Model/property release preferred. Embedded photo captions required; include location, important dates, scientific names, etc.

Making Contact Call, write or e-mail. No minimum number of images required in initial submission. Responds in 3 weeks. Photo guidelines free with SASE or download from Web site.

🖳 PHOTO EDIT

235 E. Broadway St., Suite 1020, Long Beach CA 90802. (800)860-2098. Fax: (800)804-3707. E-mail: sales@photoeditinc.com. Web site: www.photoeditinc.com. **Contact:** Kristen Sachs or Raquel Ramirez. Estab. 1987. Stock agency. 100% digital. 200,000 images online. Clients include: advertising agencies, businesses, public relations firms, book/textbook publishers, calendar companies, magazine/newspaper publishers.

Needs Digital images of babies/children/teens, couples, multicultural, families, parents, senior citizens, disasters, environment, cities/urban, education, religious, food/drink, health/fitness, hobbies, sports, travel, agriculture, business concepts, industry, medicine, political, science, technology/computers.

Specs Uses images in digital format (RAW, unmanipulated) . Send via CD as JPEG files at 300 dpi.

Payment & Terms Average price per image (to clients): $175 for color images. Enforces minimum prices. Enjoys preferred vendor status with many clients. Works with photographers on contract basis only. Offers nonexclusive contract. Contracts renew automatically with continuous submissions. Offers one-time rights. Informs photographers and allows them to negotiate when a client requests all rights. Model/property release preferred. Photo captions required.

Making Contact Send query letter by e-mail with images or link to website to view images. Does not keep samples on file. Responds immediately only if interested. Photo guidelines sheet available via e-mail.

Tips "Call to discuss interests, equipment, specialties, availability, etc."

▣ PHOTO NETWORK

P.O. Box 317, Lititz PA 17543. (717)626-0296 or (800)622-2046. Fax: (717)626-0971. E-mail: info@heilmanphoto.com. Web site: www.photonetworkstock.com or www.heilman photo.com. **Contact:** Sonia Wasco, president. Stock photo agency/library. Member of Picture Archive Council of America (PACA). Has more than 1 million photos in files. Clients include: agribusiness companies, ad agencies, textbook companies, graphic artists, public relations firms, newspapers, corporations, magazines, calendar companies, greeting card companies.

• Photo Network is now owned by Grant Heilman Photography.

Needs Wants photos of agriculture, families, couples, ethnics (all ages), animals, travel and lifestyles. Also wants photos of babies/children/teens, parents, senior citizens, disasters, environmental, wildlife, architecture, cities/urban, education, gardening, interiors/decorating, pets, religious, rural, adventure, automobiles, food/drink, health/fitness/beauty, hobbies, humor, sports, business concepts, industry, medicine, military, political, science, technology/computers. Special subject needs include people over age 55 enjoying life; medical shots (patients and professionals); children and domestic animals.

Specs Uses transparencies and digital format. Send via CD as JPEG files.

Payment & Terms Information available upon request.

Making Contact Send query letter with stock list. Send a sample of 200 images for review; include SASE for return of material. Responds in 1 month.

Tips Wants to see a portfolio "neat and well-organized and including a sampling of photographer's favorite photos." Looks for "clear, sharp focus, strong colors and good composition. We'd rather have many very good photos rather than one great piece of art. Would like to see photographers with a specialty or specialties and have it/them covered thoroughly. You need to supply new photos on a regular basis and be responsive to current trends in photo needs. Contract photographers are supplied with quarterly 'want' lists and information about current trends."

▣ PHOTO RESEARCHERS, INC.

60 E. 56th St., New York NY 10022. (212)758-3420. Fax: (212)355-0731. E-mail: portfolio@p hotoresearchers.com. Web site: www.photoresearchers.com. Stock agency. Has over 1 mil-

Stock Photo Agencies

lion photos and illustrations in files, with 250,000 images in a searchable online database. Clients include: advertising agencies; graphic designers; publishers of textbooks, encyclopedias, trade books, magazines, newspapers, calendars, greeting cards; foreign markets.

Needs Wants images of all aspects of science, astronomy, medicine, people (especially contemporary shots of teens, couples and seniors). Particularly needs model-released people, European wildlife, up-to-date travel and scientific subjects. Lifestyle images must be no older than 2 years; travel images must be no older than 5 years.

Specs Prefers images in digital format.

Payment & Terms Rarely buys outright; pay 50% commision on stock sales. General price range (to clients): $150-7,500. Works with photographers on contract basis only. Offers limited regional exclusivity. Contracts renew automatically with additional submissions for 5 years (initial term; 1 year thereafter). Charges $15 for Web placement for transparencies. Photographers allowed to review account records upon reasonable notice during normal business hours. Statements issued monthly, bimonthly or quarterly, depending on volume. Informs photographers and allows them to negotiate when a client requests to buy all rights, but does not allow direct negotiation with customer. Model/property release required for advertising; preferred for editorial. Photo captions required; include who, what, where, when. Indicate model release.

Making Contact See ''About Representation and Submission Guidelines'' on Web site.

Tips ''We seek the photographer who is highly imaginative or into a specialty (particularly in the scientific or medical fields). We are looking for serious contributors who have many hundreds of images to offer for a first submission and who are able to contribute often.''

▣ PHOTO RESOURCE HAWAII

111 Hekili St., #41, Kailua HI 96734. (808)599-7773. Fax: (808)235-5477. E-mail: prh@phot oresourcehawaii.com. Web site: www.PhotoResourceHawaii.com. **Contact:** Tami Kauakea Winston, owner. Estab. 1983. Stock photo agency. Has website with electronic delivery of over 12,000 images. Clients include: ad agencies, audiovisual firms, businesses, book/encyclopedia publishers, magazine publishers, calendar companies, greeting card companies, postcard publishers.

Needs Photos of Hawaii and the South Pacific.

Specs Accepts images in digital format only; 48MB or larger; TIFF files from RAW files preferred.

Payment & Terms Pays 50% commission. Enforces minimum prices. Offers volume discounts to customers. Discount sales terms not negotiable. Works with photographers on contract basis only. Offers nonexclusive contract. Contracts renew automatically with additional submissions. Statements issued bimonthly. Payment made bimonthly. ''Rights-managed licensing only, no royalty-free.'' Model/property release preferred. Photo captions and keywording online required.

Making Contact Send query e-mail with samples. Expects minimum initial submission of 100 images with periodic submissions at least 5 times/year. Responds in 2 weeks.

▣ ⊕ ◩ PHOTO STOCK/GRANATAIMAGES.COM

19/5 Via Wildt, Milan 20131 Italy. (39)(022)668-0702. Fax: (39)(022)668-1126. E-mail: paolo.granata@granataimages.com. Web site: www.granataimages.com. **Contact:** Paolo Granata, manager. Estab. 1985. Stock and press agency. Member of CEPIC. Has 2 million photos in files and 800,000 images online. Clients include: advertising agencies, newspapers, book publishers, calendar companies, audiovisual firms, magazine publishers, production houses.

Needs Wants photos of celebrities, people.

Specs Uses high-resolution digital files. Send via Zip, FTP, e-mail as TIFF, JPEG files.

Payment & Terms Pays 60% commission for color photos. Negotiates fees below stated minimums in cases of volume deals. Offers volume discounts to customers. Photographers can choose not to sell images on discount terms. Works with photographers on contract basis only. Offers exclusive contract only. Contracts renew automatically with additional submissions for 1 year. Statements issued monthly. Photographers allowed to review account records in cases of discrepancies only. Offers one-time rights. Model/property release preferred. Photo captions required; include location, country and any other relevant information.

Making Contact Send query letter with digital files.

⊕ ☑ PHOTOBANK-BANGKOK

Photobank-Singapore, 58/18 Soi Promsri 2, (Soi 49-19) Sukhumvit Rd., Klongton Nue, Wattana 10110 Bangkok. (66)(02)391-8185. Fax: (66)(02)391-4498. E-mail: cassio@loxinfo .co.th. Web site: www.photobangkok.com. **Contact:** Alberto Cassio. Estab. 1975. Picture library. Has 550,000 photos in files. Clients include: advertising agencies, businesses, book publishers, audiovisual firms.

Needs Wants photos of babies/children/teens, couples, families, disasters, environmental, landscapes/scenics, wildlife, cities/urban, education, interiors/decorating, pets, adventure, food/drink, health/fitness/beauty, hobbies, sports, agriculture, business concepts, industry, medicine, product shots/still life, science, technology/computers. Interested in historical/vintage.

Specs Uses 35mm, $2^1/_4 \times 2^1/_4$ transparencies; B copy videos.

Payment & Terms Pays 50% commission for color photos; 40% for videotape. Average price per image (to clients): $100-2,000 for photos; $200-3,000 for videotape. Enforces minimum prices. Offers volume discounts to customers. Works with photographers on contract basis only. Offers limited regional exclusivity. Contracts renew automatically with additional submissions. Statements issued quarterly. Photographers allowed to review account records in cases of discrepancies only. Offers one-time rights. Model release preferred. Photo captions required.

Making Contact Contact through rep. Expects minimum initial submission of 500 images with 6-month submissions of at least 200 images.

Tips "Set up an appointment and meet personally."

▣ ⊕ PHOTOLIFE CORPORATION LTD.

2012 C C Wu Building, 302 Hennessy Rd., Wanchai, Hong Kong. (852)2808 0012. Fax: (852)2808 0072. E-mail: edit@photolife.com.hk. Web site: www.photolife.com.hk. **Contact:** Serene Li, director of business development. Estab. 1994. Stock photo library. Has over 1.6 million photos in files. Clients include: advertising agencies, newspapers, book publishers, calendar companies, magazine publishers, greeting card companies, corporations, production houses, graphic design firms.

Needs Wants contemporary images of architecture, interiors, garden, infrastructure, concepts, business, finance, sports, lifestyle, nature, travel, animal, marine life, foods, medical.

Specs Accepts images in digital format only. "Use only professional digital cameras (capa-

Stock Photo Agencies

Stock Photo Agencies

ble of producing 24 MB + images) with high-quality interchangeable lenses; or images from high-end scanners producing a file up to 50 MB.''

Payment & Terms Pays 50% commission for b&w and color photos. Average price per image (to clients): $105-1,550 for b&w photos; $105-10,000 for color photos. Offers volume discounts to customers; terms specified in photographers' contracts. Works with photographers on contract basis only. Contract can be initiated with minimum 300 selected images. Quarterly submissions needed. Informs photographers and allows them to negotiate when client requests all rights. Model release required; property release preferred. Photo captions required; include destination and country.

Making Contact E-mail 50 low-res images (1,000pixels or less), or send CD with 50 images.

Tips ''Visit our website. Edit your work tightly. Send images that can keep up with current trends in advertising and print photography.''

⊕ PHOTOSOURCE NEW ZEALAND LTD.

Stock Image Group, Suite 6, Clarence House, 18 Clarence St., Devonport, Auckland New Zealand. 64 9 445 7536. Fax: 64 9 445 7537. E-mail: psi2@photosource.com. Web site: www.photosource.com. **Contact**: Rohn Engh. Estab. 1998. Picture library. Has 80,000 photos in files. Clients include: advertising agencies, businesses, postcard publishers, public relations firms, book publishers, calendar companies, government departments, magazine publishers, greeting card companies.

Needs Wants photos of babies/children/teens, celebrities, couples, multicultural, families (New Zealand only), parents, senior citizens, wildlife, disasters, environmental, landscapes/scenics, architecture, cities/urban, education, gardening, interiors/decorating, adventure, entertainment, food/drink, hobbies, performing arts, sports, travel, business concepts, industry, medicine, product shots/still life, science, technology/computers. Interested in seasonal.

Specs Uses 35mm, $2\frac{1}{4} \times 2\frac{1}{4}$, 4×5, 8×10 transparencies.

Payment & Terms Pays 50% commission for photos, film. Average price per image (to clients): $200-2,500 for photos. Offers volume discounts. Discount sales terms not negotiable. Works with photographers on contract basis only. Offers nonexclusive contract with guaranteed subject exclusivity in New Zealand. Statements issued quarterly. Payment made quarterly. Offers one-time rights. Informs photographers and allows them to negotiate when client requests all rights. Model/property release required. Photo captions preferred; include full description of location or subject.

Making Contact Contact via e-mail.

Tips ''All 35mm should be mounted with description and other relevant information on a list. Check all work thoroughly for technical faults and leave 'faulty' material out of submission. Keep subjects in order. Present slides in sleeves, not boxes. 120 format and larger, if mounted, should be labelled, too. 120 format, if unmounted, should be numbered to correspond easily with a description list.''

▣ ⊕ SYLVIA PITCHER PHOTO LIBRARY

75 Bristol Rd., Forest Gate, London E7 8HG United Kingdom. E-mail: SPphotolibrary@aol.com. Web site: www.sylviapitcherphotos.com. **Contact:** Sylvia Pitcher. Estab. 1965. Picture library. Has 70,000 photos in files. Clients include: book publishers, magazine publishers, design consultants, record and TV companies.

Needs Wants photos Musicians—blues, country, bluegrass, old time and jazz with views of America that could be used as background to this music. Also, other relevant subject matter such as recording studios, musicians' birth places, clubs etc. Please see website for a good indication of the library's contents .

Specs Accepts images in digital format.

Payment & Terms Pays 50% commission for b&w and color photos. Average price per image (to clients): $105-1,000. Negotiates fees below stated minimum for budget CDs or multiple sale. Offers volume discounts to customers; terms specified in photographers' contracts. Photographers can choose not to sell images on discount terms, if specified at time of depositing work in library. Works with photographers with or without contract; negotiable. Offers nonexclusive contract. Contracts renew automatically with additional submissions for 3 years. Statements issued quarterly. Payment made when client's check has cleared. Offers one-time rights. Model/property release preferred. Photo captions required; include artist, place/venue, date taken.

Making Contact Send query letter with CD of approximately 10 low-res sample images and stock list. Provide self-promotion piece to be kept on file. Expects minimum initial submission of 50 high-res images on CD with further submissions when available.

▣ PIX INTERNATIONAL

3600 N. Lake Shore Dr., Unit 612 Floor, Chicago IL 60613. (773)472-7457. E-mail: pixintl@yahoo.com. Web site: www.pixintl.com. **Contact:** Linda Matlow, president. Estab. 1978. Stock agency, news/feature syndicate. Has 200,000 photos in files. Clients include: advertising agencies, public relations firms, businesses, book publishers, magazine publishers, newspapers.

Needs Wants photos of celebrities, entertainment, performing arts.

Specs Accepts images in digital format only. E-mail link to Web site. ''Do not e-mail any images. Do not send any unsolicited digital files. Make contact first to see if we're interested.''

Payment & Terms Pays 50% commission for b&w or color photos, film. Average price per image (to clients): $35 minimum for b&w or color photos; $75-3,000 for film. Enforces minimum prices. Offers volume discounts to customers; terms specified in photographers' contracts. Discount sales terms not negotiable. Works with photographers with or without a contract; negotiable. Statements issued monthly. Payment made monthly. Photographers allowed to review account records in cases of discrepancies only. Offers one-time rights. Informs photographers and allows them to negotiate when client requests all rights. Model release not required for general editorial. Photo captions required; include who, what, when, where, why.

Making Contact ''E-mail us your URL with thumbnail examples of your work that can be clicked for a larger viewable image.'' Responds in 2 weeks to samples, only if interested.

Tips ''We are looking for razor-sharp images that stand up on their own without needing a long caption. Let us know by e-mail what types of photos you have, your experience, and cameras used. We do not take images from the lower-end consumer cameras—digital or film. They just don't look very good in publications. For photographers we do accept, we would only consider high-res 300-dpi at 6×9 or higher scans submitted on CDR. Please direct us to samples on your Web site.''

Ⓝ ▣ 🌐 PLANS, LTD. (Photo Libraries and News Services)

#201 Kamako Bldg., 1-8-9 Ohgi-gaya, Kamakura 248-0011 Japan. (81)(46)723-2350. Fax: (81)(46)723-2351. E-mail: yoshida@plans.jp. Web site: www.plans.jp. **Contact:** Takashi

Yoshida, president. Estab. 1982. Stock agency. Is now representing JaincoTech as Jainco-Tech Japan as a joint project for photographers in the stock photo market. Has 100,000 photos in files. Clients include: photo agencies, newspapers, book publishers, magazine publishers, advertising agencies.

Needs "We do consulting for photo agencies for the Japanese market."

Specs Accepts images in digital format, high resol ution.

Payment & Terms Pays 40-50% commission for digital data. Average price per image (to clients): $120-1,000 for b&w or color photos. Negotiates fees below standard minimum prices. Offers volume discounts to customers. Discount sales terms not negotiable. Works with photographers with or without contract; negotiable. Offers nonexclusive contract. Contracts renew automatically with additional submissions. Statements issued monthly or every 6 months. Payment made monthly or every 6 months. Photographers allowed to review account records. Offers one-time rights, electronic media rights, agency promotion rights. Model release preferred. Photo captions and keywords required; include year, states, city.

Making Contact Send query e-mail with résumé, stock list. Does not keep samples on file. Responds only if interested; send digital data samples.

Tips "We need all kinds of photographs of the world. Photographers and archival photo owners should submit stock list including subjects, themes, when, where, color or b lack & w hite, format, total amount of stock, brief profile."

POSITIVE IMAGES (STOCK PHOTOGRAPHY & GALLERY 61)

(formerly Positive Images) 61 Wingate St., Haverhill MA 01832. (978)556-9366. Fax: (978)556-9448. E-mail: pat@positiveimagesphoto.com. Web site: www.agpix.com/positiveimages. **Contact:** Pat Bruno, owner. Stock photo agency and fine art gallery. Member of ASPP, GWAA. Clients include advertising agencies, public relations firms, book/encyclopedia publishers, magazine publishers, greeting card and calendar companies, sales/promotion firms, design firms.

Needs Wants horticultural images showing technique and lifestyle, photo essays on property-released homes and gardens, travel images from around the globe, classy and funky pet photography, health & nutrition, sensitive and thought-provoking images suitable for high-end greeting cards, calendar-quality landscapes, castles, lighthouses, country churches. Model/property releases preferred.

Payment & Terms Pays 50% commission for stock photos; 60% commision for fine art. Average price per image (to clients): $250. Works with photographers on contract basis only. Offers limited regional exclusivity. Payment made quarterly. Offers one-time and electronic media rights. "We never sell all rights."

Making Contact "Positive Images Stock is accepting limited new collections; however, if your images are unique and well organized digitally, we will be happy to review online after making email contact. Our Gallery 61 will review fine art photography portfolios online as well and will consider exhibiting nonmembers' work."

Tips "Positive Images has taken on more of a boutique approach, limiting our number of photographers so that we can better service them and offer a more in-depth and unique collection to our clients. Our brand-new Gallery 61 is a storefront in a small historic arts district. Our plan is to evolve this into an online gallery as well. We are always in search of new talent, so we welcome anyone with a fresh approach to contact us!"

▣ PURESTOCK

7660 Centurion Pkwy., Jacksonville FL 32256. (800)828-4545. E-mail: info@purestock.c om. Web site: www.purestock.com. The Purestock royalty-free brand is designed to provide the professional creative community with high-quality images at high resolution and very competitve pricing. Purestock offers CDs and single-image downloads in a wide range of categories including lifestyle, business, education and sports to distributors in over 100 countries.

Needs "A variety of categories including lifestyle, business, education, medical, industry, etc."

Specs "Digital files which are capable of being output at 80MB with minimal interpolation. File must be 300 dpi, RGB, TIFF at 8-bit color."

Payment & Terms Statements issued monthly to contracted image providers. Model release required. Photo captions required.

Making Contact Submit a portfolio including a subject-focused collection of 300+ images. Photo guidelines available on website at www.purestock.com/submissions.asp.

Tips "Please review our Web site to see the style and quality of our imagery before submitting."

▣ RAINBOW

61 Entrada, Santa Fe NM 87505. (505)820-3434. E-mail: rainbow@cybermesa.com. Web site: www.rainbowimages.com. **Contact:** Coco McCoy, director. Estab. 1976. Fine art print gallery and stock photo agency. Member of American Society of Picture Professionals (ASPP). Clients include: galleries, educational publishers, advertising agencies, public relations firms, design agencies, book publishers, magazine publishers, calendar and notecard companies; 20% of sales come from overseas.

Needs "Rainbow is known for its high-quality imagery and has now opened its new fine arts division, Sky Gallery Prints. In that spirit, we are looking for outstanding images such as moody images in black and white or color, wonders of nature from micro-organisms and insects to dramatic shots of large mammals; botanica; landscapes; ancient temples; colorful Mexico and Guatemala; museum-quality artifacts; and well-known jazz and rock musicians, authors, and other creative thinkers."

Specs Accepts images in digital format only. Images must be high-res scans or shot with at least an 8-megapixel camera. Send at least 30 images as JPEGs on a CD with captions.

Payment & Terms Pays 50% commission. Contracts renew automatically with each submission; no time limit. Statements issued quarterly. Payment made quarterly. Photographers allowed to review account records to verify sales figures. Offers one-time rights. Informs photographers and allows them to negotiate when client requests all rights. Photo captions required for scientific photos or geographic locations, etc.; include simple description if not evident from photo; prefers both Latin and common names for plants and insects to make photos more valuable.

Making Contact Interested in receiving work from published photographers. "Photographers may e-mail or call us for photo guidelines or information. Arrange a personal interview to show portfolio, or send query letter with samples; include SASE for return of material. Responds in 1 month.

Tips "E-mail us describing your work or send a CD or DVD with captions. Edit your work carefully before sending. We look for luminous images."

▣ RETNA LTD.

24 W. 25th St., 12th Floor, New York NY 10010. (212)255-0622. Fax: (212)255-1224. E-mail: info@retna.com. Web site: www.retna.com. **Contact:** Jessica Daly or Walter McBride. Estab. 1978. Member of the Picture Archive Council of America (PACA). Stock photo agency, assignment agency. Has more than 2 million photos in files. Clients include advertising agencies, public relations firms, book/encyclopedia publishers, magazine publishers, newspapers, record companies.

- Retna handles shoots and assignments for clients and pulls from their talented pool of photographers.

Needs Handles photos of musicians (pop, country, rock, jazz, contemporary, rap, R&B) and celebrities (movie, film, television and politicians). Covers New York, Milan and Paris fashion shows; has file on royals. Also uses events, sports. Interested in fashion/glamour, historical/vintage.

Specs Original material required. All formats accepted. Send digital images via CD, Zip, e-mail as TIFF, JPEG files at 300 dpi.

Payment & Terms Commission varies. General price range (to clients): $200 and up. Works with photographers on contract basis only. Contracts renew automatically with additional submissions for 3 years. Statements issued monthly. Payment made monthly. Offers one-time rights; negotiable. When client requests all rights photographer will be consulted, but Retna will negotiate. Model/property release required. Photo captions required.

Making Contact Arrange a personal interview to show portfolio. Primarily concentrating on selling stock, but does assign on occasion. Does not publish "tips" sheets, but makes regular phone calls to photographers.

Tips "Wants to see strong celebrity studio shooters, some music photograhy. We are also always seeking event photographers who have great access. Photography must be creative, innovative and of the highest aesthetic quality possible."

▣ REX USA LTD.

160 Monmouth St., Red Bank NJ 07701. (732)576-1919. Fax: (732)576-1909. E-mail: chuck @rexusa.com. Web site: www.rexusa.com. **Contact:** Charles Musse, manager. Estab. 1935. Stock photo agency, news/feature syndicate. Affiliated with Rex Features in London. Member of Picture Archive Council of America (PACA). Has 1.5 million photos. Clients include: advertising agencies, public relations firms, audiovisual firms, businesses, book/encyclopedia publishers, magazine publishers, newspapers, postcard companies, calendar companies, greeting card companies and TV, film and record companies.

Needs Wants primarily editorial material: celebrities, personalities (studio portraits, candid, paparazzi), human interest, news features, movie stills, glamour, historical, geographic, general stock, sports and scientific.

Specs Digital only.

Payment & Terms Pays 50-65% commission; payment varies depending on quality of subject matter and exclusivity. "We obtain highest possible prices, starting at $100-100,000 for one-time sale." Pays 50% commission for b&w and color photos. Works with or without contract. Offers nonexclusive contract. Statements issued monthly. Payment made monthly. Photographers allowed to review account records. Offers one-time, first and all rights. Informs photographers and allows them to negotiate when client requests all rights. Model release required. Photo captions required.

Making Contact E-mail query letter with samples and list of stock photo subjects.

▣ ROBERTSTOCK

4203 Locust St., Philadelphia PA 19104. (800)786-6300. Fax: (800)786-1920. E-mail: sales@ robertstock.com. Web site: www.robertstock.com, www.classicstock.com. **Contact**: Bob Roberts, president. Estab. 1920. Stock photo agency. Member of the Picture Archive Council of America (PACA). Has 2 different Web sites: Robertstock offers contemporary rights-managed and royalty-free images; ClassicStock offers retro and vintage images. Clients include: advertising agencies, public relations firms, audiovisual firms, businesses, book/ encyclopedia publishers, magazine publishers, newspapers, postcard publishers, calendar companies, greeting card companies.

Needs Uses images on all subjects in depth.

Specs Accepts images in digital format. Send via CD, Zip at 300 dpi, 50MB or higher.

Payment & Terms Pays 45-50% commission. Works with photographers with or without a contract; negotiable. Offers various contracts. Statements issued monthly. Payment made monthly. Payment sent with statement. Photographers allowed to review account records to verify sales figures "upon advance notice." Offers one-time rights. Informs photographers when client requests all rights. Model release required. Photo captions required.

Making Contact Send query letter. Does not keep samples on file. Expects minimum initial submission of 250 images with quarterly submissions of 250 images. Responds in 1 month. Photo guidelines available.

▣ ⊕ SCIENCE PHOTO LIBRARY, LTD.

327-329 Harrow Rd., London W9 3RB United Kingdom. (44)(207)432-1100. Fax: (44)(207)286-8668. E-mail: picture.editing@sciencephoto.com. Web site: www.sciencepho to.com. **Contact**: Research Director. Stock photo agency. Clients include: book publishers, magazines, newspapers, medical journals, advertising, design, TV and the Web in the U.K. and abroad. "We currently work with agents in over 30 countries, including America, Japan, and in Europe."

Needs SPL specializes in all aspects of science, medicine and technology."

Specs Digital only via CD/DVD. File sizes at least 38 mb with no interpolation. Captions, model, and property releases required.

Payment & Terms Pays 50% commission. Works on contract basis only. Agreement made for 5 years; general continuation is assured unless otherwise advised. Offers exclusivity. Statements issued quarterly, payment made quarterly. Photographers allowed to review account records to verify sales figures; fully computerized accounts/commission handling system. Model and property release required. Photo captions required. "Detailed captions can also increase sales so please provide us with as much information as possible."

Making Contact "Please complete the enquiry form on our Web site so that we are better able to advise you on the saleability of your work for our martet. You may e-mail us low-res examples of your work. Once you have provided us with information, the editing team will be in contact within 2-3 business weeks. Full photo guidelines available on Web site."

▣ SILVER IMAGE PHOTO AGENCY

4104 NW 70th Terrace, Gainesville FL 32606. (352)373-5771. E-mail: floridalink@aol.com. Web site: www.silver-image.com. **Contact:** Carla Hotvedt, president/owner. Estab. 1988. Stock photo agency. Assignments in Florida/southern Georgia. Has 150,000 photos in files. Clients include: public relations firms, book/encyclopedia publishers, magazine publishers, newspapers.

Needs Wants photos from Florida only: nature, travel, tourism, news, people.

Specs Accepts images in digital format only. Send via CD, FTP, e-mail as JPEG files *upon request only*. No longer accepting new photographers.

Payment & Terms Pays 50% commission for image licensing fees. Average price per image (to clients): $150-600. Works with photographers on contract basis only. Offers nonexclusive contract. Payment made monthly. Statements provided when payment is made. Photographers allowed to review account records. Offers one-time rights. Informs photographer and allows them to be involved when client requests all rights. Model release preferred. Photo captions required; include name, year shot, city, state, etc.

Making Contact Send query letter via e-mail only. Do not submit material unless first requested.

Tips "I will review a photographer's work to see if it rounds out our current inventory. Photographers should review our website to get a feel for our needs. We will gladly add a photographer's e-mail address to our online photo requests list."

ⓃⒺ SILVER VISIONS

P.O. Box 2679, Aspen CO 81612. (970)923-3137. E-mail: jjohnson@rof.net. **Contact:** Joanne M. Johnson, owner. Estab. 1987. Stock photo agency. Has 10,000 photos. Clients include: book/encyclopedia publishers, magazine publishers, postcard companies, calendar companies, greeting card companies.

Needs Emphasizes lifestyles—people, families, children, couples involved in work, sports, family outings, pets, etc. Also scenics of mountains and deserts, horses, dogs, cats, cityscapes—Denver, Los Angeles., Chicago, Baltimore, New York City, San Francisco, Salt Lake City, capital cities of the USA.

Specs Uses 35mm, $2\frac{1}{4} \times 2\frac{1}{4}$ or 4×5 transparencies. Accepts images in digital format. Send via CD, e-mail, floppy disk.

Payment & Terms Pays 40-50% commission for color photos. General price range: $35-750. Offers nonexclusive contract. Charges $15/each for entries in CD-ROM catalog. Statements issued semiannually. Payment made semiannually. Offers one-time rights and English language rights. Informs photographer and allows them to negotiate when client requests all rights. Model/property release required for pets, people, upscale homes. Photo captions required; include identification of locations, species.

Making Contact Send query letter with samples, SASE. Responds in 2 weeks. Photo guidelines free with SASE.

Tips Wants to see "emotional impact or design impact created by composition and lighting. Photos must evoke a universal human interest appeal. Sharpness and good exposures—needless to say." Sees growing demand for "minority groups, senior citizens, fitness."

ⒶⒺ🌐 SKISHOOT-OFFSHOOT

Hall Place, Upper Woodcott, Whitchurch, Hants RG28 7PY United Kingdom. (44)(1635)255527. E-mail: info@skishoot.co.uk. Web site: www.skishoot.co.uk. Estab. 1986. Stock photo agency. Has over 400,000 photos in files. Clients include: advertising agencies, book publishers, magazine publishers, newspapers, greeting card companies, postcard publishers. Specializes in winter sports but also has photos from around the world (France, in particular) taken all year-round.

Needs Wants photos of skiing, snowboarding and other winter sports. Also photos of children/teens, families, landscapes/scenics, cities/urban, rural, adventure, sports.

Specs Prefers CDs with high-resolution images.

Payment & Terms Pays 50% commission for color photos. Average price per image (to clients): $100-5,000 for color. Enforces strict minimum prices. BAPLA recommended rates are used. Offers volume discounts to customers. Photographers can choose not to sell images on discount terms. Works with photographers with or without a contract; negotiable. Offers limited regional exclusivity. Contracts renew automatically with additional submissions within originally agreed time period. Payments made to photographers through PayPal. Statements issued quarterly. Photographers allowed to review account records in cases of discrepancies only. Offers one-time rights. Informs photographers when a client requests all rights. Model release preferred. Photo captions required; include location details.

Making Contact Send query letter with samples, stock list. Include SAE for return of material. Portfolio should include color. Works on assignment only. Expects minimum initial submission of 50 images. Responds in 1 month to samples.

SKYSCAN PHOTOLIBRARY

Oak House, Toddington, Cheltenham, Gloucestershire GL54 5BY United Kingdom. (44)(124)262-1357. Fax: (44)(124)262-1343. E-mail: info@skyscan.co.uk. Web site: www.skyscan.co.uk. **Contact:** Brenda Marks, library manager. Estab. 1984. Picture library. Member of the British Association of Picture Libraries and Agencies (BAPLA) and the National Association of Aerial Photographic Libraries (NAPLIB). Has more than 130,000 photos in files. Clients include: advertising agencies, public relations firms, businesses, book publishers, magazine publishers, newspapers, calendar companies, postcard publishers.

Needs Wants "anything aerial! Air-to-ground; aviation; aerial sports. As well as holding images ourselves, we also wish to make contact with holders of other aerial collections worldwide to exchange information."

Specs Uses color and/or b&w prints; any format transparencies. Accepts images in digital format. Send via CD, e-mail.

Payment & Terms Pays 50% commission for b&w and color photos. Average price per image (to clients): $100 minimum. Enforces strict minimum prices. Offers volume discounts to customers. Photographers can choose not to sell images on discount terms. Works with photographers with or without a contract; negotiable. Offers guaranteed subject exclusivity (within files); negotiable to suit both parties. Statements issued quarterly. Payment made quarterly. Photographers allowed to review account records in cases of discrepancies only. Offers one-time, electronic media and agency promotion rights. Informs photographers and allows them to negotiate when a client requests all rights. Will inform photographers and act with photographer's agreement. Model/property release preferred for "air-to-ground of famous buildings (some now insist they have copyright to their building)." Photo captions required; include subject matter, date of photography, location, interesting features/notes.

Making Contact Send query letter or e-mail. Provide résumé, business card, self-promotion piece or tearsheets to be kept on file. Agency will contact photographer for portfolio review if interested. Portfolio should include color slides and transparencies. Does not keep samples on file; include SAE for return of material. No minimum submissions. Photo guidelines sheet free with SAE. Catalog free with SAE. Market tips sheet free quarterly to contributors only.

Tips "We see digital transfer of low-resolution images for layout purposes as essential to the future of stock libraries, and we have invested heavily in suitable technology. Contact first by letter or e-mail with résumé of material held and subjects covered."

▣ SOVFOTO/EASTFOTO, INC.

263 West 20th Street #3, New York NY 10011. (212)727-8170. Fax: (212)727-8228. E-mail: research@sovfoto.com. Web site: www.sovfoto.com. **Contact:** Meredith Brosnan, researcher. Estab. 1935. Stock photo agency. Has 500,000 photos in files. Clients include: advertising firms, audiovisual firms, book/encyclopedia publishers, magazine publishers, newspapers.

Needs All subjects acceptable as long as they pertain to Russia, Eastern European countries, Central Asian countries or China.

Specs Uses b&w historical; color prints; 35mm transparencies. Accepts images in digital format. Send via CD or DVD as TIFF files.

Payment & Terms Pays 50% commission. Average price per image (to clients): $150-500 for b&w or color photos for editorial use. Statements issued quarterly. Payment made quarterly. Photographers allowed to review account records to verify sales figures or account for various deductions. Offers one-time print, electronic media, and nonexclusive rights. Model/property release preferred. Photo captions required.

Making Contact Arrange personal interview to show portfolio. Send query letter with samples, stock list. Keeps samples on file. Expects minimum initial submission of 50-100 images. Responds in 2 weeks.

Tips Looks for "news and general interest photos (color) with human element."

▣ SPORTSLIGHT PHOTO

6 Berkshire Circle, Gt. Barrington MA 01230. (413)528-8457. E-mail: stock@sportslightphoto.com. Web site: www.sportslightphoto.com. **Contact:** Roderick Beebe, director. Stock photo agency. Has 500,000 photos in files. Clients include: advertising agencies, public relations firms, corporations, book publishers, magazine publishers, newspapers, postcard companies, calendar companies, greeting card companies, design firms.

Needs "We specialize in every sport in the world. We deal primarily in the recreational sports such as skiing, golf, tennis, running, canoeing, etc., but are expanding into pro sports, and have needs for all pro sports, action and candid close-ups of top athletes. We also handle adventure-travel photos, e.g., rafting in Chile, trekking in Nepal, dogsledding in the Arctic, etc."

Specs Uses 35mm transparencies. Accepts images in digital format. Send via CD. Contact us prior to shipment.

Payment & Terms Pays 50% commission. Average price per image (to clients): $100-6,000. Contract negotiable. Offers limited regional exclusivity. Contract is of indefinite length until either party (agency or photographer) seeks termination. Charges $5/image for duping fee; $3 for catalog and digital CD-ROM insertion promotions. Statements issued quarterly. Payment made quarterly. Photographers allowed to review account records to verify sales figures "when discrepancy occurs." Offers one-time rights; sometimes exclusive rights for a period of time; and other rights, depending on client. Informs photographers and consults with them when client requests all rights. Model release required for corporate and advertising usage. (Obtain releases whenever possible.) Strong need for model-released "pro-type" sports. Photo captions required; include who, what, when, where, why.

Making Contact Interested in receiving work from newer and known photographers. Cannot return unsolicited material. Responds in 2-4 weeks. Photo guidelines free with SASE. See website for more information regarding digital transmission. For review, send JPEG files at 72 dpi via e-mail or CD; or " direct us to your website to review images for consideration."

Tips "We look for a range of sports subjects that shows photographer's grasp of the action, drama, color and intensity of sports, as well as capability of capturing great shots under all conditions in all sports. Want well-edited, perfect exposure and sharpness, good composition and lighting in all photos. Seeking photographers with strong interests in particular sports. Shoot variety of action, singles and groups, youths, male/female—all combinations; plus leisure, relaxing after tennis, lunch on the ski slope, golf's 19th hole, etc. Sports fashions change rapidly, so that is a factor. Art direction of photo shoots is important. Avoid brand names and minor flaws in the look of clothing. Attention to detail is very important. Shoot with concepts/ideas such as teamwork, determination, success, lifestyle, leisure, cooperation in mind. Clients look not only for individual sports but for photos to illustrate a mood or idea. There is a trend toward use of real-life action photos in advertising as opposed to the set-up slick ad look. More unusual shots are being used to express feelings, attitude, etc."

▣ TOM STACK & ASSOCIATES, INC.

154 Tequesta Street, Taavernier FL 33070. (305)852-5520. Fax: (305)852-5570. E-mail: tomstack@earthlink.net. **Contact:** Therisa Stack. Has 500,000 photos in files. Clients include: advertising agencies, public relations firms, businesses, audiovisual firms, book publishers, magazine publishers, encyclopedia publishers, postcard companies, calendar companies, greeting card companies.

Needs Wants photos of wildlife, endangered species, marine life, landscapes; foreign geography; photomicrogfaphy; scientific research; whales; solar heating; mammals such as weasels, moles, shrews, fisher, marten, etc.; extremely rare endangered wildlife; wildlife behavior photos; lightning and tornadoes; hurricane damage; dramatic and unusual angles and approaches to composition, creative and original photography with impact. Especially needs photos on life science, flora and fauna and photomicrography. No run-of-the-mill travel or vacation shots. Special needs include photos of energy-related topics—solar and wind generators, recycling, nuclear power and coal burning plants, waste disposal and landfills, oil and gas drilling, supertankers, electric cars, geo-thermal energy.

Specs Only accepts images in digital format. Send via CD or e-mail sample JPEGs.

Payment & Terms Pays 50-60% commission. Average price per image (to clients): $150-200 for color photos; as high as $7,000. Works with photographers on contract basis only. Contracts renew automatically with additional submissions for 3 years. Statements issued quarterly. Payment made quarterly. Offers one-time and electronic media rights. Informs photographers and allows them to negotiate when client requests all rights. Model release preferred. Photo captions preferred.

Making Contact E-mail tomstack@earthlink.net.

Tips "Strive to be original, creative and take an unusual approach to the commonplace; do it in a different and fresh way. We take on only the best so we can continue to give more effective service."

▣ STILL MEDIA

2012 Anacapa St., Santa Barbara CA 93108. (805)682-2868. E-mail: images@stillmedia.com. Web site: www.stillmedia.com. **Contact:** Jeffrey Aaronson, founder/owner. Director: Becky Green Aaronson. Photojournalism and stock photography agency. Has 500,000 photos in files. Clients include: advertising agencies, public relations firms, businesses, book/encyclopedia publishers, magazine publishers, newspapers, calendar companies.

Needs Reportage, world events, travel, cultures, business, the environment, sports, people, industry.

Specs Accepts images in digital format only. Contact via e-mail.

Payment & Terms Pays 50% commission for color photos. Works with photographers on contract basis only. Offers nonexclusive and guaranteed subject exclusivity contracts. Statements issued quarterly. Payment made quarterly. Photographers allowed to review account records. Offers one-time and electronic media rights. Model/property release preferred. Photo captions required.

Making Contact ''We are currently accepting new photographers.''

⊠ ▣ STOCK CONNECTION, INC.

110 Frederick Ave., Suite A, Rockville MD 20850. (301)251-0720. Fax: (301)309-0941. E-mail: photos@scphotos.com. Web site: www.scphotos.com. **Contact:** Cheryl Pickerell Di-Frank, president or Michael Vallarino, photographer relations. Stock photo agency. Member of the Picture Archive Council of America (PACA). Has over 125,000 photos in files. Clients include advertising agencies, graphic design firms, magazine and textbook publishers, greeting card companies.

Needs ''We handle many subject categories including lifestyles, business, concepts, sports and recreation, travel, landscapes and wildlife. We will help photographers place their images into our extensive network of over 35 distributors throughout the world. We specialize in placing images where photo buyers can find them.''

Specs Accepts images in digital format (tiff or hi-quality jpeg), minimum 50MB uncompressed, 200 dpi, Adobe RGB. Will also accept film; scanning fees apply.

Payment & Terms Pays 65% commission. Average price per image (to client): $450-500. Works with photographers on contract basis only. Offers non-exclusive contract. Contracts renew automatically with additional submissions. Photographers may cancel contract with 60 days written notice. Charges for scanning and keywording range from $4-13 per image, depending on volume. If photographer provides acceptable scans and keywords, no upload charges apply. Statements issued monthly. Photographers allowed to review account records. Offers Rights-managed and Royalty-Free. Informs photographers when a client requests exclusive rights. Model/property release required. Photo captions required.

Making Contact See website for submission guidelines. Prefer a minimum of 100 images as an initial submission.

Tips ''The key to success in today's market is wide distribution of your images. We offer an extensive network reaching a large variety of buyers all over the world. Increase your sales by increasing your exposure.''

STOCK OPTIONS®

P.O. Box 1048, Fort Davis TX 79734. (432)426-2777. Fax: (432)426-2779. E-mail: kh@stock optionsphoto.com. **Contact:** Karen Hughes, owner. Estab. 1985. Stock photo agency. Member of Picture Archive Council of America (PACA). Has 150,000 photos in files. Clients include: advertising agencies, public relations firms, audiovisual firms, corporations, book/encyclopedia and magazine publishers, newspapers, postcard companies, calendar companies, greeting card companies.

Needs Emphasizes the southern US. Files include Gulf Coast scenics, wildlife, fishing, festivals, food, industry, business, people, etc. Also western folklore and the Southwest.

Specs Uses 35mm, 2¼×2¼, 4×5 transparencies.

Stock Photo Agencies

Payment & Terms Pays 50% commission for color photos. Average price per image (to client): $300-3,000. Works with photographers on contract basis only. Offers nonexclusive contract. Contracts renew automatically with each submission for 5 years from expiration date. When contract ends photographer must renew within 60 days. Charges catalog insertion fee of $300/image and marketing fee of $10/hour. Statements issued upon receipt of payment from client. Payment made immediately. Photographers allowed to review account records to verify sales figures. Offers one-time and electronic media rights. "We will inform photographers for their consent only when a client requests all rights, but we will handle all negotiations." Model/property release preferred for people, some properties, all models. Photo captions required; include subject and location.

Making Contact Interested in receiving work from full-time commercial photographers. Arrange a personal interview to show portfolio. Send query letter with stock list. Contact by phone and submit 200 sample photos. Tips sheet distributed annually to all photographers.

Tips Wants to see "clean, in-focus, relevant and current materials." Current stock requests include industry, environmental subjects, people in up-beat situations, minorities, food, cityscapes and rural scenics.

▣ ⊕ STOCKFOOD GMBH (THE FOOD IMAGE AGENCY)

Tumblingerstr. 32, 80337 Munich Germany. (49)(89)747-20222. Fax: (49)(89)721-1020. E-mail: petra.thierry@stockfood.com. Web site: www.stockfood.com. **Contact:** Petra Thierry, manager, Photographers and Art Dept. Estab. 1979. Stock agency, picture library. Member of the Picture Archive Council of America (PACA). Has over 250,000 photos in files. Clients include: advertising agencies, businesses, newspapers, postcard publishers, public relations firms, book publishers, calendar companies, magazine publishers, greeting card companies.

Needs Wants photos of food/drink, health/fitness/food, wellness/spa, people eating and drinking, nice flowers and garden images, eating and drinking outside, table settings.

Specs Uses $2\frac{1}{4} \times 2\frac{1}{4}$, 4×5, 8×10 transparencies. Accepts images in digital format. Send via CD/DVD as TIFF files at 300 dpi, 20MB minimum (8.5 mio pixels).

Payment & Terms Pays 40% commission for rights managed images. Enforces minimum prices. Works with photographers on contract basis only. Offers limited regional exclusivity, guaranteed subject exclusivity (within files). Contracts renew automatically. Statements issued quarterly. Photographers allowed to review account records. Offers one-time rights. Model release required; photo captions required.

Making Contact Send e-mail with new examples of your work as JPEG files.

▣ STOCKYARD PHOTOS

1410 Hutchins St., Houston TX 77003. (713)520-0898. Fax: (713)227-0399. E-mail: jim@stoickyard.com. Web site: www.stockyard.com. **Contact:** Jim Olive. Estab. 1992. Stock agency. Has tens of thousands of photos in files. Clients include: advertising agencies, businesses, newspapers, postcard publishers, public relations firms, book publishers, calendar companies, audiovisual firms, magazine publishers, greeting card companies, real estate firms, interior designers, retail catalogs.

Needs Needs photos relating to Houston, Texas, and the Gulf Coast.

Specs Accepts images in digital format only. To be considered, e-mail URL to photographer's Web site, showing a sample of 20 images for review.

Payment & Terms Average price per image (to clients): $250-1,500 for color photos. Offers volume discounts to customers. Photographers can choose not to sell images on discount terms.

⊠ ▣ SUGARDADDYPHOTOS

Hanklooks Publications, P.O. Box 86776, Los Angeles CA 90086. Estab. 2000. (626)627-5127. E-mail: iphotographu@charter.net. Web site: www.sugardaddyphotos.com. **Contact:** Henry Salazar, editor-in-chief. Stock agency and picture library. Clients include: advertising agencies, businesses, newspapers, postcard publishers, public relations firms, book publishers, calendar companies, audiovisual firms, magazine publishers, greeting card companies.

Needs Wants photos of babies/children/teens, celebrities, couples, multicultural, families, parents, senior citizens, architecture, cities/urban, education, gardening, interiors/decorating, pets, religious, rural, agriculture, business concepts, industry, medicine, military, political, product shots/still life, science, technology/computers, disasters, environmental, landscapes/scenics, wildlife, adventure, automobiles, entertainment, events, food/drink, health/fitness/beauty, hobbies, humor, performing arts, sports, travel, exotic locations. Interested in alternative process, avant garde, documentary, erotic, fashion/glamour, fine art, historical/vintage, lifestyle, seasonal.

Specs Uses 35 mm, $2\frac{1}{4} \times 2\frac{1}{4}$, 4×5, 8×10 transparencies. Accepts images in digital format. Send TIFF or JPEG files at 300 dpi via CD. Buys photos, film and videotape outright; pays $5-500 for b&w photos; pays $10-1,000 for color photos; pays $20-2,000 for film; pays $30-3,000 for videotape. Pay 40-50% commission. Average price per image (to clients): $1-150 for photos and videotape. Enforces strict minimum prices. "We have set prices; however, they are subject to change without notice." Photographers can choose not to sell images on discount terms. Works with photographers with or without a contract; negotiable. Offers nonexclusive contract. Statements issued quarterly. Payments made quarterly. Offers one-time rights. Informs photographers and allows them to negotiate when a client requests all rights. Model/property release required. Photo captions required; include location, city, state, country, full description, related keywords, date image was taken.

Making Contact E-mail query letter with JPEG samples at 72 dpi. Send query letter with résumé, slides, prints, tearsheets, transparencies. Provide résumé, business card, self-promotion piece to be kept on file. Expects minimum inital submission of 50 images with submissions of at least 50 images every 2 months.

Tips "Please e-mail before sending samples. We're interested in receiving submissions from new photographers. Arrange your work in categories to view. Clients expect the very best in professional-quality material."

▣ SUPERSTOCK INC.

7660 Centurion Pkwy., Jacksonville FL 32256. (904) 565-0066. E-mail: creativeassociate@superstock.com. Web site: www.superstock.com. International stock photo agency represented in 192 countries. Extensive rights-managed and royalty-free content within 3 unique collections—contemporary, vintage and fine art. Clients include: advertising agencies, businesses, book and magazine publishers, newspapers, greeting card and calendar companies.

Needs "SuperStock is looking for dynamic lifestyle, travel, sports and business imagery, as well as fine art content and vintage images with releases."

Specs Accepts images in digital format only. Digital files must be a minimum of 50MB (upsized), 300 dpi, 8-bit color, RGB, JPEG format.

Payment & Terms Statements issued monthly to contracted contributors. "Rights offered vary, depending on image quality, type of content, and experience." Informs photographers when client requests all rights. Model release required. Photo captions required.

Making Contact Complete SuperStock's online questionnaire at www.superstock.com/expose. Photo guidelines available on at www.superstock.com/paperwork.

Tips "Please review our website to see the style and quality of our imagery before submitting."

▣ ☒ TAKE STOCK INC.

2343 Uxbridge Dr. NW, Calgary AB T2N 3Z8 Canada. (403)261-5815. E-mail: takestock@telusplanet.net. Estab. 1987. Stock photo agency. Clients include: advertising agencies, public relations firms, audiovisual firms, corporate, book/encyclopedia publishers, magazine publishers, newspapers, postcard publishers, calendar and greeting card companies, graphic designers, trade show display companies.

Needs Wants model-released people, lifestyle images (all ages), Asian people, Canadian, arts/recreation, industry/occupation, business, high-tech, illustrations. Wants photos of couples, multicultural, families, senior citizens, gardening, rural, adventure, agriculture, technology/computers with a Canadian flare or recognizable Alberta background.

Specs Uses 35mm, medium- to large-format transparencies. Accepts digital images for review only.

Payment & Terms Pays 50% commission for b&w or color photos. General price range (to clients): $300-1,000 for b&w photos; $300-1,500 for color photos. Works with photographers on contract basis only. Offers limited regional exclusivity. Contracts renew automatically with additional submissions for 3 year terms. Charges 100% duping and catalog insertion fees. Statements issued every 2 months depending on sales. Payment made every 2 months depending on sales. Photographers allowed to review account records to verify sales figures, "with written notice and at their expense." Offers one-time, exclusive and some multi-use rights; some buy-outs with photographer's permission. Model/property release required. Photo captions required.

Making Contact Send query letter with stock list. Responds in 3 weeks. Photo guidelines free with SAE/IRC. Tips sheet distributed every 2 months to photographers on file.

▣ TIMECAST PRODUCTIONS

2801 Poole Way, Carson City NV 89706. (775)883-6427. Fax: (775)883-6427. E-mail: info@timecastproductions.com. Web site: http://timecast.productions.com. **Contact:** Edward Salas, owner. Estab. 1995. Stock photo and video agency. Has 5,000 photos, 150 hours of video footage. "Timecast Productions is the leading Internet-based producer and supplier of factual and event-based stock footage for television advertising and corporate presentation." Clients include: television program content producers, advertising agencies, corporate, and multimedia producers.

Needs "We offer a wide selection of high-quality stock footage from the wild West and its infamous characters to contemporary lifestyle and culture from around the world—people, places, news, events, business, industry cities, transportation, medicine, nature, historical and more."

Specs Accepts footage in all broadcast-quality formats.

Payment & Terms Based on usage, negotiable with client. Offers royalty-free and rights-managed terms. Offers volume discounts to customers. Filmmakers can choose not to sell photos or video on discount terms. Works with filmmakers on contract basis only. Offers nonexclusive contract. Statements issued monthly. Payment made monthly. Filmmakers allowed to review account records. Offers one-time and electronic media rights. Informs filmmakers and allows them to negotiate when client requests all rights. Model, talent and property releases required. Captions and time code logs required.

Making Contact Contact us first by e-mail, through our Web site, or by telephone. Let our representative know the category and format of your material. If we are interested, we will request you send compressed samples in Quicktime format via high-speed Internet, or send material on optical disc for our review. Following our review, consideration will be given for representaion.

⊕ TRAVEL INK PHOTO LIBRARY

The Old Coach House, Goring-on-Thames, Reading, Berkshire RG8 9AR United Kingdom. (44)(149)187-3011. Fax: (44)(149)187-5558. E-mail: info@travel-ink.co.uk. Web site: www.travel-ink.co.uk. Has over 115,000 photos in files. Clients include: advertising agencies, businesses, newspapers, public relations firms, book publishers, calendar companies, audiovisual firms, magazine publishers, greeting card companies.

Needs Wants photos of multicultural, environmental, landscapes/scenics, wildlife, architecture, cities/urban, gardening, religious, rural, adventure, events, food/drink, health/fitness/beauty, hobbies, sports, travel.

Specs Uses 35mm and medium-format transparencies. Accepts images in digital format. See website for details.

Payment & Terms Pays on a commission basis. Enforces minimum prices. Offers volume discounts to customers. Works with photographers on contract basis only. Offers exclusive contract only. Statements issued quarterly. Payment made quarterly. Photographers allowed to review account records. Offers one-time rights. Model/property release required. Photo captions required.

Making Contact "Currently accepting submissions from new photographers. Please e-mail first."

▣ ⊕ TRH PICTURES/CODY IMAGES

2 Reform St., Beith, Scotland, KA15 2AE United Kingdom. (08)(45)223-5451. Fax: (08)(45)223-5452. E-mail: sam@codyimages.com. Web site: www.codyimages.com. **Contact:** Ted Nevill. Estab. 1982. Picture library. Has 100,000 photos in files. Clients include: advertising agencies, newspapers, book publishers, calendar companies, audiovisual firms, magazine publishers.

Needs Wants photos of historical/modern aviation, warfare, transport on land and sea, space.

Specs Uses color and/or b&w prints; 35mm, $2^1/_4 \times 2^1/_4$, 4×5, 8×10 transparencies. Accepts images in ditigal format.

Payment & Terms Pays commission. Average price per image (to clients): $80 minimum. Offers volume discounts to customers. Discount sales terms not negotiable. Works with photographers with or without a contract; negotiable. Offers nonexclusive contract. Contracts renew automatically with additional submissions. Statements issued quarterly. Payment made quarterly. Photographers allowed to review account records. Offers one-time rights, electronic media rights. Informs photographers and allows them to negotiate when a client requests all rights. Model/property release preferred. Photo captions preferred.

Making Contact Send query letter with résumé, slides, prints, photocopies, transparencies, stock list. Provide résumé, business card, self-promotion piece to be kept on file. Expects minimum initial submission of 1,000 images. Responds in 1 month.

▣ ⊕ TROPIX PHOTO LIBRARY

44 Woodbines Ave., Kingston-Upon-Thames, Surrey KT1 2AY United Kingdom. (44)(208)8546-0823. E-mail: photographers@tropix.co.uk. Web site: www.tropix.co.uk. **Contact:** Veronica Birley, proprietor. Picture library specialist. Has 100,000 photos in files. Clients include: advertising agencies, book/encyclopedia publishers, magazine publishers, newspapers, government departments, design groups, travel companies, calendar/card companies.

Needs "Sorry, Tropix is currently closed to new contributing photographers. But any temporary exceptions to this will be posted on our website."

Specs Uses large digital files only, minimum 25MB when sent as TIFF files.

Payment & Terms Pays 40% commission for color photos. Average price per image (to clients): $145 for b&w and color photos. Offers guaranteed subject exclusivity. Charges cost of returning photographs by insured post, if required. Statements made quarterly with payment. Photographers allowed to have qualified auditor review account records to verify sales figures in the event of a dispute but not as routine procedure. Offers one-time, electronic media and agency promotion rights. Informs photographers when a client requests all rights, but agency handles negotiation. Model release always required. Photo captions required; accurate, detailed data to be supplied in IPTC, electronically, and on paper. "It is essential to follow captioning guidelines available from agency."

Making Contact "E-mail preferred. Send no unsolicited photos or JPEGs, please."

▣ ⊕ ULLSTEIN BILD

Ullstein GmbH, Axel-Springer-Str. 65, 10888 Berlin Germany. E-mail: kontakt@ullsteinbild. de. Web site: www.ullsteinbild.de. Estab. 1900. Stock agency, picture library and news/feature syndicate. Has approximately 12 million photos in files. Clients include: advertising agencies, public relations firms, audiovisual firms, businesses, book publishers, magazine publishers, newspapers, calendar companies, greeting card companies, postcard publishers, TV companies.

Needs Wants photos of celebrities, couples, multicultural, families, parents, senior citizens, wildlife, disasters, environmental, landscapes/scenics, architecture, cities/urban, education, pets, religious, rural, adventure, automobiles, entertainment, events, health/fitness, hobbies, humor, performing arts, sports, travel, agriculture, buildings, computers, industry, medicine, military, political, portraits, science, technology/computers. Interested in digital, documentary, fashion/glamour, historical/vintage, regional, seasonal. Other specific photo needs: German history.

Specs Accepts images in digital format only. Send via FTP, CD, e-mail as TIFF, JPEG files at minimum 25MB decompressed.

Payment & Terms Pays on commission basis. Works with photographers on contract basis only. Offers nonexclusive contract for 5 years minimum. Statements issued monthly, quarterly, annually. Payment made monthly, quarterly, annually. Photographers allowed to review account records in cases of discrepancies only. Offers one-time rights. Photo captions required; include date, names, events, place.

Making Contact "Please contact Mr. Ulrich Ramershoven (Ramershoven@ullsteinbild.de) before sending pictures!"

UNICORN STOCK PHOTOS

524 Second Ave., Holdrege NE 68949. (308)995-4100. Fax: (308)995-4581. E-mail: info@uni corn-photos.com. Web site: www.unicorn-photos.com. **Contact:** Larry Durfee, owner. Has

Stock Photo Agencies

over 500,000 photos in files. Clients include: advertising agencies, corporate accounts, textbooks, magazines, calendar companies, religious publishers.

Needs Wants photos of ordinary people of all ages and races doing everyday things at home, school, work and play. Current skylines of all major cities, tourist attractions, historical, wildlife, seasonal/holiday and religious subjects. ''We particularly need images showing two or more races represented in one photo and family scenes with BOTH parents. There is a need for more minority shots including Hispanics, Asians and African-Americans.'' Also wants babies/children/teens, couples, senior citizens, disasters, landscapes, gardening, pets, rural, adventure, automobiles, events, food/drink, health/fitness, hobbies, sports, travel, agriculture.

Specs Uses 35mm color slides.

Payment & Terms Pays 50% commission for color photos. Average price per image (to clients): $200 minimum for color photos. Works with photographers on contract basis only. Offers nonexclusive contract. Contracts renew automatically with additional submissions for 4 years. Statements issued quarterly. Payment made quarterly. Informs photographers and allows them to negotiate when client requests all rights. Model release preferred; increases sales potential considerably. Photo captions required; include location, ages of people, dates on skylines.

Making Contact Write first for guidelines. ''We are looking for professionals who understand this business and will provide a steady supply of top-quality images. At least 500 images are generally required to open a file. Contact us by e-mail.''

Tips ''We keep in close, personal contact with all our photographers. Our monthly newsletter is a very popular medium for doing this.''

▣ VIEWFINDERS

Bruce Forster Photography, Inc., 1306 NW Hoyt Street #302, Portland OR 97209. (503)222-5222. Fax: (503)274-7995. E-mail: studio@viewfindersnw.com. Web site: www.viewfindersnw.com. **Contact:** Bruce Forster, owner. Estab. 1996. Stock agency. Member of the Picture Archive Council of America (PACA). Has 70,000 photos in files. Clients include: advertising agencies, public relations firms, businesses, book publishers, magazine publishers, design agencies.

• Viewfinders is currently not accepting new submissions as they overhaul and streamline their archive. They will begin accepting work as soon as the review of the archive is complete. Please check their Web site in the future for updated information regarding changes in the submission process.

Needs All images should come from the Pacific Northwest—Oregon, Washington, northern California, British Columbia and Idaho. Wants photos of babies/children/teens, couples, multicultural, families, senior citizens, environmental, landscapes/scenics, architecture, cities/urban, education, gardening, adventure, entertainment, events, health/fitness, performing arts, sports, travel, agriculture, industry, medicine, science, technology/computers and lifestyle.

Specs Prefers to review samples of photographers' work electronically, via photographer's Web site or online portfolio.

Payment & Terms Pays 50% commission for b&w and color photos. Works with photographers on contract basis only. Offers limited regional exclusivity. Statements issued monthly. Payment made monthly. Photographers allowed to review account records. Model/property release preferred. Photo captions required.

Stock Photo Agencies

▣ VIREO (VISUAL RESOURCES FOR ORNITHOLOGY)

The Academy of Natural Sciences, 1900 Benjamin Franklin Pkwy., Philadelphia PA 19103-1195. (215)299-1069. Fax: (215)299-1182. E-mail: vireo@ansp.org. Web site: www.acnatsci .org/vireo. **Contact:** Doug Wechsler, director. Estab. 1979. Picture library. "We specialize in birds only." Has 135,000 photos in files. Clients include: advertising agencies, businesses, book publishers, magazine publishers, newspapers, calendar companies, CD-ROM publishers.

Needs "Wants high-quality photographs of birds from around the world with special emphasis on behavior. All photos must be related to birds or ornithology."

Specs Uses digital format primarily. See website for specs.

Payment & Terms Pays 50% commission for b&w and color photos. Average price per image (to clients): $125. Negotiates fees below stated minimums; "we deal with many small nonprofits as well as commercial clients." Offers volume discounts to customers. Discount sales terms negotiable. Works with photographers on contract basis only. Offers nonexclusive contract. Statements issued semiannually. Payment made semiannually. Offers one-time rights. Model release preferred. Photo captions preferred; include date, location.

Making Contact Read guidelines on Web site. To show portfolio, photographer should send 10 JPEGs. Follow up with a call. Responds in 1 month to queries.

Tips "Write to us describing the types of bird photographs you have, the type of equipment you use, and where you do most of your bird photography. You may also send us a Web link to a portfolio of your work. Edit work carefully."

▣ ● VISUAL & WRITTEN

Luis Bermejo 8, 7-B, 50009 Zaragoza, Spain. (718) 715-0372 (U.S. number). E-mail: kikecalv o@gmail.com. Web site: www.vwpics.com. Contact: Kike Calvo, director. Estab. 1997. Digital stock agency and news agency. Has 500,000 photos in files. Has branch office in New York: 35-36 76th St., Suite 628, New York NY 11372. Clients include: advertising agencies, businesses, newspapers, postcard publishers, public relations firms, book publishers, calendar companies, audiovisual firms, magazine publishers, greeting card companies, zoos, aquariums.

Needs Wants photos of babies/children/teens, celebrities, couples, multicultural, families, parents, senior citizens, disasters, environmental, landscapes/scenics, wildlife, architecture, cities/urban, education, pets, religious, rural, adventure, travel, agriculture, business concepts, industry, science, technology/computers. Interested in documentary, erotic, fashion/glamour, fine art. Also needs underwater imagery: reefs, sharks, whales, dolphins and colorful creatures, divers and anything related to oceans. Images that show the human impact on the environment.

Specs Accepts images in digital format only. Send via CD or DVD, e-mail at 300 dpi, 55MB minimum, largest size: 5400 pixels; from a high-end digital camera, or scanned with a Nikon 4000 or similar scanner.

Payment & Terms Pays 50% commission for b&w photos; 50% for color photos. Enforces minimum prices. Works with photographers with or without contract; negotiable. Offers nonexclusive contract. Statements issued quarterly. Payment made quarterly. Any deductions are itemized. Offers one-time rights. Informs photographers and allows them to negotiate when client requests all rights. Model release required. Photo captions required. "Photo essays should include location, Latin name, what, why, when, how, who. Please make sure IPTC is filled correctly. It's the only way to include photo captions."

Making Contact "The best way is to send an email with some low-res images." Send an email with résumé, tearsheets, stock list. Provide self-promotion piece to be kept on file. Expects minimum initial submission of 100 images with periodic submissions of at least 50 images. Responds in 1 week to samples. "Photo guidelines available in our New Photographers link on Web site. Photographers can find all technical data there, along with contract information."

Tips "We have opened a new press division, so we are interested in daily news and event photography. Nature and animals are still a strong portion of our sales. We have a large distribution network, with partners all around the world."

▣ 🌐 WILDLIGHT PHOTO AGENCY

16 Charles St., Suite 14, Redfern NSW 2016 Australia. (61)(2)9698-8077. Fax: (61)(2)9698-2067. E-mail: images@wildlight.net. Web site: www.wildlight.net. **Contact:** Manager. Estab. 1985. Picture library. Has 300,000 photos in files. Clients include: advertising agencies, public relations firms, audiovisual firms, businesses, book/encyclopedia publishers, magazine publishers, newspapers, postcard publishers, calendar companies, greeting card companies.

Needs Wants Australian photos of babies/children/teens, couples, multicultural, families, parents, senior citizens, disasters, environmental, landscapes/scenics, wildlife, architecture, cities/urban, education, gardening, interiors/decorating, pets, religious, rural, adventure, entertainment, events, food/drink, health/fitness, hobbies, humor, performing arts, sports, travel, agriculture, business concepts, industry, medicine, military, political, product shots/still life, science, technology/computers. Interested in documentary, seasonal.

Specs Accepts images in digital format only.

Payment & Terms Pays 45% commission for color photos. Works with photographers on contract basis only. Offers image exclusive contract within Australia. Statements issued quarterly. Payment made quarterly. Offers one-time rights. Model/property release required. Photo captions required.

Making Contact Send CD to show portfolio. Expects minimum initial submission of 500 images with periodic submissions of at least 100 images/quarter. Responds in 2-3 weeks. Photo guidelines available on Web site.

▣ WINDIGO IMAGES

Kezar, Inc., 11812 Wayzata Blvd., #122, Minnetonka MN 55305. (952)540-0606. Fax: (952)540-1018. E-mail: info@windigoimages.com. Web site: www.windigoimages.com. **Contact:** Mitch Kezar, president/owner or Ellen Becker, general manager. Estab. 1982. Stock agency. Has 260,000 photos in files. Also sells fine art prints. Represents 126 photographers. Clients include: advertising agencies, businesses, newspapers, postcard publishers, public relations firms, book publishers, calendar companies, audiovisual firms, magazine publishers, greeting card companies.

Needs "We have a constant need for modern hunting, fishing, camping, hiking and mountain biking images. We seek high-quality images."

Specs Accepts images in digital format. Send via CD, e-mail as JPEG files at 72 dpi for initial consultation.

Payment & Terms Pays 50% commission for color photos. Offers volume discounts to customers; terms specified in photographers' contracts. Works with photographers on contract basis only. Offers nonexclusive contract. Statements issued monthly. Photographers allowed to review account records. Offers one-time, electronic media and agency promotion rights.

Making Contact Send query letter with résumé, stock list. Provide résumé, business card, self-promotion piece to be kept on file. Expects minimum initial submission of 100 images. Responds in 1 week.

Tips "Study the market and offer images that can compete in originality, composition, style and quality. Our clients are the best in the business, and we expect no less of our photographers."

▣ ⊕ WORLD RELIGIONS PHOTO LIBRARY

53A Crimsworth Rd., London SW8 4RJ United Kingdom. E-mail: co@worldreligions.co.uk. Web site: www.worldreligions.co.uk. **Contact:** Christine Osborne. Has 10,000 photos online. Clients include: book publishers, magazine publishers, newspapers.

Needs Religious images from anywhere in the world showing worship, rites of passage, sacred sites, shrines, food and places of pilgrimage, especially Hispanic/Mexico and from South America. Also Kabbalah, Mormon, Jehovah's Witnesses, Moonies, Aum, cults and Shamans. New associate library www.religious-tourism.com seeking images of pilgrims, anywhere, multi-fath.

Specs Images must be digital format. Inquire first. Send submissions on a CD as JPEGS, 72 dpi.

Payment & Terms Pays 50% commission. Offers volume discounts to good clients. Works with photographers with a contract. Offers one-time rights. Model release preferred if possible but not essential. Photo captions required; it is essential to include subject, place, date (if historic); descriptions are essential; no images will be considered without.

Making Contact Send query letter or e-mail. Include SAE for return of material. Expects minimum initial submission of 50 images. Responds in 2 weeks to samples.

Tips "Supply excellent captions and edit your submission very carefully."

Advertising, Design

& Related Markets

Advertising photography is always "commercial" in the sense that it is used to sell a product or service. Assignments from ad agencies and graphic design firms can be some of the most creative, exciting and lucrative that you'll ever receive.

Prospective clients want to see your most creative work—not necessarily your advertising work. Mary Virginia Swanson, an expert in the field of licensing and marketing fine art photography, says that the portfolio you take to the Museum of Modern Art is also the portfolio that Nike would like to see. Your clients in advertising and design will certainly expect your work to show, at the least, your technical proficiency. They may also expect you to be able to develop a concept or to execute one of their concepts to their satisfaction. Of course, it depends on the client and their needs: Read the tips given in many of the listings on the following pages to learn what a particular client expects.

When you're beginning your career in advertising photography, it is usually best to start close to home. That way, you can make appointments to show your portfolio to art directors.

Regions

Important

- **Northeast & Midatlantic:** Connecticut, Delaware, Maine, Maryland, Massachusetts, New Hampshire, New Jersey, New York, Pennsylvania, Rhode Island, Vermont, Washington DC.

- **Midsouth & Southeast:** Alabama, Arkansas, Florida, Georgia, Louisiana, Mississippi, North Carolina, South Carolina, Tennessee, Virginia, West Virginia.

- **Midwest & North Central:** Illinois, Indiana, Iowa, Kentucky, Michigan, Minnesota, Nebraska, North Dakota, Ohio, South Dakota, Wisconsin.

- **South Central & West:** Arizona, California, Colorado, Hawaii, Kansas, Missouri, Nevada, New Mexico, Oklahoma, Texas, Utah.

- **Northwest & Canada:** Alaska, Canada, Idaho, Montana, Oregon, Washington, Wyoming.

Meeting the photo buyers in person can show them that you are not only a great photographer but that you'll be easy to work with as well. This section is organized by region to make it easy to find agencies close to home.

When you're just starting out, you should also look closely at the agency descriptions at the beginning of each listing. Agencies with smaller annual billings and fewer employees are more likely to work with newcomers. On the flip side, if you have a sizable list of ad and design credits, larger firms may be more receptive to your work and be able to pay what you're worth.

Trade magazines such as *HOW*, *Print*, *Communication Arts* and *Graphis* are good places to start when learning about design firms. These magazines not only provide information about how designers operate, but they also explain how creatives use photography. For ad agencies, try *Adweek* and *Advertising Age*. These magazines are more business oriented, but they reveal facts about the top agencies and about specific successful campaigns. (See Publications on page 472 for ordering information.) The Web site of Advertising Photographers of America (APA) contains information on business practices and standards for advertising photographers (www.apanational.org).

NORTHEAST & MIDATLANTIC

☒ $☐ ☑ AM/PM ADVERTISING, INC.

345 Claremont Ave. #26, Montclair NJ 07042-1874. (973)824-8600. Fax: (646)366-1168. E-mail: mpt4220@aol.com. **Contact:** Robert A. Saks, president. Estab. 1962. Member of Art Directors Club, Illustrators Club, National Association of Advertising Agencies and Type Directors Club. Ad agency. Approximate annual billing: $125 million. Number of employees: 265. Firm specializes in display design, direct mail, magazine ads, packaging. Types of clients: food, industrial, retail, pharmaceutical, health and beauty and entertainment. Examples of recent clients: Cadillac (ads for TV); Oxford (ads for magazines).

Needs Works with 6 photographers/month. Uses photos for consumer and trade magazines, direct mail, P-O-P displays, catalogs, posters, newspapers and audiovisual. Subjects include: landscapes/scenics, wildlife, commercials, celebrities, couples, architecture, gardening, interiors/decorating, pets, adventure, automobiles, entertainment, events, food/drink, health/fitness, humor, performing arts, agriculture, business concepts, industry, medicine, product shots/still life. Interested in avant garde, erotic, fashion/glamour, historical/vintage, seasonal. Reviews stock photos of food and beauty products. Model release required. Photo caption preferred.

Audiovisual Needs "We use multimedia slide shows and multimedia video shows."

Specs Uses 8×10 color and/or b&w prints; 35mm, 2¼×2¼, 4×5, 8×10 transparencies; 8×10 film; broadcast videotape. Accepts images in digital format. Send via e-mail.

Making Contact & Terms Arrange personal interview to show portfolio. Send unsolicited photos by mail for consideration. Provide résumé, business card, brochure, flier or tearsheets to be kept on file. Keeps samples on file. Responds in 2 weeks. Pays $50-250/hour; $500-2,000/day; $2,000-5,000/job; $50-300 for b&w photos; $50-300 for color photos; $50-300 for film; $250-1,000 for videotape. **Pays on receipt of invoice.** Credit line sometimes given, depending upon client and use. Buys one-time, exclusive product, electronic and all rights; negotiable.

Tips In portfolio or samples wants to see originality. Sees trend toward more use of special lighting. Photographers should "show their work with the time it took and the fee."

$ $⬯ 🄰 ▣ 🖼 MARSHAD TECHNOLOGY GROUP

76 Laight St., New York NY 10013. E-mail: neal@marshad.com. Web site: www.marshad.c om. **Contact:** Neal Marshad, owner. Estab. 1983. Video, motion picture and multimedia production house. Approximate annual billing: $9 million. Number of employees: 15. Types of clients: industrial, financial, retail.

Needs Buys 20-50 photos/year; offers 5-10 assignments/year. Freelancers used for cosmetics, food, travel. Subjects include: beauty, tabletop, architectural, landscapes/scenics, wildlife, entertainment, events, food/drink, performing arts, sports, travel, business concepts, product shots/still life. Interested in avant garde, documentary, fashion/glamour, fine art. Model release required; property release preferred. Photo captions preferred.

Audiovisual Needs Uses film, video, CD for multimedia DVDs.

Specs Uses DV. Accepts images in digital format. Send via CD as TIFF, JPEG files at 300 dpi.

Making Contact & Terms Works with local freelancers on assignment only. Provide résumé, business card, self-promotion piece or tearsheets to be kept on file. "No calls!" Pays $125-250 for b&w photos; $125-450 for color photos; $125-1,000 for videotape. Pays on usage. Credit line depends on client. Buys all rights; negotiable.

$▣ MITCHELL STUDIOS DESIGN CONSULTANTS

1499 Sherwood Drive, East Meadow NY 11554. (516)832-6230. Fax: (516)832-6232. E-mail: msdcdesign@aol.com. **Contact:** Steven E. Mitchell, principal. Estab. 1922. Design firm. Number of employees: 6. Firm specializes in packaging, display design. Types of clients: industrial and retail. Examples of projects: Lipton Cup-A-Soup, Thomas J. Lipton, Inc.; Colgate Toothpaste, Colgate Palmolive Co.; Chef Boy-Ar-Dee, American Home Foods (all 3 involved package design).

Needs Works with varying number of photographers/month. Uses photographs for direct mail, P-O-P displays, catalogs, posters, signage and package design. Subjects include: products/still life. Reviews stock photos of still life/people. Model release required; property release preferred. Photo captions preferred.

Specs Uses all sizes and finishes of color and b&w prints; 35mm, $2\frac{1}{4} \times 2\frac{1}{4}$, 4×5, 8×10 transparencies. Accepts images in digital format. Send via CD, SyQuest, floppy disk, Jaz, Zip as EPS files.

Making Contact & Terms Submit portfolio for review. Provide résumé, business card, brochure, flier or tearsheets to be kept on file. Cannot return material. Responds as needed. Pays $35-75/hour; $350-1,500/day; $500 and up/job. **Pays on receipt of invoice.** Credit line sometimes given depending on client approval. Buys all rights.

Tips In portfolio, looks for "ability to complete assignment." Sees a trend toward "tighter budgets." To break in with this firm, keep in touch regularly.

◪ ▣ MONDERER DESIGN

2067 Massachusetts Ave., Cambridge MA 02140. (617)661-6125. Fax: (617)661-6126. E-mail: stewart@monderer.com. Web site: www.monderer.com. **Contact:** Stewart Monderer, president. Estab. 1981. Member of AIGA. Design firm. Approximate annual billing: $1 million. Number of employees: 4. Firm specializes in annual reports, branding, print and collateral, direct response, publication design and packaging, Web site and interactive design. Types of clients: technology, life science, industrial, financial and educational. Examples of recent clients: Brochure, Northeastern University (faces, portraits, classroom); Brochure, Makepeace (real estate, nature, landscape); ads, thermo scientific (metaphorical, conceptual).

Needs Works with 2 photographers/month. Uses photos for adverstising, annual reports, catalogs, posters and brochures. Subjects include: environmental, architecture, cities/urban, education, adventure, automobiles, entertainment, events, performing arts, sports, travel, business concepts, industry, medicine, product shots/still life, science, technology/computers, conceptual, site specific, people on location. Interested in alternative process, avant garde, documentary, historical/vintage, seasonal. Model release preferred; property release sometimes required.

Specs Accepts images in digital format. Send via CD as TIFF, EPS files at 300 dpi.

Making Contact & Terms Send unsolicited photos by mail for consideration. Keeps samples on file. Follow up from photographers recommended. Payment negotiable. **Pays on receipt of invoice.** Credit line sometimes given depending upon client. Rights always negotiated depending on use.

$ ⬚ NATIONAL BLACK CHILD DEVELOPMENT INSTITUTE

1313 L St., NW, Suite 110, Washington DC 20005. (202)833-2220. Fax: (202)833-8222. Web site: www.nbcdi.org. **Contact:** Vicki L. Davis, vice president. Estab. 1970.

Needs Uses photos in brochures, newsletters, annual reports and annual calendar. Candid action photos of black children and youth. Reviews stock photos. Model release required.

Specs Uses 5×7, 8×10 color and/or glossy b&w prints; color slides; b&w contact sheets. Accepts images in digital format. Send via CD.

Making Contact & Terms Send query letter with samples; include SASE for return of material. Pays $70 for cover; $20 for inside. Credit line given. Buys one-time rights.

Tips "Candid action photographs of one black child or youth or a small group of children or youths. Color photos selected are used in annual calendar and are placed beside an appropriate poem selected by organization. Therefore, photograph should communicate a message in an indirect way. Black & white photographs are used in quarterly newsletter and reports. Obtain sample of publications published by organization to see the type of photographs selected."

$ $ ⬚ Ⓐ ⬚ ⬚ NOVUS

121 E. 24th St., 12th Floor, New York NY 10010. (212)473-1377. Fax: (212)505-3300. E-mail: novuscom@aol.com. Web site: www.novuscommunications.com. **Contact:** Robert Antonik, owner/president. Estab. 1988. Creative marketing and communications firm. Number of employees: 5. Firm specializes in advertising, annual reports, publication design, display design, multimedia, packaging, direct mail, signage and Web site, Internet and DVD development. Types of clients: industrial, financial, retail, health care, telecommunications, entertainment, nonprofit.

Needs Works with 1 photographer/month. Uses photos for annual reports, billboards, consumer and trade magazines, direct mail, P-O-P displays, catalogs, posters, packaging and signage. Subjects include: babies/children/teens, couples, multicultural, families, parents, senior citizens, environmental, landscapes/scenics, wildlife, architecture, cities/urban, education, gardening, interiors/decorating, pets, religious, rural, adventure, automobiles, entertainment, events, food/drink, health/fitness, hobbies, humor, performing arts, sports, travel, agriculture, business concepts, industry, medicine, military, political, product shots/still life, science, technology/computers. Interested in alternative process, avant

Advertising

garde, documentary, fashion/glamour, fine art, historical/vintage, seasonal. Reviews stock photos. Model/property release required. Photo captions preferred.

Audiovisual Needs Uses film, videotape, DVD.

Specs Uses color and/or b&w prints; 35mm, $2\frac{1}{4} \times 2\frac{1}{4}$, 4×5, 8×10 transparencies. Accepts images in digital format. Send via Zip, CD as TIFF, JPEG files.

Making Contact & Terms Arrange a personal interview to show portfolio. Works on assignment only. Keeps samples on file. Cannot return material. Responds in 1-2 weeks. Pays $75-150 for b&w photos; $150-750 for color photos; $300-1,000 for film; $150-750 for videotape. Pays upon client's payment. Credit line given. Rights negotiable.

Tips "The marriage of photos with illustrations continues to be trendy. More illustrators and photographers are adding stock usage as part of their business. Send sample postcard; follow up with phone call."

$◨ ▣ POSEY SCHOOL

P.O. Box 254, Northport NY 11768. (631)757-2700. E-mail: EPosey@optonline.net. Web site: www.poseyschool.com. **Contact:** Elsa Posey, president. Estab. 1953. Sponsors a school of dance, art, music, drama; regional dance company and acting company. Uses photos for brochures, news releases and newspapers.

Needs Buys 12-15 photos/year; offers 4 assignments/year. Special subject needs include children dancing, ballet, modern dance, jazz/tap (theater dance) and "photos showing class situations in any subjects we offer. Photos must include girls and boys, women and men." Interested in documentary, fine art, historical/vintage. Reviews stock photos. Model release required.

Specs Uses 8×10 glossy b&w prints. Accepts images in digital format. Send via CD, e-mail.

Making Contact & Terms "Call us." Responds in 1 week. Pays $35 to $50 for most photos, b&w or color. Credit line given if requested. Buys one-time rights; negotiable.

Tips "We are small but interested in quality (professional) work. Capture the joy of dance in a photo of children or adults. Show artists, actors or musicians at work. We prefer informal action photos, not posed pictures. We need photos of *real* dancers dancing. Call first. Be prepared to send photos on request."

◨ ▣ ARNOLD SAKS ASSOCIATES

350 E. 81st St., 4th Floor, New York NY 10028. (212)861-4300. Fax: (212)535-2590. E-mail: afiorillo@saksdesign.com. Web site: www.saksdesign.com. **Contact:** Anita Fiorillo, vice president. Estab. 1968. Graphic design firm. Number of employees: 10. Approximate annual billing: $2 million. Types of clients: industrial, financial, legal, pharmaceutical, hospitals. Examples of recent clients: Alcoa; McKinsey; UBS; Wyeth; Xerox; Hospital for Special Surgery.

Needs Works with approximately 15 photographers during busy season. Uses photos for annual reports and corporate brochures. Subjects include corporate situations and portraits. Wants photos of babies/children/teens, couples, multicultural, families, parents, senior citizens, automobiles, health/fitness/beauty, performing arts, sports, business concepts, industry, medicine, product shots/still life, science, technology/computers. Reviews stock photos; subjects vary according to the nature of the annual report. Model release required. Photo captions preferred.

Specs Accepts images in digital format. Send via e-mail as TIFF, EPS, JPEG files.

Making Contact & Terms ''Appointments are set up during the spring for summer review on a first-come only basis. We have a limit of approximately 30 portfolios each season.'' Call to arrange an appointment. Responds as needed. Payment negotiable, ''based on project budgets. Generally we pay $1,500-2,500/day.'' **Pays on receipt of invoice** and payment by client; advances provided. Credit line sometimes given depending upon client specifications. Buys one-time and all rights; negotiable.

Tips ''Ideally a photographer should show a corporate book indicating his success with difficult working conditions and establishing an attractive and vital final product. Our company is well known in the design community for doing classic graphic design. We look for solid, conservative, straightforward corporate photography that will enhance these ideals.''

$ $ $ MARTIN THOMAS, INTERNATIONAL

Advertising & Public Relations, 42 Riverside Dr., Barrington RI 02806. (401)245-8500. Fax: (866)899-2710. E-mail: contact@martinthomas.com. Web site: www.martinthomas.com. **Contact:** Martin K. Pottle, president. Estab. 1987. Ad agency, PR firm. Approximate annual billing: $7 million. Number of employees: 5. Firm specializes in collateral. Types of clients: industrial and business-to-business. Examples of recent clients: NADCA Show Booth, Newspaper 4PM Corp. (color newspaper); Pennzoil-Quaker State ''Rescue,'' PVC Container Corp. (magazine article); ''Bausch & Lomb,'' GLS Corporation (magazine cover); ''Soft Bottles,'' McKechnie (booth graphics); ''Perfectly Clear,'' ICI Acrylics (brochure).

Needs Works with 3-5 photographers/month. Uses photos for trade magazines. Subjects include: location shots of equipment in plants and some studio. Model release required.

Audiovisual Needs Uses videotape for 5- to 7-minute capabilities or instructional videos.

Specs Uses 8×10 color and/or b&w prints; 35mm, 4×5 transparencies. Accepts images in digital format (call first). Send via CD, e-mail, floppy disk as GIF, JPEG files.

Making Contact & Terms Send stock list. Provide résumé, business card, brochure, flier or tearsheets to be kept on file. Send materials on pricing, experience. ''No unsolicited portfolios will be accepted or reviewed.'' Cannot return material. Pays $1,000-1,500/day; $300-900 for b&w photos; $400-1,000 for color photos. Pays 30 days following receipt of invoice. Buys exclusive product rights; negotiable.

Tips To break in, demonstrate you ''can be aggressive, innovative, realistic, and can work within our clients' parameters and budgets. Be responsive; be flexible.''

$ $ $ MARTIN THOMAS, INTERNATIONAL

Advertising & Public Relations, 42 Riverside Dr., Barrington RI 02806. (401)245-8500. Fax: (866)899-2710. E-mail: contact@martinthomas.com. Web site: www.martinthomas.com. **Contact:** Martin K. Pottle, president. Estab. 1987. Ad agency, PR firm. Approximate annual billing: $7 million. Number of employees: 5. Firm specializes in collateral. Types of clients: industrial and business-to-business. Examples of recent clients: NADCA Show Booth, Newspaper 4PM Corp. (color newspaper); Pennzoil-Quaker State ''Rescue,'' PVC Container Corp. (magazine article); ''Bausch & Lomb,'' GLS Corporation (magazine cover); ''Soft Bottles,'' McKechnie (booth graphics); ''Perfectly Clear,'' ICI Acrylics (brochure).

Needs Works with 3-5 photographers/month. Uses photos for trade magazines. Subjects include: location shots of equipment in plants and some studio. Model release required.

Audiovisual Needs Uses videotape for 5- to 7-minute capabilities or instructional videos.

Specs Uses 8×10 color and/or b&w prints; 35mm, 4×5 transparencies. Accepts images in digital format (call first). Send via CD, e-mail, floppy disk as GIF, JPEG files.

Making Contact & Terms Send stock list. Provide résumé, business card, brochure, flier or tearsheets to be kept on file. Send materials on pricing, experience. "No unsolicited portfolios will be accepted or reviewed." Cannot return material. Pays $1,000-1,500/day; $300-900 for b&w photos; $400-1,000 for color photos. Pays 30 days following receipt of invoice. Buys exclusive product rights; negotiable.

Tips To break in, demonstrate you "can be aggressive, innovative, realistic, and can work within our clients' parameters and budgets. Be responsive; be flexible."

[A] [E] [≈] TOBOL GROUP, INC.

14 Vanderventer Ave., Suite 250, Port Washington NY 11050. (516)767-8182. Fax: (516)767-8185. E-mail: mt@tobolgroup.com. Web site: www.tobolgroup.com. **Contact:** Mitch Tobol, president. Estab. 1981. Ad agency/design studio. Types of clients: high-tech, industrial, business-to-business, consumer. Examples of recent clients: Weight Watchers (in-store promotion).

Needs Works with up to 2 photographers and videographers/month. Uses photos for billboards, consumer and trade magazines, direct mail, P-O-P displays, catalogs, posters, newspapers, audiovisual. Subjects are varied; mostly still-life photography. Reviews business-to-business and commercial video footage. Model release required.

Audiovisual Needs DVD, CD.

Specs "Digital photos in all formats, BetaSP, digital video." Uses 4×5, 8×10, 11×14 b&w prints; 35mm, $2\frac{1}{4}\times2\frac{1}{4}$, 4×5 transparencies; $\frac{1}{2}$" videotape. Accepts images in digital format. Send via e-mail or link to Web site.

Making Contact & Terms Send query letter with samples; include SASE for return of material. Provide résumé, business card, brochure, flier or tearsheets to be kept on file; follow up with phone call. Works on assignment only. Responds in 3 weeks. Pays $100-10,000/job. Pays net 30 days. Credit line sometimes given, depending on client and price. Rights purchased depend on client.

Tips In freelancer's samples or demos, wants to see "the best—any style or subject as long as it is done well. Trend is photos or videos to be multi-functional. Show me your *best* and what you enjoy shooting. Get experience with existing company to make the transition from still photography to audiovisual."

[◻] [E] WORCESTER POLYTECHNIC INSTITUTE

100 Institute Rd., Worcester MA 01609. (508)831-6715. Fax: (508)831-5820. E-mail: charna @wpi.edu. Web site: www.wpi.edu. **Contact:** Charna Westervelt, editorial director. Estab. 1865. Publishes periodicals; promotional, recruiting and fund-raising printed materials. Photos used in brochures, newsletters, posters, audiovisual presentations, annual reports, catalogs, magazines, press releases and Web site.

Needs On-campus, comprehensive and specific views of all elements of the WPI experience.

Specs Prefers images in digital format, but will use 5×7 (minimum) glossy b&w and color prints; 35mm, $2\frac{1}{4}\times2\frac{1}{4}$, 4×5 transparencies; b&w contact sheets.

Making Contact & Terms Arrange a personal interview to show portfolio or query with Web site link. Provide résumé, business card, brochure, flier or tearsheets to be kept on file. "No phone calls." Responds in 6 weeks. Payment negotiable. Credit line given in some publications. Buys one-time or all rights; negotiable.

$ $ $ ⬚ ▣ SPENCER ZAHN & ASSOCIATES

2015 Sansom St., Philadelphia PA 19103. (215)564-5979. Fax: (215)564-6285. **Contact:** Spencer Zahn, president. Estab. 1970. Member of GPCC. Marketing, advertising and design firm. Approximate annual billing: $5 million. Number of employees: 7. Firm specializes in direct mail, electronic collateral, print ads. Types of clients: financial and retail, automotive.
Needs Works with 1-3 photographers/month. Uses photos for billboards, consumer and trade magazines, direct mail, P-O-P displays, posters and signage. Subjects include: people, still life. Reviews stock photos. Model/property release required.
Specs Uses b&w and/or color prints and transparencies. Accepts images in digital format. Send via Zip, CD.
Making Contact & Terms Send query letter with résumé of credits, stock list, samples. Submit portfolio for review. Provide résumé, business card, brochure, flier or tearsheets to be kept on file. Keeps samples on file. Responds in 1 month. Pays on publication. Credit line sometimes given. Buys one time and/or all rights; negotiable.

MIDSOUTH & SOUTHEAST

$ $ ⬚ ▣ BOB BOEBERITZ DESIGN

247 Charlotte St., Asheville NC 28801. (828)258-0316. E-mail: bobb@main.nc.us. Web site: www.bobboeberitzdesign.com. **Contact:** Bob Boeberitz, owner. Estab. 1984. Member of American Advertising Federation, Asheville Freelance Network, Asheville Creative Services Group, National Academy of Recording Arts & Sciences, Public Relations Association of Western North Carolina. Graphic design studio. Approximate annual billing: $100,000. Number of employees: 1. Firm specializes in annual reports, collateral, direct mail, magazine ads, packaging, publication design, signage, Web sites. Types of clients: management consultants, retail, recording artists, mail-order firms, industrial, nonprofit, restaurants, hotels, book publishers.
Needs Works with 1 freelance photographer "every 6 months or so." Uses photos for consumer and trade magazines, direct mail, brochures, catalogs, posters. Subjects include: babies/children/teens, couples, multicultural, families, parents, senior citizens, environmental, landscapes/scenics, wildlife, architecture, cities/urban, education, pets, rural, adventure, entertainment, events, food/drink, health/fitness/beauty, hobbies, performing arts, sports, travel, business concepts, industry, medicine, product shots/still life, science, technology/computers; some location, some stock photos. Interested in fashion/glamour, seasonal. Model/property release required.
Specs Uses 8×10 glossy b&w prints; 35mm, 4×5 transparencies. Accepts images in digital format. Send via CD, Zip, floppy disk, e-mail as TIFF, BMP, JPEG, GIF files at 300 dpi.
Making Contact & Terms Provide résumé, business card, brochure, flier or tearsheets to be kept on file. Cannot return unsolicited material. Responds "when there is a need." Pays $75-200 for b&w photos; $100-500 for color photos; $75-150/hour; $500-1,500/day. Pays on per-job basis. Buys all rights; negotiable.
Tips "Send promotional piece to keep on file. Do not send anything that has to be returned. I usually look for a specific specialty; no photographer is good at everything. I also consider studio space and equipment. Show me something different, unusual, something that sets you apart from any average local photographer. If I'm going out of town for something, it has to be for something I can't get done locally. I keep and file

Advertising

direct mail pieces (especially postcards). I do not keep anything sent by e-mail. If you want me to remember your website, send a postcard.''

$ $ ☑ Ⓐ HACKMEISTER ADVERTISING & PUBLIC RELATIONS COMPANY

2631 E. Oakland Park Blvd., Suite 204, Ft. Lauderdale FL 33306. (954)568-2511. E-mail: hackmeisterad@aol.com. **Contact:** Richard Hackmeister, president. Estab. 1979. Ad agency and PR firm. Serves industrial, electronics manufacturers who sell to other businesses.

Needs Works with 1 photographer/month. Uses photos for trade magazines, direct mail, catalogs. Subjects include: electronic products. Model release required. Photo captions required.

Specs Uses 8×10 glossy color prints; 4×5 transparencies. Digital JPG files preferred.

Making Contact & Terms ''Call on telephone first.'' Does not return unsolicited material. Pays by the day; $200-2,000/job. Buys all rights.

Tips Looks for ''good lighting on highly technical electronic products—creativity.''

$ ☑ ▣ HOWARD, MERRELL AND PARTNERS, INC.

8521 Six Forks Rd., Raleigh NC 27615. (919)848-2400. Fax: (919)845-9845. **Contact:** Ann Neely, art buyer/broadcast manager. Estab. 1945. Member of AAAA. Number of employees: 45.

Needs Works with 1-2 photographers/month. Uses photos for consumer and trade magazines, newspapers, collateral, outdoor boards and websites. Purchases stock images. Model/property release required.

Specs Uses b&w prints; 2¼×2¼, 4×5 transparencies. Accepts images in digital format.

Making Contact & Terms Provide samples to be kept on file. Work on assignment and buys stock photos. **Pays on receipt of invoice.** Buys one-time and all rights.

☑ Ⓐ ▣ MYRIAD PRODUCTIONS

P.O. Box 888886, Atlanta GA 30356. (678)417-0041. E-mail: myriad@mindspring.com. **Contact:** Ed Harris, president. Estab. 1965. Primarily involved with sports productions and events. Types of clients: publishing, nonprofit.

Needs Works with photographers on assignment-only basis. Uses photos for portraits, live-action and studio shots, special effects, advertising, illustrations, brochures, TV and film graphics, theatrical and production stills. Subjects include: celebrities, entertainment, sports. Model/property release required. Photo captions preferred; include name(s), location, date, description.

Specs Uses 8×10 b&w and/or color prints; 2¼×2¼ transparancies. Accepts images in digital format. Send via ''Mac-compatible CD or DVD. No floppy disks or Zips!''

Making Contact & Terms Provide brochure, résumé or samples to be kept on file. Send material by mail for consideration. ''No telephone or fax inquiries, please!'' Cannot return material. Response time ''depends on urgency of job or production.'' Payment negotiable. Credit line sometimes given. Buys all rights.

Tips ''We look for an imaginative photographer—one who captures all the subtle nuances. Working with us depends almost entirely on the photographer's skill and creative sensitivity with the subject. All materials submitted will be placed on file and not returned, pending future assignments. Photographers should not send us their only prints, transparencies, etc., for this reason.''

$ $⊠ SIDES & ASSOCIATES

222 Jefferson Street, Ste B., Lafayette LA 70501. (337)233-6473. Fax: (337)233-6485. E-mail: larry@sides.com. **Contact:** Larry Sides, agency president. Estab. 1976. Member of AAAA, PRSA, Association for Strategic Planning, Chamber of Commerce, Better Business Bureau. Ad agency. Number of employees: 13. Firm specializes in publication design, display design, signage, video and radio production. Types of clients: governmental, healthcare, financial, retail, nonprofit. Examples of recent clients: U.S. Dept of Homeland Security, ESF #14(web, brochure, and special event planning); Lafayette Regional Airport (signs, brochures), Our Lady of Lourdes Regional Medical Center (TV, outdoor, print ads, brochures).

Needs Works with 2 photographers/month. Uses photos for billboards, brochures, newspapers, P-O-P displays, posters, signage. Subjects include: setup shots of people. Reviews stock photos of everything. Model/property release required.

Audiovisual Needs Works with 2 filmmakers and 2 videographers/month. Uses slides and/or film or video for broadcast, TV, newspaper.

Specs Uses 35mm, $2^1/_4 \times 2^1/_4$, 4×5 transparencies.

Making Contact & Terms Provide résumé, business card, self-promotion piece or tearsheets to be kept on file. Works with local freelancers only. Responds only if interested; send nonreturnable samples. Payment determined by client and usage. Pays "when paid by our client." Rights negotiable.

$○ ▣ ⊠ SOUNDLIGHT

5438 Tennessee Ave., New Port Richey, FL 34652. (727)842-6788. E-mail: keth@awakening-healing.com. Web site: www.SoundLight.org. **Contact:** Keth Luke. Estab. 1972. Approximate annual billing: $150,000. Number of employees: 2. Firm specializes in websites, direct mail, magazine ads, model portfolios, publication design. Types of clients: businesses, astrological and spiritual workshops, books, calendars, fashion, magazines, models, nonprofit, webpages. Examples of recent clients: Sensual Women of Hawaii (calendars, post cards).

Needs Works with 1 freelance photographer every 7 months. Subjects include: women, celebrities, couples, Goddess, people in activities, landscapes/scenics, animals, religious, adventure, health/fitness/beauty, humor, alternative medicine, spiritual, travel sites and activities, exotic dance and models (art, glamour, lingerie and nude). Interested in alternative process, avant garde, erotic, fine art. Reviews stock photos, slides, computer images. Model release preferred for models and advertising people. Photo captions preferred; include who, what, where.

Audiovisual Needs Uses freelance photographers for slide sets, multimedia productions, videotapes, Web sites.

Specs Uses 4×6 to 8×10 glossy color prints; 35mm color slides. Accepts images in digital format. Send via CD, floppy disk, e-mail as TIFF, GIF, JPEG files at 70-100 dpi.

Making Contact & Terms Send query letter with résumé, stock list. Provide prints, slides, business card, computer disk, CD, contact sheets, self-promotion piece or tearsheets to be kept on file. Works on assignment; sometimes buys stock nude model photos. May not return unsolicited material. Responds in 3 weeks. Pays $100 maximum for b&w and color photos; $10-1,800 for videotape; $10-100/hour; $50-750/day; $2,000 maximum/job; sometimes also pays in "trades." Pays on publication. Credit line sometimes given. Buys one-time, all rights; various negotiable rights depending on use.

Tips In portfolios or demos, looks for "unique lighting, style, emotional involvement; beautiful, artistic, sensual, erotic viewpoints." Sees trend toward "manipulated computer images. Send query about what you have to show, to see what we can use at that time."

MIDWEST & NORTH CENTRAL

$ Ⓐ BRAGAW PUBLIC RELATIONS SERVICES

800 E. Northwest Hwy., Suite 1040, Palatine IL 60074. (847)934-5580. Fax: (847)934-5596. Web site: http://bragawpr.com. **Contact:** Richard S. Bragaw, president. Estab. 1981. Member of Publicity Club of Chicago. PR firm. Number of employees: 3. Types of clients: professional service firms, high-tech entrepreneurs.

Needs Uses photos for trade magazines, direct mail, brochures, newspapers, newsletters/news releases. Subjects include: "products and people." Model release preferred. Photo captions preferred.

Specs Uses 3×5, 5×7, 8×10 glossy prints.

Making Contact & Terms Provide résumé, business card, brochure, flier or tearsheets to be kept on file. Works with freelance photographers on assignment basis only. Payment is negotiated at the time of the assignment. **Pays on receipt of invoice.** Credit line "possible." Buys all rights; negotiable.

Tips "Execute an assignment well, at reasonable costs, with speedy delivery."

$ Ⓐ ▣ ▨ FLINT COMMUNICATIONS

101 10th St. N., Fargo ND 58102. (701)237-4850. Fax: (701)234-9680. Email: gerriL@flintcom.com or dawnk@flintcom.com. Web site: www.flintcom.com. **Contact:** Gerri Lien, creative director or Dawn Koranda, art director. Estab. 1946. Ad agency. Approximate annual billing: $9 million. Number of employees: 30. Firm specializes in display design, direct mail, magazine ads, publication design, signage, annual reports. Types of clients: industrial, financial, agriculture, health care and tourism.

Needs Works with 2-3 photographers/month. Uses photos for direct mail, P-O-P displays, posters and audiovisual. Subjects include: babies/children/teens, couples, parents, senior citizens, architecture, rural, adventure, automobiles, events, food/drink, health/fitness, sports, travel, agriculture, industry, medicine, political, product shots/still life, science, technology, manufacturing, finance, health care, business. Interested in documentary, historical/vintage, seasonal. Reviews stock photos. Model release preferred.

Audiovisual Needs Works with 1-2 filmmakers and 1-2 videographers/month. Uses slides and film.

Specs Uses 35mm, 2¼×2¼, 4×5 transparencies. Accepts images in digital format. Send via CD, Zip as TIFF, EPS, JPEG files.

Making Contact & Terms Send query letter with stock list. Submit portfolio for review. Provide résumé, business card, brochure, flier or tearsheets to be kept on file. Responds in 1-2 weeks. Pays $50-150 for b&w photos; $50-1,500 for color photos; $50-130/hour; $400-1,200/day; $100-2,000/job. **Pays on receipt of invoice.** Buys one-time rights.

$ Ⓐ ▣ ▨ IDEA BANK MARKETING

P.O. Box 2117, Hastings NE 68902. (402)463-0588. Fax: (402)463-2187. E-mail: sherma@ideabankmarketing.com, mail@ideabankmarketing.com. Web site: www.ideabankmarketing.com. **Contact:** Sherma Jones, vice president/creative director. Estab. 1982. Member of

Lincoln Ad Federation. Ad agency. Approximate annual billing: $1.5 million. Number of employees: 13. Types of clients: industrial, financial, tourism and retail.

Needs Works with 1-2 photographers/quarter. Uses photos for direct mail, catalogs, posters and newspapers. Subjects include people and products. Reviews stock photos. Model release required; property release preferred.

Audiovisual Needs Works with 1 videographer/quarter. Uses slides and videotape for presentations.

Specs Uses digital images.

Making Contact & Terms Provide résumé, business card, brochure, flier or tearsheets to be kept on file. Works with freelancers on assignment only. Responds in 2 weeks. Pays $75-125/hour; $650-1,000/day. **Pays on acceptance with receipt of invoice**. Credit line sometimes given depending on client and project. Buys all rights; negotiable.

⒜ ▣ ▨ PHOTO COMMUNICATION SERVICES, INC.

P.O. Box 9, Traverse City MI 49685-0009. (231)943-5050. E-mail: photomarket@photocomm.net. Web site: www.photocomm.net. **Contact:** M'Lynn Hartwell, president. Estab. 1970. Commercial/illustrative and multimedia firm. Types of clients: commercial/industrial, fashion, food, general, human interest.

- This firm also has an office in Hawaii: P.O. Box 458, Kapa'a HI 96746-0458. "Also see our advertising agency at www.UtopianEmpire.com."

Needs Works with varying number of photographers/month. Uses photos for catalogs, P-O-P displays, AV presentations, trade magazines and brochures, and a "large variety of subjects." Sometimes works with freelance filmmakers. Model release required.

Audiovisual Needs "Primarily industrial or training video."

Specs Uses digital, "plus some older technology" such as 8×10 (or larger) glossy (or semiglossy) b&w and/or color prints, 35mm film, transparencies, most current formats of digital videotape.

Making Contact & Terms Send query letter with résumé of credits, samples, stock list; include SASE for return of material. Works with freelance photographers on assignment basis only. Payment determined by private negotiation. Pays 30 days from acceptance. Credit line given "whenever possible."

Tips "Be professional and to the point. If I see something I can use, I will make an appointment to discuss the project in detail."

⬛ ⒜ ▣ PATRICK REDMOND DESIGN

P.O. Box 75430-PM, St. Paul MN 55175-0430. E-mail: redmond@patrickredmonddesign.com. Web site: www.patrickredmonddesign.com. **Contact:** Patrick Redmond, M.A., designer/owner/president. Estab. 1966. Design firm. Number of employees: 1. Firm specializes in publication design, book covers, books, packaging, direct mail, posters, branding, logos, trademarks, annual reports, Web sites, collateral. Types of clients: publishers, financial, retail, advertising, marketing, education, nonprofit, industrial, arts. Examples of recent clients: *Flamenco-A Touch of Spain* (Web site, Branding, Print);The Alonzo Hauser Collection (Web site launch; print); Experienced Staff, LLC (Brand identity consulting). See "portfolio" section of Web site for examples.

- Books designed by Redmond have won awards from Midwest Independent Publishers Association, Midwest Book Achievement Awards, Publishers Marketing Association Benjamin Franklin Awards.

Advertising

Needs Uses photos for books and book covers, direct mail, P-O-P displays, catalogs, posters, packaging, annual reports. Subject varies with client—may be editorial, product, how-to, etc. May need custom b&w photos of authors (for books/covers designed by PRD). "Poetry book covers provide unique opportunities for unusual images (but typically have miniscule budgets)." Reviews stock photos; subject matter varies with need. Model/property release required; varies with assignment/project. Photo captions required; include correct spelling and identification of all factual matters regarding images; names, locations, etc. to be used optionally if needed.

Specs Accepts images in digital format; type varies with need, production requirements, budgets.

Making Contact & Terms Contact through rep. Arrange a personal interview to show portfolio if requested. "Send query letter with your Web site address only via brief e-mail text message. Patrick Redmond Design will not reply unless specific photographer may be needed." Works with local freelancers on assignment only. Cannot return material. Payment negotiable. "Client typically pays photographer directly even though PRD may be involved in photo/photographer selection and photo direction." Payment depends on client. Credit line sometimes given depending upon publication style/individual projects. Rights purchased by clients vary with project; negotiable. "Clients typically involved with negotiation of rights directly with photographer. Please include note 'Photographer's Market 2009' in any correspondence (unlikely to open or respond to mail or e-mails which don't include this on envelope or in subject line)."

Tips Needs are "open—vary with project; location work, studio, table-top, product, portraits, travel, etc." Seeing "use of existing stock images when image/price are right for project, and use of black & white photos in low- to mid-budget/price books. Provide URLs and e-mail addresses. Freelance photographers need Web presence in today's market in addition to exposure via direct mail, catalogs, brochures, etc. Do not send any images/files attached to your e-mails. Briefly state/describe your work in e-mail. Do not send unsolicited print samples or digital files in any format via e-mail, traditional mail or other delivery."

🅐 🖼 🖼 VIDEO I-D, INC.

105 Muller Rd., Washington IL 61571. (309)444-4323. Fax: (309)444-4333. E-mail: videoid @videoid.com. Web site: www.videoid.com. **Contact:** Sam B. Wagner, president. Number of employees: 10. Types of clients: health, education, industry, service, cable and broadcast.

Needs Works with 2 photographers/month to shoot digital stills, multimedia backgrounds and materials, films and videotapes. Subjects "vary from commercial to industrial—always high quality." Somewhat interested in stock photos/footage. Model release required.

Audiovisual Needs Uses digital stills, videotape, DVD, DVD-ROM, CD-ROM.

Specs Uses digital still extension, Beta SP, HDV and HD. Accepts images in digital format. Send via DVD, CD, e-mail, FTP.

Making Contact & Terms Provide résumé, business card, self-promotion piece or tearsheets to be kept on file. "Also send video sample reel." Include SASE for return of material. Works with freelancers on assignment only. Responds in 3 weeks. Pays $10-65/hour; $160-650/day. Usually pays by the job; negotiable. **Pays on acceptance.** Credit line sometimes given. Buys all rights; negotiable.

Tips "Sample reel—indicate goal for specific pieces. Show good lighting and visualization skills. Show me you can communicate what I need to see, and have a willingness to put out effort to get top quality."

SOUTH CENTRAL & WEST

$ 🖳 🖼 THE ADVERTISING CONSORTIUM

10536 Culver Blvd., Suite D., Culver City, CA 90232. (310)287-2222. Fax: (310)287-2227. Email: theadco@pacbell.net. **Contact:** Kim Miyade, president. Estab. 1985. Full-service ad agency. Approximate annual billing: $1.2 million. Number of employees: 2. Firm specializes in magazine ads, direct mail. Types of clients: industrial, retail. Current clients include Bernini, Davante, Westime, Modular Communication Systems, Luxury Optical Holdings.

Needs Number of photographers used on a monthly basis varies. Uses photos for billboards, consumer and trade magazines, direct mail, posters, newspapers and signage. Subjects include: babies/children/teens, couples, families, wildlife, product shots/still life, technology/computers. Interested in fashion/glamour. Reviews stock photos. Model release required; property release preferred.

Audiovisual Needs Uses slides, film and high-res scans on disk.

Specs Uses color and b&w prints. Accepts images in digital format. Send via CD, Zip.

Making Contact & Terms Send unsolicited photos by mail for consideration. Works with local freelancers only. Provide résumé, business card, brochure, flier or tearsheets to be kept on file. Notification dependent upon opportunity. Payment negotiable. Credit line sometimes given. Buys all rights.

$ 🖉 Ⓐ 🖳 BERSON, DEAN, STEVENS INC.

P.O. Box 3997, Thousand Oaks CA 91359-3997. (818)713-0134. Fax: (818)713-0417. Web site: www.BersonDeanStevens.com. E-mail: info@bersondeanstevens.com. **Contact:** Lori Berson, owner. Estab. 1981. Design firm. Number of employees: 3. Firm specializes in annual reports, display design, collateral, packaging, direct mail and video production. Types of clients: industrial, financial, food and retail. Examples of recent clients: Dole Food Company; Charles Schwab & Co., Inc.

Needs Works with 4 photographers/month. Uses photos for billboards, trade magazines, direct mail, P-O-P displays, catalogs, posters, packaging, signage and Web. Subjects include: product shots and food. Reviews stock photos. Model/property release required.

Specs Accepts images in digital format only. Send via CD, DVD as TIFF, EPS, JPEG files at 300 dpi.

Making Contact & Terms Provide résumé, business card, brochure, flier or tearsheets to be kept on file. Works on assignment only. Responds in 1-2 weeks. Payment negotiable. Pays within 30 days after receipt of invoice. Credit line not given. Rights negotiable.

🖉 Ⓐ 🖳 BRAINWORKS DESIGN GROUP

5 Harris Court, Bldg. T, Suite A, Monterey CA 93940. (831)657-0650. Fax: (831)657-0750. E-mail: design@brainwks.com. Web site: www.brainwks.com. **Contact:** Alfred Kahn, president. Estab. 1986. Design firm. Approximate annual billing: $2 million. Number of employees: 8. Firm specializes in publication design and collateral. Types of clients: higher education, technology, science

Needs Works with 4 photographers/month. Uses photographs for direct mail, catalogs and posters. Subjects include: couples, environmental, education, entertainment, performing arts, sports, business concepts, science, technology/computers. Interested in avant garde, documentary. Wants conceptual images. Model release required.

Specs Uses 35mm, 4×5 transparencies. Accepts images in digital format. Send via CD.

Advertising

Making Contact & Terms Arrange a personal interview to show portfolio. Send unsolicited photos by mail for consideration. Works with freelancers on assignment only. Keeps samples on file. Cannot return material. Responds in 1 month. Pay negotiable. **Pays on receipt of invoice**. Credit line sometimes given, depending on client. Buys first, one-time and all rights; negotiable.

◫ ▣ ▨ BRAMSON + ASSOCIATES

7400 Beverly Blvd., Los Angeles CA 90036. (323)938-3595. Fax: (323)938-0852. E-mail: gbramson@aol.com. **Contact:** Gene Bramson, principal. Estab. 1970. Ad agency. Approximate annual billing: $2 million. Number of employees: 7. Types of clients: industrial, financial, food, retail, health care. Examples of recent clients: Sumitomo Metal and Mining: Biotech, Japan; Lawry's Restaurants, Inc.; AF Growlabs, Division of Hairraising Personal Care Products, Inc.

Needs Works with 1-2 photographers/month. Uses photos for trade magazines, direct mail, posters, newspapers, signage, Web sites, corporate brochures, and collateral. Subject matter varies; includes babies/children/teens, couples, multicultural, families, architecture, cities/urban, gardening, interiors/decorating, pets, automobiles, food/drink, health/fitness/beauty, business concepts, medicine, science. Interested in avant garde, documentary, erotic, fashion/glamour, historical/vintage. Reviews stock photos. Model/property release required. Photo captions preferred.

Audiovisual Needs Works with 1 videographer/month. Uses videotape for industrial, product.

Specs Mostly DVD and digital format.

Making Contact & Terms Submit portfolio for review. Send unsolicited photos by mail for consideration; include SASE for return of material. Works with local freelancers on assignment only. Provide résumé, business card, brochure, flier or tearsheet to be kept on file. Responds in 3 weeks. Payment negotiable, depending on budget for each project. **Pays on receipt of invoice**. Credit line not given. Buys one-time and all rights.

Tips "Innovative, crisp, dynamic, unique style—otherwise we'll stick with our photographers. If it's not great work, don't bother."

◫ ▨ DYKEMAN ASSOCIATES, INC.

4115 Rawlins St., Dallas TX 75219. (214)528-2991. Fax: (214)528-0241. E-mail: adykeman @airmail.net. Web site: www.dykemanassociates.com. **Contact:** Alice Dykeman, APR, Fellow-PRSA. Estab. 1974. Member of Public Relations Society of America. PR, marketing, video production firm. Firm specializes in Web site creation and promotion, communication plans, media training, collateral, direct marketing. Types of clients: industrial, financial, sports, technology.

Needs Works with 4-5 photographers and/or videographers. Uses photos for publicity, consumer and trade magazines, direct mail, catalogs, posters, newspapers, signage, Web sites.

Audiovisual Needs "We produce and direct video. Just need crew with good equipment and people and ability to do their part."

Making Contact & Terms Arrange a personal interview to show portfolio. Provide business card, brochure, flier or tearsheets to be kept on file. Works on assignment only. Cannot return material. Pays $800-1,200/day; $250-400/1-2 days. "Currently we work only with photographers who are willing to be part of our trade dollar network. Call if you don't understand this term." Pays 30 days after receipt of invoice.

Tips Reviews portfolios with current needs in mind. "If video, we would want to see examples. If for news story, we would need to see photojournalism capabilities."

Ⓝ $ $◨ Ⓐ ▣ ⊠ FARNAM COMPANIES, INC.

301 W. Osborn, Phoenix AZ 85013-3997. (602)207-2129. Fax: (602)207-2193. E-mail: dkuykendall@mail.farnam.com. Web site: www.farnam.com. **Contact:** Leslie Burger, creative director. Firm specializes in display design, magazine ads, packaging. Types of clients: retail.

- This company has an in-house ad agency called Charles Duff Advertising.

Needs Works with 2 photographers/month. Uses photos for direct mail, catalogs, consumer magazines, P-O-P displays, posters, AV presentations, trade magazines and brochures. Subject matter includes horses, dogs, cats, birds, farm scenes, ranch scenes, cowboys, cattle, horse shows, landscapes/scenics, gardening. Model release required.

Audiovisual Needs Uses film and videotape. Occasionally works with freelance filmmakers to produce educational horse health films and demonstrations of product use.

Specs Uses 35mm, $2\frac{1}{4} \times 2\frac{1}{4}$, 4×5 transparencies; 16mm and 35mm film and videotape. Accepts images in digital format. Send via CD, Zip.

Making Contact & Terms Send query letter with samples; include SASE for return of material. Provide résumé, business card, brochure, flier or tearsheets to be kept on file. Works with freelance photographers on assignment basis only. Pays $50-350 for color photos. Pays on publication. Credit line given whenever possible. Buys one-time rights.

Tips "Send me a number of good, reasonably priced for one-time use photos of dogs, horses or farm scenes. Better yet, send me good-quality dupes I can keep on file for *rush* use. When the dupes are in the file and I see them regularly, the ones I like stick in my mind and I find myself planning ways to use them. We are looking for original, dramatic work. We especially like to see horses, dogs, cats and cattle captured in artistic scenes or poses. All shots should show off quality animals with good conformation. We rarely use shots if people are shown and prefer animals in natural settings or in barns/stalls."

Ⓐ ▣ THE HITCHINS COMPANY

22756 Hartland St., Canoga Park CA 91307. (818)715-0510. Fax: (775)806-2687. E-mail: whitchins@socal.rr.com. **Contact:** W.E. Hitchins, president. Estab. 1985. Ad agency. Approximate annual billing: $300,000. Number of employees: 2. Firm specializes in collateral, direct mail, magazine ads. Types of clients: industrial, retail (food), auctioneers. Examples of recent clients: Electronic Expediters (brochure showing products); Allan-Davis Enterprises (magazine ads).

Needs Uses photos for trade and consumer magazines, direct mail, newspapers. Model release required.

Specs Uses b&w and/or color prints. "Copy should be flexible for scanning." Accepts images in digital format. Send via CD.

Making Contact & Terms Provide résumé, business card, brochure, flier or tearsheets to be kept on file. Works on assignment only. Cannot return material. Payment negotiable depending on job. **Pays on receipt of invoice** (30 days). Rights purchase negotiable; "varies as to project."

Tips "Wants to see shots of people and products in samples."

Advertising

☑ ▣ JUDE STUDIOS

8000 Research Forest, Suite 115-266, The Woodlands TX 77382. (281)364-9366. Fax: (281)364-9529. E-mail: jdollar@judestudios.com. Web site: www.judestudios.com. **Contact:** Judith Dollar, art director. Estab. 1994. Member of Houston Art Directors Club, American Advertising Federation. Number of employees: 2. Firm specializes in collateral, direct mail, packaging. Types of clients: industrial, high tech, medical, event marketing, service. Examples of recent clients: home builder; festivals and events; corporate collateral; various logos; banking.

Needs Works with 1 photographer/month. Uses photos for brochures, catalogs, direct mail, trade and trade show graphics. Needs photos of families, senior citizens, education, pets, business concepts, industry, product shots/still life, technology/computers. Model release required; property release preferred. Photo captions preferred.

Specs Accepts images in digital format. Send via CD as TIFF, EPS, JPEG files at 350 dpi. ''Do not e-mail attachments.''

Making Contact & Terms Send query letter with prints, photocopies, tearsheets. Provide business card, self-promotion piece to be kept on file. Responds only if interested; send nonreturnable samples. Pays by the project. **Pays on receipt of invoice.**

Ⓝ $ $☑ ▣ 🖾 LINEAR CYCLE PRODUCTIONS

Box 2608, Sepulveda CA 91393-2608. **Contact:** R. Borowy, production manager. Estab. 1980. Member of International United Photographer Publishers, Inc. Ad agency, PR firm. Approximate annual billing: $5 million. Number of employees: 20. Firm specializes in annual reports, display design, magazine ads, publication design, direct mail, packaging, signage. Types of clients: industrial, commercial, advertising, retail, publishing.

Needs Works with 7-10 photographers/month. Uses photos for billboards, consumer magazines, direct mail, P-O-P displays, posters, newspapers, audiovisual uses. Subjects include: candid photographs. Reviews stock photos, archival. Model/property release required. Photo captions required; include description of subject matter.

Audiovisual Needs Works with 8-12 filmmakers and 8-12 videographers/month. Uses slides and/or film or video for television/motion pictures. Subjects include: archival-humor material.

Specs Uses 8×10 color and/or b&w prints; 35mm, 8×10 transparencies; 16mm-35mm film; $\frac{1}{2}''$, $\frac{3}{4}''$, $1''$ videotape. Accepts images in digital format. Send via CD, floppy disk, Jaz as TIFF, GIF, JPEG files.

Making Contact & Terms Submit portfolio for review. Send query letter with résumé of credits, stock list. Provide résumé, business card, brochure, flier or tearsheets to be kept on file. Works with local freelancers on assignment and buys stock photos. Responds in 1 month. Pays $100-500 for b&w photos; $150-750 for color photos; $100-1,000/job. Prices paid depend on position. Pays on publication. Credit line given. Buys one-time rights; negotiable.

Tips ''Send a good portfolio with color images. No sloppy pictures or portfolios! The better the portfolio is set up, the better the chances we would consider it, let alone look at it!'' Seeing a trend toward ''more archival/vintage and a lot of humor pieces.''

Ⓝ $ $ $ $☑ THE MILLER GROUP

1516 Bundy Dr., Suite 200, Los Angeles CA 90025. (310)442-0101. Fax: (310)442-0107. E-mail: gary@millergroup.net. Web site: www.millergroup.net. **Contact:** Gary Bettman. Estab. 1990.

Member of WSAAA. Approximate annual billing: $12 million. Number of employees: 10. Firm specializes in print advertising. Types of clients: consumer.

Needs Uses photos for billboards, brochures, consumer magazines, direct mail, newspapers. Model release required.

Making Contact and Terms Contact through rep or send query letter with photocopies. Provide self-promotion piece to be kept on file. Buys all rights; negotiable.

Tips "Please, no calls!"

$🅰️ 🖥️ 🖼️ DANA WHITE PRODUCTIONS

2623 29th St., Santa Monica CA 90405. (310)450-9101. E-mail: dwprods@aol.com. **Contact:** Dr. Dana White, president. Estab. 1977. Full-service audiovisual, multi-image, digital photography and design, video/film production studio. Types of clients: schools and community-based nonprofit institutions, corporate, government, publishing, marketing/advertising, and art galleries . Examples of recent clients: Toyota Hybrid Synergy: Mobile Experience Tour (video production); Los Angeles County (annual report); Back Forty Feature Films; Southern California Gas Company/South Coast AQMD (Clean Air Environmental Film Trailers in 300 LA-based motion picture theaters); Glencoe/McGraw-Hill (textbook photography and illustrations, slide shows); Pepperdine University (awards banquet presentations, fundraising, biographical tribute programs); U.S. Forest Service (training programs); Venice Family Clinic (newsletter photography); Johnson & Higgins (brochure photography). "Stock photography is available through PhotoEdit: www.photoeditinc.com; locate Dana White in list of photographers."

Needs Works with 2-3 photographers/month. Uses photos for catalogs, audiovisual , books. Subjects include: people, products, still life, event documentation , architecture. Interested in reviewing 35mm stock photos by appointment. Model release required for people and companies.

Audiovisual Needs Uses all AV formats including scanned and digital images for computer-based multimedia; 35mm slides for multi-image presentations; and medium-format as needed.

Specs Uses color and/or b&w prints; 35mm, $2\frac{1}{4}\times2\frac{1}{4}$ transparencies; digital images (minimum 6mp files).

Making Contact & Terms Arrange a personal interview to show portfolio and samples. "Please do not send originals." Works with freelancers on assignment only. Will assign certain work on spec. Do not submit unsolicited material. Cannot return material. **Pays when images are shot to White's satisfaction**—never delays until acceptance by client. Pays according to job: $25-100/hour, up to $750/day; $20-50/shot; or fixed fee based upon job complexity and priority of exposure. Hires according to work-for-hire and will share photo credit when possible.

Tips In freelancer's portfolio or demo, Dr. White wants to see "quality of composition, lighting, saturation, degree of difficulty , and importance of assignment. The trend seems to be toward more video, less AV. Clients are paying less and expecting more. To break in, freelancers should diversify, negotiate, be personable and flexible, go the distance to get and keep the job. Freelancers need to see themselves as hunters who are dependent upon their hunting skills for their livelihood. Don't get stuck in one-dimensional thinking. Think and perform as a team—service that benefits all sectors of the community and process."

Advertising

$ $🖉 🖳 CREATIVE COMPANY

726 NE Fourth St., McMinnville OR 97128. (503)883-4433 or (866)363-4433. Fax: (503)883-6817. E-mail: jlmorrow@creativeco.com. Web site: www.creativeco.com. **Contact:** Jennifer L. Morrow, president, or Steve Donatelli, Creative Director. Estab. 1978. Member of American Institute of Graphic Artists. Strategic branding and communications firm. Approximate annual billing: $1.5 million. Number of employees: 12. Firm specializes in branding, collateral, direct mail, magazine ads, packaging, publication design. Types of clients: service, industrial, financial, manufacturing, food and wine, education, non-profit, business-to-business.

Needs Works with 1-2 photographers/month. Uses photos for direct mail, P-O-P displays, catalogs, posters, packaging and sales promotion packages. Subjects include: babies/children/teens, multicultural, senior citizens, gardening, food/drink, health/fitness/beauty, agriculture, business concepts, industry, product shots/still life, technology/computers. Model release preferred.

Specs Prefers high-resolution digital files. "We would like to view samples online or via e-mail."

Making Contact & Terms Arrange a personal interview to show portfolio. Works with local freelancers only. Provide resume, business card, brochure, flier or tearsheets to be kept on file. Responds "when needed." Pays $150-300 for b&w photos; $300-1,000 for color photos; $50-100/hour; $700-2,000/day; $200-15,000/job. Credit line not given. Buys one-time, one-year and all rights; negotiable.

Tips In freelancers' portfolios looks for "product shots, lighting, creative approach, understanding of sales message and reproduction." Sees trend toward "more special effect photography and manipulation of photos in computers." To break in with this firm, "do good work, be responsive, and understand how to maximize color and effect on the press."

🖽 $ $🖉 🖳 GRAFICA

P.O. Box 2758, Poulsbo WA 98370. (818)712-0071. Fax: (818)348-7582. E-mail: graficaeps @aol.com. Web site: www.graficaeps.com. **Contact:** Larry Girardi, owner. Estab. 1974. Member of Adobe Authorized Imaging Center, Quark Service Alliance, Corel Approved Service Bureau. Design studio and service bureau. Approximate annual billing: $250,000. Number of employees: 5. Firm specializes in annual reports, magazine ads, direct mail, publication design, collateral design, video graphics-titling. Types of clients: high technology, industrial, retail, publishers, entertainment.

Needs Works with 1-2 photographers/month. Uses photos for annual reports, billboards, consumer and trade magazines, P-O-P displays, catalogs, posters, packaging. Subjects include: babies/children/teens, celebrities, couples, multicultural, families, parents, senior citizens, disasters, environmental, landscapes, scenics, wildlife, architecure, cities/urban, education, gardening, interiors/decorating, pets, religious, rural, adventure, automobiles, entertainment, events, food/drink, health/fitness, hobbies, humor, performing arts, sports, travel, agriculture, business concepts, industry, medicine, military, political, product shots/still life, science, technology/computers. Interested in alternative process, avant garde, documentary, erotic, fashion/glamour, fine art, historical/vintage, seasonal. Model release required; property release preferred.

Specs Uses 35mm, 2¼×2¼, 4×5 transparencies. Accepts images in digital format. Send via CD, e-mail as JPEG files.

Making Contact & Terms Send query letter with samples. Provide résumé, business card, brochure, flier or tearsheets to be kept on file. Responds in 1-2 weeks. Pays $100-1,000 for b&w and color photos. Credit line sometimes given. Buys first, one-time, electronic and all rights; negotiable.

Tips "Send sample sheets (nonreturnable) for our files. We will contact when appropriate project arises."

$ $⬚ ⬚ HENRY SCHMIDT DESIGN

14201 SE Bunnell Street, Portland OR 97267-2631. (503)652-1114. E-mail: hank@hankink.com. Web site: www.hankink.com. **Contact:** H an k Schmidt, president. Estab. 1976. Design firm. Approximate annual billing: $250,000. Number of employees: 2. Firm specializes in branding, packaging, P-O-P display s, catalog/sales literature.

Needs Works with 1-2 photographers/month. Uses photos for catalogs and packaging. Subjects include product shots/still life. Interested in fashion/glamour. Model/property release required.

Specs Uses digital photography for almost all projects. Send digital images via CD, e-mail as TIFF, JPEG files.

Making Contact & Terms Interested in receiving work from newer, lesser-known photographers. Send query letter with samples; include SASE for return of material. Buys all rights.

$⬚ ⬚ ⬚ SUN.ERGOS: A Company of Theatre and Dance

130 Sunset Way, Priddis AB T0L 1W0 Canada. (403)931-1527. Fax: (403)931-1534. E-mail: waltermoke@sunergos.com. Web site: www.sunergos.com. **Contact:** Robert Greenwood, artistic and managing director. Estab. 1977. "A unique, professional, two-man company of theatre and dance, touring nationally and internationally as cultural ambassadors to urban and rural communities."

Needs Buys 10-30 photos/year; offers 3-5 assignments/year. Uses photos for brochures, newsletters, posters, newspapers, annual reports, magazines, press releases, audiovisual uses and catalogs. Reviews theater and dance stock photos. Property release required for performance photos for media use. Photo captions required; include subject, date, city, performance title.

Audiovisual Needs Uses slides, film and videotape for media usage, showcases and international conferences. Subjects include performance pieces/showcase materials.

Specs Uses 8×10, 8½×11 color and/or b&w prints; 35mm, 2¼×2¼ transparencies; 16mm film; NTSC/PAL/SECAM videotape.

Making Contact & Terms Arrange a personal interview to show portfolio. Send query letter with résumé of credits. Provide résumé, business card, self-promotion piece or tearsheets to be kept on file. Works on assignment only. Response time depends on project. Pays $100-150/day; $150-300/job; $2.50-10 for color or b&w photos. Pays on usage. Credit line given. Buys all rights.

Tips "You must have experience shooting dance and *live* theater performances."

⬚ ⬚ ⬚ ⬚ ⬚ WARNE MARKETING & COMMUNICATIONS

65 Overlea Blvd., Suite 112, Toronto ON M4H 1P1 Canada. (416)927-0881. Fax: (416)927-1676. E-mail: scott@warne.com. Web site: www.warne.com. **Contact:** Scott Warne, president. Estab. 1979. Ad agency. Types of clients: business-to-business.

Needs Works with 4 photographers/month. Uses photos for trade magazines, direct mail,

Internet, P-O-P displays, catalogs and posters. Subjects include: business concepts, science, technology/computers, in-plant photography and studio set-ups. Special subject needs include in-plant shots. Model release required.

Audiovisual Needs Uses PowerPoint and videotape.

Specs Uses digital images or transparencies.

Making Contact & Terms Send letter citing related experience plus 2 or 3 samples. Works on assignment only. Cannot return material. Responds in 2 weeks. Pays $1,000-1,500/day. Pays within 30 days. Buys all rights.

Tips In portfolio/samples, prefers to see industrial subjects and creative styles. ''We look for lighting knowledge, composition and imagination.''

Galleries

The popularity of photography as a collectible art form has improved the market for fine art photographs over the last decade. Collectors now recognize the investment value of prints by Ansel Adams, Irving Penn and Henri Cartier-Bresson, and therefore frequently turn to galleries for photographs to place in their private collections.

The gallery/fine art market can make money for many photographers. However, unlike commercial and editorial markets, galleries seldom generate quick income for artists. Galleries should be considered venues for important, thought-provoking imagery, rather than markets through which you can make a substantial living.

More than any other market, this area is filled with photographers who are interested in delivering a message. Many photography exhibits focus on one theme by a single artist. Group exhibits feature the work of several artists, and they often explore a theme from many perspectives, though not always. These group exhibits may be juried (i.e., the photographs in the exhibit are selected by a committee of judges who are knowledgeable about photography). Some group exhibits also may include other mediums such as painting, drawing or sculpture. In any case, galleries want artists who can excite viewers and make them think about important subjects. They, of course, also hope that viewers will buy the photographs shown in their galleries.

As with picture buyers and art directors, gallery directors love to see strong, well-organized portfolios. Limit your portfolio to 20 top-notch images. When putting together your portfolio, focus on one overriding theme. A director wants to be certain you have enough quality work to carry an entire show. After the portfolio review, if the director likes your style, then you might discuss future projects or past work that you've done. Directors who see promise in your work, but don't think you're ready for a solo exhibition, may place your photographs in a group exhibition.

HOW GALLERIES OPERATE

In exchange for brokering images, a gallery often receives a commission of 40-50 percent. They usually exhibit work for a month, sometimes longer, and hold openings to kick off new shows. And they frequently provide pre-exhibition publicity. Some smaller galleries require exhibiting photographers to help with opening night reception expenses. Galleries also may require photographers to appear during the show or opening. Be certain that such policies are put in writing before you allow them to show your work.

Gallery directors who foresee a bright future for you might want exclusive rights to represent your work. This type of arrangement forces buyers to get your images directly from the gallery that represents you. Such contracts are quite common, usually limiting the exclusive rights to specified distances. For example, a gallery in Tulsa, Oklahoma, may have exclusive rights to distribute your work within a 200-mile radius of the gallery. This would allow you to sign similar contracts with galleries outside the 200-mile range.

FIND THE RIGHT FIT

As you search for the perfect gallery, it's important to understand the different types of exhibition spaces and how they operate. The route you choose depends on your needs, the type of work you do, your long-term goals, and the audience you're trying to reach. (The following descriptions were provided by the editor of *Artist's & Graphic Designer's Market.*)

- **Retail or commercial galleries.** The goal of the retail gallery is to sell and promote artists while turning a profit. Retail galleries take a commission of 40-50 percent of all sales.
- **Co-op galleries.** Co-ops exist to sell and promote artists' work, but they are run by artists. Members exhibit their own work in exchange for a fee, which covers the gallery's overhead. Some co-ops also take a commission of 20-30 percent to cover expenses. Members share the responsibilities of gallery-sitting, sales, housekeeping and maintenance.
- **Rental galleries.** The rental gallery makes its profit primarily through renting space to artists and consequently may not take a commission on sales (or will take only a very small commission). Some rental spaces provide publicity for artists, while others do not. Showing in this type of gallery is risky. Rental galleries are sometimes thought of as "vanity galleries" and, consequently, they do not have the credibility other galleries enjoy.
- **Nonprofit galleries.** Nonprofit spaces will provide you with an opportunity to sell work and gain publicity, but will not market your work agressively, because their goals are not necessarily sales-oriented. Nonprofits normally take a commission of 20-30 percent.
- **Museums.** Don't approach museums unless you have already exhibited in galleries. The work in museums is by established artists and is usually donated by collectors or purchased through art dealers.
- **Art consultancies.** Generally, art consultants act as liaisons between fine artists and buyers. Most take a commission on sales (as would a gallery). Some maintain small gallery spaces and show work to clients by appointment.

If you've never exhibited your work in a traditional gallery space before, you may want to start with a less traditional kind of show. Alternative spaces are becoming a viable way to help the public see your work. Try bookstores (even large chains), restaurants, coffee shops, upscale home furnishings stores and boutiques. The art will help give their business a more pleasant, interesting environment at no cost to them, and you may generate a few fans or even a few sales.

Think carefully about what you take pictures of and what kinds of businesses might benefit from displaying them. If you shoot flowers and other plant life, perhaps you could approach a nursery about hanging your work in their sales office. If you shoot landscapes of exotic locations, maybe a travel agent would like to take you on. Think creatively and don't be afraid to approach a business person with a proposal. Just make sure the final agreement is spelled out in writing so there will be no misunderstandings, especially about who gets what money from sales.

COMPOSING AN ARTIST'S STATEMENT

When you approach a gallery about a solo exhibition, they will usually expect your body of work to be organized around a theme. To present your work and its theme to the public, the gallery will expect you to write an artist's statement, a brief essay about how and why you make photographic images. There are several things to keep in mind when writing your statement:

1. Be brief. Most statements should be 100-300 words long. You shouldn't try to tell your life's story leading up to this moment.
2. Write as you speak. There is no reason to make up complicated motivations for your work if there aren't any. Just be honest about why you shoot the way you do.
3. Stay focused. Limit your thoughts to those that deal directly with the specific exhibit for which you're preparing.

Before you start writing your statement, consider your answers to the following questions:

1. Why do you make photographs (as opposed to using some other medium)?
2. What are your photographs about?
3. What are the subjects in your photographs?
4. What are you trying to communicate through your work?

A.R.C. GALLERY

832 W. Superior St., #204., Chicago IL 60622. (312)733-2787. E-mail: arcgallery@yahoo.com. Web site: www.arcgallery.org. **Contact:** Pat Oho, executive director. Estab. 1973. Sponsors 5-8 exhibits/year. Average display time 1 month. Overall price range $100-1,200.
Exhibits All styles considered. Contemporary fine art photography, documentary and journalism.
Making Contact & Terms Charges no commission, but there is a space rental fee.
Submissions Must send slides, résumé and statement to gallery for review; include SASE. Reviews transparencies. Responds in 1 month.
Tips Photographers "should have a consistent body of work. Show emerging and experimental work."

ADDISON/RIPLEY FINE ART

1670 Wisconsin Ave. NW, Washington DC 20007. (202)338-5180. Fax: (202)338-2341. E-mail: addisonrip@aol.com. Web site: www.addisonripleyfineart.com. **Contact:** Christopher Addison, owner. Art consultancy, for-profit gallery. Estab. 1981. Approached by 100 artists/year; represents or exhibits 25 artists. Average display time 6 weeks. Gallery open Tuesday through Saturday from 11 to 6. Closed end of summer. Located in Georgetown in a large, open, light-filled gallery space. Overall price range $500-80,000. Most work sold at $2,500-10,000.
Exhibits Exhibits works of all media.
Making Contact & Terms Gallery provides insurance, promotion, contract. Accepted work should be framed, mounted, matted.
Submissions Mail portfolio for review. Send query letter with artist's statement, bio, photocopies, résumé, SASE. Responds in 1 month.
Tips "Submit organized, professional-looking materials."

ADIRONDACK LAKES CENTER FOR THE ARTS

Route. 28, Blue Mountain Lake NY 12812. (518)352-7715. Fax: (518)352-7333. E-mail: alca@frontiernet.net. Web site: www.adk-arts.org. **Contact:** P. Eaton Siers, executive director. Estab. 1967. "ALCA is a 501c, nonprofit organization showing national and interna-

Galleries

tional work of emerging to established artists. A tourist and second-home market, demographics profile our client as highly educated, moderately affluent, environmentally oriented and well-travelled. The busy season is June through September." Sponsors 15-20 exhibits/year. Average display time 1 month. Overall price range $100-2,000. Most work sold at $250.

Exhibits Solo, group, and call for entry exhibits of color and black & white work.

Making Contact & Terms Consignment gallery, fee structure on request. Payment for sales follows within 30 days of close of exhibit. White mat and black frame required, except under prior agreement. ALCA pays return shipping only or cover work in transit.

Submissions Apply by CD or slides, resume and bio. Must include an SASE for return of materials. Upon acceptance notification, price sheet and artist statement required.

Tips "ALCA offers a residency program, maintains a fully-equipped darkroom with 24 hour access."

◙ AKRON ART MUSEUM

One South.High St., Akron OH 44308. (330)376-9185. Fax: (330)376-1180. E-mail: mail@akronartmuseum.org. Web site: www.akronartmuseum.org. **Contact:** Barbara Tannenbaum, chief curator. The Akron Art Museum re-opened in July 2007 after expanding into a new, larger building.

- This museum annually awards the Knight Purchase Award to a living artist working with photographic media.

Exhibits To exhibit, photographers must possess "a notable record of exhibitions, inclusion in publications, and/or a role in the historical development of photography. We also feature area photographers (northeast Ohio)." Interested in innovative works by contemporary photographers; any subject matter. Interested in alternative process, documentary, fine art, historical/vintage.

Making Contact & Terms Payment negotiable. Buys photography outright.

Submissions Will review Web sites and CDs. Send material via e-mail or by mail with SASE if you want materials returned. Responds in 2 months, "depending on our workload."

Tips "Send professional-looking materials wth high-quality images, a résumé and an artist's statement. Never send original prints."

ALASKA STATE MUSEUM

395 Whittier St., Juneau AK 99801-1718. (907)465-2901. Fax: (907)465-2976. E-mail: bruce_kato@eed.state.ak.us. Web site: www.museums.state.ak.us. **Contact:** Bruce Kato, chief curator. Museum. Estab. 1900. Approached by 40 artists/year. Sponsors 1 photography exhibit every 2 years. Average display time 10 weeks. Downtown location—3 galleries.

Exhibits Interested in historical and fine art.

Submissions Finds artists through portfolio reviews.

▣ ALBANY CENTER GALLERIES

161 Washington Ave., Albany NY 12210. (518)462-4775. E-mail: director@albanycentergalleries.org. Web site: www.albanycentergalleries.org. **Contact:** Sarah Martinez, executive director. Estab. 1977. Sponsors 7 exhibits/year. Average display time 6 weeks. Sponsors openings; provides refreshments and hors d'oeuvres. Overall price range $100-1,000.

Exhibits Photographer must live within 100 miles of Albany for regular exhibits and for

Photography Regional, which is held at the Albany Center Galleries on a rotating basis. Interested in all subjects.

Making Contact & Terms Charges 35% commission. Reviews JPEGs on CD. "Work must be framed and ready to hang." Send material by mail with SASE for consideration.

THE ALBUQUERQUE MUSEUM OF ART & HISTORY

2000 Mountain Rd. NW, Albuquerque NM 87104. (505)243-7255. Fax: (505)764-6546. Web site: www.cabq.gov/museum. **Contact:** Douglas Fairfield, curator of art or Glenn Fye, photo archivist. Estab. 1967. Sponsors 7-10 exhibits/year. Average display time 3-4 months. Gallery open Tuesday through Sunday from 9 to 5. Closed Monday and city holidays.

Exhibits Considers art, historical and documentary photography for exhibition and purchase. Art related to Albuquerque, the state of New Mexico, and the Southwest.

Submissions Submit portfolio of slides, photos, or disk for review. Responds in 2 months.

AMERICAN PRINT ALLIANCE

302 Larkspur Turn, Peachtree City GA 30269-2210. E-mail: director@printalliance.org. Web site: www.printalliance.org. **Contact:** Carol Pulin, director. Nonprofit arts organization with online gallery and exhibitions, travelling exhibitions, and journal publication; Print Bin: a place on Web site that is like the unframed, shrink-wrapped prints in a bricks-and-mortar gallery's "print bin." Estab. 1992. Approached by hundreds of artists/year; represents dozens of artists/year. "We only exhibit original prints, artists' books and paperworks." Usually sponsors 2 travelling exhibits/year—all prints, paperworks and artists' books; photography within printmaking processes but not as a separate medium. Most exhibits travel for 2 years. Hours depend on the host gallery/museum/arts center. "We travel exhibits throughout the U.S. and occasionally to Canada." Overall price range for Print Bin: $150-3,200; most work sold at $300-500.

Exhibits "We accept all styles, genres and subjects; the decisions are made on quality of work."

Making Contact & Terms Individual subscription: $30-37. Print Bin is free with subscription. "Subscribers have free entry to juried travelling exhibitions but must pay for framing, shipping to and from our office." Gallery provides promotion.

Submissions Subscribe to journal, *Contemporary Impressions* (www.printalliance.org/allia nce/al_subform.html), send one slide and signed permission form (www.printalliance.org/gallery/printbin_info.html). Returns slide if requested with SASE. Usually does not respond to queries from non-subscribers. Files slides and permission forms. Finds artists through submissions to the gallery or Print Bin, and especially portfolio reviews at printmakers conferences. "Unfortunately, we don't have the staff for individual portfolio reviews, though we may—and often do—request additional images after seeing one work, often for journal articles. Generally about 100 images are reproduced per year in the journal."

Tips "See the Standard Forms area of our Web site (www.printalliance.org/library/li_forms .html) for correct labels on slides and much, much more about professional presentation."

AMERICAN SOCIETY OF ARTISTS, INC.

P.O. Box 1326, Palatine IL 60078. (847)991-4748 or (312)751-2500. E-mail: asoa@webtv.n et. Web site: www.americansocietyofartists.org. **Contact:** Helen Del Valle, membership chairman.

Exhibits Members and nonmembers may exhibit. "Our members range from internationally

Galleries

known artists to unknown artists—quality of work is the important factor. We have about 25 shows throughout the year that accept photographic art."

Making Contact & Terms Accepted work should be framed, mounted or matted.

Submissions Send SASE and 4 slides/photos representative of your work, and request membership information and application. See our Web site for on-line jury. Responds in 2 weeks. Accepted members may participate in lecture and demonstration service. Member publication: *ASA Artisan*.

⊠ ANDERSON-SOULE GALLERY

Two Capital Plaza, N. Main St., Concord NH 03301. E-mail: art@anderson-soulegallery.com. Web site: www.anderson-soulegallery.com. **Contact:** Trish Soule, gallery director. Art consultancy, for-profit gallery, rental gallery. Estab. 2002. Approached by 15 artists/year; represents or exhibits 20+ artists. Average display time 6 weeks. Open Tuesday through Saturday from 10 to 4.

Exhibits Exhibits photos of architecture, rural, landscapes/scenics. Interested in alternative process, fine art. Exhibits only artists from the Northeast US.

Making Contact & Terms Artwork is accepted on consignment, and there is a 50% commission. Mail portfolio for review; send query letter with artist's statement, bio, photocopies, résumé, CD for PC, SASE.

Submissions Mail portfolio for review. Finds artists through portfolio reviews, referrals by other artists.

Tips "Provide *all* requested materials."

ARNOLD ART

210 Thames St., Newport RI 02840. E-mail: info@arnoldart.com. Web site: www.arnoldart.com. **Contact:** William Rommel, owner. For-profit gallery. Estab. 1870. Represents or exhibits 40 artists. Average display time 1 month. Gallery open Monday through Saturday from 9:30 to 5:30; Sunday from 12 to 5. Closed Christmas, Thanksgiving, Easter. Art gallery is 17 ft×50 ft., open gallery space (3rd floor). Overall price range $100-35,000. Most work sold at $300.

Exhibits Marine (sailing), classic yachts, America's Cup, wooden boats, sailing/racing.

Making Contact & Terms Artwork is accepted on consignment, and there is a 45% commission. Gallery provides promotion. Accepted work should be framed.

Submissions E-mail to arrange personal interview to show portfolio.

▣ ART SOURCE L.A., INC.

West Coast office: 2801 Ocean Park Blvd., PMB 7, Santa Monica CA 90405. (310)452-4411. Fax: (310)452-0300. E-mail: info@artsourcela.com. Web site: www.artsourcela.com. East Coast office: 12001 Montrose Park Place, North Bethesda MD 20852. (301)230-0023. Fax: (301)230-0025. E-mail: bonniek@artsourcela.com. **Contact:** Francine Ellman, president. Estab. 1980. Overall price range $300-15,000. Most work sold at $1,000.

Exhibits Exhibits photos of multiculturual, environmental, landscapes/scenics, wildlife, architecture, cities/urban, gardening, interiors/decorating, rural, automobiles, food/drink, travel, technology/computers. Interested in alternative process, avant garde, fine art, historical/vintage, seasonal. "We do projects worldwide, putting together fine art for corporations, healthcare, hospitality, government and public space. We use a lot of photography."

Making Contact & Terms Interested in receiving work from emerging and established photographers. Charges 50% commission. Accepted work should be mounted or matted.

Submissions Prefers digital submissions via e-mail. Send a minimum of 20 slides, photographs or inkjet prints (laser copies not acceptable), clearly labeled with name, title and date of work; plus catalogs, brochures, résumé, price list, SASE. Responds in 2 months maximum.

Tips "Show a consistent body of work, well marked and presented so it may be viewed to see its merits."

ART WITHOUT WALLS, INC.

P.O. Box 341, Sayville NY 11782. (631)567-9418. Fax: (631)567-9418. E-mail: artwithoutwalls@webtv.net. **Contact:** Sharon Lippman, executive director. Nonprofit gallery. Estab. 1985. Approached by 300 artists/year; represents or exhibits 100 artists. Sponsors 3 photography exhibits/year. Average display time 1 month. Gallery open daily from 9 to 5. Closed December 22 to January 5 and Easter week. Traveling exhibits in various public spaces. Overall price range $1,000-25,000. Most work sold at $3,000-5,000. "Price varies—especially if student work."

Exhibits Exhibits photos of celebrities, multicultural, families, parents, senior citizens, disasters, environmental, landscapes/scenics, wildlife, architecture, cities/urban, education, gardening, interiors/decorating, pets, rural, adventure, automobiles, entertainment, events, food/drink, health/fitness/beauty, hobbies, humor, performing arts, sports, travel, agriculture, medicine, political, product shots/still life, science, technology/computers. Interested in alternative process, avant garde, documentary, fashion/glamour, fine art, historical/vintage, seasonal.

Making Contact & Terms Artwork is accepted on consignment, and there is a 20% commission. Gallery provides promotion, contract. Accepted work should be framed, mounted, matted.

Submissions Mail portfolio for review. Send query letter with artist's statement, brochure, photographs, résumé, reviews, SASE, slides. Responds in 1 month. Finds artists through submissions, portfolio reviews, art exhibits.

Tips "Work should be properly framed with name, year, medium, title, size."

ART@NET INTERNATIONAL GALLERY

(617)495-7451 or (359)898-448132. Fax: (359)(2)851-2838. E-mail: artnetg@yahoo.com. Web site: www.designbg.com. **Contact:** Yavor Shopov, director. For-profit Internet gallery. Estab. 1998. Approached by 100 artists/year; represents or exhibits 20 artists. Sponsors 5 photography exhibits/year. Display time permanent. "Our gallery exists only on the Internet. Each artist has individual 'exhibition space' divided into separate thematic exhibitions along with bio and statement." Overall price range $150-55,000.

Exhibits Exhibits photos of multicultural, landscapes/scenics, wildlife, architecture, cities/urban, education, adventure, beauty, sports, travel, science, buildings. Interested in avant garde, erotic, fashion/glamour, fine art, seasonal.

Making Contact & Terms Artwork is accepted on consignment; there is a 10% commission and a rental fee for space of $1/image per month or $5/image per year. First 6 images are displayed free of rental fee. Gallery provides promotion. Accepted work should be matted.

Submission "We accept computer scans only; no slides, please. E-mail us attached scans, 900×1200 px (300 dpi for prints or 900 dpi for 36mm slides), as JPEG files for IBM computers." E-mail query letter with artist's statement, bio, résumé. Responds in 6 weeks. Finds artists through submissions, portfolio reviews, art exhibits, art fairs, referrals by other artists.

Tips "E-mail us a tightly edited selection of less than 20 scans of your best work. All work must force any person to look over it again and again. Main usage of all works exhibited in our gallery is for limited edition (photos) or original (paintings) wall decoration of offices and homes, so photos must have quality of paintings. We like to see strong artistic sense of mood, composition, light, color and strong graphic impact or expression of emotions. For us, only quality of work is important, so newer, lesser-known artists are welcome."

ARTISTS' COOPERATIVE GALLERY

405 S. 11th St., Omaha NE 68102. (402)342-9617. Web site: www.artistsco-opgallery.com. Estab. 1974. Sponsors 11 exhibits/year. Average display time 1 month. Gallery sponsors all-member exhibits and outreach exhibits; individual artists sponsor their own small group exhibits throughout the year. Overall price range $100-500.

Exhibits Fine art photography only. Interested in all types, styles and subject matter.

Making Contact & Terms Charges no commission. Reviews transparencies. Accepted work should be framed work only. "Artist must be willing to work 13 days per year at the gallery. We are a member-owned-and-operated cooperative. Artist must also serve on one committee."

Submissions Send query letter with résumé, SASE. Responds in 2 months.

Tips "Write for membership application. Membership committee screens applicants August 1-15 each year. Responds by September 1. New membership year begins October 1. Members must pay annual fee of $325. Our community outreach exhibits include local high school photographers and art from local elementary schools."

ARTLINK

437 E. Berry St., Suite 202, Fort Wayne IN 46802. (260)424-7195. Fax: (260)424-8453. E-mail: deb@artlinkfw.com. Web site: www.artlinkfw.com. **Contact:** Deb Washler, executive director. Nonprofit gallery. Estab. 1978. Sponsors 1 photography exhibit every other year. Average display time 6 weeks. Gallery open Tuesday through Saturday from 12 to 5; Friday and Saturday evenings from 6 to 9; Sundays from 1 to 5. Located 2 blocks from downtown Fort Wayne. Overall price range $100-2,000. Most work sold at $250.

Making Contact & Terms Artwork of Artlink members is accepted on consignment, and there is a 35% commission. Gallery provides insurance. Accepted work should be framed.

Submissions "Please visit the artlink Web site for current call for entry, www.artlinkfw.com ."

◨ THE ARTS COMPANY

215 5th Ave., Nashville TN 37219. (615)254-2040. Fax: (615)254-9289. E-mail: art@theartsc ompany.com. Web site: www.theartscompany.com. **Contact:** Anne Brown, owner. Art consultancy, for-profit gallery. Estab. 1996. Sponsors 6-10 photography exhibits/year. Average display time 1 month. Open Tuesday through Saturday from 10 to 5. Located in downtown Nashville, the gallery has 6,000 sq. ft. of contemporary space in a historic building. Overall price range $10-35,000. Most work sold at $300-3,000.

Exhibits Exhibits photos of celebrities, architecture, cities/urban, rural, environmental, landscapes/scenics, entertainment, performing arts. Interested in documentary, fine art, historical/vintage.

Making Contact & Terms Artwork is accepted on consignment. Gallery provides insurance, contract. Accepted work should be framed. Requires exclusive representation locally.

Submissions ''We prefer an initial info packet via e-mail.'' Send query letter with artist's statement, bio, brochure, business card, photocopies, résumé, reviews, SASE, CD. Returns material with SASE. Finds artists through word of mouth, art fairs, art exhibits, submissions, referrals by other artists.

Tips ''Provide professional images on a CD along with a professional bio, résumé.''

Ⓝ ARTS ON DOUGLAS

123 Douglas St., New Smyrna Beach FL 32168. (386)428-1133. Fax: (386)428-5008. E-mail: mail@artsondouglas.net. Web site: www.artsondouglas.net. **Contact:** Meghan Martin, gallery manager. For-profit gallery. Estab. 1996. Represents 60 Florida artists in ongoing group exhibits and features 8 artists/year in solo exhibitions. Average display time 1 month. Gallery open Tuesday through Friday from 11 to 6; Saturday from 10 to 2; by appointment. Location has 5,000 sq. ft. of exhibition space. Overall price range varies.

Exhibits Exhibits photos of environmental. Interested in alternative process, documentary, fine art.

Making Contact & Terms Artwork is accepted on consignment, and there is a 50% commission. Gallery provides insurance, promotion. Accepted work should be framed. Requires exclusive representation locally. *Accepts only professional artists from Florida.*

Submissions Call in advance to inquire about submissions/reviews. Send query letter with artist's statement, bio, brochure, résumé, reviews, slides, SASE. Finds artists through referrals by other artists.

ARTWORKS GALLERY

233 Pearl St., Hartford CT 06103. (860)247-3522. Fax: (860)548-0779. E-mail: artworks.gallery@snet. Web site: www.artworksgallery.org. **Contact:** Diane Legere, executive director. Estab. 1976. Average display time 1 month. Overall price range $100-5,000. Most work sold at $500-800.

Exhibits Exhibits photos of disasters, environmental, landscapes/scenics, wildlife. Interested in contemporary work, alternative process, avant garde, documentary, erotic, fine art. ''We have juried shows; members must be voted in after interview.''

Making Contact & Terms There is a co-op membership fee plus a donation of time. There is a 30% commission.

Submissions Send for membership application. Include SASE. Responds in 1 month.

Tips ''The more energy and equipment you put into the gallery, the more you get out of it. It's a great place to network and establish yourself.''

▣ ARTWORKS GALLERY

811 Race St., Cincinnati OH 45202. (513)333-0388. Fax: (513)333-0799. E-mail: allen@artworkscincinnati.com. Web site: www.artworkscincinnati.org. **Contact:** Allen Cochran, gallery coordinator. Alternative space, cooperative gallery, nonprofit gallery, rental gallery. Estab. 2003. Average display time 1.5 months. Open Monday through Friday from 9 to 5. Closed January. Has 1,500 sq. ft of exhibition space in downtown Cincinnati. Overall price range $200-15,000. Most work sold at $1,200.

Exhibits Exhibits photos of multicultural, architecture, cities/urban, education, gardening, interiors/decorating, rural, environmental, adventure, performing arts. Interested in alter-

Galleries

native process, avant garde, documentary, fashion/glamour, fine art, lifestyle.

Making Contact & Terms Artwork is accepted on consignment, and there is a 30% commission. Gallery provides promotion, contract.

Submissions Call; send images via e-mail; mail portfolio for review; send query letter with résumé, slides, artist's statement, digital slides. Send nonreturnable samples. ''We hold on to materials for future exhibition opportunities.'' Responds to queries in 1 month. Finds artists through word of mouth, art fairs, portfolio reviews, exhibitions, submissions, referrals by other artists.

Tips ''ArtWorks is looking for strong artists who are not only talented in terms of their ability to make and create, but who can also professionally present themselves and show a genuine interest in the exhibition of their artwork. We're looking for concise statements that the artists themselves have written about their work as well as a résumé of exhibitions to help back up their written statements. Artists should continue to communicate with us beyond exhibitions and further down the line just to let us know what they're up to and how they've grown.''

N ASIAN AMERICAN ARTS CENTRE

26 Bowery, 3rd Floor, New York NY 10013. (212)233-2154. E-mail: aaacinfo@artspiral.org. Web site: www.artspiral.org. **Contact:** Robert Lee, director. Estab. 1974. Average display time 6 weeks.

Exhibits Should be Asian American or significantly influenced by Asian culture and should be entered into the archive—a historical record of the presence of Asia in the US. Interested in ''creative art pieces.''

Making Contact & Terms Requests 30% ''donation'' on works sold. Sometimes buys photos outright.

Submissions To be considered, send dupes of slides, résumé, artist's statement, bio and online form to be entered into the archive. These will be kept for users of archive to review. Recent entries are reviewed once/year for the Art Centre's annual exhibition.

N ATLANTIC GALLERY

135 W. 29th, Suite 601, New York NY 10001. (212)219-3183. Web site: www.atlanticgallery. org. Cooperative gallery. Estab. 1974. Approached by 50 artists/year; represents or exhibits 40 artists. Average display time 3 weeks. Gallery open Tuesday through Saturday from 12 to 6. Closed August. Located in Soho. Overall price range $100-13,000. Most work sold at $1,500-5,000.

Exhibits Exhibits photos of multicultural, families, environmental, landscapes/scenics, wildlife, architecture, cities/urban, rural, performing arts, travel, product shots/still life, technology/computers. Interested in fine art.

Making Contact & Terms There is a co-op membership fee plus a donation of time. Accepts mostly artists from New York, Connecticut, Massachusetts, New Jersey.

Submissions Call or write to arrange a personal interview to show portfolio of slides. Send artist's statement, bio, brochure, SASE, slides. Responds in 1 month. Views slides monthly. Finds artists through word of mouth, submissions, art exhibits, referrals by other artists.

Tips ''Submit an organized folder with slides, bio, and 3 pieces of actual work. If we respond with interest, we then review again.''

BELL STUDIO

3428 N. Southport Ave., Chicago IL 60657. E-mail: paul@bellstudio.net. Web site: www.bel lstudio.net. **Contact:** Paul Therieau, director. For-profit gallery. Estab. 2001. Approached by 60 artists/year; represents or exhibits 10 artists. Sponsors 3 photography exhibits/year. Average display time 6 weeks. Open all year; Monday through Friday from 12 to 7; weekends from 12 to 5. Located in brick storefront; 750 sq. ft. of exhibition space; high traffic. Overall price range: $150-3,500. Most work sold at $600.

Exhibits Interested in alternative process, avant garde, fine art.

Making Contact & Terms Artwork is accepted on consignment, and there is a 50% commission. Gallery provides insurance, promotion, contract. Accepted work should be framed. Requires exclusive representation locally.

Submissions Write to arrange personal interview to show portfolio; include bio and résumé. Responds to queries within 3 months, only if interested. Finds artists through referrals by other artists, submissions, word of mouth.

Tips "Send SASE; type submission letter; include show history, résumé."

◪ BENHAM STUDIO GALLERY

1216 First Ave., Seattle WA 98101. (206)622-2480. Fax: (206)622-6383. E-mail: benham@be nhamgallery.com. Web site: www.benhamgallery.com. **Contact:** Marita Holdaway, owner. Estab. 1987. Sponsors 9 exhibits/year. Average display time 6 weeks. Overall price range $250-9,750. Most work sold at $650.

Exhibits Exhibits photos of multicultural, environmental, landscapes/scenics, architecture, cities/urban, religious, rural, humor. Interested in alternative process, avant garde, documentary, fine art.

Making Contact & Terms Charges 50% commission.

Submissions See Web site for submission guidelines. "If you have a Web site with a portfolio, you can send the URL via e-mail. We will not return any unsolicited submissions. We will not be responsible for any lost or damaged materials you send us."

◪ BENNETT GALLERIES AND COMPANY

5308 Kingston Pike, Knoxville TN 37919. (865)584-6791. Fax: (865)588-6130. Web site: www.bennettgalleries.com. **Contact:** Marga Ingram, gallery director. For-profit gallery. Estab. 1985. Represents or exhibits 40 artists/year. Sponsors 1-2 photography exhibits/year. Average display time 1 month. Gallery open Monday through Saturday from 10 to 5:30. Conveniently located a few miles from downtown Knoxville in the Bearden area. The formal art gallery has over 2,000 sq. ft. and 20,000 sq. ft. of additional space. Overall price range $100-12,000. Most work sold at $400-600.

Exhibits Exhibits photos of landscapes/scenics, architecture, cities/urban, humor, sports, travel. Interested in alternative process, fine art, historical/vintage.

Making Contact & Terms Artwork is accepted on consignment, and there is a 50% commission. Gallery provides insurance, promotion, contract. Accepted work should be framed. Requires exclusive representation locally.

Submissions Mail portfolio for review. Send query letter with artist's statement, bio, photographs, SASE, CD. Responds within 1 month, only if interested . Finds artists through word of mouth, submissions, art exhibits, referrals by other artists.

Tips "When submitting material to a gallery for review, the package should include information about the artist (neatly written or typed), photographic material, and SASE if you want your materials back."

Ⓝ BONNI BENRUBI GALLERY

41 E. 57th St. #13, New York NY 10022-1908. (212)517-3766. Fax: (212)288-7815. E-mail: benrubi@bonnibenrubi.com. Web site: www.bonnibenrubi.com. **Contact:** Thom Vogel, director. Estab. 1987. Sponsors 7-8 exhibits/year. Average display time 6 weeks. Overall price range $500-50,000.

Exhibits Interested in 19th- and 20th-century photography, mainly contemporary.

Making Contact & Terms Charges commission. Buys photos outright. Accepted work should be matted. Requires exclusive representation locally. No manipulated work.

Submissions Submit portfolio for review; include SASE. Responds in 2 weeks. "Portfolio review is the first Thursday of every month. Out-of-towners can send slides with SASE, and work will be returned."

▣ MONA BERMAN FINE ARTS

78 Lyon St., New Haven CT 06511. (203)562-4720. E-mail: info@MonaBermanFineArts.com. Web site: www.MonaBermanFineArts.com. **Contact:** Mona Berman, director. Estab. 1979. Sponsors 0-1 exhibit/year. Average display time 1 month. Overall price range $500-5,000.

- "We are art consultants serving corporations, architects and designers. We also have private clients. We hold very few exhibits; we mainly show work to our clients for consideration and sell a lot of photographs."

Exhibits "Photographers must have been represented by us for over 2 years. Interested in all except figurative, although we do use some portrait work."

Making Contact & Terms Charges 50% commission. "Payment to artist 30 days after receipt of payment from client." Interested in seeing unframed, unmounted, unmatted work only.

Submissions "E-mail digital images or Web links, or send CDs. Inquire by e-mail; no calls, please. Always include retail prices." Materials returned with SASE only. Responds in 1 month.

Tips "Looking for new perspectives, new images, new ideas, excellent print quality, ability to print in *very* large sizes, consistency of vision. Digital prints must be archival. Not interested in Giclee prints."

Ⓝ BLOUNT-BRIDGERS HOUSE/HOBSON PITTMAN MEMORIAL GALLERY

130 Bridgers St., Tarboro NC 27886. (252)823-4159. Fax: (252)823-6190. E-mail: edgecombe arts@embarqmail.com. Web site: www.edgecombearts.org. Museum. Estab. 1982. Approached by 1-2 artists/year; represents or exhibits 6 artists. Sponsors 1 photography exhibit/year. Average display time 6 weeks. Gallery open Monday through Friday from 10 to 4; weekends from 2 to 4. Closed major holidays, Christmas-New Year. Located in historic house in residential area of small town. Gallery is approximately 48 ft. × 20 ft. Overall price range $250-5,000. Most work sold at $500.

Exhibits Exhibits photos of landscapes/scenics, wildlife. Interested in fine art, historical/vintage.

Making Contact & Terms Artwork is accepted on consignment, and there is a 30% commission. Gallery provides insurance, limited promotion. Accepted work should be framed. Accepts artists from the Southeast and Pennsylvania.

Submissions Mail portfolio review. Send query letter with artist's statement, bio, SASE, slides. Responds in 3 months. Finds artists through word of mouth, submissions, art exhibits, referrals by other artists.

BOOK BEAT GALLERY

26010 Greenfield, Oak Park MI 48237. (248)968-1190. Fax: (248)968-3102. E-mail: cary@thebookbeat.com. Web site: www.thebookbeat.com. **Contact:** Cary Loren, director. Estab. 1982. Sponsors 6 exhibits/year. Average display time 6-8 weeks. Overall price range $300-5,000. Most work sold at $600.

Exhibits "Book Beat is a bookstore specializing in fine art and photography. We have a backroom gallery devoted to photography and folk art. Our inventory includes vintage work from 19th- to 20th-century rare books, issues of *Camerawork*, and artist books. Book Beat Gallery is looking for couragous and astonishing image makers. Artists with no boundries and an open mind are welcome to submit a handwritten or typed proposal, artist statement, and Web site or sample images. We are especially interested in photographers who have published book works or work with originals in the artist book format, and also those who work in 'dead media' and extinct processes."

Submissions Responds in 6 weeks.

RENA BRANSTEN GALLERY

77 Geary St., San Francisco CA 94108. (415)982-3292. Fax: (415)982-1807. E-mail: info@renabranstengallery.com. Web site: www.renabranstengallery.com. For-profit gallery. Estab. 1974. Approached by 200 artists/year; represents or exhibits 12-15 artists. Average display time 4-5 weeks. Open Tuesday through Friday from 10:30 to 5:30; Saturday from 11 to 5. "We usually close the last week of August and the first week of September."

Submissions E-mail JPEG samples at 72 dpi. Finds artists through word of mouth, art exhibits, submissions, art fairs, portfolio reviews, referrals by other artists.

BUNNELL STREET GALLERY

106 W. Bunnell, Suite A, Homer AK 99603. (907)235-2662. Fax: (907)235-9427. E-mail: asia@bunnellstreetgallery.org. Web site: www.bunnellstreetgallery.org. **Contact:** Asia Freeman, director. Nonprofit gallery. Estab. 1990. Approached by 50 artists/year; represents or exhibits 35 artists. Sponsors 1 photography exhibit/year. Average display time 1 month. Gallery open Monday through Saturday from 10 to 6; Sunday from 12 to 4, summer only. Closed January. Located in 30 ft.×25 ft. exhibition space; good lighting, hardwood floors. Overall price range $50-2,500. Most work sold at $500.

Exhibits Exhibits photos of families, gardening, food/drink. Interested in alternative process, fine art.

Making Contact & Terms Artwork is accepted on consignment, and there is a 40% commission. A donation of time is requested. Gallery provides insurance, promotion, contract. Accepted work should be framed.

Submissions Call or write to arrange a personal interview to show portfolio of slides. Mail portfolio for review. Responds in 1 month. Finds artists through word of mouth, submissions, art exhibits, referrals by other artists.

🇳 BUSINESS OF ART CENTER

513 Manitou Ave., Manitou Springs CO 80829. (719)685-1861. E-mail: mburton@thebac.org. Web site: www.thebac.org. **Contact**: Mary Burton, administrative assistant. Nonprofit gallery. Estab. 1988. Sponsors 6 photography exhibits/year. Average display time 1 month. Gallery open Tuesday through Saturday from 10 to 6 (shorter winter hours; please call). Overall price range $50-3,000. Most work sold at $300.

Exhibits Exhibits photos of environmental, landscapes/scenics, wildlife, gardening, rural, adventure, health/fitness, performing arts, travel. Interested in alternative process, avant garde, documentary, fashion/glamour, fine art.

Making Contact & Terms Artwork is accepted on consignment, and there is a 40% commission. Gallery provides insurance, promotion, contract. Accepted work should be framed.

Submissions Write to arrange a personal interview to show portfolio. Send query letter with artist's statement, bio, slides. Finds artists through word of mouth, submissions, portfolio reviews, art exhibits, referrals by other artists.

THE CAMERA OBSCURA GALLERY

1309 Bannock St., Denver CO 80204. (303)623-4059. Fax: (303)893-4195. E-mail: info@CameraObscuraGallery.com. Web site: www.CameraObscuraGallery.com. **Contact:** Hal Gould, owner/director. Estab. 1980. Approached by 350 artists/year; represents or exhibits 20 artists. Sponsors 7 photography exhibits/year. Open Tuesday through Saturday from 10 to 6; Sunday from 1 to 5. Overall price range $400-20,000. Most work sold at $600-3,500.

Exhibits Exhibits photos of environmental, landscapes/scenics, wildlife. Interested in fine art.

Making Contact & Terms Charges 50% commission. Write to arrange a personal interview to show portfolio of photographs. Send bio, brochure, résumé, reviews. Responds in 1 month. Finds artists by word of mouth, submissions, portfolio reviews, art exhibits, art fairs, referrals by other artists, reputation.

Tips ''To make a professional gallery submission, provide a good representation of your finished work that is of exhibition quality. Slowly but surely we are experiencing a more sophisticated audience. The last few years have shown a tremendous increase in media reporting on photography-related events and personalities, exhibitions, artist profiles and market news.''

ℕ CAPITOL COMPLEX EXHIBITIONS

Florida Department of State, Division of Cultural Affairs, 500 S. Bronough St., R.A. Gray Bldg., 3rd Floor, Tallahassee FL 32399-0250. (850)245-6470. Fax: (850)245-6497. E-mail: lmodica@dos.state.fl.us. Web site: www.florida-arts.org. **Contact:** Lee Modica. Average display time 3 months. Overall price range $200-1,000. Most work sold at $400.

Exhibits Exhibits photos of babies/children/teens, couples, multicultural, families, parents, senior citizens, landscapes/scenics, wildlife, architecture, cities/urban, gardening, adventure, entertainment, performing arts, agriculture. Interested in avant garde, fine art, historical/vintage. ''The Capitol Complex Exhibitions Program is designed to showcase Florida artists and art organizations. Exhibitions are displayed in the Capitol Gallery (22nd floor) and the Cabinet Meeting Room in Florida's capitol. Exhibitions are selected based on quality, diversity of media, and regional representation.''

Making Contact & Terms Does not charge commission. Accepted work should be framed. *Interested only in Florida artists or arts organizations.*

Submissions Download application from Web site, complete and send with image CD. Responds in 3 weeks.

SANDY CARSON GALLERY

760 Santa Fe Dr., Denver CO 80204. (303)573-8585. Fax: (303)573-8587. E-mail: scarson@ecentral.com. Web site: www.sandycarsongallery.com. Estab. 1975. Average display time 7

weeks. Open Tuesday through Friday from 10 to 6; Saturday from 12 to 4. Gallery is available for special events.

Exhibits "We include all mediums and represent artists who are professional and committed, with an extensive body of work and continually producing more."

Submissions "We are not presently seeking new artists. Please contact us by e-mail or call the gallery."

▣ THE CENTER FOR FINE ART PHOTOGRAPHY

400 N. College Ave., Fort Collins CO 80524. (970)224-1010. E-mail: contact@c4fap.org. Web site: www.c4fap.org. **Contact:** Larry Padgett, executive director or Azarie Furlong, exhibitions manager. Nonprofit gallery. Estab. 2005. Approached by 4,500 artists/year; represents or exhibits about 500 artists. Average display time 4-5 weeks. Office open Tuesday through Friday from 10 to 5; Saturday from 1 to 5. Closed between exhibitions. Consisting of an 1,600-sq.-ft. gallery, adjoining coffee shop, and events space. Overall price range $180-3,000. Most work sold at $150-500. "The Center publishes work of selected exhibitors in its bimonthly *Artists' ShowCase*—the feature section in *CameraArts Magazine*. It also provides and markets to buyers its online gallery of artists' portfolios—*Artists' ShowCase Online*, available to all members of the Center." Workshops and forums are also offered.

Exhibits Exhibits photos of babies/children/teens, celebrities, couples, multicultural, families, parents, senior citizens, architecture, cities/urban, interiors/decorating, rural, political, environmental, landscapes/scenics, wildlife, performing arts; abstract, experimental work. Interested in alternative process, avant garde, documentary, erotic, fine art. "The Center features fine art photography that incorporates all processes, many styles and subjects."

Making Contact & Terms Art is accepted through either juried calls for entry or from portfolio review. Gallery provides insurance. Accepts only fine art photographic work.

Submissions Work accepted for exhibition via the center's juried calls for entry. Details at Web site.

Tips "Only signed archival-quality work is seriously considered by art collectors. This includes both traditional and digital prints. A certificate of archival processing should accompany the work. Signing the print rather than the mat is appropriate."

▣ CENTER FOR MAINE CONTEMPORARY ART

162 Russell Ave., Rockport ME 04856. (207)236-2875. Fax: (207)236-2490. E-mail: info@cmcanow.org. Web site: www.cmcanow.org. **Contact:** Curatorial Department. Estab. 1952. Average exhibition duration 2 months.

Exhibits Work should be recent and not previously exhibited in the area.

Making Contact & Terms Charges 40% commission.

Submissions Accepts images in digital format. See guidelines on Web site.

CENTER FOR PHOTOGRAPHIC ART

Sunset Cultural Center, P.O. Box 1100, Carmel CA 93921. (831)625-5181. Fax: (831)625-5199. E-mail: info@photography.org. Web site: www.photography.org. Estab. 1988. Nonprofit gallery. Sponsors 7-8 exhibits/year. Average display time 5-7 weeks.

Exhibits Interested in fine art photography.

Submissions Send query letter with slides, résumé, artist's statement, SASE.

Tips "Submit for exhibition consideration slides or transparencies accompanied by a concise bio and artist's statement."

Galleries

▣ CENTER FOR PHOTOGRAPHY AT WOODSTOCK

59 Tinker St., Woodstock NY 12498. (845)679-9957. Fax: (845)679-6337. E-mail: info@cpw. org. Web site: www.cpw.org. **Contact:** Ariel Shanberg, executive director. Megan Flaherty, program associate. Alternative space, nonprofit arts and education center. Estab. 1977. Approached by more than 500 artists/year. Hosts 10 photography exhibits/year. Average display time 7 weeks. Gallery open all year; Wednesday through Sunday from 12 to 5.

Exhibits Interested in presenting all aspects of contemporary creative photography including digital media, film, video, and installation by emerging and under-recognized artists. "We host 5 group exhibitions and 5 solo exhibitions annually. Group exhibitions are curated by guest jurors, curators, and CPW staff. Solo exhibition artists are selected by CPW staff. Visit the exhibition archives on our Web site to learn more."

Making Contact & Terms CPW hosts exhibition and opening reception; provides insurance, promotion, a percentage of shipping costs, installation and de-installation, and honoriaum for solo exhibition artists who give gallery talks. "We take 25% commission in exhibition-related sales." Accepted work should be framed and ready for hanging.

Submissions Send introductory letter with samples, résumé, artist's statement, SASE. Responds in 4 months. Finds artists through word of mouth, art exhibits, open calls, portfolio reviews, referrals by other artists.

Tips "Please send 10-20 slides by mail (labeled with your name, telephone number, image title, image media, size) or JPEGs on CD-ROM. Include a current résumé, statement, SASE for return. We are not responsible for unlabeled slides. We DO NOT welcome solicitations to visit Web sites. We DO advise artists to visit our Web site and become familiar with our offerings."

Ⓝ ▣ CENTER GALLERY AT OLD CHURCH

561 Piermont Rd., Demarest NJ 07627. (201)767-7160. Fax: (201)767-0497. E-mail: gallery @tasoc.org. Web site: www.tasoc.org. **Contact:** Rachael Faillace, gallery director. Nonprofit gallery. Estab. 1974. "10-exhibition season includes contemporary, emerging, and established regional artists, NJ Annual Small Works show, student and faculty group exhibitions, among others." Gallery hours: 9:30 am to 5:30 pm Monday-Friday. Call for weekend and evening hours.

Exhibits All styles and genres are considered.

Making Contact & Terms Charges 35% commission fee on all gallery sales. Gallery provides promotion and contract. Accepted work should be framed, mounted.

Submissions Guidelines are available on gallery's Web site. Small Works prospectus is available online. Mainly finds artists through referrals by other artists and artist registries.

Tips "Follow guidelines available online."

THE CHAIT GALLERIES DOWNTOWN

218 E. Washington St., Iowa City IA 52240. (319)338-4442. Fax: (319)338-3380. E-mail: info@thegalleriesdowntown.com. Web site: www.thegalleriesdowntown.com. **Contact:** Benjamin Chait, director. For-profit gallery. Estab. 2003. Approached by 100 artists/year; represents or exhibits 100 artists. Open Monday through Friday from 11 to 6; Saturday from 11 to 5; Sunday by appointment or by chance. Located in a downtown building renovated to its original look of 1882 with 14-ft.-high molded ceiling and original 9-ft. front door. Professional museum lighting and Scamozzi-capped columns complete the elegant gallery. Overall price range: $50-10,000.

Exhibits Exhibits landscapes, oil and acrylic paintings, sculpture, fused glass wall pieces, jewelry.

Making Contact & Terms Artwork is accepted on consignment, and there is a 50% commission. Gallery provides insurance, promotion and contract. Accepted work should be framed. Requires exclusive representation locally.

Submissions Call; mail portfolio for review. Responds to queries in 2 weeks. Finds artists through art fairs, art exhibits, portfolio reviews and referrals by other artists.

CHAPMAN FRIEDMAN GALLERY

624 W. Main St., Louisville KY 40202. E-mail: friedman@imagesol.com. Web site: www.chapmanfriedmangallery.com or www.imagesol.com. **Contact:** Julius Friedman, owner. For-profit gallery. Estab. 1992. Approached by 100 or more artists/year; represents or exhibits 25 artists. Sponsors 1 photography exhibit/year. Average display time 1 month. Open Wednesday through Saturday from 10 to 5. Closed August. Located downtown; approximately 3,500 sq. ft. with 15-foot ceilings and white walls. Overall price range: $75-10,000. Most work sold at more than $1,000.

Exhibits Exhibits photos of landscapes/scenics, architecture. Interested in alternative process, avant garde, erotic, fine art.

Making Contact & Terms Artwork is accepted on consignment, and there is a 50% commission. Gallery provides insurance, promotion and contract. Accepted work should be framed. Requires exclusive representation locally.

Submissions Send query letter with artist's statement, bio, brochure, photographs, résumé, slides and SASE. Responds to queries within 1 month, only if interested. Finds artists through portfolio reviews and referrals by other artists.

⊠ STEPHEN COHEN GALLERY

7358 Beverly Blvd., Los Angeles CA 90036. (323)937-5525. Fax: (323)937-5523. E-mail: info@stephencohengallery.com. Web site: www.stephencohengallery.com. Photography and photo-based art gallery. Estab. 1992. Represents 40 artists. Sponsors 6 exhibits/year. Average display time 2 months. Open Tuesday through Saturday from 11 to 6. "We are a large, spacious gallery and are flexible in terms of types of shows we can mount." Overall price range $500-20,000. Most work sold at $2,000.

Exhibits All styles of photography and photo-based art.

Making Contact & Terms Charges 50% commission. Gallery provides insurance, promotion, contract. Requires exclusive representation locally.

Submissions Mail portfolio for review. Send query letter with artist's statement, bio, brochure, business card, photographs, résumé, reviews, SASE. Responds within 3 months, only if interested. Finds artists through word of mouth, published work.

Tips "Photography is still the best bargain in 20th-century art. There are more people collecting photography now, increasingly sophisticated and knowledgeable people aware of the beauty and variety of the medium."

◼ THE CONTEMPORARY ART WORKSHOP

542 W. Grant Place, Chicago IL 60614. (773)472-4004. Fax: (773)472-4505. E-mail: info@contemporaryartworkshop.org. Web site: www.contemporaryartworkshop.org. **Contact:** Lynn Kearney, director. Nonprofit gallery. Estab. 1949. Average display time 1 month. Gallery open Tuesday through Friday from 12:30 to 5:30; Saturday from 12 to 5. Closed

holidays. "The CAW is located in Chicago's Lincoln Park neighborhood. It is housed in a converted dairy that was built in the 1800s." The CAW includes over 21 artists' studios as well as 2 galleries that show (exclusively) emerging Chicago-area artists.

Exhibits Interested in fine art.

Making Contact & Terms Artwork is accepted on consignment, and there is a 30% commission. Gallery provides promotion. *Accepts artists from Chicago area only.*

Submissions Send query letter with artist's statement, bio, résumé, reviews, samples (slides, photos or JPEGs on CD), SASE. Responds in 2 months. Finds artists through word of mouth, submissions, art exhibits, referrals by other artists.

N ▣ CONTEMPORARY ARTS CENTER

900 Camp St., New Orleans LA 70130. (504)528-3805. Fax: (504)528-3828. E-mail: info@ca cno.org. Web site: www.cacno.org. **Contact:** Johnny King, exhibitions manager. Alternative space, nonprofit gallery. Estab. 1976. Gallery open Thursday through Sunday from 11 to 4. Closed Mardis Gras, Christmas, New Year's Day. Located in the central business district of New Orleans; renovated/converted warehouse.

Exhibits Interested in alternative process, avant garde, fine art. Cutting-edge contemporary preferred.

Terms Artwork is accepted on loan for curated exhibitions. CAC provides insurance and promotion. Accepted work should be framed. "The CAC is not a sales venue, but will refer inquiries." Receives 20% commission on items sold as a result of an exhibition.

Submissions Send query letter with bio, SASE, slides or CD. Responds in 4 months. Finds artists through word of mouth, submissions, art exhibits, art fairs, referrals by other artists, professional contacts, art periodicals.

Tips "Submit only 1 slide sheet with proper labels (title, date, media, dimensions) or CD-ROM with the same information."

N THE CONTEMPORARY ARTS CENTER

44 E. Sixth St., Cincinnati OH 45202. (513)345-8400. Fax: (513)721-7418. E-mail: pr@cacma il.org. Web site: www.ContemporaryArtsCenter.org. **Contact:** Public Relations Coordinator. Nonprofit arts center. Sponsors 9 exhibits/year. Average display time 6-12 weeks. Sponsors openings; provides printed invitations, music, refreshments, cash bar.

Exhibits Photographer must be selected by the curator and approved by the board. Exhibits photos of multicultural, disasters, environmental, landscapes/scenics, gardening, technology/computers. Interested in avant garde, innovative photography, fine art.

Making Contact & Terms Photography sometimes sold in gallery. Charges 15% commission.

Submissions Send query with résumé, slides, SASE. Responds in 2 months.

CORPORATE ART SOURCE/CAS GALLERY

2960-F Zelda Rd., Montgomery AL 36106. (334)271-3772. Fax: (334)271-3772. Web site: www.casgallery.com. Art consultancy, for-profit gallery. Estab. 1990. Approached by 100 artists/year; represents or exhibits 50 artists. Sponsors 1 photography exhibit/year. Average display time 6 weeks. Gallery open Monday through Friday from 10 to 5:30; weekends from 11 to 3. Overall price range $200-20,000. Most work sold at $1,000.

Exhibits Exhibits photos of landscapes/scenics, architecture, rural. Interested in alternative process, avant garde, fine art, historical/vintage.

Making Contact & Terms Artwork is accepted on consignment, and there is a 50% commission. Gallery provides contract.

Submissions E-mail from the Web site, or mail portfolio for review. Send query letter. Responds within 6 weeks, only if interested. Finds artists through submissions, portfolio reviews, art exhibits, art fairs, referrals by other artists.

☐ ▣ CREALDÉ SCHOOL OF ART

600 St. Andrews Blvd., Winter Park FL 32792. (407)671-1886. Fax: (407)671-0311. Web site: www.crealde.org. **Contact:** Rick Lang, director of photography. ''The school's gallery holds 6-7 exhibitions/year, representing artists from regional/national stature in all media. Anyone who would like to show here may send 20 slides or digital images, resume, statement and return postage.''

▣ CROSSMAN GALLERY

University of Wisconsin-Whitewater, 950 W. Main St., Whitewater WI 53190. (262)472-5708. E-mail: flanagam@uww.edu. Web site: www.uww.edu. **Contact:** Michael Flanagan, director. Estab. 1971. Photography is frequently featured in thematic exhibits at the gallery. Average display time 1 month. Overall price range $250-3,000.

Exhibits ''We primarily exhibit artists from the Midwest but do include some from national and international venues. Works by Latino artists are also featured in a regular series at ongoing exhibits.'' Interested in all types of innovative approach to photography.

Making Contact & Terms Sponsors openings; provides food, beverage, show announcement, mailing, shipping (partial) and possible visiting artist lecture/demo.

Submissions Submit 10-20 slides or CD, artist's statement, résumé, SASE.

Tips ''The Crossman Gallery operates within a university environment. The focus is on exhibits that have the potential to educate viewers about processes and techniques and have interesting thematic content.''

ELLEN CURLEE GALLERY

1214 Washington Ave., St. Louis MO 63103. E-mail: ellen@ellencurleegallery.com. Web site: www.ellencurleegallery.com. **Contact:** Ellen Curlee, owner. For-profit gallery. Estab. 2005. Approached by 50 artists/year; represents or exhibits 7artists. Exhibits photography only. Average display time 6-8 weeks. Located in newly renovated downtown loft district; 900 sq. ft.

Exhibits Exhibits contemporary fine art photography: all procesesses, a variety of subject matters and points of view.

Making Contact & Terms Requires exclusive representation locally.

Submissions Send query letter with artist's statement, bio. Finds artists through art exhibits, submissions, portfolio reviews, referrals by other artists.

▣ THE DALLAS CENTER FOR CONTEMPORARY ART

2801 Swiss Ave., Dallas TX 75204. (214)821-2522. Fax: (214)821-9103. E-mail: info@thecon temporary.net. Web site: www.thecontemporary.net. **Contact:** Joan Davidow, director. Nonprofit gallery. Estab. 1981. Sponsors 1-2 photography exhibits/year. Other exhibits may include photography as well as other mediums. Average display time 6-8 weeks. Gallery open Tuesday through Saturday from 10 to 5.

Exhibits Exhibits a variety of subject matter and styles.

Making Contact & Terms Charges no commission. "Because we are nonprofit, we do not sell artwork. If someone is interested in buying art in the gallery, they get in touch with the artist. The transaction is between the artist and the buyer."

Submissions Reviews slides/CDs. Send material by mail for consideration; include SASE. Responds October 1 annually.

Tips "Memberships available starting at $50. See our Web site for info and membership levels."

THE DAYTON ART INSTITUTE

456 Belmonte Park N., Dayton OH 45405-4700. (937)223-5277. Fax: (937)223-3140. E-mail: info@daytonartinstitute.org. Web site: www.daytonartinstitute.org. Museum. Estab. 1919. Galleries open Tuesday through Sunday from 10 to 4, Thursdays until 8.

Exhibits Interested in fine art.

DELAWARE CENTER FOR THE CONTEMPORARY ARTS

200 S. Madison St., Wilmington DE 19801. (302)656-6466. Fax: (302)656-6944. E-mail: info@thedcca.org. Web site: www.thedcca.org. Alternative space, museum retail shop, nonprofit gallery. Estab. 1979. Approached by more than 800 artists/year; exhibits 50 artists. Sponsors 30 total exhibits/year. Average display time 6 weeks. Gallery open Tuesday, Thursday, Friday, and Saturday from 10 to 5; Wednesday and Sunday from 12 to 5. Closed on Monday and major holidays. Seven galleries located along rejuvenated Wilmington riverfront. State-of-the-art, under one-year-old, very versatile. Overall price range $500-50,000.

Exhibits Interested in alternative process, avant garde.

Making Contact & Terms Gallery provides PR and contract. Accepted work should be framed, mounted, matted. Prefers only contemporary art.

Submissions Send query letter with artist's statement, bio, SASE, 10 slides. Returns material with SASE. Responds within 6 months. Finds artists through word of mouth, submissions, portfolio reviews, art exhibits, referrals by other artists.

DEMUTH MUSEUM

120 E. King St., Lancaster PA 17602. E-mail: info@demuth.org. Web site: www.demuth.org. **Contact:** Gallery Director. Museum. Estab. 1981. Average display time 2 months. Open Tuesday through Saturday from 10 to 4; Sunday from 1 to 4. Located in the home and studio of Modernist artist Charles Demuth (1883-1935). Exhibitions feature the museum's permanent collection of Demuth's works with changing, temporary exhibitions.

SAMUEL DORSKY MUSEUM OF ART

SUNY at New Paltz, 1 Hawk Dr., New Paltz NY 12561. (845)257-3844. Fax: (845)257-3854. E-mail: sdma@newpaltz.edu. Web site: www.newpaltz.edu/museum. **Contact**: Brian Wallace, curator. Estab. 1964. Sponsors ongoing photography exhibits throughout the year. Average display time 2 months. Museum open Tuesday through Friday from 11 to 5; weekends from 1 to 5. Closed legal and school holidays "and during intersession; check Web site to confirm your visit."

Exhibits Interested in alternative process, avant garde, documentary, fine art, historical/vintage.

Submissions Send query letter with bio and SASE. Responds within 3 months, only if interested. Finds artists through art exhibits.

▣ DOT FIFTYONE GALLERY

51 NW 36 St., Miami FL 33127. (305)573-3754. Fax: (305)573-3754. E-mail: dot@dotfiftyon e.com. Web site: www.dotfiftyone.com. **Contact:** Isaac Perelman and Alfredo Guzman, directors. For-profit gallery. Estab. 2004. Approached by 40+ artists/year; represents or exhibits 10 artists. Sponsors 2 photography exhibits/year. Average display time 40 days. Open Monday through Friday from 12 to 7; Saturdays and private viewings available by appointment. Located in the Wynwood Art District; approximately 7,000 sq. ft.; 2 floors. Overall price range $600-30,000. Most work sold at $6,000.

Exhibits Exhibits photos of couples, architecture, cities/urban, interiors/decorating, landscapes/scenics. Interested in avant garde, erotic, fashion/glamour, fine art.

Making Contact & Terms Artwork is accepted on consignment, and there is a 50% commission. Requires exclusive representation locally.

Submissions E-mail with a link to photographer's Web site. Write to arrange a personal interview to show portfolio. Mail portfolio for review. Finds artists through art fairs, portfolio reviews, referrals by other artists.

Tips "Have a good presentation. Contact the gallery first by e-mail. Never try to show work during an opening, and never show up at the gallery without an appointment."

ℕ CANDACE DWAN GALLERY

24 W. 57th St., New York NY 10019. (914)232-3966. Fax: (914)232-3966. E-mail: email@can dacedwan.com. Web site: www.candacedwan.com. **Contact:** Christine Stamas, gallery manager. For-profit gallery. Estab. 1995. Approached by hundreds of artists/year; represents or exhibits hundreds of artists. Sponsors 6-8 photography exhibits/year. Average display time 6-8 weeks. NYC hours: Tuesday through Saturday from 10 to 6; July: Tuesday through Friday from 11 to 6. Closed August.

Exhibits Exhibits photos of couples, architecture, cities/urban, pets, religious, rural, landscapes/scenics, beauty, truth, love. Interested in fine art. Exhibits only photography.

Submissions *Currently not accepting submissions.*

ℕ ▣ GEORGE EASTMAN HOUSE

900 East Ave., Rochester NY 14607. (716)271-3361. Fax: (716)271-3970. Web site: www.eas tmanhouse.org. **Contact:** Alison Nordstrom, curator of photographs. Museum. Estab. 1947. Approached by more than 400 artists/year. Sponsors more than 12 photography exhibits/ year. Average display time 3 months. Gallery open Tuesday through Saturday from 10 to 5 (Thursday until 8); Sunday from 1 to 5. Closed Thanksgiving and Christmas. Museum has 7 galleries that host exhibitions, ranging from 50- to 300-print displays.

Exhibits GEH is a museum that exhibits the vast subjects, themes and processes of historical and contemporary photography.

Submissions See Web site for detailed information: http://eastmanhouse.org/inc/collecti ons/submissions.php. Mail portfolio for review. Send query letter with artist's statement, résumé, SASE, slides, digital prints. Responds in 3 months. Finds artists through word of mouth, art exhibits, referrals by other artists, books, catalogs, conferences, etc.

Tips "Consider as if you are applying for a job. You must have succinct, well-written documents; a well-selected number of visual treats that speak well with written document provided; an easel for reviewer to use.''

▣ CATHERINE EDELMAN GALLERY

300 W. Superior St., Lower Level, Chicago IL 60610. (312)266-2350. Fax: (312)266-1967. Web site: www.edelmangallery.com. **Contact:** Catherine Edelman, director. Estab. 1987. Sponsors 6 exhibits/year. Average display time 8 weeks. Open Tuesday through Saturday from 10 to 5:30. Overall price range $1,500-15,000.

Exhibits ''We exhibit works ranging from traditional photography to mixed media photo-based work.''

Making Contact & Terms Charges 50% commission. Accepted work should be matted. Requires exclusive representation within metropolitan area.

Submissions Query first. Will review unsolicited work with SASE or CD-ROM.

Tips Looks for ''consistency, dedication and honesty. Try to not be overly eager and realize that the process of arranging an exhibition takes a long time. The relationship between gallery and photographer is a partnership.''

PAUL EDELSTEIN STUDIO AND GALLERY

540 Hawthorne Street, Memphis TN 38112-5029. (901)496-8122. Fax: 901-276-1493. E-mail: henrygrove@yahoo.com. Web site: www.askart.com. **Contact:** Paul R. Edelstein, director/owner. Estab. 1985. ''Shows are presented continually throughout the year.'' Over-all price range: $300-10,000. Most work sold at $1,000.

Exhibits Exhibits photos of celebrities, children, multicultural, families. Interested in avant garde, historical/vintage, C-print, dye transfer, ever color, fine art and 20th-century photography ''that intrigues the viewer''—figurative still life, landscape, abstract—by upcoming and established photographers.

Making Contact & Terms Charges 50% commission. Buys photos outright. Reviews transparencies. Accepted work should be framed or unframed, mounted or unmounted, matted or unmatted work. There are no size limitations. Submit portfolio for review. Send query letter with samples. Cannot return material. Responds in 3 months.

Tips ''Looking for figurative and abstract figurative work.''

ENVOY

131 Chrystie Street, Ground Floor, New York NY 10002. (212)226-4555. E-mail: office@env oygallery.com. Web site: www.envoygallery.com. **Contact:** Director. Art consultancy and for-profit gallery. Estab. 2005. Approached by 120 artists/year; represents or exhibits 25 artists. Average display time 6 weeks. Open Tuesday through Saturday from 12 to 6. Closed December 23 through January 4, and July 4. Located on Lower East Side. Overall price range $1,000-35,000. Most work sold at $8,000.

Exhibits Exhibits photos of babies/children/teens, celebrities, couples, multicultural, cities/urban, pets, political, landscapes/scenics. Interested in fine art.

Making Contact & Terms Artwork is accepted on consignment, and there is a 50% commission. Requires exclusive representation locally.

Submissions Finds artists through referrals by other artists.

Tips ''Check out the gallery first to see if your work is appropriate for the gallery. Then, strictly follow the guidelines for submission of work.''

THOMAS ERBEN GALLERY

526 W. 26th St., 4th Floor., New York NY 10001. (212)645-8701. Fax: (212)941-9630. E-mail: info@thomaserben.com. Web site: www.thomaserben.com. For-profit gallery. Estab. 1996. Approached by 100 artists/year; represents or exhibits 15 artists. Average display time 5-6 weeks. Gallery open Tuesday through Saturday from 10 to 6 (Monday through Friday in July). Closed Christmas/New Year's Day and August.
Submissions Mail portfolio for review. Responds in 1 month.

Ⓝ ▣ ETHERTON GALLERY

135 S. 6th Ave., Tucson AZ 85701. (520)624-7370. Fax: (520)792-4569. E-mail: info@ethertongallery.com. Web site: www.ethertongallery.com. **Contact:** Terry Etherton, director. Estab. 1981. Sponsors 10 exhibits/year. Average display time 6 weeks. Sponsors openings; provides wine and refreshments, publicity, etc. Overall price range $400-150,000.
  ● Etherton Gallery regularly purchases 19th-century, vintage, Western survey photographs and Native American portraits.
Exhibits The gallery is interested in professional photographers with a high-quality, consistent body of work, especially artists working in the Western and Southwestern US.
Making Contact & Terms Charges 50% commission. Occasionally buys photography outright. Please send CD with no more than 20 images of best body of work, resume, and relevant artist statement for consideration or e-mail gallery with the same information. We will respond to your submission if we are interested in the work.
Tips "You should be familiar with the photo art world and with my gallery and the work I show. Please limit submissions to 20, showing the best examples of your work in a presentable, professional format; slides or digital preferred."

Ⓝ EVERSON MUSEUM OF ART

401 Harrison St., Syracuse NY 13202. (315)474-6064. Fax: (315)474-6943. E-mail: everson@everson.org. Web site: www.everson.org. **Contact:** Debora Ryan, curator. Museum. Estab. 1897. Approached by many artists/year; represents or exhibits 16-20 artists. Sponsors 2-3 photography exhibits/year. Average display time 3 months. Gallery open Tuesday through Friday from 12 to 5; Saturday from 10 to 5; Sunday from 12 to 5. "The museum features four large galleries with twenty-four foot ceilings, track lighting and oak hardwood, a sculpture court, a children's gallery, a ceramic study center and five smaller gallery spaces."
Exhibits Photos of multicultural, environmental, landscapes/scenics, wildlife. Interested in alternative process, avant garde, documentary, fine art, historical/vintage.
Submissions Send query letter with artist's statement, bio, résumé, reviews, SASE, slides. Finds artists through submissions, portfolio reviews, art exhibits.

▣ FAHEY/KLEIN GALLERY

148 N. La Brea Ave., Los Angeles CA 90036. (323)934-2250. Fax: (323)934-4243. E-mail: fkg@earthlink.net. Web site: www.faheykleingallery.com. **Contact:** David Fahey or Ken Devlin, co-owners. Estab. 1986. For-profit gallery. Approached by 200 artists/year; represents or exhibits 60 artists. Sponsors 10 exhibits/year. Average display time 5-6 weeks. Gallery open Tuesday through Saturday from 10 to 6. Closed on all major holidays. Sponsors openings; provides announcements and beverages served at reception. Overall price range $500-500,000. Most work sold at $2,500. Located in Hollywood; gallery features 2 exhibition spaces with extensive work in back presentation room.

Exhibits Interested in established work; photos of celebrities, landscapes/scenics, wildlife, architecture, entertainment, humor, performing arts, sports. Interested in alternative process, avant garde, documentary, erotic, fashion/glamour, fine art, historical/vintage. Specific photo needs include iconic photographs, Hollywood celebrities, photojournalism, music-related, reportage and still life.

Making Contact & Terms Artwork is accepted on consignment, and the commission is negotiated. Gallery provides insurance, promotion, contract. Accepted work should be unframed, unmounted and unmatted. Requires exclusive representation within metropolitan area. Photographer must be established for a minimum of 5 years; preferably published.

Submissions Prefers Web site URLs for initial contact, or send material (CD, reproductions, no originals) by mail with SASE for consideration. Responds in 2 months. Finds artists through art fairs, exhibits, portfolio reviews, submissions, word of mouth, referrals by other artists.

Tips "Please be professional and organized. Have a comprehensive sample of innovative work. Interested in seeing mature work with resolved photographic ideas and viewing complete portfolios addressing one idea."

FALKIRK CULTURAL CENTER

P.O. Box 151560, San Rafael CA 94915-1560. (415)485-3328. Fax: (415)485-3404. **Contact:** Beth Goldberg, curator. Web site: www.falkirkculturalcenter.org. Nonprofit gallery and national historic place (1888 Victorian) converted to multi-use cultural center. Approached by 500 artists /year; exhibits 300 artists. Sponsors 2 photography exhibits/year. Average display time 2 months. Gallery open Monday through Friday from 1 to 5; Saturday from 10 to 1.

Making Contact & Terms Gallery provides insurance. *Accepts only artists from San Francisco Bay area*, "especially Marin County since we are a community center."

Submissions Send query letter with artist's statement, bio, slides, résumé. Returns material with SASE. Finds artists through word of mouth, submissions, portfolio reviews, art exhibits, art fairs, referrals by other artists.

FAVA (FIRELANDS ASSOCIATION FOR THE VISUAL ARTS)

New Union Center for the Arts, 39 S. Main St., Oberlin OH 44074. (440)774-7158. Fax: (440)775-1107. E-mail: favagallery@oberlin.net. Web site: www.favagallery.org. **Contact:** Kyle Michalak, gallery director. Nonprofit gallery. Estab. 1979. Sponsors 1 photography exhibit/year. Average display time 1 month. Gallery open Tuesday through Saturday from 11 to 5; Sunday from 1 to 5. Overall price range $75-3,000. Most work sold at $200.

Exhibits Open to all media, including photography. Exhibits a variety of subject matter and styles.

Making Contact & Terms Charges 30% commission. Accepted work should be framed or matted. Sponsors 1 regional juried photo exhibit/year: Six-State Photography, open to residents of Ohio, Kentucky, West Virginia, Pennsylvania, Indiana, Michigan. Deadline for applications: March. Send annual application for 6 invitational shows by mid-December of each year; include 15-20 slides, slide list, résumé.

Submissions Send SASE for Exhibition Opportunity flier or Six-State Photo Show entry form.

Tips "As a nonprofit gallery, we do not represent artists except during the juried show. Present the work in a professional format; the work, frame and/or mounting should be clean, undamaged, and (in cases of more complicated work) well organized."

◼ FINE ARTS CENTER GALLERIES/UNIVERSITY OF RHODE ISLAND

105 Upper College Rd., Kingston RI 02881-0820. (401)874-2775. Fax: (401)874-2007. E-mail: jtolnick@uri.edu. Web site: www.uri.edu/artgalleries. **Contact:** Judith Tolnick Champa, director. Nonprofit galleries. Estab. 1968. Sponsors 4-6 photography exhibits/year. Average display time 1-3 months. There are 3 exhibition spaces: The Main and Photography Galleries, open Tuesday through Friday from 12 to 4 and weekends from 1 to 4; and The Corridor Gallery, open daily from 9 to 9. Exhibitions are curated from a national palette and regularly reviewed in the local press. Unsolicited proposals are reviewed periodically when submitted via slides or CD with SASE.

🅽 🖾 FLATFILE

217 N. Carpenter, Chicago IL 60607. (312)491-1190. Fax: (312)491-1195. E-mail: info@flatfi legalleries.com. Web site: www.flatfilegalleries.com. **Contact:** Susan Aurinko, gallery director. For-profit gallery. Estab. 2000. Exhibits over 60 emerging and established local and international artists plus guest artists. Sponsors approximately 6 photography exhibits/year. Average display time 4-5 weeks. Gallery open Tuesday through Saturday from 11 to 6. Closed between Christmas and New Year's. 8,000 sq. ft. plus 2 project rooms for video and photo-based installation. Overall price range $100-20,000. Most work sold at $400-800.

Exhibits Exhibits photos of multicultural, environmental, landscapes/scenics, architecture, rural, travel, still life, nudes, abstracts, b&w/color, Polaroid transfers and assorted other processes such as platinum prints, gold-toned prints, etc. Interested in alternative process, avant garde, fine art, video, photobased installation.

Making Contact & Terms Artwork is accepted on consignment, and there is a 50% commission. Gallery provides insurance, promotion. Accepted work should be matted and/or framed. Requires exclusive representation locally, but encourages items to be shown in shows and museums and even promotes artists to other venues.

Submissions Mail portfolio for review or send query letter with artist's statement, photocopies, photographs, résumé, reviews, slides, SASE. Finds artists through word of mouth, submissions, portfolio reviews, referrals by other artists. "They find me." Portfolio reviews run 6-8 weeks.

Tips "I like to see the following: slides or thumbnail images; work prints, collateral materials, reviews, résumé, etc. If requested, we would like to see fiber-based, finely printed work to assess print quality. No RC paper; only acid-free, archival work and matting will be accepted for exhibition."

◼ THE FRASER GALLERY

7700 Wisconsin Ave., Suite E, Bethesda MD 20814. (301)718-9651. E-mail: info@thefraserg allery.com. Web site: www.thefrasergallery.com. **Contact:** Catriona Fraser, director. Estab. 1996. Approached by 500 artists/year; represents 25 artists and sells the work of an additional 75 artists. Sponsors 4 photography exhibits/year. Average display time 1 month. Gallery open Tuesday through Saturday from 11:30 to 6. Closed Sunday and Monday except by appointment. Overall price range $200-20,000. Most work sold at under $5,000.

Exhibits Exhibits landscapes/scenics.

Making Contact & Terms Artwork is accepted on consignment, and there is a 50% commission. Gallery provides insurance, promotion, contract. Accepted work should be framed, matted to full conservation standards. Requires exclusive representation locally.

Submissions Send query letter with bio, reviews, slides or CD-ROM, SASE. Responds in 1 month. Finds artists through submissions, portfolio reviews, art exhibits, art fairs.

Tips "Research the background of the gallery, and apply to galleries that show your style of work. All work should be framed or matted to full museum standards."

ⓝ FRESNO ART MUSEUM

2233 N. First St., Fresno CA 93703. (559)441-4221. Fax: (559)441-4227. E-mail: jacquelin@fresnoartmuseum.org. Web site: www.fresnoartmuseum.org. **Contact:** Jacquelin Pilar, curator. Estab. 1948. "Approached by many California artists throughout the year." Over 25 changing exhibitions/year including at least two photography exhibitions. Average display time 8 weeks. Gallery open Tuesday through Sunday from 11 to 5 (Thursdays until 8). Closed mid-August to early September.

Exhibits Focused on Modernist and Contemporary art.

Making Contact and Terms Museum provides insurance. Send letter of inquiry through the mail with artist's statement, résumé, slides for curator to review. Studio visit arranged following review of material. "The Museum shows the work of contemporary California artists; interested in sculpture, the work of mid-career and mature artists working in photography, sculpture, painting, mixed-media, installation work. The Museum also draws exhibitions from its permanent collection."

⊡ GALLERY 110 COLLECTIVE

110 S. Washington St., Seattle WA 98104. E-mail: director@gallery110.com. Web site: www.gallery110.com. **Contact:** Molly Norris, director. Cooperative gallery. Estab. 2003. Gallery represents photography and other media. Average exhibition time 1 month. Open Wednesday through Saturday from 12 to 5. Located in the historic gallery district of Pioneer Square, the gallery shares a space with a commercial gallery-each has 1 storefront. Overall price range $125-3,000. Most work sold at $500-800.

Exhibits Photography exhibitions and installations include a variety of subject matter including portraits, still life objects, landscape, and narrative scenes. Interested in alternative and experimental process, documentary, fine art.

Making Contact & Terms Yearly active membership with monthly dues, art on consignment with 50% commission. Artwork is bought outright for 50% commission; net 60 days. Gallery provides insurance, promotion, contract (nonexclusive).

Submissions Call or write to arrange personal interview to show portfolio of slides or CD. Send query letter with artist's statement, bio, résumé, SASE, and "the reasons they've chosen us." Finds artists through word of mouth, art exhibits, submissions, referrals by other artists.

Tips "I want to know that the artist has researched us and is interested in being an active member in good standing. I want to see art I've never seen before that shows that the artist is aware of other art/history."

GALLERY 218

207 E. Buffalo St., Suite 218, Milwaukee WI 53202. (414)643-1732. E-mail: info@gallery218.com. Web site: www.gallery218.com. **Contact:** Judith Hooks, president. Estab. 1990. Sponsors 12 exhibits/year. Average display time 1 month. Sponsors openings. "If a group show, we make arrangements and all artists contribute. If a solo show, artist provides everything." Overall price range $150-5,000. Most work sold at $350.

Exhibits Interested in alternative process, avant garde, abstract, fine art. Membership dues:

$55/year plus $55/month rent. Artists help run the gallery. Group and solo shows. Photography is shown alongside fine arts painting, printmaking, sculpture, etc.

Making Contact & Terms Charges 25% commission. There is an entry fee for each month. Fee covers the rent for 1 month. Accepted work must be framed.

Submissions Send SASE for an application. "This is a cooperative space. A fee is required."

Tips "Get involved in the process if the gallery will let you. We require artists to help promote their show so that they learn what and why certain things are required. Have inventory ready. Read and follow instructions on entry forms; be aware of deadlines. Attend openings for shows you are accepted into locally."

▣ GALLERY 400

College of Architecture and the Arts, University of Illinois at Chicago, 400 S. Peoria St. (MC 034), Chicago IL 60607. (312)996-6114. Fax: (312)355-3444. E-mail: uicgallery400@gmail. co. Web site: http://gallery400.aa.uic.edu. **Contact:** Lorelei Stewart, director. Nonprofit gallery. Estab. 1983. Approached by 500 artists/year; exhibits 80 artists. Sponsors 1 photography exhibit/year. Average display time 4-6 weeks. Gallery open Tuesday through Friday from 10 to 6; Saturday from 12 to 6. Clients include local community, students, tourists, and upscale.

Making Contact & Terms Gallery provides insurance and promotion.

Submissions Check info section of Web site for guidelines. Responds in 5 months. Finds artists through word of mouth, art exhibits, referrals by other artists.

Tips "Check our Web site for guidelines for proposing an exhibition and follow those proposal guidelines. Please do not e-mail, as we do not respond to e-mails."

GALLERY M

2830 E. Third Ave., Denver CO 80206. (303)331-8400. Fax: (303)331-8522. Web site: www.g allerym.com. **Contact**: Managing Partner. For-profit gallery. Estab. 1996. Sponsors 2 photography exhibits/year. Average display time 6-12 weeks for featured artist. Overall price range $1,000-75,000.

Exhibits Primarily interested in social documentation and photojournalism.

Making Contact & Terms Gallery provides promotion. Requires exclusive regional representation.

Submissions "Artists interested in showing at the gallery should visit the Artist Submissions section of our Web site (under Site Resources). The gallery provides additional services for both collectors and artists, including our quarterly newsletter, *The Art Quarterly*."

⃞Ⓝ GALLERY M, A MICHAEL MURPHY COMPANY

(formerly Michael Murphy Gallery Inc.), 2701 S. MacDill Ave., Tampa FL 33629. (813)902-1414. Fax: (813)835-5526. E-mail: mmurphy@michaelmurphygallery.com. Web site: www. michaelmurphygallery.com. **Contact:** Michael Murphy, owner. For-profit gallery. Estab. 1988. Approached by 100 artists/year; exhibits 35 artists. Sponsors 1 photography exhibit/year. Average display time 1 month. Open all year; Monday through Saturday from 10 to 6. Overall price range $500-15,000. Most work sold at less than $1,000.

Exhibits Exhibits photos of babies/children/teens, celebrities, couples, multicultural, families, parents, senior citizens, disasters, environmental, landscapes/scenics, wildlife, architecture, cities/urban, education, gardening, interiors/decorating, pets, religious, rural, agriculture, business concepts, industry, medicine, military, political, product shots/still life, science, technology/computers. Interested in alternative process, avant garde, documentary, erotic, fashion/glamour, fine art, historical/vintage, seasonal.

Making Contact & Terms Artwork is accepted on consignment, and there is a 50% commission. Accepted work should be framed. Requires exclusive representation locally.

Submissions Send query with artist's statement, bio, brochure, business card, photocopies, photographs, résumé, reviews, slides and SASE. Responds to queries in 1 month, only if interested.

GALLERY NAGA

67 Newbury St., Boston MA 02116. (617)267-9060. Fax: (617)267-9040. E-mail: mail@gallerynaga.com. Web site: www.gallerynaga.com. **Contact:** Arthur Dion, director. For-profit gallery. Estab. 1976. Approached by 150 artists/year; represents or exhibits 40 artists. Sponsors 2 photography exhibits/year. Average display time 1 month. Gallery open Tuesday through Saturday from 10 to 5:00. Overall price range $850-35,000. Most work sold at $2,000-3,000.

Exhibits Exhibits photos of landscapes/scenics, architecture, cities/urban.

Making Contact & Terms Charges 50% commission. Gallery provides insurance. Requires exclusive representation locally. *Accepts only artists from New England/Boston.*

Submissions Send query letter with artist's statement, résumé, bio, photocopies, slides, SASE. Responds in 6 months. Finds artists through submissions, portfolio reviews, art exhibits.

Ⓝ ⊘ GERING AND LOPEZ GALLERY

730 Fifth Ave., New York NY 10011. (646)336-7183. Fax: (646)336-7185. E-mail: info@geringgallery.com. Web site: www.geringgallery.com. **Contact:** Director. For-profit gallery. Estab. 1991. Approached by 240 artists/year; represents or exhibits 12 artists. Sponsors 1 photography exhibit/year. Average display time 5 weeks. Gallery open Tuesday through Saturday from 10 to 6.

Exhibits Interested in alternative process, avant garde; digital, computer-based photography.

Making Contact & Terms Artwork is accepted on consignment.

Submissions E-mail with link to Web site or send postcard with image. Responds within 6 months, only if interested. Finds artists through word of mouth, art exhibits, art fairs, referrals by other artists. **"At this time, gallery is not actively looking for new artists."**

Tips "Most important is to research the galleries and only submit to those that are appropriate. Visit Web sites if you don't have access to galleries."

Ⓝ ANTON HAARDT GALLERY

2858 Magazine St., New Orleans LA 701115. (504)897-1172. E-mail: gallery@antonart.com. Web site: www.antonart.com. **Contact:** Anton Haardt, gallery director. For-profit gallery. Estab. 1985. Represents or exhibits 25 artists. Overall price range $500-5,000. Most work sold at $1,000.

Exhibits Exhibits photos of celebrities. Mainly photographs (portraits of folk artists).

Making Contact & Terms Prefers only artists from the South. Self-taught artists who are original and pure, specifically art created from 1945 to 1980. "I rarely take on new artists, but I am interested in buying estates of deceased artist's work or an entire body of work by artist."

Submissions Send query letter with artist's statement.

Tips "I am only interested in a very short description if the artist has work from early in his or her career."

⋈ CARRIE HADDAD GALLERY

622 Warren St., Hudson NY 12534. (518)828-1915. Web site: www.carriehaddadgallery.c om. **Contact:** Carrie Haddad, owner. Art consultancy, for-profit gallery. Estab. 1990. Approached by 50 artists/year; represents or exhibits 60 artists. Sponsors 8 photography exhibits/year. Average display time 5 weeks. Open Thursday through Monday from 11 to 5. Overall price range $350-6,000. Most work sold at $1,000.

Exhibits Exhibits photos of nudes, landscapes/scenics, architecture, pets, rural, product shots/still life.

Making Contact & Terms Artwork is accepted on consignment, and there is a 50% commission. Gallery provides insurance, promotion. Requires exclusive representation locally.

Submissions Send query letter with bio, photocopies, photographs, price list, SASE. Responds in 1 month. Finds artists through word of mouth, submissions, art exhibits, referrals by other artists.

THE HALSTED GALLERY INC.

P.O. Box 130, Bloomfield Hills MI 48303. (248)745-0062. Fax: (248)332-0227. E-mail: thalste d@halstedgallery.com. Web site: www.halstedgallery.com. **Contact:** Wendy or Thomas Halsted. Estab. 1969. Sponsors 3 exhibits/year. Average display time 2 months. Sponsors openings. Overall price range $500-25,000.

Exhibits Interested in 19th- and 20th-century photographs.

Submissions Call to arrange a personal interview to show portfolio only. Prefers to see scans. Send no slides or samples. Unframed work only.

Tips This gallery has no limitations on subjects. Wants to see creativity, consistency, depth and emotional work.

⋈ JAMES HARRIS GALLERY

312 Second Ave. S., Seattle WA 98104. (206)903-6220. Fax:(206)903-6226. E-mail: mail@ja mesharrisgallery.com. Web site: www.jamesharrisgallery.com. **Contact:** Nancy Stoaks, assistant to the director. For-profit gallery. Estab. 1999. Approached by 40 artists/year; represents or exhibits 26 artists. Average display time 6 weeks. Open Tuesday through Saturday from 11 to 5.

Exhibits Exhibits photos of cities/urban. Interested in fine art.

Submissions E-mail with JPEG samples at 72 dpi. Send query letter with artist's statement, bio, slides.

THE HARWOOD MUSEUM OF ART

238 Ledoux St., Taos NM 87571-6004. (505)758-9826. Fax: (505)758-1475. E-mail: info@ha rwoodmuseum.com. Web site: www.harwoodmuseum.org. **Contact:** Margaret Bullock, curator. Estab. 1923. Approached by 100 artists/year; represents or exhibits more than 200 artists. Sponsors "at least" 1 photography exhibit/year. Average display time 3 months. Gallery open Tuesday through Saturday from 10 to 5; Sunday from 12 to 5. Overall price range $1,000-5,000. Most work sold at $2,000.

Exhibits Interested in alternative process, avant garde, documentary, fine art.

Making Contact & Terms Artwork is accepted on consignment, and there is a 40% commission. Gallery provides insurance, contract. Accepted work should be framed, mounted, matted. "The museum exhibits work by Taos, New Mexico, artists as well as major artists from outside our region."

Submissions Mail portfolio for review. Send query letter with artist's statement, bio, brochure, résumé, reviews, SASE, slides. Responds in 3 months. Finds artists through word of mouth, submissions, art exhibits, referrals by other artists.

Tips "The gift shops accepts some art on consignment, but the museum itself does not."

N HEARST ART GALLERY, SAINT MARY'S COLLEGE

P.O. Box 5110, Moraga CA 94575. (925)631-4379. Fax: (925)376-5128. Web site: www.stma rys-ca.edu/arts/hearst-art-gallery/. College gallery. Estab. 1931. Sponsors 1 photography exhibit/year. Gallery open Wednesday through Sunday from 11 to 4:30. Closed major holidays. 1,650 sq. ft. of exhibition space.

Exhibits Exhibits photos of multicultural, landscapes/scenics, religious, travel.

Submissions Send query letter (Attn: Registrar) with artist's statement, bio, résumé, slides, SASE. Finds artists through submissions, art exhibits, art fairs, referrals by other artists.

N ⊘ HEMPHILL

1515 14th St. NW, Suite 300, Washington DC 20005. (202)234-5601. Fax: (202)234-5607. E-mail: gallery@hemphillfinearts.com. Web site: www.hemphillfinearts.com. Art consultancy and for-profit gallery. Estab. 1993. Represents or exhibits 30 artists/year. Sponsors 2-3 photography exhibits/year. Average display time 6-8 weeks. Gallery open Tuesday through Saturday from 10 to 5. Overall price range $800-200,000. Most work sold at $3,000-9,000.

Exhibits Exhibits photos of landscapes/scenics, architecture, cities/urban, rural. Interested in alternative process, fine art, historical/vintage.

Submissions Query regarding whether artist submissions are currently being accepted for consideration.

HENRY STREET SETTLEMENT/ABRONS ART CENTER

265 Henry St., New York NY 10002. (212)766-9200. E-mail: info@henrystreet.org. Web site: www.henrystreet.org. **Contact:** Martin Dust, visual arts coordinator. Alternative space, nonprofit gallery, community center. Holds 9 solo photography exhibits/year. Gallery open Monday through Friday from 9 to 6; Saturday and Sunday from 12 to 6. Closed major holidays.

Exhibits Exhibits photos of multicultural, environmental, landscapes/scenics, architecture, cities/urban, rural. Interested in alternative process, avant garde, documentary, fine art, historical/vintage.

Making Contact & Terms Artwork is accepted on consignment, and there is a 20% commission. Gallery provides insurance, space, contract.

Submissions Send query letter with artist's statement, SASE. Finds artists through word of mouth, submissions, referrals by other artists.

HERA EDUCATIONAL FOUNDATION AND ART GALLERY

327 Main St., P.O. Box 336, Wakefield RI 02880. (401)789-1488. E-mail: info@heragallery.o rg. Web site: www.heragallery.org. **Contact:** Chelsea Heffner, director. Cooperative gallery.

Estab. 1974. The number of photo exhibits varies each year. Average display time 6 weeks. Gallery open Wednesday through Friday from 1-5; Saturday from 10-4. Closed during the month of January. Sponsors openings; provides refreshments and entertainment or lectures, demonstrations and symposia for some exhibits. Call for information on exhibitions. Overall price range: $100-10,000.

Exhibits Interested in all types of innovative contemporary art that explores social and artistic issues. Exhibits photos of disasters, environmental, landscapes/scenics. Interested in fine art.

Making Contact & Terms Charges 25% commission. Works must fit inside a 6'6"×2'6" door. Photographer must show a portfolio before attaining membership.

Submissions Inquire about membership and shows. Responds in 6 weeks. Membership guidelines and application available on Web site or mailed on request.

Tip "Hera exhibits a culturally diverse range of visual and emerging artists. Please follow the application procedure listed in the Membership Guidelines. Applications are welcome at any time of the year."

GERTRUDE HERBERT INSTITUTE OF ART

506 Telfair St., Augusta GA 30901-2310. (706)722-5495. Fax: (706)722-3670. E-mail: ghia@ghia.org. Web site: www.ghia.org. **Contact:** Kim Overstreet, executive director. Nonprofit gallery. Estab. 1937. Has 5 solo or group shows annually; exhibits approximately 40 artists annually. Average display time 6-8 weeks. Open Tuesday through Friday from 10 to 5; weekends by appointment only. Closed 1st week in August, and December 17-31. Located in historic 1818 Ware's Folly mansion.

Making Contact & Terms Artwork is accepted on consignment, and there is a 35% commission.

Submissions Send query letter with artist's statement, bio, brochure, résumé, reviews, slides or CD of work, SASE. Responds to queries in 1-3 months. Finds artists through art exhibits, submissions, referrals by other artists.

Ⓝ HUNTSVILLE MUSEUM OF ART

300 Church St. S., Huntsville AL 35801. (256)535-4350. E-mail: info@hsvmuseum.org. Web site: www.hsvmuseum.org. **Contact:** Peter J. Baldaia, chief curator. Estab. 1970. Sponsors 1-2 exhibits/year. Average display time 2-3 months.

Exhibits No specific stylistic or thematic criteria. Interested in alternative process, avant garde, documentary, fine art, historical/vintage.

Making Contact & Terms Buys photos outright. Accepted work may be framed or unframed, mounted or unmounted, matted or unmatted. Must have professional track record and résumé, slides, critical reviews in package (for curatorial review). *Regional connection strongly preferred.*

Submissions Send material by mail with SASE for consideration. Responds in 3 months.

ICEBOX QUALITY FRAMING & GALLERY

1500 Jackson St. NE, Suite 443, Minneapolis MN 55413. (612)788-1790. Fax: (612)788-6947. E-mail: icebox@bitstream.net. Web site: www.iceboxminnesota.com. **Contact:** Howard M. Christopherson, owner. Exhibition, promotion and sales gallery. Estab. 1988. Represents photographers and fine artists in all media, predominantly photography. "A sole proprietorship gallery, Icebox sponsors installations and exhibits in the gallery's 1,700-sq.-ft. space in the Minneapolis Arts District.'' Overall price range $200-1,500. Most work sold at $200-800.

Exhibits Exhibits photos of multicultural, environmental, landscapes/scenics, rural, adventure, travel. Interested in alternative process, documentary, erotic, fine art, historical/vintage. Specifically wants ''fine art photographs from artists with serious, thought-provoking work.''

Making Contact & Terms Charges 50% commission.

Submissions ''Send letter of interest telling why and what you would like to exhibit at Icebox. Include only materials that can be kept at the gallery and updated as needed. Check Web site for more details about entry and gallery history.''

Tips ''We are experienced with the out-of-town artist's needs.''

ILLINOIS STATE MUSEUM CHICAGO GALLERY

100 W. Randolph, Suite 2-100, Chicago IL 60601. (312)814-5322. Fax: (312)814-3471. Web site: www.museum.state.il.us. **Contact:** Kent Smith, director. Assistant Administrator: Jane Stevens. Estab. 1985. Sponsors 2-3 exhibits/year. Average display time 4 months. Sponsors openings; provides refreshments at reception and sends out announcement cards for exhibitions.

Exhibits *Must be an Illinois photographer.* Interested in contemporary and historical/vintage, alternative process, fine art.

Submissions Send résumé, artist's statement, 10 slides, SASE. Responds in 6 months.

▣ INDIANAPOLIS ART CENTER

820 E. 67th St., Indianapolis IN 46220. (317)255-2464. Fax: (317)254-0486. E-mail: exhibs@indplsartcenter.org. Web site: www.indplsartcenter.org. **Contact:** David Kwasigroh, director of exhibitions. Estab. 1934. Sponsors 1-2 photography exhibits/year. Average display time 8 weeks. Overall price range $50-5,000. Most work sold at $500.

Exhibits Interested in alternative process, avant garde, documentary, fine art and ''very contemporary work, preferably unusual processes.'' Prefers artists who live within 250 miles of Indianapolis.

Making Contact & Terms Charges 35% commission. One-person show: $300 honorarium; 2-person show: $200 honorarium; 3-person show: $100 honorarium; plus $0.32/mile travel stipend (one way). Accepted work should be framed (or other finished-presentation formatted).

Submissions Send minimum of 20 digital images with résumé, reviews, artist's statement and SASE between July 1 and December 31. No wildlife or landscape photography. Interesting color and mixed media work is appreciated.

Tips ''We like photography with a very contemporary look that incorporates unusual processes and/or photography with mixed media. Submit excellent images with a full résumé, a recent artist's statement, and reviews of past exhibitions or projects. Please, no glass-mounted slides. Always include a SASE for notification and return of materials, ensuring that correct return postage is on the envelope. Exhibition materials will not be returned. Currently booking 2012.''

▦ INDIVIDUAL ARTISTS OF OKLAHOMA

811 N. Broadway, P.O. Box 60824, Oklahoma OK 73146. (405)232-6060. Fax: (405)232-6061. E-mail: iaogallery@coxinet.net. Web site: www.iaogallery.org. **Contact:** Jeff Stokes,

director. Alternative space. Estab. 1979. Approached by 60 artists/year; represents or exhibits 30 artists. Sponsors 10 photography exhibits/year. Average display time 3-4 weeks. Gallery open Tuesday through Friday from 11 to 4; Saturdays from 1 to 4. Closed August. Gallery is located in downtown art district, 2,300 sq. ft. with 10 ft. ceilings and track lighting. Overall price range $100-2,000. Most work sold at $400.

Exhibits Interested in alternative process, avant garde, documentary, fine art, historical/vintage photography. Other specific subjects/processes: contemporary approach to variety of subjects.

Making Contact & Terms Charges 20% commission. Gallery provides insurance, promotion, contract. Accepted work must be framed.

Submissions Mail portfolio for review with artist's statement, bio, photocopies or slides, résumé, SASE. Reviews quarterly. Finds artists through word of mouth, art exhibits, referrals by other artists.

INTERNATIONAL CENTER OF PHOTOGRAPHY

1133 Avenue of the Americas, New York NY 10036. (212)857-0000. Fax: (212)768-4688. E-mail: exhibitions@icp.org. Web site: www.icp.org. **Contact:** Department of Exhibitions & Collections. Estab. 1974.

Submissions "Due to the volume of work submitted, we are only able to accept portfolios in the form of 35mm slides or CDs. All slides must be labeled on the front with a name, address, and a mark indicating the top of the slide. Slides should also be accompanied by a list of titles and dates. CDs must be labeled with a name and address. Submissions must be limited to 1 page of up to 20 slides or a CD of no more than 20 images. Portfolios of prints or of more than 20 images will not be accepted. Photographers may also wish to include the following information: cover letter, resume or curriculum vitae, artist's statement and/or project description. ICP can only accept portfolio submissions via mail (or FedEx, etc.). Please include a SASE for the return of materials. ICP cannot return portfolios submitted without return postage."

INTERNATIONAL VISIONS GALLERY

2629 Connecticut Ave. NW, Washington DC 20008. (202)234-5112. Fax: (202)234-4206. E-mail: intvisions@aol.com. Web site: www.inter-visions.com. **Contact:** Timothy Davis, owner/director. For-profit gallery. Estab. 1997. Approached by 60 artists/year; represents or exhibits 50 artists. Sponsors 1 photography exhibit/year. Average display time 4-6 weeks. Gallery open Wednesday through Saturday from 11 to 6. Located in the heart of Washington, DC; features 1,000 sq. ft. of exhibition space. Overall price range $1,000-8,000. Most work sold at $2,500.

Exhibits Exhibits photos of babies/children/teens, multicultural.

Making Contact & Terms Artwork is accepted on consignment, and there is a 50% commission. Gallery provides insurance, promotion, contract. Accepted work should be framed. Requires exclusive representation locally.

Submissions Call. Send query letter with artist's statement, bio, photocopies, résumé, SASE. Responds in 2 months. Finds artists through word of mouth, art exhibits, referrals by other artists.

JACKSON FINE ART

3115 E. Shadowlawn Ave., Atlanta GA 30305. (404)233-3739. Fax: (404)233-1205. E-mail: info@jacksonfineart.com. Web site: www.jacksonfineart.com. **Contact:** Malia Stewart, as-

sociate director. Estab. 1990. Exhibitions are rotated every 6 weeks. Gallery open Tuesday through Saturday from 10 to 5. Overall price range $600-500,000. Most work sold at $5,000.
Exhibits Interested in innovative photography, avant garde, fine art.
Making Contact & Terms Only buys vintage photos outright. Requires exclusive representation locally. Exhibits only nationally known artists and emerging artists who show long term potential. ''Photographers must be established, preferably published in books or national art publications. They must also have a strong biography, preferably museum exhibitions, national grants.''
Submissions Send JPEG files via e-mail, or CD-ROM by mail with SASE for return. Responds in 3 months, only if interested. Unsolicited original work is not accepted.

Ⓝ ELAINE L. JACOB GALLERY AND COMMUNITY ARTS GALLERY

150 Community Arts Building, Detroit MI 48202. (313)577-2423. Fax: (313)577-8935. E-mail: s.dupret@wayne.edu. Web site: www.art.wayne.edu. **Contact:** Sandra Dupret, curator of exhibitions. Nonprofit university gallery. Estab. 1995. Approached by 30 artists/year; exhibits solo and group shows. Sponsors 1-2 photography exhibits/year. Average display time 1 month. Galleries open Tuesday through Thursday from 10 to 6; Friday from 10 to 7. Closed Mondays, Sundays, Thanksgiving weekend and Christmas. Community Arts Gallery: 3,000 sq. ft.; Elaine L. Jacob Gallery, level 1: 2,000 sq. ft., level 2: 1,600 sq. ft.
Exhibits Interested in fine art. ''The Elaine L. Jacob Gallery and the Community Arts Gallery are university galleries, displaying art appropriate for an academic environment.''
Making Contact & Terms Gallery provides insurance, promotion. Accepted work should be framed.
Submissions Send query letter with artist's statement, bio, résumé, SASE, slides, exhibition proposal, video, slide list. Responds in 3 months. Finds artists through word of mouth, portfolio reviews, art exhibits, referrals by other artists.

Ⓝ JADITE GALLERIES

413 W. 50th St., New York NY 10019. (212)315-2740. Fax: (212)315-2793. E-mail: jaditeart @aol.com. Web site: www.jadite.com. **Contact:** Roland Sainz, director. Estab. 1985. Sponsors 1-2 exhibits/year. Average display time 1 month. Open Monday through Saturday from 12 to 6. Overall price range $300-2,000. Most work sold at $500.
Exhibits Exhibits photos of landscapes/scenics, architecture, cities/urban, travel. Interested in avant garde, documentary and b&w, color and mixed media.
Making Contact & Terms Gallery receives 40% commission. There is a rental fee for space (50/50 split of expenses such as invitations, advertising, opening reception, etc.). Accepted work should be framed.
Submissions Arrange a personal interview to show portfolio. Responds in 5 weeks.

Ⓝ ▣ JAMESON GALLERY & FRAME AND THE JAMESON ESTATE COLLECTION

305 Commercial St., Portland ME 04101. (207)772-5522. Fax: (207)774-7648. E-mail: art@ja mesongallery.com. Web site: www.jamesongallery.com. **Contact:** Martha Gilmartin, gallery director. Retail gallery, custom framing, restoration, appraisals, consultation. Estab. 1992. Represents 20+ artists/year. Mounts 6 shows/year. Average display time 3-4 weeks. Open all year; Monday through Saturday from 10 to 6, and by appointment. Located on the waterfront in the heart of the shopping district; 4,000 sq. ft.; 50% of space for contemporary artists, 25% for frame shop, 25% for The Jameson Estate Collection dealing later 19th-

and 20th-century paintings, drawings and photographs. Most work sold at $1,500 and up.
Exhibits B&W photography.

Terms Gallery provides insurance, promotion and contract; artist pays shipping costs. Prefers artwork unframed, but will judge on a case-by-case basis. Artist may buy framing contract with gallery.

Submissions Send CV and artist's statement, a sampling of images on a PC-compatible CD or Zip, and SASE if you would like the materials returned. "We will not open unsolicited e-mail attachments. We do view photographers' Web sites."

🖼 🖵 JHB GALLERY

26 Grove St., Suite 4C, New York NY 10014-5329. (212)255-9286. Fax: (212)229-8998. E-mail: info@jhbgallery.com. Web site: www.jhbgallery.com. Private art dealer and consultant. Estab. 1982. Gallery open by appointment only. Overall price range $1,000-20,000. Most work sold at $2,500-5,000.

Making Contact & Terms Artwork is accepted on consignment, and there is a 50% commission. Gallery provides promotion.

Submissions "We accept submissions via Internet." Send query letter with résumé, CD, slides, artist's statment, reviews, SASE. Finds artists through submissions, portfolio reviews, art exhibits, art fairs, referrals by other curators.

STELLA JONES GALLERY

Bank One Center, 201 St. Charles, New Orleans LA 70170. (504)568-9050. Fax: (504)568-0840. E-mail: jones6941@aol.com. Web site: www.stellajones.com. **Contact:** Stella Jones. For-profit gallery. Estab. 1996. Approached by 40 artists/year; represents or exhibits 45 artists. Sponsors 1 photography exhibit/year. Average display time 6-8 weeks. Gallery open Monday through Friday from 11 to 6; Saturday from 12 to 5. Located on 1st floor of corporate 53-story office building downtown, 1 block from French Quarter. Overall price range $500-150,000. Most work sold at $5,000.

Exhibits Exhibits photos of babies/children/teens, multicultural, families, cities/urban, education, religious, rural.

Making Contact & Terms Artwork is accepted on consignment, and there is a 50% commission. Gallery provides insurance, promotion, contract. Accepted work should be framed. Requires exclusive representation locally.

Submissions Call to show portfolio of photographs, slides, transparencies. Mail portfolio for review. Send query letter with artist's statement, bio, brochure, business card, photocopies, photographs, résumé, reviews, slides, SASE. Responds in 1 month. Finds artists through word of mouth, submissions, portfolio reviews, art exhibits, referrals by other artists.

Tips "Photographers should be organized with good visuals."

KEARON-HEMPENSTALL GALLERY

536 Bergen Ave., Jersey City NJ 07304. (201)333-8855. Fax: (201)333-8488. E-mail: suzann @khgallery.com. Web site: www.khgallery.com. **Contact:** Suzann McKiernan Anderson, director. Estab. 1980. Sponsors 1 exhibit/year. Average display time 1 month. Overall price range $150-400.

Exhibits Interested in color and b&w prints.

Making Contact & Terms Charges 50% commission. Reviews transparencies. Accepted work should be mounted, matted work only. Requires exclusive representation locally.

Send material by mail for consideration. Include SASE, résumé, exhibition listing, artist's statement and price of sold work. Responds in 1 month.

Tips "Be professional: have a full portfolio; be energetic and willing to assist with sales of your work."

⊠ ▣ KENT STATE UNIVERSITY SCHOOL OF ART GALLERIES

KSU, 201 Art Building, Kent OH 44242. (330)672-7853. Fax: (330)672- 4279. E-mail: haturne r@kent.edu. Web site: www.kent.edu/art. **Contact:** Anderson Turner, director of galleries. Sponsors at least 6 photography exhibit s/year. Average display time 4 weeks.

Exhibits Interested in all types, styles and subject matter of photography. Photographer must present quality work.

Making Contact & Terms Photography can be sold in gallery. Charges 40% commission. Buys photography outright.

Submissions Will review transparencies. Write a proposal and send with slides/CD. Send material by mail for consideration ; include SASE. Responds "usually in 4 months, but it depends on time submitted."

▣ KIRCHMAN GALLERY

P.O. Box 115, 213 N. Nuget St., Johnson City TX 78636. 830-868-9290. E-mail: susan@kirch mangallery.com. Web site: www.kirchmangallery.com. **Contact**: Susan Kirchman, owner/ director. Art consultancy and for-profit gallery. Estab. 2005. Represents or exhibits 25 artists. Average display time 1 month. Sponsors 4 photography exhibits/year. Open Wednesday through Sunday from 11 to 6; any time by appointment. Located across from Johnson City's historic Courthouse Square in the heart of Texas hill country. Overall price range $250-25,000. Most work sold at $500-1,000.

Exhibits Exhibits photos of landscapes/scenics. Interested in alternative process, avant garde, fine art.

Making Contact & Terms Artwork is accepted on consignment, and there is a 50% commision.

Submissions "Send 20 digital-format examples of your work, along with a resume and artist's statement."

▣ ROBERT KLEIN GALLERY

38 Newbury St., Boston MA 02116. (617)267-7997. Fax: (617)267-5567. E-mail: inquiry@ro bertkleingallery.com. Web site: www.robertkleingallery.com. **Contact:** Robert L. Klein, owner or Eunice Hurd, director. Estab. 1978. Sponsors 10 exhibits/year. Average display time 5 weeks. Overall price range $1,000-200,000.

Exhibits Interested in fashion, documentary, nudes, portraiture, and work that has been fabricated to be photographs.

Making Contact & Terms Charges 50% commission. Buys photos outright. Accepted work should be unframed, unmmatted, unmounted. Requires exclusive representation locally. Must be established a minimum of 5 years; preferably published.

Submissions "Send materials by e-mail or mail with SASE for consideration."

ROBERT KOCH GALLERY

49 Geary St., San Francisco CA 94108. (415)421-0122. Fax: (415)421-6306. E-mail: info@ko chgallery.com. Web site: www.kochgallery.com. For-profit gallery. Estab. 1979. Sponsors 6-

8 photography exhibits/year. Average display time 2 months. Gallery open Tuesday through Saturday from 10:30 to 5:30.

Making Contact & Terms Artwork is accepted on consignment. Gallery provides insurance, promotion, contract. Requires West Coast or national representation.

Submissions Finds artists through publicatons, art exhibits, art fairs, referrals by other artists and curators, collectors, critics.

N ☐ PAUL KOPEIKIN GALLERY

6150 Wilshire Blvd., Los Angeles CA 90048. (323)937-0765. Fax: (323)937-5974. E-mail: info@PaulKopeikinGallery.com. Web site: www.PaulKopeikinGallery.com. Estab. 1990. Sponsors 7-9 exhibits/year. Average display time 4-6 weeks.

Exhibits No restrictions on type, style or subject. "Multimedia also considered."

Making Contact & Terms Charges 50% commission. Requires exclusive West Coast representation. "Must be highly professional. Quality and unique point of view also important."

Submissions Submit CDs or digital prints and support material; include SASE.

Tips "Don't waste people's time by showing work before you're ready to do so."

MARGEAUX KURTIE MODERN ART AT THE ART HOTEL

39 Yerba Buena, P.O. Box 39, Cerrillos NM 87010. (505)473-2250. E-mail: mkmamadrid@att.net. Web site: www.mkmamadrid.com. **Contact:** Jill Alikas, director. For-profit gallery and art consultancy. Estab. 1996. Approached by 200 artists/year; represents or exhibits 13 artists. Sponsors 2 photography exhibits/year. Average display time 5 weeks. Gallery open Thursday through Tuesday from 11 to 5. Closed February. Located within a historic frontier village 35 miles outside of Santa Fe, 1,020 sq. ft. Overall price range $350-15,000. Most work sold at $2,800.

Exhibits Interested in avant garde, erotic, fine art.

Making Contact & Terms Artwork is accepted on consignment, and there is a 50% commission. Requires exclusive representation locally.

Submissions Website lists criteria for review process. Mail portfolio for review. Send query letter with artist's statement, bio, résumé, reviews, SASE, slides, $25 review fee (check payable to gallery). Finds artists through art fairs, art exhibits, portfolio reviews, referrals by other artists, submissions, word of mouth.

N ☐ THE ERIK LAURITZEN GALLERY

Truckee Meadows Community College, 7000 Dandini Blvd., Reno NV 89512. (775)674-7698. Fax: (775)674-4853. E-mail: npreece@tmcc.edu. Web site: www.artgalleries.tmcc.edu. **Contact:** Nolan Preece, curator. Estab. 1990.

Exhibits Interested in all styles, subject matter, techniques—traditional, innovative and/or cutting edge.

Submissions "Call first! Submissions for national show are due by September 1, 2008. Send a powerpoint presentation with bio or résumé and statement to be reviewed by selection committee."

Tips "Images submitted should be sharp, accurate color and clearly labeled with name, title, dimensions, medium—the clearer the résumé or bio the better. Statements optional."

N ⊘ ELIZABETH LEACH GALLERY

417 NW Ninth Ave., Portland OR 97209-3308. (503)224-0521. Fax: (503)224-0844. E-mail: art@elizabethleach.com. Web site: www.elizabethleach.com. **Contact:** Daniel Peabody,

Galleries

director. Sponsors 3-4 exhibits/year. Average display time 1 month. "The gallery has extended hours every first Thursday of the month for our openings." Overall price range $300-5,000.

Exhibits Photographers must meet museum conservation standards. Interested in "high-quality concept and fine craftmanship."

Making Contact & Terms Charges 50% commission. Accepted work should be framed or unframed, matted. Requires exclusive representation locally.

Submissions Not accepting submissions at this time.

N LEEPA-RATTNER MUSEUM OF ART

P.O. Box 1545, 600 Klosterman Rd., Tarpon Springs FL 34688. (727)712-5762. Fax: (727)712-5223. E-mail: LRMA@spcollege.edu. Web site: www.spcollege.edu/museum. **Contact:** Lynn Whitelow, director. Museum. Estab. 2002. Open Tuesday through Saturday from 10 to 5; Thursday from 1 to 9; Sunday from 1 to 5. Located on the Tarpon Springs campus of St. Petersburg College.

Exhibits Exhibits photos of babies/children/teens, celebrities, couples, multicultural, families, parents, senior citizens, architecture, cities/urban, education, gardening, interiors/decorating, pets, religious, rural, agriculture, business concepts, industry, medicine, military, political, product shots/still life, science, technology/computers, disasters, environmental, landscapes/scenics, wildlife, adventure, automobiles, entertainment, events, food/drink , health/fitness/beauty, hobbies, humor, performing arts, sports, travel. Interested in alternative process, avant garde, documentary, erotic, fashion/glamour, fine art, historical/vintage, seasonal.

▣ LEHIGH UNIVERSITY ART GALLERIES

420 E. Packer Ave., Bethlehem PA 18015. (610)758-3619. Fax: (610)758-4580. E-mail: rv02@lehigh.edu. Web site: www.luag.org. **Contact:** Ricardo Viera, director/curator. Sponsors 5-8 exhibits/year. Average display time 6-12 weeks. Sponsors openings.

Exhibits Exhibits fine art/multicultural, Latin American. Interested in all types of works. The photographer should "preferably be an established professional."

Making Contact & Terms Reviews transparencies. Arrange a personal interview to show portfolio. Send query letter with SASE. Responds in 1 month.

Tips "Don't send more than 10 (top) slides, or CD."

N DAVID LEONARDIS GALLERY

1346 N. Paulina St., Chicago IL 60622. (773)278-3058. E-mail: david@dlg-gallery.com. Web site: www.dlg-gallery.com. **Contact:** David Leonardis, owner. For-profit gallery. Estab. 1992. Approached by 100 artists/year; represents or exhibits 12 artists. Average display time 30 days. Gallery open Tuesday through Saturday from 12 to 7; Sunday from 12 to 6. "One big room, four big walls." Overall price range $50-5,000. Most work sold at $500.

Exhibits Exhibits photos of celebrities. Interested in fine art.

Making Contact & Terms Artwork is accepted on consignment, and there is a 50% commission. Gallery provides promotion. Accepted work should be framed.

Submissions E-mail to arrange a personal interview to show portfolio. Mail portfolio for review. Send query letter via e-mail. Responds only if interested. Finds artists through word of mouth, art exhibits, referrals by other artists.

Tips "Artists should be professional and easy to deal with."

▣ LEOPOLD GALLERY

324 W. 63rd St., Kansas City KS 64113. E-mail: email@leopoldgallery.com. Web site: www.l eopoldgallery.com. **Contact:** Robin Elliott, assistant director. For-profit gallery. Estab. 1991. Approached by 100+ artists/year; represents or exhibits 50 artists/year. Sponsors 1 photography exhibit/year. Average display time 3 weeks. Open Sunday through Saturday from 10 to 6; weekends from 10 to 5. Closed holidays. "We are located in Brookside, a charming retail district built in 1920 with more than 70 shops, restaurants and offices. The gallery has two levels of exhibition space, with the upper level dedicated to artist openings/exhibitions." Overall price range $50-25,000. Most work sold at $1,000.

Exhibits Exhibits photos of architecture, cities/urban, rural, environmental, landscapes/scenics, wildlife, entertainment, performing arts. Interested in alternative process, avant garde, documentary, fine art.

Making Contact & Terms Artwork is accepted on consignment; there is a 50% commission. Gallery provides insurance, promotion, contract. Accepted work should be framed, mounted, matted. **Accepts artists from Kansas City area only.**

Submissions E-mail query letter with link to artist's Web site, JPEG samples at 72 dpi. Send query letter with artist's statement, bio, brochure, business card, résumé, reviews, SASE, disc with images. Responds in 2 weeks. Finds artists through word of mouth, art exhibitions, submissions, art fairs, portfolio reviews, referrals by other artists.

LIMITED EDITIONS & COLLECTIBLES

697 Haddon, Collingswood NJ 08108. (856)869-5228. E-mail: jdl697ltd@juno.com. Web site: www.ltdeditions.net. **Contact:** John Daniel Lynch, Sr., owner. For-profit online gallery. Estab. 1997. Approached by 24 artists/year; represents or exhibits 70 artists. Sponsors 20 photography exhibits/year. Overall price range $100-3,000. Most work sold at $450.

Exhibits Exhibits photos of landscapes/scenics, wildlife, adventure, automobiles, entertainment, events, food/drink, health/fitness/beauty, hobbies, humor, performing arts, sports, travel. Interested in alternative process, documentary, erotic, fashion/glamour, historical/vintage, seasonal.

Making Contact & Terms Artwork is accepted on consignment, and there is a 30% commission. Gallery provides insurance, promotion, contract.

Submissions Call or write to show portfolio. Send query letter with bio, business card, résumé. Responds in 1 month. Finds artists through word of mouth, portfolio reviews, art exhibits, referrals by other artists.

▨ LIMNER GALLERY

123 Warren St., Hudson NY 12534. (518)828-2343. E-mail: thelimner@aol.com. Web site: www.slowart.com. **Contact:** Trevor Pryce, director. Alternative space. Estab. 1987. Approached by 200-250 artists/year; represents or exhibits 90-100 artists. Sponsors 2 photography exhibits/year. Average display time 4 weeks. Open Wednesday through Sunday from 11 to 5. Closed January, July-August (weekends only). Located in the art and antiques center of the Hudson Valley. Exhibition space is 1,000 sq. ft.

Exhibits Interested in alternative process, avant garde, documentary, erotic, fine art, historical/vintage.

Submissions Artists should e-mail a link to their Web site; or download exhibition application at http://www.slowart.com/prospectus; or send query letter with artist's statement, bio, brochure or photographs/slides, SASE. Finds artists through submissions.

Tips "Artist's Web site should be simple and easy to view. Complicated animations and scripted design should be avoided, as it is a distraction and prevents direct viewing of the work. Not all galleries and art buyers have cable modems. The Web site should either work on a telephone line connection or two versions of the site should be offered—one for telephone, one for cable/high-speed Internet access."

LA ART ASSOCIATION/GALLERY 825

825 N. La Cienega Blvd., Los Angeles CA 90069. (310)652-8272. Fax: (310)652-9251. E-mail: gallery825@laaa.org. Web site: www.laaa.org. **Contact:** Peter Mays, executive director. Artistic Director: Sinead Finnerty-Pyne. Estab. 1925. Sponsors 16 exhibits/year. Average display time 4-5 weeks. Sponsors openings. Overall price range $200-5,000. Most work sold at $600.

Exhibits Considers all media and original handpulled prints. Fine art only. No crafts. Most frequently exhibits mixed media, oil/acrylic, and watercolor. Exhibits all styles.

Making Contact & Terms Retail price set by artist. Gallery provides promotion.

Submissions Submit 2 pieces during biannual screening date. Responds immediately following screening. Call for screening dates.

Tips "Bring work produced in the last three years. No commercial work (i.e. portraits or advertisements)."

N THE LOWE GALLERY

2034 Broadway, Santa Monica CA 90404. (310)449-0184. Fax:(310)449-00194. E-mail: info @lowegallery.com. Web site: www.lowegallery.com. **Contact:** Laura Clemons, director. For-profit gallery. Approached by 300 artists/year; represents or exhibits approximately 67 artists. Average display time 4-6 weeks. Open Tuesday through Friday from 10 to 5:30; Saturday from 11 to 5:30. Closed Sunday and Monday. Exhibition space is 6,000 sq. ft. with great architectural details, such as 22-ft.-high ceilings. Exhibition spaces range from monumental to intimate.

Exhibits Exhibits photos of babies/children/teens, multicultural. Interested in alternative process, mixed media.

Making Contact & Terms Artwork is accepted on consignment, and there is a 50% commission. Requires exclusive representation locally.

Submissions Send query letter with artists's statement, bio, photographs, résumé, reviews, SASE. Finds artists through word of mouth, art exhibits, submissions, art fairs, portfolio reviews, referrals by other artists, .

Tips "Look at the type of work that the gallery already represents, and make sure your work is an aesthetic fit first! Send lots of great images with dimensions and pricing."

N MACNIDER ART MUSEUM

303 Second St. SE, Mason City IA 50401. (641)421-3666. Fax: (641)422-9612. E-mail: blanchard@macniderart.org. Web site: www.macniderart.org. Nonprofit gallery. Estab. 1966. Represents or exhibits 1-10 artists. Sponsors 2-5 photography exhibits/year (1 is competitive for the county). Average display time 2 months. Gallery open Tuesday and Thursday from 9 to 9; Wednesday, Friday, Saturday from 9 to 5; Sunday from 1 to 5. Closed Monday. Overall price range $50-2,500. Most work sold at $200.

Making Contact & Terms Artwork is accepted on consignment, and there is a 40% commission. Gallery provides insurance, promotion, contract. Accepted work should be framed.

Submissions Mail portfolio for review. Responds within 3 months, only if interested. Finds artists through word of mouth, submissions, portfolio reviews, art exhibits, art fairs, referrals by other artists. Exhibition opportunities: exhibition in galleries, presence in museum shop on consignment or booth at Festival Art Market in June.

ⓝ ▣ MAIN AND THIRD FLOOR GALLERIES
Northern Kentucky University, Nunn Dr., Highland Heights KY 41099. (859)572-5148. Fax: (859)572-6501. E-mail: knight@nku.edu. Web site: www.nku.edu/~art/galleries.html. **Contact:** David J. Knight, director of collections and exhibitions. Estab. 1970. Approached by 30 artists/year; represents or exhibits 5-6 artists. Average display time 1 month. Gallery open Monday through Friday from 9 to 9; weekends by appointment. Closed between fall and spring semesters, university holidays. Main Gallery is 2,500 sq. ft.; Third Floor Gallery is 600 sq. ft. Overall price range $25-3,000. Most work sold at $500.
Making Contact & Terms Gallery provides insurance, promotion, contract. Accepted work should be framed, mounted, matted.
Submissions Mail portfolio for review. Send query letter with artist's statement, résumé, reviews, SASE, slides, CD or JPEGs. Responds in 3 months. Finds artists through word of mouth, submissions, art exhibits, referrals by other artists.
Tips "Submission guidelines, current exhibitions and complete information is available on our Web site."

▣ THE MAIN STREET GALLERY
105 Main St., P.O. Box 161, Groton NY 13073. (607)898-9010. Web site: www.mainstreetgal .com. **Contact:** Adrienne Bea Smith, director. For-profit gallery and art consultancy. Estab. 2003. Exhibits 15 artists. Sponsors 1 photography exhibit/year. Average display time 5-6 weeks. Open Thursday through Saturday from 12 to 6; Sunday from 1 to 5. Closed January and February. Located in the village of Groton in the Finger Lakes Region of New York, 20 minutes from Ithaca; 900 sq. ft. Overall price range: $120-5,000.
Exhibits Interested in fine art.
Terms Artwork is accepted on consignment, and there is a 40% commission. Gallery provides insurance, promotion and contract. Accepted work should be framed, mounted and matted. Requires exclusive representation locally.
Submissions Write to arrange a personal interview to show portfolio of photographs, slides. Send query letter with artist's statement, bio, brochure, photographs, résumé, reviews, slides/CD images, SASE. Responds to queries in 1 month, only if interested. Finds artists through art exhibits, portfolio reviews, referrals by other artists, submissions, word of mouth.
Tips After submitting materials, the artist will set an appointment to talk over work. Artists should send in up-to-date résumé and artist's statement.

MARKEIM ART CENTER
Lincoln Avenue and Walnut Street, Haddonfield NJ 08033. (856)429-8585. Fax: (856)429-8585. E-mail: markeim@verizon.net. Web site: www.markeimartcenter.org. **Contact:** Elizabeth Madden, executive director. Estab. 1956. Sponsors 10-11 exhibits/year. Average display time 4 weeks. "The exhibiting artist is responsible for all details of the opening." Overall price range $75-1,000. Most work sold at $350.
Exhibits Interested in all types work. Exhibits photos of babies/children/teens, celebrities,

couples, multicultural, families, parents, senior citizens, environmental, landscapes/scenics, wildlife, architecture, cities/urban, education, rural, adventure, automobiles, entertainment, performing arts, sports, travel, agriculture, product shots/still life. Interested in alternative process, avant garde, documentary, fine art, historical/vintage, seasonal.

Making Contact & Terms Charges 30% commission. Accepted work should be framed, mounted or unmounted, matted or unmatted. "Artists from New Jersey and Delaware Valley region are preferred. Work must be professional and high quality."

Submissions Send slides by mail for consideration. Include SASE, résumé and letter of intent. Responds in 1 month.

Tips "Be patient and flexible with scheduling. Look not only for one-time shows, but for opportunities to develop working relationships with a gallery. Establish yourself locally and market yourself outward."

Ｎ MARLBORO GALLERY

Prince George's Community College, 301 Largo Rd., Largo MD 20772-2199. (301)322-0965. Fax: (301)808-0418. E-mail: tberault@pgcc.edu. Web site: www.pgcc.edu. **Contact:** Tom Berault, gallery curator. Estab. 1976. Average display time 1 month. Overall price range $50-2,000. Most work sold at $75-350.

Exhibits Exhibits photos of celebrities, landscapes/scenics, wildlife, adventure, entertainment, events, travel. Interested in alternative process, avant garde, fine art. Not interested in commercial work.

Making Contact & Terms "We do not take commission on artwork sold." Accepted work must be framed.

Submissions "We are looking for fine art photos; we need 10-20 to make assessment. Reviews are done every 6 months. We prefer to receive submissions February through April." Send query letter with résumé, slides, photographs, artist statement, bio and SASE. Responds in 1 month.

Tips "Send examples of what you wish to display, and explanations if photos do not meet normal standards (i.e., in focus, experimental subject matter)."

THE MAYANS GALLERY LTD.

601 Canyon Rd., Santa Fe NM 87501. (505)983-8068. E-mail: arte2@aol.com. Web site: www.artnet.com/mayans.html. **Contact:** Ernesto Mayans, director. Estab. 1977. Publishes books, catalogs and portfolios. Overall price range $200-5,000. "We exhibit Photogravures by Unai San Martin; Pigment prints by Pablo Mayans, Silver Gelatin prints by Richard Faller (Vintage Southwest Works) and Johanna Saretzki and Sean McGann (Nudes)."

Making Contact & Terms Charges 50% commission. Consigns. Requires exclusive representation within area.

Submissions Size limited to 16x20 maximum. Arrange a personal interview to show portfolio. Send query by mail with SASE for consideration. Responds in 2 weeks.

Tips "Please call before submitting."

Ｎ MCDONOUGH MUSEUM OF ART

Youngstown State University, 525 Wick Ave., Youngstown OH 44555-1400. (330)941-1400. E-mail: labrothers@ysu.edu. Web site: http://mcdonoughmuseum.ysu.edu/. **Contact:** Leslie Brothers, director. A center for contemporary art, education and community. The museum supports student and faculty work through exhibitions, collaborations, courses and ongoing discussion. Estab. 1991.

Submissions Send exhibition proposal.

⚏ MESA CONTEMPORARY ARTS AT MESA ARTS CENTER

P.O. Box 1466, Mesa AZ 85211-1466. (480)644-6560. Fax: (480)644-6576. E-mail: artscenter info@mesaartscenter.com. Web site: www.mesaartscenter.com. **Contact:** Patty Haberman, curator. Not-for-profit art space. Estab. 1980.

Exhibits Exhibits photos of babies/children/teens, celebrities, couples, multicultural, families, parents, senior citizens, disasters, environmental, landscapes/scenics, wildlife, architecture, cities/urban, interiors/decorating, rural, adventure, automobiles, entertainment, events, performing arts, travel, industry, political, science, technology/computers. Interested in alternative process, avant garde, documentary, fine art, historical/vintage, seasonal, and contemporary photography.

Making Contact & Terms Charges $25 entry fee, 25% commission.

Submissions "Please view our online prospectus for further info, or contact Patty Haberman at (480)644-6561."

Tips "We do invitational or national juried exhibits. Submit professional-quality slides."

⚏ ⊘ R. MICHELSON GALLERIES

132 Main St., Northampton MA 01060. (413)586-3964. Fax: (413)587-9811. E-mail: RM@R Michelson.com. Web site: www.RMichelson.com. **Contact:** Richard Michelson, owner and president. Estab. 1976. Sponsors 1 exhibit/year. Average display time 6 weeks. Sponsors openings. Overall price range $1,200-5,000.

Exhibits Interested in contemporary, landscape and/or figure work.

Making Contact & Terms Sometimes buys photos outright. Accepted work can be framed or unframed, mounted or unmounted, matted or unmatted. Requires exclusive representation locally. Not taking on new photographers at this time.

MILL BROOK GALLERY & SCULPTURE GARDEN

236 Hopkinton Rd., Concord NH 03301. (603)226-2046. E-mail: artsculpt@mindspring.com. Web site: www.themillbrookgallery.com. For-profit gallery. Estab. 1996. Exhibits 70 artists. Sponsors 1 photography exhibit/year. Average display time 6 weeks. Gallery open Tuesday through Saturday from 11 to 5 , April 1 to December 24 ; open by appointment December 25 to March 31. Outdoor juried sculpture exhibit. Three rooms inside for exhibitions, 1,800 sq. ft. Overall price range $8-30,000. Most work sold at $500-1,000.

Making Contact & Terms Artwork is accepted on consignment , and there is a 50% commission. Gallery provides insurance, promotion, contract. Accepted work should be framed, matted.

Submissions Write to arrange a personal interview to show portfolio of photographs, slides. Send query letter with artist's statement, bio, photocopies, photographs, résumé, slides, SASE. Responds within 1 month, only if interested. Finds artists through word of mouth, submissions, art exhibits, referrals by other artists.

⚏ PETER MILLER GALLERY

118 N. Peoria St., Chicago IL 60607. (312)951-1700. Fax: (312)226-5441. E-mail: director@p etermillergallery.com. Web site: www.petermillergallery.com. **Contact:** Peter Miller and

Galleries

Natalie R. Domchenko, directors. Estab. 1979. Gallery is 3,500 sq. ft. with 12-foot ceilings. Overall price range $1,000-40,000. Most work sold at $5,000.

Exhibits Painting, sculpture, photography and new media.

Making Contact & Terms Charges 50% commission. Accepted work can be framed or unframed, mounted or unmounted, matted or unmatted. Requires exclusive representation locally.

Submissions Send 20 slides of your most recent work with SASE. Responds in 2 weeks.

Tips ''We look for work we haven't seen before; i.e., new images and new approaches to the medium.''

N MOBILE MUSEUM OF ART

4850 Museum Dr., Mobile AL 36608. (251)208-5200. Fax: (251)208-5201. Web site: www.m obilemuseumofart.com. **Contact:** Tommy McPherson, director. Estab. 1964. Sponsors 4 exhibits/year. Average display time 3 months. Sponsors openings; provides light hors d'oeuvres and wine.

Exhibits Open to all types and styles.

Making Contact & Terms Photography sold in gallery. Charges 20% commission. Occasionally buys photos outright. Accepted work should be framed.

Submissions Arrange a personal interview to show portfolio; send material by mail for consideration. Returns material when SASE is provided ''unless photographer specifically points out that it's not required.''

Tips ''We look for personal point of view beyond technical mastery.''

N MONTEREY MUSEUM OF ART

559 Pacific St., Monterey CA 93940. (831)372-5477. Fax: (831)372-5680. E-mail: info@mont ereyart.org. Web site: www.montereyart.org. **Contact:** E. Michael Whittington, executive director. Estab. 1969. Sponsors 3-4 exhibits/year. Average display time approximately 10 weeks. Open Wednesday through Saturday from 11 to 5; Sunday from 1 to 4.

• 2nd location: 720 Via Miranda, Monterey CA 93940; (831)372-3689.

Exhibits Interested in all subjects.

Making Contact & Terms Accepted work should be framed.

Submissions Send slides by mail for consideration; include SASE. Responds in 1 month.

Tips ''Send 20 slides and résumé at any time to the attention of the museum curator.''

MULTIPLE EXPOSURES GALLERY

105 N. Union St., #312, Alexandria VA 22314-3217. (703)683-2205. E-mail: multipleexposur esgallery@verizon.net. Web site: http://www.multipleexposuresgallery.com/. **Contact:** Alan Sislen, president. Cooperative gallery. Estab. 1986. Represents or exhibits 14 artists. Sponsors 12 photography exhibits/year. Average display time 1 month. Open daily from 11 to 5. Closed on 5 major holidays throughout the year. Located in Torpedo Factory Art Center; 10-ft. walls with about 40 ft. of running wall space; 1 bin for each artist's matted photos, up to 20×24 in size with space for 25 pieces.

Exhibits Exhibits photos of landscapes/scenics, architecture, beauty, cities/urban, religious, rural, adventure, automobiles, events, travel, buildings. Interested in alternative process, documentary, fine art. Other specific subjects/processes: ''We have on display roughly 300 images that run the gamut from platinum and older alternative processes through digital capture and output.''

Making Contact & Terms There is a co-op membership fee, a time requirement, a rental fee and a 15% commission. Accepted work should be matted. *Accepts only artists from Washington, DC, region.* Accepts only photography. "Membership is by jury of active current members. Membership is limited to 14. Jurying for membership is only done when a space becomes available; on average, 1 member is brought in about every 2 years."

Submissions Send query letter with SASE to arrange a personal interview to show portfolio of photographs, slides. Responds in 2 months. Finds artists through word of mouth, referrals by other artists, ads in local art/photography publications.

Tips "Have a unified portfolio of images mounted and matted to archival standards."

MUSEO DE ARTE DE PONCE

P.O. Box 9027, Ponce PR 00732-9027. (787)840-1510. Fax: (787)841-7309. E-mail: map@m useoarteponce.org. Web site: www.museoarteponce.org. **Contact**: curatorial department. Museum. Estab. 1961. Approached by 50 artists/year; mounts 3 exhibitions/year. Gallery open Monday through Sunday from 10 to 5. Closed New Year's Day, January 6, Good Friday, Thanksgiving and Christmas day.

Exhibits Interested in avant garde, fine art.

Submissions Send query letter with artist's statement, résumé, images, reviews, publications. Responds in 3 months. Finds artists through research, art exhibits, studio and gallery visits, word of mouth, referrals by other artists.

MUSEO ITALOAMERICANO

Fort Mason Center, Bldg. C, San Francisco CA 94123. (415)673-2200. Fax: (415)673-2292. E-mail: sfmuseo@sbcglobal.net. Web site: www.museoitaloamericano.org. **Contact:** Susan Filippo, administrator. Museum. Estab. 1978. Approached by 80 artists/year; exhibits 15 artists. Sponsors 1 photography exhibit/year (depending on the year). Average display time 2-3 months. Gallery open Tuesday through Sunday from 12 to 4; Monday by appointment. Closed major holidays. Gallery is located in the San Francisco Marina District, with a beautiful view of the Golden Gate Bridge, Sausalito, Tiburon and Alcatraz; 3,500 sq. ft. of exhibition space.

Exhibits Exhibits photos of babies/children/teens, celebrities, couples, multicultural, families, parents, senior citizens, environmental, landscapes/scenics, architecture, cities/urban, education, religious, rural, entertainment, events, food/drink, hobbies, humor, performing arts, sports, travel, product shots/still life. Interested in alternative process, avant garde, documentary, fine art, historical/vintage.

Making Contact & Terms "The museum rarely sells pieces. If it does, it takes 20% of the sale." Museum provides insurance, promotion. Accepted work should be framed, mounted, matted. *Accepts only Italian or Italian-American artists.*

Submissions Call or write to arrange a personal interview to show portfolio of photographs, slides, catalogs. Send query letter with artist's statement, bio, brochure, photographs, résumé, reviews, slides, SASE. Responds in 2 months. Finds artists through word of mouth, submissions.

Tips "Photographers should have good, quality reproduction of their work with slides, and clarity in writing their statements and résumés. Be concise."

▣ MUSEUM OF CONTEMPORARY PHOTOGRAPHY, COLUMBIA COLLEGE CHICAGO

600 S. Michigan Ave., Chicago IL 60605-1996. (312)663-5554. Fax: (312)344-8067. E-mail: mocp@colum.edu. Web site: www.mocp.org. **Contact:** Rod Slemmons, director or Natasha

Egan, associate director: Estab. 1984. "We offer our audience a wide range of provocative exhibitions in recognition of photography's roles within the expanded field of imagemaking." Sponsors 6 main exhibits and 4-6 smaller exhibits/year. Average display time 2 months.

Exhibits Exhibits photos of babies/children/teens, celebrities, couples, multicultural, families, parents, senior citizens, environmental, landscapes/scenics, architecture, cities/urban, rural, humor, performing arts, agriculture, medicine, political, science, technology/computers. Interested in alternative process, avant garde, documentary, fashion/glamour, fine art, photojournalism, commercial, technical/scientific, video. "All high-quality work considered."

Submissions Reviews portfolios, transparencies, images on CD. Interested in reviewing unframed work only, matted or unmatted. Submit portfolio for review; inlcude SASE. Responds in 2-3 months. No critical review offered.

Tips "Professional standards apply; only very high-quality work considered."

▣ MUSEUM OF PHOTOGRAPHIC ARTS

1649 El Prado, Balboa Park, San Diego CA 92101. (619)238-7559. Fax: (619)238-8777. E-mail: info@mopa.org. Web site: www.mopa.org. **Contact:** Deborah Klochko, director. Curator of Photography: Carol McCusker. Estab. 1983. Sponsors 12 exhibits/year. Average display time 3 months.

Exhibits Interested in the history of photography, from the 19th century to the present.

Making Contact & Terms "The criteria is simply that the photography be of advanced artistic caliber, relative to other fine art photography. MoPA is a museum and therefore does not sell works in exhibitions." Exhibition schedules planned 2-3 years in advance. Holds a private Members' Opening Reception for each exhibition.

Submissions "For space, time and curatorial reasons, there are few opportunities to present the work of newer, lesser-known photographers." Send a CD, Web site or JPEGs to curator. Curator will respond. If interested, will request materials for future consideration. Files are kept on contemporary artists of note for future reference. Send return address and postage if you wish your materials returned. Responds in 2 months.

Tips "Exhibitions presented by the museum represent the full range of artistic and journalistic photographic works. There are no specific requirements. The executive director and curator make all decisions on works that will be included in exhibitions. There is an enormous stylistic diversity in the photographic arts. The museum does not place an emphasis on one style or technique over another."

◫ MUSEUM OF PRINTING HISTORY

1324 W. Clay, Houston TX 77019. (713)522-4652. Fax: (713)522-5694. Web site: www.print ingmuseum.org. **Contact:** Ann Kasman, executive director. Estab. 1982. Represents or exhibits 4-12 artists. Sponsors 1-12 photography exhibits/year. Average display time 6-16 weeks. Gallery open Tuesday through Saturday from 10 to 5. Closed 4th of July, Thanksgiving, Christmas Eve, Christmas, New Year's Eve/Day. Three rotating exhibit galleries. Overall price range $10-1,500.

Exhibits Exhibits photos of multicultural, landscapes/scenics, architecture, cities/urban, rural. Interested in alternative process, documentary.

Making Contact & Terms Artwork is accepted on consignment, and there is a 30% commission. Gallery provides insurance. Accepted work should be mounted, matted.

Submissions Write to arrange a personal interview to show portfolio of photographs, slides. Mail portfolio for review. Send query letter with artist's statement, bio, brochure, business card, photocopies, photographs, résumé, reviews, slides, SASE. Responds within 2 months, only if interested. Finds artists through word of mouth, submissions, portfolio reviews, art exhibits, referrals by other artists.

Tips "Check our Web site for Sunday hours, e-mail addresses and additional info."

ᴺ MUSEUM OF THE PLAINS INDIAN

P.O. Box 410, Browning MT 59417. (406)338-2230. Fax: (406)338-7404. E-mail: mpi@3river s.net. Web site: www.iacb.doi.gov/museums/museum_plains.html. **Contact:** David Dragonfly, curator. Estab. 1941. Open daily from 9 to 4:45 (June-September); Monday through Friday from 10 to 4:30 (October-May). Admission is free of charge October-May. Contact for additional information.

NEVADA MUSEUM OF ART

160 W. Liberty St., Reno NV 89501. (775)329-3333. Fax: (775)329-1541. Web site: www.nev adaart.org. **Contact**: Curatorial department. Estab. 1931. Sponsors 12-15 exhibits/year in various media. Average display time 3-4 months.

Submissions "See Web site for detailed submission instructions. No phone calls, please."

Tips "The Nevada Museum of Art is a private, nonprofit institution dedicated to providing a forum for the presentation of creative ideas through its collections, educational programs, exhibitions and community outreach. We specialize in art addressing the environment and the altered landscape."

NEW GALLERY/THOM ANDRIOLA

2627 Colquitt, Houston TX 77098-2117. (713)520-7053. Fax: (713)520-1145. E-mail: info@n ewgallery.net. Web site: www.newgallery.net. **Contact:** Thom Andriola, director. For-profit gallery. Estab. 1979. Represents or exhibits 22 artists/year. Sponsors 1 photography exhibit/ year. Average display time 1 month. Open Tuesday through Saturday from 11 to 5.

Making Contact & Terms Artwork is accepted on consignment, and there is a 50% commission. Requires exclusive representation locally.

NEW MEXICO STATE UNIVERSITY ART GALLERY

MSC 3572, NMSU, P.O. Box 30001, Las Cruces NM 88001-8003. (505)646-2545. Fax: (506)646-8036. E-mail: artglry@nmsu.edu. Web site: www.nmsu.edu/~artgal. **Contact:** John Lawson, director. Museum. Estab. 1969. Average display time 2-3 months. Gallery open Tuesday through Saturday from 11 to 4; Saturday and Sunday from 1 to 5. Closed Christmas through New Year's Day and university holidays. See Web site for summer hours. Located on university campus, 3,900 sq. ft. of exhibit space.

Making Contact & Terms Artwork is accepted on consignment, and there is a 30% commission. Gallery provides insurance, promotion, contract. Accepted work should arrive ready to install.

Submissions Send query letter with artist's statement, bio, brochure, résumé, slides, SASE. Responds in 6 months.

NEXUS/FOUNDATION FOR TODAY'S ART

1400 N. American St., Suite 102, Philadelphia PA 19122. E-mail: info@nexusphiladelphia.o rg. Web site: http://nexusphiladelphia.org. **Contact:** Nick Cassway, executive director. Alternative space; cooperative, nonprofit gallery. Estab. 1975. Approached by 40 artists/year; represents or exhibits 20 artists. Sponsors 2 photography exhibits/year. Average display time 1 month. Open Wednesday through Sunday from 12 to 6; closed July and August. Located in Fishtown, Philadelphia; 2 gallery spaces, approximately 750 sq. ft. each. Overall price range: $75-1,200. Most work sold at $200-400.

Exhibits Exhibits photos of multicultural, families, environmental, architecture, rural, entertainment, humor, performing arts, industry, political. Interested in alternative process, documentary, fine art.

Submissions Send query letter with artist's statement, bio, photocopies, photographs, slides, SASE. Finds artists through portfolio reviews, referrals by other artists, submissions, and juried reviews 2 times/year. "Please visit our Web site for submission dates."

Tips "Learn how to write a cohesive artist's statement."

NICOLAYSEN ART MUSEUM & DISCOVERY CENTER

400 E. Collins Dr., Casper WY 82601. (307)235-5247. Fax: (307)235-0923. E-mail: hturner@ thenic.org. Web site: www.thenic.org. **Contact:** Holly Turner, executive director. Director of Exhibitions and Programming: Ben Mitchell. Estab. 1967. Sponsors 10 exhibits/year. Average display time 3-4 months. Sponsors openings. Overall price range $250-1,500.

Exhibits Work must demonstrate artistic excellence and be appropriate to gallery's schedule. Interested in all subjects and media.

Making Contact & Terms Charges 40% commission.

Submissions Send material by mail for consideration (slides, résumé/CV, proposal); include SASE. Responds in 1 month.

NORTHWEST ART CENTER

500 University Ave. W., Minot ND 58707. (701)858-3264. Fax: (701)858-3894. E-mail: nac@ minotstateu.edu. Web site: www.minotstateu.edu/nac. **Contact:** Avis Veikley, director. Estab. 1976. Sponsors 18-20 exhibits/year, including 2 national juried shows. Average display time 1 month. Northwest Art Center consists of 2 galleries: Hartnett Hall Gallery and the Library Gallery. Overall price range $50-2,000. Most work sold at $800 or less.

Exhibits Interested in alternative process, avant garde, documentary, fine art, historical/ vintage.

Making Contact & Terms Charges 30% commission. Accepted work must be framed.

Submissions Send material by mail with SASE or e-mail for consideration. Responds within 3 months. Prospectus for juried shows available online.

NUDOPIA GALLERY

15 Thermopilon St., 542 48 Analipsi, Thessaloniki, Greece. (30) (231)085-5950. E-mail: info@nudopiagallery.com, info@nudopia.com. Web site: www.nudopiagallery.com. **Contact:** Mary Diangelo, art director. Giannis Angelous, owner. Estab. 2007. Online commercial fine art gallery.

Exhibits Artistic and contemporary nudes exclusively.

Making Contact & Terms Charges commission for fine art prints. Other uses, such as printed media (coffee table books, limited edition posters, calendars, etc.) are negotiable. See Web site for details. Responds within 6 weeks only if interested.

Submissions Initial contact by e-mail. Provide query letter, Web site portfolio link. Ground mail submission guidelines available on Web site. Accepts digital submissions only.

ⓃO.K. HARRIS WORKS OF ART

383 W. Broadway, New York NY 10012. (212)431-3600. Fax: (212)925-4797. E-mail: okharri s@okharris.com. Web site: www.okharris.com. **Contact**: Ivan C. Karp, director. Estab. 1969. Sponsors 3-8 exhibits/year. Average display time 1 month. Gallery open Tuesday through Saturday from 10 to 6. Closed August and from December 25 to January 1. Overall price range $350-3,000.

Exhibits Exhibits photos of cities/urban, events, rural. "The images should be startling or profoundly evocative. No rocks, dunes, weeds or nudes reclining on any of the above or seascapes." Interested in urban and industrial subjects, "cogent photojournalism," documentary.

Making Contact & Terms Charges 50% commission. Accepted work should be matted and framed.

Submissions Appear in person, no appointment. Responds immediately.

Tips "Do not provide a descriptive text."

▣ OAKLAND UNIVERSITY ART GALLERY

208 Wilson Hall, Oakland University, Rochester MI 48309-4401. (248)370-3005. Fax: (248)370-4208. E-mail: goody@oakland.edu. Web site: www.oakland.edu/ouag. **Contact:** Dick Goody, director. Nonprofit gallery. Estab. 1962. Represents 10-25 artists/year. Sponsors 6 exhibits/year. Average display time 4-5 weeks. Open September-May: Tuesday through Sunday from 12 to 5; evenings during special events and theater performances (Wednesday through Friday from 7 through 1st intermission, weekends from 5 through 1st intermission). Closed Monday, holidays and June-August. Located on the campus of Oakland University; exhibition space is approximately 2,350 sq. ft. of floor space, 301-ft. linear wall space, with 10-ft. 7-in. ceiling. The gallery is situated across the hall from the Meadow Brook Theatre. "We do not sell work, but do make available price lists for visitors with contact information noted for inquiries."

Exhibits Considers all styles and all types of prints and media.

Making Contact & Terms Charges no commission. Gallery provides insurance, promotion and contract. Accepted work should be framed, mounted, matted. No restrictions on representation; however, prefers emerging Detroit artists.

Submissions E-mail bio, education, artist's statement and JPEG images. Mail portfolio for review. Send query letter with artist's statement, bio, photocopies, résumé, slides. Returns material with SASE. Responds to queries in 1-2 months. Finds artists through referrals by other artists, word of mouth, art community, advisory board and other arts organizations.

OPALKA GALLERY

The Sage Colleges, Opalka Gallery, 140 New Scotland Ave., Albany NY 12208. (518)292-7742. Fax: (518)292-1903. E-mail: opalka@sage.edu. Web site: www.sage.edu/opalka. **Contact:** Jim Richard Wilson, director. Nonprofit gallery. Estab. 2002. "The Opalka Gallery replaced Rathbone Gallery, which served The Sage Colleges for 25 years." Approached by 90-120 artists/year; represents or exhibits approximately 24 artists. Average display time 5 weeks. Open Monday through Frday from 10 to 4:30; Monday-Thursday evenings 6-8, Sundays noon-4; June-July 10-4 and by appointment. Open by appointment only between exhibitions and when classes are not in session. Closed July 4. "Located on the Sage Albany campus, The Opalka's primary concentration is on work by professional artists from outside the region. The gallery frequently features multidisciplinary projects and hosts poetry read-

Galleries

ings, recitals and symposia, often in conjunction with its exhibitions. The 7,400-sq.-ft. facility includes a vaulted gallery and a 75-seat lecture/presentation hall with Internet connectivity." Overall price range $50-260,000.

Exhibits Interested in fine art.

Making Contact & Terms Artwork is accepted on consignment; there is no commision. "We primarily accept artists from outside our region and those who have ties to The Sage Colleges. We host the local 'Photography Regional' every three years." Requires exclusive representation locally.

Submissions Send query letter with artist's statement, bio, brochure, business card, photocopies, photographs, reviews, slides, SASE; or e-mail pertinent information. Finds artists through word of mouth, art exhibits, submissions, portfolio reviews, referrals by other artists.

Tips "Submit all correspondence in a professional manner. Include an artist's statement, bio, reviews, and any pertinent information with visuals of your work (slides, CD, etc.)."

☐ ORGANIZATION OF INDEPENDENT ARTISTS

45 West 21 St., #504, New York NY 10010. (347)405-2422. E-mail: oiaonline@surfbest.net. Web site: www.oiaonline.org. **Contact:** Geraldine Cosentino, director. Estab. 1976. Sponsors several exhibits/year. Average display time 4-6 weeks.

- OIA is a nonprofit organization that provides exhibition opportunities for unaffiliated and undeserved artists at alternative public spaces in NYC and on their Web site.

Exhibits Interested in fine art.

Making Contact & Terms Membership is $75/year.

Submissions Submit slides or CD with proposal. "Write, e-mail or visit Web site for information on membership. If request is by mail, please include a SASE."

Tips "It is not required to be a member to submit a proposal, but interested photographers may want to become OIA members to be included in OIA's active artists registry that is used regularly by curators and artists. You must be a member to have your work in the registry but *not* to be considered for exhibits at OIA's Gallery 402 or public spaces."

ROBERT PARDO GALLERY

121 E. 31st St., PH12C, New York NY 10016. (917)256-1282. Fax: (646)935-0009. Email: robertpardogallery@yahoo.com. Web site: www.robertpardogallery.com. **Contact**: Dr. Giovanna Federico. For-profit gallery. Estab. 1986. Approached by 500 artists/year; represents or exhibits 18 artists. Sponsors 3 photography exhibits/year. Average display time 4-5 weeks. Gallery open Tuesday through Saturday from 10 to 6. Closed August.

Exhibits Interested in avant garde, fashion/glamour, fine art.

Submissions Arrange personal interview to show portfolio of slides, transparencies. Responds in 1 month.

PARKLAND ART GALLERY

2400 W. Bradley Ave., Champaign IL 61821. (217)351-2485. Fax: (217)373-3899. E-mail: lcostello@parkland.edu. Web site: www.parklandedu/gallery. **Contact:** Art Gallery Director. Nonprofit gallery. Estab. 1980. Approached by 130 artists /year; represents or exhibits 8 artists. Average display time 4- 6 weeks. Open Monday through Friday from 10 to 3; Saturday from 12 to 2. Closed college and official holidays. Overall price range $100-5,000. Most work sold at $300.

Exhibits Interested in alternative process, avant garde, documentary, fine art, historical/vintage.

Making Contact & Terms Gallery provides insurance, promotion. Accepted work should be framed.

Submissions Mail portfolio for review. Send query letter with artist's statement, bio, brochure, résumé, reviews, slides, SASE. Responds in 4 months. Finds artists through word of mouth, portfolio reviews, art exhibits, referrals by other artists, call for entry.

▣ LEONARD PEARLSTEIN GALLERY

The Antoinette Westphal College of Media Arts & Design, Drexel University, 33rd and Market Streets, Philadelphia PA 19104. (215)895-2548. Fax: (215)895-4917. E-mail: gallery @drexel.edu. Web site: www.drexel.edu/academics/comad/gallery. **Contact:** Ephraim Russell, director. Nonprofit gallery. Estab. 1986. Sponsors 8 total exhibits/year; 1 or 2 photography exhibits/year. Average display time 1 month. Open Monday through Friday from 11 to 5. Closed during summer.

Making Contact & Terms Artwork is bought outright. Gallery takes 20% commission. Gallery provides insurance, promotion. Accepted work should be framed, mounted, matted. "We will not pay transport fees."

Submissions Write to arrange a personal interview to show portfolio. Send query letter with artist's statement, bio, résumé, SASE. Returns material with SASE. Responds by February, only if interested. Finds artists through referrals by other artists, academic instructors.

PENTIMENTI GALLERY

145 N. Second St., Philadelphia PA 19106. (215)625-9990. Fax: (215)625-8488. E-mail: mail@pentimenti.com. Web site: www.pentimenti.com. Commercial gallery. Estab. 1992. Average display time 6 weeks. Gallery open Tuesday by appointment; Wednesday through Friday from 11 to 5; Saturday from 12 to 5. Closed August, Christmas and New Year's Day. Located in the heart of Old City Cultural District in Philadelphia. Overall price range $500-10,000. Most work sold at $3,000.

Exhibits Exhibits photos of multicultural, families, environmental, landscapes/scenics, wildlife, architecture, cities/urban, gardening, entertainment, events. Interested in avant garde, documentary, fashion/glamour, fine art, historical/vintage.

Making Contact & Terms Artwork is accepted on consignment, and there is a 50% commission. Gallery provides insurance, promotion, contract. Accepted work should be framed, mounted, matted.

Submissions Send query letter with artist's statement, bio, brochure, photocopies, photographs, résumé, reviews, slides, SASE. Responds in 3 months. Finds artists through word of mouth, portfolio reviews, art fairs, referrals by other artists, curators, etc.

▣ PETERS VALLEY CRAFT CENTER

19 Kuhn Rd., Layton NJ 07851. (973)948-5202. Fax: (973)948-0011. E-mail: mikal.store.gall ery@petersvalley.org. Web site: www.petersvalley.org. **Contact:** Mikal Brutzman, gallery manager. Nonprofit gallery and store. Estab. 1970. Approached by about 100 artists/year; represents about 350 artists. Average display time 1 month in gallery; varies for store items. Open year round; call for hours. Located in northwestern New Jersey in Delaware Water Gap National Recreation Area; 2 floors, approximately 3,000 sq. ft. Overall price range $5-3,000. Most work sold at $100-300.

Galleries

Exhibits Considers all media and all types of prints. Also exhibits non-referential, mixed media, collage and sculpture.

Making Contact & Terms Artwork is accepted on consignment, and there is a 60% commission to artist. "Retail price set by the gallery in conjunction with artist." Gallery provides insurance and promotion. Accepted work should be framed, mounted and matted. *Accepts only artists from North America.*

Submissions Submissions reviewed in March. Send query letter with artist's statement, bio, résumé and images (slides or CD of JPEGs). Returns material with SASE. Responds in 2 months. Finds artists through submissions, art exhibits, art fairs, referrals by other artists.

Tips "Submissions must be neat and well-organized throughout."

ⓃSCOTT PFAFFMAN GALLERY

35 E. First St., New York NY 10003. E-mail: scott@pfaffman.com. **Contact:** Scott Pfaffman, director. Art consultancy.

Exhibits Interested in alternative process, avant garde, documentary, erotic, fashion/glamour, fine art, historical/vintage, seasonal.

Making Contact & Terms Artwork is accepted on consignment, and there is a 40% commission.

Submissions Send query letter with SASE, photographs, reviews. Responds to queries in 2 months, only if interested. Finds artists through referrals by other artists.

ⓃPHILLIPS GALLERY

444 E. 200 S., Salt Lake City UT 84111. (801)364-8284. Fax: (801)364-8293. E-mail: meri@phillips-gallery.com. Web site: www.phillips-gallery.com. **Contact:** Meri DeCaria, director/curator. Commercial gallery. Estab. 1965. Average display time 4 weeks. Sponsors openings; provides refreshments, advertisement, and half of mailing costs. Overall price range $300-2,000. Most work sold at $600.

Exhibits Accepts all types and styles.

Making Contact & Terms Charges 50% commission. Accepted work should be matted. Requires exclusive representation locally. *Photographers must have Utah connection.* Must be actively pursuing photography.

Submissions Submit portfolio for review; include SASE. Responds in 2 weeks.

PHOENIX GALLERY

210 11th Ave. at 25th St., Suite 902, New York NY 10001. (212)226-8711. Fax: (212)343-7303. E-mail: info@phoenix-gallery.com. Web site: www.phoenix-gallery.com. **Contact:** Linda Handler, director. Estab. 1958. Sponsors 10-12 exhibits/year. Average display time 1 month. Overall price range $100-10,000. Most work sold at $3,000-8,000.

Exhibits "The gallery is an artist-run nonprofit organization; an artist has to be a member in order to exhibit in the gallery. There are 3 types of membership: active, inactive, and associate." Interested in all media; alternative process, documentary, fine art.

Making Contact & Terms Charges 25% commission.

Submissions Artists wishing to be considered for membership must submit an application form, slides and résumé. Call, e-mail or download membership application from Web site.

Tips "The gallery has a special exhibition space, The Project Room, where nonmembers can exhibit their work. If an artist is interested, he/she may send a proposal with art to the gallery. The space is free; the artist shares only in the cost of the reception with the other artists showing at that time."

▣ PHOTO-EYE GALLERY

376 Garcia St., Suite A, Santa Fe NM 87501. E-mail: elizabethavedon@photoeye.com. Web site: www.photoeye.com. **Contact:** Elizabeth Avedon, gallery director. For-profit gallery. Average display time 2 months. Open Tuesday through Saturday from 11 to 5. "We have a physical gallery, Photo-Eye Gallery, Santa Fe, located off historic Canyon Road, plus 2 online galleries—The Photographer's Showcase and Photo Bistro." Overall price range $600-4,500. Most work sold at $1,200.

Exhibits Exhibits photos of babies/children/teens, architecture, cities/urban, political, wildlife, adventure. Interested in alternative process, avant garde, documentary, fine art. Exhibits contemporary photography only, all photographic processes.

Making Contact & Terms Gallery provides insurance, promotion, contract. Accepted work should be matted. Requires exclusive representation locally.

Submissions "We only accept digital files. All work should be submitted to the Photographer's Showcase." Responds in 2-4 weeks. Finds artists through art exhibits, word of mouth, art fairs, portfolio reviews, referrals by other artists.

Tips "Approach gallery in a professional, non-pushy way. Keep it short—in the end the work will speak for itself."

PHOTOGRAPHIC RESOURCE CENTER

832 Commonwealth Ave., Boston MA 02215. (617)975-0600. Fax: (617)975-0606. E-mail: prc@bu.edu. Web site: www.prcboston.org. **Contact:** Leslie K. Brown, curator. "The PRC is a nonprofit arts organization founded in 1976 to facilitate the study and dissemination of information relating to photography." Average display time 6 weeks. Open Tuesday, Wednesday and Friday from 10 to 6; Saturday and Sunday from 12 to 5; Thursday from 10 to 8. Closed major holidays. Located in the heart of Boston University. Gallery brings in nationally recognized artists to lecture to large audiences and host workshops on photography.

Exhibits Interested in contemporary and historical photography and mixed-media work incorporating photography.

Submissions Send query letter with artist's statement, bio, slides, résumé, reviews, SASE. Responds in 3-6 months. Finds artists through word of mouth, art exhibits, portfolio reviews.

Tips "Present a cohesive body of work."

▣ PHOTOGRAPHY ART

107 Myers Ave., Beckley WV 25801. (304)252-4060 or (304)575-6491. Fax: (304)252-4060 (call before faxing). E-mail: bruceburgin@photographyart.com. Web site: www.photographyart.com. **Contact:** Bruce Burgin, owner. Internet rental gallery. Estab. 2003. "Each artist deals directly with his/her customers. I do not charge commissions and do not keep records of sales."

Exhibits Exhibits photos of landscapes/scenics, wildlife. Interested in fine art.

Making Contact & Terms There is a rental fee for space. The rental fee covers 1 year. The standard gallery is $360 to exhibit 40 images with biographical and contact info for 1 year.

No commission charged for sales. Artist deals directly with customers and receives 100% of any sale. Gallery provides promotion.

Submissions Internet sign-up. No portfolio required.

Tips "An artist should have high-quality digital scans. The digital images should be cropped to remove any unnecessary background or frames, and sized according to the instructions provided with their Internet gallery. I recommend the artist add captions and anecdotes to the images in their gallery. This will give a visitor to your gallery a personal connection to you and your work."

THE PHOTOMEDIA CENTER

P.O. Box 8518, Erie PA 16505. (617)990-7867. E-mail: info@photomediacenter.org. Web site: www.photomediacenter.org. **Contact:** Eric Grignol, executive director. Nonprofit gallery. Estab. 2004. Sponsors 12 "new" photography exhibits/year. "Previously featured exhibits are archived online. We offer many opportunities for artists, including sales, networking, creative collaboration and promotional resources; maintain an information board and slide registry for members; and hold an open annual juried show in the summer."

Exhibits Interested in alternative process, avant garde, documentary, fine art.

Making Contact & Terms Artwork is accepted on consignment, and there is a 25% commission. Gallery provides promotion. Prefers only artists working in photographic, digital and new media.

Submissions "We have a general portfolio review call in the fall for the following year's exhibition schedule. If after December 31, send query letter with artist's statement, bio, résumé, slides, SASE." Responds in 2-6 months. Finds artists through word of mouth, submissions, portfolio reviews, art exhibits, referrals by other artists.

Tips "We are looking for artists who have excellent technical skills, a strong sense of voice and cohesive body of work. Pay careful attention to our guidelines for submissions on our Web site. Label everything. Must include a SASE for reply."

PIERRO GALLERY OF SOUTH ORANGE

Baird Center, 5 Mead St., South Orange NJ 07079. (973)378-7755, ext. 3. Fax: (973)378-7833. E-mail: pierrogallery@southorange.org. Web site: www.pierrogallery.org. **Contact:** Judy Wukitsch, gallery director. Nonprofit gallery. Estab. 1994. Approached by 75-185 artists/year; represents or exhibits 25-50 artists. Average display time 7 weeks. Open Friday through Sunday from 1 to 4; by appointment. Closed mid-December through mid-January and during August. Overall price range $100-10,000. Most work sold at $800.

Exhibits Interested in fine art, "which can be inclusive of any subject matter."

Making Contact & Terms Artwork is accepted on consignment, and there is a 15% commission. Gallery provides insurance, promotion, contract. Accepted work should be framed.

Submissions Mail portfolio for review; 3 portfolio reviews/year: January, June, October. Send query letter with artist's statement, résumé, slides. Responds in 2 months from review date. Finds artists through word of mouth, submissions, portfolio reviews, referrals by other artists.

POLK MUSEUM OF ART

800 E. Palmetto St., Lakeland FL 33801-5529. (863)688-7743. Fax: (863)688-2611. E-mail: info@polkmuseumofart.org. Web site: www.polkmuseumofart.org. **Contact:** Todd Behrens, curator of art. Museum. Estab. 1966. Approached by 75 artists/year; represents or

exhibits 3 artists. Sponsors 1-3 photography exhibits/year. Galleries open Tuesday through Saturday from 10 to 5; Sunday from 1 to 5. Closed major holidays. Four different galleries of various sizes and configurations.

Exhibits Interested in alternative process, avant garde, documentary, fine art, historical/vintage.

Making Contact & Terms Museum provides insurance, promotion, contract. Accepted work should be framed.

Submissions Mail portfolio for review. Send query letter with artist's statement, bio, résumé, slides, SASE.

THE PRINT CENTER

1614 Latimer St., Philadelphia PA 19103. (215)735-6090. Fax: (215)735-5511. E-mail: info@printcenter.org. Web site: www.printcenter.org. **Contact:** Ashley Peel Pinkham, assistant director. Nonprofit gallery and Gallery Store. Estab. 1915. Represents over 75 artists from around the world in Gallery Store. Sponsors 5 photography exhibits/year. Average display time 2 months. Open all year Tuesday through Saturday 11-5:30. Closed December 21 through January 6. Three galleries. Overall price range $15-15,000. Most work sold at $200.

Exhibits Exhibits contemporary prints and photographs of all processes. Accepts original artwork only—no reproductions.

Making Contact & Terms Accepts artwork on consignment (50% commission). Gallery provides insurance, promotion, contract. Artists must be printmakers or photographers.

Submissions Must be member to submit work - member's work is reviewed by Curator and Gallery Store Manager. See Web site for membership application. Finds artists through submissions, art exhibits, and membership.

PUCKER GALLERY

171 Newbury St., Boston MA 02116 (617)267-9473. Fax: (617)424-9759. E-mail: contactus @puckergallery.com. Web site: www.puckergallery.com. **Contact:** David Winkler, art director. For-profit gallery. Estab. 1967. Approached by 100 artists/year; represents or exhibits 40 artists. Sponsors 2 photography exhibits/year. Average display time 1 month. Gallery open Monday through Saturday from 10 to 5:30; Sunday from 1 to 5. Four floors of exhibition space. Overall price range $500-75,000.

Exhibits Exhibits photos of multicultural, environmental, landscapes/scenics, architecture, cities/urban, religious, rural. Interested in fine art, abstracts, seasonal.

Making Contact & Terms Gallery provides promotion.

Submissions Send query letter with artist's statement, bio, slides/CD, SASE. "We do not accept e-mail submissions." Finds artists through submissions, referrals by other artists.

PUMP HOUSE CENTER FOR THE ARTS

P.O. Box 1613, Chillicothe OH 45601. Phone/fax: (740)772-5783. E-mail: info@pumphouse artgallery.com. Web site: www.pumphouseartgallery.com. **Contact:** Priscilla V. Smith, director. Nonprofit gallery. Estab. 1991. Approached by 6 artists/year; represents or exhibits more than 50 artists. Average display time 6 weeks. Gallery open Tuesday through Friday from 11 to 4; weekends from 1 to 4. Closed Monday and major holidays. Overall price range $150-600. Most work sold at $300. Facility is also available for rent (business, meetings, reunions, weddings, wedding receptions or rehearsals, etc.).

Exhibits Exhibits photos of landscapes/scenics, wildlife, architecture, gardening, travel, agriculture. Interested in fine art, historical/vintage.

Making Contact & Terms Artwork is accepted on consignment, and there is a 30% commission. Gallery provides insurance, promotion. Accepted work should be framed, matted, wired for hanging. Call or stop in to show portfolio of photographs, slides. Send query letter with bio, photographs, slides, SASE. Responds in 1 month. Finds artists through word of mouth, submissions, portfolio reviews, art exhibits, art fairs, referrals by other artists.

Tips "All artwork must be original designs, framed, ready to hang (wired—no sawtooth hangers)."

QUEENS COLLEGE ART CENTER

Benjamin S. Rosenthal Library, Queens College, Flushing NY 11367-1597. (718)997-3770. Fax: (718)997-3753. E-mail: suzanna.simor@qc.cuny.edu. Web site: www.qc.cuny.edu. **Contact:** Suzanna Simor, director. Curator: Alexandra de Luise. Estab. 1955. Average display time approximately 6 weeks. Overall price range $200-600.

Exhibits Open to all types, styles, subject matter; decisive factor is quality.

Making Contact & Terms Charges 40% commission. Accepted work can be framed or unframed, mounted or unmounted, matted or unmatted. Sponsors openings. Photographer is responsible for providing/arranging refreshments and cleanup.

Submissions Send query letter with résumé, samples and SASE. Responds in 1 month.

MARCIA RAFELMAN FINE ARTS

10 Clarendon Ave., Toronto ON M4V 1H9 Canada. (416)920-4468. Fax: (416)968-6715. E-mail: info@mrfinearts.com. Web site: www.mrfinearts.com. **Contact:** Marcia Rafelman, president. Gallery Director: Meghan Richardson. Semi-private gallery. Estab. 1984. Average display time 1 month. Gallery is centrally located in Toronto; 2,000 sq. ft. on 2 floors. Overall price range $800-25,000. Most work sold at $1,500.

Exhibits Exhibits photos of environmental, landscapes. Interested in alternative process, documentary, fine art, historical/vintage.

Making Contact & Terms Charges 50% commission. Gallery provides insurance, promotion, contract. Requires exclusive representation locally.

Submissions Mail or e-mail portfolio for review; include bio, photographs, reviews. Responds within 2 weeks, only if interested. Finds artists through word of mouth, submissions, art fairs, referrals by other artists.

Tips "We only accept work that is archival."

THE RALLS COLLECTION INC.

1516 31st St. NW, Washington DC 20007. (202)342-1754. Fax: (202)342-0141. E-mail: maralls@aol.com. Web site: www.rallscollection.com. For-profit gallery. Estab. 1991. Approached by 125 artists/year; represents or exhibits 60 artists. Sponsors 7 photography exhibits/year. Average display time 1 month. Gallery open Tuesday through Saturday from 11 to 4 and by appointment. Closed Thanksgiving, Christmas. Overall price range $1,500-50,000. Most work sold at $2,500-5,000.

Exhibits Exhibits photos of babies/children/teens, celebrities, parents, landscapes/scenics, architecture, cities/urban, gardening, interiors/decorating, pets, rural, entertainment, health/fitness, hobbies, performing arts, sports, travel, product shots/still life. Interested in alternative process, avant garde, documentary, fashion/glamour, fine art, historical/vintage.

Making Contact & Terms Artwork is accepted on consignment, and there is a 50% commission. Gallery provides insurance, promotion, contract. Accepted work should be framed, matted. Requires exclusive representation locally. Accepts only artists from America.

Submissions Mail portfolio for review. Send query letter with artist's statement, bio, brochure, business card, photocopies, photographs, résumé, reviews, slides, SASE. Responds in 2 months. Finds artists through word of mouth, submissions, portfolio reviews, art exhibits, art fairs, referrals by other artists.

ROCHESTER CONTEMPORARY

137 East Ave., Rochester NY 14604. (585)461-2222. Fax: (585)461-2223. E-mail: info@rochestercontemporary.org. Web site: www.rochestercontemporary.org. **Contact:** Elizabeth Switzer, programming director. Estab. 1977. Sponsors 10-12 exhibits/year. Average display time 4-6 weeks. Gallery open Wednesday through Friday from 1 to 6; weekends from 1 to 5. Overall price range $100-500.

Making Contact & Terms Charges 25% commission.

Submissions Send slides/CD, letter of inquiry, résumé and statement. Responds in 3 months.

THE ROTUNDA GALLERY

33 Clinton St., Brooklyn NY 11201. (718)875-4047. Fax: (718)488-0609. E-mail: rotunda@briconline.org. Web site: www.briconline.org/rotunda. **Contact:** Isolde Brielmaier, director/chief curator. Nonprofit gallery. Estab. 1981. Average display time 6 weeks. Open Tuesday through Friday from 12 to 5; Saturday from 11 to 4.

Exhibits Interested in contemporary works.

Making Contact & Terms Gallery provides photographer's contact information to prospective buyers. Shows are limited by walls that are 22 feet high.

Submissions Send material by mail for consideration; include SASE. "View our Web site for guidelines and Artist Registry form."

SAN DIEGO ART INSTITUTE'S MUSEUM OF THE LIVING ARTIST

1439 El Prado, San Diego CA 92101. (619)236-0011. Fax: (619)236-1974. E-mail: admin@sandiego-art.org. Web site: www.sandiego-art.org. **Contact**: Kerstin Robers, executive administrator. Art Director: K.D. Benton. Nonprofit gallery. Estab. 1941. Represents or exhibits 500 member artists. Overall price range $50-3,000. Most work sold at $700.

Exhibits Photos of babies/children/teens, couples, multicultural, families, parents, senior citizens, disasters, environmental, landscapes/scenics, wildlife, architecture, cities/urban, education, gardening, pets, rural, adventure, entertainment, events, food/drink, health/fitness/beauty, hobbies, humor, performing arts, sports, travel, agriculture, political, product shots/still life, science, technology. Interested in alternative process, avant garde, documentary, erotic, fine art, historical/vintage, seasonal.

Making Contact & Terms Artwork is accepted on consignment, and there is a 40% commission. Membership fee: $125. Accepted work should be framed. Work must be carried in by hand for each monthly show except for annual international show, jpg online submission.

Submissions Membership not required for submission in monthly juried shows, but fee required. Artists interested in membership should request membership packet. Finds artists through referrals by other artists.

Tips "All work submitted must go through jury process for each monthly exhibition. Work must be framed in professional manner. No glass; plexiglass or acrylic only."

N SCHLUMBERGER GALLERY

P.O. Box 2864, Santa Rosa CA 95405. (707)544-8356. Fax: (707)538-1953. E-mail: sande@schlumberger.org. **Contact:** Sande Schlumberger, owner. Estab. 1986. Art publisher/distributor and gallery. Publishes and distributes limited editions, posters, original paintings and sculpture. Specializes in decorative and museum-quality art and photographs.

Exhibits Interested in fine art.

Making Contact & Terms Send query letter with tearsheets and photographs. Samples are not filed and are returned by SASE if requested by artist. Publisher/distributor will contact artist for portfolio review if interested. Portfolio should include color photographs and transparencies. Negotiates payment. Offers advance when appropriate. Rights purchased vary according to project. Provides advertising, in-transit insurance, insurance while work is at firm, promotion, shipping to and from firm, written contract and shows. Finds artists through exhibits, referrals, submissions and "pure blind luck."

Tips "Strive for quality, clarity, clean lines and light. Bring spirit into your images. It translates!"

N WILLIAM & FLORENCE SCHMIDT ART CENTER

Southwestern Illinois College, 2500 Carlyle Ave., Belleville IL 62221. E-mail: libby.reuter@swic.edu. Web site: www.schmidtartcenter.com. **Contact:** Libby Reuter, executive director. Nonprofit gallery. Estab. 2002. Sponsors 3-4 photography exhibits/year. Average display time 6-8 weeks. Open Tuesday through Saturday from 11 to 5 (to 8 on Thursday). Closed during college holidays.

Exhibits Interested in fine art and historical/vintage photography.

Submissions Mail portfolio for review. Send query letter with artist's statement, bio and slides. Finds artists through art fairs and exhibits, portfolio reviews, referrals by other artists, submissions and word of mouth.

▣ SCHMIDT/DEAN GALLERY

1710 Samson St., Philadelphia PA 19103. (215)569-9433. Fax: (215)569-9434. Web site: www.schmidtdean.com. **Contact:** Christopher Schmidt, director. For-profit gallery. Estab. 1988. Sponsors 4 photography exhibits/year. Average display time 6 weeks. Gallery open Tuesday through Saturday from 10:30 to 6. August hours are Tuesday through Friday from 10:30 to 6. Overall price range $1,000-70,000.

Exhibits Interested in alternative process, documentary, fine art.

Making Contact & Terms Charges 50% commission. Gallery provides insurance, promotion. Accepted work should be framed, mounted, matted. Requires exclusive representation locally.

Submissions Call/write to arrange a personal interview to show portfolio of slides or CD. Send query letter with SASE. "Send 10 to 15 slides or digital images on CD and a résumé that gives a sense of your working history. Include a SASE."

▣ SECOND STREET GALLERY

115 Second St. SE, Charlottesville VA 22902. (434)977-7284. Fax: (434)979-9793. E-mail: ssg@secondstreetgallery.org. Web site: www.secondstreetgallery.org. **Contact:** Catherine Barber, interim director. Estab. 1973. Sponsors approximately 2 photography exhibits/year. Average display time 1 month. Open Tuesday through Saturday from 11 to 6; 1st Friday of every month from 6 to 8, with Artist Talk at 6:30. Overall price range $300-2,000.

Making Contact & Terms Charges 30% commission.

Submissions Reviews slides/CDs in fall; $15 processing fee. Submit 10 slides or a CD for review; include artist statement, cover letter, bio/résumé, and most importantly, a SASE. Responds in 2 months.

Tips Looks for work that is "cutting edge, innovative, unexpected."

SELECT ART

1025 E. Levee St., Dallas TX 75207. E-mail: selart@swbell.net. **Contact:** Paul Adelson, owner. Estab. 1986. Overall price range $250-900.

• This market deals fine art photography to corporations and sells to collectors.

Exhibits Wants photos of architectural pieces, landscapes, automobiles and buildings. Interested in fine art.

Making Contact & Terms Charges 50% commission. Accepted work should be unframed and matted.

Submissions Send e-mail with visuals.

▨ SOHO MYRIAD

1250 B Menlo Dr., Atlanta GA 30318. (404)351-5656. Fax: (404)351-8284. E-mail: sarahh@sohomyriad.com. Web site: www.sohomyriad.com. **Contact:** Sarah Hall, director of art resources. Art consulting firm and for-profit gallery. Estab. 1997. Represents and/or exhibits over 2,000 artists. Sponsors 1 photography exhibit/year. Average display time 2 months. Gallery open Monday through Friday from 9 to 5:30. Overall price range $500-20,000. Most work sold at $500-5,000.

Exhibits Exhibits photos of landscapes/scenics, architecture, floral/botanical and abstracts. Interested in alternative process, avant garde, fine art, historical/vintage.

Making Contact & Terms Artwork is accepted on consignment, and there is a 50% commission. Gallery provides insurance.

SOUTH DAKOTA ART MUSEUM

South Dakota State University, Box 2250, Brookings SD 57007. (605)688-5423 or (866)805-7590. Fax: (605)688-4445. Web site: www.SouthDakotaArtMuseum.com. **Contact**: John Rychtarik, curator of exhibits. Museum. Estab. 1970. Sponsors 1-2 photography exhibits/year. Average display time 4 months. Gallery open Monday through Friday from 10 to 5; Saturday from 10 to 4; Sunday from 12 to 4. Closed state holidays. Six galleries offer 26,000 sq. ft. of exhibition space. Overall price range $200-6,000. Most work sold at $500.

Exhibits Interested in alternative process, documentary, fine art.

Making Contact & Terms Artwork is accepted on consignment, and there is a 30% commission. Gallery provides insurance, promotion. Accepted work should be framed.

Submissions Send query letter with artist's statement, bio, résumé, slides, SASE. Responds within 3 months, only if interested. Finds artists through word of mouth, portfolio reviews, art exhibits, referrals by other artists.

Galleries

◨ SOUTHSIDE GALLERY

150 Courthouse Square, Oxford MS 38655. (662)234-9090. E-mail: southside@southsideart gallery.com. Web site: www.southsideartgallery.com. **Contact:** Wil Cook, director. For-profit gallery. Estab. 1993. Average display time 4 weeks. Gallery open Monday through Saturday from 10 to 6; Sunday from 12 to 5. Overall price range $300-20,000. Most work sold at $425.

Exhibits Exhibits photos of landscapes/scenics, architecture, cities/urban, rural, entertainment, events, performing arts, sports, travel, agriculture, political. Interested in avant garde, fine art.

Making Contact & Terms Artwork is accepted on consignment, and there is a 55% commission. Gallery provides promotion. Accepted work should be framed.

Submissions Mail portfolio for review. Responds within 4-6 weeks, only if interested. Finds artists through submissions.

B.J. SPOKE GALLERY

299 Main St., Huntington NY 11743. (631)549-5106. E-mail: managerbjs@verizon.net. Web site: www.bjspokegallery.com. **Contact:** Manager. Member-owned cooperative gallery. Average display time 1 month. Sponsors openings. Overall price range $300-2,500.

Exhibits Holds national/international juried competitions. Visit Web site for details. Interested in "all styles and genres, photography as essay, as well as 'beyond' photography."

Making Contact & Terms Charges 30% commission. Photographer sets price.

Submissions Arrange a personal interview to show portfolio. Send query letter with SASE
.

⟦N⟧ ◨ SRO PHOTO GALLERY AT LANDMARK ARTS

School of Art, Texas Tech University, Box 42081, Lubbock TX 79409-2081. (806)742-1947. Fax: (806)742-1971. E-mail: landmarkarts@ttu.edu. Web site: www.landmarkarts.org. **Contact:** Joe R. Arredondo, director. Nonprofit gallery. Estab. 1984. Hosts an annual competition to fill 8 solo photography exhibition slots each year. Average display time 2 weeks. Open Monday through Friday from 8 to 5; Saturday from 10 to 5; Sunday from 12 to 4. Closed university holidays.

Exhibits Interested in fine art.

Making Contact & Terms "Exhibits are for scholarly purposes. Gallery will provide artist's contact information to potential buyers." Gallery provides insurance, promotion, contract. Accepted work should be matted.

Submissions Exhibitions are determined by juried process. See Web site for details (under Call for Entries). Deadline for applications is end of March.

THE STATE MUSEUM OF PENNSYLVANIA

300 North St., Harrisburg PA 17120-0024. (717)783-9904. Fax: (717)783-4558. E-mail: nstev ens@state.pa.us. Web site: www.statemuseumpa.org. **Contact:** N. Lee Stevens, senior curator of art collections. Museum established in 1905; current Fine Arts Gallery opened in 1993. Number of exhibits varies. Average display time 2 months. Overall price range $50-3,000.

Exhibits Fine art photography is a new area of endeavor for The State Museum, both collecting and exhibiting. Interested in works produced with experimental techniques.

Making Contact & Terms Work is sold in gallery, but not actively. Connects artists with

interested buyers. No commission. Accepted work should be framed. *Photography must be created by a native or resident of Pennsylvania, or contain subject matter relevant to Pennsylvania.*
Submissions Send material by mail for consideration; include SASE. Responds in 1 month.

▣ STATE OF THE ART
120 W. State St., Ithaca NY 14850. (607)277-1626 or (607)277-4950. E-mail: gallery@soag.org. Web site: www.soag.org. Cooperative gallery. Estab. 1989. Sponsors 1 photography exhibit/year. Average display time 1 month. Gallery open Wednesday through Friday from 12 to 6; weekends from 12 to 5. Located in downtown Ithaca, 2 rooms about 1,100 sq. ft. Overall price range $100-6,000. Most work sold at $200-500.
Exhibits Exhibits photos in all media and subjects. Interested in alternative process, avant garde, fine art, computer-assisted photographic processes.
Making Contact & Terms There is a co-op membership fee plus a donation of time. There is a 10% commission for members, 30% for nonmembers. Gallery provides promotion, contract. Accepted work must be ready to hang. Write for membership application.
Tips Other exhibit opportunity: Annual Juried Photo Show in March. Application available on Web site in January.

STATE STREET GALLERY
1804 State St., La Crosse WI 54601. (608)782-0101. E-mail: ssg1804@yahoo.com. Web site: www.statestreetartgallery.com. **Contact:** Ellen Kallies, president. Wholesale, retail and trade gallery. Estab. 2000. Approached by 15 artists/year; exhibits 12-14 artists/quarter in gallery. Average display time 4-6 months. Gallery open Tuesday through Saturday from 10 to 3. Located across from the University of Wisconsin/La Crosse. Overall price range $50-12,000. Most work sold at $500-1,200 and above.
Exhibits Exhibits photos of environmental, landscapes/scenics, architecture, cities/urban, gardening, rural, travel, medicine.
Making Contact & Terms Artwork is accepted on consignment, and there is a 40% commission. Gallery provides insurance, promotion, contract. Accepted work should be framed, matted.
Submissions Call or mail portfolio for review. Send query letter with artist's statement, photographs, slides, SASE. Responds in 1 month. Finds artists through word of mouth, art exhibits, art fairs, referrals by other artists.
Tips "Be organized, professional in presentation, flexible."

▣ PHILIP J. STEELE GALLERY
Rocky Mountain College of Art + Design, 1600 Pierce St., Lakewood CO 80214. (303)753-6046. Fax: (303)225-8610. E-mail: lspivak.rmcad.edu. Web site: www.rmcad.edu/galleries/steelegallery.aspx. **Contact:** Lisa Spivak, director. Nonprofit gallery. Estab. 1962. Approached by 25 artists/year; represents or exhibits 6-9 artists. Sponsors 1 photography exhibit/year. Average display time 1 month. Gallery open Monday through Saturday from 12 to 5. Closed major holidays.
Exhibits No restrictions on subject matter.
Making Contact & Terms No fee or percentage taken. Gallery provides insurance, promotion. Accepted work should be framed.
Submissions Send query letter with artist's statement, bio, slides, résumé, reviews,

SASE. Reviews in May, **deadline April 15**. Finds artists through word of mouth, submissions, referrals by other artists.

THE STUDIO: AN ALTERNATIVE SPACE FOR CONTEMPORARY ART

2 Maryland Ave., Armonk NY 10504-2029. (914)273-1452. Fax: (914)219-5030. E-mail: director@thestudiony-alternative.org. Web site: www.thestudiony-alternative.org. **Contact:** Katie Stratis, director. Alternative space and nonprofit gallery. Estab. 1998. Located in Westchester County in the hamlet of Armonk, New York; approximately 500 sq. ft.; sculpture garden. ''The Studio Annex in New York City is a satellite gallery of The Studio, and it also shows up to three exhibits a year.''

Exhibits Exhibits photos of multicultural, architecture, gardening, rural, environmental, landscapes/scenics, entertainment, events, performing arts. Interested in alternative process, avant garde, documentary. ''The subject matter is left up to the artists chosen to be in the curated exhibitions.''

Making Contact & Terms Artwork is accepted on consignment, and there is a 30% commission.

Submissions ''Curated exhibitions only; no open submission policy. Once a year there is a juried exhibition, but review Juried Prospectus before sending any submissions.''

ⓝ SYNCHRONICITY FINE ARTS

106 W. 13th St., New York NY 10011. (646)230-8199. Fax: (646)230-8198. E-mail: synchspa @bestweb.net. Web site: www.synchronicityspace.com. Nonprofit gallery. Estab. 1989. Approached by hundreds of artists/year; represents or exhibits 12-16 artists. Sponsors 2-3 photography exhibits/year. Gallery open Tuesday through Saturday from 12 to 6. Closed 2 weeks in August. Overall price range $1,500-10,000. Most work sold at $3,000.

Exhibits Exhibits photos of multicultural, environmental, landscapes/scenics, architecture, cities/urban, education, rural, events, agriculture, industry, medicine, political. Interested in avant garde, documentary, fine art, historical/vintage.

Making Contact & Terms Gallery provides insurance, promotion, contract. Accepted work should be framed, mounted, matted.

Submissions Write to arrange a personal interview to show portfolio of photographs, transparencies, slides. Mail portfolio for review. Send query letter with photocopies, SASE, photographs, slides, résumé. Responds in 3 weeks. Finds artists through art exhibits, submissions, portfolio reviews, referrals by other artists.

ⓝ TALLI'S FINE ART

Pho-Tal Inc., 15 N. Summit St., Tenafly NJ 07670. (201)569-3199. Fax: (201)569-3392. E-mail: tal@photal.com. Web site: www.photal.com. **Contact:** Talli Rosner-Kozuch, owner. Alternative space, art consultancy, for-profit gallery, wholesale gallery. Estab. 1991. Approached by 38 artists/year; represents or exhibits 40 artists. Sponsors 12 photography exhibits/year. Average display time 1 month. Gallery open Monday through Sunday from 9 to 5. Closed holidays. Overall price range $200-3,000. Most work sold at $4,000.

Exhibits Exhibits photos of multicultural, architecture, cities/urban, education, gardening, interiors/decorating, pets, religious, rural, adventure, food/drink, travel, product shots/still life. Interested in alternative process, documentary, erotic, fine art, historical/vintage.

Making Contact & Terms Artwork is accepted on consignment, and there is a 50% commission. Accepted work should be framed, matted.

Submissions Write to arrange a personal interview to show portfolio of slides. Send query letter with artist's statement, bio, brochure, business card, photocopies, résumé, slides, SASE. Responds in 2 months. Finds artists through word of mouth, submissions, portfolio reviews, art exhibits, art fairs, referrals by other artists.

ⓃLILLIAN & COLEMAN TAUBE MUSEUM OF ART

2 N. Main St., Minot ND 58703. (701)838-4445. E-mail: taube@ndak.net. Web site: www.taubemuseum.org. **Contact:** Nancy Brown, executive director. Estab. 1970. Established non-profit organization. Sponsors 1-2 photography exhibits/year. Average display time 4-6 weeks. Museum is located in a newly renovated historic landmark building with room to show 2 exhibits simultaneously. Overall price range $15-225. Most work sold at $40-100.

Exhibits Exhibits photos of babies/children/teens, couples, multicultural, families, parents, senior citizens, disasters, landscapes/scenics, wildlife, beauty, rural, travel, agriculture, buildings, military, portraits. Interested in avant garde, fine art.

Making Contact & Terms Charges 30% commission for members; 40% for nonmembers. Sponsors openings.

Submissions Submit portfolio along with a minimum of 6 examples of work in slide format for review. Responds in 3 months.

Tips "Wildlife, landscapes and floral pieces seem to be the trend in North Dakota. We get many slides to review for our photography exhibits each year. We also appreciate figurative, unusual and creative photography work. Do not send postcard photos."

JILL THAYER GALLERIES AT THE FOX

1700 20th St., Bakersfield CA 93301-4329. (661)631-9711. E-mail: jill@jillthayer.com. Web site: www.jillthayer.com. **Contact:** Jill Thayer, director. For-profit gallery. Estab. 1994. Represents more than 25 "emerging, mid-career and established artists of regional and international recognition." Features 6-8 exhibits/year. Average installation: 6 weeks. Open Friday and Saturday from 1 to 4 or by appointment. Closed holidays. Located at the historic Fox Theater, built in 1930. Thayer renovated the 400-sq.-ft. space in 1994. "The gallery features large windows, high ceilings, wood floor and bare-wire halogen lighting system. Clients include southern California upscale; 25% of sales are to corporate collectors." Overall price range $250-10,000. Most work sold at $2,500.

Exhibits Considers all media. Exhibits "contemporary, abstract and representational work."

Making Contact & Terms Artwork is accepted on consignment "for duration of exhibit with 50% commission. Artist pays all shipping and must provide insurance. Retail price set by the gallery and the artist. Gallery provides marketing, mailer design and partial printing. Artist shares cost of printing, mailings and receptions."

Submissions Send query letter with artist's statement, bio, résumé, exhibition list, reviews, 12 slides, SASE. Responds in 1 month if interested. Finds artists through submissions and portfolio reviews.

Tips "When submitting to galleries, be concise, professional, send up-to-date package (art and info) and slide sheet of professionally documented work. Frame professionally if selected for exhibition. No colored mats or color laser prints. All works on paper must be archival and of museum quality."

NATALIE AND JAMES THOMPSON ART GALLERY

School of Art & Design, San José State University, San José CA 95192-0089. (408)924-4723. Fax: (408)924-4326. E-mail: jfh@cruzio.com. Web site: www.sjsu.edu. **Contact:** Jo Farb Hernandez, director. Nonprofit gallery. Approached by 100 artists/year. Sponsors 1-2 photography exhibits/year. Average display time 1 month. Gallery open Tuesday through Friday from 11 to 4; Tuesday evenings from 6 to 7:30.

Exhibits "We are open to all genres, aesthetics and techniques."

Making Contact & Terms "Works are not generally for sale." Gallery provides insurance, promotion. Accepted work should be framed and/or ready to hang.

Submissions Send query letter with artist's statement, bio, résumé, reviews, slides, SASE. Responds as soon as possible. Finds artists through word of mouth, submissions, portfolio reviews, art exhibits, art fairs, referrals by other artists.

THROCKMORTON FINE ART

145 E. 57th St., 3rd Floor, New York NY 10022. (212)223-1059. Fax: (212)223-1937. E-mail: kraige@throckmorton-nyc.com. Web site: www.throckmorton-nyc.com. **Contact:** Kraige Block, director. For-profit gallery. Estab. 1993. Approached by 50 artists/year; represents or exhibits 20 artists. Sponsors 5 photography exhibits/year. Average display time 2 months. Overall price range $1,000-10,000. Most work sold at $2,500.

Exhibits Exhibits photos of babies/children/teens, landscapes/scenics, architecture, cities/urban, rural. Interested in erotic, fine art, historical/vintage, Latin American photography.

Making Contact & Terms Charges 50% commission. Gallery provides insurance, promotion.

Submissions Write to arrange a personal interview to show portfolio of photographs/slides/CD, or send query letter with artist's statement, bio, photocopies, slides, CD, SASE. Responds in 3 weeks. Finds artists through word of mouth, portfolio reviews.

Tips "Present your work nice and clean."

TOUCHSTONE GALLERY

406 Seventh St. NW, Washington DC 20004-2217. (202)347-2787. Fax: (202)347-3339. E-mail: info@TouchstoneGallery.com. Web site: www.TouchstoneGallery.com. **Contact:** Camille Mosley-Pasley, director. Cooperative rental gallery. Estab. 1976. Approached by 240 artists/year; represents or exhibits 35 artists. Sponsors 3 photography exhibits/year. Average display time 1 month. Open Wednesday through Friday from 11 to 5; weekends from 12 to 5. Closed Christmas through New Year's Day. Located in downtown Washington, DC, on gallery row. Large main gallery with several additional exhibition areas; high ceilings. Overall price range: $100-2,500. Most artwork sold at $600.

Exhibits Exhibits photos of landscapes/scenics, architecture, cities/urban, rural, automobiles. Interested in alternative process, avant garde, documentary, erotic, fine art, historical/vintage.

Making Contact & Terms There is a co-op membership fee plus a donation of time. There is a 40% commission. There is a rental fee for space. The rental fee covers 1 month. Gallery provides contract. Accepted work should be framed and matted.

Submissions Call to arrange personal interview to show portfolio. Responds to queries in 1 month. Finds artists through referrals by other artists and word of mouth.

Tips "Visit Web site first. Read new member prospectus on the front page. Call with additional questions. Do not 'drop in' with slides or art. Do not show everything you do. Show 10-25 images that are cohesive in subject, style and presentation."

TURNER CARROLL GALLERY

725 Canyon Rd., Santa Fe NM 87501. (505)986-9800. Fax: (505)986-5027. E-mail: tcgallery @aol.com. Web site: www.turnercarrollgallery.com. **Contact:** Tonya Turner Carroll, owner. Art consultancy and for-profit gallery. Estab. 1991. Approached by 50 artists/year; represents or exhibits 15 artists. Sponsors 1 photography exhibit/year. Average display time 4-6 weeks. Open daily from 10 to 6; Friday from 10 to 7. Three salon rooms; 1,200 sq. ft. Overall price range $1,000-40,000. Most work sold at $4,000-5,000.

Exhibits Interested in fine art.

Making Contact & Terms Artwork is accepted on consignment, and there is a 50% commission. Accepts only museum track artists. Requires exclusive representation locally.

Submissions Send e-mail query with JPEG samples at 72 dpi. Send query letter with artist's statement, bio, brochure, business card. Finds artists through art fairs.

UCR/CALIFORNIA MUSEUM OF PHOTOGRAPHY

University of California, Riverside CA 92521. (951)784-3686. Fax: (951)827-4797. Web site: www.cmp.ucr.edu. **Contact:** Director. Sponsors 10-15 exhibits/year. Average display time 8-14 weeks. Open Tuesday through Saturday from 12 to 5. Located in a renovated 23,000-sq.-ft. building. "It is the largest exhibition space devoted to photography in the West."

Exhibits Interested in technology/computers, alternative process, avant garde, documentary, fine art, historical/vintage.

Making Contact & Terms Curatorial committee reviews CDs, slides and/or matted or unmatted work. Photographer must have "highest-quality work."

Submissions Send query letter with résumé, SASE. Accepts images in digital format; send via CD, Zip.

Tips "This museum attempts to balance exhibitions among historical, technological, contemporary, etc. We do not sell photos but provide photographers with exposure. The museum is always interested in newer, lesser-known photographers who are producing interesting work. We're especially interested in work relevant to underserved communities. We can show only a small percent of what we see in a year."

UNI GALLERY OF ART

University of Northern Iowa, 104 Kamerick Art Bldg., Cedar Falls IA 50614-0362. (319)273-6134. E-mail: galleryofart@uni.edu. Web site: www.uni.edu/artdept/gallery. **Contact:** Darrell Taylor, director. Estab. 1976. Sponsors 9 exhibits/year. Average display time 1 month. Approximately 5,000 sq. ft. of space and 424 ft. of usable wall space.

Exhibits Interested in all styles of high-quality contemporary art works.

Making Contact & Terms "We do not sell work."

Submissions Please provide a cover letter and proposal as well as an artist's statement, CV (curriculum vitae), and samples. Send material by mail for consideration or submit portfolio for review; include SASE for return of material. Response time varies.

UNION STREET GALLERY

1527 Otto Blvd., Chicago Heights IL 60411. (708)754-2601. E-mail: unionstreetart@sbcglobal.net. Web site: www.unionstreetgallery.org. **Contact**: Renee Klyczek Nordstrom, gallery administrator. Nonprofit gallery. Estab. 1995. Represents or exhibits more than 100 artists. "We offer group invitations and juried shows every year." Average display time 6 weeks.

Galleries

Galleries

Gallery open Wednesday through Saturday from 12 to 4; 2nd Friday of every month from 6 to 9. Overall price range $30-3,000. Most work sold at $300-600.

Submissions Finds artists through submissions, referrals by other artists, juried exhibits at the gallery. "To receive prospectus for all juried events, call, write or e-mail to be added to our mailing list. Prospectus also available on Web site. Artists interested in studio space or solo/group exhibitions should contact the gallery to request information packets."

UNIVERSITY ART GALLERY IN THE D.W. WILLIAMS ART CENTER

New Mexico State University, MSC 3572, P.O. Box 30001, Las Cruces NM 88003-8001. (505)646-2545. Fax: (505)646-5207. E-mail: artglry@nmsu.edu. Web site: www.nmsu.edu/~artgal. **Contact:** John Lawson, interim director. Estab. 1973. Sponsors 1 exhibit/year. Average display time 2 months. Overall price range $300-2,500.

Making Contact & Terms Buys photos outright.

Submissions Arrange a personal interview to show portfolio. Submit portfolio for review. Send query letter with samples. Send material by mail with SASE by end of October for consideration. Responds in 3 months.

Tips Looks for "quality fine art photography. The gallery does mostly curated, thematic exhibitions. Very few one-person exhibitions."

ⓝ UNIVERSITY OF KENTUCKY ART MUSEUM

Rose St. and Euclid Ave., Lexington KY 40506-0241. (859)257-5716. Fax: (859)323-1994. E-mail: jwelk3@email.uky.edu. Web site: www.uky.edu/artmuseum. **Contact:** Janie Welker, curator. Museum. Estab. 1979.

Exhibits Annual photography lecture series and exhibits.

Submissions Send query letter with artist's statement, résumé, reviews, slides, SASE, publications, if available. Responds in 6 months.

UNIVERSITY OF RICHMOND MUSEUMS

Richmond VA 23173. (804)289-8276. Fax: (804)287-1894. E-mail: rwaller@richmond.edu. Web site: http://museums.richmond.edu. **Contact:** Richard Waller, director. Estab. 1968. "University Museums comprises Joel and Lila Harnett Museum of Art, Joel and Lila Harnett Print Study Center, and Lora Robins Gallery of Design from Nature." Sponsors 18-20 exhibits/year. Average display time 8-10 weeks.

Exhibits Interested in all subjects.

Making Contact & Terms Charges 10% commission. Work must be framed for exhibition.

Submissions Send query letter with résumé, samples. Send material by mail for consideration. Responds in 1 month.

Tips "If possible, submit material that can be left on file and fits standard letter file. We are a nonprofit university museum interested in presenting contemporary art as well as historical exhibitions."

▣ UNTITLED [ARTSPACE]

1 NE Third St., Oklahoma City OK 73103. E-mail: untitledartspace@1ne3.org. Web site: www.1ne3.org. **Contact:** Lori Deemer, operations director. Alternative space, nonprofit gallery. Estab. 2003. Average display time 6-8 weeks. Open Tuesday, Wednesday, Thursday from 11 to 6; Friday from 11 to 8; Saturday from 11 to 4. "Located in a reclaimed industrial space abandoned by decades of urban flight. Damaged in the 1995 Murrah Federal Building

bombing, Untitled [ArtSpace] has emerged as a force for creative thought. As part of the Deep Deuce historic district in downtown Oklahoma City, Untitled [ArtSpace] brings together visual arts, performance, music, film, design and architecture. Our mission is to stimulate creative thought and new ideas through contemporary art. We are committed to providing access to quality exhibitions, educational programs, performances, publications, and to engaging the community in collaborative outreach efforts." Most work sold at $750.

Making Contact & Terms Artwork is accepted on consignment, and there is a 50% commission.

Submissions Mail portfolio for review. Send query letter with artist's statement, bio, résumé, slides, or CD of images. Prefers 10-15 images on a CD. Include SASE for return of materials or permission to file the portfolio. Reviews occur twice annually, in January and July. Finds artists through submissions, portfolio reviews. Responds to queries within 1 week, only if interested.

Tips "Review our previous programming to evaluate if your work is along the lines of our mission. Take the time to type and proof all written submissions. Make sure your best work is represented in the images you choose to show. Nothing takes away from the review like poorly scanned or photographed work."

[N] UPSTREAM GALLERY

26 Main St., Dobbs Ferry NY 10522. (914)674-8548. E-mail: upstreamgallery@aol.com. Web site: www.upstreamgallery.com. Cooperative gallery. Estab. 1990. Represents or exhibits 22 artists. Sponsors 1 photography exhibit/year. Average display time 1 month. Open all year; Thursday through Sunday from 12:30 to 5:30. Closed July and August (but an appointment can be made by calling 914-375-1693). "We have 2 store fronts, approximately 15×30 sq. ft. each." Overall price range: $300-2,000.

Exhibits Interested in fine art. Accepts all subject matters and genres for jurying.

Making Contact & Terms There is a co-op membership fee plus a donation of time. There is a 10% commission. Gallery provides insurance. Accepted work should be framed, mounted and matted.

Submissions Write to arrange a personal interview to show portfolio of photographs and slides. Send query letter with artist's statement, bio, brochure, business card, photographs, résumé, reviews, slides and SASE. Responds to queries within 2 months, only if interested. Finds artists through referrals by other artists and submissions.

UPSTREAM PEOPLE GALLERY

5607 Howard St., Omaha NE 68106. (402)991-4741. E-mail: shows@upstreampeoplegallery .com. Web site: www.upstreampeoplegallery.com. **Contact:** Larry Bradshaw, curator. For-profit Internet gallery. Estab. 1998. Approached by 13,000 artists/year; represents or exhibits 1,300 artists. Sponsors 4 photography exhibits/year. Average display time 1 or more years online. Virtual gallery open 24 hours daily. Overall price range $100-125,000. Most work sold at over $300.

Exhibits Exhibits photos of babies/children/teens, couples, multicultural, families, parents, senior citizens, disasters, environmental, landscapes/scenics, wildlife, gardening, interiors/decorating, pets, religious, adventure, automobiles, events, health/fitness/beauty, humor, performing arts, sports, travel, agriculture, military, political, product shots/still life, technology/computers. Interested in alternative process, avant garde, documentary, fine art, historical/vintage, seasonal.

Making Contact & Terms Artwork is accepted on consignment, and there is no commission if the artists sells; there is a 20% commission if the gallery sells. There is an entry fee for space; covers 1 or more years.

Submissions Mail portfolio of slides for review. Send query letter with artist's statement, bio, brochure (optional), résumé, reviews, slides, personal photo. Responds to queries in 1 week. Finds artists through art exhibits, portfolio reviews, referrals by other artists, submissions, word of mouth, Internet.

URBAN INSTITUTE FOR CONTEMPORARY ARTS

41 Sheldon Blvd. SE, Grand Rapids MI 49503. (616)454-7000. Fax: (616)459-9395. E-mail: jteunis@uica.org. Web site: www.uica.org. **Contact:** Janet Teunis, managing director. Alternative space and nonprofit gallery. Estab. 1977. Approached by 250 artists/year; represents or exhibits 20 artists. Sponsors 3-4 photography exhibits/year. Average display time 6 weeks. Gallery open Tuesday through Saturday from 12 to 10; Sunday from 12 to 7. Closed Monday, the month of August, and the week of Christmas and New Year's.

Exhibits Interested in avant garde, fine art.

Submissions Send query letter with artist's statement, bio, résumé, reviews, slides, SASE. Finds artists through submissions.

Tips "Get submission requirements at www.uica.org/visualArts.html under 'Apply for a Show.'"

VILLA JULIE COLLEGE GALLERY

1525 Greenspring Valley Rd., Stevenson MD 21153. (443)334-2163. Fax: (410)486-3552. E-mail: exhibitions@mail.vjc.edu. Web site: www.vjc.edu. **Contact:** Diane DiSalvo, director of cultural programs. College/university gallery. Estab. 1997. Sponsors at least 2 photography exhibits/year. Average display time 6 weeks. Gallery open Monday, Tuesday, Thursday, Friday from 11 to 5; Wednesday from 11 to 8; Saturday from 1 to 4. "Two beautiful spaces."

Exhibits Interested in alternative process, avant garde, documentary, fine art, historical/vintage. "We are looking for artwork of substance by artists from the mid-Atlantic region."

Making Contact & Terms "We facilitate inquiries directly to the artist." Gallery provides insurance. *Accepts artists from mid-Atlantic states only; emphasis on Baltimore artists.*

Submissions Write to show portfolio of slides. Send artist's statement, bio, résumé, reviews, slides, SASE. Responds in 3 months. Finds artists through word of mouth, submissions, portfolio reviews, referrals by other artists.

Tips "Be clear, concise. Have good representation of your images."

Ⓝ VIRIDIAN ARTISTS, INC.

530 W. 25th St., #407, New York NY 10001. (212)414-4040. Fax: (212)414-4040. Web site: www.viridianartists.com. **Contact:** Barbara Neski, director. Estab. 1968. Sponsors 11 exhibits/year. Average display time 4 weeks. Overall price range $175-10,000. Most work sold at $1,500.

Exhibits Interested in eclectic work in all fine art media including photography, installation, painting, mixed media and sculpture. Interested in alternative process, avant garde, fine art.

Making Contact & Terms Charges 30% commission.

Submissions Will review transparencies and cds only if submitted as part of membership application for representation with SASE. Request information for representation via phone or e-mail or check Web site.

Tips "Opportunities for photographers in galleries are improving. Broad range of styles being shown in galleries. Photography is getting a large audience that is seemingly appreciative of technical and aesthetic abilities of the individual artists. Present a portfolio (regardless of format) that expresses a clear artistic and aesthetic focus that is unique, individual, and technically outstanding."

Ⓝ ▣ VISUAL ARTS CENTER OF NORTHWEST FLORIDA

19 E. Fourth St., Panama City FL 32401. (850)769-4451. Fax: (850)785-9248. E-mail: visualar tscenterofnwfla@comcast.net. Web site: www.vac.org.cn. **Contact:** Exhibition Coordinator. Estab. 1988. Approached by 20 artists/year; represents local and national artists. Sponsors 1-2 photography exhibits/year. Average display time 6 weeks. Open Monday, Wednesday and Friday from 10 to 4; Tuesday and Thursday from 10 to 8; Saturday from 1 to 5. Closed major holidays. The Center features a large gallery (200 running ft.) upstairs and a smaller gallery (80 running ft.) downstairs. Overall price range $50-1,500.

Exhibits Exhibits photos of all subject matter, including babies/children/teens, couples, families, parents, senior citizens, environmental, landscapes/scenics, wildlife, architecture, product shots/still life. Interested in alternative process, avant garde, documentary, fashion/glamour, fine art, historical/vintage, seasonal, digital, underwater.

Making Contact & Terms Artwork is accepted on consignment, and there is a 30% commission. Gallery provides promotion, contract, insurance. Accepted work must be framed, mounted, matted.

Submissions Send query letter with artist's statement, bio, résumé, SASE, 10-12 slides or images on CD. Responds within 4 months. Finds artists through word of mouth, submissions, art exhibits.

VISUAL ARTS GALLERY

University of Alabama at Birmingham, 1530 Third Ave. S., Birmingham AL 35294-1260. (205)934-0815. Fax: (205)975-2836. E-mail: blevine@uab.edu. Web site: www.uab.edu/art/gallery/vag.html. **Contact:** Brett M. Levine, director/curator. Nonprofit university gallery. Sponsors 1-3 photography exhibits/year. Average display time 3-4 weeks. Gallery open Monday through Thursday from 11 to 6; Friday from 11 to 5; Saturday from 1-5. Closed major holidays and last 2 weeks of December. Located on 1st floor of Humanities Building: 2 rooms with a total of 2,000 sq. ft. and 222 running ft.

Exhibits Exhibits photos of multicultural. Interested in alternative process, avant garde, fine art, historical/vintage.

Making Contact & Terms Gallery provides insurance, promotion. Accepted work should be framed.

Submissions Does not accept unsolicited exhibition proposals. Write to arrange a personal interview to show portfolio of slides. Send query letter with artist's statement, bio, brochure, photographs, résumé, reviews, slides, SASE.

THE WAILOA CENTER GALLERY

P.O. Box 936, Hilo HI 96721. (808)933-0416. Fax: (808)933-0417. E-mail: wailoa@yahoo.com. **Contact:** Ms. Codie King, director. Estab. 1967. Sponsors 24 exhibits/year. Average display time 1 month.

Exhibits Photos must be submitted to director for approval. "All entries accepted must meet professional standards outlined in our pre-entry forms."

Making Contact & Terms Gallery receives 10% "donation" on works sold. No fee for exhibiting. Accepted work should be framed. "Photos must also be fully fitted for hanging. Expenses involved in shipping, insurance, invitations and reception, etc., are the responsibility of the exhibitor."

Submissions Submit portfolio for review. Send query letter with résumé of credits, samples, SASE. Responds in 3 weeks.

Tips "The Wailoa Center Gallery is operated by the State of Hawaii, Department of Land and Natural Resources. We are unique in that there are no costs to the artist to exhibit here as far as rental or commissions are concerned. We welcome artists from anywhere in the world who would like to show their works in Hawaii. Wailoa Center is booked 2-3 years in advance. The gallery is also a visitor information center with thousands of people from all over the world visiting."

WASHINGTON COUNTY MUSEUM OF FINE ARTS

P.O. Box 423, Hagerstown MD 21741. (301)739-5727. Fax: (301)745-3741. E-mail: info@wc mfa.org. Web site: www.wcmfa.org. **Contact:** Curator. Estab. 1929. Approached by 30 artists/year. Sponsors 1 juried photography exhibit/year. Average display time 6-8 weeks. Museum open Tuesday through Friday from 9 to 5; Saturday from 9 to 4; Sunday from 1 to 5. Closed legal holidays. Overall price range $50-7,000.

Exhibits Exhibits photos of babies/children/teens, celebrities, couples, multicultural, families, parents, senior citizens, disasters, environmental, landscapes/scenics, wildlife, architecture, cities/urban, education, gardening, interiors/decorating, pets, religious, rural, adventure, automobiles, entertainment, events, food/drink, health/fitness/beauty, hobbies, humor, performing arts, sports, travel, agriculture, business concepts, industry, medicine, military, political, product shots/still life, science, technology/computers. Interested in alternative process, avant garde, documentary, fashion/glamour, fine art, historical/vintage, seasonal.

Making Contact & Terms Museum provides artist's contact information to potential buyers. Accepted work should not be framed.

Submissions Write to show portfolio of photographs, slides. Mail portfolio for review. Responds in 1 month. Finds artists through word of mouth, portfolio reviews, art exhibits, referrals by other artists.

Tips "We sponsor an annual juried competition in photography. Entry forms are available in October each year. Send name and address to be placed on list."

◼ ⊘ WEINSTEIN GALLERY

908 W. 46th St., Minneapolis MN 55419. (612)822-1722. Fax: (612)822-1745. E-mail: weing all@aol.com. Web site: www.weinstein-gallery.com. **Contact:** Laura Hoyt, director. For-profit gallery. Estab. 1996. Approached by hundreds of artists/year; represents or exhibits 12 artists. Average display time 6 weeks. Open Tuesday through Saturday from 12 to 5. Overall price range $4,000-250,000.

Exhibits Interested in fine art. Most frequently exhibits contemporary photography.

Submissions "We do not accept unsolicited submissions."

EDWARD WESTON FINE ART AND PHOTOGRAPHY

(formerly Edward Weston Fine Art) P.O. Box 3098, Chatsworth CA 91313. (818)885-1044. Fax: (818)885-1021. **Contact:** Rachel or Anne. Estab. 1960. Approached by 50 artists/year; represents or exhibits 100 artists. Sponsors 10 photography exhibits/year. Average display time 4-6 weeks. Gallery open Monday through Friday. Overall price range $100-50,000. Most work sold at $1,000.

Exhibits Exhibits photos of celebrities, Hollywood glamour and contemporary photography.

Making Contact & Terms Artwork is accepted on consignment, and there is a 50% commission. Gallery provides contract. Accepted work should be framed, matted. Requires exclusive representation locally.

Submissions Write to arrange a personal interview to show portfolio of photographs, transparencies. Mail slides for review. Send query letter with bio, brochure, business card, photocopies, photographs, reviews.

Tips "Be thorough and complete."

WHITE CANVAS GALLERY

111 S. 14th St., Richmond VA 23219-4127. E-mail: info@whitecanvasgallery.com. Web site: www.whitecanvasgallery.com. **Contact:** Kat Hurst, director. For-profit gallery. Estab. 2004 (formerly Cudahy's Gallery, 1981-2003). Approached by 75 artists/year; represents or exhibits 50 artists. Sponsors 1 photography exhibit/year. Average display time 5 weeks. Open Tuesday through Saturday from 10 to 6; Sunday from 12 to 5. Located on a busy downtown street; free parking for customers.

Exhibits Exhibits photos of architecture, cities/urban, gardening, interiors/decorating, rural, environmental, landscapes/scenics. Interested in fine art and pinhole photography

Making Contact & Terms Artwork is accepted on consignment, and there is a 50% commission. Requires exclusive representation locally. Accepts only artists from the US.

Submissions Write to arrange a personal interview to show portfolio of photographs, slides, CDs. Mail portfolio for review. Send query letter with artist's statement, bio, brochure, business card, photocopies, photographs, résumé, slides, CD, SASE. Finds artists through word of mouth, art exhibits, submissions, art fairs, referrals by other artists. Responds to queries in 4-6 weeks.

Tips "Include list with titles, dimensions, media, price points, résumé/bio, artist's statement. Label slides and photos with title, dimensions, artist's name, media. Include SASE for return of your materials."

WISCONSIN UNION GALLERIES

800 Langdon St., Room 507, Madison WI 53706-1495. (608)262-7592. Fax: (608)262-8862. E-mail: art@union.wisc.edu. Web site: www.union.wisc.edu/art. **Contact:** Christie Wilmot, art committee director. Nonprofit gallery. Estab. 1928. Approached by 100 artists/year; represents or exhibits 20 artists. Average display time 6 weeks. Open Monday through Sunday from 10 to 8. Closed during winter break and when gallery exhibitions turn over. "See our Web site at http://www.union.wisc.edu/art/submit.html to find out more about the galleries' features."

Exhibits Exhibits photos of education. Interested in fine art. "Photography exhibitions vary based on the artist proposals submitted."

Making Contact & Terms All sales through gallery during exhibition only.

Submissions Current submission guidelines available at http://www.union.wisc.edu/

art/submit.html. Finds artists through art fairs, art exhibits, referrals by other artists, submissions, word of mouth.

WOMEN & THEIR WORK ART SPACE

1710 Lavaca St., Austin TX 78701. (512)477-1064. Fax: (512)477-1090. E-mail: info@wome nandtheirwork.org. Web site: www.womenandtheirwork.org. **Contact:** Katherine Mc-Queen, associate director. Alternative space, nonprofit gallery. Estab. 1978. Approached by more than 400 artists/year; represents or exhibits 6 solo and 1 juried show/year. Sponsors 1-2 photography exhibits/year. Average display time 5 weeks. Gallery open Monday through Friday from 9 to 6; Saturday from 12 to 5. Closed December 24 through January 2, and other major holidays. Exhibition space is 2,000 sq. ft. Overall price range $500-5,000. Most work sold at $800-1,000.

Exhibits Interested in contemporary, alternative process, avant garde, fine art.

Making Contact & Terms ''We select artists through a juried process and pay them to exhibit. We take 25% commission if something is sold.'' Gallery provides insurance, promotion, contract. Accepted work should be framed, mounted, matted. *Texas women in solo shows only.* ''All other artists, male or female, in curated show. Online Artist Slide Registry on Web site.''

Submissions Finds artists through nomination by art professional.

Tips ''Provide quality images, typed résumé and a clear statement of artistic intent.''

WOMEN'S CENTER ART GALLERY

UCSB, Student Resource Building 1220, Santa Barbara CA 93106-7190. (805)893-3778. Fax: (805)893-3289. E-mail: sharon.hoshida@sa.ucsb.edu. Web site: www.sa.ucsb.edu/women 'scenter. **Contact:** Sharon Hoshida, program director. Nonprofit gallery. Estab. 1973. Approached by 200 artists/year; represents or exhibits 50 artists. Sponsors 1 photography exhibit/year. Average display time 11 weeks. Open Monday through Thursday from 10 to 9; Friday from 10 to 5. Closed UCSB campus holidays. Exhibition space is roughly 750 sq. ft. Overall price range $10-1,000. Most work sold at $300.

Exhibits Exhibits photos of babies/children/teens, couples, multicultural, families, parents, senior citizens, disasters, environmental, landscapes/scenics, wildlife, architecture, cities/urban, education, interiors/decorating, religious, rural, adventure, entertainment, events, hobbies, humor, performing arts, sports, travel. Interested in alternative process, avant garde, documentary, erotic, fashion/glamour, fine art, historical/vintage, seasonal.

Making Contact & Terms Artwork is accepted on consignment, and there is no commission. Gallery provides insurance, promotion. Accepted work should be framed. Preference given to residents of Santa Barbara County.

Submissions Mail portfolio for review. Send query letter with artist's statement, bio, photocopies, photographs, resume, slides, SASE. Responds within 3 months, only if interested. Finds artists through word of mouth, portfolio reviews, art exhibits, e-mail and promotional calls to artists.

Tips ''Complete your submission thoroughly and include a relevent statement pertaining to the specific exhibit.''

WORLD FINE ART GALLERY

511 W. 25th St., #803, New York NY 10001-5501. (646)336-1677. Fax: (646)336- 6090. E-mail: info@worldfin eart.com. Web site: www.worldfineart.com. **Contact:** O'Delle Abney,

director. Cooperative gallery. Estab. 1992. Approached by 1,500 artists/year; represents or exhibits 50 artists. Average display time 1 month. Open Tuesday through Saturday from 12 to 6. Closed August. Located in Chelsea, NY; 1,000 sq. ft. Overall price range: $500-5,000. Most work sold at $1,500.

Exhibits Exhibits photos of landscapes/scenics, gardening. Interested in fine art.

Making Contact &Terms The re is a rental fee for space . The rental fee covers 1 month or 1 year. Gallery provides insurance, promotion and contract. Accepted work should be framed; must be considered suitable for exhibition.

Submissions Write to arrange a personal interview to show portfolio, or e-mail JPEG images. Responds to queries in 1 week. Finds artists through the Internet.

Tips "Have a Web site available for review."

YESHIVA UNIVERSITY MUSEUM

15 W. 16th St., New York NY 10011. (212)294-8330. Fax: (212)294-8335. E-mail: rwulkan@ yum.cjh.org. Web site: www.yumuseum.org. **Contact:** Sylvia A. Herskowitz, director. Estab. 1973. Sponsors 6-8 exhibits/year; at least 1 photography exhibit/year. Average display time 4-6 months. The museum occupies 4 galleries and several exhibition arcades. All galleries are handicapped accessible.

Exhibits Seeks "individual or group exhibits focusing on Jewish themes and interests; exhibition-ready work essential."

Making Contact & Terms Accepts images in digital format. Send CD and accompanying text with SASE for return. Send color slide portfolio of 10-12 slides or photos, exhibition proposal, résumé with SASE for consideration. Reviews take place 3 times/year.

Tips "We exhibit contemporary art and photography based on Jewish themes. We look for excellent quality, individuality, and work that reveals a connection to Jewish identity and/ or spirituality."

ZENITH GALLERY

413 Seventh St. NW, Washington DC 20004. (202)783-2963. Fax: (202)783-0050. E-mail: art@zenithgallery.com. Web site: www.zenithgallery.com. **Contact:** Margery E. Goldberg, owner/director. For-profit gallery. Estab. 1978. Open Tuesday through Friday from 11 to 6; Saturday from 11 to 7; Sunday from 12 to 5. Located in the heart of downtown Washington, DC—street level, 3 exhibition rooms, 2,400 sq. ft. Overall price range: $500-15,000.

Exhibits Exhibits photos of landscapes/scenics and other. Interested in avant garde, fine art.

Submissions Mail portfolio for review. Send query letter with artist's statement, bio, brochure, business card, résumé, reviews, photocopies, photographs, slides, CD, SASE. Responds to queries within 1 year, only if interested. Finds artists through art fairs and exhibits, portfolio reviews, referrals by other artists, submissions and word of mouth.

Art Fairs

Art fairs (also called art festivals or art shows) can provide photographers with a good source of income. If you like to travel and enjoy making prints, matting and framing, you might want to consider this outlet for selling your work. Art fairs are located all over the United States. Many outdoor fairs occur during the spring, summer and fall months to take advantage of warmer temperatures. However, depending on the region, temperatures could be hot and humid, and not all that pleasant! And, of course, there is always the chance of rain. Indoor art fairs held in November and December are popular because they capitalize on the holiday buying season.

To start selling your photographs at art fairs, you will need an inventory of prints. Some should be framed: Even if customers do not buy the framed pieces, at least they can get an idea of how your work looks framed, which could spur sales of your unframed prints. Ideally, all photos should be matted and stored in protective wraps or bags so that customers can look through your inventory without damaging prints and mats. You will also need a canopy or tent to protect yourself and your wares from the elements, as well as some bins in which to store the prints. A display wall will allow you to show off your best, framed prints. Generally, artists will have a 10-ft. by 10-ft. space in which to set up their tents and canopies. Most listings will specify the dimensions of the exhibition space for each artist.

If you see the "loving cup" icon ♥ before a listing, it means that this art fair is a juried event. In other words, there is a selection process artists must go through to be admitted into the fair. Many art fairs have quotas for the categories of exhibitors. For example, one art fair may accept the mediums of photography, sculpture, painting, metal work and jewelry. Once each category fills with qualified exhibitors, no more will be admitted to the show that year. The jurying process also ensures that the artists who sell their work at the fair meet the sponsor's criteria for quality. So, overall, if an art fair is juried, that is a good thing for the artists because it signals that they will be exhibiting their work with artists of equal caliber.

There are fees associated with entering art fairs. Most fairs have an application fee or a space fee, or sometimes both. The space fee is essentially a rental fee for the space your booth will occupy during the art fair's duration. These fees can vary greatly from show to show, so be sure to check this information in each listing before you apply to any art fair.

Most art fair sponsors want to exhibit only work that is handmade by the artist, no matter what medium. Unfortunately, some people try to sell work that they purchased elsewhere as their own original artwork. In the art fair trade, this is known as "buy/sell." It is an undesirable situation since it tends to bring down the quality of the whole show. Some listings will make a point to say "no buy/sell" or "no manufactured work."

AFFAIRE IN THE GARDENS ART SHOW

Greystone Park, 501 Doheny Rd., Beverly Hills CA 90210-2921. (310)550-4796. Fax: (310)858-9238. E-mail: kmclean@beverlyhills.org. Web site: www.beverlyhills.org. **Contact:** Karen Fitch McLean, art show coordinator. Estab. 1973. Fine arts & crafts show held biannulay 3rd weekend in May and 3rd weekend in October. Outdoors. Accepts photography, painting, sculpture, ceramics, jewelry, digital media. Juried. Awards/prizes: 1st Place in category, cash awards, Best in Show cash award; Mayor's Purchase Award in October show. Number of exhibitors: 225. Public attendance: 30,000-40,000. Free to public. Deadline for entry: end of February, May show; end of July, October show. Application fee: $30. Space fee: $300. Exhibition space: 10×12 ft. For more information, artists should e-mail, visit Web site, call or send SASE.

Tips "Art fairs tend to be commercially oriented. It usually pays off to think in somewhat commercial terms—what does the public usually buy? Personally, I like risky and unusual art, but the artists who produce esoteric art sometimes go hungry! Be nice and have a clean presentation."

AKRON ARTS EXPO

220 S. Balch St., Akron OH 44302. (330)375-2835. Fax: (330)375-2883. E-mail: recreation@ci.akron.oh.us. Web site: www.akronperforms.com. **Contact:** Yvette Davidson, community events coordinator. Estab. 1979. Fine art & craft show held annually in late July. Outdoors. Accepts photography, 2D art, functional craft, ornamental. Juried by 4 slides of work and 1 slide of display. Awards/prizes: $1,600 in cash awards and ribbons. Number of exhibitors: 165. Public attendance: 3,000+. Free to public. Deadline for entry: March 31. Space fee: $150-180. Exhibition space: 15×15 ft. For more information, artists should e-mail or call.

ALLENTOWN ART FESTIVAL

P.O. Box 1566, Ellicott Station, Buffalo NY 14205-1566. (716)881-4269. E-mail: allentownartfestival@verizon.net. Web site: www.allentownartfestival.com. **Contact:** Mary Myszkiewicz, president. Estab. 1958. Fine arts & crafts show held annually 2nd full weekend in June. Outdoors. Accepts photography, painting, watercolor, drawing, graphics, sculpture, mixed media, clay, glass, acrylic, jewelry, creative craft (hard/soft). Slides juried by hired professionals that change yearly. Awards/prizes: $17,925 in 40 cash prizes; Best of Show. Number of exhibitors: 450. Public attendance: 300,000. Free to public. Artists should apply by downloading application from Web site. Deadline for entry: January 31. Application fee: $15. Space fee: $250. Exhibition space: 13×10 ft. For more information, artists should e-mail, visit Web site, call or send SASE.

Tips "Artists must have attractive booth and interact with the public."

AMISH ACRES ARTS & CRAFTS FESTIVAL

1600 W Market St., Nappanee IN 46550. (574)773-4188. Fax: (574)773-4180. E-mail: jenniwysong@amishacres.com. Web site: www.amishacres.com. **Contact:** Jenni Wysong, marketplace coordinator. Estab. 1962. Arts & crafts show held annually 1st full weekend in August. Outdoors. Accepts photography, crafts, floral, folk, jewelry, oil, acrylic, sculpture, textiles, watercolors, wearable, wood. Juried by 5 images, either 35mm slides or digital images e-mailed. Awards/prizes: $10,000 cash including Best of Show and $1,500 Purchase Prizes. Number of exhibitors: 350. Public attendance: 60,000. Public admission: $6; children under 12 free. Artists should apply by sending SASE or printing application from Web site. Deadline for entry: April 1. Space fee: 10×10 ft.: $475; 15×12 ft.: $675; 20×12 ft.: $1,095; 30×12 ft.: $1,595. Exhibition space: from 120-300 sq. ft. Average gross sales/exhibitor: $7,000. For more information, artists should e-mail, visit Web site, call or send SASE.

Tips "Create a vibrant, open display that beckons to passing customers. Interact with potential buyers. Sell the romance of the purchase."

ANACORTES ARTS FESTIVAL

505 O Ave., Anacortes WA 98221. (360)293-6211. Fax: 360-299-0722 . E-mail: info@anacort esartsfestival.com. Web site: www.anacortesartsfestival.com. **Contact:** Mary Leone. Fine arts & crafts show held annually 1st full weekend in August. Accepts photography, painting, drawings, prints, ceramics, fiber art, paper art, glass, jewelry, sculpture, yard art, woodworking. Juried by projecting 3 images on a large screen. Works are evaluated on originality, quality and marketability. Each applicant must provide 3 high-quality digital images or slides—2 of the product and 1 of the booth display. Awards/prizes: over $4,000 in prizes. Number of exhibitors: 250. Artists should apply by visiting Web site for online submission or by mail (there is a $25 processing fee for application by mail). Deadline for entry: early March. Booth fee: $300. For more information, artists should see Web site.

ANN ARBOR STREET ART FAIR

P.O. Box 1352, Ann Arbor MI 48106. (734)994-5260. Fax: (734)994-0504. E-mail: production @artfair.org. Web site: www.artfair.org. **Contact:** Jeannie Uh, production coordinator. Estab. 1958. Fine arts & crafts show held annually 3rd Saturday in July. Outdoors. Accepts photography, fiber, glass, digital art, jewelry, metals, 2D and 3D mixed media, sculpture, clay, painting, drawing, printmaking, pastels, wood. Juried based on originality, creativity, technique, craftsmanship and production. Awards/prizes: cash prizes for outstanding work in any media. Number of exhibitors: 175. Public attendance: 500,000. Free to the public. Artists should apply through www.zapplication.org. Deadline for entry: January. Application fee: $30. Space fee: $595. Exhibition space: 10×20 ft. or 10×12 ft. Average gross sales/exhibitor: $7,000. For more information, artists should e-mail, visit Web site, call.

ANN ARBOR'S SOUTH UNIVERSITY ART FAIR

P.O. Box 4525, Ann Arbor MI 48106. (734)663-5300. Fax: (734)663-5303. Web site: www.a2 southu.com. **Contact:** Maggie Ladd, director. Estab. 1960. Fine arts & crafts show held annually 3rd Wednesday through Saturday in July. Outdoors. Accepts photography, clay, drawing, digital, fiber, jewelry, metal, painting, sculpture, wood. Juried. Awards/prizes: $3,000. Number of exhibitors: 190. Public attendance: 750,000. Free to public. Deadline for entry: January. Application fee: $25. Space fee: $700-1500. Exhibition space: 10×10 to 20×10 ft. Average gross sales/exhibitor: $7,000. For more information artists should e-mail, visit Web site or call.

Tips "Research the market, use a mailing list, advertise in *Art Fair Guide* (150,000 circulation)."

ANNUAL ARTS & CRAFTS ADVENTURE AND ANNUAL ARTS & CRAFTS ADVENTURE II

P.O. Box 1326, Palatine IL 60078. (847)991-4748 or (312)751-2500. E-mail: asoa@webtv.n et. Web site: www.americansocietyofartists.org. **Contact:** American Society of Artists—

"anyone in the office can help." Estab. 1991. Fine arts & crafts show held biannually in May and September. Outdoors. Accepts photography, pottery, paintings, sculpture, glass, wood, woodcarving. Juried by 4 slides or photos of work and 1 slide or photo of display; SASE (No. 10); a résumé or show listing is helpful. See our Web site for on-line jury. Number of exhibitors: 75. Free to the public. Artists should apply by submitting jury materials. If juried in, you will receive a jury/approval number. Deadline for entry: 2 months prior to show or earlier if spaces fill. Space fee: $80. Exhibition space: approximately 100 sq. ft. for single space; other sizes available. For more information, artists should send SASE, submit jury material.

● Event held in Park Ridge, Illinois.

Tips "Remember that when you are at work in your studio, you are an artist. But when you are at a show, you are a business person selling your work."

☑ ANNUAL ARTS & CRAFTS EXPRESSIONS

P.O. Box 1326, Palatine IL 60078. (847)991-4748 or (312)751-2500. E-mail: asoa@webtv.net. Web site: www.americansocietyofartists.org. **Contact:** American Society of Artists— "anyone in the office can help." Estab. 1998. Fine arts & crafts show held annually in late July. Outdoors. Accepts photography, sculpture, jewelry, glass works, woodworking and more. Juried by 4 slides or photos of your work and 1 slide or photo of your display; SASE (No. 10); a resume or show listing is helpful. Number of exhibitors: 50. Free to the public. Artists should apply by submitting jury materials. If you want to jury via internet see our Web site and follow directions given there. If juried in, you will receive a jury/approval number. Deadline for entry: 2 months prior to show or earlier if spaces fill. Space fee: $155. Exhibition space: approximately 100 sq. ft for single space; other sizes available. For more information, artsits should send SASE, submit jury material.

● Event held in Chicago, Illinois.

Tips "Remember that when you are at work in your studio, you are an artist. But when you are at a show, you are a business person selling your work."

☑ ANNUAL ARTS & CRAFTS FAIR

Pend Oreille Arts Council, P.O. Box 1694, Sandpoint ID 83864. (208)263-6139. E-mail: art@sandpoint.net. Web site: www.ArtinSandpoint.org. Estab. 1962. Arts & crafts show held annually in August. Outdoors. Accepts photography and all handmade, noncommercial works. Juried by 8-member jury. Number of exhibitors: 100. Public attendance: 5,000. Free to public. Artists should apply by sending in application. Deadline for entry: May 1. Application fee: $15. Space fee: $150-230, no commission. Exhibition space: 10×10 ft. or 10×15 ft. For more information, artists should e-mail, visit Web site, call or send SASE.

☑ ANNUAL ARTS ADVENTURE

P.O. Box 1326, Palatine IL 60078. (847)991-4748 or (312)571-2500. E-mail: asoa@webtv.net. Web site: www.americansocietyofartists.org. **Contact:** American Society of Artists— "anyone in the office can help." Estab. 2001. Fine arts & crafts show held annually the end of July. Event held in Chicago, Illinois. Outdoors. Accepts photography, paintings, pottery, sculpture, jewelry and more. Juried. Send 4 slides or photos of your work and 1 slide or photo of your display; SASE (No. 10); a resume or show listing is helpful. See our Web site for on-line jury. Number of exhibitors: 50. Free to the public. Artists should apply by submitting jury materials. If juried in, you will receive a jury/approval number. Deadline for entry: 2 months prior to show or earlier if spaces fill. Space fee: $125. Exhibition space: approximately 100 sq. ft. for single space; other sizes available. For more information, artsits should send SASE, submit jury material.

• Event held in Chicago, Illinois.

Tips "Remember that when you are at work in your studio, you are an artist. But when you are at a show, you are a business person selling your work."

☑ ANNUAL EDENS ART FAIR

P.O. Box 1326, Palatine IL 60078. (847)991-4748 or (312)2500. E-mail: asoa@webtv.net. Web site: www.americansocietyofartists.org. **Contact:** American Society of Artists—"anyone in the office can help." stab. 1995 (after renovation of location; held many years prior to renovation). Fine arts & fine selected crafts show held annually in mid-July. Outdoors. Accepts photography, paintings, sculpture, glass works, jewelry. Juried. Send 4 slides or photos of your work and 1 slide or photo of your display; SASE (No. 10); a resume or show listing is helpful. Number of exhibitors: 50. Free to the public. Artists should apply by submitting jury materials. If you wish to jury online please see our Web site and follow directions given there. If juried in, you will receive a jury/approval number. Deadline for entry: 2 months prior to show or earlier if spaces fill. Space fee: $140. Exhibition space: approximately 100 sq. ft. for single space; other sizes available. For more information, artists should send SASE, submit jury material.

• Event held in Willamette, Illinois.

Tips "Remember that when you are at work in your studio, you are an artist. But when you are at a show, you are a business person selling your work."

☑ ANNUAL HYDE PARK ARTS & CRAFTS ADVENTURE

P.O. Box 1326, Palatine IL 60078. (847)991-4748 or (312)751-2500. E-mail: asoa@webtv.net. Web site: www.americansocietyofartists.org. **Contact:** American Society of Artists—"anyone in the office can help." Estab. 2001. Arts & crafts show held twice a year in late May/early June and September. Outdoors. Accepts photography, paintings, glass, wood, fiber arts, hand-crafted candles, quilts, sculpture and more. Juried by 4 slides or photos of work and 1 slide or photo of display; SASE (No. 10); a résumé or show listing is helpful. Number of exhibitors: 50. Free to the public. Artists should apply by submitting jury materials. If juried in, you will receive a jury/approval number. See Web site for jurying on-line. Deadline for entry: 2 months prior to show or earlier if spaces fill. Space fee: $135. Exhibition space: approximately 100 sq. ft. for single space; other sizes are available. For more information, artists should send SASE, submit jury material.

• Event held in Chicago, Illinois.

Tips "Remember that when you are at work in your studio, you are an artist. But when you are at a show, you are a business person selling your work."

☑ ANNUAL OAK PARK AVENUE-LAKE ARTS & CRAFTS SHOW

P.O. Box 1326, Palatine IL 60078. (847)991-4748 or (312)751-2500. E-mail: asoa@webtv.net. Web site: www.americansocietyofartists.org. **Contact:** American Society of Artists—"anyone in the office can help." Estab. 1974. Fine arts & crafts show held annually in mid-August. Outdoors. Accepts photography, paintings, graphics, sculpture, glass, wood, paper, fiber arts, mosaics and more. Juried by 4 slides or photos of work and 1 slide or photo of display; SASE (No. 10); a resume or show listing is helpful. Number of exhibitors: 150.

Free to the public. Artists should apply by submitting jury materials. If you want to jury online please see our Web site and follow directions given there. If juried in, you will receive a jury/approval number. Deadline for entry: 2 months prior to show or earlier if spaces fill. Space fee: $160. Exhibition space: approximately 100 sq. ft. for single space; other sizes available. For more information, artists should send SASE, submit jury material.

● Event held in Oak Park, Illinois.

Tips "Remember that when you are at work in your studio, you are an artist. But when you are at a show, you are a business person selling your work."

ANNUAL VOLVO MAYFAIRE-BY-THE-LAKE

Polk Museum of Art, 800 E. Palmetto St., Lakeland FL 33801. (863)688-7743, ext. 237. Fax: (863)688-2611. E-mail: mayfaire@polkmuseumofart.org. Web site: www.PolkMuseumOfArt.org. Estab. 1971. Fine arts & crafts show held annually in May on Mother's Day weekend. Outdoors. Accepts photography, oil, acrylic, watercolor, drawing & graphics, sculpture, clay, jewelry, glass, wood, fiber, mixed media. Juried by a panel of jurors who will rank the artist's body of work based on 3 slides of works and 1 slide of booth setup. Awards/prizes: 2 Best of Show, 3 Awards of Excellence, 8 Merit awards, 10 Honorable Mentions, Museum Purchase Awards, Collectors Club Purchase Awards, which equal over $25,000. Number of exhibitors: 185. Public attendance: 65,000. Free to public. Artists should download application from Web site to apply. Deadline for entry: March 1. Application fee: $25. Space fee: $145. Exhibition space: 10×10 ft. For more information, artists should visit Web site or call.

APPLE ANNIE CRAFTS & ARTS SHOW

4905 Roswell Rd. NE, Marietta GA 30062. (770)552-6400, ext. 6110. Fax: (770)552-6420. E-mail: appleannie@st-ann.org. Web site: www.st-ann.org/appleannie. **Contact:** Show Manager. Estab.1981. Arts & crafts show held annually the 1st weekend in December. Indoors. Accepts photography, woodworking, ceramics, pottery, painting, fabrics, glass. Juried. Number of exhibitors: 135. Public attendance: 5,000. Public admission: $3. Artists should apply by visiting Web site to print an application form, or call to have one sent to them. Deadline: March 31. Application fee: $10 nonrefundable. Space fee: $120. Exhibition space: 72 sq. ft. For more information, artists should e-mail, visit Web site, call.

Tips "Have an open, welcoming booth and be accessible and friendly to customers."

APPLE CHILL & FESTIFALL

200 Plant Rd., Chapel Hill NC 27514. (919)968-2784. Fax: (919)932-2923. E-mail: lradson@townofchapelhill.org. Web site: www.applechill.com and www.festifall.com. **Contact:** Lauren Rodson, lead event coordinator. Estab. 1972. Apple Chill street fair held annually 3rd full weekend in April; Festifall street fair held annually 1st weekend in October. Estab. 1972. Outdoors. Accepts photography, pottery, painting, fabric, woodwork, glass, jewelry, leather, sculpture, tile. Juried by application process; actual event is not juried.

ART & JAZZ ON BROADWAY

P.O. Box 583, Philipsburg MT 59858. **Contact:** Sherry Armstrong at hitchinpost@blackfoot.net or (406)859-0366, or Connie Donlan at coppersok2@aol.com or (406)859-0165. Estab. 2000. Fine arts/jazz show held annually in August. Outdoors. Accepts photography and handcrafted, original, gallery-quality fine arts and crafts made by selling artist. Juried by

Flint Creek Valley Arts Council. Number of exhibitors: 75. Public attendance: 1,500-2,000. Admission fee: donation to Flint Creek Valley Arts Council. Artists should visit www.artinph ilipsburg.com, e-mail, or call for more information. Application fee: $45. Exhibtion space: 10×10 ft. For more information, artists should e-mail or call for more information.

Tips "Be prepared for temperatures of 100 degrees or rain. Display in a professional manner. Friendliness is crucial; fair pricing is essential."

✖ ART IN THE HEART OF THE CITY

171 E. State St., Ithaca NY 14850. (607)277-8679. Fax: (607)277-8691. E-mail: phil@downto wnithaca.com. Web site: www.downtownithaca.com. **Contact:** Phil White, office manager/ event coordinator. Estab. 1999. Sculpture exhibition held annually in early June. Primarily outdoors; limited indoor pieces. Accepts photography, wood, ceramic, metal, stone. Juried by Public Arts Commission. Number of exhibitors: 28-35. Public attendance: 100,000+. Free to public. Artists should apply by submitting application, artist statement, slides/ photos. Deadline for entry: May. Exhibition space depends on placement. For more information, artists should e-mail. This year we are having a "Green Exhibition, a pioneering step for public art across the country. We will focus on only (3) artists, and publicize their work broadly. The stipend has been increased to $1500. Per artist. We're creating a new online gallery and we're collaborating with area arts, sustainability and education groups for public programs. Art in the heart '09 is asking for you to use the 'Green" interpretation as a starting point- and, through your submissions, help us.

Tips "Be sure there is a market and interest for your work, and advertise early."

✖ ART IN THE PARK

P.O. Box 748, Sierra Vista AZ 85636-0247. (520)803-8981. E-mail: artinthepark@msm.com. Web site: www.huachuca-art.com. **Contact:** Vendor Committee. Estab. 1972. Fine arts & crafts show held annually 1st full weekend in October. Outdoors. Accepts photography, all fine arts and crafts created by vendor. Juried by 3-6 typical customers. Artists submit 6 photos. Number of exhibitors: 240. Public attendance: 20,000. Free to public. Artists should apply by calling, e-mailing or sending SASE between February and May; application package available online at HAA Web site. Deadline for entry: postmarked by June 27. Application fee: $10 included in space fee. Space fee: $175, includes jury fee. Exhibition space: 15×35 ft. For more information, artists should e-mail, call or send SASE.

✖ ART IN THE PARK

P.O. Box 1540, Thomasville GA 31799. (229)227-7020. Fax: (229)227-3320. E-mail: rosesho wfest@rose.net. Web site: www.downtownthomasville.com. **Contact:** Felicia Brannen, festival coordinator. Estab. 1998-1999. Arts in the park (an event of Thomasville's rose show and festival) is a 1 day arts & crafts show held annually in April. Outdoors. Accepts photography, handcrafted items, oils, acrylics, woodworking, stained glass, other varieties. Juried by a selection committee. Number of exhibitors: 60. Public attendance: 2,500. Free to public. Artists should apply by application. Deadline for entry: February 1. Space fee: $75, varies by year. Exhibition space: 20×20 ft. For more information, artists should e-mail or call.

Tips "Most important, be friendly to the public and have an attractive booth display."

✖ ART IN THE PARK

8707 Forest Ct., Warren MI 48093. (586)795-5471. E-mail: wildart@wowway.com. Web site: www.warrenfinearts.org. **Contact:** Paula Wild, chairperson. Estab. 1990. Fine arts &

crafts show held annually 2nd weekend in July. Indoors and outdoors. Accepts photography, sculpture, basketry, pottery, stained glass. Juried. Awards/prizes: 2D & 3D monetary awards. Number of exhibitors: 115. Public attendance: 7,500. Free to public. Deadline for entry: May 16. Jury fee: $20. Space fee: $125/outdoor; $175/indoor. Exhibition space: 12 × 12 ft./tent; 12 × 10 ft./atrium. For more information, artists should e-mail, visit Web site or send SASE.

ART IN THE PARK FALL FOLIAGE FESTIVAL
(formerly Art in the Park Fall Foliage Festival), sponsored by the Chaffee Center for the Visual Arts. 16 S. Main St., Rutland VT 05701. (802)775-0356. Fax: (802)773-4401. E-mail: beyondmarketing@yahoo.com. Web site: www.chaffeeartcenter.org. **Contact:** Sherri Birkheimer Rooker, event coordinator. Estab. 1961. Fine arts & crafts show held annually Columbus weekend. Outdoors. Accepts photography, clay, fiber, floral, glass, wood, jewelry, soaps and baskets. Juried by a panel of 10-15 judges. Submit 3 slides (2 of artwork and 1 of booth display). Number of exhibitors: 130. Public attendance: 7,000-9,000. Public admission: voluntary donation. Artists should apply by submitting three slides of work and one of booth (photos upon preapproval). Deadline for entry: "Ongoing jurying, but to receive discount for doing both shows, March 31." Space fee: $180-330. Exhibition space: 10 × 12 ft. and 20 × 12 ft. For more information, artists should e-mail, visit Web site or call.
Tips "Have a good presentation and variety, if possible (in pricing also), to appeal to a large group of people."

ART IN THE PARK SUMMER FESTIVAL
16 South Main St., Rutland VT 05701.802-775-0356. Fax: 802-773-4401. E-mail: beyondmarketing@yahoo.com. Web site: chaffeeartcenter.org. Sherri Birkheimer Rooker, event coordinator. Estab. 1961. Fine arts and crafts show held outdoors annually in August. 2008 dates: August 9 and 10. Accepts photography, clay, fiber, floral, glass, art, specialty foods, wood, jewelry, handmade soaps, lampshades, baskets, etc. Juried by a panel of 10-15 judges who perform a blind review of slide submissions. Number of exhibitors: 130. Public attendance: 8,000. Public admission: voluntary donation. Artists should submit three slides of work and one of booth (photos upon pre-approval). Deadline for entry: on-going but to receive discount for doing both shows, must apply by March 31; $25 late fee after that date. Space fee: $180-$330. For more information, artists should e-mail, visit Web site, or call.
Tips "Have a good presentation, variety if possible (in price ranges, too) to appeal to a large group of people."

ART'S ALIVE
200-125th St. & the Bay, Ocean City MD 21842-2247. (410)250-0125. Fax: (410)250-5409. E-mail: Bmoore@ococean.com. Web site: www.ococean.com. **Contact:** Brenda Moore, event coordinator. Estab. 2000. Fine art show held annually in mid-June. Outdoors. Accepts photography, ceramics, drawing, fiber, furniture, glass, printmaking, jewelry, mixed media, painting, sculpture, fine wood. Juried. Awards/prizes: $5,000 in cash prizes. Number of exhibitors: 110. Public attendance: 10,000. Free to pubic. Artists should apply by downloading application from Web site or call. Deadline for entry: February 28. Space fee: $75. Jury Fee: $25. Exhibition space: 10 × 10 ft. For more information, artists should e-mail, visit Web site, call or send SASE.
Tips "Apply early."

⚑ AN ARTS & CRAFTS AFFAIR, AUTUMN & SPRING TOURS

P.O. Box 184, Boys Town NE 68010. (402)331-2889. Fax: (402)445-9177. E-mail: hpifestival s@cox.net. Web site: www.hpifestivals.com. **Contact:** Huffman Productions. Estab. 1983. An arts & crafts show that tours different cities and states. The Autumn Festival tours annually October-November; Spring Festival tours annually in April. Artists should visit Web site to see list of states and schedule. Indoors. Accepts photography, pottery, stained glass, jewelry, clothing, wood, baskets. All artwork must be handcrafted by the actual artist exhibiting at the show. Juried by sending in 2 photos of work and 1 of display. Awards/ prizes: 4 $30 show gift certificates; $50, $100 and $150 certificates off future booth fees. Number of exhibitors: 300-500 depending on location. Public attendance: 15,000-40,000. Public admission: $6-8/adults; $5-7/seniors; 10 & under, free. Artists should apply by calling to request an application. Deadline for entry: varies for date and location. Space fee: $350-550. Exhibition space: 8×11 ft. up to 8×22 ft. For more information, artists should e-mail, visit Web site, call or send SASE.

Tips ''Have a nice display, make sure business name is visible, dress professionally, have different price points, and be willing to talk to your customers.''

⃞N ⚑ ARTS IN THE PARK

302 2nd Ave. East, Kalispell MT 59901. (406)755-5268. Fax: (405)755-2023. E-mail: informa tion@hackadaymuseum.org. Web site: http://www.hockadaymuseum.org/artpark.htm. Estab. 1968. Fine arts & crafts show held annually 4th weekend in July. Outdoors. Accepts photography, jewelry, clothing, paintings, pottery, glass, wood, furniture, baskets. Juried by a panel of 5 members. Artwork is evaluated for quality, creativity and originality. Jurors attempt to achieve a balance of mediums in the show. Awards/prizes: $100, Best Booth Award. Number of exhibitors: 100. Public attendance: 10,000. Public admission: $5/weekend pass; $3/day pass; under 12, free. Artists should apply by completing the application form, entry fee, a SASE and a CD containing 5 images in JPEG format; 4 images of work and 1 of booth. Deadline for entry: May 1. Application fee: $25. Space fee: $160-425 per location. Exhibition space: 10×10 ft-10×20 ft. For more information artists should e-mail, visit Web site or call.

⚑ ARTS ON FOOT

Downtown DC BID, 1250 H St., NW, Suite 1000, Washington DC 20005. (202)661-7592. E-mail: ashley@downtowndc.org. Web site: www.artsonfoot.org. **Contact:** Ashley Neeley. Fine arts & crafts show held annually in September. Outdoors. Accepts photography, painting, sculpture, fiber art, furniture, glass, jewelry, leather. Juried by 5 color images of the artwork. Send images as 35mm slides, TIFF or JPEG files on CD or DVD. Also include artist's résumé and SASE for return of materials. Free to the public. Deadline for entry: July. Exhibition space: 10×10 ft. ''Arts on Foot will pay participating artists a $25 gratuity to help cover out-of-pocket expenses (such as transportation and food) each artist may incur during Arts on Foot.'' For more information, artists should call, e-mail, visit Web site.

⚑ ARTS ON THE GREEN

P.O. Box 752, LaGrange KY 40031. 502-222-3822. Fax: 502-222-3823. E-mail: info@oldhamc ountyarts.org. Web site: www.oldhamcountyarts.org. **Contact:** Marion Gibson, show coordinator. Estab. 2001. Fine arts & crafts show held annually 1st weekend in June. Outdoors. Accepts photography, painting, clay, sculpture, metal, wood, fabric, glass, jewelry. Juried

Art Fairs

by a panel. Awards/prizes: cash prizes for Best of Show and category awards. Number of exhibitors: 100. Public attendance: 7,500. Free to the public. Artists should apply online or call. Deadline for entry: March 15, 2008. Jury fee: $15. Space fee: $125. Electricity fee: $15. Exhibition space: 12 × 12 ft. For more information, artists should e-mail, visit Web site, call.

Tips "Make potential customers feel welcome in your space. Don't overcrowd your work. Smile!"

AUTUMN FESTIVAL, AN ARTS & CRAFTS AFFAIR

P.O. Box 184, Boys Town NE 68010. (402)331-2889. Fax: (402)445-9177. E-mail: hpifestivals @cox.net. Web site: www.hpifestivals.com. **Contact:** Huffman Productions. Estab. 1986. Fine arts & craft show held annually in October. Indoors. Accepts photography, pottery, jewelry, wood. All must be handcrafted by the exhibitor. Juried by 2 photos of work and 1 of display. Awards/prizes: $420 total cash awards. Number of exhibitors: 300. Public attendance: 18,000. Public admission: $6. Artists should apply by calling for an application. Deadline: when full or by the end of September. Space fee: $400. Exhibition space: 8 × 11 ft. ("We provide pipe and drape plus 500 watts of power." For more information, artists should e-mail, visit Web site, call, send SASE.

Tips "Have a nice display; dress professionally; have various price points; be willing to talk to your customers; display your business name."

AVON FINE ART & WINE AFFAIRE

15648 N. Eagles Nest Dr., Fountain Hills AZ 85268-1418. (480)837-5637. Fax: (480)837-2355. E-mail: info@thunderbirdartists.com. Web site: www.thunderbirdartists.com. **Contact:** Denise Colter, vice president. Estab. 1993. Fine arts & crafts show and wine tasting held annually in mid-July. Outdoors. Accepts photography, painting, mixed media, bronze, metal, copper, stone, stained glass, clay, wood, paper, baskets, jewelry, scratchboard. Juried by 4 slides of work and 1 slide of booth. Number of exhibitors: 150. Public attendance: 3,000-6,000. Free to public. Artists should apply by sending application, fees, 4 slides of work, 1 slide of booth and 2 SASEs. Deadline for entry: March 27. Application fee: $20. Space fee: $360-1,080. Exhibition space: 10 × 10 ft.-10 × 30 ft. For more information, artists should visit Web site.

THE BIG ONE ARTS & CRAFTS SHOW

P.O. Box 494, Black Eagle MT 59414. (406)453-3120. Fax: (406)788-7227. E-mail: giskaasent @bresnan.net. **Contact:** Sue Giskaas, owner/promoter. Estab. 1990. Arts & crafts show held annually in mid- September. Indoors. Accepts photography, anything handmade, no resale. Juried by management selects. Number of exhibitors: 141. Public attendance: 5,000. Public admission: $2. Artists should apply by sending SASE to above address. Deadline for entry: August 15. Space fee: $125-195. Exhibition space: 10 × 10 ft-10 × 15 ft. For more information artists should e-mail, call or send SASE.

BLACK SWAMP ARTS FESTIVAL

P.O. Box 532, Bowling Green OH 43402. (419)354-2723. E-mail: info@blackswamparts.org. Web site: www.blackswamparts.org. **Contact:** Tim White, visual arts committee. Estab. 1993. Fine arts & crafts show held annually the weekend after Labor Day. Outdoors. Accepts photography, ceramics, drawing, enamel, fiber, glass, jewelry, leather, metal, mixed media, painting, paper, prints, sculpture, wood. Juried by unaffiliated, hired jurors. Awards/prizes: Best in Show, 2nd Place, 3rd Place, Honorable Mention, Painting Prize. Number of exhibitors: Juried: 110. Invitational: 40. Public attendance: 60,000. Free to the public. Artists should apply by visiting Web site. Deadline for entry: Juried: April; Invitational: June or until filled. Application fee: Juried: $225; Invitational: $120. Exhibition space: 10×10 ft. For more information, artists should visit Web site, call (voice mail only) or e-mail.

Tips "Offer a range of prices, from $5 to $500."

◙ CAIN PARK ARTS FESTIVAL

40 Severance Circle, Cleveland Heights OH 44118-9988. (216)291-3669. Fax: (216)3705. E-mail: jhoffman@clvhts.com. Web site: www.cainpark.com. **Contact:** Janet Hoffman, administrative assistant. Estab. 1976. Fine arts & crafts show held annually 2nd full week in July. Outdoors. Accepts photography, painting, clay, sculpture, wood, jewelry, leather, glass, ceramics, clothes and other fiber, paper, block printing. Juried by a panel of professional artists; submit 5 slides. Awards/prizes: cash prizes of $750, $500 and $250; also Judges' Selection, Director's Choice and Artists' Award. Number of exhibitors: 155. Public attendance: 60,000. Free to the public. Artists should apply by requesting an application by mail, visiting Web site to download application or by calling. **Deadline for entry**: March 1. Application fee: $25. Space fee: $350. Exhibition space: 10×10 ft. Average gross sales/exhibitor: $4,000. For more information, artists should e-mail, visit Web site, or call.

Tips "Have an attractive booth to display your work. Have a variety of prices. Be available to answer questions about your work."

CALABASAS FINE ARTS FESTIVAL

26135 Mureau Rd., Calabasas CA 91302. (818)878-4225, ext. 270. E-mail: artcouncil@cityof calabasas.com. Web site: www.calabasasartscouncil.com. Estab. 1997. Fine arts & crafts show held annually in late April/early May. Outdoors. Accepts photography, painting, sculpture, jewelry, mixed media. Juried. Number of exhibitors: 250. Public attendance: 10,000+. Free to public; parking: $5. For more information, artists should visit Web site or e-mail.

◙ CEDARHURST CRAFT FAIR

P.O. Box 923, Mt. Vernon IL 62864. (618)242-1236. Fax: (618)242-9530. E-mail: linda@ceda rhurst.org. Web site: www.cedarhurst.org. **Contact:** Linda Wheeler, coordinator. Estab. 1977. Arts & crafts show held annually in September. Outdoors. Accepts photography, paper, glass, metal, clay, wood, leather, jewelry, fiber, baskets, 2D art. Juried. Awards/prizes: Best of each category. Number of exhibitors: 125. Public attendance: 14,000. Public admission: $3. Artists should apply by filling out application form. Deadline for entry: March. Application fee: $25. Space fee: $275. Exhibition space: 10×15 ft. For more information, artists should e-mail, visit Web site.

CENTERVILLE/WASHINGTON TOWNSHIP AMERICANA FESTIVAL

P.O. Box 41794, Centerville OH 45441-0794. (937)433-5898. Fax: (937)433-5898. E-mail: americanafestival@sbcglobal.net. Web site: www.americanafestival.org. **Contact:** Patricia Fleissner, arts & crafts chair. Estab. 1972. Arts & crafts show held annually on the Fourth of July. Festival includes entertainment, parade, food, car show and other activities. Accepts photography and all mediums. "No factory-made items accepted." Awards/prizes: 1st

Art Fairs

Place; 2nd Place; 3rd Place; certificates and ribbons for most attractive displays. Number of exhibitors: 275-300. Public attendance: 70,000. Free to the public. Artists should send SASE for application form or apply online. Deadline for entry: June 27, 2007. "Main Street is usually full by early June." Space fee: $45. Exhibition space: 12 × 10 ft. For more information, artists should e-mail, visit Web site, call.

Tips "Artists should have moderately priced items; bring business cards; and have an eye-catching display."

CHATSWORTH CRANBERRY FESTIVAL

P.O. Box 286, Chatsworth NJ 08019-0286. (609)726-9237. Fax: (609)726-1459. E-mail: lgiamalis@aol.com. Web site: www.cranfest.org. **Contact:** Lynn Giamalis, chairperson. Estab. 1983. Arts & crafts show held annually in October. Outdoors. Accepts photography. Juried. Number of exhibitors: 200. Public attendance: 75,000-100,000. Free to public. Artists should apply by sending SASE to above address. Deadline for entry: September 1. Space fee: $200. Exhibition space: 15 × 15 ft. For more information, artists should visit Web site.

CHERRY BLOSSOM FESTIVAL OF CONYERS

1996 Centennial Olympic Parkway, Conyers GA 30013. (770)860-4190. Fax: (770)602-2500. E-mail: rebecca.hill@conyersga.com. Web site: http://www.conyerscherryblossom.com. **Contact:** Rebecca Hill, event manager. Estab. 1981. Arts & crafts show held annually in late March. Outdoors. Accepts photography, paintings. Juried. Number of exhibitors: 300. Public attendance: 40,000. Free to public; $5 parking fee. Deadline for entry: January. Space fee: $125/booth. Exhibition space: 10 × 10 ft. For more information, artists should e-mail, visit Web site or call.

CHRISTMAS CRAFTS EXPOS I & II

P O Box 227, North Granby CT 06060. (860)653-6671. Fax: (860)653-6858. E-mail: acf@handmadeinamerica.com. Web site: www.handmadeinamerica.com. **Contact:** Joanne McAulay, president. Estab. 1971. Fine arts & crafts holiday show held annually 1st 2 weekends in December. Indoors. Accepts photography, metal, fiber, pottery, glass, wood, jewelry, pen & ink. Juried by 6 product slides or photos, 1 booth photo, and 1 studio or shop photo (where the art is made). Number of exhibitors: 200. Public attendance: 10,000. Public admission: $7. Artists should apply by calling for an application or by downloading one from Web site. Deadline for entry: Applications are juried and space sold until sold out. Space fee: $420-$650. Exhibition space: 10 × 10 ft.; 10 × 15 ft.; 10 × 20 ft. For more information, artists should e-mail, visit Web site, send SASE.

Tips: "Look at current market trends and economics. Have a unique and presentable booth. Be personable and friendly to customers"

CHUN CAPITOL HILL PEOPLE'S FAIR

1290 Williams St., Denver CO 80218. (303)830-1651. Fax: (303)830-1782. E-mail: chun@chundenver.org. Web site: www.peoplesfair.com; www.chundenver.org. Estab. 1971. Arts & crafts show held annually 1st weekend in June. Outdoors. Accepts photography, ceramics, jewelry, paintings, wearable art, glass, sculpture, wood, paper, fiber. Juried by professional artisans representing a variety of mediums and selected members of fair management. The jury process is based on originality, quality and expression. Awards/prizes: Best of Show. Number of exhibitors: 300. Public attendance: 250,000. Free to public. Artists should apply by downloading application from Web site. Deadline for entry: March. Application fee: $35. Space fee: $300. Exhibition space: 10×10 ft. For more information, artists should e-mail, visit Web site or call.

☑ CHURCH STREET ART & CRAFT SHOW

P.O. Box 1409, Waynesville NC 28786. (828)456-3517. Fax: (828)456-2001. E-mail: downto wnwaynesville@charter.net. Web site: www.downtownwaynesville.com. **Contact:** Ronald Huelster, executive director. Estab. 1983. Fine arts & crafts show held annually 2nd Saturday in October. Outdoors. Accepts photography, paintings, fiber, pottery, wood, jewelry. Juried by committee: submit 4 slides or photos of work and 1 of booth display. Awards/prizes: $1,000 cash prizes in 1st, 2nd, 3rd and Honorable Mentions. Number of exhibitors: 100. Public attendance: 15,000-18,000. Free to public. Deadline for entry: August 15. Application/space fee: $95-165. Exhibition space: 10×12 ft.-12×20 ft. For more information artists should e-mail, call or send SASE.

Tips Recommends "quality in work and display."

☑ CITY OF FAIRFAX FALL FESTIVAL

4401 Sideburn Rd., Fairfax VA 22030. (703)385-7949. Fax: (703)246-6321. E-mail: klewis@f airfaxva.gov. Web site: http://www.fairfaxva.gov/SpecialEvents/FallFestival/FallFestival. asp. **Contact:** Kathy Lewis, special events coordinator. Estab. 1975. Arts & crafts show held annually 2nd Saturday in October. Outdoors. Accepts photography, jewelry, glass, pottery, clay, wood, mixed media. Juried by a panel of 5 independent jurors. Number of exhibitors: 400. Public attendance: 25,000. Public admission: $5 for age 18 and older. Artists should apply by contacting Leslie Herman for an application. Deadline for entry: March. Application fee: $10. Space fee: $150. Exhibition space: 10×10 ft. For more information, artists should e-mail.

Tips "Be on-site during the event. Smile. Price according to what the market will bear."

☑ CITY OF FAIRFAX HOLIDAY CRAFT SHOW

4401 Sideburn Rd., Fairfax VA 22030. (703)385-7949. Fax: (703)246-6321. E-mail: klewis@f airfaxva.gov. Web site: www.fairfaxva.gov. **Contact:** Leslie Herman, special events coordinator. Estab. 1985. Arts & crafts show held annually 3rd weekend in November. Indoors. Accepts photography, jewelry, glass, pottery, clay, wood, mixed media. Juried by a panel of 5 independent jurors. Number of exhibitors: 247. Public attendance: 10,000. Public admission: $5 for age 18 an older. Artists should apply by contacting Leslie Herman for an application. Deadline for entry: March. Application fee: $10. Space fee: 10×6 ft.: $175; 11×9 ft.: $250; 10×10 ft.: $250. For more information, artists should e-mail. Currently full.

Tips "Be on-site during the event. Smile. Price according to what the market will bear."

☑ COLORSCAPE CHENANGO ARTS FESTIVAL

P.O. Box 624, Norwich NY 13815. (607)336-3378. E-mail: info@colorscape.org. Web site: www.colorscape.org. **Contact:** Peggy Finnegan, festival director. Estab. 1995. Fine arts & crafts show held annually the weekend after Labor Day. Outdoors. Accepts photography and all types of mediums. Juried. Awards/prizes: $5,000. Number of exhibitors: 80-85. Public attendance: 14,000-16,000. Free to public. Deadline for entry: March. Application fee: $15/jury fee. Space fee: $150. Exhibition space: 12 × 12 ft. For more information, artists should e-mail, visit Web site, call or send SASE.

Tips Interact with your audience. Talk to them about your work and how it is created. Don't sit grumpily at the rear of your booth reading a book. People like to be involved in the art they buy and are more likely to buy if you involve them.''

COUNTRY ARTS & CRAFTS FAIR

N104 W14181 Donges Bay Rd., Germantown WI 53022. (262)251-0604. E-mail: stjohnucc53 022@sbcglobal.net. **Contact:** Mary Ann Toth, booth chairperson. Estab. 1975. Arts & crafts show held annually in September. Indoors and outdoors. Limited indoor space; unlimited outdoor booths. Accepts photography, jewelry, clothing, country crafts. Number of exhibitors: 70. Public attendance: 500-600. Free to the public. Artists should e-mail for an application and state permit. Space fee: $10 for youth; $30 for outdoor. Exhibition space: 10 × 10 ft. and 15 × 15 ft. For more information, artists should e-mail or call Mary Ann Toth or church secretary, or send SASE.

☑ CRAFT FAIR AT THE BAY

Castleberry Fairs & Festivals, 38 Charles St., Rochester NH 03867. (603)332-2616. E-mail: info@castleberryfairs.com. Web site: www.castleberryfairs.com. **Contact:** Terry Mullen, event coordinator. Estab. 1988. Arts & crafts show held annually in July in Alton Bay, New Hampshire. Outdoors. Accepts photography and all other mediums. Juried by photo, slide or sample. Number of exhibitors: 85. Public attendance: 7,500. Free to the public. Artists should apply by downloading application from Web site. Deadline for entry: until full. Space fee: $250. Exhibition space: 100 sq. ft. Average gross sales/exhibitor: ''Generally, this is considered an 'excellent' show, so I would guess most exhibitors sell ten times their booth fee, or in this case, at least $2,500 in sales.'' For more information, artists should visit Web site.

Tips ''Do not bring a book; do not bring a chair. Smile and make eye contact with everyone who enters your booth. Have them sign your guest book; get their e-mail address so you can let them know when you are in the area again. And, finally, make the sale—they are at the fair to shop, after all.''

☑ CRAFTS AT RHINEBECK

6550 Springbrook Ave., Rhinebeck NY 12572. (845)876-4001. Fax: (845)876-4003. E-mail: vimperati@dutchessfair.com. Web site: www.craftsatrhinebeck.com. **Contact:** Vicki Imperati, event coordinator. Estab. 1981. Fine arts & crafts show held biannually in late June and early October. Indoors and outdoors. Accepts photography, fine art, ceramics, wood, mixed media, leather, glass, metal, fiber, jewelry. Juried by 3 slides of work and 1 of booth display. Number of exhibitors: 350. Public attendance: 25,000. Public admission: $7. Artists should apply by calling for application or downloading application from Web site. Deadline for entry: February 1. Application fee: $20. Space fee: $300-730. Exhibition space: inside: 10 × 10 ft. and 10 × 20 ft.; outside:15 × 15 ft. For more information, artists should e-mail, visit Web site or call.

Tips ''Presentation of work within your booth is very important. Be approachable and inviting.''

◪ CUNEO GARDENS ART FESTIVAL

3417 R.F.D., Long Grove IL 60047. Phone/Fax: (847)726-8669. E-mail: dwevents@comcast. net. Web site: www.dwevents.org. **Contact:** D & W Events, Inc. Estab. 2005. Fine arts & crafts show. Outdoors. Accepts photography, fiber, oil, acrylic, watercolor, mixed media, jewelry, sculpture, metal, paper, painting. Juried by 3 jurors. Awards/prizes: Best of Show; First Place and awards of excellence. Number of exhibitors: 75. Public attendance: 10,000. Free to public. Artists should apply by downloading application from Web site, e-mail or call. Deadline for entry: March 1. Application fee: $25. Space fee: $275. Exhibition space: 100 sq. ft. For more information, artists should e-mail, visit Web site, call.

Tips "Artists should display professionally and attractively, and interact positively with everyone."

◪ DEERFIELD FINE ARTS FESTIVAL

3417 R.F.D., Long Grove IL 60047. Phone/Fax: (847)726-8669. E-mail: dwevents@comcast. net. Web site: www.dwevents.org. **Contact:** D & W Events, Inc. Estab. 2000. Fine arts & crafts show held annually in early June. Outdoors. Accepts photography, fiber, oil, acrylic, watercolor, mixed media, jewelry, sculpture, metal, paper, painting. Juried by 3 jurors. Awards/prizes: Best of Show; First Place, awards of excellence. Number of exhibitors: 150. Public attendance: 35,000. Free to public. Artists should apply by downloading application from Web site, e-mail or call. Deadline for entry: March 1. Application fee: $25. Space fee: $275. Exhibition space: 100 sq. ft. For more information artists should e-mail, visit Web site, call.

Tips "Artists should display professionally and attractively, and interact positively with everyone."

◪ DELAWARE ARTS FESTIVAL

P.O. Box 589, Delaware OH 43015. (740-)363-2695. E-mail: info@delawareartsfestival.org. Web site: www.delawareartsfestival.org. **Contact:** Tom King. Estab. 1973. Fine arts & crafts show held annually the Saturday and Sunday after Mother's Day. Outdoors. Accepts photography; all mediums, but no buy/sell. Juried by committee members who are also artists. Awards/prizes: Ribbons, cash awards, free booth for the following year. Number of exhibitors: 160. Public attendance: 25,000. Free to the public. Artists should apply by visiting Web site for application. Application fee: $10. Space fee: $125. Exhibition fee: 120 sq. ft. For more information, artists should e-mail or visit Web site.

Tips "Have high-quality stuff. Engage the public. Set up a good booth."

DOWNTOWN FESTIVAL & ART SHOW

P.O. Box 490, Gainesville FL 32602. 352)334-5064. Fax: 352)334-2249. E-mail: piperlr@city ofgainesville.org. Web site: www.gvlculturalaffairs.org. **Contact:** Linda Piper, festival director. Estab. 1981. Fine arts & crafts show held annually in November. Outdoors. Accepts photography, wood, ceramic, fiber, glass, and all mediums. Juried by 3 slides of artwork and 1 slide of booth. Awards/prizes: $14,000 in Cash Awards; $5,000 in Purchase Awards. Number of exhibitors: 250. Public attendance: 115,000. Free to the public. Artists should apply by mailing 4 slides. Deadline for entry: May. Space fee: $185. Exhibition space: 12 ft. × 12 ft. Average gross sales/exhibitor: $6,000. For more information, artists should e-mail, visit Web site, call, send SASE.

Tips "Submit the highest-quality slides possible. A proper booth slide is so important."

◨ EDWARDS FINE ART & SCULPTURE FESTIVAL

15648 N. Eagles Nest Dr., Fountain Hills AZ 85268-1418. (480)837-5637. Fax: (480)837-2355. E-mail: info@thunderbirdartists.com. Web site: www.thunderbirdartists.com. **Contact:** Denise Colter, vice president. Estab. 1999. Fine arts & sculpture show held annually in late July. Outdoors. Accepts photography, painting, drawing, graphics, fiber sculpture, mixed media, bronze, metal, copper, stone, stained glass, clay, wood, baskets, jewelry. Juried by 4 slides of work and 1 slide of booth presentation. Number of exhibitors: 115. Public attendance: 3,000-6,000. Free to public. Artists should apply by sending application, fees, 4 slides of work, 1 slide of booth labeled and 2 SASE. Deadline for entry: March 29. Application fee: $20. Space fee: $360-1,080. Exhibition space: 10×10 ft.-10×30 ft. For more information, artists should visit Web site.

◨ ◨ ELIZABETHTOWN FESTIVAL

818 Jefferson, Moundsville WV 26041. (304)843-1170. Fax: (304)845-2355. E-mail: jvhblake@aol.com. Web site: www.wvpentours.com. **Contact:** Sue Riggs at (304)843-1170 or Hilda Blake at (304)845-2552, co-chairs. Estab. 1999. Arts & crafts show held annually the 3rd weekend in May (Saturday and Sunday). Sponsored by the Moundsville Economic Development Council. Also includes heritage exhibits of 1800s-era food and entertainment. Indoors and outdoors within the walls of the former West Virginia Penitentiary. Accepts photography, crafts, wood, pottery, quilts, jewelry. "All items must be made by the craftspeople selling them; no commercial items." Juried based on design, craftsmanship and creativity. Submit 5 photos: 3 of your medium; 2 of your booth set-up. Jury fee: $10. Number of exhibitors: 70-75. Public attendance: 3,000-5,000. Public admission: $3. Artists should apply by requesting an application form by phone. Deadline for entry: May 1, 2007. Space fee: $50. Exhibition space: 100 sq. ft. For more information, artists should e-mail, visit Web site, call, send SASE.

Tips "Be courteous. Strike up conversations—do not sit in your booth and read! Have an attractive display of wares."

◨ ELMWOOD AVENUE FESTIVAL OF THE ARTS, INC.

P.O. Box 786, Buffalo NY 14213. (716)830-2484. E-mail: directoreafa@aol.com. Web site: www.elmwoodartfest.org. **Contact:** Joe DiPasquale. Estab. 2000. Arts & crafts show held annually in late-August, the weekend before Labor Day weekend. Outdoors. Accepts photography, metal, fiber, ceramics, glass, wood, jewelry, basketry, 2D media. Juried. Awards/prizes: to be determined. Number of exhibitors: 170. Public attendance: 80,000-120,000. Free to the public. Artists should apply by e-mailing their contact information or by downloading application from Web site. Deadline for entry: April. Application fee: $20. Space fee: $200. Exhibition space: 150 sq. ft. Average gross sales/exhibitor: $3,000. For more information, artists should e-mail, visit Web site, call, send SASE.

Tips "Make sure your display is well designed, with clean lines that highlight your work. Have a variety of price points—even wealthy people don't always want to spend $500 at a booth where they may like the work."

◨ A FAIR IN THE PARK

1005 Oglethorpe St., Pittsburgh PA 15201. (212)655-5796. Fax: (347)220-1181. E-mail: info@craftsmensguild.org. Web site: www.craftsmensguild.org. **Contact:** Leah Shannon, director. Estab. 1969. Contemporary fine arts & crafts show held annually the weekend after

Labor Day outdoors. Accepts photography, clay, fiber, jewelry, metal, mixed media, wood, glass, 2D visual arts. Juried. Awards/prizes: 1 Best of Show and 4 Craftsmen's Guild Awards. Number of exhibitors: 115. Public attendance: 25,000+. Free to public. Artists should apply by sending application with jury fee, booth fee and 5 digital images. Deadline for entry: May 1. Application fee: $25. Space fee: $250-300. Exhibition space: 11×12 ft. Average gross sales/exhibitor: $1,000 and up. For more information artists should e-mail, visit Web site or call.

Tips "It is very important for artists to present their work to the public, to concentrate on the business aspect of their artist career. They will find that they can build a strong customer/collector base by exhibiting their work and by educating the public about their artistic process and passion for creativity."

🅽 FAIRE ON THE SQUARE

117 W. Goodwin St., Prescott AZ 86301-1147. (928)445-2000, ext. 12. Fax: (928)445-0068. E-mail: scott@prescott.org. Web site: www.prescott.org. **Contact:** Scott or Jill Currey (Special Events—Prescott Chamber of Commerce) Estab. 1985. Arts & crafts show held annually in Labor Day weekend. Outdoors. Accepts photography, ceramics, painting, sculpture, clothing, woodworking, metal art, glass, floral, home décor . "No resale." Juried. "Photos of work and artist creating work are required." Number of exhibitors: 170. Public attendance: 10,000-12,000. Free to public. Application can be printed from Web site or obtained by phone request. Deadline: spaces are sold until show is full. Application fee: $50 deposit. Space fee: $400. Exhibition space; 10X15 ft.. For more information, artist should e-mail, visit Web site or call.

🆅 FALL CRAFTS AT LYNDHURST

P.O. Box 28, Woodstock NY 12498. (845)331-7900. Fax: (845)331-7484. E-mail: crafts@artri der.com. Web site: www.artrider.com. **Contact:** Laura Kandel. Estab. 1984. Fine arts & crafts show held annually in mid-September. Outdoors. Accepts photography, wearable and nonwearable fiber, metal and nonmetal jewelry, clay, leather, wood, glass, painting, drawing, prints mixed media. Juried by 5 images of work and 1 of booth, viewed sequentially. Number of exhibitors: 325. Public attendance: 14,000. Public admission: $10. Artists should apply by downloading application from www.artrider.com or can apply online at www.zapplication.org. Deadline for entry: January 14. Application fee: $35. Space fee: $775. Exhibition space: 10×10. For more information, artists should e-mail, visit Web site, call.

🅽 FALL FEST IN THE PARK

117 W. Goodwin St., Prescott AZ 86301-1147. (928)445-2000 ext 12. Fax: (928)445-0068. E-mail: scott@prescott.org. Web site: www.prescott.org. **Contact:** Scott or Jill Currey (Special Events—Prescott Chamber of Commerce) Estab. 1981. Arts & crafts show held annually in mid-October. Outdoors. Accepts photography, ceramics, painting, sculpture, clothing, woodworking, metal art, glass, floral, home décor . "No resale." Juried. "Photos of work and artist creating work are required." Number of exhibitors: 150. Public attendance: 6,000-7,000. Free to public. Application can be printed from Web site or obtained by phone request. Deadline: Spaces are sold until show is full. Application fee: $50 deposit. Space fee: $225. Exhibition space; 10×15 ft. For more information, artists should e-mail, visit Web site or call.

☒ FALL FINE ART & CRAFTS AT BROOKDALE PARK

Watchung Ave., Montclair NJ. (908)874-5247. Fax: (908)874-7098. E-mail: rosesquared@p atmedia.com. Web site: www.rosesquared.com. **Contact:** Janet Rose, president. Estab.1997. Fine arts & craft show held annually in mid-October. Outdoors. Accepts photography and all other mediums. Juried. Number of exhibitors: 180. Public attendance: 14,000. Free to the public. Artists should apply by downloading application from Web site or call for application. Deadline: 1 month before show date. Application fee: $15. Space fee: $310. Exhibition space: 120 sq. ft. For more information, artists should e-mail, visit Web site, call.

Tips "Create a professional booth that is comfortable for the customer to enter. Be informative, friendly and outgoing. People come to meet the artist."

☒ FALL FINE ART & CRAFTS AT NOMAHEGAN PARK

Springfield Ave, Cranford NJ. (908)874-5247. Fax: (908)874-7098. E-mail: rosesquared@pat media.com. Web site: www.rosesquared.com. **Contact:** Janet Rose, president. Estab.1986. Fine arts & craft show held annually in October. Outdoors. Accepts photography and all other mediums. Juried. Number of exhibitors: 100. Public attendance: 14,000. Free to the public. Artists should apply by downloading application from Web site or call for application. Deadline: 1 month before show date. Application fee: $20. Space fee: $325. Exhibition space: 120 sq. ft. For more information, artists should e-mail, visit Web site, call.

Tips "Create a professional booth that is comfortable for the customer to enter. Be informative, friendly and outgoing. People come to meet the artist."

Ⓝ ☒ FARGO'S DOWNTOWN STREET FAIR

203 4th St., Fargo ND 58102. (701)241-1570. Fax: (701)241-8275. E-mail: steph@fmdownto wn.com. Web site: www.fmdowntown.com. **Contact:** Stephanie, events & membership. Estab. 1975. Fine arts & crafts show held annually in July. Outdoors. Accepts photography, ceramics, glass, fiber, textile, jewelry, metal, paint, print/drawing, sculpture, 3D mixed media, wood. Juried by a team of artists from the Fargo-Moorehead area. Awards/prizes: Best of Show and best in each medium. Number of exhibitors: 300. Public attendance: 130,000-150,000. Free to pubic. Artists should apply online or by mail. Deadline for entry: February 18. Space fee: $275/booth; $50/corner. Exhibition space: 10×10 ft. For more information, artists should e-mail, visit Web site or call.

Ⓝ ☒ FAUST FINE ARTS & FOLK FESTIVAL

15185 Olive St., St. Louis MO 63017. (636)391-0900, ext.27. Fax: (636)527-2259. E-mail: toconnell@stlouisco.com. Web site: www.stlouisco.com/parks. **Contact:** Tonya O'Connell, recreation supervisor. Fine arts & crafts show held biannually in May and September. Outdoors. Accepts photography, oil, acrylic, clay, fiber, sculpture, watercolor, jewelry, wood, floral, baskets, prints, drawing, mixed media, folk art. Juried by a committee. Awards/prizes: $100. Number of exhibitors: 90-100. Public attendance: 5,000. Public admission: $5. Deadline for entry: March, spring show; July, fall show. Application fee: $15. Space fee: $75. Exhibition space: 10×10 ft. For more information, artists should call.

☒ FERNDALE ART SHOW

Integrity Shows, 2102 Roosevelt, Ypsilanti MI 48197. (734)216-3958. Fax: (734)482-2070. E-mail: mark@integrityshows.com. Web site: www.downtownferndale.com. **Contact:** Mark

Loeb, president. Estab. 2004. Fine arts & crafts show held annually in September. Outdoors. Accepts photography and all fine art and craft mediums; emphasis on fun, funky work. Juried by 3 independent jurors. Awards/prizes: Purchase Awards and Merit Awards. Number of exhibitors: 90. Public attendance: 30,000. Free to the public. Application is available in March. Deadline for entry: July. Application fee: $15. Space fee: $250. Exhibition space: 10X12 ft. For more information,.artists should e-mail or call.

Tips "Enthusiasm. Keep a mailing list. Develop collectors."

⚑ FESTIVAL IN THE PARK

1409 East Blvd., Charlotte NC 28203. (704)338-1060. Fax: (704)338-1061. E-mail: festival@f estivalinthepark.org. Web site: www.festivalinthepark.org. **Contact:** Julie Whitney Austin, executive director. Estab. 1964. Fine arts & crafts/arts & crafts show held annually 3rd Thursday after Labor Day. Outdoors. Accepts photography, decorative and wearable crafts, drawing and graphics, fiber and leather, jewelry, mixed media, painting, metal, sculpture, wood. Juried by slides or photographs. Awards/prizes: $4,000 in cash awards. Number of exhibitors: 150. Public attendance: 85,000. Free to the public. Artists should apply by visiting Web site for application. Application fee: $25. Space fee: $345. Exhibition space: 10×10 ft. For more information, artists should e-mail, visit Web site, call.

⚑ FILLMORE JAZZ FESTIVAL

P.O. Box 15107, San Rafael CA 94915. (800)310-6563. Fax: (414)456-6436. E-mail: art@fillm orejazzfestival.com. Web site: www.fillmorejazzfestival.com. Estab. 1984. Fine arts & crafts show and jazz festival held annually 1st weekend of July in San Franciso, between Jackson & Eddy Streets. Outdoors. Accepts photography, ceramics, glass, jewelry, paintings, sculpture, metal clay, wood, clothing. Juried by prescreened panel. Number of exhibitors: 250. Public attendance: 90,000. Free to public. Deadline for entry: ongoing. Space fee: $350-600. Exhibition space: 8×10 ft. or 10×10 ft. Average gross sales/exhibitor: $800-11,000. For more information, artists should e-mail, visit Web site or call.

⚑ FINE ART & CRAFTS AT ANDERSON PARK

N. Mountain Ave., Upper Montclair NJ. (908)874-5247. Fax: (908)874-7098. E-mail: rosesqu ared@patmedia.net. Web site: www.rosesquared.com. **Contact:** Janet Rose, president. Estab.1984. Fine arts & craft show held annually in mid-September. Outdoors. Accepts photography and all other mediums. Juried. Number of exhibitors: 190. Public attendance: 16,000. Free to the public. Artists should apply by downloading application from Web site or call for application. Deadline: 1 month before show date. Application fee: $15. Space fee: $310. Exhibition space: 120 sq. ft. For more information, artists should e-mail, visit Web site, call.

Tips "Create a professional booth that is comfortable for the customer to enter. Be informative, friendly and outgoing. People come to meet the artist."

⚑ FINE ART & CRAFTS AT NOMAHEGAN PARK

Springfield Ave., Cranford NJ. (908)874-5247. Fax: (908)874-7098. E-mail: rosesquared@pa tmedia.com. Web site: www.rosesquared.com. **Contact:** Janet Rose, president. Estab. 1987. (908)874-5247. Fax: (908)874-7098. e-mail rosesquared@patmedia.net. Fine arts & craft show held annually in early June. Outdoors. Accepts photography and all other mediums. Juried. Number of exhibitors: 110. Public attendance: 12,000. Free to the public. Artists should apply by downloading application from Web site or call for application. Deadline: 1 month before show date. Application fee: $15. Space fee: $310. Exhibition space: 120 sq. ft. For more information, artists should e-mail, visit Web site, call.

Tips "Create a professional booth that is comfortable for the customer to enter. Be informative, friendly and outgoing. People come to meet the artist."

☑ FINE ART & CRAFTS FAIR AT VERONA PARK

Verona Park NJ. (908)874-5247. Fax: (908)874-7098. E-mail: rosesquared@patmedia.net. Web site: www.rosesquared.com. **Contact:** Janet Rose, president. Estab.1986. Fine arts & craft show held annually in May. Outdoors. Accepts photography and all other mediums. Juried. Number of exhibitors: 140. Public attendance: 14,000. Free to the public. Artists should apply by downloading application from Web site or call for application. Deadline: 1 month before show date. Application fee: $15. Space fee: $310. Exhibition space: 120 sq. ft. For more information, artists should e-mail, visit Web site, call.

Tips "Create a professional booth that is comfortable for the customer to enter. Be informative, friendly and outgoing. People come to meet the artist."

☑ FOOTHILLS CRAFTS FAIR

2753 Lynn Rd. #A, Tryon NC 28782-7870. (828)859-7427. E-mail: bbqfestival@azztez.net. Web site: www.BlueRidgeBBQFestival.com. **Contact:** Julie McIntyre. Estab. 1994. Fine arts & crafts show and Blue Ridge BBQ Festival/Championship held annually 2nd Friday and Saturday in June. Outdoors. Accepts photography, arts and handcrafts by artist only; nothing manufactured or imported. Juried. Number of exhibitors: 50. Public attendance: 25,000+. Public admission: $8; 12 and under free. Artists should apply by downloading application from Web site or sending personal information to e-mail or mailing address. Deadline for entry: March 30. Jury fee: $25 nonrefundable. Space fee: $150. Exhibition space: 10×10 ft. For more information, artists should visit Web site.

Tips "Have an attractive booth, unique items, and reasonable prices."

N ☑ FORD CITY HERITAGE DAYS

P.O. Box 205, Ford City PA 16226-0205. (724)763-1617. Fax: (724)763-1763. E-mail: pendletonhomer@hotmail.com. Estab. 1980. Arts & crafts show held annually on the Fourth of July. Outdoors. Accepts photography, any handmade craft. Juried by state. Awards/prizes: 1st & 2nd place plaques for best entries. Public attendance: 35,000-50,000. Free to public. Artists should apply by requesting an application by e-mail or telephone. Deadline for entry: April 15. Application fee: $200. Space fee included with application fee. Exhibition space: 12×17 ft. For more information, artists should e-mail, call or send SASE.

Tips "Show runs for six days. Have quality product, be able to stay for length of show, and have enough product."

N ☑ 49TH ARTS EXPERIENCE

P.O. Box 1326, Palatine IL 60078. (847)991-4748 or (312)751-2500. E-mail: asoa@webtv.net. Web site: www.americansocietyofartists.org. Estab. 1979. Fine arts & crafts show held in summer. Outdoors. Accepts photography, paintings, graphics, sculpture, quilting, woodworking, fiber art, hand-crafted candles, glass works, jewelry, etc. Juried by 4 slides/photo representative of work being exhibited; 1 photo of display set-up, #10 SASE, résumé with 7 show listings helpful. Number of exhibitors: 50. Free to public. Artists should apply by submitting jury material and indicate you are interested in this particular show. If you wish to jury online please see our Web site and follow directions given there. When you pass the jury, you will receive jury approval number and application you requested. Deadline for entry: 2 months prior to show or earlier if space is filled. Space fee: to be announced. Exhibition space: 100 sq. ft. for single space; other sizes are available. For more information, artists should send SASE to submit jury material.

● Event held in Chicago, Illinois.

Tips "Remember that at work in your studio, you are an artist. When you are at a show, you are a business person selling your work."

✦ FOUR RIVERS ARTS & CRAFTS HARVEST HOME FESTIVAL

112 S. Lakeview Dr., Petersburg IN 47567. (812)354-6808, ext. 112. Fax: (812)354-2785. E-mail: rivers4@sigecom.net. Web site: http://www.fourriversrcd.org/gpage.html4.html. **Contact:** Denise Tuggle, program assistant. Estab. 1976. Arts & crafts show held annually the 3rd weekend in October. Indoors. Juried. Board of Directors are assigned certain buildings to check for any manufactured items. Crafts are not judged. Awards/prizes: $30-50; 3 display awards based on display uniqueness and the correlation of the harvest theme. Number of exhibitors: 200. Public attendance: 5,000. Free to public; $2 parking fee. Artists should apply by calling with information. Application will be mailed along with additional information. Deadline for entry: July 30. Space fee: $55, 2 per applicant. Exhibition space: 10×10 ft. For more information, artists should call.

✦ FOURTH AVENUE SPRING STREET FAIR

329 E. 7th St., Tucson AZ 85705.(520)624-5004. Fax: (520)624-5933. E-mail: kurt@fourthav enue.org. Web site: www.fourthavenue.org. **Contact:** Kurt Tallis, event director. Estab. 1970. Arts & crafts fair held annually in March. 2009 dates March 20-22. Outdoors. Accepts photography, drawing, painting, sculpture, arts and crafts. Juried by 5 jurors. Awards/prizes: Best of Show. Number of exhibitors: 400. Public attendance: 300,000. Free to the public. Artists should apply by completing the online application. Deadline for entry: December 17, 2008. Application fee: $35. Space fee: $470. Exhibition space: 10×10 ft. Average gross sales/exhibitor: $3,000. For more information, artists should e-mail, visit Web site, call, send SASE.

✦ FOURTH AVENUE WINTER STREET FAIR

329 E. 7th St., Tucson AZ 85705. (520)624-5004. Fax: (520)624-5933. E-mail: kurt@fourtha venue.org. Web site: www.fourthavenue.com. **Contact:** Kurt Tallis, event director. Estab. 1970. Arts & crafts fair held annually in December. 2008 dates December 12-14. Outdoors. Accepts photography, drawing, painting, sculpture, arts and crafts. Juried by 5 jurors. Awards/prizes: Best of Show. Number of exhibitors: 400. Public attendance: 300,000. Free to the public. Artists should apply by completing the online application. Deadline for entry: September. Application fee: $35. Space fee: $470. Exhibition space: 10×10 ft. Average gross sales/exhibitor: $3,000. For more information, artists should e-mail, visit Web site, call, send SASE.

✦ FOURTH OF JULY STREET FAIR, AUTUMN FEST IN THE PARK AND HOLIDAY STREET FESTIVAL

501 Poli St. #226, Ventura CA 93002. (805)654-7830. Fax: (805)648-1030. E-mail: mgoody@

ci.ventura.ca.us. Web site: www.venturastreetfair.com. **Contact:** Michelle Goody, cultural affairs coordinator. Estab. 1976. Fine arts & crafts show held annually in July, September and December. Outdoors. Accepts photography. Juried by a panel of 3 artists who specialize in various mediums; photos of work required. Number of exhibitors: 75-300. Public attendance: 1,000-50,000. Free to public. Artists should apply by downloading application from Web site or call to request application. Space fee: $100-175. Exhibition space: 10×10 ft. For more information, artists should e-mail, visit Web site or call.

Tips "Be friendly, outgoing; know the area for pricing."

FOURTH STREET FESTIVAL FOR THE ARTS & CRAFTS

P.O. Box 1257, Bloomington IN 47402. (812)335-3814. Web site: www.4thstreet.org. Estab. 1976. Fine arts & crafts show held annually Labor Day weekend. Outdoors. Accepts photography, clay, glass, fiber, jewelry, painting, graphic, mixed media, wood. Juried by a 4-member panel. Awards/prizes: Best of Show, 1st, 2nd, 3rd in 2D and 3D. Number of exhibitors: 105. Public attendance: 25,000. Free to public. Artists should apply by sending requests by snail mail, e-mail or download application from Web site. Deadline for entry: April 1. Application fee: $15. Space fee: $175. Exhibition space: 10×10 ft. Average gross sales/exhibitor: $2,700. For more information, artists should e-mail, visit Web site, call or send for information with SASE.

Tips "Be professional."

FRANKFORT ART FAIR

P.O. Box 566, Frankfort MI 49635.(231)352-7251. Fax: (231)352-6750. E-mail: fcofc@frankf ort-elberta.com. Web site: www.frankfort-elberta.com. Estab. 1976. **Contact:** Joanne Bartley, art fair director. Fine Art Fair held annually in August. Outdoors. Accepts photography, clay, glass, jewelry, textiles, wood, drawing/graphic arts, painting, sculpture, baskets, mixed media. Juried by 3 photos of work, one photo of booth display and one photo of work in progress. Prior exhibitors are not automatically accepted. No buy/sell allowed. Artists should apply by downloading application from Web site, e-mailing or calling. Deadline for entry: May 1. Jury fee: $15. Space fee: $105 for Friday and Saturday. Exhibition space: 12×12 ft. For more information, artists should e-mail, see Web site.

GARRISON ART CENTER FINE ART & CRAFT FAIR

P.O. Box 4, 23 Camison's Landing, Garrison NY 10524. (845)424-3960. Fax: (845)424-3960. E-mail: gac@highlands.com. Web site: www.garrisonartcenter.org. Estab. 1969. **Contact:** Libby Turnock, executive director. Fine arts & crafts show held annually 3rd weekend in August. Outdoors. Accepts all mediums. Juried by a committee of artists and community members. Number of exhibitors: 75. Public attendance: 10,000. Public admission: suggested donation of $5. Artists should call for application form or download from Web site. Deadline for entry: April. Application fee: $15. Space fee: $245; covered corner booth: $265. Exhibition space: 10×10 ft. For more information, artists should e-mail, visit Web site, call, send SASE.

Tips "Have an inviting booth and be pleasant and accessible. Don't hide behind your product—engage the audience."

GERMANTOWN FESTIVAL

P.O. Box 381741, Germantown TN 38183. (901)757-9212. E-mail: gtownfestival@aol.com. **Contact:** Melba Fristick, coordinator. Estab. 1971. Arts and crafts show held annually the weekend after Labor Day. Outdoors. Accepts photography, all arts & crafts mediums. Number of exhibitors: 400+. Public attendance: 65,000. Free to public. Artists should apply by sending applications by mail. Deadline for entry: until filled. Application/space fee: $190-240. Exhibition space: 10×10 ft. For more information, artists should e-mail, call or send SASE.

Tips "Display and promote to the public. Price attractively."

⛵ GLOUCESTER WATERFRONT FESTIVAL

Castleberry Fairs & Festivals, 38 Charles St., Rochester NH 03867. (603)332-2616. E-mail: info@castelberryfairs.com. Web site: www.castleberryfairs.com. **Contact:** Terry Mullen, events coordinator. Estab. 1971. Arts & crafts show held 3rd weekend in August in Gloucester, Massachusettes. Outdoors. Accepts photography and all other mediums. Juried by photo, slide or sample. Number of exhibitors: 300. Public attendance: 50,000. Free to the public. Artists should apply by downloading application from Web site. Deadline for entry: until full. Space fee: $350. Exhibition space: 100 sq. ft. Average gross sales/exhibitor: "Generally, this is considered an 'excellent' show, so I would guess most exhibitors sell ten times their booth fee, or in this case, at least $3,500 in sales." For more information, artists should visit Web site.

Tips "Do not bring a book; do not bring a chair. Smile and make eye contact with everyone who enters your booth. Have them sign your guest book; get their e-mail address so you can let them know when you are in the area again. And, finally, make the sale—they are at the fair to shop, after all."

Ⓝ GOLD RUSH DAYS

P.O. Box 774, Dahlonega GA 30533. (706)864-7247. Web site: www.dahlonegajaycees.com. **Contact:** Gold Rush Chairman. Arts & crafts show held annually the 3rd full week in October. Accepts photography, paintings and homemade, handcrafted items. No digitally originated art work. Outdoors. Number of exhibitors: 300. Public attendance: 200,000. Free to the public. Artists should apply online at www.dahlonegajaycees.com under "Gold Rush," or send SASE to request application. Deadline: March. Space fee: $225, "but we reserve the right to raise the fee to cover costs." Exhibition space: 10×10 ft. Artists should e-mail, visit Web site for more information.

Tips "Talk to other artists who have done other shows and festivals. Get tips and advice from those in the same line of work."

⛵ GOOD OLD SUMMERTIME ART FAIR

P.O. Box 1753, Kenosha WI 53141-1753. (262)654-0065. E-mail: kaaartfairs@yahoo.com. Web site: www.KenoshaArtAssoc.org. **Contact:** Karen Gulbransen, art fair coordinator. Estab. 1975. Fine arts show held annually the 1st Sunday in June. Outdoors. Accepts photography, paintings, drawings, mosaics, ceramics, pottery, sculpture, wood, stained glass. Juried by a panel. Photos or slides required with application. Awards/prizes: Best of Show, 1st, 2nd and 3rd Places, plus Purchase Awards. Number of exhibitors: 100. Public attendance: 3,000. Free to public. Artists should apply by completing application form, and including fees and SASE. Deadline for entry: April 1. Application/space fee: $60-65. Exhibition space: 12×12 ft. For more information, artists should e-mail, visit Web site or send SASE.

Tips "Have a professional display, and be friendly."

N GRADD ARTS & CRAFTS FESTIVAL

3860 US Hwy 60 W., Owensboro KY 42301. (270)926-4433. Fax: (270)684-0714. E-mail: bethgoetz@gradd.com. Web site: www.gradd.com. **Contact:** Beth Goetz, festival coordinator. Estab. 1972. Arts & crafts show held annually 1st full weekend in October. Outdoors. Accepts photography taken by crafter only. Number of exhibitors: 180-200. Public attendance: 15,000+. Free to public; $3 parking fee. Artists should apply by calling to be put on mailing list. Space fee: $100-150. Exhibition space: 10×12 ft. For more information, artists should e-mail, visit Web site or call.

Tips "Be sure that only hand-crafted items are sold. No buy/sell items will be allowed."

N ☑ GRAND FESTIVAL OF THE ARTS & CRAFTS

P.O. Box 429, Grand Lake CO 80447-0429. (970)627-3372. Fax: (970)627-8007. E-mail: glinfo@grandlakechamber.com. Web site: www.grandlakechamber.com. **Contact:** Cindy Cunningham, events coordinator; Elaine Arguien, office chamber. Fine arts & crafts show held annually 1st weekend in June. Outdoors. Accepts photography, jewelry, leather, mixed media, painting, paper, sculpture, wearable art. Juried by chamber committee. Awards/ prizes: Best in Show and Peoples' Choice. Number of exhibitors: 50-55. Public attendance: 1,000+. Free to public. Artists should apply by submitting slides or photos. Deadline for entry: May 1. Application fee: $125, includes space fee, security deposit and business license. Exhibition space: 10×10 ft. For more information, artists should e-mail or call.

N ☑ GREAT NECK STREET FAIR

P.O. Box 477, Smithtown NY 11787-0477. (631)724-5966. Fax: (631)724-5967. E-mail: showtiques@aol.com. Web site: www.showtiques.com. **Contact:** Eileen. Estab. 1978. Fine arts & crafts show held annually in May. Outdoors. Accepts photography, all arts & crafts made by the exhibitor. Juried. Number of exhibitors: 250. Public attendance: 50,000. Free to public. Deadline for entry: until full. Space fee: $150-175. Exhibition space: 10×10 ft. For more information, artists should e-mail, visit Web site or call.

☑ GUNSTOCK SUMMER FESTIVAL

Castleberry Fairs & Festivals, 38 Charles St., Rochester NH 03867. (603)332-2616. E-mail: info@castelberryfairs.com. Web site: www.castleberryfairs.com. **Contact:** Terry Mullen, events coordinator. Estab. 1971. Arts & crafts show held annually in July in Gilford, New Hampshire. Indoors and outdoors. Accepts photography and all other mediums. Juried by photo, slide or sample. Number of exhibitors: 100. Public attendance: 10,000. Free to the public. Artists should apply by downloading application from Web site. Deadline for entry: until full. Space fee: $200. Exhibition space: 100 sq. ft. For more information, artists should visit Web site.

Tips "Do not bring a book; do not bring a chair. Smile and make eye contact with everyone who enters your booth. Have them sign your guest book; get their e-mail address so you can let them know when you are in the area again. And, finally, make the sale—they are at the fair to shop, after all."

N ☑ HIGHLAND MAPLE FESTIVAL

P.O. Box 223, Monterey VA 24465-0223. (540)468-2550. Fax:(540)468-2551. E-mail: highcc @cfw.co. Web site: www.highlandcounty.org. **Contact:** Carolyn Pottowsky, executive director. Estab. 1958. Fine arts & crafts show held annually the 2nd and 3rd weekends in

March. Indoors and outdoors. Accepts photography, pottery, weaving, jewelry, painting, wood crafts, furniture. Juried by 3 photos or slides. Number of exhibitors: 150. Public attendance: 35,000-50,000. Public admission: $2. Deadline for entry: "There is a late fee after December 20, 2006. Vendors accepted until show is full." Space fee: $125-$150. Exhibition space: 10×10 ft. For more information, artists should e-mail, visit Web site, call.
Tips "Have quality work and good salesmanship."

☘ HINSDALE FINE ARTS FESTIVAL
22 E. First St., Hinsdale IL 60521. (630)323-3952. Fax: (630)323-3953. E-mail: janet@hindsd alechamber.com. Web site: www.hinsdalechamber.com. **Contact:** Jan Anderson, executive director. Fine arts show held annually in mid-June. Outdoors. Accepts photography, ceramics, painting, sculpture, fiber arts, mixed media, jewelry. Juried by 3 slides. Awards/prizes: Best in Show, Presidents Award and 1st, 2nd and 3rd Place in 7 categories. Number of exhibitors: 150. Public attendance: 2,000-3,000. Free to public. Artists should apply by mailing or downloading application from Web site. Deadline for entry: March 2. Application fee: $25. Space fee: $250. Exhibition space: 10×10 ft. For more information, artists should e-mail or visit Web site.
Tips "Original artwork sold by artist. Artwork should be appropriately and reasonably priced."

☘ HOLIDAY ARTS & CRAFTS SHOW
60 Ida Lee Dr., Leesburg VA 20176. (703)777-1368. Fax: (703)737-7165. E-mail: lfountain@l eesburgva.gov. Web site: www.idalee.org. **Contact:** Linda Fountain, program supervisor. Estab. 1990. Arts & crafts show held annually 1st weekend in December. Indoors. Accepts photography, jewelry, pottery, baskets, clothing, accessories. Juried. Number of exhibitors: 100. Public attendance: 4,000. Free to public. Artists should apply by downloading application from Web site. Deadline for entry: August 31. Space fee: $100-150. Exhibition space: 10×7 ft. For more information, artists should e-mail or visit Web site.

☘ HOLIDAY CRAFTS AT MORRISTOWN
P.O. Box 28, Woodstock NY 12498. (845)331-7900. Fax: (845)331-7484. E-mail: crafts@artri der.com. Web site: www.craftsatmorristown.com; www.artrider.com. **Contact:** Laura Kandel. Estab. 1990. Fine arts & crafts show held annually in early December. Indoors. Accepts photography, wearable and nonwearable fiber, metal and nonmetal jewelry, clay, leather, wood, glass, painting, drawing, prints, mixed media. Juried by 5 images of work and 1 of booth, viewed sequentially. Number of exhibitors: 165. Public attendance: 5,000. Public admission: $7. Artists should apply by downloading application from www.artrider.com or can apply online at www.zapplication.org. Deadline for entry: August 1. Application fee: $35. Space fee: $475. Exhibition space: 10×10. For more information, artists should e-mail, visit Web site, call.

☘ HOLLY ARTS & CRAFTS FESTIVAL
P.O. Box 2122, Pinehurst NC 28370. (910)295-7462. E-mail: sbharrison@earthlink.net, pbg uild@pinehurst.net. Web site: www.pinehurstbusinessguild.com. **Contact:** Susan Harrison, Holly Arts & Crafts committee. Estab. 1978. Arts & crafts show held annually 3rd Saturday in October. Outdoors. Accepts quality photography, arts, and crafts. Juried based on uniqueness, quality of product, and overall display. Awards/prizes: plaque given to

Best in Show; 2 Honorable Mentions receive ribbons. Number of exhibitors: 200. Public attendance: 7,000. Free to the public. Artists should apply by filling out application form. Deadline for entry: March 31, 2008. Space fee: $75. Exhibition space: 10×10 ft. For more information, artists should e-mail, visit Web site, call, send SASE. Applications accepted after deadline if available space.

HOME DECORATING & REMODELING SHOW

P.O. Box 230699, Las Vegas NV 89105-0699. (702)450-7984 or (800)343-8344. Fax: (702)451-7305. E-mail: spvandy@cox.net. Web site: www.nashvillehomeshow.com. **Contact:** Vandy Richards, manager member. Estab. 1983. Home show held annually in September. Indoors. Accepts photography, sculpture, watercolor, oils, mixed media, pottery. Awards/prizes: Outstanding Booth Award. Number of exhibitors: 300-350. Public attendance: 25,000. Public admission: $8. Artists should apply by calling. Marketing is directed to middle and above income brackets. Deadline for entry: open until filled. Space fee: $850+. Exhibition space: 9×10 ft. or complement of 9×10 ft. For more information, artists should call.

HOME, CONDO AND GARDEN ART & CRAFT FAIR

P.O. Box 486, Ocean City MD 21843. (410)524-7020. Fax: (410)524-0051. E-mail: oceanpromotions@beachin.net. Web site: www.oceanpromotions.info. **Contact:** Mike, promoter; Starr, assistant. Estab. 1984. Fine arts & crafts show held annually in March. Indoors. Accepts photography, carvings, pottery, ceramics, glass work, floral, watercolor, sculpture, prints, oils, pen & ink. Number of exhibitors: 125. Public attendance: 18,000. Public admission: $7/adults; $6/seniors & students; 13 and under free. Artists should apply by e-mailing request for info and aplication. Deadline for entry: Until full. Space fee: $250. Exhibition space: 10×8 ft. For more information, artists should e-mail, visit Web site or call.

N ☑ STAN HYWET HALL & GARDENS WONDERFUL WORLD OF OHIO MART

714 N. Portage Path, Akron OH 44303-1399. (330)836-5533. Web site: www.stanhywet.org. **Contact:** Lynda Grieves, exhibitor chair. Estab. 1966. Arts & crafts show held annually 1st full weekend in October. Outdoors. Accepts photography and all mediums. Juried 2 Saturdays in January and via mail application. Awards/prizes: Best Booth Display. Number of exhibitors: 115. Public attendance: 15,000-20,000. Public admission: $7. Deadline for entry: Mid-February. Space fee: $450. Exhibition space: 10×10 ft. For more information, artists should visit Web site or call.

☑ INTERNATIONAL FOLK FESTIVAL

P.O. Box 318, Fayetteville NC 28302-0318. (910)323-1776. Fax: (910)323-1727. E-mail: kelvinc@theartscouncil.com. Web site: www.theartscouncil.com. **Contact:** Kelvin Culbreth, director of special events. Estab. 1978. Fine arts & crafts show held annually in late September. Outdoors. Accepts photography, painting of all mediums, pottery, woodworking, sculptures of all mediums. "Work must be original." Juried. Awards/prizes: $2,000 in cash prizes in several categories. Number of exhibitors: 120+. Public attendance: 70,000. Free to public. Artists should apply on the Web site. Deadline for entry: September 1. Application fee: $60; includes space fee. Exhibition space: 10×10 ft. Average gross sales/exhibitor: $500. For more information, artists should e-mail or visit Web site.
Tips "Have reasonable prices."

Art Fairs

N ☑ ISLE OF EIGHT FLAGS SHRIMP FESTIVAL

18 N. Second St., Ferninda Beach FL 32034. (904)271-7020. Fax: (904)261-1074. E-mail: islandart@net-magic.net. Web site: www.islandart.org. **Contact:** Shrimp Festival Committee Chairperson. Estab. 1963. Fine arts & crafts show and community celebration held annually the 1st weekend in May. Outdoors. Accepts photography and all mediums. Juried. Awards/prizes: $9,700 in cash prizes. Number of exhibitors: 425. Public attendance: 150,000. Free to public. Artists should apply by downloading application from Web site. Deadline for entry: January 1. Application fee: $30. Space fee: $200. Exhibition space: 10 × 12 ft. Average gross sales/exhibitor: $1,500 + . For more information, artists should visit Web site.

Tips "Quality product and attractive display."

N ☑ JOHNS HOPKINS UNIVERSITY SPRING FAIR

3400 N Charles Street, Mattin Suite 210, Baltimore MD 21218. (410)513-7692. Fax: (410)516-6185. E-mail: springfair@gmail.com. Web site: www.jhuspringfair.com. **Contact:** Catalina McCallum, arts & crafts chair. Estab. 1972. Fine arts & crafts, campus-wide, festival held annually in April. Outdoors. Accepts photography and all mediums. Juried. Number of exhibitors: 80. Public attendance: 20,000 + . Free to public. Artists should apply via Web site. Deadline for entry: March 1. Application fee: $200. Space fee: $200. Exhibition space: 10 × 10 ft. For more information, artists should e-mail, visit Web site or call.

Tips "Artists should have fun displays, good prices, good variety and quality pieces."

JUBILEE FESTIVAL

P.O. Drawer 310, Daphne AL 36526. (251)621-8222. Fax: (251)621. E-mail: office@eschamber.com. Web site: www.eschamber.com. **Contact:** Angela Kimsey, event coordinator. Estab. 1952. Fine arts & crafts show held in September in Olde Towne of Daphne, Alabama. Outdoors. Accepts photography and fine arts and crafts. Juried. Awards/prizes: ribbons and cash prizes. Number of exhibitors: 258. Public attendance: 200,000. Free to the public. Application fee: $25. Space fee: $265. Exhibition space: 10 ft. × 10 ft. For more information, artists should e-mail, call, see Web site.

N ☑ KETNER'S MILL COUNTY ARTS FAIR

P.O. Box 322, Lookout Mountain TN 37350. (243)267-5702. Fax: (423)757-1343. **Contact:** Sally McDonald. Estab. 1977. Arts & crafts show held annually the 3rd weekend in October. Outdoors. Accepts photography, painting, prints, dolls, fiber arts, baskets, folk art, wood crafts, jewelry, musical instruments, sculpture, pottery, glass. Juried. Prizes: 1st: $75 and free booth for following year; 2nd: $50 and free booth for following year; 3rd: free booth for following year; People's Choice Award. Number of exhibitors: 150. Number of attendees: 10,000/day, depending on weather. Public admission: $5.00. Artists should call or send SASE to request a prospectus/application. Deadline for entry: August 1, 2007. Space fee: $125. Exhibition space: 15 × 15 ft. Average gross sales/exhibitor: $1,500.

Tips "Display your best and most expensive work, framed. But also have smaller unframed items to sell. Never underestimate a show: Someone may come forward and buy a large item."

☑ KIA ART FAIR (KALAMAZOO INSTITUTE OF ARTS)

314 S. Park St., Kalamazoo MI 49007-5102. (269)349-7775. Fax: (269)349-9313. E-mail: sjrodia@yahoo.com. Web site: www.kiarts.org. **Contact:** Steve Rodia, artist coordinator.

Estab. 1951. Fine arts & crafts show held annually the 1st Friday and Saturday in June. Outdoors. Accepts photography, prints, pastels, drawings, paintings, mixed media, ceramics (functional and nonfunctional), sculpture/metalsmithing, wood, fiber, jewelry, glass, leather. Juried by no fewer than 3 and no more than 5 art professionals chosen for their experience and expertise. See prospectus for more details. Awards/prizes: 1st prize: $500; 2nd prize: 2 at $300 each; 3rd prize: 3 at $200 each. 10 category prizes at $100 each. Number of exhibitors: 200. Public attendance: 40,000-50,000. Free to the public. Artists should apply by filling out application form and submitting 3 digital images of their art and 1 digital image of their booth display. Deadline for entry: March 1. Application fee: $25, nonrefundable. Space fee: $110. Exhibition space: 10×12 ft. Height should not exceed 10 ft. in order to clear the trees in the park. For more information, artists should e-mail, visit Web site, call.

KINGS MOUNTAIN ART FAIR

13106 Skyline Blvd., Woodside CA 94062. (650)851-2710. E-mail: kmafsecty@aol.com. Web site: www.kingsmountainartfair.org. **Contact:** Carrie German, administrative assistant. Estab. 1963. Fine arts & crafts show held annually Labor Day weekend. Fundraiser for volunteer fire dept. Accepts photography, ceramics, clothing, 2D, painting, glass, jewelry, leather, sculpture, textile/fiber, wood. Juried. Number of exhibitors: 135. Public attendance: 10,000. Free to public. Deadline for entry: January 30. Application fee: $10. Space fee: $100 plus 15%. Exhibition space: 10×10 ft. Average gross sales/exhibitor: $3,000. For more information, artists should e-mail, visit Web site, call or send SASE.

LAKE CITY ARTS & CRAFTS FESTIVAL

P.O.Box 1147, Lake City CO 81235. (970)944-2706. E-mail: jlsharpe@centurytel.net. Web site: www.lakecityarts.org. **Contact:** Laura Sharpe, festival director. Estab. 1975. Fine arts/arts & craft show held annually 3rd Tuesday in July. One-day event. Outdoors. Accepts photography, jewelry, metal work, woodworking, painting, handmade items. Juried by 3-5 undisclosed jurors. Prize: Winners are entered in a drawing for a free both space in the following year's show. Number of Exhibitors: 85. Public Attendance: 500. Free to the public. Deadline for entry: entries must be postmarked April 25. Application fee: $75; nonrefundable jury fee: $10. Exhibition space: 12×12 ft. Average gross sales/exhibitor: $500-$1,000. For more information, artists should visit Web site.

Tips ''Repeat vendors draw repeat customers. People like to see their favorite vendors each year or every other year. If you come every year, have new things as well as your best-selling products.''

LES CHENEAUX FESTIVAL OF ARTS

P.O. Box 30, Cedarville MI 49719. (906)484-2821. Fax: (906)484-6107. E-mail: lcha@cedarville.net. Contact: A. Goehring, curator. Estab. 1976. Fine arts & crafts show held annually 2nd Saturday in August. Outdoors. Accepts photography and all other media; original work and design only; no kits or commercially manufactured goods. Juried by a committee of 10. Submit 4 slides (3 of the artwork; 1 of booth display). Awards/prizes: monetary prizes for excellent and original work. Number of exhibitors: 70. Public attendance: 8,000. Public admission: $7. Artists should fill out application form to apply. Deadline for entry: April 1. Application fee: $65. Exhibition space: 10×10 ft. Average gross sales/exhibitor: $5-$500. For more information, artists should call, send SASE.

ⓝ ⓥ LILAC FESTIVAL ARTS & CRAFTS SHOW

171 Reservoir Ave., Rochester NY 14620. (585)256-4960. Fax: (585)256-4968. E-mail: info@ lilacfestival.com. Web site: www.lilacfestival.com. **Contact:** Sue LeBeau, art show coordinator. Estab. 1985. Arts & crafts show held annually in May. Outdoors. Accepts photography, painting, ceramics, woodworking, metal sculpture, fiber. Juried by a panel. Number of exhibitors: 150. Public attendance: 25,000. Free to public. Deadline for entry: March 1. Application fee: $190. Space fee: $190. Exhibition space: 10×10 ft. For more information, artists should visit Web site or send SASE.

ⓥ LITCHFIELD LIBRARY ARTS & CRAFTS FESTIVAL

101 W Wigwam Blvd., Litchfield Park AZ 85340. (623)393-7820. E-mail: cvermill@apsc.c om. **Contact:** Candy Vermillion, promoter. Estab. 1970. Fine arts and select crafts show held annually 1st weekend in November. Outdoors. Accepts photography and all mediums. Juried. Number of exhibitors: 300. Public attendance: 90,000. Free to public. Artists should apply by calling for application. Deadline for entry: August 1, 2008. Space fee: $300. Exhibition space: 10×15 ft. For more information, artists should call.

Tips "Professional display and original art."

ⓝ ⓥ LOMPOC FLOWER FESTIVAL

P.O. Box 723, Lompoc CA 93438. (805)735-9501. Web site: www.lompocvalleyartassociatio n.com. **Contact:** Marie Naar, chairman. Estab. 1942. Fine arts & crafts show held annually last week in June. Event includes a parade, food booths, entertainment, beer garden and commercial center, which is not located near arts & crafts. Outdoors. Accepts photography, fine art, woodworking, pottery, stained glass, fine jewelry. Juried by 5 members of the Lompoc Valley Art Association. Vendor must submit 5 photos of their craft and a description on how to make the craft. Number of exhibitors: 95. Public attendance: 95,000+. Free to public. Artists should apply by calling the contact person for application or download application from Web site. Deadline for entry: April 1. Application fee: $173 plus insurance. Exhibition space: 16×16 ft. For more information, artists should visit Web site, call or send SASE.

Tips "Artists should have prices that are under $100 to succeed."

ⓥ MASON ARTS FESTIVAL

P.O. Box 381, Mason OH 45040. (513)573-9376. E-mail: pgast@cinci.rr.com. for Inside City Gallery; e-mail: mraffel@cinci.rr.com for outdoor art festival. Web site: www.masonarts.o rg. **Contact:** Pat Gastreich, City Gallery Chairperson. Fine arts and crafts show held annually in September. Indoors and outdoors. Accepts photography, graphics, printmaking, mixed media; painting and drawing; ceramics, metal sculpture; fiber, glass, jewelry, wood, leather. Juried. Awards/prizes: $3,000+. Number of exhibitors: 75-100. Public attendance: 3,000-5,000. Free to the public. Artists should apply by visiting Web site for application, e-mailing mraffel@cinci.rr.com, or calling (513)573-0007. Deadline for entry: June. Application fee: $25. Space fee: $75 for single space; $135 for adjoining spaces. Exhibition space: 12×12 ft.; artist must provide 10×10 ft. pop-up tent.

● City Gallery show is held indoors; these artists are not permitted to participate outdoors and vice versa. City Gallery is a juried show featuring approximately 30-50 artists who may show up to 2 pieces.

Tips "Photographers are required to disclose both their creative and printing processes. If digital manipulation is part of the composition, please indicate."

⚓ MEMORIAL WEEKEND ARTS & CRAFTS FESTIVAL

Castleberry Fairs & Festivals. 38 Charles St., Rochester NH 03867. (603)332-2616. E-mail: info@castleberryfairs.com. Web site: www.castleberryfairs.com. **Contact:** Terry Mullen, event coordinator. Estab. 1989. Arts & crafts show held annually on Memorial Day weekend in Meredith, New Hampshire. Outdoors. Accepts photography and all other mediums. Juried by photo, slide or sample. Number of exhibitors: 85. Public attendance: 7,500. Free to the public. Artists should apply by downloading application from Web site. Deadline for entry: until full. Space fee: $300. Exhibition space: 100 sq. ft. Average gross sales/exhibitor: "Generally, this is considered an 'excellent' show, so I would guess most exhibitors sell ten times their booth fee, or in this case, at least $3,000 in sales." For more information, artists should visit Web site.

Tips "Do not bring a book; do not bring a chair. Smile and make eye contact with everyone who enters your booth. Have them sign your guest book; get their e-mail address so you can let them know when you are in the area again. And, finally, make the sale—they are at the fair to shop, after all."

⚓ MICHIGAN STATE UNIVERSITY SPRING ARTS & CRAFTS SHOW

322 MSU Union, East Lansing MI 48824. (517)355-3354. E-mail: artsandcrafts@uabevents.com. Web site: www.uabevents.com. Contact: Kate Lake, assistant manager. Estab. 1963. Arts & crafts show held annually in mid-May. Outdoors. Accepts photography, basketry, candles, ceramics, clothing, sculpture, soaps, drawings, floral, fibers, glass, jewelry, metals, painting, graphics, pottery, wood. Juried by a panel of judges using the photographs submitted by each vendor to eliminate commercial products. They will evaluate on quality, creativity and crowd appeal. Number of exhibitors: 329. Public attendance: 60,000. Free to public. Artists can apply online beginning in February. Online applications will be accepted until show is filled. Application fee: $240. Exhibition space: 10×10 ft. For more information, artists should visit Web site or call.

⚓ MID-MISSOURI ARTISTS CHRISTMAS ARTS & CRAFTS SALE

P.O. Box 116, Warrensburg MO 64093. (660)747-6092. E-mail: bjsmith@iland.net or rlimback@iland.net. **Contact:** Beverly Smith. Estab. 1970. Holiday arts & crafts show held annually in November. Indoors. Accepts photography and all original arts and crafts. Juried by 3 good-quality color photos (2 of the artwork, 1 of the display). Number of exhibitors: 50. Public attendance: 1,200. Free to the public. Artists should apply by e-mailing or calling for an application form. Deadline for entry: November 1. Space fee: $50. Exhibition space: 10×10 ft. For more information, artists should e-mail or call.

Tips "Items under $100 are most popular."

⚓ MOUNT GRETNA OUTDOOR ART SHOW

P.O. Box 637, Mount Gretna PA 17064. (717)964-3270. Fax: (717)964-3054. E-mail: mtgretnaart@comcast.net. Web site: www.mtgretnaarts.com. **Contact:** Linda Bell, show committee chairperson. Estab. 1974. Fine arts & crafts show held annually 3rd full weekend in August. Outdoors. Accepts photography, oils, acrylics, watercolors, mixed media, jewelry, wood, paper, graphics, sculpture, leather, clay/porcelain. Juried by 4 professional artists who assign each applicant a numeric score. The highest scores in each medium are accepted. Awards/prizes: Judges' Choice Awards: 30 artists are invited to return the following year, jury exempt; the top 10 are given a monetary award of $250. Number of exhibitors: 275. Public attendance: 15,000-19,000. Public admission: $7; children under 12: free. Artists should apply via www.zapplication.org. Deadline for entry: April 1. Application fee: $20 jury fee. Space fee: $300. Exhibition space: 10×10 ft. For more information, artists should e-mail, visit Web site, call.

Ⓝ Ⓥ NAPA WINE & CRAFTS FAIRE

1556 First St., Suite 102, Napa CA 94559. (707)257-0322. Fax: (707)257-1821. E-mail: info@napadowntown.com. Web site: www.napadowntown.com. **Contact:** Craig Smith, executive director. Wine and crafts show held annually in September. Outdoors. Accepts photography, jewelry, clothing, woodworking, glass, dolls, candles and soaps, garden art. Juried based on quality, uniqueness, and overall craft mix of applicants. Number of exhibitors: over 200. Public attendance: 20,000-30,000. Artists should apply by contacting the event coordinator, Marla Bird, at (707)299-0712 to obtain an application form. Application forms are also available on Web site. Application fee: $15. Space fee: $200. Exhibition space: 10×10 ft. For more information, artists should e-mail, visit Web site or call.

Tips "Electricity is available, but limited. There is a $40 processing fee for cancellations."

Ⓥ NEW ENGLAND ARTS & CRAFTS FESTIVAL

Castleberry Fairs & Festivals, 38 Charles St., Rochester NE 03867. (603)322-2616. E-mail: info@castleberryfairs.com. Web site: www.castleberryfairs.com. **Contact:** Terry Mullen, event coordinator. Estab. 1988. Arts & crafts show held annually on Labor Day weekend in Topsfield, Massachusettes. Indoors and outdoors. Accepts photography and all other mediums. Juried by photo, slide or sample. Number of exhibitors: 250. Public attendance: 25,000. Public admission: $6.00 for adults: free for 13 and under. Artists should apply by downloading application from Web site. Deadline for entry: until full. Space fee: $350. Exhibition space: 100 sq. ft. Average gross sales/exhibitor: "Generally, this is considered an 'excellent' show, so I would guess most exhibitors sell ten times their booth fee, or in this case, at least $3,500 in sales." For more information, artists should visit Web site.

Tips "Do not bring a book; do not bring a chair. Smile and make eye contact with everyone who enters your booth. Have them sign your guest book; get their e-mail address so you can let them know when you are in the area again. And, finally, make the sale—they are at the fair to shop, after all."

Ⓥ NEW ENGLAND CRAFT & SPECIALTY FOOD FAIR

Castleberry Fairs & Festivals, 38 Charles Rd., Rochester NH 03867. (603)332-2616. E-mail: info@castleberryfairs.com. Web site: www.castleberryfairs.com. **Contact:** Terry Mullen, event coordinator. Estab. 1995. Arts & crafts show held annually on Veteran's Day weekend in Salem, New Hampshire. Indoors. Accepts photography and all other mediums. Juried by photo, slide or sample. Number of exhibitors: 200. Public attendance: 15,000. Admissions: $6. Artists should apply by downloading application from Web site. Deadline for entry: until full. Space fee: $300. Exhibition space: 100 sq. ft. Average gross sales/exhibitor: "Generally, this is considered an 'excellent' show, so I would guess most exhibitors sell ten times their booth fee, or in this case, at least $3,000 in sales." For more information, artists should visit Web site.

Tips "Do not bring a book; do not bring a chair. Smile and make eye contact with everyone who enters your booth. Have them sign your guest book; get their e-mail address so you can let them know when you are in the area again. And, finally, make the sale—they are at the fair to shop, after all."

⚑ NEW MEXICO ARTS & CRAFTS FAIR

P.O. Box 7279, Albuquerque NM 87194. (505)884-9043. Fax: (505)247-0608. E-mail: info@ nmartsandcraftsfair.org. Web site: www.nmartsandcraftsfair.org. **Contact:** Corey Dzenko, office manager. Estab. 1962. Fine arts & craft show held annually in June. Indoors and outdoors. Accepts photography, ceramics, fiber, digital art, drawing, jewelry—precious and nonprecious, printmaking, sculpture, wood, mixed media. **Only New Mexico residents 18 years and older are eligible.** Juried by submitting 5 slides; 5 New Mexico artists are chosen each year to jury. Awards/prizes: Total cash awards exceed $4,500. Best of Show: $1,500; First Lady's Choice; Jury Awards; Artist's Choice Award; Creativity Award; First-Time Exhibitor Award. Number of exhibitors: 220. Public admission: $10 for 3-day adult & senior pass; $5 for adult & senior daily admission; free to youth 12 and under. Artists should apply by downloading application from Web site or e-mail for application. Deadline: January. Application fee: Jury fee of $25 per category entered. Space fee: 10×10 ft. (outdoor-1 exhibitor): $350; 10×10 ft. (indoor-1 exhibitor): $400; 10×10 ft. (outdoor, 2 exhibitors): $425; 10×10 ft. (indoor, 2 exhibitors): $450; corner booth fee: $60. For more information, artists should e-mail, visit Web site, call.

NEW SMYRNA BEACH ART FIESTA

210 Sams Ave., New Smyrna Beach FL 32168. (386)424-2175. Fax: (386)424-2177. Web site: www.cityofnsb.com. **Contact:** Kimla Shelton, program coordinator. Estab. 1952. Arts & crafts show held annually the last full weekend in February. Outdoors. Accepts photography, oil, acrylics, pastel, drawings, graphics, sculpture, crafts, watercolor. Awards/prizes: $14,000 prize money; $1,500/category; Best of Show. Number of exhibitors: 250. Public attendance: 14,000. Free to public. Artists should apply by calling to get on mailing list. Applications are always mailed out the day before Thanksgiving. Deadline for entry: until full. Application/space fee: $135 plus tax. Exhibition space: 10×10 ft. For more information, artists should call.

ℕ NEW WORLD FESTIVAL OF THE ARTS

PO Box 994, Manteo NC 27954. (252)473-2838. Fax: (252)473-6044. E-mail: Edward@outer bankschristmas.co. **Contact:** Owen Holleran, event registrar. Estab. 1963. Fine arts &crafts show held annually in August. Outdoors. Juried. Accepts photography, watercolor, oil, mixed media, drawing printmaking, graphics, pastel, ceramic, sculpture, fiber, handwoven wearable art, wood, glass, hand-crafted jewelry, metalsmithing, leather. "No commercial molds or kids will be accepted. All work must be signed by the artist." Juror reviews slides to select participants; then selects winners on the 1st day of exhibit. Awards/prizes: cash awards totaling $3,000. Number of exhibitors: 80. Public attendance: 4,500-5000. Free to pubic. Artists should apply by sending for application. Deadline for entry: June 10. Application fee: $10 jury fee. Space fee: $80. Exhibition space: 10×10 ft. For more information, artists should e-mail or call.

⚑ OFFICIAL TEXAS STATE ARTS & CRAFTS FAIR

4000 Riverside Dr., Kerrville TX 78028. (830)896-5711. Fax: (830)896-5569. E-mail: fair@tac ef.org. Web site: www.tacef.org. **Contact:** Penni Carr. Estab.1972. Fine arts & crafts show held annually on Memorial Day weekend. Outdoors. Accepts photography, ceramics, fiber, glass, graphics/drawing, jewelry, leather, metal, mixed media, painting, sculpture, wood. Juried by a panel of professional artists and college art professors. Number of exhibitors: 160+. Public attendance: 16,000. Public admission: $10 for a 4-day pass. Artists should apply by downloading application from Web site. Deadline: December. Application fee: $20. Space fee: $300-600. Exhibition space: 10×10. ft. and 10×20 ft. For more information, artists should visit Web site.

Tips "Market and advertise."

⚑ ORCHARD LAKE FINE ART SHOW

P.O. Box 79, Milford MI 48381-0079. (248)684-2613. Fax: (248)684-0195. E-mail: patty@hot works.org. Web site: www.hotworks.org. **Contact:** Patty Narozny, show director. Estab. 2002. Fine arts & crafts show held annually late July/early August. Outdoors. Accepts photography, clay, glass, fiber, wood, jewelry, painting, prints, drawing, sculpture, metal, multimedia. Juried by 3 art professionals who view 3 slides of work and 1 of booth. Awards/prizes: $2,500 in awards: 1 Best of Show: $1,000; 2 Purchase Awards: $500 each; 5 Awards of Excellence: $100 each. Free to the public; parking: $5. Artists can obtain an application on the Web site, or they can call the show director who will mail them an application. Deadline for entry: March. Application fee: $25. Space fee: starts at $300. Exhibition space: 12×3 ft. "We allow room on either side of the tent, and some space behind the tent." For more information, artists should e-mail, visit Web site, call, send SASE.

Tips "Be attentive to your customers. Do not ignore anyone."

⚑ PANOPLY ARTS FESTIVAL, PRESENTED BY THE ARTS COUNCIL, INC.

700 Monroe St. SW, Suite 2, Huntsville AL 35801. (256)519-2787. Fax: (256)533-3811. E-mail: tac@panoply.org. Web site: www.panoply.org; www.artshuntsville.org. Estab. 1982. Fine arts show held annually the last weekend in April. Also features music and dance. Outdoors. Accepts photography, painting, sculpture, drawing, printmaking, mixed media, glass, fiber. Juried by a panel of judges chosen for their in-depth knowledge and experience in multiple mediums, and who jury from slides or disks in January. During the festival 1 judge awards the various prizes. Awards/prizes: Best of Show: $1,000; Award of Distinction: $500; Merit Awards: 5 awards, $200 each. Number of exhibitors: 60-80. Public attendance: 140,000+. Public admission: weekend pass: $10; 1-day pass: $5; children 12 and under: free. Artists should e-mail, call or write for an application form, or check online through November 1. Deadline for entry: January 2008. Application fee: $30. Space fee: $175 for space only; $375 including tent rental. Exhibition space: 10×10 ft. Average gross sales/exhibitor: $2,500. For more information, artists should e-mail.

⚑ PARADISE CITY ARTS FESTIVALS

30 Industrial Dr. E., Northampton MA 01060-2351. (800)511-9725. Fax: (413)587-0966. E-mail: artist@paradisecityarts.com. Web site: www.paradisecityarts.com. **Contact:** Katherine Sanderson. Estab. 1995. Five fine arts & crafts shows held annually in March, April, May, October and November. Indoors. Accepts photography, all original art and fine craft media. Juried by 5 slides or digital images of work and an independent board of jury

advisors. Number of exhibitors: 150-275. Public attendance: 5,000-20,000. Public admission: $12. Artists should apply by submitting name and address to be added to mailing list or print application from Web site. Deadline for entry: August 25 and April 1. Application fee: $30. Space fee: $650-1,500. Exhibition space: 8' to 10' deep; 10; to 20' wide. For more information, artists should e-mail, visit Web site or call.

PASEO ARTS FESTIVAL

3022 Paseo, Oklahoma City OK 73103. (405)525-2688. Web site: www.ThePaseo.com. **Contact:** Lori Oden, executive director. Estab. 1976. Fine arts & crafts show held annually Memorial Day weekend. Outdoors. Accepts photography and all fine art mediums. Juried by submitting 3 slides or CD. Awards/prizes: $1,000, Best of Show; $350, 2D; $350, 3D; $350, Best New Artist. Number of exhibitors: 75. Public attendance: 50,000-60,000. Free to public. Artists should apply by calling for application form. Deadline for entry: March 1. Application fee: $25. Space fee: $250. Exhibition space: 10×10 ft. For more information, artists should visit Web site, call or send SASE.

PATTERSON APRICOT FIESTA

P.O. Box 442, Patterson CA 95363. (209)892-3118. Fax: (209)892-3388. E-mail: patterson-apricot-fiesta@hotmail.com. Web site: www.patterson-ca.com. **Contact:** Chris Rodriguez, chairperson. Estab. 1984. Arts & crafts show held annually in May/June. Outdoors. Accepts photography, oils, leather, various handcrafts. Juried by type of product; number of artists already accepted; returning artists get priority. Number of exhibitors: 140-150. Public attendance: 25,000. Free to the public. Deadline for entry: approximately April 15. Application fee/space fee: $130. Exhibition space: 12×12 ft. For more information, artists should call, send SASE.

Tips "Please get your applications in early!"

PETERS VALLEY ANNUAL CRAFT FAIR

19 Kuhn Rd., Layton NJ 07851. (973)948-5200. Fax: (973)948-0011. E-mail: info@petersvalley.org. Web site: www.petersvalley.org. **Contact:** Mikal Brutzman, craft fair coordinator. Estab. 1970. Arts & crafts show held annually in late September at the Sussex County Fair Grounds in Augusta, New Jersey. Indoors. Accepts photography, ceramics, fiber, glass, basketry, metal, jewelry, sculpture, printmaking, paper book art, drawing, painting. Juried. Awards/prizes: cash awards. Number of exhibitors: 180. Public attendance: 8,000-10,000. Public admission: $7. Artists should apply by downloading application from Web site. Deadline for entry: May 15. Jury fee: $25. Space fee: $375. Exhibition space: 10×10 ft. Average gross sales/exhibitor: $2,000-5,000. For more information artists should e-mail, visit Web site, call or send SASE.

Tips "Have fun, have an attractive booth design and a diverse price range."

PUNGO STRAWBERRY FESTIVAL

P.O. Box 6158, Virginia Beach VA 23456. (757)721-6001. Fax: (757)721-9335. E-mail: pungofestival@aol.com. Web site: www.PungoStrawberryFestival.info. **Contact:** Janet Dowdy, secretary of board. Estab. 1983. Arts & crafts show held annually on Memorial Day Weekend. Outdoors. Accepts photography and all media. Number of exhibitors: 60. Public attendance: 120,000. Free to Public; $5 parking fee. Artists should apply by calling for application or downloading a copy from the Web site and mail in. Deadline for entry: March 1; applications accepted from that point until all spaces are full. Application fee: $50 refundable deposit. Space fee: $175. Exhibition space: 10 × 10 ft. For more information, artists should e-mail, visit Web site or call.

◪ QUAKER ARTS FESTIVAL

P.O. Box 202, Orchard Park NY 14127. (716)677-2787. **Contact:** Randy Kroll, chairman. Estab. 1961. Fine arts & crafts show held annually in September. Outdoors. Accepts photography, painting, graphics, sculpture, crafts. Juried by 4 panelists during event. Awards/prizes: over $10,000 total cash prizes. Number of exhibitors: 330. Public attendance: 75,000. Free to the public. Artists should apply by sending SASE. Deadline for entry: August. Space fee: $175. Exhibition space: 10 × 12 ft. For more information, artists should call, send SASE. **Tips** "Have an inviting booth and be pleasant and accessible. Don't hide behind your product—engage the audience."

◪ RILEY FESTIVAL

312 E. Main St. #C, Greenfield IN 46140. (317)462-2141. Fax: (317)467-1449. E-mail: info@rileyfestival.com. Web site: www.rileyfestival.com. **Contact:** Sarah Kesterson, office manager. Estab. 1970. Fine arts & crafts show held October 2-5, 2008. Outdoors. Accepts photography, fine arts, home arts, quilts. Juried. Awards/prizes: small monetary awards and ribbons. Number of exhibitors: 450. Public attendance: 75,000. Free to public. Artists should apply by downloading application on Web site. Deadline for entry: September 15. Space fee: $165. Exhibition space: 10 × 10 ft. For more information, artists should visit Web site. **Tips** "Keep arts priced for middle-class viewers."

◪ ◪ RIVERBANK CHEESE & WINE EXPOSITION

3429 Harpers Ferry Dr., Stockton CA 95219. (209)955-1310. Fax: (209)955-1028. E-mail: info@riverbankcheeseandwine.org. Web site: www.riverbankcheeseandwine.org. **Contact:** Suzi DeSilva. Estab. 1977. Arts & crafts show and food show held annually 2nd weekend in October. Outdoors. Accepts photography, other mediums depends on the product. Juried by pictures and information about the artists. Number of exhibitors: 400. Public attendance: 70,000-80,000. Free to public. Artists should apply by calling and requesting an application. Deadline for entry: June 30. Space fee: $260/arts & crafts; $380/commercial. Exhibition space: 10 × 12 ft. For more information, artists should e-mail, visit Web site, call or send SASE.
Tips "Make sure your display is pleasing to the eye."

◪ RIVERFRONT MARKET

P.O. Box 565, Selma AL 36702-0565.(334)874-6683. **Contact:** Ed Greene, chairman. Estab. 1972. Arts & crafts show held annually the 2nd Saturday in October. Outdoors. Accepts photography, painting, sculpture. Number of exhibitors: 200. Public attendance: 8,000. Public admission: $2. Artists should apply by calling or mailing to request application. Deadline for entry: September 1. Space fee: $40; limited covered space available at $60. Exhibition space: 10 × 10 ft. For more information, artists should call.

◪ RIVERSIDE ART FESTIVAL

2623 Herschel St., Jacksonville FL 32204. (904)389-2449. Fax: (904)389-0431. E-mail: info@riversideavondale.org. Web site: www.Riverside-Avondale.com. **Contact:** Bonnie Grissett, executive director. Estab. 1972. Fine arts & crafts show held annually the weekend after Labor Day. Outdoors. Accepts photography and all fine art. Juried. Awards/prizes: $10,000/ cash. Number of exhibitors: 150. Public attendance: 25,000. Free to public. Artists should apply by sending name and address or by e-mailing for an application. Deadline for entry: June 15. Jury fee: $25 (nonrefundable). Space fee: $175. Exhibition space: 10 × 10 ft. For more information, artists should call or e-mail.

⊠ ROYAL OAK OUTDOOR ART FAIR

PO Box 64, Royal Oak MI 48068-0064. (248)246-3180. Fax: (248)246-3007. E-mail: artfaire@ ci.royal-oak.mi.us. Web site: http://www.ci.royal-oak.mi.us/rec/r7.html. **Contact**: Recreation Office Staff. Events & Membership. Estab. 1970. Fine arts & crafts show held annually in July. Outdoors. Accepts photography, collage, jewelry, clay, drawing, painting, glass, wood, metal, leather, soft sculpture. Juried. Number of exhibitors: 110. Public attendance: 25,000. Free to pubic. Artists should apply with application form and 3 slides of current work. Deadline for entry: March 1. Application fee: $20. Space fee: $300. Exhibition space: 15 × 15 ft. For more information, artists should e-mail or call.

Tips ''Be sure to label your slides on the front with name, size of work and 'top'.''

⊠ ⊠ SACO SIDEWALK ART FESTIVAL

P.O. Box 336, 146 Main St., Saco ME 04072. (207)286-3546. E-mail: sacospirit@hotmail.c om. Web site: www.sacospirit.com. **Contact:** Ann-Marie Mariner, downtown director. Estab. 1970. Fine arts/crafts show held annually the last Saturday in June. Outdoors. Accepts photography, sculpture, mixed media, painting, silk screening, graphics. Juried by a committee of judges with an art/media background. Awards/prizes: Best of Show, First Runner-up, Merit Awards, People's Choice Award, Purchase Prizes. Number of exhibitors: 115-125. Public attendance: 5,000. Free to the public. Space fee: $50. Exhibition space: 10 × 10 ft. Artists should e mail, call for more information.

Tips ''Offer a variety of pieces priced at various levels.''

⊠ SANDY SPRINGS FESTIVAL

135 Hilderbrand Dr., Sandy Springs GA 30328-3805. (404)851-9111. Fax: (404)851-9807. E-mail: info@sandyspringsfestival.com. Web site: www.sandyspringsfestival.com. **Contact:** Christy Nickles, special events director. Estab. 1985. Fine arts & crafts show held annually in mid-September. Outdoors. Accepts photography, painting, sculpture, jewelry, furniture, clothing. Juried by area professionals and nonprofessionals who are passionate about art. Awards/prizes: change annually; usually cash with additional prizes. Number of exhibitors: 100 +. Public attendance: 20,000. Public admission: $5. Artists should apply via application on Web site. Application fee: $10 ($35 for late registration). Space fee: $150. Exhibition space: 10 × 10 ft. Average gross sales/exhibitor: $1,000. For more information, artists should visit Web site.

Tips ''Most of the purchases made at Sandy Springs Festival are priced under $100. The look of the booth and its general attractiveness are very important, especially to those who might not 'know' art.''

⊠ SANTA CALI GON DAYS FESTIVAL

P.O. Box 1077, Independence MO 64051. (816)252-4745. Fax: (816)252-4917. E-mail: tfreela nd@independencechamber.org. Web site: www.santacaligon.com. **Contact:** Teresa Freeland, special projects assistant. Estab. 1973. Market vendors show held annually Labor Day weekend. Outdoors. Accepts photography, all other mediums. Juried by committee. Number of exhibitors: 240. Public attendance: 225,000. Free to public. Artists should apply by requesting application. Application requirements include completed application, application fee, 4 photos of product/art and 1 photo of display. Deadline for entry: March 6-April 7. Application fee: $20. Space fee: $330-430. Exhibition space: 8×8 ft.-10×10 ft. For more information, artists should e-mail, visit Web site or call.

⚑ SAUSALITO ART FESTIVAL

P.O. Box 10, Sausalito CA 94966. (415)332-3555. Fax: (415)331-1340. E-mail: info@sausalit oartfestival.org. Web site: www.sausalitoartfestival.org. **Contact:** Tracy Bell Redig, festival coordinator. Estab. 1952. Fine arts & crafts show held annually Labor Day weekend. Outdoors. Accepts painting, photography, 2D and 3D mixed media, ceramics, drawing, fiber, functional art, glass, jewelry, printmaking, sculpture, watercolor, woodwork. Juried. Jurors are elected by their peers from the previous year's show (1 from each category). They meet for a weekend at the end of March and give scores of 1, 2, 3, 4 or 5 to each applicant (5 being the highest). Awards/prizes: $500 for each 1st and 2nd Place in each category; optional $1,000 for Best in Show. Number of exhibitors: 270. Public attendance: 40,000. Public admission: $20; seniors (age 62+): $10; children (under 6): $5. Artists should apply by visiting Web site for instructions and application (http://www.sausalitoartfestival.org/artis ts.html). Applications are through Juried Art Services. Deadline for entry: March. Application fee: $50. Space fee: $1050-2,800. Exhibition space: 100 or 200 sq. ft. Average gross sales/exhibitor: $14,000. For more information, artists should visit Web site.

Ⓝ ⚑ SCOTTSDALE ARTS FESTIVAL

7380 E. 2nd St., Scottsdale AZ 85251. (480)874-4686. Fax: (480)874-4699. E-mail: festival@ sccarts.org. Web site: www.scottsdaleartsfestival.org. **Contact:** Debbie Rauch, artist coordinator. Estab. 1970. Fine arts & crafts show held annually in March. Outdoors. Accepts photography, jewelry, ceramics, sculpture, metal, glass, drawings, fiber, paintings, printmaking, mixed media, wood. Juried. Awards/prizes: 1st, 2nd, 3rd Places in each category and Best of Show. Number of exhibitors: 200. Public attendance: 40,000. Public admission: $7. Artists should apply through www.zapplication.org. Deadline for entry: October. Application fee: $25. Space fee: $415. Exhibition space: 100 sq. ft. For more information, artists should visit Web site.

Ⓝ SIDEWALK ART SHOW

One Market Square, Roanoke VA 24011-143. (540)342-5760. E-mail: info@artmuseumroan oke.org. Web site: www.artmuseumroanoke.org. **Contact:** Mickie Kagey, registration chair. Estab. 1958. Fine arts show held annually in early June. Outdoors. Accepts photography, watercolor, oils, acrylic, sculpture, prints. Awards/prizes: $6,500 total cash awards. Number of exhibitors: 175-200. Public attendance: 10,000. Free to public. Deadline for entry: April 15th. Application fee: $25. Space fee: $90-175. Exhibition space: 10×10 ft./tent; 8 ft./fence. For more information, artists should e-mail or visit Web site.

⚑ SIERRA MADRE WISTARIA FESTIVAL

37 Auburn Ave., Suite 1, Sierra Madre CA 91024.(626)355-5111. Fax: (626)306-1150. E-mail: info@sierramadrechamber.com. Web site: www.SierraMadrechamber.com. Estab.

100 years ago. Fine arts, crafts and garden show held annually in March. Outdoors. Accepts photography, anything handcrafted. Juried. Craft vendors send in application and photos to be juried. Most appropriate are selected. Awards/prizes: Number of exhibitors: 175. Public attendance: 12,000. Free to public. Artists should apply by sending completed and signed application, 3-5 photographs of their work, application fee, license application, space fee and 2 SASEs. Deadline for entry: December 20. Application fee: $25. Space fee: $175 and a city license fee of $29. Exhibition space: 10×10 ft. For more information, artists should e-mail, visit Web site or call.

Tips "Have a clear and simple application. Be nice."

SOLANO AVENUE STROLL

1563 Solano Ave. #PMB 101, Berkeley CA 94707. (510)527-5358. E-mail: saa@solanoave.org. Web site: www.solanoave.org. **Contact:** Allen Cain, executive director. Estab. 1974. Fine arts & crafts show held annually 2nd Sunday in September. Outdoors. Accepts photography and all other mediums. Juried by board of directors. Jury fee: $10. Number of exhibitors: 140 spaces for crafts; 600 spaces total. Public attendance: 300,000. Free to the public. Artists should apply online after April 1, or send SASE. Deadline for entry: June 1. Space fee: $10. Exhibition space: 10×10 ft. For more information, artists should e-mail, visit Web site, send SASE.

Tips "Artists should have a clean presentation; small-ticket items as well as large-ticket items; great customer service; enjoy themselves."

SPRING CRAFTS AT LYNDHURST

P.O. Box 28, Woodstock NY 12498. (845)331-7900. Fax: (845)331-7484. E-mail: crafts@artrider.com. Web site: www.craftsatlyndhurst.com; www.artrider.com. **Contact:** Laura Kandel. Estab. 1984. Fine arts & crafts show held annually in early May. Outdoors. Accepts photography, wearable and nonwearable fiber, metal and nonmetal jewelry, clay, leather, wood, glass, painting, drawing, prints, mixed media. Juried by 5 images of work and 1 of booth, viewed sequentially. Number of exhibitors: 300. Public attendance: 14,000. Public admission: $10. Artists should apply by downloading application from www.artrider.com or can apply online at www.zapplication.org. Deadline for entry: January 14. Application fee: $35. Space fee: $750. Exhibition space: 10×10. For more information, artists should e-mail, visit Web site, call.

SPRING CRAFTS AT MORRISTOWN

P.O. Box 28, Woodstock NY 12498. (845)331-7900. Fax: (845)331-7484. E-mail: crafts@artrider.com. Web site: www.craftsatmorristown.com; www.artrider.com. **Contact:** Laura Kandel. Estab. 1990. Fine arts & crafts show held annually end of March. Indoors. Accepts photography, wearable and nonwearable fiber, metal and nonmetal jewelry, clay, leather, wood, glass, painting, drawing, prints, mixed media. Juried by 5 images of work and 1 of booth, viewed sequentially. Number of exhibitors: 165. Public attendance: 5,000. Public admission: $7. Artists should apply by downloading application from www.artrider.com or apply online at www.zapplication.org. Deadline for entry: January 14. Application fee: $35. Space fee: $475. Exhibition space: 10×10 ft. For more information, artists should e-mail, visit Web site, call.

⚐ SPRING FINE ART & CRAFTS AT BROOKDALE PARK

Watchung Ave., Montclair NJ. (908)874-5247. Fax: (908)874-7098. E-mail: rosesquared@p atmedia.net. Web site: www.rosesquared.com. **Contact:** Janet Rose, president. **Contact:** Estab.1988. Fine arts & craft show held annually in mid-June. Outdoors. Accepts photography and all other mediums. Juried. Number of exhibitors: 180. Public attendance: 16,000. Free to the public. Artists should apply by downloading application from Web site or call for application. Deadline: 1 month before show date. Application fee: $15. Space fee: $310. Exhibition space: 120 sq. ft. For more information, artists should e-mail, visit Web site, call.

Tips "Create a professional booth that is comfortable for the customer to enter. Be informative, friendly and outgoing. People come to meet the artist."

SPRINGFEST

P.O. Box 831, Southern Pines NC 28388. (910)315-6508. E-mail: spba@earthlink.net. Web site: www.southernpines.biz. **Contact:** Susan Harrison, booth coordinator. Estab. 1979. Arts & crafts show held annually last Saturday in April. Outdoors. Accepts photography and crafts. Number of exhibitors: 200. Public attendance: 8,000. Free to the public. Artists should apply by filling out application form. Deadline for entry: March 15, 2009. Space fee: $60. Exhibition space: 10×12 ft. For more information, artists should e-mail, visit Web site, call, send SASE. Application online in fall 2008.

SPRINGFEST AND SEPTEMBERFEST

PO Box 677, Nyack NY 10960-0677. (845)353-2221. Fax: (845)353-4204. Web site: www.ny ack-ny.com. **Contact:** Lorie Reynolds, executive director. Estab. 1980. Arts & crafts show held annually in April and September. Outdoors. Accepts photography, pottery, jewelry, leather, clothing. Number of exhibitors: 220. Public attendance: 30,000. Free to public. Artists should apply by submitting application, fees, permits, photos of product and display. Deadline for entry: 15 days before show. Space fee: $175. Exhibition space: 10×10 ft. For more information, artists should visit Web site, call or send SASE.

⚐ ST. CHARLES FINE ART SHOW

213 Walnut St., St. Charles IL 60174. (630)513-5386. Fax: (630)513-6310. E-mail: bethany@ dtown.org. Web site: www.stcharlesfineartshow.com. **Contact:** Bethany McFarland, marketing coordinator. Estab. 1999. Fine art fair held annually in late May. Outdoors. Accepts photography, painting, sculpture, glass, ceramics, jewelry, nonwearable fiber art. Juried by committee: submit 4 slides of art and 1 slide of booth/display. Awards/prizes: Cash awards of $2,500+ awarded in several categories. Purchase Award Program: $14,000 of art has been purchased through this program since its inception in 2005. Number of exhibitors: 100. Free to the public. Artists should apply by downloading application from Web site or call for application. Deadline for entry: February. Jury fee: $25. Space fee: $200. Exhibition space: 12×12 ft. For more information, artists should e-mail, visit Web site, call.

⚐ ST. GEORGE ART FESTIVAL

86 S. Main St., St. George UT 84770. (435)634-5850. Fax: (435)634-0709. E-mail: leisure@sg city.org. Web site: www.sgcity.org. **Contact:** Carlene Garrick, administrator assistant. Estab. 1979. Fine arts & crafts show held annually Easter weekend in either March or April.

Outdoors. Accepts photography, painting, wood, jewelry, ceramics, sculpture, drawing, 3D mixed media, glass. Juried from slides. Awards/prizes: $5,000 Purchase Awards. Art pieces selected will be placed in the city's permanent collections. Number of exhibitors: 110. Public attendance: 20,000/day. Free to public. Artists should apply by completing application form, nonrefundable application fee, slides or digital format of 4 current works in each category and 1 of booth, and SASE. Deadline for entry: January 6. Application fee $20. Space fee: $125. Exhibition space: 10×11 ft. For more information, artists should e-mail.

Tips "Artists should have more than 50% originals. Have quality booths and set-up to display art in best possible manner. Be outgoing and friendly with buyers."

ST. JAMES COURT ART SHOW

P.O. Box 3804, Louisville KY 40201. (502)635-1842. Fax: (502)635-1296. E-mail: mesrock@ stjamescourtartshow.com. Web site: www.stjamescourtartshow.com. **Contact:** Marguerite Esrock, executive director. Estab. 1957. Annual fine arts & crafts show held the first full weekend in October. Accepts photography; has 16 medium categories. Juried in March; there is also a street jury held during the art show. Awards/prizes: Best of Show—3 places; $7,500 total prize money. Number of exhibitors: 340. Public attendance: 275,000. Free to the public. Artists should apply by visiting Web site and printing out an application or via www.zapplication.org. Deadline for entry in 2009 show: March 1, 2009. Application fee: $30. Space fee: $500. Exhibition space: 10×12 ft. For more information, artists should e-mail or visit Web site.

Tips "Have a variety of price points. Don't sit in the back of the booth and expect sales."

STEPPIN' OUT

P.O. Box 233, Blacksburg VA 24063. (540)951-0454. E-mail: dmob@downtownblacksburg. com. Web site: www.downtownblacksburg.com. **Contact:** Laureen Blakemore, director. Estab. 1981. Arts & crafts show held annually 1st Friday and Saturday in August. Outdoors. Accepts photography, pottery, painting, drawing, fiber arts, jewelry, general crafts. Number of exhibitors: 170. Public attendance: 45,000. Free to public. Artists should apply by e-mailing, calling or by downloading application on Web site. Space fee: $150. For more information, artists should e-mail, visit Web site or call.

Tips "Visit shows and consider the booth aesthetic—what appeals to you. Put the time, thought, energy and money into your booth to draw people in to see your work."

STOCKLEY GARDENS FALL ARTS FESTIVAL

801 Boush St., Norfolk VA 23510.(757)625-6161. Fax: (757)625-7775. E-mail: jlong@hope-house.org. Web site: www.hope-house.org. **Contact:** Jenny Long, development coordinator. Estab. 1984. Fine arts & crafts show held annually 3rd weekend in October. Outdoors. Accepts photography and all major fine art mediums. Juried. Number of exhibitors: 150. Public attendance: 30,000. Free to the public. Artists should apply by submitting application, jury and booth fees, 5 slides. Deadline for entry: July. Application fee: $15. Space fee: $225. Exhibition space: 10×10 ft. For more information, artists should e-mail, visit Web site, call.

STONE ARCH FESTIVAL OF THE ARTS

219 Main St. SE, Suite 304, Minneapolis MN 55414. (612)378-1226. E-mail: mplsriverfront@ msn.com. Web site: www.stonearchfestival.com. **Contact:** Sara Collins, manager. Estab.

1994. Fine arts & crafts show and culinary arts show held annually Father's Day weekend. Outdoors. Accepts photography, painting, ceramics, jewelry, fiber, printmaking, wood, metal. Juried by committee. Awards/prizes: free booth the following year; $100 cash prize. Number of exhibitors: 230. Public attendance: 80,000. Free to public. Artists should apply by application found on Web site or through www.zapplication.org. Deadline for entry: March 15. Application fee: $20 jury. Space fee: $250-300. Exhibition space: 10 × 10 ft. For more information, artists should e-mail, visit Web site, call or send SASE.
Tips ''Have an attractive display and variety of prices.''

STRAWBERRY FESTIVAL

2815 2nd Ave. N., Billings MT 59101. (406)259-5454. Fax: (406)294-5061. E-mail: lisaw@downtownbillings.com. Web site: www.strawberryfun.com. **Contact:** Lisa Woods, executive director. Estab. 1991. Fine arts & crafts show held annually 2nd Saturday in June. Outdoors. Accepts photography. Juried. Number of exhibitors: 76. Public attendance: 15,000. Free to public. Artists should apply by application available on the Web site. Deadline for entry: April 14. Exhibition space: 12 × 12 ft. For more information, artists should visit Web site.

STREET FAIRE AT THE LAKES

PO Box 348, Detroit Lakes MN 56502. (800)542-3992. Fax: (218)847-9082. E-mail: dlchamber@visitdetroitlakes.com. Web site: www.visitdetroitlakes.com. **Contact:** Sue Braun, artist coordinator. Estab. 2001. Fine arts & crafts show held annually 1st weekend after Memorial Day. Outdoors. Accepts photography, handmade/original artwork, wood, metal, glass, painting, fiber. Juried by anonymous scoring. Submit 5 slides, 4 of work and 1 of booth display. Top scores are accepted. Number of exhibitors: 125. Public attendance: 15,000. Free to public. Artists should apply by downloading application from Web site. Deadline for entry: January 15. Application fee: $150-175. Exhibition space: 11 × 11 ft. For more information, artists should e-mail or call.

SUMMER ARTS & CRAFTS FESTIVAL

Castleberry Fairs & Festivals, 38 Charles St., Rochester NH 03867. (603)332-2616. E-mail: info@castleberryfairs.com. Web site: www.castleberryfairs.com. **Contact:** Terry Mullen, events coordinator. Estab. 1992. Arts & crafts show held annually 2nd weekend in August in Lincoln, New Hampshire. Outdoors. Accepts photography and all other mediums. Juried by photo, slide or sample. Number of exhibitors: 100. Public attendance: 7,500. Free to the public. Artists should apply by downloading application from Web site. Deadline for entry: until full. Space fee: $200. Exhibition space: 100 sq. ft. For more information, artists should visit Web site.
Tips ''Do not bring a book; do not bring a chair. Smile and make eye contact with everyone who enters your booth. Have them sign your guest book; get their e-mail address so you can let them know when you are in the area again. And, finally, make the sale—they are at the fair to shop, after all.''

SUMMER ARTS AND CRAFTS FESTIVAL

UW-Parkside, 900 Wood Rd., Box 2000, Kenosha WI 53141. (262)595-2457. E-mail: eichner @uwp.edu. **Contact:** Mark Eichner, coordinator. Estab. 1990. Arts & crafts show held annually 3rd week in June. Outdoors. Accepts photography, painting, glass, sculpture, woodwork, metal, jewelry, leather, quilts. Number of exhibitors: 200. Public attendance: 4,000.

Free to the public. Artists should apply by calling or e-mailing for an application form. Deadline for entry: May. Space fee: $100. Exhibition space: 10×10 ft. For more information, artists should e-mail, call.

Tips "Items priced less than $100 are excellent sellers."

◘ SUMMERFAIR

7850 Five Mile Road, Cincinnati OH 45230. (513)531-0050. Fax:(513)531-0377. E-mail: exhibitors@summerfair.org. Web site: www.summerfair.org. **Contact:** Sharon Strubbe. Estab. 1968. Fine arts & crafts show held annually the weekend after Memorial Day. Outdoors. Accepts photography, ceramics, drawing/printmaking, fiber/leather, glass, jewelry, painting, sculpture/metal, wood. Juried by a panel of judges selected by Summerfair, including artists and art educators with expertise in the categories offered at Summerfair. Submit 5 slides of artwork, including artist's name, dimensions of work, and arrow indicating top of work. "Do not submit a booth slide." Awards/prizes: $10,000 in cash awards. Number of exhibitors: 300. Public attendance: 25,000. Public admission: $10. Artists should apply by downloading application from Web site (available in December) or by e-mailing for an application. Deadline: February. Application fee: $30. Space fee: $375, single single; $750, double space; $75 canopy fee (optional—exhibitors can rent a canopy for all days of the fair.). Exhibition space: 10×10 ft. for single space; 10×20 for double space. For more information, artists should e-mail, visit Web site, call.

🅽 ◘ THREEFOOT ART FESTIVAL & CHILI COOKOFF

P.O. Box 1405, Meridian MS 39302. (601)693-ARTS. E-mail: debbie0708@comcast.net. Web site: www.meridianarts.org. **Contact:** Debbie Martin, president. Estab. 2002. Fine arts & crafst show held annually the 2nd Saturday in October. Outdoors. Accepts photography and all mediums. Juried by a panel of prominent members of the arts community on day of show. Awards/prizes: $1,000, Best in Show; $500, 2 Awards of Distinction; up to 10 Merit Awards. Number of exhibitors: 50-75. Public attendance: 5,000. Free to public. Artists should apply by downloading application from Web site or request to be added to mailing list. Deadline for entry: August 1, 2008. Application fee: $10. Space fee: $85. Exhibition space: 10×10 ft. Average gross sales/exhibitors: $1,000. For more information, artists should visit Web site or send SASE.

Tips "Price points are relative to the market. Booth should be attractive."

◘ TUBAC FESTIVAL OF THE ARTS

P.O. Box 1866, Tubac AZ 85646. (520)398-2704. Fax: (520)398-1704. E-mail: artfestival@tu bacaz.com. Web site: www.tubacaz.com. Estab. 1959. Fine arts & crafts show held annually in early February. Outdoors. Accepts photography and considers all fine arts and crafts. Juried. A 7-member panel reviews digital images and artist statement. Jury process is blind—applicants' names are withheld from the jurists. Number of exhibitors: 170. Public attendance: 80,000. Free to the public; parking: $6. Applications for the 2009 festival will be available and posted on Web site mid-summer 2008. Deadline for entry: October 31. Application fee: $25. Space fee: $575 for 10×10 ft. space. For more information, artists should e-mail, visit Web site, call, send SASE.

◘ TULIP FESTIVAL STREET FAIR

P.O. Box 1801, Mt. Vernon WA 98273. (360)226-9277. E-mail: dwntwnmv@cnw.com. Web site: www.downtownmountvernon.com. **Contact:** Executive Director. Estab. 1984. Arts &

crafts show held annually 3rd weekend in April. Outdoors. Accepts photography and original artists' work only. No manufactured work. Juried by a board. Jury fee: $10 with application and prospectus. Number of exhibitors: 215-220. Public attendance: 20,000-25,000. Free to public. Artists should apply by calling or e-mailing. Deadline for entry: January 30. Application fee: $10. Flat fee: $300. Exhibition space: 10×10 ft. Average gross sales/exhibitor: $2,500-4,000. For more information, artists should e-mail, visit Web site, call or send SASE.

Tips "Keep records of your street fair attendance and sales for your résumé. Network with other artists about which street fairs are better to return to or apply for."

◪ TULSA INTERNATIONAL MAYFEST

321 S. Boston #101, Tulsa OK 74103. (918)582-6435. Fax: (918)587-7721. E-mail: comments @tulsamayfest.org. Web site: www.tulsamayfest.org. Estab. 1972. Fine arts & crafts show annually held in May. Outdoors. Accepts photography, clay, leather/fiber, mixed media, drawing, pastels, graphics, printmaking, jewelry, glass, metal, wood, painting. Juried by a blind jurying process. Artists should apply online at www.zapplication.org and submit 4 photos of work and 1 of booth set-up. Awards/prizes: Best in Category and Best in Show. Number of exhibitors: 120. Public attendance: 350,000. Free to public. Artists should apply by downloading application in late November. Deadline for entry: January 16. Application fee: $35. Space fee: $300. Exhibition space: 10×10 ft. For more information, artists should e-mail or visit Web site.

◪ UPTOWN ART FAIR

1406 West Lake St., Suite 202, Minneapolis MN 55408. (612)823-4581. Fax: (612)823-3158. E-mail: info@uptownminneapolis.com. Web site: www.uptownminneapolis.com. **Contact:** Cindy Fitzpatrick. Estab. 1963. Fine arts & crafts show held annually 1st full weekend in August. Outdoors. Accepts photography, painting, printmaking, drawing, 2D and 3D mixed media, ceramics, fiber, sculpture, jewelry, wood. Juried by 4 images of artwork and 1 of booth display. Awards/prizes: Best in Show in each category; Best Artist. Number of exhibitors: 350. Public attendance: 350,000. Free to the public. Artists should apply by visiting www.zapplication.com. Deadline for entry: March. Application fee: $30. Space fee: $450 for 10×10 space; $900 for 10×20 space. For more information, artists should call or visit Web site.

◪ A VICTORIAN CHAUTAUQUA

1101 E Market St., P.O. Box 606, Jeffersonville IN 47131-0606. (812)283-3728. Fax: (812)283-6049. E-mail: hsmsteam@aol.com. Web site: www.steamboatmuseum.org. **Contact:** Yvonne Knight, administrator. Estab. 1993. Fine arts & crafts show held annually 3rd weekend in May. Outdoors. Accepts photography, all mediums. Juried by a committee of 5. Awards/prizes: $100, 1st Place; $75, 2nd Place; $50, 3rd Place. Number of exhibitors: 80. Public attendance: 3,000. Public admission: $3. Deadline for entry: March 31. Space fee: $40-60. Exhibition space: 12×12 ft. For more information, artists should e-mail or call.

◪ VIRGINIA CHRISTMAS SHOW

P.O. Box 305, Chase City VA 23924. (434)372-3996. Fax: (434)372-3410. E-mail: vashowsinc @aol.com. **Contact:** Patricia Wagstaff, coordinator. Estab. 1986. Holiday arts & crafts show held annually 1st week in November in Richmond, Virginia. Indoors at the showplace.

Accepts photography and other arts and crafts. Juried by 3 slides of artwork and 1 of display. Awards/prizes: Best Display. Number of exhibitors: 350. Public attendance: 25,000. Public admission: $7. Artists should apply by writing or e-mailing for an application. Space fee: $400. Exhibition space: 10×10 ft. For more information, artists should e-mail, send SASE.

Tips "If possible, attend the show before you apply. 21st Virginia Spring show March 13-15, 2009 is held at the same facility. Fee is $300. Requirements same as above."

WASHINGTON SQUARE OUTDOOR ART EXHIBIT
115 East 9th St., #7C, New York NY 10003. (212)982-6255. Fax: (212)982-6256. Web site: www.washingtonsquareoutdoorartexhibit.org. **Contact:** Margot J. Lufitg, executive director. Estab. 1931. Fine arts & crafts show held semiannually Memorial Day weekend and the following weekend in May/early June and Labor Day weekend and following weekend in September. Outdoors. Accepts photography, oil, watercolor, graphics, mixed media, sculpture, crafts. Juried by submitting 5 slides of work and 1 of booth. Awards/prizes: certificates, ribbons and cash prizes. Number of exhibitors: 200. Public attendance: 200,000. Free to public. Artists should apply by sending a SASE or downloading application from Web site. Deadline for entry: March, Spring Show; July, Fall Show. Application fee: $20. Exhibition space: 10×5 ft. For more information, artists should call or send SASE.

Tips "Price work sensibly."

WELCOME TO MY WORLD PHOTOGRAPHY COMPETITION
319 Mallery St., St. Simons Island GA 31522.(912)638-8770. E-mail: glynnart@bellsouth.net. Web site: www.glynnart.org. **Contact:** Ann Marie Dalis, executive director. Estab. 1991. Seasonal photography competition annually held in July. Indoors. Accepts only photography. Juried. Awards/prizes: 1st, 2nd, 3rd in each category. Number of exhibitors: 50. Artists should apply by visiting Web site. Deadline for entry: June. Application fee: $35. For more information, artists should e-mail, visit Web site or call.

WESTMORELAND ART NATIONALS
252 Twin Lakes Rd., Latrobe PA 15650-3554. (724)834-7474. E-mail: info@artsandheritage.com. Web site: www.artsandheritage.com. **Contact:** Donnie Gutherie, executive director. Estab. 1975. Fine arts & crafts show held annually in July. Photography displays are indoors. Accepts photography, all mediums. Juried: 2 jurors review slides. Awards/prizes: $5,000+ in prizes. Number of exhibitors: 200. Public attendance: 100,000. Free to public. Artists should apply by downloading application from Web site. Application fee: $35/craft show vendors; $25/fine art/photography exhibitors. Space fee: $325. Vendor/exhibition space: 10×10 ft. For more information, artists should visit Web site.

WHITE OAK CRAFTS FAIR
The Arts Center, 1424 John Bragg, Woodbury TN. (625)563-2787. Fax: (615)563-2788. E-mail: carol@artcenterofcc.com. Web site: www.artscenterofcc.com. **Contact:** Carol Reed, publicity. Estab. 1985. Arts & crafts show held annually in September. Outdoors. Accepts photography; all handmade crafts, traditional and contemporary. Must be handcrafted displaying "excellence in concept and technique." Juried by committee. Send 3 slides or photos. Awards/prizes: more than $1,000. Number of exhibitors: 80. Public attendance:

6,000. Free to public, $2 parking fee. Applications can be downloaded from Web site. Deadline for entry: June 1. Space fee: $60. Exhibition space: 15 ft. For more information, artists should e-mail mary@artscenterofcc.com.

☙ WHITEFISH ARTS FESTIVAL

P.O. Box 131, Whitefish MT 59937. (406)862-5875. Fax: (406)862-3515. Web site: www.whi tefishartsfestival.org. **Contact:** Rachael Knox, coordinator. Estab. 1979. Fine arts & crafts show held annually 1st full weekend in July. Outdoors. Accepts photography, pottery, jewelry, sculpture, paintings, woodworking. Juried. Art must be original and handcrafted. Work is evaluated for creativity, quality and originality. Awards/prizes: Best of Show awarded half-price booth fee for following year with no application fee. Number of exhibitors: 100. Public attendance: 3,000. Free to public. Deadline for entry: April 14. Application fee: $20. Space fee: $195. Exhibition space: 10 × 10 ft. For more information, artists should e-mail, visit Web site or call.

Tips Recommends ''variety of price range, professional display, early application for special requests.''

☙ WILD WIND FOLK ART & CRAFT FESTIVAL

719 Long Lake, New York NY 12847. (814)723-0707 or (518)624-6404. E-mail: wildwindcraf tshow@yahoo.com. Web site: www.wildwindfestival.com. **Contact:** Liz Allen or Carol Jilk, promoters. Estab. 1979. Fine arts & traditional crafts show held annually the weekend after Labor Day at the Warren County Fairgrounds in Pittsfield, Pennsylvania. Barn locations and outdoors. Accepts photography, paintings, pottery, jewelry, traditional crafts, prints, stained glass. Juried by promoters. Three photos or slides of work plus one of booth, if available. Number of exhibitors: 140. Public attendance: 8,000. Public admission: $6/adult; $4/seniors; 12 & under free. Artists should apply by visiting Web site and filling out application request, calling or sending a written request.

☙ WILMETTE FESTIVAL OF FINE ARTS

P.O. Box 902, Wilmette IL 60091-0902. Phone/fax: (847)256-2080. E-mail: wilmetteartsguil d@aol.com. Web site: www.wilmetteartsguild.org. **Contact:** Julie Ressler, president. Estab. 1992. Fine arts & crafts show held annually in September. Outdoors. Accepts photography, paintings, prints, jewelry, sculpture, ceramics, and any other appropriate media; no wearable. Juried by a committee of 6-8 artists and art teachers. Awards/prizes: 1st Place: $1,000; 2nd Place: $750; 3rd Place: $500; People's Choice: $50; local merchants offer purchase awards. Number of exhibitors: 100. Public attendance: 4,000. Free to the public. Deadline for entry: April. Application fee: $120. Space fee: $195. Exhibition space: 12 × 12 ft. For more information, artists should e-mail, visit Web site, call, send SASE.

Tips ''Maintain a well-planned, professional appearance in booth and person. Greet viewers when they visit the booth. Offer printed bio with photos of your work. Invite family, friends and acquaintances.''

☙ WINNEBAGOLAND ART FAIR

South Park Avenue/South Park, Oshkosh WI 54902. (920)303-1503. E-mail: shelling1230@ charter.net. Estab. 1957. Fine arts show held annually. Outdoors. Accepts photography, watercolor, oils & acrylics, 3D large, 3D small, drawing, pastels. Juried. Applicants send in slides to be reviewed. Awards/prizes: monetary awards, Purchase, Merit and Best of Show awards. Number of exhibitors: 125-160. Public attendance: 5,000-7,000. Free to public. Deadline for entry: April 30. Application fee: $60, but may increase next year. Exhibition space: 20×20 ft. For more information, artists should e-mail or call.

Tips "Have a nice-looking exhibit booth."

WYANDOTTE STREET ART FAIR

3131 Biddle Ave., Wyandotte MI 48192. (734)324-4505. Fax: (734)324-4505. E-mail: info@ wyan.org. Web site: www.wyandottestreetartfair.net. **Contact:** Lisa Hooper, executive director, Wyandotte Downtown Development Authority. Estab. 1961. Fine arts & crafts show held annually 2nd week in July. Outdoors. Accepts photography, 2D mixed media, 3D mixed media, painting, pottery, basketry, sculpture, fiber, leather, digital cartoons, clothing, stitchery, metal, glass, wood, toys, prints, drawing. Juried. Awards/prizes: Best New Artist: $500; Best Booth Design Award: $500; Best of Show: $1,200. Number of exhibitors: 300. Public attendance: 200,000. Free to the public. Artists may apply online or request application. Deadline for entry: February. Application fee: $20 jury fee. Space fee: $225/single space; $450/double space. Exhibition space: 10×10 ft. Average gross sales/exhibitor: $2,000-$4,000. For more information, artists should e-mail, visit Web site, call, send SASE.

Contests

Whether you're a seasoned veteran or a newcomer still cutting your teeth, you should consider entering contests to see how your work compares to that of other photographers. The contests in this section range in scope from tiny juried county fairs to massive international competitions. When possible, we've included entry fees and other pertinent information in our limited space. Contact sponsors for entry forms and more details.

Once you receive rules and entry forms, pay particular attention to the sections describing rights. Some sponsors retain all rights to winning entries or even *submitted* images. Be wary of these. While you can benefit from the publicity and awards connected with winning prestigious competitions, you shouldn't unknowingly forfeit copyright. Granting limited rights for publicity is reasonable, but you should never assign rights of any kind without adequate financial compensation or a written agreement. If such terms are not stated in contest rules, ask sponsors for clarification.

If you're satisfied with the contest's copyright rules, check with contest officials to see what types of images won in previous years. By scrutinizing former winners, you might notice a trend in judging that could help when choosing your entries. If you can't view the images, ask what styles and subject matters have been popular.

AFI FEST

2021 N. Western Ave., Los Angeles CA 90027-1657. (323)856-7600 or (866)AFI-FEST. Fax: (323)467-4578. E-mail: AFIfest@AFI.com. Web site: www.afifest.com. **Contact:** Director, festivals. Cost: $40 shorts; $50 features. "LA's most prominent annual film festival." Various cash and product prizes are awarded. Open to filmmakers of all skill levels. **Annual July deadline.** Photographers should write, call or e-mail for more information.

ALEXIA COMPETITION

Syracuse University Newhouse School, Syracuse NY 13244-2100. (315)443-2304. E-mail: dcsuther@syr.edu. Web site: www.alexiafoundation.org. **Contact:** David Sutherland. Annual contest. Provides financial ability for students to study photojournalism in England, and for professionals to produce a photo project promoting world peace and cultural understanding. Students win cash grants plus scholarships to study photojournalism at Syracuse University in London. A professional wins $15,000 cash grant. **February 1 student deadline. January 16 professional deadline**. Photographers should e-mail or see Web site for more information.

ANNUAL COLLEGE PHOTOGRAPHY CONTEST

Serbin Communications, 813 Reddick St., Santa Barbara CA 93103. (805)963-0439 or (800)876-6425. Fax: (805)965-0496. E-mail: admin@serbin.com. Web site: www.serbin.com. Annual student contest. Sponsored by *Photographer's Forum Magazine* (see separate listing in the Consumer Publications section) and Nikon. Winners and finalists have their photos published in *The Best of College Photography Annual*. See Web site for entry form.

ANNUAL EXHIBITION OF PHOTOGRAPHY

San Diego County Fair Entry Office, 2260 Jimmy Durante Blvd., Del Mar CA 92014. (858)792-4207. E-mail: entry@sdfair.com. Web site: www.sdfair.com/entry. Sponsor: San Diego County Fair (22nd District Agricultural Association). Annual event for still photos/prints. **Pre-registration deadline:** April/May. Access the dates and specifications for entry on Web site. There are 3 divisions: Photography, Digital Arts, and Photojournalism. Entry form can be submitted online.

ANNUAL INTERNATIONAL PHOTOGRAPHY COMPETITION

Fraser Gallery, 7700 Wisconsin Ave., Suite E, Bethesda MD 20814. (301)718-9651. Fax: (301)718-9652. E-mail: info@thefrasergallery.com. Web site: www.thefrasergallery.com. **Contact:** Catriona Fraser, director. Cost: $25. Annual contest. Provides an exhibition opportunity in the greater Washington, D.C., area in a highly respected independent commercial fine arts gallery. Nearly $1,000 in cash awards and inclusion in group shows for all award winners. **December deadline.** Photographers should send SASE for more information or print the prospectus and entry form from the Web site, www.thefrasergallery.com/photocomp.html.

ANNUAL JURIED PHOTOGRAPHY EXHIBITION

Perkins Center for the Arts, 395 Kings Hwy., Moorestown NJ 08057. (856)235-6488 or (800)387-5226. Fax: (856)235-6624. E-mail: create@perkinscenter.org. Web site: www.per

kinscenter.org. Cost: $8/entry; up to 3 entries. Regional juried photography exhibition. Works from the exhibition are considered for inclusion in the permanent collection of the Philadelphia Museum of Art, the Woodmere Art Museum, and the Johnson & Johnson Corporate Art Collection. Past jurors include Merry Foresta, former curator of photography at the Smithsonian American Art Museum; Katherine Ware, curator of photographs at the Philadelphia Museum of Art; and photographers Emmett Gowin, Ruth Thorne-Thomsen, Matthew Pillsbury, and Vik Muniz. All work must be framed with wiring in back and hand-delivered to Perkins Center. Photographers should call, e-mail or see Web site for prospectus in November.

ANNUAL SPRING PHOTOGRAPHY CONTEST

Serbin Communications, 813 Reddick St., Santa Barbara CA 93103 . (805)963-0439 or (800)876-6425. Fax: (805)965-0496. E-mail: admin@serbin.com. Web site: www.serbin.com. Annual amateur contest. Sponsored by *Photographer's Forum Magazine* (see separate listing in the Consumer Publications section) and Canon. Winners and finalists have their photos published in Best of Photography Annual. See Web site for entry form.

APOGEE PHOTO MAGAZINE BIMONTHLY PHOTO CONTEST

11749 Zenobia Loop, Westminster CO 80031. (303)838-4848. Fax: (303)463-2885. E-mail: mfulks@apogeephoto.com. Web site: www.apogeephoto.com. **Contact:** Michael Fulks, publisher. Bimonthly contest. Themes and prizes change with each contest. Photographers should see Web site (www.apogeephoto.com/contest.shtml) for more information.

ARC AWARDS

500 Executive Blvd., Ossining-on-Hudson NY 10562. (914)923-9400. Fax: (914)923-9484. E-mail: info@mercommawards.com. Web site: www.mercommawards.com. Cost: $165-270. Annual contest. The purpose of the contest is to honor outstanding achievement in annual reports. Major category for annual report photography—covers and interiors. "Best of Show" receives a personalized trophy. Grand Award winners receive personalized award plaques. Gold, silver, bronze and finalists receive a personalized award certificate. Every entrant receives complete judge score sheets and comments. **May deadline.** Photographers should see Web site, write, call or e-mail for more information.

THE ART OF DIGITAL SHOW

3830 Valley Centre Dr., Suite 705-833, San Diego CA 92130. (858)793-0900. E-mail: steven@artofdigitalshow.com. Web site: www.artofdigitalshow.com. **Contact:** Steven Churchill, curator. Cost: $25 for 1st entry; $10 for each additional entry; $45 for video art. This competition accepts art created or manipulated via any form of digital technology, including digital painting, computer-based illustration, digitally manipulated photography, digital video art, etc. It does not include photographic images that are simply made with a digital camera or printed with a digital printer. Upload via Web site (preferred), e-mail to entries@artofdigitalshow.com, or mail CD. Award/prize: 1st Place: $1,000; 2nd Place: $750; 3rd Place: $500; 4th Place: $250; Honorable Mention: $100. Photographers should e-mail, visit Web site for more information.

ARTIST FELLOWSHIP GRANTS

% Oregon Arts Commission, 775 Summer St. NE, Salem OR 97310. (503)986-0082. Fax: (503)986-0260. E-mail: oregon.artscomm@state.or.us. Web site: http://www.oregonart

scommission.org/main.php. A juried grant process offering cash awards to Oregon visual artists, in **odd-numbered years**.

ARTIST FELLOWSHIPS/VIRGINIA COMMISSION FOR THE ARTS

223 Governor St., Richmond VA 23219-2010. (804)225-3132. Fax: (804)225-4327. E-mail: arts@arts.virginia.gov. Web site: www.arts.virginia.gov. Applications accepted in alternating years. The purpose of the Artist Fellowship program is to encourage significant development in the work of individual artists, to support the realization of specific artistic ideas, and to recognize the central contribution professional artists make to the creative environment of Virginia. Grant amounts: $5,000. Emerging and established artists are eligible. Open only to photographers who are legal residents of Virginia and at least 18 years of age. Applications are available in June. See *Guidelines for Funding* and application forms on the Web site or write for more information.

ARTISTS ALPINE HOLIDAY

P.O. Box 167, Ouray CO 81427. Web site: http://ourayarts.org/aah.html. **Contact**: Gary Wade, business director, (970)252-9095; Registration: DeAnn McDaniel, (970)626-3212. Cost: $20 1st entry; $5 2nd entry; $5 3rd entry. Annual fine arts show. Juried. Cash awards for 1st, 2nd and 3rd prizes in all categories total $4,300. Best of Show: $500; People's Choice Award: $300. Open to all skill levels. Photographers should write or call for more information.

ARTSLINK PROJECTS

435 Hudson Street, New York NY 10014. (212)643-1985, ext. 22. Fax: (212)643-1996. E-mail: al@cecartslink.org. Web site: www.cecartslink.org. **Contact:** Chelsey Morell. Cost: free. Annual travel grants. ArtsLink Projects accepts applications from individual artists, curators and nonprofit arts organizations who intend to undertake projects in Central and Eastern Europe, Russia, Central Asia, and the Caucasus. Grants range from $2,500 10,000. Open to advanced photographers. **January deadline.** Photographers should e-mail or call for more information.

ASTRID AWARDS

500 Executive Blvd., Ossining-on-Hudson NY 10562. (914)923-9400. Fax: (914)923-9484. E-mail: info@mercommawards.com. Web site: www.mercommawards.com. Annual contest. The purpose of the contest is to honor outstanding achievement in design communications. Major category for photography, including books, brochures and publications. "Best of Show" receives a personalized trophy. Grand Award winners receive personalized award plaques. Gold, silver, bronze and finalists receive a personalized award certificate. Every entrant receives complete judge score sheets and comments. **January deadline.** Photographers should see Web site, write, call or e-mail for more information.

◼ ATLANTA PHOTOJOURNALISM SEMINAR CONTEST

PMB 301, 541 Tenth St. NW, Atlanta GA 30318-5713. (404)982-9359. E-mail: contest@photojournalism.org. Web site: www.photojournalism.org. Annual contest. This is an all-digital contest with several different categories (all related to news and photojournalism). Photographs may have been originally shot on film or with a digital camera, but the entries must be submitted in digital form. Photographs do not have to be published to qualify. No slide or print entries are accepted. Video frame grabs are not eligible. Rules are very specific. See Web site for official rules. More than $5,000 in prizes, including $1,000 and Nikon camera gear for Best Portfolio. Open to all skill levels. **November deadline.**

⚃ BANFF MOUNTAIN PHOTOGRAPHY COMPETITION

Box 1020, 107 Tunnel Mountain Dr., Banff AB T1L 1H5 Canada. (403)762-6347. Fax: (403)762-6277. E-mail: BanffMountainPhotos@banffcentre.ca. Web site: www.BanffMountainFestivals.ca. **Contact:** Competition Coordinator. Annual contest. Up to 5 images (prints or slides) in each of 5 categories: Mountain Landscape, Mountain Adventure, Mountain Flora/Fauna, Mountain Culture, and Mountain Environment. Entry form available on Web site. Approximately $6, 000 in cash and prizes to be awarded. Open to all skill levels. Photographers should write, e-mail or fax for more information.

▣ THE CENTER FOR FINE ART PHOTOGRAPHY

400 North College Ave., Fort Collins CO 80524. (907)224-1010. E-mail: exhibitions@c4fap.org. Web site: www.c4fap.org. **Contact:** Grace Norman, exhibitions director. Cost: typically $35 for first 3 entries; $10 for each additional entry. Competitions held 10 times/year. ''The Center's competitions are designed to attract and exhibit quality fine art photography created by emerging and established artists working in traditional, digital and mixed-media photography. The themes for each exhibition vary greatly. The themes, rules, details and entry forms for each call for entry are posted on the Center's Web site.'' All accepted work is exhibited in the Center gallery. Additionally, the Center offers monetary awards, scholarships, solo exhibitions and other awards. Awards are stated with each call for entry. Open to all skill levels and to all domestic and international photographers working with digital or traditional photography or combinations of both. Photographers should see Web site for deadlines and more information.

COLLEGE PHOTOGRAPHER OF THE YEAR

109 Lee Hills Hall, Columbia MO 65211-1370. (573)882-4882. Fax: (573)884-4999. E-mail: info@cpoy.org. Web site: www.cpoy.org. **Contact:** Angel Anderson, coordinator. Annual contest to recognize excellent photography by currently enrolled college students. Portfolio winner receives a plaque, cash and camera products. Other category winners receive cash and camera products. Open to beginning and intermediate photographers. **Fall deadline.** Photographers should see Web site for more information.

COMMUNICATION ARTS ANNUAL PHOTOGRAPHY COMPETITION

110 Constitution Dr., Menlo Park CA 94025-1107. (650)326-6040. Fax: (650)326-1648. E-mail: competition@commarts.com. Web site: www.commarts.com. Entries must be accompanied by a completed entry form. ''Entries may originate from any country. Explanation of the function in English is very important to the judges. The work will be chosen on the basis of its creative excellence by a nationally representative jury of designers, art directors and photographers.'' Categories include interactive design, illustration, photography, design, advertising. **Deadline: March 6, 2009**. ''For further information regarding our competitions, please visit our Web site.''

⚃ ⚃ DANCE ON CAMERA FESTIVAL

48 W. 21st St., #907, New York NY 10010. Phone/fax: (212)727-0764. E-mail: dfa5@earthlink.net; info@dancefilms.org. Web site: www.dancefilms.org. **Contact:** Artistic Director.

Contests

Sponsored by Dance Films Association, Inc. The oldest annual dance festival competition in the world for films and videotapes on all aspects of dance. Co-presented by the Film Society of Lincoln Center in New York City; also tours internationally. Entry forms available on Web site.

ⓝ DIRECT ART MAGAZINE PUBLICATION COMPETITION

(formerly New Art Showcase Exhibition), 59 Main St., Box 503, Phoenicia NY 12464. (845)688-7129. E-mail: slowart@aol.com. Web site: www.slowart.com. **Contact:** Tim Slow-inski, director. Cost: $30. Biannual contest. National magazine publication of new and emerging art in all medias. Cover and feature article awards. Open to all skill levels. **April/October deadlines.** Photographers should send SASE for more information.

ⓒ ENERGY GALLERY ART CALL

info@energygallery.com. Web site: www.energygallery.com. Cost: $30 for 5 images; additional images $5/each. A jury selects artworks for the online exhibition at Energy Gallery's Web site for a period of 3 months and archived in Energy Gallery's Web site permanently. Selected artists also qualify to participate in Energy Gallery's annual exhibit. Photographers should visit Web site for submission form and more information.

ⓝ EXCELLENCE IN PHOTOGRAPHIC TEACHING AWARD

Santa Fe Center for Photography, P.O. Box 2483, Santa Fe NM 87504. (505)984-8353. E-mail: info@visitcenter.org. Web site: www.visitcenter.org. **Contact:** Laura Wzorek, pro-grams director. Cost: $20 members, $25 non-members. Annual contest. $2,500 cash award. Rewards educators for their dedication and passion for photographic teaching. Educators in all areas of photographic teaching are eligible. **Deadline:** May 2009. Photographers should see Web site for more information.

FIFTYCROWS INTERNATIONAL FUND FOR DOCUMENTARY PHOTOGRAPHY

FiftyCrows, 49 Geary St., Suite 225, San Francisco CA 94108. Web site: www.fiftycrows.org. Grants, career and distribution assistance to emerging and mid-career documentary photog-raphers to help complete a long-term documentary project of social, political, ethical, envi-ronmental or economic importance. FiftyCrows maintains a by-appointment gallery and reference library, and creates short films about documentary photographers. To receive call-for-entry notification and updates, enter e-mail address in the sign-up area on the home page of the Web site .

FIRELANDS ASSOCIATION FOR THE VISUAL ARTS

39 S. Main St., Oberlin OH 44074. (440)774-7158. E-mail: favagallery@oberlin.net. Web site: www.favagallery.org. **Contact:** Betsy Manderen, executive director. Cost: $15/photog-rapher; $12 for FAVA members. Annual juried photography contest for residents of Ohio, Kentucky, Indiana, Michigan, Pennsylvania and West Virginia. Both traditional and experi-mental techniques welcome. Photographers may submit up to 3 works completed in the last 3 years. **Annual entry deadline: March-April (date varies).** Photographers should call or e-mail for entry form.

N ⊕ **HUMANITY PHOTO AWARDS (HPA)**

P.O. Box 8006, Beijing 100082 China. (86)(106)225-2175. E-mail: hpa@china-fpa.org. Web site: www.china-fpa.org. **Contact:** Organizing Committee HPA. Cost: free. Biennial contest. Open to all skill levels.

N **INFOCUS**

Palm Beach Photographic Centre, 55 NE Second Ave., Delray Beach FL 33444. (561)276-9797. Fax: (561)276-1932. E-mail: info@fotofusion.org. Web site: www.workshop.org. **Contact**: Fatima NeJame, executive director. Cost: $25 nonrefundable entry fee. Annual contest. Best of Show: $750. Merit awards of free tuition for a PBPC photography workshop of choice. Open to members of the Palm Beach Photographic Centre. Interested parties can obtain an individual membership for $45. Photographers should write or call for more information.

N ⊕ **KRASZNA-KRAUSZ PHOTOGRAPHY AND MOVING IMAGE BOOK AWARDS**

National Museum of Photograhy, Film & Television, Bradford, West Yorkshire BD1 1NQ United Kingdom. E-mail: awards@k-k.org.uk. Web site: www.k-k.org.uk. **Contact:** Margaret Brown, awards coordinator. Awards made to encourage and recognize outstanding achievements in the writing and publishing of books on the art, history, practice and technology of photography and the moving image (film, television, video). **Entries from publishers only.** Announcement of winners in March every year.

LAKE CHAMPLAIN MARITIME MUSEUM'S SPRING JURIED PHOTOGRAPHY EXHIBIT

4472 Basin Harbor Rd., Vergennes VT 05491. (802)475-2022, ext. 107. E-mail: eloiseb@lcmm.org. Web site: www.lcmm.org. **Contact:** Eloise Beil. Annual exhibition, images of Lake Champlain. "Amateur and professional photographers are invited to submit framed prints in color or black & white. Professional photographers will judge and comment on the work." Call for entries begins in June, photograph delivery in August, on view September and October. Photographers should call, e-mail, or visit Web site for registration form.

LAKE CHAMPLAIN THROUGH THE LENS: JURIED PHOTOGRAPHY EXHIBIT

4472 Basin Harbor Rd., Vergennes VT 05491. (802)475-2022, ext. 107. E-mail: eloiseb@lcmm.org. Web site: www.lcmm.org. **Contact:** Eloise Beil. Annual exhibition, images of Lake Champlain. "Amateur and professional photographers are invited to submit framed prints in color or black and white. Professional photographers will judge and comment on the work." Call for entries begins in June; photo delivery in August, on view September and October. Photographers should call, e-mail, or visit Web site for registration form.

■ **LAKE SUPERIOR MAGAZINE AMATEUR PHOTO CONTEST**

P.O. Box 16417, Duluth MN 55816-0417. (218)722-5002. Fax: (218)722-4096. E-mail: edit@lakesuperior.com. Web site: www.lakesuperior.com. **Contact:** Konnie LeMay, editor. Annual contest. Photos must be taken in the Lake Superior region and should be labeled for categories: lake/landscapes, nature, people/humor. Accepts up to 10 b&w and/or color images—prints no larger than 8×10, and transparencies. Digital images can be submitted as prints with accompanying CD. Grand Prize: $200 prize package to select Lake Superior region hotels and restaurants, plus a 1-year subscription and calendar. Other prizes include subscriptions and calendars. **October deadline**. Photographers should write, e-mail or see Web site for more information.

LARSON GALLERY JURIED BIENNIAL PHOTOGRAPHY EXHIBITION

Yakima Valley Community College, P.O. Box 22520, Yakima WA 98907. (509)574-4875. Fax: (509)574-6826. E-mail: gallery@yvcc.edu. Web site: www.larsongallery.org. **Contact:** Denise Olsen, assistant gallery director. Cost: $12/entry (limit 4 entries). National juried competition with approximately $3,500 in prize money. Held annually in April. **First jurying held in February.** Photographers should write, fax, e-mail or visit the Web site for prospectus.

LOS ANGELES CENTER FOR DIGITAL JURIED COMPETITION

107 W. Fifth St., Los Angeles CA 90013. (323)646-9427. E-mail: lacda@lacda.com, rexbruce @lacda.com. Web site: www.lacda.com. **Contact:** Rex Bruce, gallery director and principal curator. LACDA is dedicated to the propagation of all forms of digital art, supporting local, international, emerging and established artists in our gallery. Its Juried Competition is open to digital artists around the world. It also sponsors other competitions throughout the year. Photographers should visit Web site, e-mail, call for more information.

MERCURY AWARDS

500 Executive Blvd., Ossining-on-Hudson NY 10562. (914)923-9400. Fax: (914)923-9484. E-mail: rwitt@mercommawards.com. Web site: www.mercommawards.com. **Contact:** Ms. Reni L. Witt, president. Cost: $190-250/entry (depending on category). Annual contest. The purpose of the contest is to honor outstanding achievement in public relations and corporate communications. Major category for photography, including ads, brochures, magazines, etc. "Best of Show" receives a personalized trophy. Grand Award winners receive award plaques (personalized). Gold, silver, bronze and finalists receive a personalized award certificate. All nominators receive complete judge score sheets and evaluation comments. **November 11 deadline.** Photographers should write, call or e-mail for more information.

N ⚬ THE MOBIUS ADVERTISING AWARDS

713 S. Pacific Coast Hwy., Suite A, Redondo Beach CA 90277-4233. (310)540-0959. Fax: (310)316-8905. E-mail: mobiusinfo@mobiusawards.com. Web site: www.mobiusawards.c om. Annual international awards competition founded in 1971 for TV and radio commercials, print advertising, outdoor, specialty advertising, online, mixed media campaigns and package design. Student/spec work welcome. **October 1 deadline**. Awards presented in February each year in Los Angeles.

MYRON THE CAMERA BUG, "Photography's Official Mascot" ™

(featuring The Digital Shutterbugs & The Foto Critters Family), % Educational Dept., 2106 Hoffnagle St., Philadelphia PA 19152-2409. E-mail: cambug8480@aol.com. **Contact:** Len Friedman, director. Sponsored by Luvable Characters EduTainment Workshop. Open to all photography students and educators. Photographers should e-mail for details.

NEW YORK STATE FAIR PHOTOGRAPHY COMPETITION AND SHOW

581 State Fair Blvd., Syracuse NY 13209.(315)487-7711, ext. 1264 or 12. Web site: www.nys fair.org. See Web site for entry forms and submission guidelines.

⊞ ⊕ NORTHERN COUNTIES INTERNATIONAL COLOUR SLIDE EXHIBITION

9 Cardigan Grove, Tynemouth, Tyne & Wear NE30 3HN United Kingdom. (44)(191)252-2870. E-mail: jane@hall-black.fsnet.co.uk. Web site: www.ncpf.co.uk. **Contact:** Mrs. J.H. Black, honorary exhibition chairman, ARPS, Hon. PAGB, APSA. Judges 35mm slides—4 entries per person. 3 categories: general, nature and photo travel. PSA and FIAP recognition and medals.

THE GORDON PARKS PHOTOGRAPHY COMPETITION

Fort Scott Community College, 2108 S. Horton, Fort Scott KS 66701-3140. (620)223-2700. Fax: (620)223-6530. E-mail: photocontest@fortscott.edu. Web site: www.fortscott.edu. **Contact:** Jill Warford. Cost: $15 for each photo up to 4 entries. Photos should reflect the important themes in the life and works of Gordon Parks. Awards: $800 1st Place, $400 2nd Place, $200 3rd Place and up to 3 honorable mentions with prizes of $100 each. Open to all skill levels. Winners will be announced during annual Gordon Parks celebration held each October. Photographers should see Web site for more information.

⊞ THE PHOTO REVIEW ANNUAL PHOTOGRAPHY COMPETITION

140 E. Richardson Ave., Suite 301, Langhorne PA 19047. (215)891-0214. E-mail: info@photoreview.org. Web site: www.photoreview.org. **Contact:** Stephen Perloff, editor. Cost: $30 for up to 3 images; $5 each for up to 2 additional images. National annual contest. All types of photographs are eligible—b&w, color, nonsilver, computer-manipulated, etc. Submit slides or prints (unmatted, unframed, 16×20 or smaller), or images on CD. All entries must be labeled. Awards include a Microtek i800 scanner; $350 in gift certificates from Calumet Photographic; 2 Lensbaby 2.0 SLR selective focus lenses with macro kits; 2 $100 gift certificates from Sprint Systems; a professional-level membership in Women in Photography International (worth $235) and $250 in cash prizes. All winners reproduced in summer issue of *Photo Review* magazine and exhibited at photography gallery of the University of Arts/Philadelphia. Open to all skill levels. **May 15 deadline**. Photographers should send SASE or see Web site for more information.

PHOTOGRAPHY NOW

% The Center for Photography at Woodstock, 59 Tinker St., Woodstock NY 12498. (845)679-9957. Fax: (845)679-6337. E-mail: info@cpw.org. Web site: www.cpw.org. **Contact**: CPW program associate. Two annual contests: 1 for exhibitions, 1 for publication. Juried annually by renowned photographers, critics, museum and gallery curators. Deadlines vary. General submission is ongoing. Photographers must call or write for guidelines.

⊞ PHOTOSPIVA

Spiva Center for the Arts, 222 W. Third St., Joplin MO 64801. (417)623-0183. E-mail: spiva@spivaarts.org. Web site: www.spivaarts.org. **Contact:** Executive director. 33rd annual, national fine art photography competition. Over $2,000 cash awards. Open to all photographers in the U.S. and its territories; any photographic process welcome. Enter online at www.photospiva.org beginning December 5, 2008. Juror: TBA. **Deadline:** January 9, 2009. Exhibition: March 7-May 3, 2009.

PICTURE.COM FREE PHOTO CONTEST

The International Library of Photography, 3600 Crondall Lane, Suite 101-3111, Owings Mills MD 21117.Web site: www.picture.com. Prize/award: $67,000 in prizes. Apply online

Contests

or by mail. Send 1 photo in only 1 of the following categories: action, children, humor, nature, people, animals/pets, portraiture, sports, travel or other. Photographers retain all rights to their photographs. Photographers should visit Web site for more information.

PICTURES OF THE YEAR INTERNATIONAL

109 Lee Hills Hall, Columbia MO 65211-1370. (573)882-4882. Fax: (573)884-4999. E-mail: shawrf@missouri.edu. Web site: www.poyi.org. **Contact:** Rick Shaw, director. Cost: $50/ entrant. Annual contest to reward and recognize excellence in photojournalism, sponsored by the Missouri School of Journalism and the Donald W. Reynolds Journalism Institute. Over $20,000 in cash and product awards. Open to all skill levels. **January deadline.** Photographers should write, call or e-mail for more information.

- The Missouri School of Journalism also sponsors College Photographer of the Year. See Web site for details.

THE PROJECT COMPETITION

Center, P.O. Box 2483, Santa Fe NM 87504. E-mail: info@visitcenter.org. Web site: www.visitcenter.org. **Contact:** Laura Wzorek, programs director. Cost: $35. Annual contest. The Project Competition honors committed photographers working on long-term documentary projects and fine-art series. Three jurors reach a consensus on the 1st Prize and 3 Honorable Mentions. Each individual juror also selects a project to receive 1 of the 3 Juror's Choice awards. $5,000 cash award; full-tuition scholarship for a weeklong workshop of winner's choice at the Santa Fe Workshops; and complimentary participation in Review Santa Fe. Open to all skill levels. **Deadline:** September, 2008. Photographers should see Web site for more information.

- Center, the organization that sponsors this competition, was formerly known as The Santa Fe Center for Photography.

RHODE ISLAND STATE COUNCIL ON THE ARTS FELLOWSHIPS

One Capitol Hill, 3rd Floor, Providence RI 02908. (401)222-3880. Fax: (401)222-3018. E-mail: Cristina@arts.ri.gov. Web site: www.arts.ri.gov. **RI residents only.** Cost: free. Annual contest "to encourage the creative development of Rhode Island artists by enabling them to set aside time to pursue their work and achieve specific career goals." Awards $5,000 fellowship; $1,000 merit award. Open to advanced photographers. **April 1 deadline.** Photographers should send SASE, e-mail or see Web site for more information.

THE SINGULAR IMAGE

Center, P.O. Box 2483, Santa Fe NM 87504. (505)984-8353. E-mail: info@visitcenter.org. Web site: www.visitcenter.org. **Contact**: Laura Wzorek, programs director. Cost: $35. Annual contest. Recognizes outstanding individual photographs in color and b&w. Photographers are invited to submit their most compelling images. Open to all skill levels. **Deadline:** January 2009. Photographers should see Web site for more information.

- Center, the organization that sponsors this competition, was formerly known as The Santa Fe Center for Photography.

N W. EUGENE SMITH MEMORIAL FUND, INC.

% ICP, 1133 Avenue of the Americas, New York NY 10036. (212)857-0038. Fax: (212)768-4688. Web site: www.smithfund.org. Annual contest. Promotes humanistic traditions of

W. Eugene Smith. Grant of $30,000; secondary grant of $5,000. Open to photographers with a project in the tradition of W. Eugene Smith. Photographers should send SASE (60¢) for application information.

TEXAS PHOTOGRAPHIC SOCIETY, THE NATIONAL COMPETITION

6338 N. New Braunfels #174, San Antonio TX 78209. (210)824-4123. E-mail: clarke@texasphoto.org. Web site: www.texasphoto.org. **Contact:** Clarke Evans, TPS president. Cost: $35 for 5 images, plus $5 for each image over 5, and membership fee if joining Texas Photographic Society. You do not have to be a member to enter. See Web site or call for information on membership fees. TPS has a membership of 1,300 from 49 states and 12 countries. Contest held annually. Cash awards: 1st Place: $1,000; 2nd Place: $650; 3rd Place: $350; 5 honorable mentions at $150 each. TPS 16: The National Competition will be juried by Michelled Dunn Marsh, Director of Aperture West. The exhibition will open at St. Edward's University Art Gallery and be exhibited at galleries in Odessa, Houston (as part of FotoFest International); New York and San Francisco. Open to all skill levels. See Web site or call Clarke for more information.

N ◨ U.S. INTERNATIONAL FILM AND VIDEO FESTIVAL

713 S. Pacific Coast Hwy., Suite A, Redondo Beach CA 90277-4233. (310)540-0959. Fax: (310)316-8905. E-mail: filmfestinfo@filmfestawards.com. Web site: www.filmfestawards.com. **Contact:** Lee W. Gluckman, Jr., chairman. Annual international awards competition founded in 1968 for business, television, industrial, entertainment, documentary and informational film and video. **March 1 deadline.** Awards presented in early June each year in Los Angeles.

UNLIMITED EDITIONS INTERNATIONAL JURIED PHOTOGRAPHY COMPETITIONS

% Competition Chairman, 319 E. Shay Circle, Hendersonville NC 28791. (828)489-9609. E-mail: UltdEditionsIntl@aol.com. **Contact:** Gregory Hugh Leng, president/owner. Sponsors juried photography competitions several times yearly offering cash, award certificates and prizes. Photography accepted from amateurs and professionals. Open to all skill levels and ages. Prizes awarded in different categories or divisions such as commercial, portraiture, journalism, landscape, digital imaging, and retouching. We accept formats in print film, transparencies and digital images. Black and white, color, and digital imaging CD's or DVD's may be submitted for consideration. Prints and large transparencies may be in mats, no frames. All entries must be delivered in a reusable container with prepaid postage to insure photography is returned. Unlimited Editions International also offers teh unique opportunity to purchase photography from those photographers who wish to sell their work. All images submitted in competition remain the property of the photographer/entrants unless an offer to purchase their work is accepted by the photographer. All photographers must send SASE (.92 USA and $2.25 international) for entry forms, contest dates, and detailed information on how to participate in our International juried photography competitions.

WRITERS' JOURNAL PHOTO CONTEST

Val-Tech Media, P.O. Box 394, Perham MN 56573. (218)346-7921. Fax: (218)346-7924. E-mail: writersjournal@writersjournal.com. Web site: www.writersjournal.com. **Contact:** Leon Ogroske. Cost: $3/entry. No limit on number of entries. Photos can be of any subject matter, with or without people. Model releases must accompany all photos of people. 1st Prize: $25; 2nd Prize: $15; 3rd Prize: $10; winners will be published in *WRITERS' Journal* magazine. **May 30/November 30 deadlines**. Photographers should send SASE for guidelines.

YOUR BEST SHOT

Popular Photography. E-mail: yourbestshot@hfmus.com. Web site: www.PopPhoto.com. Monthly contest; submit up to 5 entries/month. Cash awards: 1st Place: $300; 2nd Place: $200; 3rd Place: $100; Honorable Mentions: $50. Photographers should see Web site for more information on how to enter.

Photo Representatives

Many photographers are good at promoting themselves and seeking out new clients, and they actually enjoy that part of the business. Other photographers are not comfortable promoting themselves and would rather dedicate their time and energy solely to producing their photographs. Regardless of which camp you're in, you may need a photo rep.

Finding the rep who is right for you is vitally important. Think of your relationship with a rep as a partnership. Your goals should mesh. Treat your search for a rep much as you would your search for a client. Try to understand the rep's business, who they already represent, etc., before you approach them. Show you've done your homework.

When you sign with a photo rep, you basically hire someone to get your portfolio in front of art directors, make cold calls in search of new clients, and develop promotional ideas to market your talents. The main goal is to find assignment work for you with corporations, advertising firms, or design studios. And, unlike stock agencies or galleries, a photo rep is interested in marketing your talents rather than your images.

Most reps charge a 20-to 30-percent commission. They handle more than one photographer at a time, usually making certain that each shooter specializes in a different area. For example, a rep may have contracts to promote three different photographers—one who handles product shots, another who shoots interiors, and a third who photographs food.

DO YOU NEED A REP?

Before you decide to seek out a photo representative, consider these questions:

- Do you already have enough work, but want to expand your client base?
- Are you motivated to maximize your profits? Remember that a rep is interested in working with photographers who can do what is necessary to expand their businesses.
- Do you have a tightly edited portfolio with pieces showing the kind of work you want to do?
- Are you willing to do what it takes to help the rep promote you, including having a budget to help pay for self-promotional materials?
- Do you have a clear idea of where you want your career to go, but need assistance in getting there?
- Do you have a specialty or a unique style that makes you stand out?

If you answered yes to most of these questions, perhaps you would profit from the expertise of a rep. If you feel you are not ready for a rep or that you don't need one, but you still want some help, you might consider a consultation with an expert in marketing and/or self-promotion.

As you search for a rep, there are numerous points to consider. First, how established is the rep you plan to approach? Established reps have an edge over newcomers in that they know the territory. They've built up contacts in ad agencies, magazines and elsewhere. This is essential since most art directors and picture editors do not stay in their positions for long periods of time. Therefore, established reps will have an easier time helping you penetrate new markets.

If you decide to go with a new rep, consider paying an advance against commission in order to help the rep financially during an equitable trial period. Usually it takes a year to see returns on portfolio reviews and other marketing efforts, and a rep who is relying on income from sales might go hungry if he doesn't have a base income from which to live.

Whatever you agree upon, always have a written contract. Handshake deals won't cut it. You must know the tasks that each of you is required to complete, and having your roles discussed in a contract will guarantee there are no misunderstandings. For example, spell out in your contract what happens with clients that you had before hiring the rep. Most photographers refuse to pay commissions for these ''house'' accounts, unless the rep handles them completely and continues to bring in new clients.

Also, it's likely that some costs, such as promotional fees, will be shared. For example, photographers often pay 75 percent of any advertising fees (such as sourcebook ads and direct mail pieces).

If you want to know more about a specific rep, or how reps operate, contact the Society of Photographers and Artists Representatives, 60 E. 42nd St., Suite 1166, New York NY 10165, (212)779-7464, www.spar.org. SPAR sponsors educational programs and maintains a code of ethics to which all members must adhere.

ROBERT BACALL REPRESENTATIVES INC.
16 Penn Plaza, Suite 731, New York NY 10001. (212)695-1729. E-mail: rob@bacall.com. Web site: www.bacall.com. **Contact:** Robert Bacall. Commercial photography and artist representative. Estab. 1988. Represents 12 photographers. Agency specializes in digital, food, still life, fashion, beauty, kids, corporate, environmental, portrait, lifestyle, location, landscape. Markets include advertising agencies, corporations/clients direct, design firms, editorial/magazines, publishing/books, sales/promotion firms.

Terms Rep receives 30% commission. Exclusive area representation required. For promotional purposes, talent must provide portfolios, cases, tearsheets, prints, etc. Advertises in *Creative Black Book*, *Workbook*, *Le Book*, *Alternative Pick*, *PDN-Photoserve*, *At-Edge*.

How to Contact Send query letter/e-mail, direct mail flier/brochure. Responds only if interested. After initial contact, drop off or mail materials for review.

Tips ''Seek representation when you feel your portfolio is unique and can bring in new business.''

RANDY COLE REPRESENTS, LLC
115 West 30th St. Ste. 404, New York NY 10001. (212)760-1212. Fax: (212)760-1199. E-mail: randy@randycole.com. Web site: www.randycole.com. Commercial photography representative. Estab. 1989. Member of SPAR. Represents 9 photographers. Staff includes an assistant. Markets include advertising agencies, editorial/magazines, direct mail firms, corporate/client direct, design firms, publishing/books.

Handles Photography.

Terms Rep receives commission on the creative fees; dependent upon specific negotiation. Advertises in *At Edge, Archive* and *Le Book* , as well as online creative directories i.e.*Workbook* and Photoserve, etc.

Photo Representatives

How to Contact Send e-mail or promo piece and follow up with call. Portfolios may be dropped off; set up appointment.

Tips Finds new talent through submissions and referrals.

LINDA DE MORETA REPRESENTS

1511 Union Street, Alameda CA 94501. (510)769-1421. Fax: (510)892-2955. E-mail: linda@li ndareps.com. Web site: www.lindareps.com. **Contact:** Linda de Moreta. Commercial photography and illustration representative. Estab. 1988. Member of Graphic Artists Guild. Represents 1 photographer and 10 illustrators. Markets include advertising agencies, design firms, corporations/client direct, editorial/magazines, paper products/greeting cards, publishing/books, sales/promotion firms.

Handles Photography, illustration, lettering.

Terms Exclusive representation requirements and commission arrangements vary. Advertising costs are handled by individual agreement. Materials for promotional purposes vary with each artist. Advertises in *Workbook*, *Directory of Illustration*.

How to Contact E-mail or send direct mail flier/brochure. "Please do *not* send original art. Include SASE for any items you wish returned." Responds to any inquiry in which there is an interest. Portfolios are individually developed for each artist.

Tips Obtains new talent primarily through client and artist referrals, some solicitation. "I look for a personal vision and style of photography, and exceptional creativity combined with professionalism, maturity, and commitment to career advancement."

FRANÇOISE DUBOIS/DUBOIS REPRESENTS

305 Newbury Lane, Newbury Park CA 91320. (805)376-9738. Fax: (805)376-9729. E-mail: fdubois@francoisedubois.com. Web site: www.francoisedubois.com. **Contact**: Françoise Dubois, owner. Commercial photography representative and creative and marketing consultant. Represents 3 photographers. Staff includes Andrew Bernstein (sports and sports celebrities), Michel Dubois (still life/people) and Michael Baciu (photo impressionism). Agency specializes in commercial photography for advertising, editorial, creative, marketing consulting. Markets include advertising agencies, corporations/clients direct, design firms, editorial/magazines, publishing/books, sales/promotion firms.

Handles Photography.

Terms Rep receives 25% commission. Charges FedEx expenses (if not paid by advertising agency or other potential client). Exclusive area representation required. Advertising costs are paid by talent. For promotional purposes, talent must provide "3 portfolios, advertising in national sourcebook, and 3 or 4 direct mail pieces per year. All must carry my name and number."

How to Contact Not looking at portfolios at this time. Send e-mail with link to site.

Tips "Do not look for a rep if your target market is too small a niche. Do not look for a rep if you're not somewhat established. Hire a consultant to help you design a consistent and unique portfolio and marketing strategy, and to make sure your strengths are made evident and you remain focused."

▧ MICHAEL GINSBURG & ASSOCIATES, INC.

345 East 94th St., New York NY 10128. (212)369-3594 or (212) 369-3595. E-mail: mg@mich aelginsburg.com. Web site: www.michaelginsburg.com. **Contact:** Michael Ginsburg. Commercial photography representative. Estab. 1978. Represents 9 photographers. Agency spe-

cializes in advertising and editorial photographers. Markets include advertising agencies, corporations/clients direct, design firms, editorial/magazines, sales/promotion firms.
Handles Photography.
Terms Rep receives 30% commission. Charges for messenger costs, FedExp expenses. Exclusive area representation required. Advertising costs are paid 100% by talent. For promotional purposes, talent must provide a minimum of 5 portfolios—direct mail pieces 2 times per year—and at least 1 sourcebook per year. Advertises in *Workbook*, source books and online source books.
How to Contact Send query letter, direct mail flier/brochure, or e-mail. Responds only if interested within 2 weeks. After initial contact, call for appointment to show portfolio of tearsheets, slides, photographs.
Tips Obtains new talent through personal referrals and solicitation.

BARBARA GORDON

165 E. 32nd St., New York NY 10016. (212)686-3514. Fax: (212)532-4302. **Contact:** Barbara Gordon. Commercial illustration and photography representative. Estab. 1969. Member of SPAR, Society of Illustrators, Graphic Artists Guild. Represents illustrators and photographers. "I represent only a small select group of people and therefore give a great deal of personal time and attention to each." Also does coaching and consulting.
Terms Rep receives 25% commission. No geographic restrictions in continental US.
How to Contact Send direct mail flier/brochure. Responds in 2 weeks. After initial contact, drop off or mail appropriate materials for review. Portfolio should include tearsheets, slides, photographs; "if you want materials or promotion piece returned, include SASE."
Tips Obtains new talent through recommendations from others, solicitation, art conferences, etc. "I have obtained talent from all of the above. I do not care if an artist or photographer has been published or is experienced. I am essentially interested in people with a good, commercial style. Don't send résumés and don't call to give me a verbal description of your work. Send promotion pieces. *Never* send original art. If you want something back, include a SASE. Always label your slides in case they get separated from your cover letter. And always include a phone number where you can be reached."

CAROL GUENZI AGENTS, INC.

865 Delaware, Denver CO 80204-4533. (303)820-2599 or (800)417-5120. Fax: (303)820-2598. E-mail: art@artagent.com. Web site: www.artagent.com. **Contact:** Carol Guenzi. Commercial illustration, photogoraphy, new media, film/animation representative. Estab. 1984. Member of Art Directors Club of Denver, AIGA and ASMP. Represents 30 illustrators, 8 photographers, 6 computer multimedia designers. Agency specializes in a "worldwide selection of talent in all areas of visual communications." Markets include advertising agencies, corporations/clients direct, design firms, editorial/magazine, paper products/greeting cards, sales/promotions firms.
Handles Illustration, photography, new media, film and animation. Looking for unique styles and applications and digital imaging.
Terms Rep receives 25-30% commission. Exclusive area representation required. Advertising costs are split: 70-75% paid by talent; 25-30% paid by representative. For promotional purposes, talent must provide "promotional material after 6 months, some restrictions on portfolios." Advertises in *Directory of Illustration*, *Black Book* and *Workbook*.
How to Contact E-mail JPEGs or send direct mail piece, tearsheets. Responds in 2-3 weeks,

Photo Representatives

only if interested. After initial contact, call or e-mail for appointment or to drop off or ship materials for review. Portfolio should include tearsheets, prints, samples and a list of current clients.

Tips Obtains new talent through solicitation, art directors' referrals and active pursuit by individual. "Show your strongest style and have at least 12 samples of that style before introducing all your capabilities. Be prepared to add additional work to your portfolio to help round out your style. We do a large percentage of computer manipulation and accessing on network. All our portfolios are both electronic and prints."

PAT HACKETT/ARTIST REPRESENTATIVE

7014 N. Mercer Way, Mercer Island WA 98040. (206)447-1600. Fax: (206)447-0739. E-mail: pat@pathackett.com. Web site: www.pathackett.com. **Contact:** Pat Hackett. Commercial illustration and photography representative. Estab. 1979. Member of Graphic Artists Guild. Represents 12 illustrators and 1 photographer. Markets include advertising agencies, corporations/client direct, design firms, editorial/magazines.

Handles Illustration, photography.

Terms Rep receives 25-33% commission. Exclusive area representation required. No geographic restrictions. Advertising costs are split: 75% paid by talent; 25% paid by representative. For promotional purposes, talent must provide "standardized portfolio, i.e., all pieces within the book are the same format." Advertises in *Showcase* and *Workbook* (www.portfolios.com and www.theispot.com).

How to Contact Send direct mail flier/brochure or e-mail. Responds within 3 weeks if interested.

TRICIA JOYCE INC

79 Chambers St., New York NY 10007. (212)962-0728. E-mail: info@triciajoyce.com. Web site: www.triciajoyce.com. **Contact**: Tricia Joyce or Jann Johnson. Commercial photography representative. Estab. 1988. Represents photographers and stylists. Agency specializes in fashion, advertising, lifestyle, still life, travel, cosmetics/beauty, interiors, portraiture. Markets include advertising agencies, corporations/clients direct, design firms, editorial/magazines and sales/promotion firms.

Handles Photography and fine art.

Terms Agent receives 25% commission for photography; 20% for stylists, 50% for stock.

How to Contact Send query letter, résumé, direct mail flier/brochure and photocopies. Responds only if interested. After initial contact, "wait to hear—please don't call."

LEE + LOU PRODUCTIONS INC.

211 N Dianthus St., Manhattan Beach CA 90266. (310)374-1918. Fax: (310)374-1918. E-mail: leelou@earthlink.net. Web site: www.leelou.com. Commercial illustration and photography representative, digital and traditional photo retouching. Estab. 1981. Represents 2 retouchers, 5 photographers, 5 film directors, 2 visual effects com, 1CGI com. Specializes in automotive. Markets include advertising agencies.

Handles Photography, commercial film, CGI, visual effects.

Terms Rep receives 25% commission. Charges for shipping, entertainment. Exclusive area representation required. Advertising costs are paid by talent. For promotional purposes, talent must provide direct mail advertising material. Advertises in *Creative Black Book*, *Workbook* and *Single Image, Shoot, Boards*.

How to Contact Send direct mail flier/brochure, tearsheets. Responds in 1 week. After initial contact, call for appointment to show portfolio of photographs.

Tips Obtains new talent through recommendations from others, some solicitation.

THE BRUCE LEVIN GROUP

305 Seventh Ave., Suite 1101, New York NY 10001. (212)627-2281. Fax: (212)627-0095. E-mail: brucelevin@mac.com. Web site: www.brucelevingroup.com. **Contact:** Bruce Levin, president. Commercial photography representative. Estab. 1983. Member of SPAR and ASMP. Represents 10 photographers. Agency specializes in advertising, editorial and catalog; heavy emphasis on fashion, lifestyle and computer graphics.

Handles Photography. Looking for photographers who are "young and college-educated."

Terms Rep receives 25% commission. Exclusive area representation required. Advertising costs are split: 75% paid by talent; 25% paid by representative. Advertises in *Workbook* and other sourcebooks.

How to Contact Send brochure, photos; call. Portfolios may be dropped off every Monday through Friday.

Tips Obtains new talent through recommendations, research, word of mouth, solicitation.

JUDITH MCGRATH

P.O. Box 133, 32W040 Army Trail Rd., Wayne IL 60184. (630)762-8451. Fax: 630-524-9126. E-mail: judy@judymcgrath.net. Web site: www.judymcgrath.net. Commercial photography representative. Estab. 1980. Represents photographers. Markets include advertising agencies, corporate/client direct, design firms, editorial/magazines, paper products/greeting cards, publishing/books, direct mail firms.

Handles Photography.

Terms Rep receives 25% commission. Exclusive area representation required. Advertising costs paid by talent. Advertises in *Workbook*.

How to Contact Send query letter, bio, tearsheets, photocopies. Rep will contact photographer for portfolio review if interested.

MUNRO GOODMAN ARTISTS REPRESENTATIVES

630 N. State St., #2109, Chicago IL 60610. (312)335-8925. E-mail: steve@munrocampagna.com. Web site: www.munrocampagna.com. **Contact:** Steve Munro, president. Commercial photography and illustration representative. Estab. 1987. Member of SPAR, CAR (Chicago Artist Representatives). Represents 4 photographers, 30 illustrators. Markets include advertising agencies, corporations/clients direct, design firms, publishing/books.

Handles Illustration, photography.

Terms Rep receives 25% commission. Exclusive area representation required. Advertising costs are split: 75% paid by talent; 25% paid by representative. For promotional purposes, talent must provide 2 portfolios, leave-behinds, several promos. Advertises in *Creative Black Book*, *Workbook*, other sourcebooks.

How to Contact Send query letter, bio, tearsheets, SASE. Responds within 2 weeks, only if interested. After initial contact, write to schedule an appointment.

Tips Obtains new talent through recommendations, periodicals. "Do a little homework and target appropriate rep. Try to get a referral from an art buyer or art director."

NPN WORLDWIDE

The Roland Group, Inc., 4948 St. Elmo Ave., Suite 201, Bethesda MD 20814. (301)718-7955. Fax: (301)718-7958. E-mail: info@npnworldwide.com. Web site: www.npnworldwide.com. Photography broker. Member of SPAR. Markets include advertising agencies, corporate/client direct, design firms.

Handles Photography.

Terms Rep receives 35% commission.

How to Contact "Go to our Web site. The 'contact us' section has a special talent recruitment form with further instructions on how to submit your work." Rep will contact photographer for portfolio review if interested.

Tips Finds new talent through submissions. "Go to our Web site and take a look around to see what we are all about."

ⓃJACKIE PAGE

219 E. 69th St., New York NY 10021. (212)772-0346. E-mail: jackiepage@pobox.com. **Contact:** Jacqueline Page. Commercial photography representative. Estab. 1985. Represents 6 photographers. Markets include advertising agencies.

Handles Photography. "I have represented many photographers for 20+ years in the New York City Advertising industry. I now prefer to do consulting for photographers wanting to obtain major campaign work in the national market."

Terms "Details given at a personal interview." Advertises in *Workbook*.

How to Contact Send direct mail, promo pieces or e-mail with 2-3 sample pictures in JPEG format (under 200kb total). After initial contact, call for appointment to show portfolio of tearsheets, prints, chromes.

Tips Obtains new talent through recommendations from others and mailings.

PHOTOKUNST

725 Argyle Ave., Friday Harbor WA 98250. (360)378-1028. Fax: (360)370-5061. E-mail: info@photokunst.com. Web site: www.photokunst.com. **Contact:** Barbara Cox, principal. Consulting and marketing of photography archives and fine art photography, nationally and internationally. Estab. 1998. "Accepting select number of photographers on our new website. Works with artists on Lecensing, Photo Sales, Curating and traveling exhibitions, book projects."

Handles Emphasis on photojournalism, documentary and ethnographic photography. Vintage and contemporary photography.

Terms Charges for consultation, hourly/daily rate; for representation, website fee and percentage of sales.

How to Contact Send website information. Responds in 2 months.

Tips Finds new talent through submissions, recommendations from other artists, publications, art fairs, portfolio reviews. "In order to be placed in major galleries, a book or catalog must be either in place or in serious planning stage."

PHOTOTHERAPY: CONSULTANTS

(formerly Phototherapy: Rhoni Epstein + Susan Baraz), 11977 Kiowa Ave., Los Angeles CA 90049-6119. E-mail: rhoni@phototherapists.com. Web site: www.phototherapists.com. **Contact:** Rhoni Epstein. Commercial and fine art photography consultants. Expert in imagery/portfolio development, design, branding/ marketing and business plans. Estab. 1983.

"We show you how to differentiate yourself from the myriad of other photographers. Customized portfolios, marketing programs, branding materials and Web site design are developed to be compatible with you and your photography. Your imagery will be focused and tell memorable stories that will last in the viewer's mind long after your portfolio has been seen. We'll guide you to recognize and embrace your own personal style, which will fulfill you and your market." Rhoni Epstein is a photography panel moderator, portfolio reviewer, lecturer and contest judge.

How to Contact Via e-mail.

Tips "Consulting with a knowledgeable and well-respected industry insider is a valuable way to get focused and advance your career in a creative and cost-efficient manner. Always be true to your own personal vision! When researching a representative's agency, research their photographers to understand if they prefer to rep similar styles or experts in a specific area. Remain persistent and enthusiastic; there is always a market for creative and talented people."

MARIA PISCOPO

2973 Harbor Blvd., #341, Costa Mesa CA 92626-3912. Phone/fax: (888)713-0705. E-mail: maria@mpiscopo.com. Web site: www.mpiscopo.com. **Contact:** Maria Piscopo. Commercial photography representative. Estab. 1978. Member of SPAR, Women in Photography, Society of Illustrative Photographers. Markets include advertising agencies, design firms, corporations.

Handles Photography. Looking for "unique, unusual styles; established photographers only."

Terms Rep receives 25% commission. Exclusive area representation required. No geographic restrictions. Advertising costs are split: 50% paid by talent; 50% paid by representative. For promotional purposes, talent must have a website and provide 3 traveling portfolios, leave-behinds and at least 6 new promo pieces per year. Plans web, advertising and direct mail campaigns.

How to Contact Send query letter, bio, promo piece and SASE. Responds within 2 weeks, only if interested.

Tips Obtains new talent through personal referral and photo magazine articles. "Do lots of research. Be very businesslike, organized, professional and follow the above instructions!"

ALYSSA PIZER

13121 Garden Land Rd., Los Angeles CA 90049. (310)440-3930. Fax: (310)440-3830. E-mail: alyssapizer@earthlink.net. Web site: www.alyssapizer.com. **Contact:** Alyssa Pizer. Commercial photography representative. Estab. 1990. Member of APCA. Represents 10 photographers. Agency specializes in fashion, beauty and lifestyle (catalog, image campaign, department store, beauty and lifestyle awards). Markets include advertising agencies, corporations/clients direct, design firms, editorial/magazines.

Handles Photography. Established photographers only.

Terms Rep receives 25% commission. Photographer pays for FedEx and messenger charges. Talent pays 100% of advertising costs. For promotional purposes, talent must provide 10 portfolios, leave-behinds and quarterly promotional pieces.

How to Contact Send query letter or direct mail flier/brochure or e-mail Web site address.

Responds in a couple of days. After initial contact, call to schedule an appointment or drop off or mail materials for review.

Tips Obtains new talent through recommendations from clients.

THE ROLAND GROUP, INC.

4948 St. Elmo Ave., Suite 201, Bethesda MD 20814. (301)718-7955. Fax: (301)718-7958. E-mail: info@therolandgroup.com. Web site: www.therolandgroup.com. **Contact:** Rochel Roland. Commercial photography and illustration representatives and brokers. Estab. 1988. Member of SPAR, Art Directors Club and Ad Club. Represents 300 photographers, 10 illustrators. Markets include advertising agencies, corporations/clients direct, design firms and sales/promotion firms.

Handles Illustration, photography.

Terms Agent receives 35% commission. For promotional purposes, talent must provide transparencies, slides, tearsheets and a digital portfolio.

How to Contact Go to www.npnworldwide.com and complete talent recruitment form on contact page. Responds only if interested.

Tips "The Roland Group provides the NPN Worldwide Service, a global network of advertising and corporate photographers." (See separate listing in this section.)

Ⓝ VICKI SANDER/FOLIO FORUMS

48 Gramercy Park N., New York NY 10010. (212)420-1333. E-mail: vicki@vickisander.com. Web site: www.vickisander.com. Commercial photography representative. Estab. 1985. Member of SPAR, The One Club for Art and Copy, The New York Art Directors Club. Represents photographers. Markets include advertising agencies, corporate/client direct, design firms, editorial/magazines, paper products/greeting cards. "Folio Forums is a company that promotes photographers by presenting portfolios at agency conference rooms in catered breakfast reviews. Accepting submissions for consideration on a monthly basis."

Handles Photography, fine art. Looking for lifestyle, fashion, food.

Terms Rep receives 30% commission. Exclusive representation required. Advertising costs are paid by talent. For promotional purposes, talent must provide direct mail and sourcebook advertising. Advertises in *Workbook*.

How to Contact Send tearsheets. Responds in 1 month. To show portfolio, photographer should follow up with a call and/or letter after initial query.

Tips Finds new talent through recommendation from other artists, referrals. Have a portfolio put together and have promo cards to leave behind, as well as mailing out to rep prior to appointment.

TM ENTERPRISES

P.O. Box 18644, Beverly Hills CA 90209. E-mail: tmarquesusa@yahoo.com. **Contact:** Tony Marques. Commercial photography representative and photography broker. Estab. 1985. Member of Beverly Hills Chamber of Commerce. Represents 50 photographers. Agency specializes in photography of women only: high fashion, swimsuit, lingerie, glamour and fine (good taste) *Playboy*-style pictures, erotic. Markets include advertising agencies, corporations/clients direct, editorial/magazines, paper products/greeting cards, publishing/books, sales/promotion firms, medical magazines.

Handles Photography.

Terms Rep receives 50% commission. Advertising costs are paid by representative. "We promote the standard material the photographer has available, unless our clients request something else." Advertises in Europe, South and Central America, and magazines not known in the U.S.

How to Contact Send everything available. Responds in 2 days. After initial contact, drop off or mail appropriate materials for review. Portfolio should include slides, photographs, transparencies, printed work.

Tips Obtains new talent through worldwide famous fashion shows in Paris, Rome, London and Tokyo; by participating in well-known international beauty contests; recommendations from others. "Send your material clean and organized (neat). Do not borrow other photographers' work in order to get representation. Always protect yourself by copyrighting your material. Get releases from everybody who is in the picture (or who owns something in the picture)."

DOUG TRUPPE

121 E. 31st St., New York NY 10016. (212)685-1223. E-mail: doug@dougtruppe.com. Web site: www.dougtruppe.com. **Contact:** Doug Truppe, president. Commercial photography representative. Estab. 1998. Member of SPAR, Art Directors Club. Represents 8 photographers. Agency specializes in lifestyle, food, still life, portrait and children's photography. Markets include advertising agencies, corporate, design firms, editorial/magazines, publishing/books, direct mail firms.

Handles Photography. "Always looking for great commercial work." Established, working photographers only.

Terms Rep receives 25% commission. Exclusive area representation required. Advertising costs are paid by talent. For promotional purposes, talent must provide directory ad (at least 1 directory per year), direct mail promo cards every 3 months, website. Advertises in *Workbook*.

How to Contact Send e-mail with website address. Responds within 1 month, only if interested. To show portfolio, photographer should follow up with call.

Tips Finds artists through recommendations from other artists, source books, art buyers. "Please be willing to show some new work every 6 months. Have 4-6 portfolios available for representative. Have website and be willing to do direct mail every 3 months. Be professional and organized."

THE WILEY GROUP

1535 Green St., # 301, San Francisco CA 94123. (415)441-3055. Fax: (415)520-0999. E-mail: office@thewileygroup.com. Web site: www.thewileygroup.com. **Contact:** David Wiley. Commercial artist representative. Estab. 1984 "as an artist agency that promotes and sells the work of illustrators for commercial use worldwide. He has over 24 years of experience in the industry, and extensive knowledge about the usage, pricing, and marketing of commercial art. Currently represents 13 illustrators. The artists' work ranges from traditional to digital. The agency services accounts in advertising, design, and publishing as well as corporate accounts." Clients include Disney, Coca Cola, Smithsonian, Microsoft, Nike, Oracle, Google, Random House, Eli Lilly Pharmaceuticals, National Geographic, Super Bowl XLII, FedEx, Nestle Corp., and Apple Computers.

Terms Rep receives 25% commission with a bonus structure. No geographical restriction. Artist pays 75% of online agencies (Workbook.com or Theispot.com), postcards. Agent will reimburse artist for 25% of costs. Each year the artists are promoted using online agencies, monthly postcard mailings, and weekly eMailers from Adbase.com.

How to Contact For first contact, e-mail URL and one visual image representing your style. If interested, agent will e-mail or call back to discuss representation.

Tips "The bottom line is that a good agent will get you more work at better rates of pay."

Workshops & Photo Tours

Taking a photography workshop or photo tour is one of the best ways to improve your photographic skills. There is no substitute for the hands-on experience and one-on-one instruction you can receive at a workshop. Besides, where else can you go and spend several days with people who share your passion for photography?

Photography is headed in a new direction. Digital imaging is here to stay and is becoming part of every photographer's life. Even if you haven't invested a lot of money into digital cameras, computers or software, you should understand what you're up against if you plan to succeed as a professional photographer. Taking a digital imaging workshop can help you on your way.

Outdoor and nature photography are perennial workshop favorites. Creativity is another popular workshop topic. You'll also find highly specialized workshops, such as underwater photography. Many photo tours specialize in a specific location and the great photo opportunities that location affords.

As you peruse these pages, take a good look at the quality of workshops and the skill level of photographers the sponsors want to attract. It is important to know if a workshop is for beginners, advanced amateurs or professionals. Information from a workshop organizer can help you make that determination.

These workshop listings contain only the basic information needed to make contact with sponsors, and a brief description of the styles or media covered in the programs. We also include information on costs when possible. Write, call or e-mail the workshop/photo tour sponsors for complete information. Most have Web sites with extensive information about their programs, when they're offered, and how much they cost.

A workshop or photo tour can be whatever the photographer wishes—a holiday from the normal working routine, or an exciting introduction to new skills and perspectives on the craft. Whatever you desire, you're sure to find in these pages a workshop or tour that fulfills your expectations.

Workshops

⊠ EDDIE ADAMS WORKSHOP

P.O. Box 1458, Peter Stuyvesant Station NY 10009. (212)358-1818. Fax: (212)388-1713. E-mail: producer@eddieadamsworkshop.com. Web site: www.eddieadamsworkshop.com. **Contact:** Mirjam Evers, workshop producer. Annual tuition-free photojournalism workshop. The Eddie Adams Workshop brings together 100 promising young photographers with over 150 of the most influential picture journalists, picture editors, managing editors and writers from prestigious organizations such as the Associated Press, CNN, The White House, *Life, National Geographic, Newsweek, Time, Parade, Entertainment Weekly, Sports Illustrated, The New York Times, The Los Angeles Times* and *The Washington Post.* Pulitzer-prize winning photographer Eddie Adams created this program to allow young photographers to learn from experienced professionals about the story-telling power and social importance of photography. Participants are divided into 10 teams, each headed by a photographer, editor, producer, or multimedia person. Daily editing and critiquing help each student to hone skills and learn about the visual, technical, and emotional components of creating strong journalistic images. Open to photography students and professional photographers with 3 years or less of experience. Photographers should e-mail for more information.

ALASKA'S SEAWOLF ADVENTURES

P.O. Box 312, Gustavus AK 99826. (907)957-1438. E-mail: seawolfadventures@earthlink.net. Web site: www.seawolfadventures.net. **Contact**: Kimber Owen. Cost: $3,180/6 days. ''Photograph glaciers, whales, bears, wolves, incredible scenics, etc., while using the Seawolf, a 97-foot, 12-passenger expedition ship, as your base camp in the Glacier Bay area.''

ALDERMAN'S SLICKROCK ADVENTURES

19 W. Center St., Kanab UT 84741. (435)644-5981. E-mail: fotomd@xpressweb.com. Web site: www.utahcameras.com. **Contact:** Terry G. Alderman, master photographer. Cost: $85/day; 2-person minimum. Covers landscape photography of ghost towns, arches, petroglyphs and narrow canyons in the back country of Southern Utah and the Arizona Strip.

ANCHELL PHOTOGRAPHY WORKSHOPS

879 Cottage Street NE, Salem OR 97301. (503)375-2163. Fax: (503)588-4003. E-mail: info@anchellworkshops.com. Web site: www.anchellworkshops.com. **Contact:** Steve Anchell. Cost: $250-2,500. Film or digital, group or private workshops held throughout the year, including large-format, 35mm, studio lighting, figure, darkroom, both color and b&w, travel. Open to all skill levels. Photographers should write, call or e-mail for more information.

ANDERSON RANCH ARTS CENTER

P.O. Box 5598, Snowmass Village CO 81615. (970)923-3181. Fax: (970)923-3871. E-mail: reg@andersonranch.org. Web site: www.andersonranch.org. Digital media and photography workshops, June through September, feature distinguished artists and educators from around the world. Classes range from traditional silver and alternative photographic processes to digital formats and use of the computer as a tool for time-based and interactive works of art. Program is diversifying into video, animation, sound and installations.

ARIZONA HIGHWAYS PHOTO WORKSHOPS

Friends of Arizona Highways, P.O. Box 6106, Phoenix AZ 85005-6106. (888)790-7042. E-mail: Rnoll@azdot.gov. Web site: www.friendsofazhighways.com. **Contact:**Robyn Noll, director. Offers photo adventures to the American West's most spectacular locations with top professional photographers whose work routinely appears in *Arizona Highways* magazine.

ARROWMONT SCHOOL OF ARTS AND CRAFTS

556 Parkway, Gatlinburg TN 37738. (865)436-5860. E-mail: info@arrowmont.org. Web site: www.arrowmont.org. Tuition ranges from $365-435 per week. Housing and meal packages begin at $285 (1 week) and $608 (2 weeks). Offers weekend, 1- and 2-week spring, summer and fall workshops in photography, drawing, painting, clay, metals/enamels, kiln glass, fibers, surface design, wood turning and furniture. Residencies, studio assistantships, work study, and scholarships are available.

⊠ ART NEW ENGLAND SUMMER WORKSHOPS @ BENNINGTON VT

Massachusetts College of Art, 621 Huntington Avenue, 2nd Floor, Tower Building, Boston MA 02115. (617)879-7200. Fax: (617)879-7171. E-mail: continuing_education@massart.edu. Web site: www.massartplus.org. **Contact:** Nancy McCarthy, coordinator. Weeklong workshops in August, run by Massachusetts College of Art. Areas of concentration include b&w, alternative processes, digital printing and many more. Photographers should call, e-mail or see Web site for more information.

⊠ ART OF NATURE PHOTOGRAPHY WORKSHOPS

3581 Schooner Ridge Dr., Alpharetta GA 30005-4289. (770)752-8566. Fax: (770)752-7080. E-mail: charles@charlesneedlephoto.com. Web site: www.charlesneedlephoto.com. **Contact:** Charles Needle, founder/instructor. Cost: $125-1,5000 depending on the workshop; U.S. and international locations; includes personalized one-on-one field and classroom instruction and supportive image evaluations. Emphasis on creative camera techniques in the field and digital darkroom, allowing students to express "the art of nature" with unique personal vision. Topics include creative macro, intimate landscapes and scenics, dynamic composition and lighting, etc. Open to all skill levels. Photographers should call, e-mail, see Web site for more information.

ART WORKSHOPS IN GUATEMALA

4758 Lyndale Ave. S., Minneapolis MN 55419-5304. (612)825-0747. E-mail: info@artguat.org. Web site: www.artguat.org. **Contact:** Liza Fourre, director. Cost: $1,825; includes tuition, lodging, breakfast, ground transport. Annual workshops held in Antigua, Guatemala. Workshops include Adventure Travel Photo with Steve Northup, Portraiture/Photographing the Soul of Indigenous Guatemala with Nance Ackerman, Photography/Capturing Guatemala's Light and Contrasts with David Wells, Travel Photography/Indigenous Peoples, and Spirit of Place with Doug Beasley.

BACHMANN TOUR OVERDRIVE

P.O. Box 950833, Lake Mary FL 32746. (407)333-9988. E-mail: bill@billbachmann.com. Web site: www.billbachmann.com. **Contact:** Bill Bachmann, owner. Cost varies; see Web site for prices. Bill Bachmann shares his knowledge and adventures with small groups

Workshops

several times a year. Past trips have been to China, Tibet, South Africa, Antarctica, India, Nepal, Australia, New Zealand, New Guinea, Guatemala and Honduras. Future trips will be to Cuba, Italy, Greece, Peru, Brazil, Argentina and other destinations. Programs are designed for adventure travelers who love photography and want to learn stock photography from a top stock photographer. Open to all skill levels. Photographers should write, call or e-mail after seeing Web site for information, times and prices.

NOELLA BALLENGER & ASSOCIATES PHOTO WORKSHOPS

P.O. Box 457, La Canada CA 91012. (818)954-0933. Fax: (818)954-0910. E-mail: Noella1B@ aol.com. Web site: www.noellaballenger.com. **Contact:** Noella Ballenger. Travel and nature workshops/tours, West Coast locations. Individual instruction in small groups emphasizes visual awareness, composition, and problem-solving in the field. All formats and levels of expertise welcome. Call or write for information.

FRANK BALTHIS PHOTOGRAPHY WORKSHOPS

P.O. Box 255, Davenport CA 95017. (831)426-8205. E-mail: frankbalthis@yahoo.com. Web site: http://www.digitalrailroad.net/FrankBalthis. **Contact:** Frank S. Balthis, photographer/owner. Cost depends on the length of program and travel costs. "Workshops emphasize natural history, wildlife and travel photography, often providing opportunities to photograph marine mammals." Worldwide locations range from Baja California to Alaska. Frank Balthis runs a stock photo business and is the publisher of the Nature's Design line of cards and other publications.

BETTERPHOTO.COM ONLINE PHOTOGRAPHY COURSES

16544 NE 79th St., Redmond WA 98052. (888) 927-9992. Fax: (425)881-0309. E-mail: bpsupport@betterphoto.com. Web site: www.betterphoto.com. **Contact:** Jim Miotke, president. Cost: Online courses including personal critiques from professional photographers cost $198-348 for 4- and 8-week sessions. BetterPhoto.com is the worldwide leader in online photography education, offering an approachable resource for photographers who want to improve their skills, share their photos, and learn more about the art and technique of photography. BetterPhoto offers over 100 photography courses that are taught by top professional photographers. Courses begin the 1st Wednesday of every month. Courses range in skill level from beginner to advanced and consist of inspiring weekly lessons and personal feedback on students' photos from the instructors. "We provide Web sites for photographers, photo sharing solutions, free online newsletters, lively Q&A and photo discussions, a free monthly contest, helpful articles and online photography courses." Open to all skill levels.

BIRDS AS ART/INSTRUCTIONAL PHOTO-TOURS

P.O. Box 7245, 4041 Granada Dr., Indian Lake Estates FL 33855. (863)692-0906. E-mail: birdsasart@verizon.net. Web site: www.birdsasart.com. **Contact:** Arthur Morris, instructor. Cost: varies, approximately $300/day. The tours, which visit the top bird photography hot spots in North America, feature evening in-classroom lectures, breakfast and lunch, in-the-field instruction, 6 or more hours of photography, and most importantly, easily approachable yet free and wild subjects.

BLACK AND WHITE PHOTOGRAPHIC WORKSHOPS

P.O. Box 27555, Seattle WA 98165. (206)367-6864. Fax: (206)367-8102. E-mail: mark@infin ityworkshops.com. Web site: www.infinityworkshops.com. **Contact:** Mark Griffith, director. Cost: $795. Lodging and food are not included in any workshop fee. Location workshops on the Oregon coast and Southern Utah. Open to all digital and film users, color or black and white. Call, e-mail, or see Web site for information.

BLUE PLANET PHOTOGRAPHY WORKSHOPS AND TOURS

1526 W. Charlotte Ct., Suite 107, Nampa ID 83687. (208)466-9340. E-mail: inquire@bluepla netphoto.com. Web site: www.blueplanetphoto.com. **Contact:** Mike Shipman, owner/photographer. Cost: varies depending on type and length of workshop ($250-5,000; average: $1,900). Award-winning professional photographer and former wildlife biologist Mike Shipman conducts small group workshops/tours emphasizing individual expression and "vision-finding" by Breaking the Barriers to Creative Vision™. Workshops held in beautiful locations away from crowds and the more-often-photographed sites. Some workshops are semi-adventure-travel style, using alternative transportation such as hot air balloons, horseback, llama, and camping in remote areas. Group feedback sessions, digital presentations and film processing whenever possible. Workshops and tours held in western U.S., Alaska, Canada and overseas. Onsite transportation and lodging during workshop usually included; meals included on some trips. Specific fees, optional activities and gear list outlined in tour materials. Digital photographers welcome. Workshops and tours range from 2 to 12 days, sometimes longer; average is 9 days. Custom tours and workshops available upon request. Open to all skill levels. Photographers should write, call, e-mail or see Web site for more information.

NANCY BROWN HANDS-ON WORKSHOPS

381 Mohawk Lane, Boca Raton FL 33487. (561)988-8992. Fax: (561)988-1791. E-mail: nbro wn50@bellsouth.net. Web site: www.nancybrown.com. **Contact:** Nancy. Cost: $2,000. Offers one-on-one intensive workshops all year long in studio and on location in Florida. You work with Nancy, the models and the crew to create your images. Photographers should call, fax, e-mail or see Web site for more information.

⊕ BURREN COLLEGE OF ART WORKSHOPS

Burren College of Art, Newton Castle, Ballyvaughan, County Clare, Ireland. (353)(65)707-7200. Fax: (353)(65)707-7201. E-mail: anna@burrencollege.ie. Web site: www.burrencolle ge.ie. **Contact:** Admissions Officer. "These workshops present unique opportunities to capture the qualities of Ireland's western landscape. The flora, prehistoric tombs, ancient abbeys and castles that abound in the Burren provide an unending wealth of subjects in an ever-changing light." Photographers should e-mail for more information.

CALIFORNIA PHOTOGRAPHIC WORKSHOPS

2500 N. Texas St., Fairfield CA 94533. (888)422-6606. E-mail: cpwschool@sbcglobal.net. Web site: www.CPWschool.com. **Contact:** James Inks. 3 and ½ day workshops in professional photography at the Chaminade Resort.

⊕ CAMARGO FOUNDATION VISUAL ARTS FELLOWSHIP

1, Avenue Jermini, 13260 Cassis, France. E-mail: apply@camargofoundation.org. Web site: www.camargofoundation.org. **Contact**. Applications Coordinator. Semester-long residencies awarded to visual artists, creative writers, composers, and academics. Artists may work on a specific project, develop a body of work, etc. Fellows must live on-site at foundation headquarters for the duration of the term. One-semester residential grants (September-December or January-May). Each fellow receives a $2,500 stipend. Open to advanced photographers. **January 12 deadline.** Photographers should visit Web site to apply.

Ⓝ CAMERA BUG TOURS & WORKSHOPS

2106 Hoffnagle Street, Philadelphia PA 19152.215-742-5515. E-mail: cambug8480@aol.com. Web site: www.shutterbugstv.com. **Contact:** Nick or Len, coordinators. Cost: Day excursions: $75-125, includes meal. Transportation may or may not be included, depending on destination and group size. Also cruises out of Philadelphia to Bermuda starting at $609 per person for a double occupancy cabin, plus insurance, taxes, and fuel charges. Next excursions scheduled for Fall 2008 and Spring 2009.Open to all skill levels. Photographers should e-mail. Provides basic photo tips in Nature and Environmental Photography and birding photos with Dwight Molotsky.

JOHN C. CAMPBELL FOLK SCHOOL

One Folk School Rd., Brasstown NC 28902. (800)365-5724 or (828)837-2775. Fax: (828)837-8637 Web site: www.folkschool.org. Cost: $250-442 tuition; room and board available for additional fee. The Folk School offers weekend and weeklong courses in photography year-round. "Please call for free catalog."

Ⓝ CAPE COD PHOTO WORKSHOPS

46 Main St., P.O. Box 1687, Orleans MA 02653. (508)255-5202. E-mail: bob@bobkornimaging.com. Web site: www.bobkornimaging.com. **Contact:** Bob Korn, director. Cost: $365-575. Photography workshops for the digital photographer. All skill levels. Workshops run year round. Photographers should call, e-mail or see Web site for more information.

THE CENTER FOR FINE ART PHOTOGRAPHY

400 N. College Ave., Fort Collins CO 80524. (907)224-1010. Web site: www.c4fap.org/workshops_intro.asp. Cost: varies depending on workshop, $10-195. Offers worshops and forums by photographers who have skills in the subject they present, including Photoshop; photography basics with film and digital; studio lighting. Open to all skill levels. Photographers should write, call, see Web site for more information.

CENTER FOR PHOTOGRAPHY AT WOODSTOCK

59 Tinker St., Woodstock NY 12498. (845)679-9957. Fax: (845)679-6337. E-mail: info@cpw.org. Web site: www.cpw.org. **Contact**: Ariel Shanberg, executive director. A not-for-profit arts and education organization dedicated to contemporary creative photography, founded in 1977. Programs in education, exhibition, publication, and services for artists. This includes year-round exhibitions, summer/fall Woodstock Photography Workshop and Lecture Series, artist residencies, PHOTOGRAPHY Quarterly magazine, annual call for entries, permanent print collection, slide registry, library, darkroom, fellowship, membership, portfolio review, film/video screenings, internships, gallery talks and more.

🌐 CATHY CHURCH PERSONAL UNDERWATER PHOTOGRAPHY COURSES

P.O. Box 479, Grand Cayman, KY1-1106 Cayman Islands. (345)949-7415. Fax: (345)949-9770. E-mail: cathy@cathychurch.com. Web site: www.cathychurch.com. **Contact:** Cathy

Church. Cost: $125/hour. Hotel/dive package available at Sunset House Hotel. Private and group lessons available for all levels throughout the year; classroom and shore diving can be arranged. Lessons available for professional photographers expanding to underwater work. Photographers should e-mail for more information.

CLICKERS & FLICKERS PHOTOGRAPHY NETWORK—LECTURES & WORKSHOPS

P.O. Box 6094, Malibu CA 90264-6094 and P.O. Box 60508, Pasadena CA 91116-6508. (626)794-7447. E-mail: photographer@ClickersAndFlickers.com. Web site: www.ClickersAndFlickers.com. **Contact:** Dawn Stevens, organizer. Estab. 1985. Cost: depends on particular event. Monthly networking dinners with outstanding guest speakers (many award winners, including the Pulitzer Prize), events and free activities for members. "Clickers & Flickers Photography Network, Inc., was created to provide people with an interest and passion for photography (cinematography, filmmaking, image making) the opportunity to meet others with similar interests for networking and camaraderie. It creates an environment in which photography issues, styles, techniques, enjoyment and appreciation can be discussed and viewed as well as experienced with people from many fields and levels of expertise (beginners, students, amateur, hobbyist, or professionals, gallery owners and museum curators). We publish a bimonthly color magazine listing thousands of activities for photographers and lovers of images." Most of its content is not on our Web site for a reason. Membership and magazine subscriptions help support this organization. Clickers & Flickers Photography Network, Inc., is a 21-year-old professional photography network association that promotes information and offers promotional marketing opportunities for photographers, cinematographers, individuals, organizations, businesses, and events. "C&F also provides referrals for photographers. Our membership includes photographers, videographers, and cinematographers who are skilled in the following types of photography: outdoor and nature, wedding, headshots, fine art, sports, events, products, news, glamour, fashion, macro, commercial, landscape, advertising, architectural, wildlife, candid, photojournalism, marquis gothic—fetish, aerial and underwater; using the following types of equipment: motion picture cameras (Imax, 70mm, 65mm, 35mm, 16mm, 8mm), steadicam systems, video, high-definition, digital, still photography—large format, medium format and 35mm." Open to all skill levels. Photographers should call or e-mail for more information.

COMMUNITY DARKROOM

713 Monroe Ave., Rochester NY 14607. (585)271-5920. E-mail: darkroom@geneseearts.org. Web site: www.geneseearts.org. **Contact:** Sharon Turner, director. Associate Director: Marianne Pojman and Karlie Cary Lanni, program assistant. Costs $65-210, depending on type and length of class. "We offer 30 different photography and digital classes for all ages on a quarterly basis utilizing digital and vintage processes. Classes include 35mm and digital camera techniques; black & white darkroom techniques; composition; studio lighting and available light; Photoshop, Dreamweaver, InDesign, and Illustrator; wet plate collodion, cyanotype, salt printing, liquid emulsion, and gum biochromate, and many special topics including nature, sports, architecture, night photography, photojournalism, and portraiture."

CONE EDITIONS WORKSHOPS

17 Powder Spring Rd., East Topsham VT 05076. (802)439-5751, ext. 101. Fax: (802)439-6501. E-mail: cathy@cone-editions.com. Web site: www.coneeditions.com. **Contact:** Cathy

Cone. Cost: varies per workshop. See Web site for details on workshop dates and prices. Workshops in Piezography b&w digital printing, digital cameras, various workshops with Jon Cone, George DeWolfe, Larry Danque, Tyler Boley, Amaduo Diallo, Phil Bard, Clyde Butcher. Open to all skill levels. Photographers should call, e-mail, see Web site for more information.

THE CORPORATION OF YADDO RESIDENCIES

P.O. Box 395, Saratoga Springs NY 12866-0395. (518)584-0746. Fax: (518)584-1312. E-mail: yaddo@yaddo.org. Web site: www.yaddo.org. **Contact:** Candace Wait, program director. No fee; room, board, and studio space are provided. Deadlines to apply are January 1 and August 1—residencies are offered year round. Yaddo is a working artists' community on a 400-acre estate in Saratoga Springs, New York. It offers residencies of 2 weeks to 2 months to creative artists in a variety of fields. The mission of Yaddo is to encourage artists to challenge themselves by offering a supportive environment and good working conditions. Open to advanced photographers. Photographers should write, send SASE (63¢ postage), call or e-mail for more information.

⊕ THE CORTONA CENTER OF PHOTOGRAPHY, ITALY

P.O. Box 550894, Atlanta GA 30355. (404)872-3264. E-mail: allen@cortonacenter.com. Web site: www.cortonacenter.com. **Contact:** Allen Matthews, director. Robin Davis and Allen Matthews lead a personal, small-group photography workshop in the ancient city of Cortona, Italy, centrally located in Tuscany, once the heart of the Renaissance. Dramatic landscapes; Etruscan relics; Roman, Medieval and Renaissance architecture; and the wonderful and photogenic people of Tuscany await. Photographers should write, e-mail or see Web site for more information.

CORY PHOTOGRAPHY WORKSHOPS

P.O. Box 42, Signal Mountain TN 37377. (423)886-1004. E-mail: tompatcory@aol.com. Web site: www.tomandpatcory.com. **Contact:** Tom or Pat Cory. Small workshops/field trips (8-12 maximum participants) with some formal instruction, but mostly one-on-one instruction in the field. "Since we tailor this instruction to each individual's interests, our workshops are suitable for all experience levels. Participants are welcome to use film or digital cameras or even video. Our emphasis is on nature and travel photography. We spend the majority of our time in the field, exploring our location. Cost and length vary by workshop. Many of our workshop fees include single-occupancy lodging, and some also include home-cooked meals and snacks. We offer special prices for 2 people sharing the same room, and, in some cases, special non-participant prices. Workshop locations vary from year to year but include the Eastern Sierra of California, Colorado and Arches National Park, Olympic National Park, Acadia National Park, the Upper Peninsula of Michigan, Death Valley National Park, Smoky Mountain National Park, and Glacier National Park. We offer international workshops in Ireland, Scotland, Provence, Brittany, Tuscany, New Zealand, Newfoundland, Wales, Iceland, Costa Rica and Panama. We also offer a number of short workshops throughout the year in and around Chattanooga, Tennessee—individual instruction and custom-designed workshops for groups." Photographers should write, call, e-mail or see Web site for more information.

COUPEVILLE ARTS CENTER/PHOTOGRAPHY

15 NW Birch St., Coupeville WA 98239. (360)678-3396. Tollfree: (877)678-3396. E-mail: info@coupevillearts.org. Web site: www.coupevillearts.org. **Contact:** Registrar. Cost: varies. Workshops are held on Whidbey Island and at various other locations. Topics are new and varied every year .

CREALDÉ SCHOOL OF ART

600 St. Andrews Blvd., Winter Park FL 32792. (407)671-1886. Web site: www.crealde.org. **Contact:** Peter Schreyer, executive director. Director of Photography: Rick Lang. Cost: Membership fee begins at $35/individual. Offers classes covering traditional and digital photography; b&w darkroom techniques; landscape, portrait, documentary, travel, wildlife and abstract photography; and educational tours.

CREATIVE ARTS WORKSHOP

80 Audubon St., New Haven CT 06511. (203)562-4927. E-mail: hshapiro8@aol.com. Web site: www.creativeartsworkshop.org. **Contact:** Harold Shapiro, photography department head. Offers advanced workshops and exciting courses for beginning and serious photographers. Traditional darkroom and digital classes.

⬛ ⬛ DAWSON COLLEGE CENTRE FOR TRAINING AND DEVELOPMENT

4001 de Maisonneuve Blvd. W., Suite 2G.1, Montreal QC H3Z 3G4 Canada. (514)933-0047. Fax: (514)937-3832. E-mail: ctd@dawsoncollege.qc.ca. Web site: www.dawsoncollege.qc .ca/ctd. **Contact:** Roula Koutsoumbas. Cost: $90-595. Workshop subjects include imaging arts and technologies, computer animation, photography, digital imaging, desktop publishing, multimedia, and web publishing and design.

THE JULIA DEAN PHOTO WORKSHOPS

801 Ocean Front Walk, Studio 8, Venice CA 90291. (310)392-0909. Fax: (310)664-0809. E-mail: workshops@juliadean.com. Web site: www.juliadean.com. **Contact:** Brandon Gannon, general manager. Photography workshops of all kinds held throughout the year, including alternative and fine art, photography fundamentals, digital photography and travel workshops. Now offering workshops in Los Angeles, Santa Ana, Oceanside, Escondido and San Diego. Open to all skill levels. Photographers should call, e-mail or see Web site for more information.

CYNTHIA DELANEY PHOTO WORKSHOPS

168 Maple St., Elko NV 89801. (775)753-5833. E-mail: cynthia@cynthiadelaney.com. Web site: www.cynthiadelaney.com. **Contact:** Cynthia Delaney, owner/photographer. Cost: $250-4,000. Held in periodically throughout the year. Workshops focus on outdoor, travel and creative photography. Destinations include several locations in the western U.S. and tours abroad, including Peru, Costa Rica, and Nevada." e are continuing to add new itineraries to the schedule. We welcome both film and digital shooters. The group size is kept small so that each participant will have plenty of one-on-one instruction." Open to all skill levels. Photographers should see Web site for more information.

DIGITAL WILDLIFE PHOTOGRAPHY FIELD SCHOOL

P.O. Box 236, South Wellfleet MA 02663. (508)349-2615. E-mail: mlowe@massaudubon.o rg. **Contact:** Melissa Lowe, program coordinator. Cost: $325-350. Four-day course on Cape

Cod focusing on wildlife photography using digital technology. Course covers fundamentals of shooting wildlife in a natural setting and an introduction to editing images using photoshop. Taught by Shawn Carey and Eric Smith. Sponsored by Massachusetts Audubon Society.

⃞Ⓝ ELOQUENT LIGHT PHOTOGRAPHY WORKSHOPS

903 W. Alameda Street, No. 115, Santa Fe NM 87501. (505) 983-2934. E-mail: cindylane@eloquentlight.com. Web site: www.eloquentlight.com. **Contact:** Cindy Lane, managing director. "Step into the light! While our name is new, we have been offering photography workshops in the southwest for over 20 years. What was once the prestigious New Mexico Photography Field School has become the exciting new Eloquent Light Photography Workshops. We absolutely know the southwest. We know how to guide you to the best locations - to capture that special atmosphere at just the right moment. We're experts and enjoy sharing our passion for making photographs. We offer small groups with lots of individual attention. A photography workshop should be about helping you become a better photographer and helping you make great photographs. It should be about you and how photography fits into your world." Field school director and instructor Craig Varjabedian has been teaching photography for over 25 years. His photographs are known for their interpretation of light and place in the Southwest. His works are widely exhibited and collected. A workshop catalogue is available upon request.

JOE ENGLANDER PHOTOGRAPHY WORKSHOPS & TOURS

P.O. Box 1261, Manchaca TX 78652. (512)922-8686. E-mail: info@englander-workshops.com. Web site: www.englander-workshops.com. **Contact:** Joe Englander. Cost: $275-8,000. Instruction in beautiful locations throughout the world, all formats and media, color/b&w/digital, photoshop instruction. Locations include Europe, Asia with special emphasis on Bhutan and the Himalayas and the US. See Web site for more information.

EUROPA PHOTOGENICA PHOTO TOURS TO EUROPE

(formerly France Photogenique/Europa Photogenica Photo Tours to Europe), 3920 W. 231st Place, Torrance CA 90505. Phone/fax: (310)378-2821. E-mail: FraPhoto@aol.com. Web site: www.europaphotogenica.com. **Contact:** Barbara Van Zanten-Stolarski, owner. Cost: $2,700-3,600; includes meals, transportation, hotel accommodation. Tuition provided for beginners/intermediate and advanced level. Workshops held in spring (3-5) and fall (1-3). Five- to 11-day photo tours of the most beautiful regions of Europe. Shoot landscapes, villages, churches, cathedrals, vineyards, outdoor markets, cafes and people in Paris, Provence, southwest France, England, Italy, Greece, etc. Open to all skill levels. Photographers should call or e-mail for more information.

EXPOSURE36 PHOTOGRAPHY

805 SE 17th Place, Portland OR 97233. (866)368-6736. E-mail: info@exposure36.com. Web site: www.exposure36.com. Cost: varies, depending on workshop Open to all skill levels. Workshops offered at prime locations in the U.S. and Canada, including Yosemite, Smoky Mountains, Bryce Canyon, the Oregon coast. Also offers classes on the basics of photography in Portland, Oregon (through the Experimental College or Mt. Hood Community College) and Seattle, Washington (through the Experimental College of the University of Washington). Photographers should write, call, e-mail, see Web site for more information.

FINDING & KEEPING CLIENTS

2973 Harbor Blvd., Suite 341, Costa Mesa CA 92626-3912. Phone/fax: (888)713-0705. E-mail: maria@mpiscopo.com. Web site: www.mpiscopo.com. **Contact:** Maria Piscopo, instructor. "How to find new photo assignment clients and get paid what you're worth! See Web site for schedule or send query via e-mail." Maria Piscopo is the author of *The Photographer's Guide to Marketing & Self Promotion*, 3rd edition(Allworth Press).

FINE ARTS WORK CENTER

24 Pearl St., Provincetown MA 02657. (508)487-9960, ext. 103. Fax: (508)487-8873. E-mail: workshops@fawc.org. Web site: www.fawc.org. **Contact:** Dorothy Antczak, summer program director. Cost: $700/week, $625/week (housing). Faculty includes Constantine Manos, David Graham, Amy Arbus, Marian Roth, Gabe Greenburg, Joanne Dugan, David Hilliard, and Connie Imboden. Write, call or e-mail for more information.

FIRST LIGHT PHOTOGRAPHIC WORKSHOPS AND SAFARIS

P.O. Box 240, East Moriches NY 11940. (631)581-0400. Web site: www.firstlightphotography.com. **Contact**: Bill Rudock, president. Photo workshops and photo safaris for all skill levels held on Long Island, NY, and specializing in national parks, domestic and international; also presents workshops for portrait and wedding photographers .

FIRST LIGHT PHOTOGRAPHY WORKSHOP TOURS

P.O. Box 36201, Lakewood CO 80227. (720)962-5929. E-mail: andy@firstlighttours.com. Web site: www.firstlighttours.com. **Contact:** Andy Long, owner. Cost: $1,095-4,395, depending on tour; hotels, meals and ground transportaion included. Tours are held in a variety of locations, including Penguins of Falkland Islands, Tasmania, Oregon coast, southwest Alaska, Alaskan northern lights, Florida, south Texas birds, Glacier National Park, historic Taos and Santa Fe, Bosque del Apache Wildlife Preserve, and more. See Web site for more information on locations, dates and prices. Open to all skill levels. Photographers should call, e-mail, see Web site for more information.

FLORENCE PHOTOGRAPHY WORKSHOP

Washington University, College of Art, Campus P.O. Box 1031, St. Louis MO 63130. (314)935-6500. E-mail: strembicki@wustl.edu. Web site: www.artsci.wustl.edu/~photo/florenc.html. **Contact**: Stan Strembicki, professor. "Four-week intensive photographic study of urban and rural landscape of Florence and Tuscany. Digital darkroom, field trips within Florence, housing available."

FOCUS ADVENTURES

P.O. Box 771640, Steamboat Springs CO 80477. Phone/fax: (970)879-2244. E-mail: karen@focusadventures.com. Web site: www.focusadventures.com. **Contact:** Karen Gordon Schulman, owner. Photo workshops and tours emphasize the art of seeing and personal photographic vision. Summer digital photo workshops in Steamboat Springs, Colorado. Field trips to working ranches, the rodeo and wilderness areas. New fall digital workshop offered at Focus Ranch, a private guest ranch in NW Colorado. Customized private and small-group lessons available year-round. International photo tours and workshops to various destinations including Ecuador, the Galapagos Islands, Morocco and western Ireland.

FOTOFUSION

55 NE Second Ave., Delray Beach FL 33444. (561)276-9797. Fax: (561)276-9132. E-mail: info@fotofusion.org. Web site: www.fotofusion.org. **Contact:** Fatima NeJame, executive director. America's foremost festival of photography and digital imaging is held each January. Learn from more than 90 master photographers, picture editors, picture agencies, gallery directors, and technical experts, over 5 days of field trips, seminars, lectures and Adobe Photoshop CS workshops. January 15-19, 2008. Open to all skill levels. Photographers should write, call or e-mail for more information.

GAĹPAGOS TRAVEL

783 Rio Del Mar Blvd., Suite 49, Aptos CA 95003. (800)969-9014. E-mail: info@galapagostravel.com. Web site: www.galapagostravel.com. Cost: $4,500 plus fuel surcharges; includes lodging and most meals. Landscape and wildlife photography tour of the islands with an emphasis on natural history. Three nights in a first-class hotel in Quito, Ecuador, and 11 or 14 nights aboard a yacht in the GaĹpagos. See Web site for more information.

🅽 📷 ANDRÉ GALLANT/FREEMAN PATTERSON PHOTO WORKSHOPS

Shampers Bluff NB Canada. (506)763-2189. E-mail: freepatt@nbnet.nb.ca. Web site: www.freemanpatterson.com. Cost: $1900 plus13% HST (Canadian) for 6-day course including accommodations and meals. All workshops are for anybody interested in photography and visual design, from the novice to the experienced amateur or professional. "Our experience has consistently been that a mixed group functions best and learns the most."

GERLACH NATURE PHOTOGRAPHY WORKSHOPS & TOURS

P.O. Box 642, Ashton ID 83420. (208)652-4444. E-mail: michele@gerlachnaturephoto.com. Web site: www.gerlachnaturephoto.com. **Contact:** Michele Smith, office manager. Costs vary. Professional nature photographers John and Barbara Gerlach conduct intensive field workshops in the beautiful Upper Peninsula of Michigan in August and during October's fall color period. They lead a photo safari to the best game parks in Kenya during late-August/early-September every year. They also lead winter, summer and fall photo tours of Yellowstone National Park and conduct high-speed flash hummingbird photo workshops in British Columbia in late May. Barbara and John work for an outfitter a couple weeks a year leading photo tours into Yellowstone Back Country with the use of horses. This is a wonderful way to experience Yellowstone. Photographers should see Web site for more information.

GLOBAL PRESERVATION PROJECTS

P.O. Box 30866, Santa Barbara CA 93130. (805)682-3398 or (805)455-2790. E-mail: TIMorse@aol.com. Web site: www.GlobalPreservationProjects.com. **Contact:** Thomas I. Morse, director. Offers photographic workshops and expeditions promoting the preservation of environmental and historic treasures. Produces international photographic exhibitions and publications. GPP workshops include the ghost town of Bodie, CA; Digital Basics for Photographers held in Santa Barbara, CA; expeditions to Arches and Canyonlands; Durango Fall and Winter, Big Sur; Slot Canyons; White Sands; Death Valley and other places. GPP uses a 34-ft. motor home with state-of-the art digital imaging and printer systems for participants use. Photographers should call, e-mail or see Web site for more information.

GOLDEN GATE SCHOOL OF PROFESSIONAL PHOTOGRAPHY

P.O. Box F, San Mateo CA 94402-0018. (650)548-0889. E-mail: goldengateschool@yahoo.com. Web site: www.goldengateschool.org. **Contact:** Julie Olson, director. Offers 1- to 4-day workshops in traditional and digital photography for professional and aspiring photographers in the San Francisco Bay Area.

ROB GOLDMAN CREATIVE WORKSHOPS

55 West Main St., Oyster Bay NY 11771. (631)424-1650. Fax: (631)424-1650. E-mail: rob@rgoldman.com. Web site: www.rgoldman.com. **Contact:** Rob Goldman, photographer. Cost varies depending on type and length of workshop. 1-on-1 customized photography lessons for all levels, plus intensive workshops held 2-3 times/year. Purpose is artistic and personal growth for photographers. Open to all skill levels. Photographers should call or e-mail for more information.

HALLMARK INSTITUTE OF PHOTOGRAPHY

P.O. Box 308, Turners Falls MA 01376. (413)863-2478. E-mail: info@hallmark.edu. Web site: www.hallmark.edu. **Contact:** George J. Rosa III, president. Director of Admissions: Andy Vecellio. Tuition: $49,450. Offers an intensive 10-month resident program teaching the technical, artistic and business aspects of traditional and digital professional photography for the career-minded individual.

🄽 JOHN HART PORTRAIT SEMINARS

344 W. 72nd St., New York NY 10023. (212)873-6585. E-mail: johnhartstudio1@mac.com; johnharth@aol.com. Web site: www.johnhartpics.com. One-on-one advanced portraiture seminars covering lighting and other techniques. John Hart is a New York University faculty member and author of *50 Portrait Lighting Techniques*, *Professional Headshots*, *Lighting For Action* and *Art of the Storyboard*.

HAWAII PHOTO SEMINARS

Changing Image Workshops, P.O. Box 280, Kualapuu, Molokai HI 96757. (808)567-6430. E-mail: hui@aloha.net. Web site: www.huiho.org. **Contact:** Rik Cooke. Cost: $2,150; includes lodging, meals and ground transportation. Seven-day landscape photography workshop for beginners to advanced photographers. Workshops taught by 2 *National Geographic* photographers and a multimedia producer.

🄽 HAWAII PHOTO TOURS, POLAROID, FUJI & DIGITAL TRANSFERS, DIGITAL INFRARED, DIGITAL PHOTOGRAPHY, PHOTOSHOP WORKSHOPS & PRIVATE TOURS AND SESSIONS

P.O. Box 335, Honaunau HI 96726. (808)328-2162. E-mail: kcarr@kathleencarr.com. Web site: www.kathleencarr.com. **Contact:** Kathleen T. Carr. Cost: $85-100/day plus $30 for materials. Carr, author of *Polaroid Transfers* and *Polaroid Manipulations: A Complete Visual Guide to Creating SX-70, Transfer and Digital Prints* (Amphoto Books), and *To Honor the Earth*, offers her expertise on the subjects for photographers of all skill levels. Programs last 1-7 days in various locations in Hawaii, California, Montana and other locales.

HEART OF NATURE PHOTOGRAPHY WORKSHOPS

P.O. Box 1214, Volcano HI 96785. (808)345-7179. E-mail: info@heartofnature.net. Web site: www.heartofnature.net. **Contact:** Robert Frutos or Jenny Thompson. Cost: $345-2,695,

Workshops

depending on workshop/tours. "Experience beautiful Hawaii and capture dynamic images that convey the wonder, beauty, and spirit of the islands." Photographers should call or see Web site for more information.

⃞N⃞ HORIZONS: ARTISTIC TRAVEL

P.O. Box 634, Leverett MA 01054. (413)367-9200. Fax: (413)367-9522. E-mail: horizons@horizons-art.com. Web site: www.horizons-art.com. **Contact:** Jane Sinauer, director. One-of-a-kind small-group travel adventures: 1- and 2-week programs in the American Southwest, Italy, Amsterdam, Prague, Scandinavia, Mexico, Ecuador, Laos, Vietnam, Cambodia, Southern Africa, Northern India.

IN FOCUS WITH MICHELE BURGESS

20741 Catamaran Lane, Huntington Beach CA 92646. (714)536-6104. E-mail: maburg5820 @aol.com. Web site: www.infocustravel.com. **Contact:** Michele Burgess, president. Cost: $4,500-8,000. Offers overseas tours to photogenic areas with expert photography consultation at a leisurely pace and in small groups (maximum group size: 20).

INTERNATIONAL CENTER OF PHOTOGRAPHY

1114 Avenue of the Americas, New York NY 10036. (212)857-0001. E-mail: education@icp. org. Web site: www.icp.org. **Contact:** Donna Ruskin, education associate. "The cost of our weekend workshops range from $255 to $720 plus registration and lab fees. Our 5- and 10-week courses range from $360 to $770 plus registration and lab fees." ICP offers photography courses, lectures and workshops for all levels of experience—from intensive beginner classes to rigorous professional workshops.

INTERNATIONAL EXPEDITIONS

One Environs Park, Helena AL 35080. (800)633-4734 (US/Canada); (205)428-1700 (worldwide). Fax: (205)428-1714. E-mail: nature@ietravel.com. Web site: www.ietravel.com. **Contact:** Ralph Hammelbacher, president. Cost: $1,800-$4,898; includes scheduled transportation during expeditions unless otherwise specified; services of experienced English-speaking local guides; all accommodations; meals as specified in the respective itineraries; transfer and luggage handling when taking group flights. Guided nature expeditions all over the world: Costa Rica, Machu Picchu, Galapagos, Kenya, Patagonia and many more. Open to all skill levels. Photographers should write, call, e-mail, see Web site for more information.

JIVIDEN'S NATURALLY WILD PHOTO ADVENTURES

P.O. Box 333, Chillicothe OH 45601. (800)866-8655 or (740)774-6243. E-mail: mail@naturallywhild.net. Web site: www.naturallywild.net. **Contact:** Jerry or Barbara Jividen. Cost: $149 and up depending on length and location. Workshops held throughout the year; please inquire. All workshops and photo tours feature comprehensive instruction, technical advice, pro tips and hands-on photography. Many workshops include lodging, meals, ground transportation, special permits and special guest rates. Group sizes are small for more personal assistance and are normally led by 2 photography guides/certified instructors. Subject emphasis is on photographing nature, wildlife and natural history. Supporting emphasis is on proper techniques, composition, exposure, lens and accessory use. Workshops range from 1-7 days in a variety of diverse North American locations. Open to all skill levels. Free information available upon request. Free quarterly journal by e-mail upon request. Photographers should write, call or e-mail for more information.

JORDAHL PHOTO WORKSHOPS

P.O. Box 3998, Hayward CA 94540. (510)785-7707. E-mail: kate@jordahlphoto.com. Web site: www.jordahlphoto.com. **Contact:** Kate or Geir Jordahl, directors. Cost: $150-700. Intensive 1- to 5-day workshops dedicated to inspiring creativity and community among artists through critique, field sessions and exhibitions.

ART KETCHUM HANDS-ON MODEL WORKSHOPS

2215 S. Michigan Ave., Chicago IL 60616. (773)866-2803. E-mail: ketch22@ix.netcom.com. Web site: www.artketchum.com. **Contact:** Art Ketchum, owner. Cost: $160 for 1-day workshops in Chicago studio; $125 for repeaters; and a special price of $100 fro participants that attend at least 6 workshops. Photographers should call, e-mail or visit Web site for more information.

WELDON LEE'S ROCKY MOUNTAIN PHOTO ADVENTURES

P.O. Box 487, Allenspark CO 80510-0487. Phone/fax: (303)747-2074. E-mail: wlee@Rocky MountainPhotoAdventures.com. Web site: www.RockyMountainPhotoAdventures.com. **Contact:** Weldon Lee. Cost: $695-5,995; includes transportation and lodging. Workshops held monthly year round. Wildlife and landscape photography workshops featuring hands-on instruction with an emphasis on exposure, composition, and digital imaging. Participants are invited to bring a selection of images to be critiqued during the workshops. Photographers should write, call or e-mail for more information.

LEPP INSTITUTE OF DIGITAL IMAGING

1062 Los Osos Valley Rd., Los Osos CA 93402. (805)528-7385. Fax: (805)528-7387. E-mail: info@LeppPhoto.com. Web site: www.LeppPhoto.com. **Contact:** Mary Sylvester, registrar. Offers small groups. "New focus on digital tools to optimize photography, make the most of your images and improve your photography skills at the premier digital imaging school on the West Coast."

◪ THE LIGHT FACTORY

Spirit Square, Suite 211, 345 N. College St., Charlotte NC 28202. (704)333-9755. E-mail: info@lightfactory.org. Web site: www.lightfactory.org. **Contact:** Marcie Kelso, executive director. The Light Factory is "a nonprofit arts center dedicated to exhibition and education programs promoting the power of photography and film." Classes are offered throughout the year in SLR and digital photography and filmmaking.

⃞ ⃟ PETER LLEWELLYN PHOTOGRAPHY WORKSHOPS & FIELD TOURS

645 Rollo Road, Gabriola BC VOR 1X3 Canada. (250)247-9109. E-mail: peter@peterllewelly n.com. Web site: www.peterllewellyn.com. **Contact:** Peter Llewellyn. Cost varies. "All workshops and field trips feature small groups, maximum 6 for workshops and 12 for field trips to allow maximum personal attention. Workshops include basic Photoshop skills, digital photography and digital workflow. Field trips are designed to provide maximum photographic opportunities to participants with the assistance of a professional photogra-

pher. Trips include several South American destinations, including Brazil, Guatemala, and Peru, and various venues in Canada and U.S.'' Open to all skill levels. For further information, e-mail or see Web site.

C.C. LOCKWOOD WILDLIFE PHOTOGRAPHY WORKSHOP

P.O. Box 14876, Baton Rouge LA 70898. (225)769-4766. Fax: (225)767-3726. E-mail: cactusc lyd@aol.com. Web site: www.cclockwood.com. **Contact:** C.C. Lockwood, photographer. Cost: Lake Martin Spoonbill Rookery, $800; Atchafalaya Swamp, $290; Yellowstone, $ 3,775; Grand Canyon, $2,450. Workshop at Lake Martin is 3 days plus side trip into Atchafalaya, February and April. Each April and October, C.C. conducts a 2-day Atchafalaya Basin Swamp Wildlife Workshop. It includes lecture, canoe trip into the swamp, and critique session. Every other year, C.C. does a 7-day winter wildlife workshop in Yellowstone National Park. C.C. also leads an 8-day Grand Canyon raft trip photo workshop in May.

LONG ISLAND PHOTO WORKSHOP

(516)221-4058. E-mail: jerry@jsmallphoto.com. Web site: www.liphotoworkshop.com. **Contact:** Jerry Small, director. Annual 4-day workshop covering professional wedding, portrait, and digital photography and photographic skills. Open to all skill levels.

THE MACDOWELL COLONY

100 High St., Peterborough NH 03458. (603)924-3886. Fax: (603)924-9142. E-mail: admissio ns@macdowellcolony.org. Web site: www.macdowellcolony.org. Founded in 1907 to provide creative artists with uninterrupted time and seclusion to work and enjoy the experience of living in a community of gifted artists. Residencies of up to 8 weeks for writers, playwrights, composers, film/video makers, visual artists, architects and interdisciplinary artists. Artists in residence receive room, board and exclusive use of a studio. Average length of residency is 5 weeks. Ability to pay for residency is not a factor. There are no residency fees. Limited funds available for travel reimbursement and artist grants based on need. Application deadlines: January 15: summer (June-September); April 15: fall/winter (October-January); September 15: winter/spring (February-May). Photographers should write, call or see Web site for application and guidelines. Questions should be directed to the admissions director.

ⓝ THE MAINE MEDIA WORKSHOPS

(877)577-7700 or (207)236-8581. Fax: (207)236-2558. E-mail: info@TheWorkshops.com. Web site: www.TheWorkshops.com. For over 34 years this international school has been offering hundreds of one- and two- week workshops for photographers, filmmakers, and media artists in Rockport, Maine. Programs are available for working professionals, serious amateurs, and high school and college students. Destination workshop locations include Venice, Paris, Rome, Istanbul, Greece, and India. Professional certificate and MFA programs are also available through Rockport College, www.rockportcollege.edu.

WILLIAM MANNING PHOTOGRAPHY

6396 Birchdale Court, Cincinnati OH 45230. (513)624-8148. E-mail: william@williammanni ng.com. Web site: www.williammanning.com. **Contact:** William Manning, director. Cost: $1,200-4,000. Offers small group tours. Four programs worldwide, with emphasis on landscapes, wildlife and culture.

JOE & MARY ANN MCDONALD WILDLIFE PHOTOGRAPHY WORKSHOPS AND TOURS

73 Loht Rd., McClure PA 17841-9340. (717)543-6423. Fax: (717)543-6423. E-mail: info@hoothollow.com. Web site: www.hoothollow.com. **Contact**: Joe McDonald, owner. Cost: $1,200-8,500. Offers small groups, quality instruction with emphasis on nature and wildlife photography.

MEXICO PHOTOGRAPHY WORKSHOPS

Otter Creek Photography, Hendricks WV 26271. (304)478-3586. E-mail: OtterCreekPhotography@yahoo.com. **Contact:** John Warner, instructor. Cost: $1,400. Intensive weeklong, hands-on workshops held throughout the year in the most visually rich regions of Mexico. Photograph snow-capped volcanoes, thundering waterfalls, pre-Columbian ruins, botanical gardens, fascinating people, markets and colonial churches in jungle, mountain, desert and alpine environments.

MID-ATLANTIC REGIONAL SCHOOL OF PHOTOGRAPHY

666 Franklin Ave., Nutley NJ 07110. (888)267-MARS (6277). E-mail: marschool@nac.net. Web site: www.photoschools.com. Contact: Jim Bastinck, director. Cost: $985; includes lodging and most meals. Annual 5-day workshop covering many aspects of professional photography from digital to portrait to wedding. Open to photographers of all skill levels.

ⓝ MIDWEST PHOTOGRAPHIC WORKSHOPS

28830 W. Eight Mile Rd., Farmington Hills MI 48336. (248)471-7299. E-mail: bryce@mpw.com. Web site: www.mpw.com. **Contact:** Bryce Denison, owner. Cost: varies per workshop. "One-day weekend and weeklong photo workshops, small group sizes and hands-on shooting seminars by professional photographers/instructors on topics such as portraiture, landscapes, nudes, digital, nature, weddings, product advertising and photojournalism."

MISSOURI PHOTOJOURNALISM WORKSHOP

109 Lee Hills Hall, Columbia MO 65211. (573)882-4882. Fax: (573)884-4999. E-mail: reesd@missouri.edu. Web site: www.mophotoworkshop.org. **Contact:** Angel Anderson, coordinator. Cost: $600. Workshop for photojournalists. Participants learn the fundamentals of documentary photo research, shooting, and editing.

MOUNTAIN WORKSHOPS

Western Kentucky University, 1906 College Heights Blvd., 11070, Bowling Green KY 42101-1070. (270)745-8927. E-mail: mountainworkshops@wku.edu. Web site: www.mountainworkshops.org. **Contact:** Jim Bye, workshops coordinator. Cost: Photojournalism and Picture editing: $595 plus expenses, Multimedia: $750 plus expenses. Annual weeklong documentary photojournalism workshop held September 30 - October 5, 2008. Open to intermediate and advanced shooters.

ⓝ NATURAL HABITAT ADVENTURES

P.O. Box 3065, Boulder CO 80307. (800)543-8917. E-mail: info@nathab.com. Web site: www.nathab.com. Cost: $2,195-20,000; includes lodging, meals, ground transportation and expert expedition leaders. Guided photo tours for wildlife photographers. Tours last 5-27 days. Destinations include North America, Latin America, Canada, the Arctic, Galápagos Islands, Africa, the Pacific and Antarctica.

NATURAL TAPESTRIES

1208 State Rt. 18, Aliquippa PA 15001. (724)495-7493. E-mail: nancyrotenberg@aol.com. Web site: www.naturaltapestries.com. **Contact:** Nancy Rotenberg, owner. Cost: varies by workshop; $500-600 for weekend workshops in Pennsylvania. "We offer small groups with quality instruction and an emphasis on nature. Garden and macro workshops are held on our farm in Pennsylvania, and others are held in various locations in North America." Open to all skill levels. Photographers should call or e-mail for more information.

NATURE PHOTOGRAPHY WORKSHOPS, GREAT SMOKY MOUNTAINS INSTITUTE AT TREMONT

Great Smoky Mountains National Park, 9275 Tremont Rd., Townsend TN 37882. (865)448-6709. E-mail: mail@gsmit.org. Web site: www.gsmit.org. **Contact:** Registrar. Workshop instructors: Bill Lea, Will Clay and others. Cost: $540. Offers workshops April 24 - 27, 2009 and October 23 - 26, 2009 emphasizing the use of natural light in creating quality scenic, wildflower and wildlife images.

NEVERSINK PHOTO WORKSHOP

P.O. Box 641, Woodbourne NY 12788. (212)929-0008 or (845)434-0575. E-mail: lou@louja witz.com. Web site: www.loujawitz.com/neversink.html. **Contact:** Louis Jawitz, owner. Offers weekend workshops in digital and film, teaching scenic, travel, location and stock photography during the last 2 weeks of August in the Catskill Mountains. See Web site for more information.

N NEW ENGLAND SCHOOL OF PHOTOGRAPHY

537 Commonwealth Ave., Boston MA 02215. (617)437-1868 or (800)676-3767. Fax: (617)437-0261. E-mail: info@nesop.com. Web site: www.nesop.com. **Contact:** Academic Director. Instruction in professional and creative photography.

NEW JERSEY HERITAGE PHOTOGRAPHY WORKSHOPS

124 Diamond Hill Rd., Berkeley Heights NJ 07922. (908)790-8820. Fax: (908)790-0074. E-mail: nancyori@comcast.net. Web site: www.nancyoriphotography.com. **Contact:** Nancy Ori, director. Estab. 1990. Cost: $295-450. Workshops held every spring. Nancy Ori, well-known instructor, freelance photographer and fine art exhibitor of landscape and architecture photography, teaches how to use available light and proper metering techniques to document the man-made and natural environments of Cape May. A variety of film and digital workshops taught by guest instructors are available each year and are open to all skill levels, especially beginners. Topics include hand coloring of photographs, creative camera techniques with Polaroid materials, intermediate and advanced digital, landscape and architecture with alternative cameras, environmental portraits with lighting techniques, street photography; as well as pastel, watercolor and oil painting workshops. All workshops include an historic walking tour of town, location shooting or painting, demonstrations and critiques. Scholarships available annually.

NEW JERSEY MEDIA CENTER LLC WORKSHOPS AND PRIVATE TUTORING

124 Diamond Hill Rd., Berkeley Heights NJ 07922. (908)790-8820. Fax: (908)790-0074. E-mail: nancyori@comcast.net. Web site: www.nancyoriworkshops.com. **Contact:** Nancy Ori, director. **1. Tuscany Photography Workshop** by Nancy Ori. Explore the Tuscan coun-

tryside, cities and small villages, with emphasis on architecture, documentary, portrait and landscape photography. The group will venture in non-tourist areas. Cost: call for this year's price; includes tuition, accommodations at a private estate, breakfasts and some dinners. Open to all skill levels. Held September 13-20, 2008. **2. Private Photography and Darkroom Tutoring** with Nancy Ori in Berkeley Heights, New Jersey. This unique and personalized approach to learning photography is designed for the beginning or intermediate student who wants to expand his/her understanding of the craft and work more creatively with the camera, develop a portfolio, create an exhibit or learn darkroom techniques. The goal is to refine individual style while exploring the skills necessary to make expressive photographs. The content will be tailored to individual needs and interests. Cost: $350 for a total of 8 hours; $450 for the darkroom sessions. **3. Capturing the Light of the Southwest**, a painting, sketching and photography workshop with Nancy Ori and a different painting instructor each year, held every other year in October, will focus on the natural landscape and man-made structures of the area around Santa Fe and Taos. Participants can be at any level in their media. All will be encouraged to produce a substantial body of work worthy of portfolio or gallery presentation. Features special evening guest lecturers from the photography and painting community in the Santa Fe area. Artists should e-mail for more information. **4. Cape May Photography Workshops** are held annually in April and May. Also, a variety of subjects such as photojournalism, environmental portraiture, landscape, alternative cameras, Polaroid techniques, creative digital techniques, on-location wedding photography, large-format, and how to photograph birds in the landscape are offered by several well-known East-Coast instructors. Open to all skill levels. Includes critiques, demonstrations, location shooting of Victorian architecture, gardens, seascapes, and, in some cases, models in either film or digital. E-mail for dates, fees and more information. Workshops are either 3 or 4 days.

NIKON SCHOOL DIGITAL SLR PHOTOGRAPHY

1300 Walt Whitman Rd., Melville NY 11747. (631)547-8666. Fax: (631)547-0309. Web site: www.nikonschool.com. Weekend seminars traveling to 30 major cities in the U.S. **Intro to Digital SLR Photography**—Cost: $119; covers composition, exposure, menu reviews, reading LCD for histograms and highlights, basic editing and printing. **Next Steps in Digital Photography: Streamlined Workflow Technique**—Cost: $159; covers the entire workflow process, benefits of RAW files, live wireless, multiple flash demo, color management, advanced editing and printing techniques, and archiving of image files.

NORTHERN EXPOSURES

4917 Evergreen Way #383, Everett WA 98203. (425)347-7650. E-mail: abenteuerbc@yahoo.com. **Contact:** Linda Moore, director. Cost: $300-750 for 3- to 5-day workshops (U.S. and Canada); $175-400/day for tours in Canada. Offers 3- to 5-day intermediate to advanced nature photography workshops in several locations in Pacific Northwest and western Canada; spectacular settings including coast, alpine, badlands, desert and rain forest. Also, 1- to 2-week Canadian Wildlife and Wildlands Photo Adventures and nature photo tours to extraordinary remote wildlands of British Columbia, Alberta, Saskatchewan, Yukon and Northwest Territories.

NYU TISCH SCHOOL OF THE ARTS

721 Broadway, 8th Floor, New York NY 10003. (212)998-1930. E-mail: photo.tsoa@nyu.edu. Web site: www.photo.tisch.nyu.edu. **Contact:** Department of Photography and Im-

aging. Summer classes offered for credit and noncredit covering digital imaging, career development, basic to advanced photography, and darkroom techniques. Open to all skill levels.

OREGON COLLEGE OF ART AND CRAFT

8245 SW Barnes Rd., Portland OR 97225. (503)297-5544 or (800)390-0632. Web site: www. ocac.edu. Offers workshops and classes in photography throughout the year: b&w, color, alternative processes, studio lighting, digital imaging. Also offers MFA in photography. For schedule information, call or visit Web site.

⊕ STEVE OUTRAM'S TRAVEL PHOTOGRAPHY WORKSHOPS

D. Katsifarakis St., Galatas, Chania 73100 Crete, Greece. E-mail: mail@steveoutram.com. Web site: www.steveoutram.com. **Contact:** Steve Outram, workshop photographer. **Brazil:** 13 days every March and October. **Western Crete:** 9 days in the Venetian town of Chania, every May and October. **Lesvos:** 14 days on Greece's 3rd-largest island, every October. **Slovenia**: 11 days exploring the charming towns of Ljubljana and Piran, every June. **Zanzibar:** 14 days on this fascinating Indian Ocean island, every February and September. Learn how to take more than just picture postcard-type images on your travels. Workshops are limited to 8 people.

PALM BEACH PHOTOGRAPHIC CENTRE

55 NE Second Ave., Delray Beach FL 33444. (561)276-9797. Fax: (561)276-1932. E-mail: cs@workshop.org. Web site: www.workshop.org. **Contact:** Fatima NeJame, executive director. Cost: $75-1,300 depending on class. The center is an innovative learning facility offering 1- to 5-day seminars in photography and digital imaging year round. Also offered are travel workshops to cultural destinations such as South Africa, Bhutan, Cambodia, Peru, and India. Emphasis is on photographing the indigenous cultures of each country. Also hosts the annual Fotofusion event (see separate listing in this section). Photographers should call for details.

⊕ PAN HORAMA

Puskurinkatu 2, FIN-33730, Tampere Finland. Fax: 011-358-3-364-5382. E-mail: info@panh orama.net. Web site: www.panhorama.net. **Contact:** Rainer K. Lampinen, chairman. Annual panorama photography workshops. International Panorama Photo Exhibition held annually in autumn in Finland and retrospective exhibitions abroad. Awards: Master of Panorama Art, opportunity to exhibit at Underground Photo Gallery (http://www.iisalmi .fi/?deptid+12149), other awards.

ⓝ RALPH PAONESSA PHOTOGRAPHY WORKSHOPS

509 W. Ward Ave., Suite B-108, Ridgecrest CA 93555-2542. (800)527-3455. E-mail: ralph@r pphoto.com. Web site: www.rpphoto.com. **Contact:** Ralph Paonessa, director. Cost: starting at $1,675; includes 1 week or more of lodging, meals and ground transport. Various workshops repeated annually. Nature, bird and landscape trips to Death Valley, Falkland Islands, Alaska, Costa Rica, Ecuador, and many other locations. Open to all skill levels. Photographers should write, call or e-mail for more information.

PETERS VALLEY CRAFT CENTER

19 Kuhn Rd., Layton NJ 07851. (973)948-5200. Fax: (973)948-0011. E-mail: photography@ petersvalley.org. Web site: www.petersvalley.org. Offers workshops May, June, July, August and September; 3-6 days long. Offers instruction by talented photographers in a wide range of photographic disciplines—from daguerrotypes to digital and everything in between. Also offers classes in blacksmithing/metals, ceramics, fibers, fine metals, weaving and woodworking. Located in northwest New Jersey in the Delaware Water Gap National Recreation Area, 70 miles west of New York City. Photographers should call for catalog or visit Web site or more information.

N PHOTO ADVENTURE TOURS

2035 Park St., Atlantic Beach NY 11509-1236. (516)371-0067 or (800)821-1221. Fax: (516)371-1352. E-mail: info@photoadventuretours.com. **Contact:** Richard Libbey, manager. Offers photographic tours to Finland, Iceland, India, Nepal, Norway, Ireland, Mexico, South Africa, and domestic locations such as New Mexico, Albuquerque Balloon Fiesta, Navajo Indian regions, Alaska and New York.

PHOTO EXPLORER TOURS

2506 Country Village, Ann Arbor MI 48103-6500. (800)315-4462 or (734)996-1440. E-mail: decoxphoto@aol.com. Web site: www.PhotoExplorerTours.com. **Contact:** Dennis Cox, director. Cost: $3,195; all-inclusive. Photographic explorations of China, southern Africa, India, Turkey, Burma, Iceland, Croatia, Bhutan, and Vietnam. "Founded in 1981 as China Photo Workshop Tours by award-winning travel photographer and China specialist Dennis Cox, Photo Explorer Tours has expanded its tours program since 1996. Working directly with carefully selected tour companies at each destination who understand the special needs of photographers, we keep our groups small, usually from 5 to 16 photographers, to ensure maximum flexibility for both planned and spontaneous photo opportunities." On most tours, individual instruction is available from professional photographer leading tour. Open to all skill levels. Photographers should write, call or e-mail for more information.

PHOTO WORKSHOPS BY COMMERCIAL PHOTOGRAPHER SEAN ARBABI

San Francisco Bay Area, California. Phone/fax: (925)855-8060. E-mail: workshops@seanarbabi.com. Web site: www.seanarbabi.com/workshops.html. **Contact:** Sean Arbabi, photographer/instructor. Cost: $85-3,000 for workshops only; some meals, lodging included - airfare and other services may be included, depending on workshop. Online and seasonal workshops held in spring, summer, fall, winter. Taught around the world via online, and in US locations including California New Mexico, Colorado, and Maine. Sean Arbabi teaches through computer presentations and slide shows, field instruction and hands-on demonstrations. All levels of workshops are offered from beginner to advanced; subjects include exposure, digital photography, composition, technical aspects of photography, lighting, how to fine-tune your personal vision, equipment to pack and use, a philosophical approach to the art, as well as how to run a photography business.

PHOTOGRAPHERS' FORMULARY

P.O. Box 950, 7079 Hwy. 83 N, Condon MT 59826-0950. (800)922-5255. Fax: (406)754-2896. E-mail: lynnw@blackfoot.net; formulary@blackfoot.net. Web site: www.photoformulary.com. **Contact:** Lynn Wilson, workshops program director. Photographers' Formulary workshops include a wide variety of alternative processes, and many focus on the traditional darkroom. Located in Montana's Swan Valley, some of the best wilderness lands in the Rocky Mountains. See Web site for details on costs and lodging. Open to all skill levels.

PHOTOGRAPHIC ARTS CENTER
Fresh Meadows, Queens NY. Phone/Fax: (718)969-7924. E-mail: photocenter48@yahoo.com. **Contact:** Beatriz Arenas, president. Offers workshops on basics to advanced, b&w and color; Mac computers, Photoshop, Pagemaker, Canvas, CD recording and digital photography. Gives lessons in English and Spanish.

PHOTOGRAPHIC ARTS WORKSHOPS
P.O. Box 1791, Granite Falls WA 98252. (360)691-4105. E-mail: photoartswkshps@aol.com. Web site: www.barnbaum.com. **Contact:** Bruce Barnbaum, director. Offers a wide range of workshops across the US, Mexico, Europe and Canada. Instructors include masters of both tradional and digital images. Workshops feature instruction in the understanding and use of light, composition, exposure, development, printing, photographic goals and philosophy. Includes reviews of student portfolios. Sessions are intense but highly enjoyable, held in field, darkroom and classroom with various instructors. Ratio of students to instructors is always 8:1 or fewer, with detailed attention to problems students want solved. All camera formats, color and b&w.

PHOTOGRAPHIC CENTER NORTHWEST
900 12th Ave., Seattle WA 98122. (206)720-7222. E-mail: pcnw@pcnw.org. Web site: www.pcnw.org. **Contact:** Annie Van Avery, executive director. Day and evening classes and workshops in fine art photography (b&w, color, digital) for photographers of all skill levels; accredited certificate program.

PHOTOGRAPHS II
P.O. Box 4376, Carmel CA 93921. (831)624-6870. E-mail: rfremier@redshift.com. Web site: www.starrsites.com/photos2 or www.photographsII.com. **Contact:** Roger Fremier. Cost: Starts at $2,945 for International Photography Retreats. Offers 4 programs/year. Previous locations include France, England, Spain and Japan.

PHOTOGRAPHY AT THE SUMMIT: JACKSON HOLE
Rich Clarkson & Associates LLC, 1099 18th St., Suite 2840, Denver CO 80202. (303)295-7770 or (800)745-3211. E-mail: info@richclarkson.com. Web site: www.photographyatthesummit.com. **Contact:** Brett Wilhelm, administrator. Annual workshops held in spring (May) and fall (October). Weeklong workshops with top journalistic, nature and illustrative photographers and editors. See Web site for more information.

🌐 PHOTOGRAPHY IN PROVENCE
La Chambre Claire, Rue du Buis, Ansouis 84240 France. E-mail: andrew.squires@photography-provence.com. Web site: www.photographie.-provence.com. **Contact:** Mr. Andrew Squires, M.A. Cost: €540-620; accommodations €255-315. Workshops May to October. Theme: What to Photograph and Why? Designed for people who are looking for a subject and an approach they can call their own. Explore photography of the real world, the uni-

verse of human imagination, or simply let yourself discover what touches you. Explore Provence and photograph on location. Possibility to extend your stay and explore Provence if arranged in advance. Open to all skill levels. Photographers should send SASE, call or e-mail for more information.

PRAGUE SUMMER SEMINARS
Metropolitan College, ED 118, University of New Orleans, 2000 Lakeshore Dr., New Orleans LA 70148. (504)280-7318. E-mail: prauge@uno.edu. Web site: http://inst.uno.edu/prague. **Contact:** Irene Ziegler, program coordinator. Cost: $3,395; includes lodging. Challenging seminars, studio visits, excursions within Prague; field trips to Vienna, Austria and Brno, Moravia; film and lecture series. Open to beginners and intermediate photographers. Photographers should call, e-mail or see Web site for more information.

PROFESSIONAL PHOTOGRAPHER'S SOCIETY OF NEW YORK STATE PHOTO WORKSHOPS
2175 Stuyvesant St., Niskayuna NY 12309. (518)377-5935. E-mail: Linda@ppsnysworkshop .com. Web site: www.ppsnysworkshop.com. **Contact:** Tom Mack, director. Cost: $675 or $775. Weeklong, specialized, hands-on workshops for professional photographers in July.

PROFESSIONAL PHOTOGRAPHY AT DAYTONA BEACH COMMUNITY COLLEGE
Southeast Center for Photographic Studies, Daytona Beach College, P.O. Box 2811, Daytona Beach FL 32120-2811. (386)506-3581. Fax: (386)506-3112. E-mail: biferid@dbcc.edu. Web site: http://go.dbcc.edu/photography. **Contact:** Dan Biferie, chair. Full-range professional photography coursework and periodic workshops available leading to an A.S. in Photographic Technology from Daytona Beach College and a B.Sc. degree in photography from University of Central Florida. Skills: commercial, editorial, fine art. Open to all. E-mail or call for more information.

⊕ PYRENEES EXPOSURES
20, rue du Soleil, 66190 Collioure, France. E-mail: explorerimages@yahoo.com. Web site: www.explorerimages.com. **Contact:** Martin N. Johansen, director. Cost: varies by workshop; starts at $150 for tuition; housing and meals extra. Workshops held year round. Offers 2- to 7-day workshops and photo expeditions in the French and Spanish Pyrenees, including the Andorra, with emphasis on landscapes, wildlife and culture. Workshops and tours are limited to small groups. Open to all skill levels. Photographers should e-mail or see Web site for more information.

◪ QUETICO PHOTO TOURS
P.O. Box 593, Atikokan ON P0T 1C0 Canada. (807)597-2621(summer), (807)737-8196 (winter). E-mail: jdstradiotto@canoemail.com. Web site: www.nwconx.net/~jdstradi. **Contact:** John Stradiotto, owner/operator/instructor. Cost: $750 U.S.; food and accommodation provided. Annual workshop/conference. Tours depart every Monday morning, May to October. "Nature photography skills, portrait photography, and telephoto work will be undertaken during a gentle wilderness tour. Guests additionally enjoy the benefits of fine outdoor food. We provide the support necessary for photographers to focus on observing nature and developing their abilities."

Workshops

JEFFREY RICH WILDLIFE PHOTOGRAPHY TOURS

PO Box 493921, Redding CA 96049. (530)410-8428. E-mail: jrich@jeffrichphoto.com. Web site: www.jeffrichphoto.com. **Contact:** Jeffrey Rich, owner. Leading wildlife photo tours in Alaska and western U.S. since 1990: bald eagles, whales, birds, Montana babies and predators, Brazil's Pantanal, Borneo, and Japan's winter wildlife. Photographers should call or e-mail for brochure.

ROCKY MOUNTAIN FIELD SEMINARS

1895 Fall River Rd., Estes Park CO 80517. (970)586-3262 or (800)748-7002. E-mail: fieldsemi nars@rmna.org. Web site: www.rmna.org. **Contact:** Seminar coordinator. Cost: $85-200. Daylong and weekend seminars covering photographic techniques for wildlife and scenics in Rocky Mountain National Park. Professional instructors include David Halpern, W. Perry Conway, Don Mammoser, Glenn Randall, Allan Northcutt and Lee Kline. Call or e-mail for a free seminar catalog listing over 50 seminars.

ROCKY MOUNTAIN SCHOOL OF PHOTOGRAPHY

210 N. Higgins, Suite 101, Missoula MT 59802. (800)394-7677. Fax: (406) 721-9133. E-mail: rmsp@rmsp.com. Web site: www.rmsp.com. **Contact:** Jeanne Chaput de Saintonge, co-director. Cost: $90-6,000. "RMSP offers professional career training in an 11-week 'Summer Intensive' program held each year in Missoula, Montana." Program courses include: basic and advanced color and b&w, studio and natural lighting, portraiture, marketing, stock, landscape, portfolio and others. Offers 7-day advanced training programs in nature, commercial, wedding, portraiture and documentary photography. "We also offer over 40 workshops year round, including field workshops and digital and b&w darkroom printing. Instructors include David Muench, David Middleton, Brenda Tharp, Alison Shaw, George DeWolfe, John Paul Caponigro and others."

SANTA FE PHOTOGRAPHIC WORKSHOPS

P.O. Box 9916, Santa Fe NM 87504-5916. (505)983-1400. E-mail: info@santafeworkshops.c om. Web site: www.santafeworkshops.com. **Contact:** Registrar. Cost: $850-1,150 for tuition; lab fees, housing and meals extra; package prices for workshops in Mexico start at $2,250 and include ground transportation, most meals and accommodations. Over 120 weeklong workshops encompassing all levels of photography and more than 35 digital lab workshops and 12 weeklong workshops in Mexico—all led by top professional photographers. The Workshops campus is located near the historic center of Santa Fe. Call or e-mail to request a free catalog.

SELLING YOUR PHOTOGRAPHY

2973 Harbor Blvd., #341, Costa Mesa CA 92626-3912. (888)713-0705. E-mail: maria@mpisc opo.com. Web site: www.mpiscopo.com. **Contact:** Maria Piscopo. Cost: $25-100. One-day workshops cover techniques for marketing and selling photography services. Open to photographers of all skill levels. See Web site for dates and locations. Maria Piscopo is the author of *Photographer's Guide to Marketing & Self-Promotion*, 3rd edition (Allworth Press).

SELLPHOTOS.COM

Pine Lake Farm, 1910 35th Rd., Osceola WI 54020. (715)248-3800, ext. 21. Fax: (715)248-7394. E-mail: info@photosource.com. Web site: www.sellphotos.com. **Contact:** Rohn

Engh. Offers half-day workshops in major cities. Marketing critique of attendees' slides follows seminar.

JOHN SEXTON PHOTOGRAPHY WORKSHOPS

P.O. Box 30, Carmel Valley CA 93924. (831)659-3130. Fax: (831)659-5509. E-mail: info@joh nsexton.com. Web site: www.johnsexton.com. **Contact:** Laura Bayless, administrative assistant. Director: John Sexton. Cost: $800-900. Offers a selection of intensive workshops with master photographers in scenic locations throughout the US. All workshops offer a combination of instruction in the aesthetic and technical considerations involved in making expressive black and white prints.

BOB SHELL PHOTO WORKSHOPS

P.O. Box 808, Radford VA 24141. (540)639-4393. E-mail: bob@bobshell.com. Web site: www.bobshell.com. **Contact**: Bob Shell, owner. Cost: $750 and up. Glamour and nude photography workshops in exciting locations with top models. Taught by Bob Shell, one of the world's top glamour/nude photographers and technical editor of Digital Camera magazine. Full details on Web site.

◼ THE SHOWCASE SCHOOL OF PHOTOGRAPHY

1135 Sheridan Rd. NE, Atlanta GA 30324. (404)965-2205. E-mail: staff@theshowcaseschool .com. Web site: www.theshowcaseschool.com. **Contact:** Jan Fields, director. Cost: $30-330 depending on class. Offers photography classes to the general public, including beginning digital camera, people photography, nature photography, and Adobe Photoshop. Open to beginner and intermediate amateur photographers. Photographers should see Web site for more information.

SMOKY MOUNTAIN LEARNING CENTER

414 Whittier School Rd., Whittier NC 28789. (828)497-3637. E-mail: info@mountainlearnin g.com. Web site: www.mountainlearning.com. Cost: $595; includes breakfast, lunch and dinner. Offers workshops on portraiture and wedding photography, Photoshop and Painter. Open to all skill levels. Photographers should write, call, see Web site for more information.

SOUTH SHORE ART CENTER

119 Ripley Rd., Cohasset MA 02025. (781)383-2787. Fax: (781)383-2964. E-mail: info@ssac. org. Web site: www.ssac.org. Cost: $50-175. Offers workshops and classes in introductory and advanced digital photography, landscape photography, travel photography, portrait photography, and darkroom. Photographers should call, e-mail, or visit Web site for more information.

SOUTHEAST MUSEUM OF PHOTOGRAPHY AT DAYTONA COLLEGE

1200 W. International Speedway Blvd., Daytona Beach FL 32114. (386)506-4475. Fax: (386)506-4487. E-mail: museum@dpcc.edu. Web site: www.smponline.org. Contact: Kevin Miller, director. Photographic exhibitions, workshops and lecture series.

◼ SOUTHEAST PHOTO ADVENTURE SERIES WORKSHOPS

1143 Blakeway Street, Daniel Island SC 29492. (518)432-9913. E-mail: images@peterfinger. com. Web site: www.peterfinger.com/photoworkshops.html. **Contact:** Peter Finger, presi-

Workshops

dent. Cost: ranges from $150 for a weekend to $895 for a weeklong workshop. Offers over 20 weekend and weeklong photo workshops, held in various locations. Workshops planned include Charleston, Savannah, Carolina Coast, Outer Banks, and the Islands of Georgia. "Group instruction from dawn till dusk." Write for additional information.

SPORTS PHOTOGRAPHY WORKSHOP: COLORADO SPRINGS, CO

Rich Clarkson & Associates LLC, 1099 18th St., Suite 1840, Denver CO 80202. (303)295-7770 or (800)745-3211. E-mail: info@richclarkson.com. Web site: www.sportsphotography workshop.com. **Contact:** Brett Wilhelm, administrator. Annual workshop held in June. Weeklong workshop in sports photography at the U.S. Olympic Training Center with *Sports Illustrated* and Getty Images photographers and editors. See Web site for more information.

▣ STRABO PHOTO TOUR COLLECTION

P.O. Box 580, Dryden NY 13053. (607)756-8676. Fax: (208)545-4119. E-mail: info@staboto urs.com. Web site: www.phototc.com. **Contact:** Jacque Steedle, president. Cost: varies for destination locations—some all meals included, lodging included. See tour descriptions. Held annually. Photography tours designed by and for photographers. "Strabo Tours is dedicated to enriching your life, helping you see the world with new eyes, and creating images that express your unique experience to others. We're a leader in the field of wildlife and landscape photography tours: clients attest to this by traveling with us year after year. Open to all skill levels. Photographers should see Web site for more information.

SUMMIT PHOTOGRAPHIC WORKSHOPS

P.O. Box 67459, Scotts Valley CA 95067. (831)440-0124. E-mail: b-and-k@pacbell.net. Web site: www.summitphotographic.com. **Contact:** Barbara Brundege, owner. Cost: $99-200 for workshops; $1,500-6,000 for tours. Offers several workshops per year, including nature and landscape photography; wildlife photography classes; photo tours from 5 days to 3 weeks. Open to all skill levels. Photographers should see Web site for more information.

SUPERIOR/GUNFLINT PHOTOGRAPHY WORKSHOPS

P.O. Box 19286, Minneapolis MN 55419. E-mail: photoworkshop@laynekennedy.com. **Contact:** Layne Kennedy, director. Cost: $300-1,300; includes meals/lodging for all adventure-related workshops; lodging and meals for North Shore session are paid for by participants. Offers wilderness adventure photo workshops 3 times/year. Winter session includes driving your own dogsled team in northeastern Minnesota. Summer sessions include kayaking/camping trip in the Apostle Islands with first and last nights in lodges, and a new session along Minnesota's North Shore, at the famed North House Folk School, covering Lake Superior's north shore. All trips professionally guided. Workshops stress how to shoot effective and marketable magazine photos in a story-telling format. Write for details on session dates.

SYNERGISTIC VISIONS WORKSHOPS

P.O. Box 2585, Grand Junction CO 81502. Phone/fax: (970)245-6700. E-mail: steve@synvis.com. Web site: www.synvis.com. **Contact:** Steve Traudt, director. Offers a variety of digital photography and Photoshop classes at 13 Photography Gallery (www.13photo.com). Destinations include Slot Canyons, Colorado Wildflowers, Bosque del Apache, Rock Art, Arches, Canyonlands and more. Customized private field trips in Colorado, New Mexico, Utah and

Arizona. "Steve is also available to present day-long photo seminars to your group." Visit Web site for more information.

TAKE A PHOTOGRAPHIC JOURNEY OF A LIFETIME

(888)676-6468. E-mail: mcast@hfmus.com. Web site: www.mentorseries.com. **Contact:** Michelle Cast. Workshops that build not only your skill as a photographer but your sense of the world around you. Enjoy many days of photo activities led by world-renown professional shooters, all experienced and charismatic photographers who will offer in-the-field advice, lectures, slide shows and reviews. "The chance of getting good photos is high because we have invested in getting great teachers and permits for private access to some cool places. Some of our upcoming destinations include Greenland, Turkey, Ireland, New York City, South Carolina, Egypt, and the Everglades." Open to all skill levels. Photographers should call, e-mail or see Web site for more information.

TEXAS SCHOOL OF PROFESSIONAL PHOTOGRAPHY

1501 W. Fifth St., Plainview TX 79072. (806)296-2276. E-mail: don@texasschool.org. Web site: http://texasschool.org/index.html. **Contact:** Don Dickson, director. Cost: $435 for TPPA members. Twenty-five different classes offered, including portrait, wedding, marketing, background painting and video.

TRAVEL IMAGES

P.O. Box 2434, Eagle ID 83616. (800)325-8320. E-mail: phototours@travelimages.com. Web site: www.travelimages.com. **Contact:** John Baker, owner/guide. Small-group photo tours. Locations include U.S, Canada, Wales, Scotland, Ireland, England, New Zealand, Tasmania, Galapagos Islands, Provence, Tuscany, Cinque Terre, Venice, Austria, Switzerland, Germany, and Greece.

JOSEPH VAN OS PHOTO SAFARIS, INC.

P.O. Box 655, Vashon Island WA 98070. (206)463-5383. Fax: (206)463-5484. E-mail: info@photosafaris.com. Web site: www.photosafaris.com. **Contact:** Joseph Van Os, director. Offers over 50 different photo tours and workshops worldwide.

VIRGINIA CENTER FOR THE CREATIVE ARTS

154 San Angelo Dr., Amherst VA 24521. (434)946-7236. Fax: (434)946-7239. E-mail: vcca@vcca.com. Web site: www.vcca.com. **Contact:** Sheila Gulley Pleasants, artists services director. The Virginia Center for the Creative Arts (VCCA) is an international working retreat for writers, visual artists and composers. Located on 450 acres in the foothills of the Blue Ridge Mountains in central Virginia, the VCCA provides residential fellowships ranging from 2 weeks to 2 months. The VCCA can accommodate 22 fellows at a time and provides separate working and living quarters and all meals. There is 1 fully equipped black & white darkroom at the VCCA. Artists provide their own materials. Cost: $30/day suggested contribution. VCCA application and work samples required. Photographers should call or see Web site for more information. Application deadlines are January 15, May 15, and September 15 each year.

VISION QUEST PHOTO WORKSHOP CENTER

2370 Hendon Ave., St. Paul MN 55108-1453. (651)644-1400. Fax: (651)644-2122. E-mail: info@douglasbeasley.com. Web site: www.douglasbeasley.com. **Contact:** Doug Beasley, director. Cost: $495-1,995; includes food and lodging. Annual workshops held February through November. Hands-on photo workshops that emphasize content, vision and creativity over technique or gimmicks. Workshops are held in a variety of locations such as The Badlands of South Dakota, Oregon, Hawaii, Ireland, Norway and Guatemala. Open to all skill levels. Photographers should call or e-mail for more information.

VISUAL ARTISTRY & FIELD MENTORSHIP PHOTOGRAPHY WORKSHOP SERIES

P.O. Box 963, Eldersburg MD 21784. (410)552-4664. Fax: (410)552-3332. E-mail: tony@ton ysweet.com. Web site: http://tonysweet.com. **Contact:** Tony Sweet or Susan Milestone, susan@tonysweet.com. Cost: $795-$1,000 for instruction; all other costs are the responsibility of participant. Five-day workshops, limit 8-10 participants. Formats: 35mm film; digital; xpan. Extensive personal attention and instructional slide shows. Post-workshop support and image critiques for 6 months after the workshop (for an additional fee). Frequent attendees discounts and inclement weather discounts on subsequent workshops. Dealer discounts available from major vendors. ''The emphasis is to create in the participant a greater awareness of composition, subject selection, and artistic rendering of the natural world using the raw materials of nature: color, form and line.'' Open to intermediate and advanced photographers.

WILD WINGS PHOTO ADVENTURES

2035 Buchanan Rd. Manning SC 29102. (803)473-3414. E-mail: doug@totallyoutdoorspubli shing.com. Web site: www.douggardner.com. **Contact:** Doug Gardner, founder/instructor. Cost: $200-$450 (some adventures include meals and lodging). Annual workshops held various times throughout the year in North and South Carolina: Waterfowl (Ducks, Snow Geese, Tundra Swan), Osprey & Swamp Critters. ''The purpose of Wild Wings Photo Adventures is to offer one on one instruction and great opportunities to photograph 'wild' animals up close. Students will learn valuable techniques in the field with internationally recognized wildlife photographer Doug Gardner. Be sure to view the all new TV series, 'Wild Photo Adventures' online at www.wildphotoadventures.com.''

WILDERNESS ALASKA

P.O. Box 113063, Anchorage AK 99511. (907)345-3567. Fax: (907)345-3967. E-mail: macgill @alaska.net. Web site: www.wildernessalaska.com. **Contact:** MacGill Adams. Offers custom photography trips featuring natural history and wildlife to small groups.

WILDERNESS PHOTOGRAPHY EXPEDITIONS

402 S. Fifth, Livingston MT 59047. (406)222-2986 or (406)222-2302. E-mail: tom@tmurphy wild.com. Web site: www.tmurphywild.com. **Contact:** Tom Murphy, president. Offers programs in wildlife and landscape photography in Yellowstone National Park and special destinations.

ROBERT WINSLOW PHOTO, INC.

P.O. Box 334, Durango CO 81302-0334. (970)259-4143. Fax: (970)259-7748. E-mail: rwinslo w@mydurango.net. Web site: www.robertwinslowphoto.com. **Contact:** Robert Winslow, president. Cost: varies depending on workshop or tour. ''We arrange and lead custom wildlife and natural history photo tours to most destinations around the world.''

WOODSTOCK PHOTOGRAPHY WORKSHOPS

The Center for Photography at Woodstock, 59 Tinker St., Woodstock NY 12498. (845)679-9957. E-mail: info@cpw.org. Web site: www.cpw.org. **Contact:** Liz Unterman, CPW Education Coordinator. Cost: $120-625. Offers annual lectures and workshops in all topics in photography from June through October. Faculty includes numerous top professionals in fine art, documentary and commercial photography. Topics include still life, landscape, portraiture, lighting, alternative processes and digital. Offers 1-, 2- and 4-day events. Free catalog available by request.

WORKING WITH ARTISTS

445 S. Saulsbury, Studios C-D/Main Gallery, Lakewood CO 80226. (303)837-1341. E-mail: info@workingwithartists.org. Web site: www.workingwithartists.org. Cost: varies, depending on workshop, $95-995. Offers workshops on Photoshop, digital, alternative process, portraiture, landscape, creativity, studio lighting and more. Travels with Artists Workshops are held in Bali; Tuscany, Italy; San Miquel de Allende, Mexico; Spain. Open to all skill levels. They also have a gallery with changing juried photo exhibits. Photographers should call, e-mail, see Web site for more information.

THE HELENE WURLITZER FOUNDATION OF NEW MEXICO

218 Los Pandos Rd., P.O. Box 1891, Taos NM 87571. (505)758-2413. E-mail: hwf@taosnet.com. **Contact:** Michael A. Knight, executive director. The foundation offers residencies to artists in the creative fields-visual, literary, and music composition. There are three thirteen week sessions from mid-January through November annually. Application deadline: January 18 for following year. For application, request by e-mail or visit Web site to download.

YELLOWSTONE ASSOCIATION INSTITUTE

P.O. Box 117, Yellowstone National Park WY 82190. (307)344-2294. Fax: (307)344-2485. E-mail: registrar@YellowstoneAssociation.org. Web site: www.YellowstoneAssociation.org. **Contact:** Registrar. Offers workshops in nature and wildlife photography during the summer, fall and winter. Custom courses can be arranged. Photographers should see Web site for more information.

YOSEMITE OUTDOOR ADVENTURES

P.O. Box 230, El Portal CA 95318. (209)379-2321. E-mail: pdevine@yosemite.org. Web site: www.yosemite.org. **Contact:** Pete Devine, educational programs director. Cost: more than $200. Offers small (8-15 people) workshops in Yosemite National Park in outdoor field photography and natural history year-round. Photographers should see Web site for more information.

Stock Photography Portals

These sites market and distribute images from multiple agencies and photographers.

AGPix www.agpix.com

Alamy www.alamy.com

Digital Railroad www.digitalrailroad.net

Find a Photographer www.asmp.org/findaphotographer

Independent Photography Network (IPNStock) www.ipnstock.com

PhotoServe www.photoserve.com

PhotoSource International www.photosource.com

Portfolios.com www.portfolios.com

Shutterpoint Photography www.shutterpoint.com

Veer www.veer.com

Workbook Stock www.workbook.com

Portfolio Review Events

Portfolio review events provide photographers the opportunity to show their work to a variety of photo buyers including photo editors, publishers, art directors, gallery representatives, curators and collectors.

Art Director's Club, International Annual Awards Exhibition, New York City, www.adcglobal.org

Atlanta Celebrates Photography, held annually in October, Atlanta GA, www.acpinfo.org

Center for Photography at Woodstock, New York City, www.cpw.org

Festival of Light International Directory of Photography Festivals, an international collaboration of 16 countries and 22 photography festivals, www.festivaloflight.net

Fotofest, March, Houston TX, www.fotofest.org. Biennial—held in even-numbered years.

Fotofusion, January, Delray Beach FL, www.fotofusion.org

North American Nature Photographers Association, annual summit held in January. Location varies. www.nanpa.org

Photo LA, January, Los Angeles CA, www.photola.com.

Photo Miami, held annually in December, Miami FL, http://artfairsinc.com

Photo San Francisco, July, San Francisco CA, www.photosanfrancisco.net

Photolucida, March, Portland OR, www.photolucida.org. Biennial—held in odd-numbered years.

The Print Center, events held throughout the year, Philadelphia PA, www.printcenter.org

Review Santa Fe, July, Santa Fe NM, www.sfcp.org. The only juried portfolio review event.

Rhubarb-Rhubarb, July, Birmingham UK, www.rhubarb-rhubarb.net

Society for Photographic Education National Conference, March, different location each year, www.spenational.org

Grants

State, Provincial & Regional

Arts councils in the United States and Canada provide assistance to artists (including photographers) in the form of fellowships or grants. These grants can be substantial and confer prestige upon recipients; however, **only state or province residents are eligible**. Because deadlines and available support vary annually, query first (with a SASE) or check Web sites for guidelines.

UNITED STATES ARTS AGENCIES

Alabama State Council on the Arts, 201 Monroe St., Montgomery AL 36130-1800. (334)242-4076. E-mail: staff@arts.alabama.gov. Web site: www.arts.state.al.us.

Alaska State Council on the Arts, 411 W. Fourth Ave., Suite 1-E, Anchorage AK 99501-2343. (907)269-6610 or (888)278-7424. E-mail: aksca_info@eed.state.ak.us. Web site: www.eed.state.ak.us/aksca.

Arizona Commission on the Arts, 417 W. Roosevelt St., Phoenix AZ 85003-1326. (602)771-6501. E-mail: info@azarts.gov. Web site: www.azarts.gov.

Arkansas Arts Council, 1500 Tower Bldg., 323 Center St., Little Rock AR 72201. (501)324-9766. E-mail: info@arkansasarts.com. Web site: www.arkansasarts.com.

California Arts Council, 1300 I St., Suite 930, Sacramento CA 95814. (916)322-6555. E-mail: info@caartscouncil.com. Web site: www.cac.ca.gov.

Colorado Council on the Arts, 1625 Broadway, Suite 2700, Denver CO 80202. (303)892-3802. E-mail: online form. Web site: www.coloarts.state.co.us.

Connecticut Commission on Culture & Tourism, Arts Division, One Financial Plaza, 755 Main St., Hartford CT 06103. (860)256-2800. Web site: www.cultureandtourism.org.

Delaware Division of the Arts, Carvel State Office Bldg., 4th Floor, 820 N. French St., Wilmington DE 19801. (302)577-8278 (New Castle Co.) or (302)739-5304 (Kent or Sussex Counties). E-mail: delarts@state.de.us. Web site: www.artsdel.org.

District of Columbia Commission on the Arts & Humanities, 410 Eighth St. NW, 5th Floor, Washington DC 20004. (202)724-5613. E-mail: cah@dc.gov. Web site: http://dcarts.dc.gov.

Florida Arts Council, Division of Cultural Affairs, R.A. Gray Building, Third Floor, 500 S. Bronough St., Tallahassee FL 32399-0250. (850)245-6470. E-mail: info@florida-arts.org. Web site: www.florida-arts.org.

Georgia Council for the Arts, 260 14th St., Suite 401, Atlanta GA 30318. (404)685-2787. E-mail: gaarts@gaarts.org. Web site: www.gaarts.org.

Guam Council on the Arts & Humanities Agency, P.O. Box 2950, Hagatna GU 96932. (671)646-2781. Web site: www.guam.net.

Hawaii State Foundation on Culture & the Arts, 2500 S. Hotel St., 2nd Floor, Honolulu HI 96813. (808)586-0300. E-mail: ken.hamilton@hawaii.gov. Web site: www.state.hi.us/sfca.

Idaho Commission on the Arts, 2410 N. Old Penitentiary Rd., Boise ID 83712. (208)334-2119 or (800)278-3863. E-mail: info@arts.idaho.gov. Web site: www.arts.idaho.gov.

Illinois Arts Council, James R. Thompson Center, 100 W. Randolph, Suite 10-500, Chicago IL 60601. (312)814-6750. E-mail: iac.info@illinois.gov. Web site: www.state.il.us/agency/iac.

Indiana Arts Commission, 150 W. Market St., Suite 618, Indianapolis IN 46204. (317)232-1268. E-mail: IndianaArtsCommission@iac.in.gov. Web site: www.in.gov/arts.

Iowa Arts Council, 600 E. Locust, Des Moines IA 50319-0290. (515)281-6412. Web site: www.iowaartscouncil.org.

Kansas Arts Commission, 700 SW Jackson, Suite 1004, Topeka KS 66603-3761. (785)296-3335. E-mail: KAC@arts.state.ks.us. Web site: http://arts.state.ks.us.

Kentucky Arts Council, 21st Floor, Capital Plaza Tower, 500 Mero St., Frankfort KY 40601-1987. (502)564-3757 or (888)833-2787. E-mail: kyarts@ky.gov. Web site: http://artscouncil.ky.gov.

Louisiana Division of the Arts, Capitol Annex Bldg., 1051 N. 3rd St., 4th Floor, Room #420, Baton Rouge LA 70804. (225)342-8180. Web site: www.crt.state.la.us/arts.

Maine Arts Commission, 193 State St., 25 State House Station, Augusta ME 04333-0025. (207)287-2724. E-mail: MaineArts.info@maine.gov. Web site: www.mainearts.com.

Maryland State Arts Council, 175 W. Ostend St., Suite E, Baltimore MD 21230. (410)767-6555. E-mail: msac@msac.org. Web site: www.msac.org.

Massachusetts Cultural Council, 10 St. James Ave., 3rd Floor, Boston MA 02116-3803. (617)727-3668. E-mail: mcc@art.state.ma.us. Web site: www.massculturalcouncil.org.

Michigan Council for Arts & Cultural Affairs, 702 W. Kalamazoo St., P.O. Box 30705, Lansing MI 48909-8205. (517)241-4011. E-mail: artsinfo@michigan.gov. Web site: www.michigan.gov/hal/0,1607,7-160-17445_19272---,00.html.

Minnesota State Arts Board, Park Square Court, 400 Sibley St., Suite 200, St. Paul MN 55101-1928. (651)215-1600 or (800)866-2787. E-mail: msab@arts.state.mn.us. Web site: www.arts.state.mn.us.

Mississippi Arts Commission, 501 N. West St., Suite 701B, Woolfolk Bldg., Jackson MS 39201. (601)359-6030. Web site: www.arts.state.ms.us.

Missouri Arts Council, 815 Olive St., Suite 16, St. Louis MO 63101-1503. (314)340-6845 or (866)407-4752. E-mail: moarts@ded.mo.gov. Web site: www.missouriartscouncil.org.

Montana Arts Council, 316 N. Park Ave., Suite 252, Helena MT 59620-2201. (406)444-6430. E-mail: mac@mt.gov. Web site: www.art.state.mt.us.

Resources

National Assembly of State Arts Agencies, 1029 Vermont Ave. NW, 2nd Floor, Washington DC 20005. (202)347-6352. E-mail: nasaa@nasaa-arts.org. Web site: www.nasaa-arts.org.

Nebraska Arts Council, 1004 Farnam St., Plaza Level, Omaha NE 68102. (402)595-2122 or (800)341-4067. Web site: www.nebraskaartscouncil.org.

Nevada Arts Council, 716 N. Carson St., Suite A, Carson City NV 89701. (775)687-6680. E-mail: online form. Web site: http://dmla.clan.lib.nv.us/docs/arts.

New Hampshire State Council on the Arts, 2½ Beacon St., 2nd Floor, Concord NH 03301-4974. (603)271-2789. Web site: www.nh.gov/nharts.

New Jersey State Council on the Arts, 225 W. State St., P.O. Box 306, Trenton NJ 08625. (609)292-6130. Web site: www.njartscouncil.org.

New Mexico Arts, Dept. of Cultural Affairs, P.O. Box 1450, Santa Fe NM 87504-1450. (505)827-6490 or (800)879-4278. Web site: www.nmarts.org.

New York State Council on the Arts, 175 Varick St., New York NY 10014. (212)627-4455. Web site: www.nysca.org.

North Carolina Arts Council, 109 East Jones St., Cultural Resources Building, Raleigh NC 27601. (919)807-6500. E-mail: ncarts@ncmail.net. Web site: www.ncarts.org.

North Dakota Council on the Arts, 1600 E. Century Ave., Suite 6, Bismarck ND 58503. (701)328-7590. E-mail: comserv@state.nd.us. Web site: www.state.nd.us/arts.

Commonwealth Council for Arts and Culture (Northern Mariana Islands), P.O. Box 5553, CHRB, Saipan MP 96950. (670)322-9982 or (670)322-9983. E-mail: galaidi@vzpacifica.net. Web site: www.geocities.com/ccacarts/ccacwebsite.html.

Ohio Arts Council, 727 E. Main St., Columbus OH 43205-1796. (614)466-2613. Web site: www.oac.state.oh.us.

Oklahoma Arts Council, Jim Thorpe Building, 2101 N. Lincoln Blvd., Suite 640, Oklahoma City OK 73105. (405)521-2931. E-mail: okarts@arts.ok.gov. Web site: www.arts.state.ok.us.

Oregon Arts Commission, 775 Summer St. NE, Suite 200, Salem OR 97301-1280. (503)986-0082. E-mail: oregon.artscomm@state.or.us. Web site: www.oregonartscommission.org.

Pennsylvania Council on the Arts, 216 Finance Bldg., Harrisburg PA 17120. (717)787-6883. Web site: www.pacouncilonthearts.org.

Institute of Puerto Rican Culture, P.O. Box 9024184, San Juan PR 00902-4184. (787)724-0700. E-mail: www@icp.gobierno.pr. Web site: www.icp.gobierno.pr.

Rhode Island State Council on the Arts, One Capitol Hill, Third Floor, Providence RI 02908. (401)222-3880. E-mail: info@arts.ri.gov. Web site: www.arts.ri.gov.

American Samoa Council on Culture, Arts and Humanities, P.O. Box 1540, Office of the Governor, Pago Pago AS 96799. (684)633-4347. Web site: www.prel.org/programs/pcahe/PTG/terr-asamoa1.html.

South Carolina Arts Commission, 1800 Gervais St., Columbia SC 29201. (803)734-8696. E-mail: info@arts.state.sc.us. Web site: www.southcarolinaarts.com.

South Dakota Arts Council, 711 E. Wells Ave., Pierre SD 57501-3369. (605)773-3301. E-mail: sdac@state.sd.us. Web site: www.artscouncil.sd.gov.

Tennessee Arts Commission, 401 Charlotte Ave., Nashville TN 37243-0780. (615)741-1701. Web site: www.arts.state.tn.us.

Texas Commission on the Arts, E.O. Thompson Office Building, 920 Colorado, Suite 501, Austin TX 78701. (512)463-5535. E-mail: front.desk@arts.state.tx.us. Web site: www.arts. state.tx.us.

Utah Arts Council, 617 E. South Temple, Salt Lake City UT 84102-1177. (801)236-7555. Web site: http://arts.utah.gov.

Vermont Arts Council, 136 State St., Drawer 33, Montpelier VT 05633-6001. (802)828-3291. E-mail: online form. Web site: www.vermontartscouncil.org.

Virgin Islands Council on the Arts, 5070 Norre Gade, St. Thomas VI 00802-6872. (340)774-5984. Web site: http://vicouncilonarts.org.

Virginia Commission for the Arts, Lewis House, 223 Governor St., 2nd Floor, Richmond VA 23219. (804)225-3132. E-mail: arts@arts.virginia.gov. Web site: www.arts.state.va.us.

Washington State Arts Commission, 711 Capitol Way S., Suite 600, P.O. Box 42675, Olympia WA 98504-2675. (360)753-3860. E-mail: info@arts.wa.gov. Web site: www.arts.wa.gov.

West Virginia Commission on the Arts, The Cultural Center, Capitol Complex, 1900 Kanawha Blvd. E., Charleston WV 25305-0300. (304)558-0220. Web site: www.wvculture. org/arts.

Wisconsin Arts Board, 101 E. Wilson St., 1st Floor, Madison WI 53702. (608)266-0190. E-mail: artsboard@arts.state.wi.us. Web site: www.arts.state.wi.us.

Wyoming Arts Council, 2320 Capitol Ave., Cheyenne WY 82002. (307)777-7742. E-mail: ebratt@state.wy.us. Web site: http://wyoarts.state.wy.us.

CANADIAN PROVINCES ARTS AGENCIES

Alberta Foundation for the Arts, 10708 - 105 Ave., Edmonton AB T5H 0A1. (780)427-9968. Web site: www.cd.gov.ab.ca/all_about_us/commissions/arts.

British Columbia Arts Council, P.O. Box 9819, Stn. Prov. Govt., Victoria BC V8W 9W3. (250)356-1718. E-mail: BCArtsCouncil@gov.bc.ca. Web site: www.bcartscouncil.ca.

The Canada Council for the Arts, 350 Albert St., P.O. Box 1047, Ottawa ON K1P 5V8. (613)566-4414 or (800)263-5588 (within Canada). Web site: www.canadacouncil.ca.

Manitoba Arts Council, 525-93 Lombard Ave., Winnipeg MB R3B 3B1. (204)945-2237 or (866)994-2787 (in Manitoba). E-mail: info@artscouncil.mb.ca. Web site: www.artscouncil.mb.ca.

New Brunswick Arts Board (NBAB), 634 Queen St., Suite 300, Fredericton NB E3B 1C2. (506)444-4444 or (866)460-2787. Web site: www.artsnb.ca.

Newfoundland & Labrador Arts Council, P.O. Box 98, St. John's NL A1C 5H5. (709)726-2212 or (866)726-2212. E-mail: nlacmail@nfld.net. Web site: www.nlac.nf.ca.

Nova Scotia Department of Tourism, Culture, and Heritage, Culture Division, 1800 Argyle St., Suite 601, P.O. Box 456, Halifax NS B3J 2R5. (902)424-4510. E-mail: cultaffs@gov.ns. ca. Web site: www.gov.ns.ca/dtc/culture.

Resources

Resources

Ontario Arts Council, 151 Bloor St. W., 5th Floor, Toronto ON M5S 1T6. (416)961-1660 or (800)387-0058 (in Ontario). E-mail: info@arts.on.ca. Web site: www.arts.on.ca.

Prince Edward Island Council of the Arts, 115 Richmond St., Charlottetown PE C1A 1H7. (902)368-4410 or (888)734-2784. E-mail: info@peiartscouncil.com. Web site: www.peiart scouncil.com.

Québec Council for Arts & Literature, 79 boul. René-Lévesque Est, 3e étage, Québec QC G1R 5N5. (418)643-1707 or (800)897-1707. E-mail: info@calq.gouv.qc.ca. Web site: www.calq. gouv.qc.ca.

The Saskatchewan Arts Board, 2135 Broad St., Regina SK S4P 1Y6. (306)787-4056 or (800)667-7526 (Saskatchewan only). E-mail: sab@artsboard.sk.ca. Web site: www.artsbo ard.sk.ca.

Yukon Arts Section, Cultural Services Branch, Dept. of Tourism & Culture, Government of Yukon, Box 2703 (L-3), Whitehorse YT Y1A 2C6. (867)667-8589 or (800)661-0408 (in Yukon). E-mail: arts@gov.yk.ca. Web site: www.btc.gov.yk.ca/cultural/arts.

STATE AND REGIONAL GRANTS AND AWARDS

The following opportunities are arranged by state since most of them grant money to artists in a particular geographic region. Because deadlines vary annually, check Web sites or call for the most up-to-date information. Note: not all states are listed; see the list of state and provincial arts agencies on page 456 for state-sponsored arts councils.

California

Flintridge Foundation Awards for Visual Artists, 1040 Lincoln Ave., Suite 100, Pasadena CA 91103. (626)449-0839 or (800)303-2139. Fax: (626)585-0011. Web site: www.flintridge foundation.org. *For artists in California, Oregon and Washington only.*

James D. Phelan Award in Photography, Kala Art Institute, Don Porcella, 1060 Heinz Ave., Berkeley CA 94710. (510)549-6914. Web site: www.kala.org. *For artists born in California only.*

Connecticut

Martha Boschen Porter Fund, Inc., 145 White Hallow Rd., Sharon CT 06064. *For artists in northwestern Connecticut, western Massachusetts and adjacent areas of New York (except New York City).*

Idaho

Betty Bowen Memorial Award, % Seattle Art Museum, 100 University St., Seattle WA 98101. (206)654-3131. Web site: www.seattleartmuseum.org/bettybowen/. *For artists in Washington, Oregon and Idaho only.*

Illinois

Illinois Arts Council, Artists Fellowship Program, James R. Thompson Center, 100 W. Randolph, Suite 10-500, Chicago IL 60601. (312)814-6750. Web site: www.state.il.us/agency/ iac/Guidelines/guidelines.htm. *For Illinois artists only.*

Kentucky

Kentucky Foundation for Women Grants Program, 1215 Heyburn Bldg., 332 W. Broadway, Louisville KY 40202. (502)562-0045. Web site: www.kfw.org/grants.html. *For female artists living in Kentucky only.*

Massachusetts

See Martha Boschen Porter Fund, Inc., under Connecticut.

Minnesota

McKnight Photography Fellowships Program, University of Minnesota Dept. of Art, Regis Center for Art, E-201, 405 21st Ave. S., Minneapolis MN 55455. (612)626-9640. Web site: www.mcknightphoto.umn.edu. *For Minnesota artists only.*

New York

A.I.R. Gallery Fellowship Program, 511 W. 25th St., Suite 301, New York NY 10001. (212)255-6651. E-mail: info@airnyc.org. Web site: www.airnyc.org. *For female artists from New York City metro area only.*

Arts & Cultural Council for Greater Rochester, 277 N. Goodman St., Rochester NY 14607. (585)473-4000. Web site: www.artsrochester.org.

Constance Saltonstall Foundation for the Arts Grants and Fellowships, P.O. Box 6607, Ithaca NY 14851 (include SASE). (607)277-4933. E-mail: info@saltonstall.org. Web site: www.saltonstall.org. *For artists in the central and western counties of New York.*

New York Foundation for the Arts: Artists' Fellowships, 155 Avenue of the Americas, 14th Floor, New York NY 10013-1507. (212)366-6900, ext. 217. E-mail: nyfaafp@nyfa.org. Web site: www.nyfa.org. *For New York artists only.*

Oregon

See Flintridge Foundation Awards for Visual Artists, under California.

Pennsylvania

Leeway Foundation—Philadelphia, Pennsylvania Region, 123 S. Broad St., Suite 2040, Philadelphia PA 19109. (215)545-4078. E-mail: info@leeway.org. Web site: www.leeway. org. *For female artists in Philadelphia only.*

Texas

Individual Artist Grant Program—Houston, Texas, Cultural Arts Council of Houston and Harris County, 3201 Allen Pkwy., Suite 250, Houston TX 77019-1800. (713)527-9330. E-mail: info@cachh.org. Web site: www.cachh.org. *For Houston artists only.*

Washington

See Flintridge Foundation Awards for Visual Artists, under California.

Resources

Professional Organizations

Advertising Photographers of America, National, 28 E. Jackson, Bldg. #10-A855, Chicago IL 60604-2263. (800)272-6264. E-mail: office@apanational.com. Web site: www.apanational.com.

Advertising Photographers of America, Atlanta, P.O. Box 20471, Atlanta GA 30325. (888)889-7190, ext. 50. E-mail: info@apaatlanta.com. Web site: www.apaatlanta.com.

Advertising Photographers of America, Los Angeles, 5455 Wilshire Blvd., Suite 1709, Los Angeles CA 90036. (323)933-1631. Fax: (323)933-9209. E-mail: office@apa-la.org. Web site: www.apa-la.org.

Advertising Photographers of America, Midwest, 28 E. Jackson, Bldg. #10-A855, Chicago IL 60604. (877)890-7375. E-mail: ceo@apa-m.com. Web site: www.apamidwest.com.

Advertising Photographers of America, New York, 27 W. 20th St., Suite 601, New York NY 10011. (212)807-0399. Fax: (212)727-8120. E-mail: info@apany.com. Web site: www.apany.com.

Advertising Photographers of America, San Diego, P.O. Box 84241, San Diego CA 92138. (619)417-2150. E-mail: membership@apasd.org. Web site: www.apasd.org.

Advertising Photographers of America, San Francisco, 560 Fourth St., San Francisco CA 94107. (415)882-9780. Fax: (415)882-9781. E-mail: info@apasf.com. Web site: www.apasf.com.

American Society of Media Photographers (ASMP), 150 N. Second St., Philadelphia PA 19106. (215)451-2767. Fax: (215)451-0880. Web site: www.asmp.org.

American Society of Picture Professionals (ASPP), 117 S. St. Asaph St., Alexandria VA 22314. Phone/fax: (703)299-0219. Web site: www.aspp.com.

The Association of Photographers, 81 Leonard St., London EC2A 4QS United Kingdom. (44)(207)739-6669. Fax: (44)(207)739-8707. E-mail: general@aophoto.co.uk. Web site: www.the-aop.org.

British Association of Picture Libraries and Agencies, 18 Vine Hill, London EC1R 5DZ United Kingdom. (44)(207)713-1780. Fax: (44)(207)713-1211. E-mail: enquiries@bapla.org.uk. Web site: www.bapla.org.uk.

British Institute of Professional Photography (BIPP), Fox Talbot House, Amwell End, Ware, Hertsfordshire SG12 9HN United Kingdom. (44)(192)046-4011. Fax: (44)(192)0487056. E-mail: info@bipp.com. Web site: www.bipp.com.

Canadian Association of Journalists, Algonquin College, 1385 Woodroffe Ave., B224, Ottawa ON K2G 1V8 Canada. (613)526-8061. Fax: (613)521-3904. E-mail: caj@igs.net. Web site: www.caj.ca.

Canadian Association of Photographers & Illustrators in Communications, The Case Goods Building, Suite 302, 55 Mill St., Toronto ON M5A 3C4 Canada. (416)462-3677. Fax: (416)462-9570. E-mail: info@capic.org. Web site: www.capic.org.

Canadian Association for Photographic Art, 31858 Hopedale Ave., Clearbrook BC V2T 2G7 Canada. (604)855-4848. Fax: (604)855-4824. E-mail: capa@capacanada.ca. Web site: www.capacanada.ca.

The Center for Photography at Woodstock (CPW), 59 Tinker St., Woodstock NY 12498. (845)679-9957. Fax: (845)679-6337. E-mail: info@cpw.org. Web site: www.cpw.org.

Evidence Photographers International Council (EPIC), 229 Peachtree St. NE, Suite 2200, Atlanta GA 30303. (886)868-3742. E-mail: EPICheadquarters@verizon.net. Web site: www.epic-photo.org.

International Association of Panoramic Photographers, 8855 Redwood St., Las Vegas NV 89139. (702)260-4608. E-mail: iappsecretary@aol.com. Web site: www.panoramicassociation.org.

International Center of Photography (ICP), 1133 Avenue of the Americas at 43rd St., New York NY 10036. (212)857-0000. E-mail: info@icp.org. Web site: www.icp.org.

The Light Factory (TLF), Spirit Square, Suite 211, 345 N. College St., Charlotte NC 28202. (704)333-9755. E-mail: info@lightfactory.org. Web site: www.lightfactory.org.

National Association of Photoshop Professionals (NAPP), 333 Douglas Rd. E., Oldsmar FL 34677. (813)433-5006. Fax: (813)433-5015. Web site: www.photoshopuser.com.

National Press Photographers Association (NPPA), 3200 Croasdaile Dr., Suite 306, Durham NC 27705. (919)383-7246. Fax: (919)383-7261. E-mail: info@nppa.org. Web site: www.nppa.org.

North American Nature Photography Association (NANPA), 10200 W. 44th Ave., Suite 304, Wheat Ridge CO 80033-2840. (303)422-8527. Fax: (303)422-8894. E-mail: info@nanpa.org. Web site: www.nanpa.org.

Photo Marketing Association International, 3000 Picture Place, Jackson MI 49201. (517)788-8100. Fax: (517)788-8371. E-mail: PMA_Information_Central@pmai.org. Web site: www.pmai.org.

Photographic Society of America (PSA), 3000 United Founders Blvd., Suite 103, Oklahoma City OK 73112-3940. (405)843-1437. Fax: (405)843-1438. E-mail: hq@psa-photo.org. Web site: www.psa-photo.org.

Picture Archive Council of America (PACA). (949)460-4531. Fax: (949)460-4532. E-mail: pacnews@pacoffice.org. Web site: www.stockindustry.org.

Professional Photographers of America (PPA), 229 Peachtree St. NE, Suite 2200, Atlanta GA 30303. (404)522-8600. Fax: (404)614-6400. E-mail: csc@ppa.com. Web site: www.ppa.com.

Professional Photographers of Canada (PPOC), 371 Dundas St., Woodstock ON N4S 1B6 Canada. (519)537-2555. Fax: (519)537-5573. E-mail: ppoc@rogers.com. Web site: www.ppoc.ca.

The Royal Photographic Society, Fenton House, 122 Wells Rd., Bath BA2 3AH United Kingdom. (44)(122)546-2841. Fax: (44)(122)544-8688. E-mail: reception@rps.org. Web site: www.rps.org.

Society for Photographic Education, 126 Peabody, The School of Interdisciplinary Studies, Miami University, Oxford OH 45056. (513)529-8328. Fax: (513)529-9301. E-mail: speoffice @spenational.org. Web site: www.spenational.org.

Society of Photographers and Artists Representatives (SPAR), 60 E. 42nd St., Suite 1166, New York NY 10165. E-mail: info@spar.org. Web site: www.spar.org.

Volunteer Lawyers for the Arts, 1 E. 53rd St., 6th Floor, New York NY 10022. (212)319-2787, ext. 1. Fax: (212)752-6575. Web site: www.vlany.org.

Wedding & Portrait Photographers International (WPPI), P.O. Box 2003, 1312 Lincoln Blvd., Santa Monica CA 90406. (310)451-0090. Fax: (310)395-9058. Web site: www.wppionline.com.

White House News Photographers' Association (WHNPA), 7119 Ben Franklin Station, Washington DC 20044-7119. Web site: www.whnpa.org.

Resources

Publications

PERIODICALS

Advertising Age, Crain Communications, 711 Third Ave., New York NY 10017-4036. (212)210-0100. Web site: www.adage.com. Weekly magazine covering marketing, media and advertising.

Adweek, VNU Business Publications, 770 Broadway, New York NY 10003. (646)654-5421. Fax: (646)654-5365. E-mail: info@adweek.com. Web site: www.adweek.com. Weekly magazine covering advertising agencies.

American Photo, 1633 Broadway, 43rd Floor, New York NY 10019. (212)767-6000. Web site: www.americanphotomag.com. Monthly magazine emphasizing the craft and philosophy of photography.

Art Calendar, 1500 Park Center Dr., Orlando FL 32835. (877)415-3955. Fax: (407)563-7099. E-mail: info@ArtCalendar.com. Web site: www.artcalendar.com. Monthly magazine listing galleries reviewing portfolios, juried shows, percent-for-art programs, scholarships and art colonies.

ASMP Bulletin, 150 N. Second St., Philadelphia PA 19106. (215)451-2767. Fax: (215)451-0880. Web site: www.asmp.org. Newsletter of the American Society of Media Photographers published 5 times/year. Subscription with membership.

Communication Arts, 110 Constitution Dr., Menlo Park CA 94025. (650)326-6040. Fax: (650)326-1648. Web site: www.commarts.com. Trade journal for visual communications.

Editor & Publisher, VNU Business Publications, 770 Broadway, New York NY 10003-9595. (800)336-4380 or (646)654-5270. Fax: (646)654-5370. Web site: www.editorandpublisher. com. Monthly magazine covering latest developments in journalism and newspaper production. Publishes an annual directory issue listing syndicates and another directory listing newspapers.

Folio, Red 7 Media, LLC, 33 S. Main St., Norwalk CT 06854. (203)854-6730. Fax: (203)854-6735. Web site: www.foliomag.com. Monthly magazine featuring trends in magazine circulation, production and editorial.

Graphis, 307 Fifth Ave., 10th Floor, New York NY 10016. (212)532-9387. Fax: (212)213-3229. E-mail: info@graphis.com. Web site: www.graphis.com. Magazine for the visual arts.

HOW, F + W Media, Inc., 4700 E. Galbraith Rd., Cincinnati OH 45236. (513)531-2690. Web site: www.howdesign.com. Bimonthly magazine for the design industry.

News Photographer, 6677 Whitemarsh Valley Walk, Austin TX 78746-6367. (919)383-7246. Fax: (919)383-7261. E-mail: magazine@nppa.org. Web site: www.nppa.org. Monthly news tabloid published by the National Press Photographers Association. Subscription with membership.

Outdoor Photographer, Werner Publishing, 12121 Wilshire Blvd., 12th Floor, Los Angeles CA 90025-1176. (310)820-1500. Fax: (310)826-5008. Web site: www.outdoorphotographe r.com. Monthly magazine emphasizing equipment and techniques for shooting in outdoor conditions.

Photo District News, VNU Business Publications, 770 Broadway, 7th Floor, New York NY 10003. (646)654-5780. Fax: (646)654-5813. Web site: www.pdn-pix.com. Monthly magazine for the professional photographer.

Photosource International, Pine Lake Farm, 1910 35th Rd., Osceola WI 54020-5602. (800)624-0266, ext. 21. E-mail: info@photosource.com. Web site: www.photosource.c om. This company publishes several helpful newsletters, including *PhotoLetter, PhotoDaily* and *PhotoStockNotes.*

Popular Photography & Imaging, 1633 Broadway, New York NY 10019. (212)767-6000. Fax: (212)767-5602. Web site: www.popphoto.com. Monthly magazine specializing in technical information for photography.

Print, F + W Media, Inc., 4700 E. Galbraith Rd., Cincinnati OH 45236. (513)531-2690. E-mail: info@printmag.com. Web site: www.printmag.com. Bimonthly magazine focusing on creative trends and technological advances in illustration, design, photography and printing.

Professional Photographer, Professional Photographers of America (PPA), 229 Peachtree St. NE, Suite 2200, Atlanta GA 30303. (404)522-8600. Fax: (404)614-6400. Web site: www. ppa.com. Monthly magazine emphasizing technique and equipment for working photographers.

Publishers Weekly, 360 Park Ave. S., New York NY 10010. (646)746-6758. Fax: (646)746-6631. Web site: www.publishersweekly.com. Weekly magazine covering industry trends and news in book publishing; includes book reviews and interviews.

Rangefinder, P.O. Box 1703, 1312 Lincoln Blvd., Santa Monica CA 90406. (310)451-8506. Fax: (310)395-9058. Web site: www.rangefindermag.com. Monthly magazine covering photography technique, products and business practices.

Selling Stock, 110 Frederick Ave., Suite A, Rockville MD 20850. (301)251-0720. Fax: (301)309-0941. E-mail: sellingstock@chd.com. Web site: www.pickphoto.com. Newsletter for stock photographers; includes coverage of trends in business practices such as pricing and contract terms.

Shutterbug, Primedia, 1419 Chaffee Dr., Suite 1, Titusville FL 32780. (321)269-3212. Fax: (321)225-3149. Web site: www.shutterbug.net. Monthly magazine of photography news and equipment reviews.

Studio Photography, Cygnus Business Media, 3 Huntington Quadrangle, Suite 301N, Melville NY 11747. (631)845-2700. Fax: (631)845-7109. Web site: www.imaginginfo.com/ spd/. Monthly magazine showcasing professional photographers. Also provides guides, tips and tutorials.

BOOKS & DIRECTORIES

Adweek Agency Directory, VNU Business Publications, 770 Broadway, New York NY 10003. (646)654-5421. E-mail: info@adweek.com. Web site: www.adweek.com. Annual directory of advertising agencies in the U.S.

Adweek Brand Directory, VNU Business Publications, 770 Broadway, New York NY 10003. (646)654-5421. E-mail: info@adweek.com. Web site: www.adweek.com. Directory listing top 2,000 brands, ranked by media spending.

ASMP Copyright Guide for Photographers, American Society of Media Photographers, 150 N. Second St., Philadelphia PA 19106. (215)451-2767. Fax: (215)451-0880. Web site: www.asmp.org.

ASMP Professional Business Practices in Photography, 6th Edition, American Society of Media Photographers, 150 N. Second St., Philadelphia PA 19106. (215)451-2767. Fax: (215)451-0880. Web site: www.asmp.org. Handbook covering all aspects of running a photography business.

Bacon's Media Directories, Cision, 332 S. Michigan Ave., Suite 900, Chicago IL 60604. (866)639-5087. Web site: www.cision.com/media-directories.asp.

The Big Picture: The Professional Photographer's Guide to Rights, Rates & Negotiation, by Lou Jacobs, Writer's Digest Books, F + W Media, Inc., 4700 E. Galbraith Rd., Cincinnati OH 45236. (513)531-2690. Web site: www.writersdigest.com. Essential information on understanding contracts, copyrights, pricing, licensing and negotiation.

Business and Legal Forms for Photographers, 3rd Edition, by Tad Crawford, Allworth Press, 10 E. 23 St., Suite 510, New York NY 10010. (212)777-8395. Fax: (212)777-8261. E-mail: PUB@allworth.com. Web site: www.allworth.com. Negotiation book with 28 forms for photographers.

The Business of Commercial Photography, by Ira Wexler, Amphoto Books, Watson-Guptill Publications, 770 Broadway, New York NY 10003. (800)278-8477. E-mail: info@watsonguptill.com. Web site: http://amphotobooks.com. Comprehensive career guide including interviews with 30 leading commercial photographers.

The Business of Photography: Principles and Practices, by Mary Virginia Swanson, available through her Web site (www.mvswanson.com) or by calling (520)742-6311.

The Business of Studio Photography, Revised Edition, by Edward R. Lilley, Allworth Press, 10 E. 23 St., Suite 510, New York NY 10010. (212)777-8395. Fax: (212)777-8261. E-mail: PUB@allworth.com. Web site: www.allworth.com. A complete guide to starting and running a successful photography studio.

Children's Writers & Illustrator's Market, Writer's Digest Books, F + W Media, Inc., 4700 E. Galbraith Rd., Cincinnati OH 45236. (513)531-2690. Web site: www.writersdigest.com. Annual directory including photo needs of book publishers, magazines and multimedia producers in the children's publishing industry.

Color Confidence: The Digital Photographer's Guide to Color Management, by Tim Grey, Sybex, 10475 Crosspoint Blvd., Indianapolis IN 46256. Web site: www.sybex.com.

Color Management for Photographers: Hands-On Techniques for Photoshop Users, by Andrew Rodney, Focal Press. Web site: www.focalpress.com.

Resources

Creative Black Book, 740 Broadway, 2nd Floor, New York NY 10003. (800)841-1246. Fax: (212)673-4321. Web site: www.blackbook.com. Sourcebook used by photo buyers to find photographers.

How to Shoot Stock Photos That Sell, 3rd Edition, by Michal Heron, Allworth Press, 10 E. 23 St., Suite 510, New York NY 10010. (212)777-8395. Fax: (212)777-8261. E-mail: PUB@allworth.com. Web site: www.allworth.com. Comprehensive guide to producing, marketing and selling sock photos.

How You Can Make $25,000 a Year With Your Camera, by Larry Cribb, Writer's Digest Books, F+W Media, Inc., 4700 E. Galbraith Rd., Cincinnati OH 45236. (513)531-2690. Web site: www.writersdigest.com. Newly revised edition of the popular book on finding photo opportunities in your own hometown.

LA 411, 411 Publishing, 5700 Wilshire Blvd., Suite 120, Los Angeles CA 90036. (800)545-2411. Fax: (323)965-2052. Web site: www.la411.com. Music industry guide, including record labels.

Legal Guide for the Visual Artist, 4th Edition, by Tad Crawford, Allworth Press, 10 E. 23 St., Suite 510, New York NY 10010. (212)777-8395. Fax: (212)777-8261. E-mail: PUB@allworth.com. Web site: www.allworth.com. The author, an attorney, offers legal advice for artists and includes forms dealing with copyright, sales, taxes, etc.

Literary Market Place, Information Today, 143 Old Marlton Pike, Medford NJ 08055-8750. (800)300-9868. Fax: (609)654-4309. E-mail: custserv@infotoday.com. Web site: www.infotoday.com or www.literarymarketplace.com. Directory that lists book publishers and other book publishing industry contacts.

Negotiating Stock Photo Prices, by Jim Pickerell and Cheryl Pickerell DiFrank, 110 Frederick Ave., Suite A, Rockville MD 20850. (301)251-0720. Fax: (301)309-0941. E-mail: sellingstock@chd.com. Web site: www.pickphoto.com. Hardbound book that offers pricing guidelines for selling photos through stock photo agencies.

Newsletters in Print, Thomson Gale, 27500 Drake Rd., Farmington Hills MI 48331. (248)699-4253 or (800)877-GALE. Fax: (800)414-5043. E-mail: gale.galeord@thomson.com. Web site: www.gale.com. Annual directory listing newsletters.

O'Dwyer's Directory of Public Relations Firms, J.R. O'Dwyer Company, 271 Madison Ave., #600, New York NY 10016. (212)679-2471. Fax: (212)683-2750. E-mail: john@odwyerpr.com. Web site: www.odwyerpr.com. Annual directory listing public relations firms, indexed by specialties.

Photo Portfolio Success, by John Kaplan, Writer's Digest Books, F+W Media, Inc., 4700 E. Galbraith Rd., Cincinnati OH 45236. (513)531-2690. Web site: www.writersdigest.com.

The Photographer's Guide to Marketing & Self-Promotion, 3rd Edition, by Maria Piscopo, Allworth Press, 10 E. 23 St., Suite 510, New York NY 10010. (212)777-8395. Fax: (212)777-8261. E-mail: PUB@allworth.com. Web site: www.allworth.com. Marketing guide for photographers.

The Photographer's Internet Handbook, Revised Edition, by Joe Farace, Allworth Press, 10 E. 23 St., Suite 510, New York NY 10010. (212)777-8395. Fax: (212)777-8261. E-mail: PUB@allworth.com. Web site: www.allworth.com. Covers the many ways photographers can use the Internet as a marketing and informational resource.

Photographer's Market Guide to Building Your Photography Business, by Vic Orenstein, Writer's Digest Books, F + W Media, Inc., 4700 E. Galbraith Rd., Cincinnati OH 45236. (513)531-2690. Web site: www.writersdigest.com. Practical advice for running a profitable photography business.

Pricing Photography: The Complete Guide to Assignment & Stock Prices, 3rd Edition, by Michal Heron and David MacTavish, Allworth Press, 10 E. 23 St., Suite 510, New York NY 10010. (212)777-8395. Fax: (212)777-8261. E-mail: PUB@allworth.com. Web site: www.allworth.com.

Real World Color Management: Industrial-Strength Production Techniques, by Bruce Fraser, Chris Murphy and Fred Bunting, Peachpit Press, 1248 8th St., Berkeley CA 94710. Web site: www.peachpit.com.

Sell & Resell Your Photos, 5th Edition, by Rohn Engh, Writer's Digest Books, F + W Media, Inc., 4700 E. Galbraith Rd., Cincinnati OH 45236. (513)531-2690. Web site: www.writersdigest.com. Revised edition of the classic volume on marketing your own stock.

SellPhotos.com, by Rohn Engh, Writer's Digest Books, F + W Media, Inc., 4700 E. Galbraith Rd., Cincinnati OH 45236. (513)531-2690. Web site: www.writersdigest.com. A guide to establishing a stock photography business on the Internet.

Shooting & Selling Your Photos, by Jim Zuckerman, Writer's Digest Books, F + W Media, Inc., 4700 E. Galbraith Rd., Cincinnati OH 45236. (513)531-2690. Web site: www.writersdigest.com.

Songwriter's Market, Writer's Digest Books, F + W Media, Inc., 4700 E. Galbraith Rd., Cincinnati OH 45236. (513)531-2690. Web site: www.writersdigest.com. Annual directory listing record labels.

Standard Rate and Data Service (SRDS), 1700 Higgins Rd., Des Plains IL 60018-5605. (847)375-5000. Fax: (847)375-5001. Web site: www.srds.com. Directory listing magazines and their advertising rates.

Workbook, Scott & Daughter Publishing, 940 N. Highland Ave., Los Angeles CA 90038. (800)547-2688. Fax: (323)856-4368. E-mail: press@workbook.com. Web site: www.workbook.com. Numerous resources for the graphic arts industry.

Writer's Market, Writer's Digest Books, F + W Media, Inc., 4700 E. Galbraith Rd., Cincinnati OH 45236. (513)531-2690. Web site: www.writersmarket.com. Annual directory listing markets for freelance writers. Many listings include photo needs and payment rates.

Resources

Web Sites

PHOTOGRAPHY BUSINESS

The Alternative Pick www.altpick.com

Black Book www.blackbook.com

Copyright Web site www.benedict.com

EP: Editorial Photographers www.editorialphoto.com

MacTribe www.mactribe.com

ShootSMARTER.com www.shootsmarter.com

Small Business Administration www.sba.gov

MAGAZINE AND BOOK PUBLISHING

American Journalism Review's News Links http://newslink.org

Bookwire www.bookwire.com

STOCK PHOTOGRAPHY

Global Photographers Search www.photographers.com

PhotoSource International www.photosource.com

Stock Photo Price Calculator www.photographersindex.com/stockprice.htm

Selling Stock www.pickphoto.com

Stock Artists Alliance www.stockartistsalliance.org

The STOCKPHOTO Network www.stockphoto.net

ADVERTISING PHOTOGRAPHY

Advertising Age www.adage.com

Adweek, Mediaweek and Brandweek www.adweek.com

Communication Arts Magazine www.commarts.com

FINE ART PHOTOGRAPHY

The Art List www.theartlist.com

Art Support www.art-support.com

Art DEADLINES List www.artdeadlineslist.com

Photography in New York International www.photography-guide.com

Mary Virginia Swanson www.mvswanson.com

PHOTOJOURNALISM

The Digital Journalist www.digitaljournalist.org

Foto8 www.foto8.com

National Press Photographers Association www.nppa.org

MAGAZINES

Afterimage www.vsw.org

Aperture www.aperture.org

Art Calendar www.artcalendar.com

Art on Paper www.artonpaper.com

Black and White Photography www.bandwmag.com

Blind Spot www.blindspot.com

British Journal of Photography www.bjphoto.co.uk

Camera Arts www.cameraarts.com

Lens Work www.lenswork.com

Photo District News www.pdnonline.com

Photograph Magazine www.photography-guide.com

Photo Insider www.photoinsider.com

The Photo Review, The Photography Collector, and The Photographic Art Market Magazines www.photoreview.org

Shots Magazine www.shotsmag.com

View Camera www.viewcamera.com

Resources

E-ZINES

The following publications exist online only. Some offer opportunities for photographers to post their personal work.

Apogee Photo www.apogeephoto.com

American Photo Magazine www.americanphotomag.com

American Photography Museum www.photographymuseum.com

Art in Context www.artincontext.org

Art Business News www.artbusinessnews.com

Art Support www.art-support.com

Artist Register http://artistsregister.com

Digital Journalist www.digitaljournalist.org

En Foco www.enfoco.org

Fotophile www.fotophile.com

Handheld Magazine www.handheldmagazine.com/index.html

Musarium www.musarium.com

Fabfotos www.fabfotos.com

Foto8 www.foto8.com

One World Journeys www.oneworldjourneys.com

PhotoArts www.photoarts.com

Pixel Press www.pixelpress.org

Photo Imaging Information Council www.takegreatpictures.com

Photo Links www.photolinks.com

Online Photo Workshops www.photoworkshop.com

Picture Projects www.pictureprojects.com

Sight Photo www.sightphoto.com

Zone Zero www.zonezero.com

TECHNICAL

About.com www.photography.about.com

FocalFix.com www.focalfix.com

Photo.net www.photo.net

The Pixel Foundry www.thepixelfoundry.com

Shoot Smarter www.shootsmarter.com

Wilhelm Imaging Research www.wilhelm-research.com

HOW TO

Adobe Tutorials www.adobe.com.designcenter/tutorials/

Digital Photographers www.digitalphotographers.net

Digital Photography Review www.dpreview.com

Fred Miranda www.fredmiranda.com/forum/index.php

Imaging Resource www.imaging-resource.com

Lone Star Digital www.lonestardigital.com

The National Association of Photoshop Professionals www.photoshopuser.com

PC Photo Review www.pcphotoreview.com

Steve's Digicams www.steves-digicams.com

Glossary

Absolute-released images. Any images for which signed model or property releases are on file and immediately available. For working with stock photo agencies that deal with advertising agencies, corporations and other commercial clients, such images are absolutely necessary to sell usage of images. Also see Model release, Property release.

Acceptance (payment on). The buyer pays for certain rights to publish a picture at the time it is accepted, prior to its publication.

Agency promotion rights. Stock agencies request these rights in order to reproduce a photographer's images in promotional materials such as catalogs, brochures and advertising.

Agent. A person who calls on potential buyers to present and sell existing work or obtain assignments for a client. A commission is usually charged. Such a person may also be called a *photographer's rep*.

All rights. A form of rights often confused with work for hire. Identical to a buyout, this typically applies when the client buys all rights or claim to ownership of copyright, usually for a lump sum payment. This entitles the client to unlimited, exclusive usage and usually with no further compensation to the creator. Unlike work for hire, the transfer of copyright is not permanent. A time limit can be negotiated, or the copyright ownership can run to the maximum of 35 years.

Alternative Processes. Printing processes that do not depend on the sensitivity of silver to form an image. These processes include cyanotype and platinum printing.

Archival. The storage and display of photographic negatives and prints in materials that are harmless to them and prevent fading and deterioration.

Artist's statement. A short essay, no more than a paragraph or two, describing a photographer's mission and creative process. Most galleries require photographers to provide an artist's statement.

Assign (designated recipient). A third-party person or business to which a client assigns or designates ownership of copyrights that the client purchased originally from a creator such as a photographer. This term commonly appears on model and property releases.

Assignment. A definite OK to take photos for a specific client with mutual understanding as to the provisions and terms involved.

Assignment of copyright, rights. The photographer transfers claim to ownership of copyright over to another party in a written contract signed by both parties.

Audiovisual (AV). Materials such as filmstrips, motion pictures and overhead transparencies which use audio backup for visual material.

Automatic renewal clause. In contracts with stock photo agencies, this clause works on the concept that every time the photographer delivers an image, the contract is automatically renewed for a specified number of years. The drawback is that a photographer can be bound by the contract terms beyond the contract's termination and be blocked from marketing the same images to other clients for an extended period of time.

Avant garde. Photography that is innovative in form, style or subject matter.

Biannual. Occurring twice a year. Also see Semiannual.

Biennial. Occurring once every two years.

Bimonthly. Occurring once every two months.

Bio. A sentence or brief paragraph about a photographer's life and work, sometimes published along with photos.

Biweekly. Occurring once every two weeks.

Blurb. Written material appearing on a magazine's cover describing its contents.

Buyout. A form of work for hire where the client buys all rights or claim to ownership of copyright, usually for a lump sum payment. Also see All rights, Work for hire.

Caption. The words printed with a photo (usually directly beneath it), describing the scene or action.

CCD. Charged Coupled Device. A type of light detection device, made up of pixels, that generates an electrical signal in direct relation to how much light strikes the sensor.

CD-ROM. Compact disc read-only memory; non-erasable electronic medium used for digitized image and document storage and retrieval on computers.

Chrome. A color transparency, usually called a slide.

Cibachrome. A photo printing process that produces fade-resistant color prints directly from color slides.

Clips. See Tearsheet.

CMYK. Cyan, magenta, yellow and black—refers to four-color process printing.

Color Correction. Adjusting an image to compensate for digital input and output characteristics.

Commission. The fee (usually a percentage of the total price received for a picture) charged by a photo agency, agent or gallery for finding a buyer and attending to the details of billing, collecting, etc.

Composition. The visual arrangement of all elements in a photograph.

Compression. The process of reducing the size of a digital file, usually through software. This speeds processing, transmission times and reduces storage requirements.

Consumer publications. Magazines sold on newsstands and by subscription that cover information of general interest to the public, as opposed to trade magazines, which cover information specific to a particular trade or profession. See Trade magazine.

Contact Sheet. A sheet of negative-size images made by placing negatives in direct contact with the printing paper during exposure. They are used to view an entire roll of film on one piece of paper.

Contributor's copies. Copies of the issue of a magazine sent to photographers in which their work appears.

Copyright. The exclusive legal right to reproduce, publish and sell the matter and form of an artistic work.

Cover letter. A brief business letter introducing a photographer to a potential buyer. A cover letter may be used to sell stock images or solicit a portfolio review. Do not confuse cover letter with query letter.

C-print. Any enlargement printed from a negative.

Credit line. The byline of a photographer or organization that appears below or beside a published photo.

Cutline. See Caption.

Resources

Day rate. A minimum fee that many photographers charge for a day's work, whether a full day is spent on a shoot or not. Some photographers offer a half-day rate for projects involving up to a half-day of work.

Demo(s). A sample reel of film or sample videocassette that includes excerpts of a filmmaker's or videographer's production work for clients.

Density. The blackness of an image area on a negative or print. On a negative, the denser the black, the less light that can pass through.

Digital Camera. A filmless camera system that converts an image into a digital signal or file.

DPI. Dots per inch. The unit of measure used to describe the resolution of image files, scanners and output devices. How many pixels a device can produce in one inch.

Electronic Submission. A submission made by modem or on computer disk, CD-ROM or other removable media.

Emulsion. The light-sensitive layer of film or photographic paper.

Enlargement. An image that is larger than its negative, made by projecting the image of the negative onto sensitized paper.

Exclusive property rights. A type of exclusive rights in which the client owns the physical image, such as a print, slide, film reel or videotape. A good example is when a portrait is shot for a person to keep, while the photographer retains the copyright.

Exclusive rights. A type of rights in which the client purchases exclusive usage of the image for a negotiated time period, such as one, three or five years. May also be permanent. Also see All rights, Work for hire.

Fee-plus basis. An arrangement whereby a photographer is given a certain fee for an assignment—plus reimbursement for travel costs, model fees, props and other related expenses incurred in completing the assignment.

File Format. The particular way digital information is recorded. Common formats are TIFF and JPEG.

First rights. The photographer gives the purchaser the right to reproduce the work for the first time. The photographer agrees not to permit any publication of the work for a specified amount of time.

Format. The size or shape of a negative or print.

Four-color printing, four-color process. A printing process in which four primary printing inks are run in four separate passes on the press to create the visual effect of a full-color photo, as in magazines, posters and various other print media. Four separate negatives of the color photo—shot through filters—are placed indentically (stripped) and exposed onto printing plates, and the images are printed from the plates in four ink colors.

GIF. Graphics Interchange Format. A graphics file format common to the Internet.

Glossy. Printing paper with a great deal of surface sheen. The opposite of matte.

Hard Copy. Any kind of printed output, as opposed to display on a monitor.

Honorarium. Token payment—small amount of money and/or a credit line and copies of the publication.

Image Resolution. An indication of the amount of detail an image holds. Usually expressed as the dimension of the image in pixels and the color depth each pixel has. Example: a 640×480, 24-bit image has higher resolution than a 640×480, 16-bit image.

IRC. International Reply Coupon. IRCs are used with self-addressed envelopes instead of stamps when submitting material to buyers located outside a photographer's home country.

JPEG. Joint Photographic Experts Group. One of the more common digital compression methods that reduces file size without a great loss of detail.

Licensing/Leasing. A term used in reference to the repeated selling of one-time rights to a photo.

Manuscript. A typewritten document to be published in a magazine or book.

Matte. Printing paper with a dull, nonreflective surface. The opposite of glossy.

Model release. Written permission to use a person's photo in publications or for commercial use.

Multi-image. A type of slide show that uses more than one projector to create greater visual impact with the subject. In more sophisticated multi-image shows, the projectors can be programmed to run by computer for split-second timing and animated effects.

Multimedia. A generic term used by advertising, public relations and audiovisual firms to describe productions using more than one medium together—such as slides and full-motion, color video—to create a variety of visual effects.

News release. See Press release.

No right of reversion. A term in business contracts that specifies once a photographer sells the copyright to an image, a claim of ownership is surrendered. This may be unenforceable, though, in light of the 1989 Supreme Court decision on copyright law. Also see All rights, Work for hire.

On spec. Abbreviation for "on speculation." Also see Speculation.

One-time rights. The photographer sells the right to use a photo one time only in any medium. The rights transfer back to the photographer on request after the photo's use.

Page rate. An arrangement in which a photographer is paid at a standard rate per page in a publication.

Photo CD. A trademarked, Eastman Kodak-designed digital storage system for photographic images on a CD.

PICT. The saving format for bit-mapped and object-oriented images.

Picture Library. See Stock photo agency.

Pixels. The individual light-sensitive elements that make up a CCD array. Pixels respond in a linear fashion. Doubling the light intensity doubles the electrical output of the pixel.

Point-of-purchase, point-of-sale (P-O-P, P-O-S). A term used in the advertising industry to describe in-store marketing displays that promote a product. Typically, these highly-illustrated displays are placed near checkout lanes or counters, and offer tear-off discount coupons or trial samples of the product.

Portfolio. A group of photographs assembled to demonstrate a photographer's talent and abilities, often presented to buyers.

PPI. Pixels per inch. Often used interchangeably with DPI, PPI refers to the number of pixels per inch in an image. See DPI.

Press release. A form of publicity announcement that public relations agencies and corporate communications staff people send out to newspapers and TV stations to generate news coverage. Usually this is sent with accompanying photos or videotape materials.

Property release. Written permission to use a photo of private property or public or government facilities in publications or for commercial use.

Public domain. A photograph whose copyright term has expired is considered to be "in the public domain" and can be used for any purpose without payment.

Publication (payment on). The buyer does not pay for rights to publish a photo until it is actually published, as opposed to payment on acceptance.

Query. A letter of inquiry to a potential buyer soliciting interest in a possible photo assignment.

Rep. Trade jargon for sales representative. Also see Agent.

Resolution. The particular pixel density of an image, or the number of dots per inch a device is capable of recognizing or reproducing.

Résumé. A short written account of one's career, qualifications and accomplishments.

Royalty. A percentage payment made to a photographer/filmmaker for each copy of work sold.

R-print. Any enlargement made from a transparency.

SAE. Self-addressed envelope.

SASE. Self-addressed, stamped envelope. (Most buyers require a SASE if a photographer wishes unused photos returned to him, especially unsolicited materials.)

Self-assignment. Any project photographers shoot to show their abilities to prospective clients. This can be used by beginning photographers who want to build a portfolio or by photographers wanting to make a transition into a new market.

Self-promotion piece. A printed piece photographers use for advertising and promoting their businesses. These pieces generally use one or more examples of the photographer's best work, and are professionally designed and printed to make the best impression.

Semiannual. Occurring twice a year. Also see Biannual.

Semigloss. A paper surface with a texture between glossy and matte, but closer to glossy.

Semimonthly. Occurring twice a month.

Serial rights. The photographer sells the right to use a photo in a periodical. Rights usually transfer back to the photographer on request after the photo's use.

Simultaneous submissions. Submission of the same photo or group of photos to more than one potential buyer at the same time.

Speculation. The photographer takes photos with no assurance that the buyer will either purchase them or reimburse expenses in any way, as opposed to taking photos on assignment.

Stock photo agency. A business that maintains a large collection of photos it makes available to a variety of clients such as advertising agencies, calendar firms and periodicals. Agencies usually retain 40-60 percent of the sales price they collect, and remit the balance to the photographers whose photo rights they've sold.

Stock photography. Primarily the selling of reprint rights to existing photographs rather than shooting on assignment for a client. Some stock photos are sold outright, but most are rented for a limited time period. Individuals can market and sell stock images to individual clients from their personal inventory, or stock photo agencies can market photographers' work for them. Many stock agencies hire photographers to shoot new work on assignment, which then becomes the inventory of the stock agency.

Subsidiary agent. In stock photography, this is a stock photo agency that handles marketing of stock images for a primary stock agency in certain US or foreign markets. These are usually affiliated with the primary agency by a contractual agreement rather than by direct ownership, as in the case of an agency that has its own branch offices.

SVHS. Abbreviation for Super VHS. Videotape that is a step above regular VHS tape. The number of lines of resolution in a SVHS picture is greater, thereby producing a sharper picture.

Tabloid. A newspaper about half the page size of an ordinary newspaper that contains many photos and news in condensed form.

Tearsheet. An actual sample of a published work from a publication.

TIFF. Tagged Image File Format. A common bitmap image format developed by Aldus.

Trade magazine. A publication devoted strictly to the interests of readers involved in a specific trade or profession, such as beekeepers, pilots or manicurists, and generally available only by subscription.

Transparency. Color film with a positive image, also referred to as a slide.

Unlimited use. A type of rights in which the client has total control over both how and how many times an image will be used. Also see All rights, Exclusive rights, Work for hire.

Unsolicited submission. A photograph or photographs sent through the mail that a buyer did not specifically ask to see.

Work for hire. Any work that is assigned by an employer who becomes the owner of the copyright. Stock images cannot be purchased under work-for-hire terms.

World rights. A type of rights in which the client buys usage of an image in the international marketplace. Also see All rights.

Worldwide exclusive rights. A form of world rights in which the client buys exclusive usage of an image in the international marketplace. Also see All rights.

Geographic Index

This index lists photo markets by the state in which they are located. It is often easier to begin marketing your work to companies close to home. You can also determine with which companies you can make appointments to show your portfolio, near home or when traveling.

Geographic Index

INDIANA

Geographic Index

Geographic Index

Geographic Index

NEW MEXICO

NEW YORK

Geographic Index

Geographic Index

NORTH CAROLINA

NORTH DAKOTA

OHIO

Geographic Index

WASHINGTON

WEST VIRGINIA

WISCONSIN

WYOMING

International Index

This index lists photo markets outside the United States. Most of the markets are located in Canada and the United Kingdom. To work with markets located outside your home country, you will have to be especially professional and patient.

Subject Index

This index can help you find buyers who are searching for the kinds of images you are producing. Consisting of markets from the Publications, Book Publishers, Greeting Cards, Posters & Related Products, Stock Photo Agencies, Advertising, Design & Related Markets, and Galleries sections, this index is broken down into 48 different subjects. If, for example, you shoot outdoor scenes and want to find out which markets purchase this material, turn to the categories Landscapes/Scenics and Environmental.

Adventure

Agriculture

Subject Index

Subject Index

Alternative Process

Subject Index

Architecture

Subject Index

Babies/Children/Teens

Business Concepts

Celebrities

Cities/Urban

Couples

Disasters

Documentary

Subject Index

Entertainment

Subject Index

Environmental

Erotic

Events

Fashion/Glamour

Fine Art

Subject Index

Food/Drink

Gardening

Health/Fitness/Beauty

Historical/Vintage

Subject Index

Hobbies

Subject Index

Humor

Industry

Interiors/Decorating

Landscapes/Scenics

Subject Index

Subject Index

Lifestyle

Subject Index

Medicine

Military

Multicultural

Parents

Subject Index

Performing Arts

Subject Index

Pets

Subject Index

Political

Product Shots/ Still Life

Religious

Rural

Science

Subject Index

Seasonal

Senior Citizens

Sports

Subject Index

Technology/ Computers

Travel

Wildlife

Subject Index

Subject Index

General Index

This index lists every market appearing in the book; use it to find specific companies you wish to approach.

General Index

General Index

NOTES

NOTES

NOTES

NOTES

NOTES

NOTES

NOTES

NOTES

NOTES

NOTES

NOTES

NOTES

NOTES

NOTES

TR 12 .P515 2008

2009 photographer's market

DEMCO